ANTIQUES

SOURCE | 2003
BOOK | 2004

THIS IS A CARLTON BOOK

Copyright © 2003 Martin Miller

This edition published by Carlton Books Limited 2003
20 Mortimer Street
London W1T 3JW

Edited and designed for Carlton Books by Bluefrog and PAGEOne

A CIP catalogue for this book is available from the British Library.

ISBN 1 84222 823 4

ANTIQUES

SOURCE BOOK | 2003–2004

The Definitive Guide to Retail
Prices for Antiques and Collectables

MARTIN MILLER

CARLTON
BOOKS

Contents

ACKNOWLEDGEMENTS

GENERAL EDITOR
Martin Miller

EDITORS
Marianne Blake
Peter Blake
Simon Blake
Richard Bundy
Abigail Zoe Martin
Michael Spilling
Charlotte Stock

EDITORIAL ASSISTANTS
Lisa Bailey
Vicky Blake
Liz Cox
Jasper Graham
Ozlem Gunay
Gemma Martin
Cara Miller

EDITORIAL CO-ORDINATORS
Marianne Blake
Kim Khahn
Abigail Zoe Martin
Elizabeth Roebig

CREATIVE DIRECTOR
Bob Gordon

PHOTOGRAPHIC/PRODUCTION
CO-ORDINATORS
Marianne Blake
Garry Lewis
Warren Philbey
Megan Smith

PHOTOGRAPHERS
Neil Fox
Anders Gramer
Ryan Green
Carmen Klammer
Anna Malni
Abigail Zoe Martin
Chris Smailes
James Beam Van Etten
Lee Walsh

DESIGNERS
Gill Andrews
Jessica Barr
Pauline Hoyle
Alexandra Huchet
Louise Kerby
Robert Law
Michelle Pickering
Tim Stansfield
Mark Tattham

How to Use This Book

by Martin Miller

This is the fourth edition of the first full-colour antiques retail price guide published in the United Kingdom, a distinction that possibly deserves a little explanation. I started publishing antiques price guides in 1969 – and they have always been very successful – but one criticism that I have heard is from people saying, rather wistfully, 'I loved the book, but what a pity that everything in it was already sold'. And it was perfectly true, the books were designed more as compilations of information from auction sales that had already taken place than as immediate guides; as reference books rather than handbooks.

The difference with this book is that here we have used retailers, rather than auction houses, as our sources of information. Everything in this book is actually for sale at the time of going to press and many items, certainly some of the more arcane, will remain so for the lifespan of the book. As the introduction explains, a reputable and experienced dealer's assessment of the price of an antique is at least as reliable – and usually a great deal more reasoned – than a price achieved at auction, and so even when the item you wish to purchase from the book turns out to have been sold, you have a reliable guide to the price you should pay when you happen upon another.

The book is designed for maximum visual interest and appeal. The Contents and Index will tell you in which area to find items that you are specifically seaking, but the collector, enthusiast or interior designer will profit most from reading through a section or several sections and gathering information and inspiration as they go.

Should you happen upon something that you wish to purchase, simply note the dealer reference to the bottom right of the entry and look up the dealer's full name and details in the Directory of Dealers section towards the back of the book. You can telephone, fax and, in many cases, visit the dealer's website. All the dealers who have helped us with the book will be happy to assist you, and if the piece you wish to buy has already been sold, they will almost certainly be able to help you find another. The price shown against an entry is per individual item, unless the heading and description refer to more than one item, a set, or a pair. Should you wish to sell an item, the relevant section and dealer reference will again be of help, but do not expect to be offered the same price at which the dealer is selling.

Since the first *Antiques Source Book* was published, the way in which we look for antiques has remained almost the same, whether it is from the large fairs such as the D.M.G. Palm Beach International Art and Antique Fair run by David Lester, the Grosvenor House and Olympia antiques fairs in London, the N.E.C in Birmingham or the relaxed Coopers Antique Fair in Snape, Suffolk; they are all part of the same global antique market.

The internet has also considerably helped the international antiques market – we can now find with ease the prices of antiques sold at auction across the world, and view an antique dealer's website to search for that special piece.

We hope you find these instructions easy to follow. Good luck and enjoy your journey into the world of antiques.

Introduction

A contemporary and practical guide to antiques and collectables

With the rise in property prices over the past three years how have the prices of antiques in general performed? For example, since the 1970s furniture has out-performed the property market, certainly in the south-east of England. However, recently it has not been keeping up in investment terms.

It has been reported that antiques price increases over the last three years have been in single figures and that last year they remained static. However, stagnation set against a stock market where values dropped 30 percent last year doesn't seem so bad. Since the tragic events of 11th September 2001 the market has stayed gloomy and the lack of American buyers seems set to continue. So, this may be a great time to start buying, especially in the bottom to middle market. Prices of exceptional items are always strong.

Arguably there is no better place to put your spare cash than into antiques to enhance your home. House prices will probably remain stable and may fall. Shares may suffer a similar fate. Antiques on the other hand have already hit rock bottom and have one great bonus – they are finite. Houses can be built and shares created, but they are no longer making genuine Chippendales.

There really is no comparison in terms of aesthetics between a collection of fine Georgian silver and an entry on a stockbroker's statement. However, collecting antiques, works of art and collectables can have one major drawback: converting them to cash is time-consuming and difficult. It's "sod's law" that when you want to sell, you will hear the same old excuses from a dealer; "sorry, overstocked"; "the market's dead"; "out of fashion" and so on. Even if you have purchased a piece from a dealer offering a buy-back at a specified price after an agreed time, it may not be that simple.

However, help is at hand! The Internet has opened up a completely new market for the antique dealer. Now, at virtually no cost, you can put anything up for auction on sites like www.ebay.com – you will be amazed at the results and the cash comes quickly. Of course, there's no real substitute for visiting an antiques shop or market. Many people are still wary of buying "unseen" but it is catching on. Most good dealers have a website with an e-mail alert system, which notifies customers as soon as an item of particular interest comes into stock. Antique dealers who specialize in small and rare items are really benefiting from the internet – many now consider the web to be their new shop-front to the world.

The last couple of years have also spawned a host of TV shows devoted to antiques and the home. As television executives remain besotted with bargain hunt and home improvement series, it is surprising that auction rooms are not awash with seas of waving hands. However, most people appear to be content with the second hand experience from the armchair. The *Antiques Source Book* is the perfect "armchair guide" with most buyers still feeling more comfortable buying from a reputable dealer. You may in some cases pay a little more than at auction, but the benefits are all too clear: no buyer's premium; recourse to the dealer or their trade association in case of dispute; no restoration normally needed and if you build a relationship with a good dealer you can often get an exclusive on a piece. In many cases a dealer will buy at auction for you for a small commission and you may even negotiate a part exchange – you really do get the best of all worlds.

The 2003–4 edition of the *Antiques Source Book* is packed with antiques and

collectables together with a directory of recommended dealers and specialists. Remember, if what you are looking for is not in the guide you can always contact one of the specialists, as they may be able to help you. The *Source Books* are fast becoming a valuable price and identification reference library in their own right.

However, even the best price guide cannot replace legwork as a part of the learning process. Although there is unfortunately no way of becoming an "overnight" expert, there are ways to fast-track your knowledge base. Visit museums and houses open to the public, go to auctions, attend courses and beyond this read, read, read. I have a friend who within an incredibly short time became an expert in sixteenth and seventeenth century Chinese porcelain. He sucked dealers dry of information, viewed every auction and visited as many collections as he could. Then he started buying. His expertise was so much greater than the average generalist or market stall-holder that he was already ahead of the game. He amassed a collection of broken and repaired porcelain second to none – his reference collection. He had focus and gained enormous fun and profit from his single-minded passion. He became hooked in a big way – beware, it can creep up on you!

Antiquities

The artefacts of long dead civilisations have, for centuries, made a fascinating field of study for both the collector and the forger.

The sixteenth-century art historian, Vasari, apparently used to regale his audience with a story about the young and keen Michelangelo. According to Vasari, Michelangelo made a sculpture of a fawn in imitation of the antique, then broke a tooth to make it look more authentic. Whether the story is true or not, it highlights the point that many sculptors learned their trade by copying the earlier work of others. A sculpture that has stood outside for several generations may look more worn and ancient than one that has been better protected, so that only a specialist who really knows his subject can tell whether a piece is Greek, Roman, Renaissance or merely an eighteenth- or nineteenth-century copy – and even then he may be wrong. There are scientific tests that can be employed to date some antiquities – at a price. But, on the whole, be warned: this is one of the most rewarding of collecting areas, but it is also the one where some of the most expensive mistakes can be made.

Roman Bronze Lamp
- *1st century BC*
A fine Roman bronze oil lamp with dolphin finial, stylised bird adornment and fan-tail scrolled handle.
- *length 15cm*
- £2,800
- Pars

Byzantine Oil Lamp
- *7th–8th century AD*
Terracotta oil lamp from the Holy Land, with an inscription in Greek around the filling hole.
- *length 11cm*
- £1,000
- Pars

Roman Garnet Ring
- *circa 1st century AD*
A Roman ring with a garnet engraved with a figure of Herakles leaning on his club, with the skin of the Nemean lion draped over his other arm. The original intaglio is set in a new band.
- *diameter 1.5cm*
- £600
- Pars

Egyptian Female Divinity
- *27th Dynasty, 525–404 BC*
The hippopotamus goddess Taurt, shown standing upright on her hind legs. She was the Protectress of childbirth. The amulet is executed in black faience.
- *height 8cm*
- £500
- Pars

Roman Earrings ▼

- *2nd–3rd century AD*
Pair of Roman earrings with
circular garnets set in gold roped
banding, with suspended gold
strands and beads.
- *length 3cm*
- £2,000   • Pars

Alabaster Drinking Vessel ▼

- *circa 2nd millennium BC*
Bactrian Afghanistan alabaster
cylindrical drinking vessel, with
engraved circular designs and
turned lip.
- *height 10.5cm*
- £650   • Rasoul Gallery

Islamic Pendant ▲

- *circa 9th–10th century AD*
Islamic gold pendant in the shape
of a bird with beautiful intricate
work.
- *height 0.5cm*
- £3,000   • Pars

Roman Gold Earrings ▲

- *circa 1st–3rd century AD*
Pair of late roman gold earrings of
tear drop form with beaded
circular design.
- *height 3cm*
- £2,000   • Pars

Roman Gold Pendant ▼

- *7th–8th century AD*
Late Roman square gold pendant
set with one amethyst lozenge
shaped stone and flanked by two
circular turquoise stones.
- *width 1.4cm*
- £450   • Pars

Gold Pendant ▲

- *circa 15th century AD*
Lozenge shaped green stone set
within a circular gold pendant
with a herringbone design.
- *width 1cm*
- £200   • Pars

Bactrian Vessel ▲

- *circa 2nd millennium BC*
Bactrian alabaster drinking vessel
of cylindrical form from
Afghanistan.
- *height 12cm*
- £550   • Rasoul Gallery

Green Glass Flask ▼
- *4th century AD*

Translucent green glass flask of bottle shaped form, with a cylindrical neck, splayed rim, strap handle and good iridescence.
- *height 11cm*
- £1,000 • **Pars**

Perfume Bottle ▲
- *7th century AD*

Perfume bottle of globular form, with silver iridescence and pinched surface.
- *height 8.5cm*
- £1,000 • **Pars**

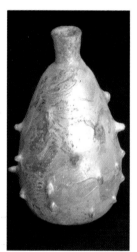

Translucent Glass Flask ▼
- *4th century AD*

Small translucent blue glass flask with applied handle and thumb support, with a flattened globular body and dark blue spiral threads on the neck.
- *height 8cm*
- £800 • **Pars**

Amphoriskos ▲
- *5th century AD*

Feather patterned long-necked amphoriskos with a turquoise ground, yellow and dark blue threads and amber colour glass handles.
- *height 14cm*
- £4,000 • **Pars**

Cedonian Amphoriskos ▲
- *1st century AD*

Cedonian, mould-blown, amber glass Amphoriskos, the handles in cream glass, with a long cylindrical neck with inverted rim, the ovoid body incorporating a central frieze of geometric designs.
- *height 8.5cm*
- £2,500 • **Pars**

Expert Tips

Considering its age, beauty and fragility, Roman glass is a relatively affordable investment for the antiquities collector, and is a good place to start with.

Byzantine Flask ▲
- *Byzantine 7th century AD*

Byzantine translucent pale green hexagonal flask with strap handle. The surface of the glass has shallow indentations and is decorated with Christian symbols.
- *height 21.5cm*
- £6,000 • **Pars**

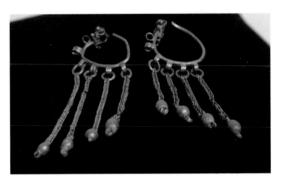

Egyptian Sculptured Relief ▼
- **650–30 BC**
A limestone sculptor's model of a male head which has been sculptured in raised relief, from the Late Period to the Ptolemaic Period.
- *14cm x 10.5cm x 2cm*
- **£1,500**　　　　• Pars

Gold Earrings ▲
- **2nd–3rd century AD**
Gold pendulous earrings, probably Sassanium, from the Zoroastrian Persian Empire.
- *length 7cm*
- **£1,000**　　　　• Pars

Roman Bronze Figure ▲
- **1st–3rd century AD**
A bronze Roman figure of Jupiter with one arm raised and a cloak draped over his shoulder, mounted on a wooden plinth.
- *height 12cm*
- **£2,800**　　　　• Pars

Roman Terracotta Head ◄
- **1st century BC/AD**
A Roman terracotta head of Dionysus showing the god with a full beard and mounted on a wooden plinth.
- *height 10cm*
- **£700**　　　　• Pars

Anthropomorphic Janus Figure ▲
- **1000 BC**
A Luristan bronze anthropomorphic Janus tube in the form of a stylised human figure.
- *height 12cm*
- **£900**　　　　• Pars

Luristan Dagger ▶
- **1000 BC**
A Luristan bronze dagger with oval pommel and a pierced hilt, in fine condition with good patination.
- *length 40cm*
- **£900**　　　　• Yazdani

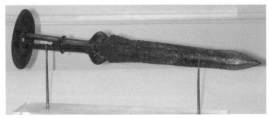

Roman Leopard ▲
- *1st century AD*
Roman bronze leopard with raised paw and head slightly turned, standing on a circular base.
- *height 4.5cm*
- £2,500 • Pars

Egyptian Mace Head ▲
- *late 4th millennium BC*
Egyptian black stone mace head.
- *height 10cm*
- £1,000 • Pars

Bronze Cat ▲
- *635–525 BC*
Bronze cat from the Saite period dynasty or late bronze dynasty (625-525BC).
- *height 9.5cm*
- £6,000 • Pars

Venetian Flask ▲
- *5th century BC*
Venetian flask with a pinched lip and strap handle, raised on a pedestal base, with a yellow and green diagonal design on a black ground.
- *height 10cm*
- £2,000 • Pars

Aubergine Glass Flask ▲
- *7th century AD*
Aubergine glass flask with a single handle, a narrow neck and a bulbous body with applied circular raised design.
- *height 9cm*
- £700 • Pars

Translucent Bowl ▼
- *1st century AD*
Roman, translucent, green pillar-moulded glass bowl of shallow form with vertical ribbing, the tondo with three wheel-cut concentric circles.
- *diameter 15cm*
- £2,000 • Pars

Pottery Candleholder ▼
- *circa 8th century AD*
Byzantine pottery candle holder modelled as a church, with carved arches and openings with a geometric design.
- *height 29cm*
- £2,000 • Pars

Babylonian Terracotta Statues ▲

- *1900–1750 BC*
A group of statues all relating to fertility, modelled in the form of female figures with emphasis on the breast.
- *average height 8cm*
- **£100 each** • Shiraz

Roman Deep Dish ▲

- *2nd century AD*
Decorated with iridescent olive glaze. With a bevelled lip, standing on a raised base.
- *height 10cm*
- **£500** • Shiraz

Spearhead ▲

- *8th century BC*
Bronze, trowel-shaped spearhead, in fine condition. Persian from Luristan, Western Iran.
- *length 33cm*
- **£150** • Pars

Animal Figure ▼

- *9th–8th century BC*
Bronze model of a double-headed animal figure on four legs, with head at each end. From Luristan.
- *height 6cm*
- **£400** • Pars

Pair of Roman Beakers ▼

- *3rd–1st century BC*
Pair of Roman beakers with a green iridescence.
- *height 9.5cm*
- **£800** • Shahdad

Isis and Osiris ▼

- *664–30 BC*
Late to Ptolemaic period bronze statue of Isis and Osiris, the King of the Underworld and his wife/sister. Isis is shielding Osiris.
- *height 13cm*
- **£5,500** • Pars

Earrings ▼

- *circa 600 AD*
Gold, pendulous earrings, probably Sassanian, from the Zoroastrian Persian Empire.
- *length 7cm*
- **£1,000** • Pars

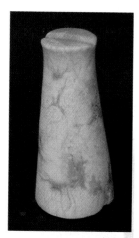

Proto-Bactrian Limestone Idol ▲

- *circa 2nd millennium BC*
Proto-Bactrian limestone fertility column idol.
- *height 14.5cm*
- £1,500 • Rasoul Gallery

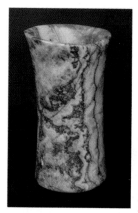

Alabaster Vessel ▲

- *circa 2nd millennium BC*
Bactrian alabaster cylindrical drinking vessel with red marbling.
- *height 16cm*
- £1,300 • Rasoul Gallery

Stone Inkwell ▼

- *circa 2nd millennium BC*
Bactrian stone inkwell with two receptacles, carved with circular designs between triple banding.
- *9cm x 10cm*
- £1,200 • Rasoul Gallery

Bactrian Inkwell ▼

- *3rd millennium BC*
Bactrian stone inkwell with a geometric design around the neck, above a square base with an engraved circular pattern.
- *height 4cm*
- £250 • Rasoul Gallery

Bactrian Bronze Weight ▲

- *circa 3rd millennium BC*
Bactrian bronze weight with two handles in the form of leopard heads.
- *height 7.5cm*
- £1,000 • Rasoul Gallery

Bactrian Inkwell ▲

- *circa 3rd millennium BC*
Stone inkwell from the Bactrian period of conical form with an inverted conical base.
- *height 7.5cm*
- £450 • Rasoul Gallery

Bronze Lion ▼

- *4th century AD*
Bronze figure of a lion with a truncated body in a crouching position with his mouth open.
- *height 6cm*
- £2,300 • Rasoul Gallery

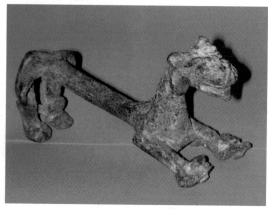

Roman Bone Doll

- *6th century AD*
A Roman hollow bone doll with articulated arms showing a female figure. Late Roman, early Byzantine period.
- *height 12cm*
- £900 • Pars

Roman Glass Bowl ▲

- *5th century AD*
A pale green late Roman bowl with trailed dark blue concentric rings, and three vertical decorations.
- *8.5cm x 11cm*
- £2,000 • Pars

Expert Tips

Always make sure you have an export licence and a museum certificate that confirms the authenticity and origin of the antique.

Glass Aryballos ▼

- *500 BC*
A Greek sand core-formed glass Aryballos with a dark blue ground, yellow line and zigzag pattern over a spherical body. Applied "Duck head" handles.
- *height 13cm*
- £3,800 • Pars

Roman Tar Bottle ▶

- *1st–3rd century AD*
Roman, ribbed-body tear bottle with handle and splaying lip. With good iridescence.
- *height 12cm*
- £680 • Shahdad

Old Babylonian Seal ▼

- *1900–1700 BC*
Cylinder seal, late Old Babylonian, with inscription, "So meeting, Beane son of Warad, Amoro servant of Amoro".
- *height 7cm*
- £700 • Pars

Sassanian Earrings ▲

- *7th century AD*
Late Roman, Sassanian earrings in the form of flat, semicircular bases with three garnets, the whole in solid gold.
- £1,500 • Pars

Amuletic Rings ▼

- *1470–750 BC*
Two faience amuletic rings. The oval panels have moulded designs under a turquoise glaze.
- *length 1.5cm*
- £3,000 • Pars

Architectural &
Garden Furniture

The television and the revival in all things Victorian have led to a boom in what used to be regarded as builders' scrap.

Over the last twenty years, the architectural antique has gradually made its way from the junkyard to the saleroom. Architectural reclamation has become much more a branch of the antiques trade than the building business, and things that would once have been hidden in corners of builders' yards are now highly polished and taking pride of place in auction houses and showrooms. The rise in value of the architectural antique has been accelerated by numerous television programmes on interior design. Items such as Victorian lamp-posts, fireplaces, doors, bricks, tiles, chimney pots, lavatory pans, rainwater hoppers and radiators, along with smaller pieces such as coat hooks, curtain rails and rings, door furniture, shelf brackets and bootscrapers are much in demand. The situation is very similar with garden artefacts, furniture and statuary. Victorian and Regency cast- and wrought-iron furniture now fetch very good prices. The knock-on effect of these relatively ordinary items selling so well is that the really good pieces – old and in marble – fetch astronomical prices. Make sure these items are included when you buy the house!

Statue of Neptune ▼
- *circa 1765*

A finely carved stone figure of the god Neptune in traditional pose, with broken hand.
- *height 205cm*
- £4,850   • Drummonds

Stone Sundial ▲
- *circa 1870*

Stone sundial with a circular marble top supported on a hexagonal column, raised on a splayed foot.
- *height 129cm*
- £2,100   • Drummonds

Stone Torso ▼
- *circa 1920*

A French stone statue of the torso and thighs of a woman, with attention to form.
- *height 1.5m*
- £3,600   • Drummonds

19

Christening Font ▼
- *circa 1930*
An unusual 20th century carved stone christening font in the Fothic style with octagonal oak lid from a church in Farnham Surrey.
- *height 130cm*
- £1,950   • Drummonds

Sandstone Finials ▼
- *circa 1880*
A pair of finely carved Victorian sandstone finials with moulded decoration on a square base.
- *height 96cm*
- £1,250   • Drummonds

Cast-Iron Stove ▼
- *circa 1880*
A fine French stove, highly decorated with fan-shaped motif and scrolled decoration to legs, and "Pied Selle Noel" inscription.
- *58cm x 52cm*
- £340   • Drummonds

Stone Bench ▲
- *1860*
Stone bench with lead frieze, including allegorical figures of above average size. Formerly belonged to Lloyd George.
- *121cm x 185cm x 61cm*
- £9,598   • Drummonds

Decorated Urns ▲
- *18th century*
A pair of eighteenth century highly decorative, ornate sandstone urns with lids. Decorated with a swags of flowers and heads in excellent condition.
- *height 190cm*
- £1,475   • Drummonds

Italian Water Fountain ▲

- *early 20th century*

Charming Italian Rosso Verona marble and bronze fountain by Rafffaello Romanelli. The marble bowl is supported on the shoulders of a bronze satyr crouching on a marble base. A laughing cherub stands with arms raised in the centre of the bowl, while being squirted by a frog crouching on the rim.

- *height 170cm, diameter of bowl 92cm*
- **£35,000** ● Crowthers

Stoneware Urns ▲

- *mid 19th century*

One of a pair of stoneware urns, each semi-lobed body with a frieze of stylised foliage beneath a rope twist and lobed rim, on a circular foot and square base stamped, 'Pulhams Terra Cotta Boxbourne'.

- *height 67cm*
- **£9,500** ● Crowthers

Pair of Urns ▼

- *1910*

Pair of cast iron urns with egg and dart moulded rim above a lobed body, raised on a fluted, splayed foot on a square base.

- *58.5cm diameter*
- **£460** ● Drummonds

Stone Finials ▼

- *circa 1880*

One of a pair of English sandstone finials, finely carved with scrolled and leaf designs, surmounted with a stylised acorn finial.

- *height 200cm*
- **£7,500** ● Drummonds

Sir Walter Raleigh ▶

- *circa 1880*

Stone statue of Sir Walter Raleigh dressed in a tunic and breeches and holding his cloak.

- *height 120cm*
- **£23,000** ● Drummonds

Carved Stone Lions ▲

- *circa 1890*

One of a pair of late 19th-century stone lions in a crouching position, with tail swept onto one side and a finely carved expression.

- *44cm x 100cm*
- **£14,000** ● Drummonds

Cast Iron Fountain ▲

- *19th century*

Cast iron fountain from Ardennes, France, in the form of a young boy holding a staff in one hand and pointing with the other.

- *height 122cm*
- **£3,400** ● Drummonds

Brass Lantern ▼

- 1880

Brass lantern with glass front and sides with pagoda top and small round brass finials.
- *height 45cm*
- £110   • Myriad

Chinese Garden Seat ▶

- 1880

Chinese ceramic garden seat with a cream glaze, pierced lattice panels, and lion mask decoration.
- *height 39cm*
- £350   • Ormonde

Galvanised Flower Bucket ▲

- 1960

French flower vendors galvanised display bucket with carrying handles.
- *height 48cm*
- £22   • Myriad

Galvanised Tub ▲

- 1880

One of a pair of galvanised water butts with an inverted linear design.
- *height 54cm*
- £95   • Myriad

Ceramic Garden Seat ▶

- 1880

Chinese ceramic garden seat, in a green glaze, with black floral designs and a repeating pattern of spots.
- *height 39cm*
- £350   • Ormonde

Enamel Bucket ▼

- 1920

French enamelled water bucket with a red rim, pale green body, hand painted strawberries and original handle.
- *height 29cm*
- £78   • Myriad

Expert Tips

Garden, unlike interior furniture, does not need to be perfect in order to create a beautiful garden, as some wear and distress can add mystery and delight to any design. All that is needed is a little imagination.

Green Stucco Pot ◀

- 1950

Stoneware urn of ovoid form with green glazed lip and neck with rusticated finish to the body.
- *height 44cm*
- £240   • Myriad

Brass Urns ▼
- *circa 1910*

One of a pair of brass urns from the modern movement, with unusual angular double handles, the whole on a pedestal foot resting on a square base.
- *height 48cm*
- £880
- Myriad

Zinc Urns ▼
- *1920*

One of a pair of French urns made from zinc with unusual angular designs and a marbled finish.
- *height 31cm*
- £680
- Myriad

Garden Folding Stool ▲
- *1950*

Folding picnic stool with a candy striped linen seat supported by four teak legs.
- *height 41cm*
- £78
- Myriad

Stone Flower Pot ▲
- *1970*

Stone flower pot with a fluted body with carved designs in relief.
- *height 24cm*
- £24
- Myriad

Pink Pottery Bucket ▼
- *1910*

French ceramic pail with salmon pink glaze and white interior with a raffia covered handle.
- *height 24cm*
- £18
- Myriad

Expert Tips

Unglazed period pottery of any value should be covered up and protected if left outside in the winter, as ice can destroy it as it expands in the cracks.

Salt Glazed Urn ▼
- *1910*

French salt glazed pottery urn with pinched lip and banding, the body centred with a flower motif in relief on a pedestal base.
- *height 41cm*
- £120
- Myriad

Watering Can ◄
- *1920*

Zinc watering can with an elongated spout.
- *height 26cm*
- £34
- Myriad

Pottery Urn ▲
- *circa 1940*
One of a pair of pottery urns with
lobed designs around the body
and egg and dart motif to the
splayed lip, standing on a pedestal
base.
- *height 43cm*
- £480   • Myriad

French Chair ▲
- *circa 1950*
One of a set of four French
wrought iron garden chairs with
pierced geometric designs to back
splat and seat.
- *height 87cm*
- £680   • Myriad

Mythical Yarli Lions ▼
- *18th century*
One of a pair of Mythical Yarli
lions with elephant trunks,
standing on top of human heads.
Has traces of original paint
remaining in excellent condition.
Vellore Tamil Naou.
- *height 166cm*
- £7,800   • Gordon Reece

Indian Jarli Window ▼
- *17th century*
Indian Mughal Jarli window
carved from red sandstone
flanked by four cartouches in the
form of Mirabs arches. The
central Jarli of interlocking
honeycomb is topped by a floral
finial with a flower to left and
right from Northern Rajastan.
- *83cm x 115cm*
- £5,800   • Gordon Reece

Wicker Chair ▶
- *circa 1920*
French provincial wicker
conservatory chair painted
pistachio green with a deep
horseshoe back, apron front and
splayed legs.
- *height 67cm*
- £240   • Myriad

Wrought Iron Chair ▲
- *circa 1950*
Set of four French wrought iron
patio chairs with a heart shaped
back scrolled arms and original
white enamel paint.
- *height 87cm*
- £680 for set of four • Myriad

Carved Ceiling Panel ▲
- *circa 1850*
Carved rosewood ceiling panel
with central flower within a
stylised leaf motif, from Southern
India.
- *length 56cm*
- £310   • Gordon Reece

Garden Rocker ▼

- *circa 1920*
A cast-iron garden rocking chair with floral designs and new beechwood slats.
- *height 82cm*
- **£560**   • Fiona McDonald

Sandstone Carving ▼

- *circa 1870*
A 19th-century sandstone carving of a naturalistic wolverine head.
- *height 30cm*
- **£650**   • Annette Puttnam

Metal Arch ▲

- *circa 1870*
Decorative, wrought-iron, over-door arch of Gothic form with scrolled, foliate decoration inside and an outer arch with scrolled decoration within the border.
- *height 1.02m*
- **£385**   • Drummonds

Corbel ▲

- *circa 1840*
A terracotta corbel, used in the support of a projecting ledge, with acanthus-leaf and scrolled decoration to surface and architectural mouldings to sides.
- *height 40cm*
- **£80**   • Drummonds

Expert Tips

Belfast sinks – the deep white ones – are relatively inexpensive because so many were made for labs, school kitchens etc. They are virtually indestructible.

Stone Frieze ▶

- *circa 1870*
A 19th-century carved stone frieze, with bulls and cherubs among heavily carved leaf designs.
- *length 2.49m*
- **£5,200**   • Drummonds

Chairs ▼

- *circa 1880*
A pair of white-painted bentwood armchairs with curved, slatted seats.
- *height 78cm*
- **£585**   • Drummonds

Garden Gate ▼

- *circa 1865*
A Victorian, iron, pedestrian garden gate with Gothic architectural forms.
- *height 1.05m*
- **£625**   • Drummonds

Victorian Iron Gates ▲
- *circa 1880*
Pair of Victorian iron gates,
heavily constructed with ball and
spike finial designs.
- *200cm x 300cm*
- **£5,100** • Drummonds

Expert Tips

*Decorative fireplaces were
mass-produced from the
1840s, so it is important to
check the grate is complete
with basket and hood, as
perfect replacements are
difficult to find.*

Oak Bar ▲
- *circa 1920s*
Circular oak bar with moulded
panelled doors, consisting of a
four door fridge unit, marble
surround and surfaces.
- *length 635cm*
- **£5,900** • Drummonds

Architectural Fireplace ▶
- *circa 1800–1900*
Carved wooden fireplace flanked
by two architectural columns
surmounted by a moulded mantle.
With traces of white paint.
- *height 128cm*
- **£2,350** • Drummonds

Gothic Window ▼
- *circa 1800s*
Carved gothic sandstone window.
- *89cm x 69cm*
- **£675** • Drummonds

Fire Dogs and Grate ▶
- *circa 1900s*
Victorian serpentine–fronted
cast-iron grate and fire back with
a raised design of tulips,
surmounted by two cherubs
holding a wreath.
- *75cm x 80cm*
- **£3,600** • Drummonds

English Rococo Chimneypiece ▲
- *circa 1840*
An English white marble
chimneypiece signed D Aí.
The serpentine shaped shelf
with moulded edge above an
elaborately carved frieze
decorated with scrolled
acanthus leaves, with a central
scallop carved shell above the
hearth opening and a double
moulded surround with relief
flower heads above three small
acanthus motifs terminating in
scrolled leaves.
- *122cm x 193cm*
- **£38,000** • Anthony Outred

Victorian Fire Fender ▼

- *1830*

A Victorian cast-iron fire fender
in the Jacobean style with ball
and finial decoration.

- *176cm x 42cm*
- **£3,500** • **Old World**

George III Steel Fender ▲

- *1800*

A George III steel fender with
brass claw feet.

- *21cm x 113cm x 26cm*
- **£950** • **Old World**

Regency Fender ▼

- *1800*

A Regency serpentine steel
fender, with urns and floral swag
pierced decoration.

- *12cm x 102cm x 12cm*
- **£750** • **Old World**

Fire Place ◄

- *1750*

Stove Carron foundry designed
by Robert Adam, cast by
Oldham of London for George III
when he was Prince of
Wales. Reputed to have come
from Carlton House.

- *175cm x 40cm*
- **£25,000** • **Old World**

Stone Window ▼

- *17th century*

An Indian Mogul window of red
sandstone with a central lattice
panel, and floral decoration to
side panels and borders.

- *109cm x 69cm*
- **£5,800** • **Gordon Reece**

Garden Lantern ▼

- *1920*

An oval wirework Chinoiserie
garden lantern, lined with
decorative parchment on a
circular wooden base.

- *height 60cm*
- **£210** • **Myriad**

Expert Tips

*Check that an antique fireplace
is genuine as there are many
good reproductions around.*

Door Surround and Door ▲

- *Late 19th century*
Carved door surround and door,
consisting of two panel doors,
door surround and frieze, carved
with amorphic and foliate
designs.
- *224cm x 125cm*
- £1,250 • Drummonds

Oak Fireplace ▼

- *circa 1890s*
Victorian mahogany fire place
with carved architectural pillars
surmounted by a carved frieze
with moulded cornice.
- *270cm x 90cm*
- £9,200 • Drummonds

Mahogany Door Surround ▶

- *Circa 1890*
Mahogany door frame with
moulded designs and beading,
surmounted by a carved frieze.
- *224cm x 125cm*
- £1,250 • Drummonds

Gothic Archway ▼

- *circa 1800s*
Carved Gothic sandstone window
consisting of two arched windows
with Gothic tracery .
- *274cm x 137cm*
- £1,975 • Drummonds

Glazed Doors ▲

- *circa 1890s*
Victorian glazed double doors
within a moulded frame
surmounted by an arched
moulded fanlight.
- *200cm x 125cm*
- £675 • Drummonds

Chimney Pot ▼

- *19th century*

A glazed terracotta chimney pot. With banding and fluted design around the neck tapering to a square chamfered base.

- *125cm x 30cm*
- £80
- Old School

Carved Shutters ▼

- *early 19th century*

A pair of carved shutters with Oriental paintwork.

- *74cm x 106cm*
- £425
- Gordon Reece

Lion Mask ◄

- *1800*

An iron lion mask with terracotta patination.

- *diameter 35cm*
- £250
- R. Conquest

Coal Scuttle ▲

- *circa 1890*

English cast-iron coal scuttle with lion's head surrounded by heavily moulded edging.

- *45cm x 51xm*
- £295
- Drummonds

Park Bench ▼

- *1940s*

English garden seat with scrolled arm rests in original condition.

- *184cm x 88cm x 69cm*
- £299
- Old School

Mahogany Jardinière ▼

- *1760*

A George III mahogany jardinière with carved apron.

- *length 70cm*
- £2,950
- Dial Post House

Elmwood Planter ◄

- *1850*

Elmwood planter with brass inlay.

- *length 30cm*
- £1,950
- Dial Post House

Shanks Canopy Bath ▼

- *circa 1910*

Shanks, cast iron canopy bath, with original nickel fittings including numerous water-jets and large shower rose.
- *height 32cm*
- £9,800　　• Drummonds

Copper Tub ▲

- *circa 1860s*

Large 19th century, circular copper tub, supported on a steel frame.
- *diameter 174cm*
- £16,500　　• Drummonds

Italian Marble Bath ▼

- *circa 1890s*

Late 19th century Italian marble bath, with a carved frieze of stylised acanthus leaves.
- *length 188cm*
- £13,800　　• Drummonds

London Ceramic Trap ▼

- *circa 1910*

London porcelain trap with bracket and seat, with rose and leaf decoration, to the inside and outside of the unit.
- *height 46cm*
- £1,125　　• Drummonds

Lounge Bath ◀

- *circa 1910*

Lounge bath with ball and claw feet with original nickel plated fittings including built in waist and plunger units.
- *width 86cm*
- £1,950　　• Drummonds

Arms & Armour

From suits of English Civil War armour, through early firearms, edged weapons and World War II medals, the collection of militaria remains a fascination.

There will always be a fascination with the engines of war, be they large and complicated or small, sharp and extremely basic, because of their historical interest, their high-quality craftsmanship and because of man's atavistic interest in things that can destroy his fellow man. The collectables that come under the broad heading of Arms and Armour – or Militaria – include such diverse items as armour, edged weapons, medals, badges, uniforms and firearms and even extend into the areas of prints and cigarette cards. Edged weapons, which include swords, sabres, dirks, daggers and bayonets, come up for sale very often and are probably the least expensive way to start a collection. Firearms, from match- and flintlocks onwards, tend to require a greater outlay and more arcane knowledge. One thing they all have in common is that they must be useable and well-made, so practice in handling in important, as is the ability to spot a 'marriage' or a fake.

Officer's Peaked Cap ▶
- *1940*

Officer's peaked cap of the Kriegsmarine Administration Service, with silver wire eagle cockade and braid, in excellent condition. Items of this branch of the Kriegsmarine are rarely seen!
- *size 8*
- **£795** • Gordon's

Kriegsmarine Colani Jacket ▲
- *1940*

A rare Kriegsmarine Colani Jacket-Haupt Feldwebel, Coxwain rank, complete with breast eagle, shoulder boards and all original buttons.
- *medium*
- **£315** • Gordon's

Tap Action Pistol ▼
- *1790*

Flintlock tap action pistol, screw-off barrels by Spencer of London. London proofed 45 calibre with walnut grip.
- *length 19cm*
- **£575** • C.F. Seidler

Naval Officer's Sword ▼
- *1880*

Royal Naval Officer's sword retailed by Ashdown, 106 St. Georges Street, Portsmouth, with original gilding to guard and mounts and gilt brass lion's head on handle.
- *length 112cm*
- **£500** • C.F. Seidler

Pith Helmet ▶

- *circa 1915*
Turn of the century linen pith
helmet for the overseas campaign
in India, in fine original
condition.
- *size 7*
- £120 • Bentleys

Officers Belt Pistol ◀

- *circa 1840*
Officers 16 bore percussion pistol,
with double back action locks, by
Roper of Halifax.
- *length 30cm*
- £875 • C.F. Seidler

Luftwaffe Belt ▶

- *1940*
Luftwaffe other ranks late pattern
standard leather belt, with some
wear, but complete.
- *5cm x 3cm*
- £45 • Gordon's

SS Steel Helmet ▼

- *1940*
SS M-44 Steel helmet, a rare
early double decal version
complete with inner lining and
chin strap, stamped '54' on lining
and a maker's stamp on inside of
helmet, with most of original
finish still present.
- *Size 8*
- £1,195 • Gordon's

Khula–Khad Helmet ▶

- *circa 1800*
Fine Indo Persian Khula-Khad
helmet formed as a face with
horns, with chiselled steel
designs, gold inlays and chain
mail neck guard.
- *height 30cm*
- £3,200 • Michael German

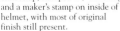

Japanese N.C.O. Sword ▶

- *circa 1939*
Japanese N.C.O. Katena sword
with polished folded steel blade
and original paintwork to handle.
No. 79275, with matching
scabbard number.
- *length 59cm*
- £290 • C.F. Seidler

Japanese Dagger ▼

- *circa 1870*
A Japanese Tanto dagger with
cloisonne hilt and scabbard, the
blade is unsigned.
- *length 35cm*
- £1,800 • Michael German

Pinfire Revolver ▼

- *circa 1870*
Continental pinfire carbine
revolver with 'Fabrique de Le
Page Freres a Liege, Maison a
Paris 12 Rue de Eugieue' etched
on barrel .
- *length 66cm*
- £1,200 • Michael German

German Crossbow

- *circa 1620*

Fine early German hunting crossbow, stock inlaid with numerous engraved stag horn plaques, depicting a hunting lodge. The steel bow struck with armourer's mark. Original cord with set trigger.
- *length 71cm*
- £4,600 • Michael German

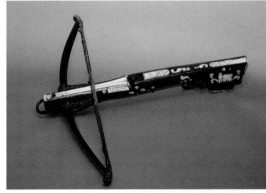

Adams Percussion Pistol

- *1848*

A fine double-barrelled percussion cap and ball travelling pistol. Made by Adams of London with back action locks and swivel ram rod.
- *length 24cm*
- £1,200 • Michael German

Indian Dagger

- *18th century*

Indian water blade with signature of the maker. Menooher intricate floral gilding. Bone handle and shark skin scabbard with stylised floral silver mounts.
- *length 36cm*
- £1,500 • Shahdad

British Cavalry Helmet

- *1910*

British Cavalry Helmet 1st Dragoon Guards. Black plume representing a farrier. Nickel skull with eight metal mounts and linked chin strap leaf with leaf decoration.
- £1,200 • Michael German

Japanese Kabuto

- *circa 1810*

An early 19th-century red lacquer kabuto with doe skin visor. Three come-mons in gilt. Four lame shikiro wide-splayed neck guard.
- £2,000 • Don Bayney

Bristol Tipstaff

- *1819*

Bristol tipstaff dated and inscribed "Saint Ewins Ward No 4" with typical bull finial and ash or elm shaft.
- *length 36cm*
- £650 • C.F. Seidler

English Civil War Piece

- *1640*

English Civil War piece found in a castle moat. A Linstock or Gunner's head. A touching off stick for lighting cannon.
- *length 42cm*
- £200 • C.F. Seidler

33

Belgian Courtier's Sword ▼

- *circa 1860*

Belgian courtier's sword with mother of pearl grip and brass gilt guard, with foliate designs together with a black leather scabbard with gilt mounts. Inscribed 'Docteur Lorthioir' and the maker's mark 49 Rue des Fabrique, Brussels.
- *length 85cm*
- £200   • C.F. Seidler

Royal Engineers Busby ▼

- *circa 1910*

Royal engineers officers bear fur busby with the gilt flaming bomb incorporating the Regiments insignia, and patent leather chinstrap.
- *height 14cm*
- £375   • C.F. Seidler

Fintlock Pistol ▲

- *circa 1790*

English flintlock three barrel tap action pistol made by Clarke of London. 62 Cheapside London.
- *length 21cm*
- £1,900   • Michael German

Captain's Jacket and Hat ▼

- *1855*

Scarlet tunic of a Captain in the First Royal Tower Hamlets Miliita (The King's Own Light Infantry). Collar insignia of Crown and Pip with tin case by Flight Military Tailors, Winchester, containing belts and sashes. Plus an Officer's shako (without plume) with K.O.L.I plate.
- *large*
- £1,650   • Gordon's

General's Aiguilettes ▼

- *1940*

Third Reich General's aiguilettes, in good condition with only minor damage to parts of the gilt wiring.
- *length 42cm*
- £185   • Gordon's

32 Calibre Percussion Revolver ◀

- *1860*

32 calibre double action Adams revolver, with hexagonal barrel, made under licence by Mass Arms. Co. U.S.A. with modern bullet mould.
- *length 21.5cm*
- £550   • C.F. Seidler

Islamic Stirrups ▲

- *17th century*

A pair of bronze Islamic stirrups which are finely engraved with floral designs.
- *height 15cm*
- £150　　　　　• Ghaznavid

French Fireman's Helmet ▲

- *1895*

A highly ornate late nineteenth century brass French fireman's helmet, complete with red feather plume.
- £225　　　• Chelsea (OMRS)

World War II RAF Ashtray ▼

- *World War II*

An aluminum ashtray made from the piston of a Rolls Royce Merlin engine. Includes RAF emblem and Churchill dedication.
- *diameter 31cm*
- £25　　　• Chelsea (OMRS)

Girl's Hitler Youth Uniform ▶

- *circa 1940*

A blouson from a girl's uniform of the Hitler Youth, dating from the beginning of World War II and emblazoned with the insignia of the National Socialist party.
- *length 34cm*
- £150　　　• Chelsea (OMRS)

World War II German Paratrooper's Helmet ◀

- *1944*

A World War II paratrooper's helmet with single German airforce emblem, carrying decal camouflage painted for Normandy.
- £2,000　　• Chelsea (OMRS)

British SAS Uniform ▼

- *1990*

A British SAS sergeant's uniform and medals for the Falklands and Gulf War period (medals are replacements).
- £250　　　• Chelsea (OMRS)

Expert Tips

Weapons must be cleaned very carefully in order to maintain them, and should be stored in a dry, well-ventilated place. Always wear cotton gloves when handling fine weapons and armour to prevent the formation of rust deposits.

Victorian Pioneers Sword ▼

- *1890*

A late Victorian side-arm sword with sheath, the blade in steel and the hilt in brass, with the sheath mounted in brass and leather. From the Regiment of Pioneers.
- *length 58cm*
- £200　　　• Chelsea (OMRS)

Katena Sword ▼

- **circa 17th century**
17th-century katena sword. The
blade is 17th century, unsigned,
probably mino den. Lacquer and
wood scabbard
with manta-ray skin hilt.
- **£2,500**   • Don Bayney

Japanese Kabuto ▼

- **circa 18th century**
Sixty-two plate 18th-century
Japanese kabuto with mempi face
mask, maidate crest of a demon
and gilded lacquer neck bard.
- *height 51cm*
- **£3,500**   • Don Bayney

Officer's Dispatch Pouch ▼

- **1842**
Officer's dress dispatch pouch. A
cartridge box of 1st Dragoons
with silver flap. Hallmarked,
London 1842. Leather backed
with detailing of an eagle taken
from French Pensinsular War.
- *length 19cm*
- **£575**   • C.F. Seidler

Marching Drum ▼

- **circa 1950**
1st Battalion Coldstream Guards
marching drum. Good condition.
Painted and enamelled.
- *height 40cm*
- **£1,200**   • The Armoury

Expert Tips

*Complete sets of armour
virtually never appear on sale
these days, and helmets,
breastplates and even good
19th-century reproductions are
very collectable. Armour should
be protected with wax
after polishing.*

Rootes Colt ◀

- **1855**
.28 calibre Rootes colt. Five
shot cap and ball revolver.
Hexagonal barrel with a
sheath trigger.
- *length 21cm*
- **£495**   • C.F. Seidler

SMF Solinger German Dirk ▲

- **1937**
German Luftwaffe flying
personnel dirk. Bakelite handle,
plain blade with hanging straps
and epée portepée. Made by SMF
Solinger.
- *length 42cm*
- **£350**   • C.F. Seidler

Japanese Dagger ▲

- **1900**
Profusely carved elephant ivory
aikuichi showing scholarly scenes
with kodzukea and hrrimono
dragon carved on the reverse.
- *length 23cm*
- **£1,600**   • Don Bayney

Georgian Sword ▼
- *circa 1800*

Georgian officer's sabre with blue and gilt blade. Maker Johnston late Bland and Foster Sword Cutler and belt maker to his Majesty, 68 St. James' Street London.
- *length 92cm*
- £1,700   • Michael German

Fighting Axe ▼
- *circa 15th century*

Gothic fighting axe with iron blade and steel insert, with a later wooden shaft for display purposes.
- *length 158cm*
- £900   • C.F. Seidler

Jade Dagger ▲
- *circa 1800*

Indian dagger with mutton fat jade handle, inlaid with semi - precious stones, water steel blade and red cloth covered scabbard.
- *length 41cm*
- £3,800   • Michael German

Tibetan Helmet ▲
- *circa 1540*

15th century Tibetan helmet fashioned from iron plates, with plume holder.
- *height 32cm*
- £1,900   • Michael German

Luftwaffe Flying Helmet ▲
- *1940*

Luftwaffe flying helmet. Summer issue version, with canvas hood, straps, leads and sockets still present. Stamped inside earpiece. Ln 26602.
- *height 19cm*
- £245   • Gordon's

Pin Fire Revolver ▼
- *circa 1817*

Ten shot ll mil. pin fire revolver made in Belgium and proofed in Birmingham with matching numbers.
- *length 29cm*
- £800   • C.F. Seidler

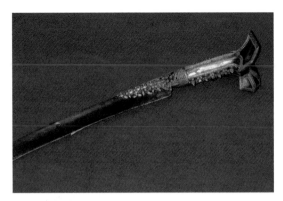

Turkish Sword ▲

- *circa 1840*
Turkish Yataghan sword with large ornate silver hilt with extending ears and blade with maker's stamp.
- *length 77cm*
- £1,400   • Michael German

Airforce Honour Dagger ▼

- *1937*
Airforce honour dagger 1st pattern known as Bordoich, complete with hanging chains.
- *length 39cm*
- £295   • Gordon's

Helmet Plate ▼

- *1914*
Baden Reservists gilt metal helmet plate, modelled as a griffin centered with shield and cross swords.
- *width 14cm*
- £65   • C.F. Seidler

Artillery Parade Tunic ▼

- *1936*
Waffenrock Gebirgsjaeger artillery parade tunic, complete with ribbon bar of 5 and breast eagle shoulder boards.
- *medium*
- £325   • Gordon's

Regimental Sash Plate ▼

- *circa 1900*
South Lancashire colour sash plate commemorating all the battles that the regiment had served, with a blue enamelled and gilt foliate design below the fleur de lys.
- *diameter 10cm*
- £495   • C.F. Seidler

Light Infantry Buckle ▲

- *1881*
Duke of Somerset's Light Infantry officers belt buckle. With worn gilt, 1881 patent.
- *width 13cm*
- £120   • C.F. Seidler

Indian Axe ▲

- *circa 1830*
Ornate Indian battle axe with concealed dagger in handle, with ornate copper and brass chiselled overlay and steel blade with elephants and lion finials.
- *length 57cm*
- £1,100   • Michael German

Breech-Loading Cannon ▶

- *1880*
Rare bronze breech-loading
cannon on oak stand by Astley.
- *length 120cm*
- £15,000
- Holland & Holland

Lifeguard Boots ▲

- *1950s*
A pair of post-World War II dress
boots of a trooper from the Royal
Regiment of Lifeguards.
- *height 43cm*
- £150   • Chelsea (OMRS)

Japanese Stirrups ▲

- *19th century*
Pair of bronze Japanese stirrups,
with red leather interior from the
Tokugawa period.
- *width 12cm*
- £895   • Japanese Gallery

Great War
Commemorative Frame ▲

- *circa 1918*
A World War I commemorative
picture frame in bronze, modelled
as a relief map of France and
Belgium, with a circular glass
portal displaying the photograph
of a soldier.
- *height 16cm*
- £85   • Chelsea (OMRS)

English Copper
Powder Flask ▲

- *circa 1800*
An English copper powder flask,
used for the storage of powder
for guns.
- *length 12cm*
- £180   • Holland & Holland

World War II German
Red Cross Dagger ◀

- *World War II*
A World War II German red
cross man's "heuer" dress dagger,
with serrated edge and blood
gutter.
- *length 30cm*
- £375   • Chelsea (OMRS)

WWII German
Airforce Tunic ▲

- *1940*
A flight blouse of a German
airforce signals section, from the
Battle of Britain period, complete
with insignia and collar flashes.
- £395   • Chelsea (OMRS)

Army Officer's Home Service Helmet ▲

- *Edwardian*
A Royal West Kent Regiment
officer's blue cloth home service
helmet, with brass insignia and
embellishments including spiked
finial top.
- £450 • Chelsea (OMRS)

World War I German Helmet Badge ▲

- *1914*
The helmet badge of a Prussian
soldier from the beginning of
World War I, with the crowned
eagle of the emperor and the
inscription, "Mitt Gott fur
Koenig und Vaterland".
- *height 9cm*
- £50 • Chelsea (OMRS)

Cigarette Gift Tin ▶

- *1914*
An example of a gift tin sent by
Queen Mary to the troops
fighting in France for the first
Christmas of World War I.
Complete with photographs,
monogrammed cigarettes and all
the original contents.
- *18cm x 11cm*
- £125 • Chelsea (OMRS)

Child's Replica Guard's Uniform ▼

- *1936*
A child's replica uniform with the
insignia of a lieutenant and
complete with medals, brass
buttons and cuffs.
- £250 • Chelsea (OMRS)

World War II German Army Helmet ▼

- *1940*
A World War II German army
1935 pattern helmet with single
army decal. With evocative bullet
hole sustained in battle.
- £175 • Chelsea (OMRS)

German Pilot's Log Books ▲

- *1936–1939*
Completed pilot's log books
covering the years 1936 to 1939.
Details the flights taken by a
German pilot.
- £175 • Chelsea (OMRS)

World War I German Helmet ▲

- *1916*
A World War I camouflaged
German army helmet of 1916
design, with original camouflage
paint and chinstrap fittings.
- £200 • Chelsea (OMRS)

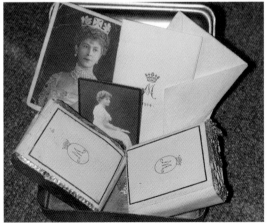

Automobilia

There is still a romance about the motor car – especially harking back to the time when there really was an open road.

Since the motor car is usually the second most expensive purchase that most people ever make, there is obviously a great deal of ancillary material – be it commemorative, promotional or aspirational – surrounding it. Models, children's pedal cars, badges, helmets, goggles, clothing, posters, paintings, photographs, autographs, clocks, lights, hub caps, radiator caps, garage equipment, cigar lighters, cigarette boxes, match strikers, log books and much more. They all haved their collectors and so they all have a price. Rarity and condition are obviously

important in the field of automobilia. Arcane knowledge is essential in establishing what is rare – some oil pouring cans were made in great numbers; some are unique. Much of automobilia collecting is based around the cult of the personality. The helmet worn by Sir Malcolm Campbell when winning the land speed record, for instance, properly authenticated, is valuable. Today's heroes, on the other hand, have a different cap for every occasion – and many of them. Invest with care.

Rolls Royce Pedal Car ▼
- 1980–90
A 12-volt, electric powered Sharna Rolls Royce Corniche convertible made by Tri-Ang.
- *122cm x 53cm*
- £700 • C.A.R.S.

Bugatti Pedal Car ▲
- *late 1920s*
A Bugatti Eureka made in France. Two-seater replica of the type 35 Grand Prix Sports with very fine chrome and leather detailing.
- *165cm x 56cm*
- £3,500 • C.A.R.S.

Tri-Ang Convertible ▲
- *mid 1960s*
A plastic Rolls Royce convertible with chrome detailing, made by Tri-Ang.
- *122cm x 46cm*
- £650 • C.A.R.S.

Expert Tips

Collecting brochures of new motor cars could be a wise investment for the future, since this kind of memorabilia increases in value.

Pedal Car ◄
- 1980–90
A Tri-Ang Sharna Rolls Royce Corniche convertible. Pedal-powered car in plastic.
- *122cm x 53cm*
- £500 • C.A.R.S.

Bentley Pedal Car ▲
- **mid 1960s**
A Tri-Ang Bentley continental convertible. Plastic body with chrome detailing.
- *122cm x 46cm*
- **£950**
- ● C.A.R.S.

Jaguar Pedal Car ▲
- **1950s–mid 1960s**
A Jaguar XK-120 open Roadster. Fibreglass body with chrome detailing, pedal powered car.
- *length 150cm, width 53cm*
- **£950**
- ● C.A.R.S.

Morgan Pedal Car ▼
- **1980**
A Morgan 4/4 Roadster with a fibreglass body and chrome detailing, and has working headlights and horn.
- *122cm x 50cm*
- **£950**
- ● C.A.R.S.

Ford Pedal Car ▼
- **Early 1960s**
A Tri-Ang Ford Zephyr-style police car with working siren and chrome detailing.
- *84cm x 36cm*
- **£300**
- ● C.A.R.S.

Fire Truck Pedal Car ▼
- **1940**
An American fire truck replica from the 1940s period. A pedal-powered car with very fine chrome detailing.
- *96cm x 38cm*
- **£200**
- ●C.A.R.S.

Massiot Locomotive ▲
- **1900**
Locomotive by Radiguet Massiot.
- *39cm x 42cm*
- **£1,900**
- ● Langfords Marine

Speed Award Badge ▲
- **1920–1930**
A Brookland's B.A.R.C. 130mph speed award badge. Converted to a trophy with enamelled decoration, showing cars banking round the Brookland's circuit.
- *height 16cm*
- **£3,500**
- ● C.A.R.S.

Chrysler Pedal Car ▲
- **late 1920s**
An American-made Chrysler "Airflow" with an all-pressed steel body and chrome detailing. Built by Steelcraft.
- *120cm x 55cm*
- **£3,000**
- ● C.A.R.S.

Japanese Cadillac ▲

- *1950*

A tin-plate Japanese 50s Marysan Cadillac, cream and green with working lights. Forward and reverse, very rare, in original box.
- *length 30cm*
- £250 • Langfords Marine

Zephyr/Zodiac Pedal Car ▲

- *mid 1950s*

A Tri-Ang Zephyr/Zodiac with a pressed-steel body and chrome detailing.
- *115cm x 42cm*
- £650 • C.A.R.S.

Wolesley Pedal Car ▲

- *late 1950s*

A Tri-Ang pressed-steel bodied model of a Wolesley with chrome detailing and working headlights.
- *105cm x 43cm*
- £450 • C.A.R.S.

Moscouich Pedal Car ▲

- *early 1980s–mid 1990s*

A Moscouich pressed-steel pedal car with working lights and horn.
- *109cm x 44cm*
- £350 • C.A.R.S.

Pedal Fire Truck ▲

- *early 1920s*

An American-made fire truck with fine detailing. Wooden ladder with mascot on bonnet.
- *105cm x 52cm*
- £3,500 • C.A.R.S.

F3 Racing Pedal Car ▼

- *early 1970s*

A Tri-Ang plastic-bodied F3 racing car with dummy rear engine.
- *122cm x 63cm*
- £150 • C.A.R.S.

Brookland's Badge ▲

- *1920*

A Brookland's B.A.R.C 120mph speed award badge.
- *height 13cm*
- £3,000 • C.A.R.S.

Expert Tips

Rarity and condition are important in the field of automobilia. Some knowledge is essential in establishing what is rare as well as documentation to authenticate provenance.

MG Pedal Car ▼

- *1950s*

An MG TD pedal-powered car with a fibreglass body and chrome detailing.
- *122cm x 51cm*
- £650 • C.A.R.S.

Morgan Club Badge ▲

- *2001*

Morgan Sports Car Club present day membership badge, known as 'Sex Mog.' Cut brass with plastic based enamel colours.
- *diameter 7cm*
- £25   • C.A.R.S.

Jaguar Mascot ▲

- *circa 1925–30*

Jaguar leaping cat car mascot by Desmo, after a design by Frederick Gordon Crosby, cast brass, chrome plated and mounted on a radiator cap. An after sales accessory mascot popular during the inter-war period.
- *length 20cm*
- £300   • C.A.R.S.

Rolls-Royce Mascot ▶

- *circa 1920s*

Rolls-Royce flying lady known as 'The Spirit of Ecstasy' designed by Charles Sykes and patented in 1911. This very tall example is from the pre World War 1 period. In cast brass, nickel plated sometimes silver plated
- *height 17cm*
- £1,250   • C.A.R.S.

R. A. C. Silver Jubilee Badge ▼

- *1977*

R.A.A Queen's Silver Jubilee 1977 specially produced limited edition commemorative badge sold with certificate. Die struck brass chrome plated with plastic based enamel colours.
- *diameter 10cm*
- £200   • C.A.R.S.

British Motor Racing Badge ▲

- *circa 1940s*

British Motor Racing Marshall's badge produced in die struck brass, chrome plated with vitreous enamel colours.
- *12cm x 9cm*
- £150   • C.A.R.S.

B. A. R. C. Badge ▲

● *1920–30s*
Brookland Automobile Racing Club. Special speed award for attaining a timed lap speed of 120 mph or more on the outer circuit. The red vitreous enamel label riveted beneath the wings.
● *height 14cm*
● **£5,500**   ● **C.A.R.S.**

B. A. R. C. Badge ▲

● *circa 1930s*
Brookland Automobile Racing Club committee members' badge (a standard issue badge with the legend 'Committee' on a yellow label beneath the wings, only a very few were issued) 1,500.
● *height 14cm*
● **£2,000**   ● **C.A.R.S.**

Expert Tips

The most famous car mascot is the Spirit of Ectasy, which was created for Rolls Royce by Charles Sykes in 1910. The earliest and most prized mascot is that for the Vulcan Motor Company from 1903.

B. A. R. C. Badge ▼

● *From 1907*
Brookland Automobile Racing Club member's and guests brooches. Every year on joining a member would be issued with a pin brooch tag in gilt brass with vitreous coloured enamel centre with two smaller versions on coloured string for the guests. These were sent to the member in an official box with the matching year date shown. The dates issued were from the opening of the circuit in 1910.
● *height 14cm*
● **boxed sets £200**   ● **C.A.R.S.**

Brooklands Aero Club Badge ▼

● *circa 1930s*
Brooklands Aero Club membership badge issued during the inter-war period up until the closure of the circuit in 1939. Die cast brass, chrome plated and vitreous coloured enamels. Produced by Spencer of London.
● *height 14cm*
● **£550**   ● **C.A.R.S.**

M. S. C. C. Badge ▲

● *circa 1970–80*
M.S.C.C. Morgan Sports Car Club shield shape membership badge of the 4/4 owner's (special anniversary issue dates thereon) Die struck with vitreous coloured enamels.
● *height 14cm*
● **£75**   ● **C.A.R.S.**

Steering Wheel Ashtray ▲

● *circa 1950s*
Ashtray in the form of a steering wheel in moulded porcelain produced by Beswick, England for Les Leston (Motoring Suppliers).
● *diameter 19cm*
● **£55**   ● **C.A.R.S.**

J.C.C. Ashtray ▲

● *circa 1920s*
Ashtray of the J.C.C. Junior Car Club produced in epns, with the club badge positioned in the centre.
● *diameter 14cm*
● **£75**   ● **C.A.R.S.**

Bentley Mascot ▲

- *circa 1955*
The Bentley 'Flying B' mascot, on the pressure cap of an "S" series Bentley.
- £250 • C.A.R.S.

Measuring Cans ▲

- *circa 1930*
A two-gallon and a five-gallon metering vessel with copper bodies and heavy-duty brass banding. The cans show funnel tops and brass spouts, positioned to prevent over-filling. The five-gallon vessel with hinged carrying-handle.
- £195; £180 • Castlegate

Expert Tips

Rolls Royce's success with the Schneider Trophy led them to offer models of the Supermarine S.6B aeroplane as alternative mascots to the Spirit of Ecstasy. These were unpopular and are, consequently, highly collectable.

Formula I Book ▶

- *circa 1999*
A pop-up book entitled *The Formula I Pack*, by Van der Meer.
- *height 32cm*
- £30 • Motor

Badge / Trophy ▼

- *circa 1930*
A Brooklands Automobile Racing Club badge converted to a trophy, with enamelled decoration showing cars banking.
- £450 • C.A.R.S.

Bugatti Book ▼

- *circa 1997*
Memoirs of a Bugatti Hunter by Antoine Raffaëlli.
- *height 42cm*
- £32.50 • Motor

Bentley Emblem ▲

- *circa 1935*
Bentley 'Flying B' designed by Joseph Fraey for the Derby open roadster. In nickel-plated bronze mounted on a marble base.
- *width 20cm*
- £500 • C.A.R.S.

Carrera RS ▲

- *circa 1992*
Illustrated Porsche book entitled *Carrera RS*, by T. A. G. Verlag. Printed in Austria.
- *height 34cm*
- £139 • Motor

Books, Maps & Atlases

Most books are more prized for their binding than for their contents. Where the contents were most prized, the print dealers have usually benefitted.

The first real books were produced during the fifth century AD, after the fall of the Roman Empire. Much of the old writing in the form of scrolls and tablets had been destroyed, but many were saved by monks who hid them in their monasteries and continued with the writings on parchment, often adding drawings or paintings to decorate the sheets. As the sheets grew in numbers, they were sewn together in sections so that the sequence of writing was maintained. Later, several sections were gathered together and bound between wooden boards, the outer surfaces of which were often beautifully carved. In the unlikely event of

your coming across one of these, it will make you very rich indeed. The real production of books in any quantities started in the middle of the fifteenth century, but they were not available to the masses until much later – basically, when books became cheaper and the masses could read. By the nature of the materials used in their manufacture, books have not lasted well. As with almost all antiques, it is unwise to pay heavily for books that have been considerably restored. On the other hand, books with good interiors, but broken bindings or torn boards, can be rebound by hand relatively cheaply, and this is a practice that can only enhance the book's value.

The Great River ▼
- 1911
The Great River by Frederick Oakes Sylvester. The book contains poetry and illustrations throughout and has an embossed and gilded leather binder.
- *15cm x 21cm*
- £350 • Chelsea Gallery

The Lion, the Witch and the Wardrobe ▲
- 1950
The Lion, the Witch and the Wardrobe by C.S. Lewis. First edition. Illustrations and colour frontispiece by Pauline Baynes. The first and best known of the Narnia chronicles. Post 8vo. Bound in an elegant recent green quarter-morocco, banded and gilt. Published by Geoffrey Bles.
- £850 • Ash Books

Antique Globe ▼
- 1862
Antique terrestrial globe by Malby. Brass meridian ring, horizon circle on four upright mahogany legs.
- 43cm x 48cm
- £6,400 • Langfords Marine

David Robert's Spain ▲

- *1837*

First edition of David Robert's first set of published views of Spain. Finely bound in half dark green morocco with gilt tooled green moire cloth, hand coloured tinted lithograph title and 25 hand coloured tinted lithograph plates by Thomas Allom, W. Gauchi, Thomas Shotter boys, Louis Hage and T. S. Cooper after David Robert.
- *height 56cm*
- **£6,000**   • Peter Harrington

Expert Tips

Leather binding needs care and regular inspection – a wipe with a cloth smeared with Vaseline will help prevent the leather from drying out.

The Fairy Tales of the Brothers Grimm ▲

- *1909*

A beautiful copy of *The Fairy Tales of the Brothers Grimm*, limited edition: number 41 of 750, signed on the limitation page by Arthur Rackham. Originally bound by Bayntun Riviere of Bath and more recently in full burgundy morocco, with gilt titles.
- *height 29.5cm*
- **£4,950**   • Peter Harrington

Alhambra ▼

- *1835*

John F. Lewis's sketches and drawings of the *Alhambra*, made during a residence in Granada, in the years 1833-4. Published in London by Hogson, Boys & Graves. Bound in recent half dark brown morocco with gilt title, ruling to the spine and 25 tinted lithograph plates by Lewis, Harding, Lane & Gauchi.
- *height 55cm*
- **£2,750**   • Peter Harrington

Bill the Minder ▼

- *1912*

Bill the Minder by W. Heath Robinson. Limited edition of 380 copies, of which this is no.167. Signed on the limitation page by Arthur Rackham. Bound by the Chelsea Bindery, others untrimmed. With sixteen colour plates and many monochrome illustrations by W. Heath Robinson.
- *height 29.5cm*
- **£2,750**   • Peter Harrington

The Old Regime Court, Salons, and Theatres ▶

- *1880*

The Old Regime Court, Salons, and Theatres by Lady Catherine Charlotte. Published by Richard Bentley & Son, London - Vol.II, with Madam Geoffrin. From the library of W. A. Foyle with ex-libris.
- *height 20cm*
- **£9,750**   • Peter Harrington

The Wind in the Willows ▲

- *1908*

First edition of *The Wind in the Willows*, by Kenneth Grahame. With a frontispiece by Graham Robertson. Methuen & Co. Ltd. London. Publisher's blue cloth with gilt titles and illustrations.
- *height 20cm*
- **£4,500**   • Peter Harrington

Ulysses ▲

- *1922*

First edition of *Ulysses* by James Joyce. Limited to 1000 copies on Dutch handmade paper. This is one of 750 printed on handmade paper and numbered 501 (of 251 - 1000). Published by Shakespeare and Company, 12, Rue de L'Odeon, Paris.
- *height 26cm*
- **£23,500**   • Peter Harrington

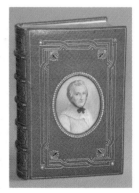

Life of Wellington ▼
• *1914*
Life of Wellington by W.H.
Maxwell. Leather bound and
gilded and signed on the binding.
• *15cm x 22cm*
• £190   • Chelsea Gallery

Map of London ▼
• *mid 18th century*
A map of London and
surrounding environs with
vignettes covering Chelsea,
Greenwich, Kensington,
Hampton Court and Windsor,
by J.B. Homamm.
• *51cm x 60cm*
• £900   • Chelsea Gallery

The Compleat Angler ▼
• *1931*
The Compleat Angler by Izaak
Walton with fine, hand-coloured
illustrations of rural themes by
Arthur Rackham. Limited
edition.
• *27cm x 20cm*
• £750   • Chelsea Gallery

Voyages de Cook ▼
• *1774*
A first edition complete set of
thirteen volumes in French.
Illustrated throughout including
the "Death of Cook".
• *height 30cm*
•£13,000   • Chelsea Gallery

Coxe's Travels in Poland ◀
• *1784*
A two-volume set with a full calf
binding, with various illustrations
and maps. The book includes
travels to Poland, Russian,
Sweden and Denmark.
• £600   • Chelsea Gallery

Descriptions de L'Egypte ▲
• *circa 1820*
A second edition complete set,
comprising eleven volumes and
almost a thousand copper
engraved plates of various studies
of Egypt. Subjects include
architecture, natural history,
geography, views and city life.
Commissioned by Napoleon and
published by C.L.F. Panckouke.
Half Moroccan binding.
• *72cm x 55cm*
• £35,000   • Chelsea Gallery

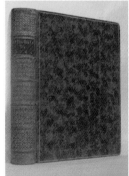

Antichita Di Roma ▲
• *1763*
A book of the antiquities of
Rome by Ridolfino Venuti
Cortonese and published by
Bernabo & Lazzarini. This is a
first edition and consists of 96
copper engraved plates depicting
architectural views and Roman
ruins. Leather bound and gilded.
• *28cm x 22cm*
• £2,400   • Chelsea Gallery

49

Sense and Sensibility ▼

- *1811*

First edition of Jane Austen's masterpiece, *Sense and Sensibility*. Published in London by T. Egerton, 1811. Three volumes, finely bound in contemporary mottled calf.
- *18.5cm x 11.4cm*
- **£60,000** • **Peter Harrington**

How the Grinch Stole Christmas ▼

- *1957*

First edition of *How the Grinch Stole Christmas* by Dr. Seuss. Published by Random House, New York. Original pictorial paper covered boards. Housed in a red cloth solander box with a green gilt lettered label. Illustrated by the author. Inscribed in the first blank page, 'for Pamela Benepe! Dr. Seuss'.
- *29cm x 20cm*
- **£6,500** • **Peter Harrington**

Doctor Zhivago ▶

- *1958*

First edition of *Doctor Zhivago* by Boris Pasternak translated from the Russian by Max Hayward and Manya Harari. Collins and Harvill Press, London. Original publisher's red cloth, felt lettered spine, complete with dust wrapper.
- *21cm x 14cm*
- **£150** • **Peter Harrington**

Arabian Nights ▲

- *1937*

The Arabian Nights by Parish Maxfield. Edited by Kate Douglas Wiggin and Nora A. Smith published in New York by Charles Scribner and Sons. Illustrated by Maxfield Parish with 9 colour illustrations.
- *24cm x 17cm*
- **£75** • **Peter Harrington**

Omar Khayyam ▲

- *1884*

Rubiyat of Omar Khayyam rendered into English verse by Edward Fitzgerald with drawings by Elihu Vedder. Published by Houghton Mifflin and Company, Boston.
- *40cm x 33cm*
- **£475** • **Peter Harrington**

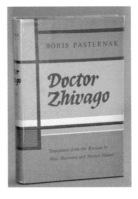

Poems by Christina Rossetti ▼

- *circa 1920*

Poems by Christina Rossetti with illustrations by Florence Harrison published by Blackie and Son.
- *26cm x 21cm*
- **£475** • **Peter Harrington**

Winnie the Pooh ▼

- *1924-8*

Set of books by A.A. Milne including: 'When We Were Very Young', 'Winnie the Pooh', 'Now We Are Six', and 'The House at Pooh Corner'.
- *22cm x 15cm*
- **£12,000** • **Peter Harrington**

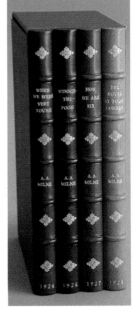

Harry Potter ▼

- **1997–2000**

An extremely scarce set of first editions of the *Harry Potter* series by J.K. Rowling, which includes: 'The Philosopher's Stone', 'The Chamber of Secrets', 'The Prisoner of Azkaban' and 'The Goblet of Fire'. Published by Bloomsbury, London. All signed.
- *20cm x 13cm*
- **£27,500** • Peter Harrington

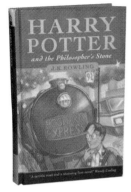

The Cat in the Hat ▼

- **1957**

First edition of *The Cat in the Hat* by Dr. Seuss. Original pictorial paper covered boards complete with dust wrapper. Illustrated throughout by the author.
- *29cm x 21cm*
- **£8,500** • Peter Harrington

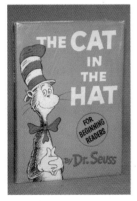

Peter Rabbit ▶

- **1902**

The Tale of Peter Rabbit by Beatrix Potter. First edition, and first issue of the flat spine.
- *14cm x 10cm*
- **£50,000** • Peter Harrington

Three Guineas ▲

- **1938**

First edition of *Three Guineas* by Virginia Woolf. Published by The Hogarth Press, London. Pale yellow cloth, gilt titles to spine, complete with dust wrapper. Illustrated with photographic plates.
- *18cm x 12cm*
- **£500** • Peter Harrington

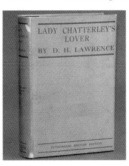

Lady Chatterley's Lover ▲

- **1932**

First authorised UK edition of *Lady Chatterley's Lover* by D.H Lawrence. Publisher's brown cloth with gilt title to spine. Complete with dust wrapper. Published by Martin Secker, London.
- *19cm x 12.4cm*
- **£450** • Peter Harrington

Little Lord Fauntleroy ▼

- **1886**

First UK edition of *Little Lord Fauntleroy* by Francis Hodgson Burnett. London: Frederick, Warne and Co. With 26 illustrations after Reginald B. Birch.
- *22cm x 14.5cm*
- **£210** • Peter Harrington

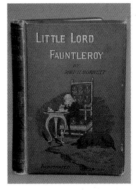

The Hound of Death and Other Stories ▼

- **1933**

The Hound of Death and Other Stories by Agatha Christie. First edition. Published by Odhams Press Limited, London.
- *18.5cm x 13cm*
- **£350** • Peter Harrington

Expert Tips

Most paper items are susceptible to damage from ultraviolet (UV) and visible light. If UV is present it should be eliminated using filters over windows and bulbs.

Mappe Monde ▶

- *circa 1730*
Double hemisphere world map by
M. Seutter. Hand coloured and
copper engraved.
- *63cm x 55cm*
- £3,800   • Chelsea Gallery

The Old Curiosity Shop ▼

- *1841*
First edition of Dickens novel
in good condition. Full calf
binding and gilt floral decoration
by Rowler.
- *height 16cm*
- £400   • Chelsea Gallery

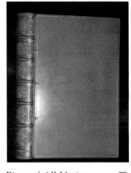

Pipes of All Nations ▼

- *1890*
Review of various pipes around
the world, by R.T. Pritchett.
Complete with 46 plates and
original binder. Slightly worn.
- *height 28cm*
- £700   • Chelsea Gallery

Journal of a Residence ▶

- *date 1824*
Account of life in nineteenth
century Chile published by John
Murray. In English, including 14
aquaintant plates. Fine condition.
- £1,200   • Paul Orssich

Gallery of the Graces ▶

- *1837*
The *Gallery of the Graces* is a
book of portraits and contains 36
copper engravings by Finden and
was published by Charles Tilt.
- *29cm x 22 cm*
- £350   • Chelsea Gallery

The Loves of the Poets ◀

- *1860*
Twelve steel plate engravings by
the most eminent artists of the
day. Published by W. Kent & Co
(Late D. Bogue).
- *30cm x 23 cm*
- £120   • Chelsea Gallery

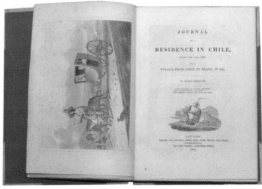

Moore's Poetical Works ◀

- *circa 1850*

A beautifully bound book of poetry entitled *Moore's Poetical Works*, containing 48 steel engraved portraits. Published by The London Printing and Publishing Company.
- *34cm x 26cm*
- £850   • Chelsea Gallery

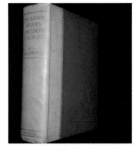

The Salmon Rivers and Lochs of Scotland ▲

- *1909*

The Salmon Rivers and Lochs of Scotland by W.L. Calderwood with original binder and in good condition. A limited edition book, only 250 produced.
- *height 23cm*
- £550   • Chelsea Gallery

Celestial Chart ▼

- *1742*

A celestial map by Doppelmayr of the northern hemisphere. It has been hand coloured and engraved by Honann, and shows the celestial sky and the heroes of mythology.
- *64cm x 55cm*
- £1,400   • Chelsea Gallery

Bartolozzi ▲

- *19th century*

Stipple engravings of the mythological characters Cupid and Psyche, in original frames.
- *diameter 40cm*
- £1,600   • Chelsea Gallery

The Children's Natural History Scrap Album ▲

- *1887*

A 55-page book of collected stickers with original binder and gilding.
- *height 42cm*
- £280   • Chelsea Gallery

Mobile Etude ▲

• ***1962***

Mobile Etude pour une Representation des Etats Unis. by Michel Butor. Published in Paris by Gallimard. One of 25 numbered copies with contemporary black leather backed dark grey boards and an intricate mosaic onlay of coloured paper cubes. Preserved in original grey board cover with perspex back, t.e.g., matching grey board slipcase. This work is dedicated to Jackson Pollock.

• *23.6cm x 18.7cm*

• **£5,000** • **Bernard Shapero**

Bronze Book Box ▲

• ***mid-19th century***

A set of three household books including cash accounts, journal, and visitor and address book. London, 3 vols. Uniformly bound in red morocco, red morocco labels on spine. Preserved in the original red morocco brass box, each side decorated with 3 large banded chalcedony in cabochon setting, the clasps with one large cabochon, the whole can be locked, with original key in side.

• *18cm x 11cm*

• **£2,500** • **Bernard Shapero**

Tacitus ▼

• ***1809***

Folding engraved frontispiece map, with contemporary vellum, in the style of Edwards of Halifax. The covers are decoratively bordered in gilt, the front cover with a watercolour of Buckingham Palace and the back cover with a watercolour of Garrick's Villa At Hampton. With the inscription,"De Moribus Germanorum, et de Vita Agricolae. Ex editione Gabrielis Brotier. Locis annalium et historiarum ab eo citatis, selectis et additis, cura Richardi Relhan Cambridge".

• *24.4cm x 15cm*

• **£6,000** • **Bernard Shapero**

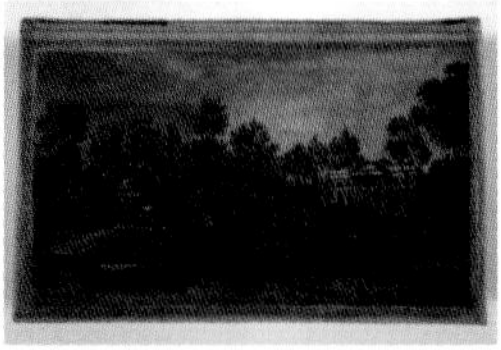

Rosalind and Helen ▼

• ***1820***

Rosalind and Helen by Shelley, Percy Bysshe. London, Ollie. First edition. Magnificently bound by Sangorski & Sutcliffe in dark blue morocco, richly gilt, adorned with 92 jewels, the upper cover with gilt border decorated with foliage and dot-work, with red fruit onlays, around panel of white morocco within which is an elaborate design of interleaved hearts in different colours around a large gilt fleur-de-lys, interspersed with floral designs. The back cover with gilt border surrounding a panel inlaid with a mother-of-pearl lyre. The back liner with a flat panel containing a mother-of-pearl heart, both these panels surrounded by an inlaid design of vines and grapes.

• *22.5cm x 13.5cm*

• **£30,000** • **Bernard Shapero**

Bible ▲

• ***1690–1700***

Biblia Das Is De Gantsche H. Schrifture. Published in Amsterdam by N. Burgers, 1681. Title within architectural border, tortoiseshell binding, (1690-1700), with engraved silver book furniture, corner pieces, two small hinges to each joint, clasps, one clasp with initials of the owner engraved on the inside.

• *14cm x 8cm*

• **£5,000** • **Bernard Shapero**

The Tempest ▲

• ***1926***

The Tempest by William Shakespeare, illustrated by Arthur Rackham. London, William Heinemann. In contemporary full deep-blue morocco du cap, the lower board and decorated doublure are decorated in an elaborate grolieresque retrospective design consisting of onlaid, interlaced strapwork in three colours, red, saffron and tan, all edged in gilt. The book itself is one of 520 copies, reserved for America and signed in ink by Arthur Rackham.

• *29.5cm x 23cm*

• **£2,500** • **Bernard Shapero**

Early Binding for Pillone ▼

• *15 April 1507*
Extremely rare early 16th century North Italian binding of half blind-stamped morocco over bevelled wooden boards, leather clasps at top and bottom and two at fore-edge. The title and Pillone arms are painted on the upper board, and the leaf of a large format legal work is used as front endpaper. The binding is preserved in a modern cloth covered box and comes from the library of Odorico Pillone.
• *45cm x 29cm*
• **£20,000**   • **Bernard Shapero**

Miniature Renaissance Binding ▼

• *1621*
French Missal binding in gold, glass, enamel and one emerald. Missel. Troyes, C. de Villiers. Contains calendar for the years 1621-37, bound in a preserved contemporary binding of green glass cut in imitation of rose emeralds, each attached by 4 gold clasps to a gold enamelled white background. This binding contains one emerald, but where it is in the binding, no-one has recorded.
• *5cm x 3.5cm*
• **£65,000**   • **Bernard Shapero**

Scribbling Pad ▲

• *circa 1580*
German scribbling pad, (possibly Dresden). This fine 16th century binding has been attributed to Jakob Krause, who was active in Dresden during the last quarter of the 16th century, working predominantly for elector Augustus of Saxony (one of the foremost patrons for book bindings of the Renaissance). In spite of the provenance of the binding, the surviving entries in the book are in Italian. Some of Krause's works are known to have been presented to foreign rulers. German renaissance bindings are of the greatest rarity.
• *14.5cm x 10cm*
• **£6,750**   • **Bernard Shapero**

Book of Common Prayer ▲

• *1638*
The book of Common Prayer and Administration of the Sacraments: and other Rites and Ceremonies of the Church of England [and] the New Testament . Published in London by Robert Barker and in Edinburgh by Robert Young, 1638. This is a presentation of prayers by Queen Anne. Preserved in the J.R. Abbey collection, with large morocco gilt label describing its royal provenance.
• *17cm x 11.5cm*
• **£22,500**   • **Bernard Shapero**

The Old Regime Court, Salons, and Theatres ▼

• *1880*
The Old Regime Court, Salons, and Theatres by Lady Catherine Charlotte. Published by Richard Bentley & Son, London. Full tan morocco with full gilt decorated spine and covers. Enhanced with hand painted oval portraits, Vol 1. With La Duchess de Berri. The portrait is surrounded with seed-pearls.
• *height 20cm*
• **£9,750**   • **Peter Harrington**

The Beautiful and the Damned ▼

• *1922*
Presentation copy of *The Beautiful and the Damned* inscribed twice by F. Scott Fitzgerald. The first inscription reads:- 'Sincerely F Scott Fitzgerald' and the later reads: 'Believe it or not this was in this book when it came to me from the Tyron bookshop. I must have autographed it for some book-seller and it fell into a stock of remainders. Such is fame.' Charles Scribner and Sons.
• *height 19cm*
• **£22,500**   • **Peter Harrington**

The Mill on the Floss ▼
- **1860**
By George Eliot. William Blackwood & Sons, Edinburgh and London. First edition, in the more elaborate gilt binding. Three volumes. Original cloth gilt, expertly recased and refurbished.
- *20cm x 13cm*
- **£750**   • **Ash Books**

Map by Ortelius ▼
- **1586**
Ortelius was the first person to publish a map. Shows Iberian peninsula in full contemporary colour. The language text, page number and pagination signature are the key to dating the copper engraving on paper.
- *38cm x 50cm*
- **£250**   • **Paul Orssich**

Six Volumes of Spain ▶
- **1725**
An 18th-century set of six volumes by Mariana. Covers the history of Spain. With contemporary binders and four engraved maps.
- **£600**   • **Paul Orssich**

Terrestrial and Celestial Globes ▲
- **1783–85**
Accurate and complete terrestrial and celestial globes with turned mahogany stands. Made in London, celestial date 1785.
- *diameter 23cm, height 33cm*
- **£19,500**   • **The Map House**

Book of Mexico ▲
- **1855**
A 19th-century copy by Carl Christian Sartorius. Written in Germanand entitled 'Land Shafesbilden und Skizzer'. Contains 18 plates. A good quality copy.
- *23cm x 15cm*
- **£800**   • **Paul Orssich**

Expert Tips
The value of globes was determined by the quality of the stand. Globes were relatively inexpensive.

A Grammar of Japanese Ornament and Design ▼
- **1880**
Japanese. By Thomas Cutler, with introductory text.
- *32cm x 38cm*
- **£450**   • **Bernard Shapero**

Book by Baron Taylor ▲
- 1853
Book on the Alhambra showing one plan and 10 lithographs.
- *45cm x 62cm*
- £2,500   • Paul Orssich

The Panorama.
A Traveller's Instructive Guide ▲
- 1620
17th-century book, 'A Traveller's Instructive Guide'. Published in London by J. Wallis & W.H. Reid. Original cover. 40 English county maps, 12 Welsh county maps. Clean and complete copy.
- *12cm x 9cm*
- £250   • Russell Rare Books

Spain ▼
- 1881
By Davellier. This book belonged to Isadora Duncan's lover. Attractive cloth binding with gilt. Illustrated by Gustave Dore.
- £320   • Paul Orssich

Koran ▼
- 16th–17th century
Persian Koran, illuminated double page. Many illuminations. Sura headings. Illuminated leather binding.
- *20cm x 14cm*
- £800   • Oasis

Castle and Andolucia ◄
- 1853
Lady Louisa Tennyson. With gate-folding frontispiece and 23 lithographs showing panorama of Alhambra.
- £650   • Paul Orssich

Aart Van America ▲
- late 18th century
Nieuwe K. Aart Van America. Published by D.M. Tangueld. Copper line engraving on paper with original hand colour. Dutch school.
- *22cm x 18cm*
- £195   • Ash Books

Atlas National Illustre... 1852 ▲
- 1852
By V. Levasseur. 98 handcoloured maps of France. Attractive and very decorative atlas.
- *38cm x 55cm*
- £600   • Russell Rare Books

Bambi ▼

● *1928*

Bambi: A Life in the Wood by Felix Salten. Published in London by Jonathan Cape. First edition in English. Translated from the original German by Whittaker Chamber, with an introduction by John Galsworthy. Crown 8vo. Bound in a smart recent half green morocco, banded and gilt retaining the original pictorial endpapers.

● £350   ● Ash Books

Frederick de Wit ▼

● *17th century*

Fine seventeenth-century map of the British Isles from the engraver and mapseller Frederick de Wit (1630-1706). Decorated with the arms of England, Ireland and Scotland and an attractive title-piece of frolicking nymphs. Original hand colour.

● £600   ● Ash Books

Crimson Fairy Book ▼

● *circa 1890*

First edition of the *Crimson Fairy Book* by Andrew Lang.

● £350   ● Ash Books

Chichester ▲

● *1676*

Sussex described and divided into rapes with the situation of Chichester by John Speed. Copper line engraving on paper by Jodocus Hondius.

● £750   ● Ash Books

Map of London ▲

● *1658*

Map of London by Abraham Saur. Frankfurt: Johan Bayern, Johann Willhelm Ammon & Wilhelm Serlin 1658. A scarce and previously unrecorded miniature woodcut plan of London, deriving from known sixteenth-century precursor, originally produced to illustrate *Saur's Parvum, Thetrum Urbuim*.

● £500   ● Ash Books

Map of the Americas ▲

● *1782*

Map of the Americas, published in Amsterdam: Arend Fokke 1782. Pleasant and scarce antique map of the Americas, drawn and engraved by H. Klockhoff bearing the Amsterdam imprint of Arend Fokke. Copper line engraving on paper, original hand colour.

● £125   ● Ash Books

British Isles ▼

● *circa 1706*

A map of the British Isles produced for Oorlogs Tabetten, published by Daniel de la Feuille. Copper line engraving on paper, with full original hand colour.

● £200   ● Ash Books

The World ▼

● *1777*

The World. A scarce map of the world in hemispheres, drawn and engraved by H. Knockhoff. 1777-1784, bearing the Amsterdam imprint of Arend Fokke. Published in Amsterdam 1777. Copper line engraving on paper.

● £195   ● Ash Books

Monde ▼

● *1706*

A very attractive antique map of the world in hemispheres by Daniel de la Feuille. This was originally produced for Oorlogs Tabetten and published in Amsterdam in 1706.

● £500   ● Ash Books

Map by J. Mettullus ▼
- *1601*

Very rare. Includes the Canary Islands. Showing galleons with slight lines and inset of Madiera.
- **£220**   • **Paul Orssich**

World Map ▶
- *1662*

Double hemisphere world map. Published by Johannius Blaeu, Amsterdam. Hand coloured and copper engraved. At the top, outside the twin hemispheres are celestial figures seated amid clouds.
- **£9,850**   • **The Map House**

Scrambles Amongst the Alps ▲
- *1900*

'Scrambles Amongst the Alps in the Years 1860–69' by Edward Whymper. John Murray, London. Fifth edition. 8vo, numerous maps and illustrations throughout. Original blue cloth gilt, slight wear.
- **£220**   • **Bernard Shapero**

Views in Palestine ▲
- *1803*

By Luigi Mayer. Two works in one volume. First editions. Titles and text in English and French. Historical and descriptive account of the country. 48 handcoloured aquatint plates. Spine gilt in compartments.
- **£3,500**   • **Bernard Shapero**

A History of the River Thames ◀
- *1794–96*

Published by John and Josiah Boydell, London. Spine with single gilt rubs on raised bands. Printed by W. Bulmer & Co. for John and Sonia Boydell.
- *height 40cm x 32cm*
- **£3,200**
- **Russell Rare Books**

Le Relatiani Universali di Giovanni Botero Beines ▼
- *1605*

By Giovanni Botero, Venice. Renaissance geographical and anthropological 'relatives' of Giovanni Butero. With maps and illustrations.
- *14.5cm x 20cm*
- **£1,450**   • **Ash Books**

La Terre Sainte ◀
- *1843*

Original half green morocco, folio, Brussels. Tinted lithograph title, thirty half-page and thirty full-page plates. A little foxing and marginal damp staining but a good copy.
- *38cm x 55cm*
- **£2,900**
- **Russell Rare Books**

Map of Huntingdonshire ▲

- **1645**

Map of Huntingdonshire by J.
Willem Blaeu with the
inscription, "Hvntingdo-Nensis
Comitatvs, Huntington- shire".
Published in Amsterdam.
Decorated with a ribanded
display of coats or arms, the
Stuart Royal Arms, and a hunters
and hounds title-piece, with
stags, falcon, boar, hare and
rabbit. Originally produced by
Blaeu in1645.

- **£350**　　　● Ash Books

City of London, Westminster and Southwark ▼

- **1720**

*A New Plan Of The City Of
London, Westminster And
Southwark.* Published in London:
in 1720. Originally produced to
accompany John Strype's revised
edition of John Stow's 'Survey of
London'. The map is dedicated to
Sir George Thorold, Lord Mayor
in 1719-1720.
- *48.5cm x 66cm*
- **£950**　　　● Ash Books

Map of Northumberland ▼

- **1645**

Map Of Northumberland by J.
Willem Blaeu, entitled,
"Comitatvs Northvmbria;
Vernacule Northumberland" and
produced in Amsterdam in1645.
Decorated with shields, the Royal
Arms, a draped title-piece, ships,
cherubs, and a scale-bar showing
a 17th-century surveyor at work.
Copper line engraving on paper.
Full contemporary hand colour.
- *41cm x 49cm*
- **£350**　　　● Ash Books

Map of Lothian ◄

- **circa 1500s**

A map depicting the area of
Lothian in Scotland, by the
Dutch cartographer Joannes
Janssonius, 1646, Amsterdam. A
fine example of this well-known
map of the Edinburgh region.
- *36.5 cm 54cm*
- **£400**　　　● Ash Books

Binding Fit for a King ▼

- **1620-1630**

Extremely rare Renaissance
gold binding, jewelled and
enamelled. Possibly made for
King Christian IV of Denmark.
Enamelled with a design of
different flowers, and a central
plaque with the nativity, as
decorated with 52 diamonds.
- *9.1cm x 6.4cm*
- **£85,000**　　● Bernard Shapero

Map of the Orkney & Shetland Isles ▲

- **1654**

*Map of the Orkney and Shetland
Isles* by Willem Janszoon Blaeu,
Amsterdam, 1645. With the
inscription, "Oradvm Et
SchetandiE Insvlarvm
Accuatissima Descriptio". The
maps are finely decorated.
- *40.5cm x 53cm*
- **£350**　　　● Ash Books

London ▲

- **1673**

An early map of London by
Wenceslas Hollar, with the coat
of arms of the City of London,
fifteen of the great Livery and
Merchant Companies and those
of Sir Robert Vyner of Viner.
- **£400**　　　● Ash Books

Map of Essex ▲

- **1636**

The rare first issue of the Janssonius map showing Essex, entitled,"Essexi Descriptio. The Description Of Essex". First published in Amsterdam, Holland, by the Dutch master Janssonius (1588-1664) in the 'Atlas Appendix' of 1636. With copper line engravings on paper. In full contemporary hand colour.
- *38cm x 49cm*
- **£550**　　　　● Ash Books

Map of Norfolk ▼

- *circa 1646*

A fine seventeenth century map of the county of Norfolk, England, from the Dutch master Joannes Janssonius (1588-1664). The map is highly decorated with a pastoral cartouche, shields, putti, sailing ships and a sea monster. This was originally produced for the 'inovus atlas ...' (Amsterdam 1646).
- *38cm x 49cm*
- **£395**　　　　● Ash Books

Map of Scotland ▼

- *circa 1630s*

A decorative map of Scotland by the Dutch cartographer Janssonius entitled, "Scotia Regnvm, Amsterdam" and dated1636. This map was originally produced for the 'Janssonius Atlas Appendix' of 1636. It is decorated with the royal arms, sailing ships, and a cartouche featuring unicorns, sheep and thistles.
- *38cm x 49.5cm*
- **£495**　　　　● Ash Books

Seutter British Isles ◀

- *18th century*

Original hand coloured map of the British Isles by Matthaeus Seutter. A scarce antique map of the British Isles, with an elegant military lion and unicorn cartouche. In another corner an angel with a trumpet bears aloft the arms of the four nations, and sailing ships off the coast. Originally engraved by Tobias Conrad Lotter (1717-1777) for Seutter's Atlas Minor in the 1740s.
- **£250**　　　　● Ash Books

Map of Somerset ▲

- *circa 1630s*

An amorial map of the county of Somerset, in England by Janssonius entitled "Somerset-Tensis Comitatvs Somerset Shire". Amsterdam: G.Valk & P. Schenk, 1636. This was first published by Janssonius (1588-1664).The map appears here in its final form, with the addition of grid lines to the original Janssonius image.
- *37.5cm x 49cm*
- **£395**　　　　● Ash Books

Merian Map of the British Isles ▼

- *mid 17th century*

Map of the British Isles from Mathaus Merian the Elder (1593-1650). With a baroque title piece draped in cornucopia, the Royal Arms, sailing ships etc. Originally produced for the 'Neuwe Archontolgia Cosmica' (Frankfurt 1638) and here in a later issue, with Merian's name removed.
- **£400**　　　　● Ash Books

Expert Tips

With old books and maps, look out for foxing or orange stains because these kinds of blemishes can be expensive to rectify.

Carpets & Rugs

Oriental carpets and rugs have been collected by Europeans for many centuries and need not be prohibitively expensive.

The older the civilisation, the better the carpets and rugs. In the West, the Romans invented the dome, which allowed for vast spaces within rooms and, with light pouring in from all the windows, gave some point to decorative floor covering – it was nice to look at and it kept their feet warm. During the European Dark Ages, there was a flourishing carpet industry in the Near and Middle East, creating floor coverings, wall hangings and canopies. Oriental carpets have been collected in Europe for several centuries, but somewhat

sporadically. Even in this century there was little interest until the 1960s, when a new generation of travellers started to revere the wisdom of all things Eastern. European needlework carpets of the nineteenth century have become an interesting area for the collector over the past few years, and carpets from Aubusson, where the first workshop was set up under the auspices of Louis XIV, fetch serious prices. Frequent handling, observation and buying according to your taste are the rules. Good antique carpets and rugs need not be prohibitively expensive.

Indian Rug ▶

- *circa 1998*

A rug from Rajput with an old Mughal design, using all natural dyes and clay washing.
- *length 159cm, width 91cm*
- **£575**
- Oriental Rug

Persian Rug ▲

- *circa 1940*

A Persian bidjar kilim, the blue ground woven with geometric patterns, with a strong border.
- *length 212cm, width 120cm*
- **£770**
- Oriental Rug

Expert Tips

Silk rugs are the most expensive, followed by silk/wool mix. But even wool rugs can command high prices. Look to the reverse of the rug to ascertain the tightness and fineness of the knots. This is not only an indication of the quality, but also of the longevity. More knots last longer.

Tibetan Cushion ▼

- *circa 1995*

A modern Tibetan cushion with a traditional design of stylised lotus flower in part silk.
- *40cm x 40cm*
- **£90**
- Oriental Rug

Turkish Cushion ▼

- *circa 1960*

A Turkish (Anatolia) kilim cushion, the cover of which originally came from a rug.
- *40cm x 40cm*
- **£39**
- Oriental Rug

Persian Kilim ▼

- *early 20th century*
A rare kilim from a dowry
treasure found in Luristan. Little-
used, with fine naive design in
natural dyes.
- *length 198cm, width 128cm*
- **£1,200** • Gordon Reece

Persian Rug ▼

- *circa 1998*
A fine vegetable-dyed Persian
jajim, originally used to cover the
bedding of nomadic people.
- *length 247cm, width 157cm*
- **£1,100** • Oriental Rug

Bag End Panel ▶

- *19th century*
End panel from a maprush bag.
From the Shirvan area of the
Caucusus. Slit-woven with
natural dyes.
- *length 55cm, width 32cm*
- **£310** • Gordon Reece

Persian Rug ▲

- *circa 1950*
A Karaja Persian rug.
- *length 137cm, width 107cm*
- **£550** • Oriental Rug

Persian Cushion ▲

- *circa 1960*
A Persian cushion with cover
woven by the Shasavan into
geometric, polychromatic designs
with a hexagonmal central panel.
- *40cm x 40cm*
- **£69** • Oriental Rug

Indian Rug ▼

- *circa 1996*
A vegetable-dyed Indian kilim
rug with squared, polychrome
pattern, with the red colouring
derived from the madder plant.
- *length 269cm, width 188cm*
- **£950** • Oriental Rug

Shahsavan Cushion ▼

- *circa 1940*
A Persian Shahsavan kilim
cushion. Woven by the nomadic
Shahsavan people.
- *40cm x 40cm*
- **£69** • Oriental Rug

Heriz Carpet ◀

1880

A section of antique woollen heriz with a centre medallion design and a dragon border.
- *300cm x 400cm*
- **£6,600**   • A. Rezai Persian

Dhurrie ◀

- **19th century**

Cotton wool rug, the warp and weft dyed with indigo and turmeric. Woven by Indian prisoners (code QT9775).
- *195cm x 116cm*
- **£695**   • Gordon Reece

Silk Persian Carpet ▲

- *1820*

A silk Persian carpet of a traditional Mothsham design.
- *198cm x 127cm*
- **£6,600**   • A. Rezai Persian

Tapestry Cushions ▲

- **1880**

A selection of needlepoint tapestry cushions.
- **£1,800**   • A. Rezai Persian

Gabbeh Carpet ▼

- *circa 1880*

Luri Gabbeh carpet coloured with natural dyes, showing a strong geometric pattern on a blue ground (code NZ00165).
- *215cm x 170cm*
- **£2,250**   • Gordon Reece

Expert Tips

Look out for wear and repair as this can affect the value of the carpet or rug, as can the cutting or trimming of the fringe. If a design is rare it can still fetch a high price as it can be used as a template by rug makers. It is also valuable because of its historical importance.

Tapestry ▲

- **1880**

A beautiful tapestry with stags, monkeys, a leopard, pheasants and red roses. In excellent condition.
- *180cm x 140cm*
- **£3,300**   • A. Rezai Persian

Karabagh Cushion ▲
- *1920*
Karabagh kilim converted into a
cushion cover.
- *35cm square*
- £50   ● Oriental Rug

Turkish Yurik Runner ▲
- *1870*
A section of a Turkish Yurik
runner with four hexagonal
designs of blue, red, green, and
gold in the centre panel,
surrounded by a pink border with
blue flowers.
- *length 300cm*
- £1,800   ● David Black

Bakhtiari Rug ▶
- *circa 1940*
Bakhtiari rug with a glorious
central medallion design in blue,
green, coral and cream. The
reverse of the carpet shows a very
open weaving technique with
wefts which may have a bluish
hue.
- *127cm x 207cm*
- £490   ● Oriental Rug

Luri Gabbeth Rug ▲
- *mid 20th century*
A Luri Gabbeth rug from the
Zagros mountains of southern
Persia. With bold design of red,
blue, brown and cream, the
borders with red squares and
cream centres.
- *length 180cm*
- £1,450   ● Gordon Reece

Kilim Stool ▲
- *1930*
Anotonian kilim upholstered
stool.
- *30cm x 40cm*
- £125   ● Oriental Rug

Turkaman Cushion ▲
- *1860*
Fragment of a Turkaman used as a
cushion cover.
- *47cm square*
- £150   ● David Black

Bownat Marriage Rug ▲
- *circa 1920*
Bownat marriage rug, produced
by a small tribe in Southern Iran.
The rug shows courting birds and
the name and date in Arabic of
the couple to be married. These
rugs are some of the most
beautiful tribal weaving produced
today.
- *210cm x 293cm*
- £1,650   ● Oriental Rug

Turkaman Utensils Bag ▲
- **1880**
Unusual bag for kitchen utensils
from the Turkaman tribe in
brown and cream with a
geometric design, with green and
pink tassels.
- 65cm x 36cm
- £200   • Oriental Rug

Chinese Carpet ▲
- **1850**
Section of a Chinese carpet from
the Ning Xia Province.
- 68cm *square*
- £800   • David Black

Tibetan Rug ▲
- *circa 1880*
Tibetan rug with three central
medallions and a key border in
indigo dye.
- *length 168cm*
- £1,200   • Gordon Reece

Belouch Rug ▲
- *circa 1920*
Belouch rug from western
Afghanistan and eastern Iran,
where lions from the nomadic
and semi-nomadic Belouch
Tribes represent courage. All
Belouch rugs are made with
woollen warps and wefts with
lustrous wool pile, and the
Belouch are noted for their
"prayer rug" designs. Typical
Botay design.
- 92cm x 184cm
- £420   • Oriental Rug

Needlepoint Panel ▲
- *circa 19th century*
Needlepoint panel of floral design
made into a footstool.
- *diameter 30.5cm*
- £258   • Classic Fabrics

Shahsavan Kilim ▲
- **1890**
Shahsavan kilim with broad
geometric designs in blue, red,
cream and gold.
- *width 350cm*
- £3,250   • David Black

Persian Runner ▲

- *1880*

Northwest Persian camel hair . runner with paisley design on the border. The centre features an unusual diamond-shaped geometrical design.
- *550cm x 110cm*
- £3,000 • A. Rezai Persian

Persian Rug ▲

- *early 20th century*

Persian Quashquai Gabbeh rug incorporating a strong central design within a geometric border on a red ground (code NZ00174).
- *165cm x 104cm*
- £760 • Gordon Reece

Geometric Carpet ▲

- *1820*

An unusual carpet with a dramatic geometric design incorporating a lion, cat and scorpion with stars on the border.
- *300cm x 122cm*
- £3,300 • A. Rezai Persian

Woollen Runner ▼

- *1880*

Woollen Tulish short runner of geometric design. The border design incorporating leaves.
- *240cm x 120cm*
- £2,200 • A. Rezai Persian

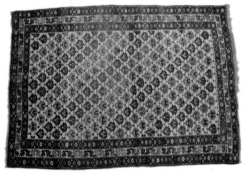

Expert Tips

Moths love a good carpet, so keep them well sprayed with anti-moth repellant.

Russian Chichi Rug ▲

- *1880*

A Russian Chichi rug with central desert flower design.
- *180cm x 120cm*
- £3,300 • A. Rezai Persian

Persian Rug ◄

- *early 20th century*
Luri Gabbeh rug from southwest
Persia. Includes a strong
geometric pattern in blue
and red and an alternating
zig-zag border.
- *200cm x 147cm*
- **£950**   • Gordon Reece

Gabbeh Carpet ▲

- *20th century*
Luri Gabbeh carpet from the
Zagros mountains, southern
Persia.
- *148cm x 121cm*
- **£770**   • Gordon Reece

Tibetan Rug ▼

- *1880*
Tibetan rug with an indigo
background and delicately
embroidered butterflies around a
central floral design (code
TEX0048).
- *77cm x 54cm*
- **£280**   • Gordon Reece

Persian Wool Carpet ►

- *1820*
A Persian wool carpet with floral
design on a rust coloured ground
with cobalt blue borders, by
Zigla Mahal.
- *120cm x 150cm*
- **£3,300**   • A. Rezai Persian

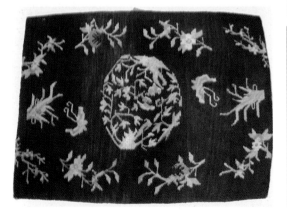

Expert Tips

*Cleaning should be done by
vacuum or by hand. By rotating
the rug you can avoid uneven
wear. Try to avoid direct
sunlight on the rug as this will
affect the colours.
In the seventeenth century the
fashion was to hang rugs on
walls or to cover tables with
good examples. This is
something carpet and rug
collectors could recommend as
this also helps to prolong the life
of the rug or carpet.*

Tent Trappings ▲

- *1940*
Tent trappings in red, purple, orange and cream with beaded tassels.
- *55cm x 13cm*
- £65   • Oriental Rug

Sarouk Rug ▲

- *circa 1940*
Typical Harati design with a large medallion in the centre, the ground colour is coral with blue, pink and cream. Sarouk is a small village of approximately 1000 houses, west of Iran.
- *89cm x 118cm*
- £1,100   • Oriental Rug

Tibetan Wool Rug ▲

- *circa 1890*
Tibetan rug of natural dyes with a red background with three circles in the centre. Wool on warp and weft.
- *length 145cm*
- £950   • Gordon Reece

Hammadan Runner ▲

- *1870*
Section of a Hammadan runner.
- *length 300cm*
- £1,500   • David Black

Kilim Cushion ◀

- *1870*
Fragment of a kilim from Turkey used as a cushion cover.
- *47cm x 38cm*
- £150   • David Black

Indian Dhurrie ▲

- *circa 1860*
Indian cotton dhurrie with a blue background with pink and yellow geometric designs and a pink key pattern design, on a yellow background with a yellow border.
- *269cm x 251cm*
- £2,800   • David Black

Indian Dhurrie ▲

- *1850*
Indian dhurrie, a blue foliate design and gold torchieries, on a pink background.
- *156cm x 230cm*
- £950   • David Black

Ceramics

Pottery and porcelain need to be perfect to command top prices. Converseley, great pleasure can be derived by the enthusiast in finding slightly flawed bargains.

The term 'ceramics' is used to cover all artefacts that are fired in a kiln. Ceramics can be divided into two main groups: pottery and porcelain. The distinction between these can be easily identified by holding them up to the light; pottery is opaque, porcelain translucent. Porcelain has long been highly prized and tends to be more expensive than pottery. Unfortunately, particularly with European porcelain, makers' marks are no guarantee of authenticity, since many factories copied each other's marks. Value is usually a matter of size, age, rarity and, above all, condition. Because fine pottery and porcelain have been produced in China for longer than anywhere else, it is a mistake to believe that all of it is wildly out of your price range. It is, in fact, not hard to find pieces that are both decorative and inexpensive. The Dutch first imported Chinese porcelain into Europe in the seventeenth century and, because of the quality unattainable in Europe, there was a huge demand, leading to the manufacture in China of 'export wares', which were in more varied colour schemes than the traditional blue and white, with which all Chinese porcelain had hitherto been decorated.

English Ceramics

Quatralobe Tea Set ▼
- *circa 1890*
English quatralobe cup, saucer and plate, gilded with a delicate floral design. Part of a set of four.
- *height of cup 6cm*
- £65   • A. Piotrowski

Crown Derby Cup and Saucer ▲
- *circa 1880*
Royal Crown Derby cup and saucer decorated with pink roses, and wild flowers, with raised gilding.
- *height 7cm*
- £65   • A. Piotrowski

Staffordshire Piper ▼
- *1800*
Staffordshire pottery figure of a piper crisply moulded and decorated with pastel and matt black enamel colours.
- *height 22cm*
- £620   • Dando

Coalport Cup and Saucer ◀
- *circa 1864*
Coalport cup and saucer of lobed design, with stylised floral designs and profuse gilding, with ear shaped handle.
- *height 8cm*
- £125   • A. Piotrowski

King of Prussia Teapot ▶
- *1765*

Staffordshire salt glaze teapot with black arrow pattern, and a cartouche of the King of Prussia with stylised twig handle, spout and finial top.
- *height 9cm*
- £3,850 • Jonathan Horne

Creamware Teapot ▲
- *1765*

English creamware teapot with farm hands resting in a pastoral setting, and a cottage on the reverse, with leaf designs to the handle and spout.
- *height 10cm*
- £1,100 • Jonathan Horne

Staffordshire Creamer ▼
- *circa 1765*

Early Staffordshire creamer with the inscription 'William Dixson' within a cartouche of flowers. The side of the jug is a painted figure of a musician wearing a red jacket and black tri-cornered hat.
- *height 18.4cm*
- £6,850 • Jonathan Horne

Staffordshire Sauceboat ▼
- *circa 1745*

Staffordshire sauce boat with a scrolled handle, decorated with a pink house and clouds, with shaped rim and foot.
- *height 8cm*
- £1,850 • Jonathan Horne

Saltglaze Teapot ▲
- *circa 1765*

Staffordshire salt glaze teapot decorated with pink wild flowers on a crimson ground, with twig handle and spout.
- *height 10cm*
- £2,100 • Jonathan Horne

Saltglazed Stand with Teapot ▼
- *circa 1755*

Staffordshire teapot decorated with green and yellow vases and foliate design around the handle and spout, and standing on three raised feet.
- *height 8cm*
- £3,950 • Jonathan Horne

Staffordshire Teapot ▲
- *circa 1765*

Staffordshire salt glazed teapot with a musician wearing a pink jacket and a black hat, in chinioserie style, playing a flute, whilst seated on a riverbank.
- *height 9.4cm*
- £3,650 • Jonathan Horne

Sauce Tureen ▼
- *circa 1896*
A blue and white tureen made by the Empire Porcelain Company.
- *height 8cm*
- **£65**   • **A.D. Antiques**

Staffordshire Jug ▼
- *1860*
Mid nineteenth century moulded Staffordshire jug with pewter lid.
- *height 32cm*
- **£125**   • **A.D. Antiques**

Muffin Dish ▶
- *1872*
Minton muffin dish with Japanese crane design applied to the base of the cover and dish.
- *height 10cm*
- **£125**   • **A.D. Antiques**

Jug and Bowl ▼
- *circa 1900*
Jug and bowl, with moulded shell design.
- *height 35cm*
- **£185**   • **A.D. Antiques**

Worcester Plate ▼
- *1811*
Worcester plate with hand-painted polychrome decoration.
- *diameter 22cm*
- **£65**   • **A.D. Antiques**

Victorian Jug ▶
- *1880*
A Victorian lustre jug, with scrolled handle and painted decoration of a classical urn with floral sprays.
- *height 54cm*
- **£65**   • **A.D. Antiques**

Water Jug ▲
- *1890*
Copeland Spode water jug with scrolled handle and painted decoration to the body and lip.
- *height 56cm*
- **£75**   • **A.D. Antiques**

Worcester Bowl ▲

- 1765–70

Worcester 'Queen Charlotte' pattern waste bowl with dark blue and white panels with floral designs and gilding.
- *diameter 12cm*
- £275
- Dando

English Ceramics Jug ▲

- *circa 1840*

Large English ceramics milk jug with painted floral decoration and gilding.
- *height 16cm*
- £420
- Dando

Bow Candlestick ▲

- 1765

A large Bow porcelain double figure group of Columbine and a young boy, seated with a dog in front of an elaborate floral bocage. Fitted with two candle sconces with metal supports.
- *height 23cm*
- £1,850
- Dando

Derby Dish ▼

- *circa 1815–20*

Derby lozenge shape dessert dish of Trotter pattern, with cartouches of hand painted flowers.
- *length 28cm*
- £580
- Dando

Worcester Cup and Saucer ▲

- *circa 1770*

Faceted Worcester coffee cup and saucer decorated with panels of polychrome flowers and gilding between underglaze blue bands.
- *diameter of saucer 5.25cm*
- £795
- Dando

Worcester Heart Shaped Dish ▲

- 1780

Worcester attractive heart shaped dish decorated with sprays of flowers within an underglaze blue border with gilt foliate pattern. Crescent mark in underglaze blue.
- *length 27cm*
- £875
- Dando

Spode Miniature Basket ▼

- *circa 1825*

Miniature spode porcelain basket decorated with an exotic bird and foliage in raised gilding against a mazarin blue ground.
- *length 10cm*
- £475
- Dando

Derby Vases ▶

- *1830*

A pair of small bottle-shaped Derby vases, gilded with flower encrustation.
- *height 11cm*
- £285 ● London Antique

Royal Worcester Cup and Saucer ▲

- *1936*

An English Royal Worcester cup and saucer, with interlaced scroll decoration.
- *height 9cm*
- £150 ● London Antique

Staffordshire Deer with Dog ▼

- *1870*

A spill holder showing a group depicting a deer leaping through a woodland setting with a hound giving chase, on an oval base.
- *height 18cm*
- £795 ● Jesse Davis

Pagoda Cup and Saucer ▼

- *circa 1785*

Cup and saucer with a pagoda pattern.
- *height 4cm*
- £135 ● London Antique

One of Pair of Greyhounds with Prey ▲

- *1865*

One of a pair of Staffordshire greyhounds, each with a rabbit in its mouth. Painted in iron red, brown and gilt, and raised on a rock moulded base.
- *height 20cm*
- £258 ● Jesse Davis

Poodle Group ▲

- *1860*

A Staffordshire dog group with poodles and their puppies, on blue cushion bases.
- *height 13cm*
- £595 ● Jesse Davis

Chinoiserie Plate ◀

- **1780**

An English blue and white oval plate decorated with a Chinoiserie scene.
- N/A   • Ashcombe House

Pair of Perching Birds ▼

- **1865**

A pair of Staffordshire figures, showing two resplendent birds, on a stylised tree base.
- *height 32cm*
- £1,995   • Jesse Davis

Staffordshire Spaniel ▲

- **1750**

One of a pair of Staffordshire King Charles spaniels in an alert pose, splashed with iron red, and each with a gilt collar.
- *height 14cm*
- £750   • Jesse Davis

Staffordshire Pony ▲

- **1860**

An unusual moulded Staffordshire pony with cheshnut colouration and a black mane, on a moulded rock oval base with gilt banding.
- *height 8cm*
- £249   • Jesse Davis

King Charles Spaniel ▼

- **1880**

An unusual small King Charles spaniel, recumbent on a mazarin blue cushion base .
- *height 13cm*
- £498   • Jesse Davis

Pair of Spill Holders ◀

- **1850**

Pair of Staffordshire spill holders showing a ram and a ewe, with bocage and flower encrustation on rock moulded base.
- *height 13cm*
- £895   • Jesse Davis

Figure of Young Lady ▲

- **1977**

A Royal Doulton figure of a young lady standing posed in an evening dress, entitled "Harmony".
- *height 29cm*
- **£125**　　● London Antique

Figure of a Seated Lady ▲

- **1950**

A figure of a young girl in nineteenth century dress on a garden seat accompanied by a macaw. The whole on an oval moulded base with gilding.
- *19cm x 18cm*
- **£195**　　● London Antique

Art Deco Plate ▼

- **1930**

An Art Deco Shelley ceramic cake plate and side plate with swallow and foliate design.
- *width 25cm*
- **£55**　　● London Antique

Figure in White Gown ▼

- **1983**

A Royal Doulton figurine of young girl in a flowing white gown with her hands clasped and her head tilted to one side.
- *height 20cm*
- **£120**　　● London Antique

Victorian Goblet ▼

- **1860**

A Victorian copper lustre goblet with floral decoration on a sandy ground.
- *height 13cm*
- **£56**　　　　　　● Cekay

Haddon Hall Set ▼

- **1940**

A polychrome Minton Haddon Hall cup and saucer, with profuse floral decoration.
- *height 11cm*
- **£45**　　● London Antique

Ralph Wood Group ▲
- *1785*

Fine quality Ralph Wood group of the 'Vicar and Moses' showing two seated figures, painted in brown and grey hues.
- *height 23.5cm*
- £1,650   • Dando

Samuel Alcock Spaniel ▲
- *circa 1835*

Samuel Alcock model of a brown and white spaniel sitting attentively on a yellow base.
- *height 14cm*
- £440   • Dando

Staffordshire Group ▼
- *circa 1850*

Early Staffordshire brown and white spaniel with puppy, resting on an oval white base with gilding.
- *height 8.5cm*
- £460   • Dando

Copper Lustre Jug ▼
- *circa 1840*

Large copper lustre jug with moulded band of shamrocks and thistles in pale blue relief.
- *height 19cm*
- £210   • Dando

Staffordshire Stag ▼
- *1810*

Fine quality Staffordshire pottery stag shown recumbent on a naturally formed oval base.
- *height 19cm*
- £740   • Dando

Staffordshire Figure ▲
- *circa 1810*

Staffordshire pottery figure of Iphegenia shown gathering her skirts with her head to one side.
- *height 18.5cm*
- £850   • Dando

Musician ▲
- *circa 1840*

Small figure of a boy musician, playing a penny whistle with a poodle at his side.
- *height 16cm*
- £215   • Dando

St Mark ▲
- 1850

Staffordshire figure of St Mark with a lion recumbent at his side, on a rock moulded base.
- *height 24cm*
- £450   • J. Oosthuizen

Queen Victoria's Children ▲
- 1880

Staffordshire group depicting Queen Victoria's children.
- *height 41cm*
- £275   • J. Oosthuizen

Expert Tips

Some Staffordshire figures were inspired by the famous Newfoundland dog rescuing a child from a river – one of the many faithful and heroic hounds who abound in Victorian literature and art.

Spill Vases ▼
- 1860

Pair of Staffordshire spill vases modelled as foxes with chickens in there mouths, standing on a foliate base.
- *height 25cm*
- £1,600   • J. Oosthuizen

Little Red Riding Hood ▼
- 1860

Staffordshire figure of Little Red Riding Hood seated with a fox.
- *height 26cm*
- £185   • J. Oosthuizen

Staffordshire Zebras ▲
- 1865

Pair of prancing Staffordshire zebras on a foliate oval base with gilding.
- *height 16cm*
- £725   • J. Oosthuizen

Staffordshire Actor ▲
- 1855

Man in theatrical dress sitting on a branch, with a parrot on his shoulder and a spaniel at his side, with gilding on a green foliate base.
- *height 37cm*
- £450   • J. Oosthuizen

Staffordshire Children ▲
- 1850

Pair of Staffordshire figures modelled as children playing with rats, raised on oval moulded bases with gilding.
- *height 15cm*
- £800   • J. Oosthuizen

Staffordshire Group ▲
- 1880

Ivory Staffordshire group modelled as a cow with her calf, standing on an oval moulded base with gilding.
- *16cm x 21cm*
- £350   • J. Oosthuizen

Pirate Figure ◄
- *1880*

A Staffordshire figure of man in the theatrical dress of a pirate with a parrot on his shoulder.
- *height 12cm*
- £89 • Cekay

Staffordshire Cottage ▲
- *1820*

A Staffordshire pink cottage with a white flower-encrusted roof.
- *height 11cm*
- £135 • Cekay

Staffordshire Lady ▼
- *1880*

A Staffordshire figure of a lady in theatrical dress with a bird on her shoulder.
- *height 12cm*
- £89 • Cekay

Romantic Group ▼
- *1880*

A Staffordshire romantic group with bocage and a swan below a bridge.
- *20cm x 13cm*
- £150 • Cekay

Empress Eugenie ◄
- *1880*

A Staffordshire figure of Empress Eugenie of France on horseback, riding side saddle.
- *height 29cm*
- £155 • Cekay

Wedgwood Candlesticks ▶
- *circa 1768–1800*

A pair of black Wedgwood candlesticks of cylindrical form on a wide splayed base with moulded relief and "Etruria" inscribed on the base.
- *height 20cm*
- £250 • London Antique

Creamware Shoe Buckles ▶
- *circa 1770*
A pair of creamware shoe buckles with floral decoration. Item has been restored.
- *height 8cm*
- £600 • Garry Atkins

Basket With Kittens ▼
- *circa 1880*
English Staffordshire basket with kittens,'Charles Ford' model.
- *height 20cm*
- £850 • David Brower

Worcester Cup and Saucer Set ◀
- *circa 1782–92*
Worcester cup and saucer, French influenced, of the flight period. Marked with blue crescent moon and gilded with floral decoration.
- *height 8cm*
- £185 • London Antique

Creamware Jug ▲
- *circa 1780–90*
A creamware jug by James Sculthorp with ribbing and floral decoration. Restored.
- *height 23cm*
- £1,850 • Garry Atkins

Expert Tips

Printed wares were introduced by English factories to capitalise on the popularity of blue and white porcelain. The value of these wares is dependent on the skills of the copper engraver who made the template.

Small Floral House ▼
- *circa 1870*
Late 19th-century Staffordshire house decorated with colourful flowers. Shows chimney and front door, with steps leading to it.
- *height 13cm*
- £250 • J. Oosthuizen

Crown Derby Cup and Saucer Set ◀
- *circa 1931*
Early 20th-century Crown Derby cup and saucer set, decorated with an Imari pattern. Both pieces have gilding around the edges.
- *height 6cm*
- £95 • London Antique

Terracotta Tile ▲
- *circa 14th century*
English terracotta tile with
grotesque design.
- *dimensions 11cm x 11cm*
- £435 • Jonathan Horne

Royal Worcester Cup & Saucer Set ▲
- *circa 1877*
An English Royal Worcester
'Honeycomb' cup and saucer
with jewelled detailing with an
intermittant rosette motif and
raised decoration to the outside
of the cup. Gilded rim to cup
and saucer.
- *height 6cm*
- £1,500 • David Brower

Cup and Saucer ▲
- *circa 1780*
A cup and saucer with matching
floral decoration. The cup has a
cross-over strap handle.
- *height 7cm*
- £225 • Garry Atkins

Worcester Plate ▲
- *circa 18th century*
Worcester plate with mixed
oriental influence, showing
Kakieman and birds of paradise
with oriental floral decoration.
- *diameter 16cm*
- £585 • London Antique

A Soup Ladle ▼
- *circa 1780*
A creamware soup ladle with a
scallop design. The item is
slightly cracked.
- *height 29cm*
- £195 • Garry Atkins

Pastille-Burner Cottage ▼
- *circa 1850*
Pastille-burner cottage with floral
design. Working chimney.
- *height 12cm*
- £295 • J. Oosthuizen

Drinking Cup ▼
- *circa 18th century*
An English lead-glazed drinking
cup with handle.
- *height 10cm*
- £220 • Jonathan Horne

Worcester Cup & Saucer ◄
- *circa 1765*
Worcester cup and saucer of the
first period. Open crescent
marking with ribbed design to
cup and saucer.
- *height 6.5cm*
- £265 • Jonathan Horne

Earthenware Jug ▲
- *13th century*
English earthenware jug of
bulbous form with incised
banding and a burnt orange glaze.
- *height 20cm*
- £2,950 • Jonathan Horne

English Earthenware Jug ▲
- *13th century*
English earthenware jug of
bulbous form with handle, in
good condition.
- *height 28cm*
- £2,200 • Jonathan Horne

Earthenware Vessel ▼
- *1270–1350*
Earthenware elongated vessel
with a light green glaze and
thumb prints around the base and
top of handle, from Mill Green,
Essex.
- *height 30cm*
- £4,400 • Jonathan Horne

Red-Ware Tea Kettle ▲
- *circa 1770*
Red-ware tea kettle with double
rope twist handle, and mask
decoration to the base of the
spout.
- *height 23cm*
- £3,950 • Jonathan Horne

Earthenware Vessel ▲
- *circa 14th century*
Earthenware vessel with a green
glaze, found in the foundations of
a house in Grace Church Street,
London in 1873.
- *height 21.5cm*
- £1,950 • Jonathan Horne

Earthenware Jug ▲
- *16th century*
Small earthenware jug of bulbous
proportions, with moulded
handle, splayed lip and a green
glaze.
- *height 14cm*
- £780 • Jonathan Horne

Teapot ▲

- *circa 1780*

A creamware teapot, probably Wedgwood, with a cabbage spout design. Decorations of a church and a house by a river, with decoration to the lid. Some restoration evident.
- *height 13.5cm*
- £995　　● Garry Atkins

Balm Pot ▲

- *circa 1826*

Lead-glazed balm pot, possibly Halifax, with repetitive dot and wave pattern, inscribed 'JW'.
- *height 12cm*
- £350　　● Garry Atkins

Money Box ▼

- *circa 1850*

A Sussex pottery money box. Lead glaze in inverted baluster form with wide slot.
- *height 17.5cm*
- £150　　● Garry Atkins

Worcester Vase ▼

- *circa 1872*

Royal Worcester vase with spiralling terrapins.
- *height 9cm*
- £575　　● David Brower

Staffordshire Cottage ◄

- *circa 1860*

Staffordshire cottage with flower encrustation and triple bower front.
- *height 18cm*
- £240　　● J. Oosthuizen

Cabaret Set ▲

- *circa 1920*

Royal Worcester cabaret set by Harry Stinton, with spoons by Henry James Hulbert. Porcelain gilded and painted with fruit designs; spoons engraved with fruit designs.
- £3,850　　● London Antique

Expert Tips

Porcelain and all forms of ceramics need to be exciting and in near-perfect condition to attract top buyers. The desirability gulf between the good and the ordinary is growing all the time – and is reflected in the prices.

Drinking Cup ▼

- *circa 17th century*

English double-handled, fluted and lead-glazed cup.
- *height 16cm*
- £1,150　　● Jonathan Horne

Spode Figure ▼
- **1910**
A Spode figure of a lady in courtly dress with chinoiserie design, holding an extended fan to her side.
- *height 12cm*
- **£268**   • London Antique

Stephanie ▲
- **1975**
A Royal Doulton figurine entitled "Stephanie" showing a young girl dancing in period costume.
- *height 28cm*
- **£125**   • London Antique

Reticulated Vase ▲
- **1870–89**
A Grainger Worcester reticulated oval vase and cover with pierced decoration.
- *height 21cm*
- **£485**   • London Antique

Plate and Bowl ▲
- **1930–40**
A Susie Cooper twin-handled bowl with plate with a graduated green glaze with floral design.
- *diameter 16cm*
- **£45**   • London Antique

Royal Doulton Lady ◄
- **1982**
A Royal Doulton figurine of a young lady in a yellow dress with green waistband, holding a parasol over her shoulder and gazing upwards.
- *height 20cm*
- **£100**   • London Antique

Royal Doulton Figurine ▲
- **1950**
A Royal Doulton ceramic figure of a young girl in a red and white dress and bonnet, holding a posy.
- *height 13cm*
- **£95**   • London Antique

Staffordshire Castle ▲
- 1855

Very rare Staffordshire model commemorating Malakoff Castle from the Crimean War.
- *22cm x 24cm*
- £750   • J. Oosthuizen

Staffordshire Group ▲
- 1850

Staffordshire group depicting Uncle Tom and Little Eva.
- *height 21cm*
- £360   • J. Oosthuizen

Staffordshire Spill Vases ▲
- 1880

Pair of Staffordshire spill vases modelled as two white stallions, standing on an oval moulded base.
- *height 30cm*
- £1,500   • J. Oosthuizen

Baden Powell ▼
- 1899

Staffordshire figure of Baden Powell, founder of the Scout Movement and the leader of the British Troops of the Siege of Mafeking.
- *height 42cm*
- £450   • J. Oosthuizen

Staffordshire Cavalry Officer ▼
- 1880

Staffordshire model of a mounted cavalry officer on a very fine horse.
- *height 30cm*
- £450   • J. Oosthuizen

Duke of Wellington ▲
- 1845

Staffordshire figure of the Duke of Wellington wearing full uniform of blue and gold.
- *height 23cm*
- £380   • J. Oosthuizen

Shepherd and Shepherdess ▲
- 1790

Early salt glaze group depicting a shepard and shepherdess with a goat, sheep and dog at their feet. He is playing on the flute for his female companion.
- *height 28cm*
- £2,400   • J. Oosthuizen

Staffordshire Group ◀
- 1855

Staffordshire group depicting two lovers under a green bower.
- *height 24cm*
- £300   • J. Oosthuizen

Creamware Teapot ▶

- *circa 1775*

Small creamware teapot with red
and black mottled design, twig
spout and handle and a red finial
cover.
- *14cm*
- £750   • Libra

Davenport Tureen and Cover ▲

- *circa 1820*

Davenport polychrome sauce
tureen and cover, on fixed stand
with chinoiserie designs within a
key pattern border, with gilt
banding and a leaf shaped finial.
- *height 17cm*
- £228   • Libra

Wedgwood Teapot ▲

- *circa 1790*

Small Wedgwood teapot
decorated with a tulip pattern in
magenta, with designs on spout
and handle with a flower finial
cover.
- *height 12.5cm*
- £420   • Libra

Swansea Pinwheel Pepperpot ▲

- *1870*

Swansea blue and white
'Pinwheel' pepperpot of bulbous
form raised on a splayed foot.
- *height 11cm*
- £270   • Libra

Stone China Vase ◀

- *circa 1825*

One of a set of four stone china
vases decorated with an apple
blossom design with gilt banded
decoration.
- *height 11cm*
- £360   • Libra

Swansea Moulded Jug ▼

- *circa 1825*

Swansea daisy pattern moulded
jug, with C scroll handle and
shaped lip with red, blue, green
and white stripes and a black
diagonal stripe across the body.
- *height 22cm*
- £150   • Libra

Pearlware Jug ▼

- *circa 1815*

Pearlware moulded jug decorated
with pink roses, cornflowers and
leaves, with black banded
decoration.
- *height 12cm*
- £125   • Libra

Davenport Calceony Teapot ▲

- *circa 1805*
Davenport silver-form teapot in the Grecian style with a leaf pattern and black banding.
- *height 14cm*
- £595   • Libra

Davenport Sauce Tureen ▲

- *circa 1810*
Davenport sauce tureen and cover on a fixed stand in the form of overlapping oak leaves, with black handles and finial.
- *height 18cm*
- £560   • Libra

Ridgway Puzzle Jug ▲

- *circa 1820*
Ridgway blue and white puzzle jug, with pierced decoration to the neck and rim, painted with a rural landscape.
- *height 22cm*
- £750   • Libra

Creamware Jug ▲

- *circa 1790*
Creamware milk jug decorated with a compass with the inscription 'Come box the compass' with a man with a rope in hand and the words 'Invented by Murphy a Dutchman'.
- *height 15cm*
- £340   • Libra

English Delft Jug ▼

- *1730*
Small English delft jug with original cover, painted with flowers and a stylised leaf design.
- *height 18cm*
- £295   • Libra

Blue and White Cup ▼

- *circa 1820*
Blue and white cup and saucer decorated with apples, blossom and leaves.
- *height 6cm*
- £190   • Libra

Spode Basket ▼

- *circa 1810*
Spode lattice work basket with shaped rim, painted with a delicate green and red foliate design, raised on four ochre feet.
- *width 27cm*
- £175   • Libra

Royal Worcester Cabaret Set

• *1918–19*

A Royal Worcester cabaret set with six cups, saucers and spoons in a presentation box. Signed by Stinton, with spoons by Henry James Hulbert.

• **£2,850** • **London Antique**

Porcelain Figurines

• *1850*

Pair of miniature porcelain figures of an English lady and gentleman.

• *height 12cm*

• **£135** • **Cekay**

Double-Handled Goblet ▼

• *1830*

An English double-handled silver lustre goblet.

• *height 56cm*

• **£56** • **Cekay**

Derby Jug ▲

• *1820–40*

A Derby water jug of oval form with flower encrusted cartouches on a blue ground, with gilding to the handle and splayed lip.

• *height 17cm*

• **£235** • **London Antique**

Worcester Bowl ▼

• *1755–90*

A Worcester bowl of a fluted design with gilded floral decoration and a blue and gilded pattern around the rim..

• *height 18cm*

• **£80** • **London Antique**

Staffordshire Castle ▼

• *1890*

Victorian Staffordshire pink castle with a red door and arched leaded light window.

• *height 24cm*

• **£111** • **Cekay**

Susie Cooper Milk Jug ▼
- *circa 1930s*
A Susie Cooper milk jug with graduated banding and stylised bird lip. Stamped "698 83".
- *height 20cm*
- £63   • **London Antique**

Minton Cup and Saucer ▼
- *1912–50*
A Minton cup and saucer made in New York by Cilman Collamore & Co., 5th Avenue and 30th Street, New York.
- £85   • **London Antique**

Quatrolobe Set ◄
- *1890*
A Coalport Quatrolobe cup and saucer with pink and gold floral decoration.
- *height 2.5cm*
- £185   • **London Antique**

Coalport Gilded Cup and Saucer Set ▲
- *circa 1883*
A Coalport cup and saucer with lobed rim and gilded floral decoration on a cobalt-blue ground.
- *height 3cm*
- £175   • **London Antique**

Butter Dish ▼
- *1870*
Ceramic butter dish with a sitting cow on lid.
- *21cm x 14cm*
- £1,295   • **Jesse Davis**

Staffordshire Greyhounds ▶
- *1840*
A pair of Staffordshire greyhounds seated upon oval bases with floral decoration.
- *height 13cm*
- £495   • **Jesse Davis**

Cream Ware Jug ▼

- *1790*

A Cream Ware jug for milk or beer, with a transfer print depicting a gentleman in period costume within a vine border.
- *height 25cm*
- **£4,950**　　• Jonathan Horne

Staffordshire Spill Holder ▼

- *1820*

A Staffordshire spill holder modelled with bocage showing a young boy and two recumbent leopards on a naturalistically formed base.
- *height 25cm*
- **£4,950**　　• Jonathan Horne

Minton Plate ▶

- *1863*

A Minton white plate with a turquoise rim, with a cherub depicted in the centre sitting by a tree with a bird basket.
- *diameter 24cm*
- **£100**　　• London Antique

Wedgwood Plate ▶

- *1860*

A tullic design Wedgwood plate showing a leaf pattern on a basket weave base with a green glaze.
- *height 23cm*
- **£149**　　• Jesse Davis

Bull with Dog ▼

- *1820*

A Staffordshire group showing a tethered bull with a farmer and his dog on a rectangular base.
- *23cm x 36cm*
- **£6,600**　　• Jonathan Horne

Cruet Set ◀

- *1865*

A most unusual English or Scottish cruet set consisting of salt and pepper. The gentleman is shown with a tri-cornered hat, a red overcoat and a wry expression.
- *height 91cm*
- **£295**　　• Jesse Davis

English Cup and Saucer ◄

- *1930*

An English cup and saucer colourfully decorated with a pastoral scene.

- £130 • London Antique

Shelly Jug ►

- *1930*

A porcelain Shelly milk jug with swallow and pastoral scene with a yellow handle.

- *height 10cm*
- £55 • London Antique

Susie Cooper Trio ▼

- 1930–40

A Susie Cooper trio comprising a white teacup, blue saucer and plate with a moulded rim.

- *diameter 19cm/plate; 9cm/saucer*
- £75 • London Antique

Soup Bowl ◄

- 1930–40

A Susie Cooper soup bowl with a variegated pink glaze and a central pink rose.

- *diameter 23cm*
- £85 • London Antique

Vegetable Dish ▼

- 1930–40

A Susie Cooper vegetable dish with a graduated pale blue glaze with flower designs and banding.

- *18cm x 9cm*
- £78
- London Antique

Minton Cup and Saucer ▲

- 1950

Cup and saucer with a Minton white and blue leaf pattern.

- £25 • London Antique

Soup Tureen ▶

- *1827*

Soup tureen manufactured by
Jones to celebrate the Coronation
of George IV.
- *height 31cm*
- £1,273   • Libra

Leeds Egg Cup ▲

- *1820*

Leeds blue and white egg cup
decorated with two boys fishing
beside a river within a parkland
setting.
- *height 7cm*
- £195   • Libra

Dresden Sauceboat ▲

- *1225*

Dresden sauceboat with scrolled
handle, shaped lip, vase and floral
decoration, raised on a moulded,
splayed foot.
- *height 8cm*
- £120   • Libra

Platter ▶

- *1820*

Blue and white platter with a
moonlit naval battle scene
surrounded by tropical shells and
fauna.
- *width 53cm*
- £1,350   • Libra

Tea Bowl and Saucer ▲

- *1790*

Pearlware tea bowl and saucer,
with finely fluted decoration,
painted with a dark blue trailing
band with stylised flowers.
- *diameter 8.5cm*
- £195   • Libra

Ewer and Bowl ▼

- *1820*

Blue and white ewer and bowl
decorated with a view of
Worcester, and the word
'Worcester' inscribed on the base.
- *height of jug 20cm*
- £490   • Libra

English Chinoiserie Mug ▲
- *circa 1790*
English blue and white mug decorated with a chinoiserie design, with turned decoration and ear shaped handle.
- *height 8.5cm*
- £180   • Libra

Goldfinch Sugar Bowl ▲
- *1820*
Blue and white sugar bowl with twin handles, moulded rim and finial lid, decorated with floral designs and centred with a goldfinch.
- *height 10cm*
- £280   • Libra

Spittoon ▲
- *1820*
Rare spittoon with moulded decoration and spout, decorated with floral designs and a rural scene.
- *height 10cm*
- £325   • Libra

Pepperpot ▼
- *1795*
Underglazed blue and white pepperpot painted freely with groups of flowers, raised on a splayed foot.
- *height 3cm*
- £115   • Libra

Salopian Tea Bowl ▼
- *1810*
Salopian polychrome tea bowl and saucer pictured with a woodcutter and his wife seated holding a baby, with a gate and church in the background.
- *diameter 8cm*
- £170   • Libra

Sugar Shaker ▲
- *1820*
Unusually shaped blue and white sugar shaker with floral designs to the neck and a chinoiserie style landscape on the body, raised on a splayed foot.
- *height 11cm*
- £50   • Libra

Hall Cup Plate ▲
- *1820*
Cup-plate manufactured by 'Hall' centred with a hyena within a floral border with urn decoration.
- *diameter 11cm*
- £185   • Libra

Liverpool Bottle ▶
- *circa 1760*

An English Delftware Liverpool bottle, with blue and white floral decoration.
- *height 25cm*
- £650　　• Garry Atkins

Terracotta Tile ▲
- *circa 19th century*

Part of a set of four English terracotta tiles, this decorated with a coat of arms.
- *15cm x 15cm*
- £440　　• Jonathan Horne

Expert Tips

Identification can be difficult with much sought-after, early Victorian teawares, since few pieces bear a factory mark. Learning shapes and styles used by individual factories – and frequent handling – helps.

Staffordshire Dogs ▼
- *circa 1850*

A pair of Staffordshire pipe-smoking dogs.
- £6,000　　• J. Oosthuizen

Prattware Jug ▼
- *circa 1810*

Showing a touching farewell scene between a man and a woman. Decorated with acanthus leaf with blue bands around base and lip.
- *height 13cm*
- £395　　• Constance Stobo

Prince of Wales ▼
- *circa 1862*

A slim, young Prince of Wales with hound.
- *height 36cm*
- £475　　• J. Oosthuizen

Delftware Tile ▼
- *circa 1720–30*

Delftware tile depicting the biblical scene of Judith with the head of Holofernes.
- *height 14cm*
- £95　　• Jonathan Horne

Salt-glazed Sauceboat ▼
- *circa 1760*

A salt-glazed sauceboat with pear design in relief.
- *height 8cm*
- £275　　• Garry Atkins

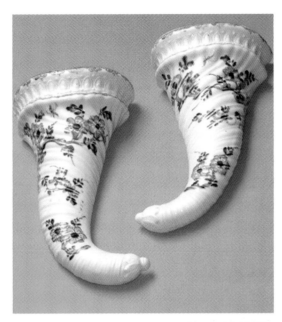

Worcester Cornocuperies ◄

- *circa 1756-8*

Pair of blue and white moulded
Worcester cornocuperies
decorated with small blue flowers.
Workman's mark.
- *height 22cm*
- £4,500   • Stockspring

Large Worcester Mug ▲

- *circa 1805*

Large Worcester mug, with two
yellow enamel bands between gilt
banding and a central repetitive
design of stylised feathers.
- *height 12cm*
- £680   • Stockspring

Minton Cup ▼

- *circa 1805*

Minton cup decorated with three
cartouches and a foliate design in
terracotta, set amongst profuse
gilding. With mark on base:
M.205.
- *height 6.5cm*
- £139   • Stockspring

Minton Bowl ▶

- 1860

Minton bowl with polychrome
floral and gilt decoration, raised
on a large footpad.
- *height 15cm*
- £225   • A.D. Antiques

Lowestoft Tea Bowl ▲

- *circa 1760*

Lowestoft tea bowl decorated
with a blue and white chinsoserie
scene depicting a house behind a
wall with a tree and birds.
- *height of bowl 5cm*
- £690   • Stockspring

Worcester Tea Bowl ▲

- *circa 1740*

Worcester octagonal tea bowl
with finely painted sprays of
flowers and insects with gilding,
from the studio of James Giles.
- *height 5cm*
- £420   • Stockspring

Minton Barometer ▼
- 1835

A Minton barometer with a frame encrusted with flowers.
- *height 18cm*
- £235 • London Antique

Elephant Spill Holders ▼
- 1865

A pair of Staffordshire elephant spill holders shown standing on a bocage oval base.
- *height 14cm*
- £1,095 • Jesse Davis

Staffordshire Cottage ▲
- 1890

A Staffordshire cottage with recess for a time piece, with additional floral decoration and two lead-lined windows either side of the front door.
- *height 13cm*
- £168 • Jesse Davis

Pair of Staffordshire Spill Holders ▼
- 1870

One of a pair of Staffordshire spill holders modelled as mother and calf with bocage, raised on a naturalistically moulded oval base.
- *height 28cm*
- £895 • Jesse Davis

Hunting Pair ▲
- 1865

One of a pair of Staffordshire harlequin greyhounds with a hare on a bocage base.
- *height 29cm*
- £2,450 • Jesse Davis

English Ewer ▲
- 1810

An English Ewer with a moulded Bacchanal face about the body, decorated with a band of vines and floral sprays. Includes a stylised handle in the form of a monkey with a splayed lip on a circular pedestal base.
- *height 18cm*
- £395 • Jesse Davis

Staffordshire Figure ▼
- *1863*

A Staffordshire figure of Bonnie Prince Charles in a woodland setting.
- *height 23cm*
- £225 • Jesse Davis

Staffordshire Group ▲
- *1866*

A Staffordshire group showing Royal children in Scottish dress with sheep, on a naturalistically formed oval base.
- *height 20cm*
- £695 • Jesse Davis

Minton Cup and Saucer ▲
- *1850*

A Minton cup and saucer with polychrome floral decoration and cobalt blue banding with gilt meanderings.
- *height 5cm; diameter 10cm resp.*
- £139 • Jesse Davis

Polychrome Set ▼
- *1860*

A polychrome cup and saucer with an Edward pattern, decorated with sunflowers and yellow ochre banding with pink interior to the cup.
- *height 8cm; diameter 11cm resp.*
- £295 • Jesse Davis

Royal Worcester Set ▼
- *1951*

A Royal Worcester cup and saucer with large, colourful fruit decoration. Includes gilding inside the cup, base and handle.
- *height 7cm*
- £335 • London Antique

Expert Tips

Staffordshire figures remain as popular as ever but as they were produced in large numbers they were not always treated with care, so keep a sharp eye out for damages and repairs. The best period for Staffordshire figures is 1854–6.

Pot Pourri Vases ▼

- *circa 1765*

A pair of Chelsea pot pourri vases with pierced lids. Gold Anchor period., with finial top and pierced lid, Mazarin blue gilding and notable gilt floral swags. The pots stand on three goat legs on a gilt base. Also feature three outward looking goat heads.

- *height 120cm*
- **£ 5,500** • **E. & H. Manners**

Tureen ▼

- *circa 1780*

A creamware tureen and cover, probably Staffordshire. Some restoration has been made to the body of the tureen.

- *height 25cm*
- **£850** • **Garry Atkins**

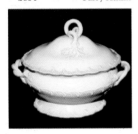

Sunderland Mug ▶

- *circa 1810*

Sunderland pink lustre mug, showing sailor's farewell to his family in pastoral setting with his ship in the distance. Anecdote on reverse.

- *height 13cm*
- **£295** • **Constance Stobo**

Pair of Copeland Vases ▲

- *circa 1880*

With covers depicting courtly scenes in a woodland setting to the front and cherub panels to rear, decorated with gilded, interlaced knob on the cover and ribbon handles.

- *height 31cm*
- **£2,250** • **David Brower**

A Creamware Dish ▲

- *circa 1780–1800*

A creamware dish with a hyacinth design.

- *diameter 22cm*
- **£275** • **Garry Atkins**

Monkey Teapot ▼

- *circa 1875*

A Minton monkey teapot in majolica. Torquoise/green glaze.

- *height 16cm*
- **£675** • **London Antique**

Wedgwood Jam Pot ▼

- *circa 1880*

A Wedgwood jam pot shown with silver-plated handle. Lilac and sage green with floral swirls and goat-heads decoration with classical cameos.

- *height 18.5cm*
- **£520** • **R.A. Barnes**

Expert Tips

Early bone china was suitable only for small-scale objects. Some of the best examples were by Minton, but do not usually carry a Minton mark. They can be identified by the impressed shape number.

European Ceramics

Coffee Pot and Teapot ▲
- *circa 1800*

Meissen coffee and teapot, part of
a set including milk jug, sugar
bowl, cups and saucers, cake
plates and one large plate.
- *height 27cm*
- **£2,550** • London Antique

Meissen Figurative
Group ▲
- *circa 1880*

Meissen figurative group of Diana
the Huntress seated on a lion
holding a cornucopia of flowers,
with cherubs holding a key and
garlands.
- *26cm x 24cm*
- **£1,580** • London Antique

Westerwald Storage Jar ▶
- *17th Century*

Rhineland blue salt glazed
stainwear jar, with pewter cover
and handle, with a cartouche on
each side depicting William III,
within a raised floral design.
- *height 27cm*
- **£4,850** • Jonathan Horne

Dresden Europa and
The Bull ▲
- *circa 1860*

Dresden group of Europa and the
Bull, the lady wearing a lilac
tunic, and the bull with a garland
of flowers around its neck.
- *height 22cm*
- **£350** • Gloria Sinclair

Neptune ▲
- *1760*

Meissen figure of Neptune astride
a sea-horse with trident.
- *height 15cm*
- **£980** • Stockspring Antiques

Dresden Cup and Saucer ▲
- *circa 1880*

Dresden cup standing on three
paw feet and saucer decorated
with orange borders and a central
cartouche of boats in a harbour.
- *height 10cm*
- **£285** • London Antique

Expert Tips

*Originating in the Kangxi period
famille vert is a palette of
enamels in which a strong green
predominates. It influenced the
decoration of English soft paste
porcelain in the 18th century,
before being overtaken by
famille rose colours.*

Floral Sugar Bowl ▶

- *1750*

Meissen sugar bowl with floral sprays to the cover and body.
- *height 8cm*
- **£235** • **London Antique**

Meissen Cup and Saucer ▲

- *1750*

Meissen teacup and saucer with a moulded body and scrolled handle. Decorated with floral designs and gilding around rim.
- *height 9cm/cup*
- **£885** • **London Antique**

Helena Wolfsohn Set ▲

- *1880*

Helena Wolfsohn cup and saucer of quartra-lobed form. Shepherd and shepherdess and floral sprays are shown in gilt cartouches.
- *height 5cm/cup*
- **£255** • **London Antique**

Expert Tips

Always inspect floral sprays on Chelsea and Meissen porcelain, as they are often damaged or have been repaired.

Meissen Teapot ▼

- *1765*

Meissen teapot with a lobed cartouche of harbour scenes within gilt borders. Part of a set comprising milk jug, sugar bowl, tea cup and saucer.
- *height 14cm*
- **£3,550** • **London Antique**

Encrusted Cup ▼

- *1814*

A flower and bird encrusted cup and saucer, decorated with flower detailing under the saucer, and a bird nestled within foliage on the cup.
- *diameter 3cm/cup*
- **£885** • **London Antique**

Swan-Handled Cup ▲

- *1860*

Sèvres-style cylindrical cup and saucer, with a swan handle and paw feet, and decorated with floral sprays and gilding.
- *height 7cm*
- **£355** • **London Antique**

Cherub Figure ▲

- *1880*

Meissen figure of a cherub sharpening his arrow on a grindstone. Heavily scrolled and gilded.
- *height 12cm*
- **£895** •**London Antique**

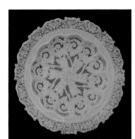

Kauffman Self Portrait ▲

- *circa 1985*

Ceramic self portrait by Angelica
Kauffman from Germany, set in a
carved oval giltwood frame with
deep moulding and central
ribbon.

- *17.5cm x 12cm*
- £985 • London Antique

Berlin Cup and Saucer ▲

- *circa 1850*

Berlin cup and saucer, with gilt
foliate medallions on a pale
salmon pink ground.

- *height 6cm*
- £235 • London Antique

Hochst Group ▶

- *1780*

A group depicting figures of
children playing set on a
naturalistically formed base.

- *height 14cm*
- £1,700 • Stockspring Antiques

Meissen Moulded Dish ◀

- *circa 1835-40*

Meissen dish relief-moulded with
gothic leaves and scrolls emanating
from a central flower head within
a foliate under glaze in gold on a
green ground.

- *diameter 32.5cm*
- £275 • London Antique

Sèvres Tray ▼

- *1767*

A scalloped edged Sèvres tray
with blue banding and gilding,
the centre of the tray decorated
with flowers, by Francois le
Vavassaur.

- *length 28cm*
- £780 • Stockspring Antiques

Berlin Luisentasse ◀

- *circa 1890s*

Berlin cabinet cup and saucer
(Luisentasse), the cup applied
with a biscuit profile bust of
Queen Louise of Prussia to
sinister, on a vermiculated gilt
oval medallion, the rims with a
gilt formal foliate border.

- *height 10cm*
- £995 • London Antique

Dresden Coffee Cup ▲
• 1890
Dresden coffee cup and saucer painted with cartouches showing a romantic scene of floral sprays on a pink ground within gilded borders.
• *height 8cm*
• £235   • London Antique

Lady's Writing Set with Candle Holders ▲
• 1880
Lady's glazed desktop writing set with ink well and candle holders designed with an oriental theme.
• *height 15cm*
• £3,500   • London Antique

Gilded Cup and Saucer ▲
• 1890
Porcelain cup and saucer by Sampson. Decorated with a chinoiserie-influenced design. Both the cup and saucer have gilded rims.
• *height 8cm*
• £45   • London Antique

Picasso Bowl ▲
• 1952
A Picasso bowl with a wide rim. The centre of the bowl is hand painted in a charcoal and grey wash, with a stylised picture of a raven with stones at its feet.
• *diameter 15cm*
• £755   • London Antique

Dresden Coffee Cup and Saucer ▲
• 1880
Dresden coffee cup and saucer with scrolled decoration and gilding. The cup has a barley twist handle and stands on three paw feet. Decorated with a central lobed cartouche showing a romantic setting.
• *height 8cm*
• £285   • London Antique

Meissen Decorative Column ▶
• 1870
Meissen column converted for use as an electric lamp. Featuring cherub adornment and flower encrustation with scrolled asymmetric designs about the base.
• *height 50cm*
• £485   • London Antique

Royal Copenhagen Ware ▲
• 1945
Royal Copenhagen blue and white cup and saucer, with interlaced banding and foliate designs.
• *height 10cm*
• £35   •London Antique

Meissen Shell Salt ▲

- *circa 1755*

Meissen shell salt in the form of an upturned shell the interior painted with a spray of puce, iron-red and yellow flowers with scattered sprigs, on scroll moulded feet, blue crossed swords mark.
- *diameter 10.2cm*
- £1,200 • London Antique

French Cup and Saucer ▲

- *circa 1860*

French cup, saucer and plate, centred with a cartouche of a chateau with gilt banding.
- *plate diameter 18.5cm*
- £140 • A. Piotrowski

Nudenmiller Sauce Boat ▲

- *1780*

Nudenmiller sauce boat with scrolled handle and shaped rim, with floral sprays and gilding.
- *width 15cm*
- £400 • Stockspring Antiques

Dutch Delft Kylins ▼

- *1860*

One of a pair of Dutch Delft Kylins decorated with a blue and white floral design, seated with their mouths open.
- *height 32cm*
- £795 • Gloria Sinclair

Limoges plate ▲

- *1895*

Limoges plate enamelled with a floral spray of crimson and pink flowers with green and gold leaves, within a heavily gilded border.
- *diameter 23cm*
- £115 • A. Piotrowski

Irish Belleek Basket ▲

- *circa 1880*

Irish Belleek moulded cream latticework basket with three bunches of roses and daisies.
- *height 5cm*
- £155 • London Antique

Sèvres Dinner Plate ▲

- *circa 1814*

Sèvres dinner plate decorated with cherubs holding roses, on the side is the royal crest of M Imple de Sèvres, lst Empire.
- *diameter 24cm*
- £225 • London Antique

Meissen Salts ◀

- *circa 1736-40*
Meissen salts modelled by J.F. Eberlein, basket shaped bowl with rope twist handles painted with a bird, supported by three male caryatid figures terminating in gilt-edged double scroll feet. Completed by Eberlein for the Sulkowsky service. Listed in the factory records of June 1736.
- *height 10cm*
- **£1,950**   • London Antique

Saltglazed Stainwear Tankard ▲

- *1690*
Westerwald saltglazed stainwear tankard with a pewter cover and cartouches decorating the body showing portraits of royalty.
- *height 17cm*
- **£1,650**   • Jonathan Horne

Dresden Goblet ▶

- *circa 1880*
Dresden goblet with saucer decorated with cherubs and children playing, with a blue iridescent interior and gilt leaves circling the base and saucer marked with a Crown and Dresden.
- *height 9cm*
- **£465**   • London Antique

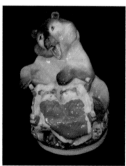

Russian Bear ▲

- *circa 1890*
Russian mother bear with two baby bears in a cradle covered with an orange cover with white spots, set on a circular floral and green base.
- *height 20cm*
- **£250**   • Gloria Sinclair

Parisian Porcelain Plates ▲

- *1830*
Part of a set of six Parisian porcelain plates with a green border and gilt foliate designs with dragon flies and a central cartouche of painted rose and tulips, cornflowers and pansies.
- *diameter 16cm*
- **£980**   • Stockspring Antiques

Dresden Group ▲

- *circa 1870*
Dresden group of young girl and two men around a pillar with a cherub holding a rose, on the base is a basket overflowing with pink roses and garlands.
- *height 30cm*
- **£675**   • Gloria Sinclair

Vase ▼

- *circa 1910*
Very large, Galileo Chini
lustre with decoration from
Manfactura Di Fontebuoni.
- *height 55cm*
- £6,000–£8,000 • Bazaart

Fruit Basket ▲

- *circa 1870*
Signed Galle on the underside.
With cross twig handles,
butterfly and moth decoration
and grass and flower designs.
With gilding.
- *height 18cm*
- £2,800 • Cameo Gallery

Slipware Dish ▲

- *1740–60*
A feathered slipware dish in lead
glaze from the northern Rhine
with distinctive wavy pattern.
- *diameter 18cm*
- £135 • Garry Atkins

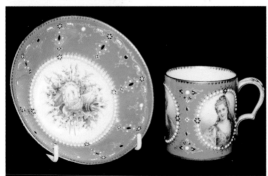

German Jug ▼

- *circa 1480*
A German pottery jug. Rare
with incised face pattern and
banding with handle.
- *height 19cm*
- £850 • Garry Atkins

Stoneware Jug ▼

- *13th century*
A German stoneware jug,
showing the effects of having
partially collapsed in kiln when
being fired, with throwing lines.
- *height 19cm*
- £550 • Garry Atkins

Sèvres Cup and Saucer ◄

- *circa 1880*
Sèvres-style 'jewelled' cup and
saucer. Cup painted with named
portraits on three panels. Saucer
with floral decoration to centre.
- *height 9cm*
- £1,850 • David Brower

Dresden Dancing Figure ▼

• *1945*

Dresden figurine depicting a
Flamenco dancer, standing on an
oval moulded base with gilding.

• *height 12cm*

• **£65**   • **London Antique**

Earthenware Beer Jug ▶

• *circa 1600*

Rare German earthenware beer
jug with stamped and incised
decoration, together with pewter
lid and thumb piece.

• *height 18cm*

• **£3,750**   • **Jonathan Horne**

German Dessert Plate ▼

• *1765*

Nymphenburg dessert plate with
trellis border and birds and flower
design at centre (tulips/roses) and
gilt border.

• *diameter 23cm*

•**£1,400**   • **E. & H. Manners**

Alborelli Vases ▲

• *circa 1700*

Pair of Alborelli vases from
Sciacca, Sicily. Predominantly
blue with cartouches showing
maritime scene framed with
leaf design.

• *height 22cm*

• **£3,000–£4,000**   • **Bazaart**

Alberello Vase ▼

• *circa 1670*

Probably Bassano vase, of
dumbbell form with floral swags
from mask decoration.

• *height 27cm*

• **£1,200–£1,500**   • **Bazaart**

Gallé Cat ▲
- circa 1890

Highly decorated model of a cat with painted gems and scrolled design. Russian crest on hindquarters. Glass eyes, Gallé marked.
- height 34cm
- £4,000 • Constance Stobo

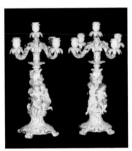

Meissen Candelabra ▲
- 1860

Pair of Meissen candelabra, flower encrusted with detachable arms and cherub decoration. Figures depicting the four seasons.
- height 46cm
- £4,250 • David Brower

Asparagus Dish ▼
- 1870

French asparagus dish with cradle of ceramic asparagus tips.
- height 19cm
- £495 • Jesse Davis

Armorial Alborello ▼
- circa 1580

One of a pair of Armorial alborelli. Naples or Sciacca polychrome with castle motif.
- height 3cm
- £8,000–£12,000 • Bazaart

Vincennes Sucrier ◄
- 1754

Early Vincennes sucrier painted with birds on cartouches on a blue lapis ground. A chrysanthemum finial gilt decoration. With interlaced 'L' and the date letter 'B'.
- height 10cm
- £5,000 • E. & H. Manners

Porcelain Vase ▲
- circa 1870

One of a pair of ormolu mounted Sèvres porcelain vases, with hand painted galant scenes.
- height 62cm
- £14,000 • Judy Fox

Expert Tips

Never lift any piece by its handle. Remove the lid and grip with the finger inside and the thumb outside. The piece may have been weakened by an invisible crack or bad luting.

Vienna Dish ▼
- mid 19th century

A silver mounted Vienna dish with painted panels of maidens and swans at play by a river, entitled 'Sommer Lust'.
- diameter 36cm
- £1,880 • David Brower

107

Majolica Twin-Handled Vase ◄

- **1875**

Majolica twin-handled urn shaped vase with a central frieze showing classical figures above acanthus leaf design on a pedestal foot, by Thomes Sargent.
- *height 49cm*
- **£695**　　　● **Jesse Davis**

Duck Tureens ▲

- **1875**

Pair of polychrome continental soup tureens, probably French, naturalistically formed as a duck and drake in a seated pose.
- *height 11cm*
- **£395**　　　● **Jesse Davis**

Flemish Jug ▲

- **17th century**

Flemish stoneware jug of oval form with silver mounts.
- *height 22cm*
- **£1,400** ● **P. Boyd-Carpenter**

Pineapple Teapot ▲

- **1865**

Majolica teapot, with the body styled as a pineapple with leaf designs, and pineapple finial applied to the cover.
- *height 21cm*
- **£395**　　　● **Jesse Davis**

Majolica Jug ◄

- **1865**

Majolica jug of ovoid form with a pewter lid and thumb piece. Features moulded decoration depicting a forest scene under a green glaze.
- *height 9cm*
- **£195**　　　● **Jesse Davis**

Italian Jug ▲

- **1870**

Italian Majolica palm-leaf jug, with vertical stylised palm leaf decoration to the body of the jug, with a pinched lip and the whole on a splayed foot.
- *height 19cm*
- **£295**　　　● **Jesse Davis**

Islamic Ceramics

Turquoise Glazed Bowl ▼

- **16th century**

Large bowl with banding and geometric chevron designs and floral medallions under a turquoise glaze.
- *diameter 38cm*
- **£2,800**
- Yazdani

Persian Bowl ▶

- **13th century**

A polychrome Persian bowl with a geometric design consisting of seven panels surrounding a central leaf pattern.
- *diameter 18cm*
- **£100**
- Pars

Minai Pottery Bowl ▼

- **circa 1200**

A fine polychrome Minai pottery bowl showing a courtly scene depicting a seated figure in the centre flanked by two attendants. Both the interior and exterior of the rim is decorated with a continuous band of inscriptions.
- *diameter 18cm*
- **£5,500**
- Yazdani

Kashan Bowl ▼

- **11th–13th century**

A Kashan turquoise-glazed conical bowl from central Persia.
- *10cm x 17.5cm*
- **£1,800**
- Pars

Persian Bowl ◀

- **10–11th century AD**

Persian pottery bowl with a cream glaze and two concentric bands bearing inscriptions in a cobalt blue glaze.
- *diameter 20cm*
- **£1,000**
- Pars

Bamiyan Dish ▼

- **12th century**

An Islamic Bamiyan plate with concentric designs surrounding the outline of a bird in the centre of the dish under a green glaze.
- *diameter 23cm*
- **£3,800**
- Yazdani

Gazelle Motif Bowl ▼

- *10th–11th century*
A polychrome bowl from
Nishapur with designs to the
lip surrounding a stylised
gazelle motif.
- *diameter 15.5cm*
- £400 • Pars

Geometric Wall Tile ▼

- *13th century*
A polychrome Islamic wall tile
with repeating geometric pattern.
- *width 12cm*
- £290 • Ghaznavid

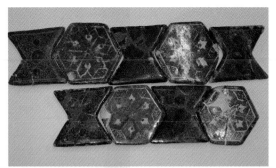

Islamic Tiles ▲

- *12th century*
A group of Islamic tiles in
original condition with a cobalt-
blue and gold glaze showing a
repeating geometric pattern.
- *height 11cm*
- £800 • Ghaznavid

Expert Tips

*When displaying early or
ancient ceramics always make a
prominent statement. Do not
crowd the subject as this will
diminish its impact.*

Turkish Wine Jug ▲

- *1900*
A ceramic Turkish wine ewer
with strap handle in a green glaze.
- *height 33cm*
- £300 • Sinai

Signed Vase ▼

- *19th century*
A very finely patterned Islamic
vase signed by "T.D.".
- *34cm x 23cm*
- £5,500 • Sinai

Large Pottery Tile ◄

- *mid 19th century*
The glazed decoration on this
large tile depicts a lady listening
to musicians.
- *33cm x 43cm*
- £2,500 • Arthur Millner

Gold Lustre Bowl ▶

- *circa 12th century*

Gold lustre bowl with ten panels decorated with a floral design, and a lady seated in the centre.
- *diameter 17cm*
- £4,500 • Sultani

Kashan Vase ▲

- *circa 12th century*

An Islamic vase of bulbous proportions with thumb piece. The body with circular bands of writing and floral designs, raised on a pedestal foot, with stops to the base.
- *height 13cm*
- £1,200 • Solamani Gallery

Terracotta Ewer ▲

- *circa 12th century*

Terracotta small ewer of baluster form, with a long upturned spout and strap handle, with a chevron design running around the middle of the body, raised on a circular foot.
- *height 19.5cm*
- £400 • Rasoul Gallery

Lead-Glazed Bowl ▲

- *11–13th century AD*

Nishapur earthenware glazed bowl decorated with a stylised leaf design, in a ochre, green and brown glaze.
- *diameter 19cm*
- £300 • Pars

Bamiyan Bowl ▼

- *12th century*

Bamiyan pottery bowl decorated with a green and brown star, and stylised leaf designs, over a cream underglaze.
- *diameter 17.5cm*
- £600 • Rasoul Gallery

Six-Sided Star Bowl ▲

- *circa 12th century*

Small brown glazed bowl with a six-sided star in a cream glaze inside, with scrolling around the inside of the rim.
- *diameter 14cm*
- £800 • Sultani

Persian Pottery Dish ▲

- *10–11th century AD*

Large pottery dish decorated with a green and brown glaze with an inscribed circular design with beading.
- *diameter 34cm*
- £1,500 • Pars

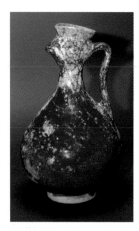

Kashan Water Jug ▲
- *11–12th century*
Cockerel-headed water jug with lajvar glaze and strap handle.
- *height 29cm*
- £5,500 • Yacobs

Tiled Panel ▲
- *circa 1760*
A North African, hand-painted, tiled panel showing with floral and leaf meanderings.
- *height 88cm*
- £2,000 • Sinai

Expert Tips

Half-glazed pieces are not failures or rejects; that is how they are made.

Clay Goddess ▼
- *3000 BC*
Mother goddess statue from Tel-Halaf in Syria offering fruitfulness.
- *height 17cm*
- £3,000 • Aaron

Drug Jar ▼
- *12th century*
Persian drug jar with floral design on black and blue glaze.
- *height 23cm*
- £3,200 • Samiramis

Kushan Tile ▶
- *13th century*
Eight-pointed star with phoenix and floral decoration.
- *height 21cm*
- £700 • Samiramis

Nishapur Dish ▲
- *11–13th century*
Nishapur polychrome dish with stylised deer.
- *diameter 18cm*
- £300 • Pars

Kushan Bottle ▲
- *13th century*
Balloon body with long neck and cup-shaped lip. Turquoise glaze with Kufic writing.
- *height 28cm*
- £3,405 • Samiramis

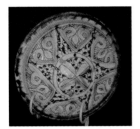

Bamiyan Pottery Bowl ▲
- *12th century*
Bamiyan pottery bowl decorated
with a green and brown star
pattern with a cream underglaze.
- *diameter 19cm*
- £1,000   • Rasoul Gallery

Bamiyan Turquoise Bowl ▼
- *circa 12th century*
Small Bamiyan turquoise bowl,
centered with a small bird, with a
ribbed design radiating from the
centre.
- *height 6cm*
- £500   • Rasoul Gallery

Persian Dish ▲
- *circa 10th century*
Persian bowl with three panels
with Kufic inscriptions in blue
and yellow ochre.
- *diameter 29cm*
- £3,000   • Sultani

Guazin Water Jug ◄
- *circa 12th century*
Pottery water jug from Guazin
with unusual brown, black and
sandstone glaze.
- *height 21cm*
- £1,200   • Sultani

Nishapur Vessel ▲
- *11–13th century AD*
Nishapur pottery dish known as
silhouette ware, decorated with a
green glaze and a cream lotus
design in the centre, raised on a
splayed foot.
- *diameter 22cm*
- £550   • Pars

Kashan Jar ▲
- *12–13th century*
A small Kasham jar of bulbous
form with strap handle and acorn
thumb piece in a cobalt-blue
glaze.
- *height 13cm*
- £800   • Pars

Expert Tips

*The French art nouveau glass,
by makers such as Gallé,
was heavily influenced by
the technique and style of
early Islamic potters, in
particular their use of
translucent and iridescent
decoration and enamelling.*

Kufic Bowl ▶

- *11–13 century AD*
Turquoise pottery bowl with
Kufic script running around the
body, with turned decoration and
a wide splayed lip.
- *diameter 22cm*
- £1,200   • Pars

Samakan Bowl ▼

- *circa 11th century*
Central Asian bowl, probably
Samakan, with a floral pattern
and Kufic inscriptions, translated
as, "Prosperity and Health to the
owner of the bowl".
- *diameter 19cm*
- £1,200   • Rasoul Gallery

Water Jug ◀

- *circa 12th century*
Persian small water vessel, of
conical form with strap handle,
brown circular designs, and raised
on a circular foot.
- *height 14.4cm*
- £250   • Rasoul Gallery

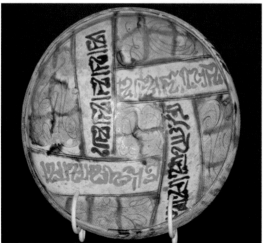

Persian Bowl ◀

- *12th century*
Persian bowl decorated with a
central figure of a lady and
inscribed with Kufic and Persian
writing.
- *diameter 21cm*
- £2,20   • Sultani

Persian Water Vessel ▲

- *circa 12th–13th century*
Persian water vessel of baluster
form with strap handle and
thumb piece, decorated with birds
and circular designs, with Kufic
and Arabic inscriptions with a
pink lustre glaze.
- *height 21cm*
- £6,500   • Sultani

Timori Bowl ▲

- *circa 15–16th century*
Timori bowl decorated with a
blue glazed hexagonal design
around the inside, with a central
blue, white and black flower in
the center.
- *diameter 19cm*
- £1,000   • Rasoul Gallery

Sandcore Ure ▼
- **2nd century BC**
Pinchel lip with a comb design
overglaze, in brown and cream.
- *height 12cm*
- £4,000 • Aaron

Kashan Sprinkler ▼
- **11th–13th century**
Turquoise, monochrome glaze
sprinkler with bosses to neck.
- *height 11cm*
- £550 • Pars

Persian Vases ▶
- **19th century**
A pair of baluster-form vases
decorated with flora, birds and
animals in a blue glaze.
- *height 27cm*
- £800 • Shahdad

Terracotta Pipe ▲
- **circa 1855**
Silver and gold gilded Tophane
pipe with gilded floral base.
- *height 5cm*
- £850 • Sinai

Parthian Pitcher ▲
- **1st–3rd century**
Pre-Islam earthenware pitcher of
concial, teardrop form, with
green glaze and iridescence.
- *height 20cm*
- £800 • Pars

Tiled Panel ▼
- **circa 1760**
A North African, hand-painted,
tiled panel showing urn with
floral and leaf meanderings.
- *height 88cm*
- £2,000 • Sinai

Damascus Pottery Tile

- *17th century*
Pottery tile decorated with arabesque and iris motif.
- *20cm x 22cm*
- **£400**   • **Arthur Millner**

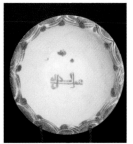

Kashan Jug

- *12th–13th century*
A Kashan jug of bulbous form with a splayed neck and strap handle in a turquoise and black glaze with stops to the base.
- *height 22cm*
- **£1,000**   • **Pars**

Pre-Ottoman Vase

- *12th century*
A green monochrome vase from the pre-Ottoman Empire period. Of a baluster form with a wide lip and two handles to the shoulders with extensive openwork decoration to the body. The whole is raised on a circular foot ring.
- *height 35cm*
- **£400**   • **Pars**

Nishapur Bowl

- *13th century*
A Nishapur bowl with the Kufic calligraphic inscription "healthy and long life".
- *diameter 30cm*
- **£2,000**   • **Shiraz**

Ceramic Bowl

- *circa 9th century*
A blue and white, tin-glazed ceramic bowl of the Abbasid period, the rim with blue swags.
- *diameter 21cm*
- **£15,000**   • **Axia**

Kashan Vase

- *13th century*
A small Kashan vase with balloon body and long neck with fine iridescence and stops to base.
- *height 14cm*
- **£950**   • **Yazdani**

Oriental Ceramics

Imari Vases ▼
- 1890

Pair of cylindrical Imari vases of famille verte, each with a splayed lip.
- *height 17cm*
- **£1, 890** • **Japanese Gallery**

Amari Bowl ▲
- 1880

Amari fluted bowl with famille vert floral decoration and lattice border, set in ormolu mounts.
- *height 20cm*
- **£2,885** • **Japanese Gallery**

Octagonal Vase ▲
- 1890

Octagonal Satsuma vase of famille verte, with alternating panels of stylised floral decoration and gilding
- *height 24cm*
- **£2,980** • **Japanese Gallery**

Pair of Satsuma Vases ▼
- 1890

Pair of Satsuma bottle vases in the shape of double gourds. Each vase is decorated with two figures at the base of the neck embellished with profuse gilding.
- *height 24cm*
- **£2,980** • **Japanese Gallery**

Expert Tips

When purchasing Satsuma and Amari ware, the general rule of thumb is that the larger the item the better the price. As always, good condition is fundamental. In the last twenty years these oriental wares have become so popular that it has heralded a flood of reproductions into the market.

Gilded Vase ◄
- 1910

Satsuma vase of baluster form, showing figures in a garden setting, and decorated with gilded and stylised floral patterns.
- *height 21cm*
- **£355** • **Japanese Gallery**

Covered Imari Pot ▲
- late 18th century

Imari pot and cover, with a pair of gilded handles and ornate dog finial.
- *height 30cm*
- **£1,950** • **Japanese Gallery**

Cylindrical Hat Stand ▲
- *circa 19th century*

Cylindrical shape porcelain hat stand painted with a pink cherry blossom tree with a song bird, sitting above a pond, with a poem dedicated to the owner with leaf shape openings for airing. Seal of manufacturer on the base. Ex Guonxi period.
- *height 29cm*
- £385 • Iren Rakosa

Chinese Sauce Tureen ▶
- *circa 1760*

Very rare Chinese export sauce tureen and cover, modelled as a sitting quail on its nest and painted in iron red, black and green. Qianlong period.
- *height 9cm*
- £6,700 • Cohen & Cohen

Expert Tips

To authenticate a piece of Ming blue and white ware, it is necessary to study the following aspects of the piece: painting techniques, wash methods, lines, brush strokes, form and shape, clay and glazes used and the evolution of motifs.

Chinese Vase ▼
- *circa 1770*

A fine quality Chinese export porcelain, two handled vase, decorated with a turquoise chicken skin ground and bright 'Mandarin' panels. Quianlong Period.
- *height 24cm*
- £420 • Dando

Famille Rose Teapot ◀
- *circa 1790*

Famille rose teapot with a scene after Watteau of Europe, in a garden watched by Pierot. Qianlong Period.
- *height 12cm*
- £1,000 • Cohen & Cohen

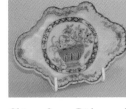

Chinese Spoon Dish ▲
- *circa 1760*

Miniature Chinese export spoon dish with shaped rim and a central panel of fruit and flowers in a bowl.
- *length 13cm*
- £240 • Dando

Annamese Dish ▲
- *12th century*

Annamese dish with scalloped edge with a bold chrysanthemum in the centre, under a olive-green glaze.
- *diameter 15cm*
- £250 • Ormonde Gallery

Famille Verte Bowl ◄
- *1662–22*

Chinese export bowl decorated on the exterior with overglaze enamels in the famille verte palette with birds flying amid prunus plants, issuing from stylised rockwork.
- *diameter 22cm*
- £980   • A. & S. Gray

Pair of Baluster Jars ▲
- *1740*

Important pair of baluster jars and covers of famille rose, painted with three medallions of scenes from a romance on an elaborate floral ground.
- *height 62cm*
- £55,000   • Cohen & Cohen

Chinese Teapot ▼
- *1730*

Unusual Chinese export teapot and cover in the style of a European silver shape, with loop handle and zoomorphic spout, decorated in rose/verte enamels.
- *height 14cm*
- £3,200   • Cohen & Cohen

Christening Bowl ▲
- *1750*

Massive and exceptionally rare christening bowl painted with four bands of lotus petals in green, purple, blue and rose, with four floral reserves.
- *24.5cm x 55cm*
- £43,000   • Cohen & Cohen

Oil and Vinegar Cruet ▲
- *1740*

Chinese Imari oil and vinegar cruet, comprising two lidded sparrow-beak jugs in a stand with a loop handle. All with floral decoration.
- *16cm x 14cm*
- £2,750   • Cohen & Cohen

Famille Rose Bowl ◄
- *1760*

Famille Rose punchbowl with two large panels of pagodas by a lake and surrounded by mountains on a soufflé blue and gilt ground.
- *diameter 39cm*
- £5,000   • Cohen & Cohen

Japanese Bowl ◀

- 1890

Japanese bowl decorated in gold with painted figures.
- *height 8cm*
- £1,250 • Japanese Gallery

Valentine Charger ▼

- 1760

Famille Rose charger decorated with a version of the valentine pattern above which are arms of an English family.
- *diameter 25cm*
- £2250 • Cohen & Cohen

Satsuma Teapot ▼

- 1890

Satsuma teapot, decorated with scholarly figures in a garden setting with rocks and foliage.
- *height 11cm*
- £155 • Japanese Gallery

Figure of Kwanyin ▼

- 1700

Biscuit figure in famille verte of Kwanyin seated on a throne fronted by lotus leaves. The group comprises two pieces.
- *height 44cm*
- £6,850 • Cohen & Cohen

Yenyen Vases ▶

- 1690

One of a pair of large Chinese export blue and white Yenyen vases, decorated with panels of flowers in jardiniers between rows of floral lappets.
- *height 54cm*
- £35,000 • Cohen & Cohen

Moon Flask Ewer ▲

- *circa 1750*

Exceptionally rare polychrome ewer and cover of moon flask form, with panels within borders of bats and cranes and cell diaper.
- *height 30cm*
- £50,000 • Cohen & Cohen

Quenti Pot ▲

- *Mid 20th century*

Very large impressively constructed Quenti pot, with diagrammatic decoration.
- *65cm x 45cm*
- £1,800 • Gordon Reece

Famille Rose Soup Plate ▼
- *1735*

A pair of soup plates of famille rose style painted with arms of Rose of Kilvarock within a border of flowers and inner rim diaper of trelis en grisaille.
- *diameter 23cm*
- £2,600 • Cohen & Cohen

Blue and White Kangxi Dish ▼
- *circa 1690*

Fine deep dish decorated with panels of mounted warriors in underglaze blue with six-character reign mark on the reverse and ruyi-heads on rim underside.
- *diameter 24cm*
- £1,650 • Cohen & Cohen

Famille Rose Style Dish ▲
- *1740*

A Qianlong famille rose style dish enamelled with peonies inside an unfolded scroll on a diaper ground strewn with floral sprays.
- *diameter 35cm*
- £1,900 • Cohen & Cohen

Armorial Milk Jug ▲
- *circa 1740*

Export armorial milk jug with the Dutch arms of van Zandijk of Zeeland, a rouge de fer and gilt spearhead border to rim.
- *height 10cm*
- £1,400 • Cohen & Cohen

Small Pair of Fine Chinese Mandarin Vases ▼
- *Qianlong period 1736–95*

Qianlong vases of flattened baluster form, moulded with fluted, flaring neck and two side handles. Decorated in the mandarin palette.
- *height 15.4cm*
- £1,100 • A. & S. Gray

Blue and White Stemcup ▼
- *Kangxi period 1662–1722*

Standing on a domed base, the stem with raised middle section, decorated around the body with flowers and foliage, with bands of stiff leaves at the stem.
- *height 15cm*
- £850 • A. & S. Gray

Famille Verte Bowl ◄
- *Kangxi period 1662–1722*

Decorated with four cartouches of kylins and deer with a border of four bird cartouches. The inside rim has a border of four floral cartouches reserved on a diaper ground.
- *height 8cm*
- £650 • A. & S. Gray

Expert Tips

Copies made by Böttger at Meissen, in c.1710, of the first Chinese porcelain to reach Europe, are few in number and have a very much higher historical and financial value than the originals which he copied.

Teacup and Saucer ▶

- *1720*

Chinese teacup and saucer.
Decorated with strong famille
rose enamels showing an East
Indiaman under full sail.
Yongzheng period.
- *height 4cm*
- £800   • Cohen & Cohen

Chinese Coffee Pot ▼

- *1750*

Unusual and rare Chinese export
coffee pot. Meissen with closed
cover and dragonhead spout. Blue
underglaze decorated with
peonies. Qianlong period.
- *height 28cm*
- £4,500   • Cohen & Cohen

Chinese Imari Vase ◀

- *Kangxi Period 1662–1722*

Moulded ribbed body and flanged
neck. Underglaze blue and
overglaze iron red. Four floral
sprays of peony.
- *height 26.5cm*
- £2,200   • A. & S. Gray

Famille Verte Fluted Bowl ▲

- *Kangxi Period 1662–1722*

Decorated in underglaze blue and
famille verte enamels with four
different pairs of designs in
alternating panels. The interior is
in famille verte enamels.
- *diameter 15cm*
- £750   • J.A.N. Fine Art

Earthenware Bowl ▲

- *19th century*

Satsumaware. Made in Japan.
19th-century earthenware.
Painted with goldfish interior.
- *height 9cm*
- £1,700   • J.A.N. Fine Art

Chinese Famille Rose Tankard ▼

- *Qianlong period 1736–95*

Tankard of barrel form. Decorated
in bright enamels in the
Mandarin palette; the front of the
body with a large cartouche.
- *height 12.2cm*
- £700   • A. & S. Gray

Okimono Porcelain Puppy ▼

- *19th century*

Aritaware Okimono of a
porcelain puppy scratching his
ears. With painted polychrome
ruff painted eyes
- *height 12.5cm*
- £2,000   • Gregg Baker

Armorial Plates ▼

- *1745*

Pair of Chinese porcelain plates
decorated in bright enamels with
the arms of 'Minchin of
Monnegall'.
- *diameter 22.5cm*
- £3,500   • A. & S. Gray

Chinese Tankard ▼

- *circa 1770*

Export Chinese porcelain tankard with 'Mandrin' style panel depicting a courtly scene.
- *height 24cm*
- £235
- Dando

Oriental Cup ▼

- *16th century*

Blue and white cup with a wide splayed rim, with a blue lattice design running around the exterior, above a song bird with prunus blossom.
- *height 5cm*
- £450
- Ormonde Gallery

Sauce Tureen and Cover ▶

- *circa 1765*

Rare Chinese export sauce tureen, cover and stand of English creamware form. Painted with the arms of Parker imp. Nesbitt, within a diaper border. Qianlong period. Made for the widow of the second Earl of Macclesfield (Parker), she was a Nesbitt.
- *height of tureen 13cm*
- £16,000
- Cohen & Cohen

Desk Set ▲

- *circa 1760*

Rare and unusual famille rose desk set from the Qianlong period. Comprising five quill holders, two inkwells with pewter liners and a covered box.
- *height 6cm*
- £4,800
- Cohen & Cohen

Chinese Marriage Plate ▲

- *circa 1750*

Exceptionally rare Chinese export marriage plate made for the Dutch market, with a polychrome depiction of the ship Slooten, from the Qianlong period.
- *diameter 36cm*
- £12,500
- Cohen & Cohen

Tea Bowl and Saucer ▲

- *circa 1735*

Chinese export porcelain tea bowl and saucer, profusely gilded with floral sprays and cartouches of prunus with a central panel of a Chinese gentleman.
- *diameter of cup 6cm*
- £225
- Dando

Nanking Bowl and Saucer ▲

- *1790*

Nanking blue and white bowl and saucer with pagoda scenes and later English gilding.
- *diameter of saucer 13cm*
- £125
- Dando

Nankin Tureen ▲

- *1736–95*
Elongated, octagonal blue-and-white Nankin tureen. Decorated with tiny figures among pagodas and bridges over waterways. Well-modelled fruit as knob and handles
- *length 35cm*
- £1,200 • A. & S. Gray

Chinese Cloisonné Vase ▶

- *early 18th century*
Cloisonné enamel vase of yan yan form, from the Qing Dynasty period. High-shouldered tapering body with two gilt monster mask and lotus leaf handles, standing on a flared foot. Decorated in colourful enamels on a turquoise and lapis blue ground filled with scrolling lotus, dragon designs, bats, and flower heads, with gilt trim on base and rim.
- *height 67.3cm*
- £18,000 • Gerard Hawthorn

Porcelain Tureen ▼

- *17th century*
Japanese Imari porcelain tureen and underdish, featuring a bird fruit and flower decoration.
- £12,000 • Gerard Hawthorn

Swatow Dish ▼

- *early 17th century*
Circular dish painted to the centre with a circular panel of two kylins playing with a broaded ball, surrounded by symbolic objects and scrollwork
- *diameter 37cm*
- £1,600 • A. & S. Gray

Octagonal Bowl ▼

- *18th century*
Octagonal bowl from the Kukieman Edo period, decorated with a central design of birds with floral border.
- *5cm x 13cm*
- £1,550 • Japanese Gallery

Porcelain Punchbowl ◀

- *18th century*
Finely decorated Chinese punchbowl in famille rose, from the Quing Dynasty period. Decorated with enamel figures set in a garden landscape.
- *17cm x 40cm*
- £8,000 • Gerard Hawthorn

Chinese Chocolate Pot ◀
- *circa 1775*
Unusual Chinese export bulbous chocolate pot.
- *height 19.5cm*
- £9,000   • Cohen & Cohen

Tea Bowl and Saucer ▲
- *circa 1770*
Famille rose tea bowl and saucer, decorated with a group of European figures in a garden within a gilt, pink and grisaille border. Qianlong period.
- *height of cup 4.5cm diameter of saucer 13cm*
- £950   • Cohen & Cohen

Famille Rose Plate ▼
- *circa 1740*
One of a pair of fine and rare famille rose botanical plates, each vividly painted with a cornucopia of European flowers, made in the Qianlong period.
- *diameter 23cm*
- £10,700   • Cohen & Cohen

Chinese Export Plate ▲
- *circa 1760*
Chinese export famille rose porcelain plate with floral sprays and gilding.
- *diameter 15cm*
- £375   • Dando

Chinese Hat Stand ▶
- *circa 19th century*
Porcelain hat stand of cylindrical form with a polychrome glaze of scholarly objects, flora and Buddhist symbols. The stand has a six leaf shape opening for airing. Seal at the base. Ex-Guonxi period.
- *height 29cm*
- £350   • Iren Rakosa

Kutani Jar and Cover ▼

- *circa 19th century*
Kutani jar and cover, two panels with river setting. Dragon decoration on base and finial.
- *height 20cm*
- £490   • J.A.N. Fine Art

Blue and White Mustard Pot ▲

- *Kangxi period 1662–1722*
The moulded body decorated with alternating panels of maidens and baskets of flowers, between borders of stylised flowerheads. The base with an artemisia leaf.
- *height 10cm*
- £850   • A. & S. Gray

Kangxi Famille Verte Dish ▼

- *circa 1700*
Decorated with a basket of flowers at the centre. Radiating panels of flowers and rock work. Rim border with cartouches of peaches.
- *diameter 35cm*
- £2,500   • Guest & Gray

Joss-Stick Holders ▶

- *circa 1662–1722*
A pair of Chinese egg and spinach biscuit joss-stick holders, modelled in the shape of Dogs of Fo Buddhist lions
- *height 8.5cm*
- £2,300   • Guest & Gray

Fluted Bowls ▼

- *circa 1700*
Pair of Kangxi fluted bowls, decorated with panels of flowers and mythological beasts.
- *diameter 18.5cm*
- £2,500   • Guest & Gray

Kangxi Famille Verte Dish

- *circa 1700*
Polychrome lobed dish with scholarly items and flowers with gilding. Central panel shows woman in domestic setting with butterflies.
- *height 22cm*
- £850   • J.A.N. Fine Art

Qianlong Vase ◀

- *Qianlong period 1736–96*
Quinlong Chinese coral monochrome glaze vase. Globular body with narrow flared neck, splayed foot
- *height 19cm*
- £1,250   • Guest & Gray

Clocks, Watches & Scientific Instruments

This category includes all forms of clock from carriage to longcase, fine watches to the antiques of the future and all scientific artefacts.

Scientific – and, particularly, timekeeping instruments – have never been more popular. Perhaps the change of millennium and the chaos it was supposed to cause among those reliant on high technology has re-engendered a love of those accurate instruments which sailed through the millennium barrier without missing a beat. In any case, man will always be fascinated by the ingenuity of his forebears. At the top end of the market, prices are high, largely because there have

been very few really good English clocks coming onto the market. Rare English longcase specimens by good makers are fetching very much higher prices than they were two or three years ago. Lower down the market, mahogany longcases with painted dials have almost caught up in value with earlier, brass-dialled specimens. This is largely because the clock market is now no longer dominated by serious collectors, but is catering for those who desire them as beautiful objects to adorn the home.

Clocks

English Longcase Clock ◀
- *circa 1800*
Flame mahogany English 8-day longcase clock with brass square dial and subsidiary silvered second ring, the florally engraved centre dial inscribed, 'John Smith, Chester'.
- *220cm x 56cm*
- £5,900   • Gütlin Clocks

Chagrin Mantle Clock ▲
- *1920*
English made chagrin leather cased clock, with a white face and white ivory stringing, the whole resting on ivory feet.
- *height 14cm*
- £2,750   • Bentleys

Scottish Longcase Clock ▲
- *circa 1830*
Flame mahogany belly door longcase clock by Christie and Barrie of Abroath, with Scottish 8- day, break arch, painted dial. 'The Cotters Saturday Night' painted in the break arch with four seasons to the corner spandrels. 8- day movement with subsidiary seconds and date.
- *220cm x 38cm*
- £6,500   • Gütlin Clocks

Gilt Bronze Clock ▲
- *circa 1880*
A gilt bronze ormolu French mantel clock with blue porcelain panels. The fine ormolu case depicts a woman rested on a rock with her dog with original mercury gilding. The porcelain panels include pictures of flowers, eight day movement with hour and half hour strikes on a bell. White enamel dial with black roman numerals. Dial signed by the retailers "Maitrot à Dijon". movement by Vincenti and Cie.
- *45cm x 50cm x 10cm*
- **£2,900**   • Gütlin Clocks

French Mantel Clock ▲
- *circa 1870*
A decorative late nineteenth century French mantel clock with simulated red tortoiseshell and engraved brass boulle work. The top of the case is surmounted by a seated maiden holding a bunch of flowers with figures of children to sides of case. Eight day movement by "'Hry Marc", Paris. Thirteen pieces, enamel cartouche gilt ormolu dial enclosed by a heavily chiselled front bezel with a very thick front glass.
- *63cm x 35.5cm x 16.5cm*
- **£2,500**   • Gütlin Clocks

George III Bracket Clock ▼
- *circa 1780*
A George III London-made bracket clock in figured mahogany case with pagoda top. Eight day movement with fully engraved backplate and original verge escapement. Unusually for an eighteenth century English clock, it strikes on the hour and half hour. Dial with centre calendar, strike/silent in the arch and signed by the maker.
- *height 58cm*
- **£8,900**   • Clock Clinic

Hallmarked Clock ▼
- *1904*
Small, red leather and silver-fronted mantel clock with silver hallmark "Birmingham 1904". Eight day movement on platform escapement in very original condition, white enamel dial with roman black numerals and black spade hands.
- *20cm x 10cm x 5cm*
- **£850**   • Gütlin Clocks

English Moonroller Clock ▲
- *circa 1830*
An English all-mahogany moonroller longcase clock by "Carruthers" of Carlisle. Painted flower spandrels with globes below break arch. The moonroller disc includes scenes of a French galleon at sea and a country chapel. The case with canted corners, square flamed mahogany door and flame mahogany base with ebony and boxwood stringing sitting on ogée feet.
- *233cm x 53cm x 51cm*
- **£8,500**   • Gütlin Clocks

Lyre Clock ▲
- *circa 1900*
Attractive French lyre clock, the strings forming the moving pendulum. Paste brillants surround the floral enamel dial. *Bleu de Roi* porcelain case with gilded mounts and Medusa head in a sunray to top. Eight day movement striking the hours on a bell. The whole in excellent condition, overhauled and guaranteed.
- *height 49cm*
- **£6,600**   • Clock Clinic

First Empire Mantle Clock ▼

• *circa 1830*
Gilt ormolu and bronze first empire French mantle clock by 'Douillon'. The case with two cherubs holding the face with gilt swag mounts in the centre. 8-day silk suspension movement, silvered waterslik dial signed by retailer. Chimes hours & half hours on a bell.
• *46cm x 47cm*
• **£2,400**　　• Gütlin Clocks

French Clock ▼

• *circa 1880*
French gilt brass glass clock with signed ivory miniature pendulum surrounded by diamonte stones. The pendulum with a hand painted miniature ivory portrait of a maiden. 8-day movement by 'Mougin'.
• *30.5cm x 18.5cm*
• **£1,500**　　• Gütlin Clocks

Gilt Ormulu Mantle Clock ▲

• *circa 1860*
Gilt ormulu French mantle clock with 8-day movement chiming hours and half hours on a bell. The case in the form of a wine barrel with cherubs sitting on the barrel, supported by male figures. 12 piece white enamel cartouche dial with fleur de leys hands and black Roman numerals.
• *51cm x 36cm*
• **£2,800**　　• Gütlin Clocks

'Le Paute' Fils Clock ▲

• *circa 1812*
Birds-eye maple and ebony strung French wooden mantle clock. The fine quality silk suspension movement by 'Le Paute' & Fils. Hrs du Roi (Horologer to the King). Signed silvered dial.
• *35.5cm x 15cm*
• **£2,500**　　• Gütlin Clocks

First Empire Clock ▼

• *circa 1870*
French gilt ormolu and bronze mantle clock in the form of an oil lamp with an angel being warmed by the lamp. 8-day movement with hour and half hour strike on a bell. White enamel dial with black roman numerals and finely chiselled gilt brass hands.
• *35.5cm x 20cm*
• **£2,800**　　• Gütlin Clocks

Propeller Blade Clock ▲

• *circa 1900*
An industrial timepiece propeller blade clock with ships capstan containing a compass, gilded lifebelt, apothec and anchor. An 8-day cylinder escapement timepiece French movement, gilded dial with black roman numerals and fleurs de lys hands.
• *33.5cm x 34.5cm*
• **£1,600**　　• Gütlin Clocks

Expert Tips

The springs from which pendulums are suspended are fragile and easily broken in transit. Secure or remove pendulums on long journeys.

French Lyre Clock ▼

- *circa 1900*

A satinwood and gilt ormolu mounted French timepiece lyre clock retailed by 'Howell and James', Paris. 8-day French movement with original English lever escapement, convex cream enamel dial with hand painted swags of roses boarding black arabic numerals.
- *25.5cm x 12.5cm*
- **£1,600**   • Gütlin Clocks

Three Piece Clock Garniture ▼

- *circa 1870*

French gilt bronze and cloisonne enamelled three piece clock garniture. 8-day movement chiming hours and half hours on a bell. The gilt bronze and blue porcelain case with fine cloisonne enamelling and urn shaped side pieces.
- *40.5cm x 22.5cm*
- **£3,700**   • Gütlin Clocks

3 Piece Clock Garniture ▲

- *circa 1860*

A gilt bronze and jewelled pink porcelain French 3 piece clock garniture, gilt bronze case with porcelain panels surmounted by an urn with gilt bronze mounts, 8-day French movement chiming hours and half hours on the bell.
- *43cm x 30.5cm*
- **£5,500**   • Gütlin Clocks

Mantle Clock ▲

- *circa 1890*

A white Paris Bisque French timepiece mantle clock with small French 8-day timepiece movement, white convex enamel dial with roman numerals and counter poised moon hands.
- *25.5cm x 15.5cm*
- **£750**   • Gütlin Clocks

Black Marble Clock ▼

- *circa 1860*

French black marble mantle clock with a gilt bronze figure of a maiden reading a book resting on a column with a lyre beside her, 8-day French movement. Hour and half hour strike on a bell.
- *61cm x 56cm*
- **£3,500**   • Gütlin Clocks

French Four Glass Clock ▼

- *circa 1870*

A polished brass French four day glass clock with diamonte bezel, 8-day movement with hour and half hour strike on a gong and mercury pendulum, the white enamelled dial painted with pink music sheets.
- *25.5cm x 5cm*
- **£1,600**   • Gütlin Clocks

Mantle Clock ◄

- *circa 1880*

French gilt metal and porcelain mantle clock, the gilt ormolu case swags to the sides, acanthus cast gallery to the base raised on toupie feet. The pink porcelain panels with gilt- bordered white reserves painted with flowers.
- *51cm x 25.5cm*
- **£2,300**   • Gütlin Clocks

English Bracket Clock ▲
- *circa 1840*
A finely figured flame mahogany
English bracket clock. The twin
gut fusée movement with
shoulder plates and hour strike on
a bell. White painted convex dial
signed "Taylor of Bristol" with
black spade hands within a finely
figured rectangular mahogany
case sitting on ball feet.
- *53cm x 30.5cm*
- **£3,500**   • Gütlin Clocks

French Mantel Clock ▲
- *circa 1900*
A good quality gilt bronze and
blue porcelain panelled French
mantel clock. White convex
enamel dial with black roman
numerals and eight day
movement chiming hours and
half hours on a bell signed by
"Raingo Freres".
- *34cm x 24cm x 10cm*
- **£3,100**   • Gütlin Clocks

Expert Tips

*Always check to see if the name
of the clock maker has been
engraved on the back plate –
many a bargain has been
found this way.*

Three-Train Bracket Clock ▼
- *circa 1850*
An English three train, quarter
striking, ebonised and gilt ormolu
mounted bracket clock standing
on its original bracket. The arch
topped case has finely chiselled
mounts, caryatids to sides of case
and ormolu mounted side frets.
The movement is of high quality
with engraved back plate chiming
on nine bells with hour strike on
a large nickeled bell. Engraved
silver chapter ring with black
roman numerals and matted
centre to dial with finely
chiselled ormolu spandrels and
two subsidiary dials in break arch.
- *55cm x 33cm*
- **£5,500**   • Gütlin Clocks

Oak Bracket Clock ▼
- *circa 1840*
A carved oak English bracket
clock by the famous "Walker" of
London with blue spade hands.
English eight day chain fusée
movement of fine quality with
original pendulum holdfast.
- *43cm x 35.5cm x 20cm*
- **£1,900**   • Gütlin Clocks

Austrian Bracket Clock ▲
- *circa 1750*
A well-made oak-cased original
Austrian grand sonnerie bracket
clock. The very finely foliate
engraved dial has Dutch-type
silvered, chapter ring, date
aperture and two subsidiary dials
with makers name plaque signed
"Augustin Heckel". The triple
fusee Austrian movement is of
short duration (30 hours).
Chimes the hours and quarters on
two original nickeled bells.
- *53cm x 27cm*
- **£3,900**   • Gütlin Clocks

Painted Dial Clock ▲
- *circa 1830*
Country-cased oak English
longcase clock with readed,
canted columns to case. Unusual
pierced fretwork making swan
neck of hood with ball and spire
finials,a nd featuring dentistry
around hood throat. The painted
dial includes a scene of bird in
break arch and flowers to
spandrels. Subsidiary seconds and
date ring chiming on a bell.
Maker "W.C. Clark" of Morpeth.
- *226cm x 51cm x 25cm*
- **£5,50**   • Gütlin Clocks

French Mantel Clock ◀

- *circa 1870*

A late nineteenth century French gilt bronze three-piece clock garniture. Eight day movement chiming hours and half hours on a bell. The gilt bronze and blue porcelain case with fine cloisonné enamelling and egg-shaped urn side pieces.
- *40.5cm x 23cm x 13cm*
- **£3,700** • **Gütlin Clocks**

Carrera Mantel Clock ▼

- *circa 1870*

A large impressive Carrera white marble and gilt bronze French mantel Clock. Carrera white marble case with two cherubs and a dolphin, ram's head to sides of case. Eight day movement with hour and half hour strikes on a bell, white enamel dial with blue enamel numerals.
- *40.5cm x 58cm x 18cm*
- **£4,500** • **Gütlin Clocks**

American Calendar Clock ▼

- *1860*

An unusual American calendar clock by Seth Thomas, having a pine carcass, and two dials. The top dial marks the time, and the lower one is for the date.
- *107cm x 79cm*
- **£2,800** • **Lacquer Chest**

Industrial Mantel Clock ◀

- *circa 1890*

A gilt bronze French industrial mantel clock by "Hry Marc à Paris", with two week movement in the form of an open-plated bed. Strikes hours and half hours on a bell surmounted on the top of the case.
- *63.5cm x 26.5cm x 15cm*
- **£3,900** • **Gütlin Clocks**

Victorian Desk Clock ▲

- *circa 1860*

Victorian ship's wheel eight-day desk clock of fine quality. Agate handles to the wheel. Signed "J. and M. Boyd, Greenock".
- *height 34cm*
- **£925** • **Clock Clinic**

Third Republic Clock ▲

- *1880*

A French Third Republic lyre-shaped ormulu and gilt clock, with a Champs-Levée platform movement by G. Jamieson. Seated at the base are two gilt cherubs holding lyres.
- *height 40cm*
- **£1,400** • **Barham Antiques**

Muse of Learning Clock ▼

- *circa 1805*

French patinated bronze, ormolu and green marble mantel clock showing a muse of learning.
- *height 53cm*
- £7,750   • Gavin Douglas

George II Longcase Clock ▼

- *circa 1760*

English lacquer, with pagoda hood. Painted scenes to front door and base of stories from the Bible. Five-pillar London-made eight-day movement.
- *height 2.36m*
- £9,500   • Gütlin Clocks

Musical Longcase Clock ▶

- *circa 1850*

Cuban mahogany, eight-bell quarter striking, by Herbert Blockley. Brass dial and subsidiary dials for chime/silent. Whittington and Cambridge tune changer with subsidiary silvered second ring.
- *height 2.39m*
- £12,500   • Gütlin Clocks

Marine Chronometer ▼

- *circa 1840*

By Owen Owens, Liverpool. Two-day marine chronometer in brass-bound mahogany case.
- *height 19cm*
- £5,500   • Raffety Walwyn

Striking Carriage Clock ◀

- *circa 1800*

Rococo gilt ormolu with ornate design. Highly decorative gilt case with caryatid figures to sides and a well-cast cherub carrying handle. Two train French movement, chiming hours and half hours.
- *height 20.5cm*
- £2,900   • Gütlin Clocks

French Mystery Clock ▲

- *1870*

French mystery clock with crystal pendulum, black marble and bronze case with spelter figure.
- *height 57cm*
- £2,750
- Old Father Time Clock Centre

French Mantel Clock ▲

- *circa 1830*

Gilt ormolu, First Empire. By Lugrunge à Paris. Finely chiselled gilt bronze case with a maiden and Cupid. Convex enamel dial.
- *height 42cm*
- £2,300   • Gütlin Clocks

Large Longcase Clock ▼

- *circa 1790*

George III flame-mahogany Moonroller longcase clock, with fan-shell satinwood inlay and cross-and-feather banding in a Gothic case. Reeded Corinthian columns with matching reeded Corinthian columns to hood. Engraved plaque reads, "Peter Fearnley of Wigan Tempest Fugit".
- *254cm x 45cm x 23cm*
- **£12,500**   • Gütlin Clocks

Desk Compendium ▼

- *circa 1902*

A gilt bronze and green enamel French desk compendium in an original leather travelling case. Eight day movement with original silvered English lever platform escapement. Presented to "VWL Parnett Botfield Esq" by the servants of the Hut on his coming of age, December 29, 1902.
- *15cm x 16.5cm x 6cm*
- **£2,300**   • Gütlin Clocks

Hopwood Clock ▼

- *circa 1800*

Country-style oak and mahogany 30 hour moonroller longcase clock sitting on ogée feet, by "Hopwood" of Rochdale. The painted dial includes scenes of two birds. The moonroller disc is painted with a galleon at sea and a fox hunt. Reeded square columns with diamond inlay to tops, with brass capitals on hood with inlayed central swan neck.
- *223cm x 52cm x 24cm*
- **£3,900**   • Gütlin Clocks

Mantel Clock ◄

- *circa 1875*

A French mantel clock by "J.B. Delettrez". Finely waisted green boulle case with gilt bronze ormolu mounts. Eight day French square plate movement with hour and half hour strikes on a gong. Twenty-five-piece cartouche dial with blued hands. Signed "J.B. Delettrez No.21174" with "J.B.D." stamp.
- *43cm x 23cm x 15cm*
- **£4,500**   • Gütlin Clocks

English Mahogany Clock ◄

- *circa 1830*

Flat-topped mahogany English longcase clock with break arch painted dial and leafy carved blind fretwork to hood. Eight day painted dial with masonic secotros to corner spandrels. Painted moonroller disc with scene of galleon at sea and country cottage scene. Made by "John P. Campbell" of Govan, Glasgow.
- *208cm x 51cm x 25cm*
- **£6,500**   • Gütlin Clocks

George III Clock ▲

- *circa 1790*

George III black-lacquered, pagoda-hooded, English eight day longcase clock. Chinoiserie decorated case with original hood housing a brass dial with four pillar movement. Sunburst engraving to center of dial and strike/silent in break arch.
- *238cm x 35.5cm x 18cm*
- **£8,500**   • Gütlin Clocks

German Brass Clock ▼
- *circa 1900*
Elephant mystery clock with spelter figure and swinging brass clock by Junghans.
- *height 22cm*
- £700
- Old Father Time Clock Centre

English Bracket Clock ▼
- *circa 1715*
Striking bracket clock in ebony. Veneered case with rise and fall regulation and eight-day fusée. Five-pillar movement. Signed.
- *height 54cm*
- £16,000   • Clock Workshop

Expert Tips

Brass and silvered dials are protected with lacquer and no attempt should ever be made to clean them with water or detergent.

Greek Figurative Clock ▲
- *circa 1720*
Gilt and bronze clock by Robert Molyneux, London. With Greek figures of Sappho and Cupid.
- *height 60cm*
- £3,500   • Clock Workshop

Lighthouse Mantel Clock ▲
- *1890–1900*
Oak four-sided cased French eight-day timepiece. Unusual French movement with original English lever escapement within the base. Signed Hry.
- *height 41cm*
- £1,500   • Gütlin Clocks

Art Nouveau Timepiece ▼
- *circa 1900*
French, polished brass. Cream white dial, faint pale blue arabic numerals and gilt hour markers. Eight-day French movement.
- *height 15.5cm*
- £450   • Gütlin Clocks

English Mantel Clock ▼
- *circa 1805*
Marble and ormolu mantel clock, neoclassical style, showing Cupid and Venus. Fusée movement by Graite, London. Bronze panels.
- *height 45cm*
- £6,250   • Gavin Douglas

Horse and Jockey Mantel Clock ◄
- *circa 1860*
Victorian black slate and rouge marble French mantel clock, with bronze model. Eight-day French movement, chiming the hours and half hours on bell.
- *height 46cm*
- £1,700   • Gütlin Clocks

Mantle Clock ▲
- *1904*
A small red leather and silver fronted timepiece mantle clock. Silver hallmarked Birmingham 1904. 8-day movement on platform escapement in very original condition, white enamel dial with Roman black numerals and black spade hands.
- *20cm x 10cm*
- £850 • Gütlin Clocks

French Mantle Clock ▲
- *circa 1830*
First empire French ormolu and bronze mantle clock by 'Gaullin', Paris. With 8-day silk suspension movement. The arched case depicting pomegranates, torches and an oil lamp, flanked by figures of Cupid & Psyche in a romantic pose, the rectangular plinth with stylised leaf mouldings, applied with a butterfly mount.
- *78cm x 48cm*
- £5,900 • Gütlin Clocks

Ormulu Mantle Clock ▼
- *circa 1880*
A Gilt bronze ormolu French mantle clock with blue porcelain panels. The Fine ormolu case depicting a woman rested on a rock with her dog with original mercury gilding.The porcelain panels of fine quality with pictures of flowers, 8-day movement with hour and half hour strike on a bell. White enamel dial with black Roman numerals. Dial signed by the retailers 'Maitrot a Dijon'. The movement is by Vincenti and Cie.
- *46cm x 51cm*
- £2,900 • Gütlin Clocks

Gilt Bronze Clock ▼
- *circa 1870*
Gilt bronze French clock. The finely chiselled case with maidens to sides surmounted by an urn with draping ormolu swags. With 8-day French movement with hour and half hour strike on a bell. The back door of this clock is engraved, 'Antony Bailly & LYON'.
- *63.5cm x 38cm*
- £4,500 • Gütlin Clocks

Tortoiseshell Boulle Clock ▲
- *circa 1880*
An ormolu mounted French tortoiseshell boulle clock in a Renaissance style. 8-day French square plate movement chiming hours and half hours on the bell with gilt ormolu 12 piece dial and enamel cartouches showing black Roman numerals.
- *58.5cm x 33cm*
- £1,900 • Gütlin Clocks

French Mantle Clock ▲
- *circa 1830*
Gilt ormolu first empire French mantle clock by Lugrunge & Paris. The finely chiselled gilt bronze case with a maiden and cupid and a laurel wreath to bottom of case. Convex enamel dial with black Roman numerals. 8-day silk-suspension movement chiming hours and half hours on a bell.
- *40.5cm x 30.5cm*
- £2,300 • Gütlin Clocks

Victorian Bracket Clock ▲
- *circa 1890-1900*
Small Victorian mahogany
balloon style, English bracket
clock, with a boxwood inlay. The
8- day numbered and stamped
French movement chiming the
hours and half hours on a gong,
- *28cm x 17.5cm*
- **£1,200**   • **Gütlin Clocks**

English Bracket Clock ▲
- *circa 1880-90*
English ebonised and gilt bronze
mounted substantial 3-train 10-
bell or 4-gongs (Westminster
chime) bracket clock. Retailed in
Scotland by 'Hamilton, Crighton
& Co, 41 George Street,
Edinburgh.
- *68.5cm x 33cm*
- **£6,500**   • **Gütlin Clocks**

Oak Bracket Clock ▼
- *circa 1870*
English oak quarter striking 8-bell
bracket clock retailed by
'Christie', Cannon Street,
London. The 8-day 6-pillar chain
fusee signed Victorian movement
of large size chiming the quarters
every 15-minutes on 8-bells with
hour strike on a large gong.
- *71cm x 43cm*
- **£4,500**   • **Gütlin Clocks**

Cathedral Clock ▼
- *circa 1880-90*
Victorian yellow oak, Gothic
English substantial 3-train, 8-bell
(Westminster chime) bracket
clock, modelled as a cathedral
with English three train, 6-pillar,
chain fusee movement.
- *81.5cm x 25cm*
- **£6,500**   • **Gütlin Clocks**

Ting-Tang Bracket Clock ▲
- *circa 1890*
Oak German quarter striking
ting-tang bracket clock by W. &
H. with 8-day quarter striking
German movement. The silvered
dial with separate chapter ring
subsidiaries and retailers plaque
engraved 'Bonner', Brighton.
- *35.5cm x 28cm*
- **£1,600**   • **Gütlin Clocks**

Expert Tips
*A specialist should carry out the
cleaning and oiling of a clock's
mechanism. Wheels and pinions
should never be oiled.*

Mahogany Bracket Clock ▲
- *circa 1900*
Mahogany and gilt mounted
English quarter (Westminster
chime) bracket clock, the
substantial triple chain fusee
movement chiming on 8-bells or
4-gongs.
- *84cm x 43.5cm.*
- **£13,300**   • **Gütlin Clocks**

Longcase Clock ▲

- *circa 1810*
Mahogany longcase clock with moonroller sweep. Second hand and centre date with quarter strike on two bells. By W. Reece.
- *height 2.5m*
- **£8,500**
- **Ronald G. Chambers**

Miniature Longcase Clock ▲

- *circa 1890–1900*
Jacobean-style oak, weight driven. Eight-day duration with brass dial. Chimes hours and half hours on a gong.
- *height 153cm*
- **£3,800**
- **Gütlin Clocks**

William IV Mantel Clock ▼

- *circa 1830*
Fine quality William IV mantel timepiece in mahogany.
- *height 32cm*
- **£4,400**
- **Raffety Walwyn**

Boudoir Balloon Clock ▼

- *circa 1903*
Silver and enamel, French and English hallmarked, Birmingham. Signed L. Leroy & Cie of Paris.
- *height 16cm*
- **£1,600**
- **Gütlin Clocks**

Hobnail Mantel Clock ◀

- *circa 1840*
French First Empire cut-glass. clock. Eight-day movement, knife-edge suspension.
- *height 51cm*
- **£4,500**
- **Gütlin Clocks**

Charles X Clock ▲

- *1820–25*
A very fine French Charles X clock in patinated bronze ormolu and marble vert. Showing 'Diana the Huntress'. Signed by Ravrio Bronzien. Eight-day escapement. Bell strike, with silk suspension.
- *height 64cm*
- **£5,750**
- **Gavin Douglas**

Bracket Clock ▲

- *1770*
Mahogany inverted bell, double fusée. Brass dial, calendar, with recessed name plate by Thomas Grinnard. Ormolu mountings.
- *height 53cm*
- **£ 14,000**
- **Pendulum of Mayfair**

Watches

Masonic Watch ▶
- *circa 1950*
A gold-plated watch with masonic symbols as numerals.
- £150   • AM-PM

Cartier Cocktail ▲
- *circa 1930*
Cartier lady's cocktail watch, in platinum with diamonds.
- £1,000   • Sugar

Repeating Watch ▶
- *circa 1891*
Keyless half-hunter in 18ct. gold, with lever minute repeating movement.
- *diameter 53mm*
- £6,750   • C. Frodsham

Omega Dynamic ▲
- *circa 1968*
Omega Dynamic automatic day and date watch.
- £350   • AM-PM

Pocket Watch ▲
- *circa 1910*
A 14ct. gold-filled pocket watch, with top-wind button set, by Thomas Russell.
- £800   • Sugar

Waterproof Watch ▼
- *circa 1930*
Omega rare, double-case waterproof wristwatch.
- £3,250   • Anthony Green

Expert Tips

There is a difference between watches that appreciate and ones that simply depreciate more slowly than expected.

Gold Watch ◀
- *circa 1960*
Jaeger LeCoultre 18ct. gold movement watch, designed by Kutchinsky, with nine diamonds and seven graded rubies on either side of the band.
- £3,250   • Emmy Abé

Omega Watch ▼

- **1950s**

Gentleman's Omega watch set in 9ct gold on a white dial with gold Arabic numerals and auxiliary sweep seconds.
- *diameter 2.9cm*
- **£350** • AM-PM

Lemania ▲

- **1953**

An Air Ministry RAF issue, pilots high grade one button chronograph with a steel case. The dial signed Lemania & with MOD Arrow, with minute recording dial and sweep second dial. The case with fixed bar lugs and back with ordinance marks: Arrow AM/6B/551 333/53.
- **£1,800** • Anthony Green

Romer Wristwatch ▲

- **1950s**

Ladies Swiss made Romer wristwatch set in 9ct gold on a 9ct gold bracelet with safety chain. White dial with 3,6,9,12 Arabic numerals.
- *diameter 1.2cm*
- **£250** • AM-PM

Vacheron Constantin Watch ▼

- **1960s**

Gentleman's Vacheron Constantin 18ct white gold wristwatch with oblong design black dial with white gold digits.
- *diameter 1.9cm*
- **£1.300** • AM-PM

Omega Seamaster Watch ▲

- **1950s**

Gentleman's Omega seamaster wristwatch set in stainless steel with a black dial with white Roman numerals. Mechanical movement and a screw back case. Red second hand.
- *Diameter 2.9cm*
- **£300** • AM-PM

Bulova Wristwatch ▲

- **1920s**

Ladies Bulova wristwatch set in 18ct gold with white dial. 3,6,9,12 Arabic numerals with serrated lugs, on a black leather cocktail strap.
- *diameter 1.1cm*
- **£200** • AM-PM

Universal Geneve ▶

- **circa 1939**

An early 18ct gold 'Compax' two button chronograph with subsidiary seconds, minute and hour recording dials.
- **£3,900** • Anthony Green

**Rolex Earl
Wrist Watch** ▲
- *1930*
A gentleman's Rolex Earl
manual-wind wrist watch, with
a stainless steel case and a white
dial with clear digits and
subsidiary seconds.
- *diameter 3cm*
- £375   • The Swan

Vintage Lady's Watch ▲
- *circa 1910*
An 18ct. gold lady's watch set
with demantoid garnets and
diamonds around the bezel.
White porcelain face with black
numerals and red number 12,
decorated with gold pips with an
18ct. expandable bracelet.
- *diameter 2.2cm*
- £1,275   • Westminster

**Lady's Cocktail
Watch** ▼
- *circa 1940s*
A gas-tube bracelet lady's watch,
inset with natural Burma rubies,
with jointed finials on a circular
silvered dial with black numerals.
Mechanical movement.
- *width 1.2cm*
- £2,100   • Westminster

**Demi-Hunter
Pocket Watch** ▼
- *1905*
A 9ct. gold demi-hunter pocket
watch by Wilson and Sharp of
Edinburgh. With three-quarter
plate movement.
- *diameter 4cm*
- £495   • Sugar

White Gold Watch ▲
- *circa 1950s*
Lady's Rolex watch in 18ct. white
gold. Integral strap with a square
white dial with silvered batons
and black hands. Leaver
movement, Rolex case and
named movement.
- *1.5cm square*
- £875   • Westminster

Expert Tips

Watch straps can suffer wear and damage, and gold or metal straps can be expensive to repair, so do inspect any potential purchases closely before deciding to buy.

Signed Rolex Watch ▼

- **1940**

A 9ct. gold lady's Rolex watch, with a linked gold bracelet strap. Back plate signed "MA".
- *2.5cm square*
- **£275**   • The Swan

Hamilton Watch ▲

- **1930**

A rectangular gentleman's gold-plated manual wind watch by Hamilton with gold roman numerals on a white enamel dial with subsidiary seconds.
- *3.5cm x 2.5 cm*
- **£375**   • The Swan

Military Issue Watch ▲

- **1940**

A military issue pocket watch by Waltman, with white Arabic numerals on a black dial with subsidiary seconds.
- *3.5cm diameter*
- **£75**   • The Swan

Bulova Wrist Watch ▼

- **1930**

A gentleman's rectangular, gold plated and curved, manual wind wrist watch by Bulova. White dial with gold Arabic numerals and subsidiary seconds.
- *3.5cm x 2cm*
- **£295**   • The Swan

Lady's Platinum and Diamond Watch ▲

- *circa 1930s*

A lady's platinum and diamond watch by Longines, with Arabic numerals on a white face and a gold integral twin snake bracelet. Swiss movement with an English case.
- *diameter 1.5cm*
- **£895**   • Westminster

Rolex Oyster Perpetual ◀

- *circa 1952*

18ct. gold Rolex Perpetual wristwatch with moon-phase calendar.
- **£35,000**   • Somlo

Omega Watch ▼

- *circa 1915*

A First World War officers large size wristwatch with original mesh 'Trench Guard'. The white enamel dial with subsidiary seconds, signed Omega. The case struck Omega Depose No. 9846 case # 5425073. The movement with Swan Neck Micro Reg. Signed Omega # 211504.

- *diameter 4.2cm*
- **£2,250**   • Anthony Green

Rolex Watch ▼

- *1924*

Gentleman's silver cushion shaped wristwatch. The movement signed 'Rolex 15 Jewels Swiss Made' Cal 507 Rebberg Depose. The case back signed RWC Ltd. (Rolex Watch Company). The case frame #655. The dial signed 'Rolex Swiss Made' Lug size 22.5mm.

- *width 2.3cm*
- **£2,850**   • Anthony Green

Rolex Watch ▲

- *1935*

A 9ct gold gentleman's Rolex wristwatch. The dial signed Rolex Swiss Made, with subsidiary seconds. The case signed Rolex 25 World Records Geneva Suisse R.W.C. Ltd. #19736 ref#2356 Movement Sig Rolex Precision 17 Rubis Patented Superbalance Swiss Made.

- **£4,500**   • Anthony Green

Rolex Watch ▲

- *circa 1947*

An Oyster 'Royal' waterproof Rolex wristwatch, with centre seconds. The case signed 'Rolex Geneve Suisse' with screw down Oyster button and case # 506021 Ref# 4444.

- **£1,550**   • Anthony Green

Pocket Watch ▶

- *circa 1920*

A high grade fully jewelled minute repeating open face pocket watch, with dial with subsidiary seconds. The case with Swiss control marks for 18ct gold and case # 62837. Repeating activated by a slide on the band.

- **£4,800**   • Anthony Green

Peerless Wristwatch ▼

- *1934*

A gentleman's wristwatch, the movement jewelled to the centre signed 'Peerless' Swiss Made # 332257 with S & Co Logo. The case # 331618-2 & FB fo Francis Baumgartner Borgelle case designer Enamel dial subsidiary seconds.

- *diameter 3.3cm*
- **£2,750**   • Anthony Green

Rolex Officer's Wristwatch ▼

- *circa 1916*

An early First World War 'Officer's' wristwatch. The silvered dial signed Rolex & Swiss Made. The movement #4636 and signed Rolex Swiss 15 Jls. Case signed with 'W & D' for Wilsdorf & Davis, the original founders of the Rolex empire. Case # 769936.

- **£2,500**   • Anthony Green

Chronograph Watch ▼

- *circa 1905*

An 18ct. gold hunter, keyless
lever, minute-repeating
chronograph watch with register,
enamel dial and thief-proof
swivel bow, by Dent, London.
- *height 53mm*
- £11,500   • C. Frodsham

Cylinder Watch ▼

- *circa 1800*

An 18ct. gold, open-face, keyless
lever, minute-repeating, split
seconds chronograph watch with
original box and certificate, by
Patek Philippe of Geneva;
retailed by Spaulding & Co of
Chicago.
- *diameter 45mm*
- £14,750   • C. Frodsham

Oyster Submarine Diving Watch ▲

- *circa 1964*

Oyster Perpetual Submariner
automatic diver's wristwatch, on
Rolex steel 'flip-lock' bracelet.
- £2,950   • Anthony Green

Pocketwatch ▲

- *circa 1940*

Silver/steel. By Movado. With
triple date and moon phase. Case
with winding mechanism
operating when opening and
closing. Covered in crocodile
skin.
- £1,850   • Anthony Green

Keyless Lever Watch ▲

- *circa 1908*

An 18ct. gold open-face watch
with split seconds chronograph
and register. By Dent of London.
- *diameter 54mm*
- £4,750   • C. Frodsham

Rolex Oyster Waterproof ▼

- *circa 1937*

Fine example of an early Oyster
waterproof gentleman's
'Chronometer' wristwatch, the
case with the original, screw-
down 'Oyster' button.
- £2,650   • Anthony Green

Cylinder Watch ▼

- *circa 1800*

A Swiss-made, gold and enamel
double-dialled watch with visible
diamond-set escapement and
calendar.
- *diameter 43mm*
- £8,000   • C. Frodsham

Expert Tips

*It is principally the efficacy
of the wristwatch as a timekeeping instrument that
determines its value. The Rolex
Oyster first appeared in 1927
and was the first model to be
waterproofed and able to
withstand climatic changes.
Technically years in advance,
it is its sheer reliability that
has kept it collectable.*

Olympics Commemorative Watch ▲
- **1972**
A rare, limited edition commemorative wrist watch by Longines, which features a stamp from the Olympic games in Munich. With silvered baton numerals on a white dial.
- *diameter 3cm*
- **£295**   • The Swan

Open-Face Pocket Watch ▲
- *circa 1830*
A fine quality open-face pocket watch, the cylindrical case with turned sides. The engine-turned dial with roman chapter ring and signed "Simmons Finsbury London". English lever movement with fusée signed and numbered "778". The balance has a diamond endstone.
- **£1,500**   • Anthony Green

Expert Tips

Rolex is not the only sought-after make: watches made by Patek Philippe are just as keenly pursued but are not so readily found.

Lord Elgin Wrist Watch ▼
- **1950**
A rectangular, gold-plated Lord Elgin gentleman's wrist watch with subsidiary seconds by the Elgin National Watch Company.
- *width 3.5cm*
- **£275**   • The Swan

Longines Wrist Watch ▼
- **1980**
A rectangular lady's 9ct. gold quartz Longines wrist watch with a diamond-set linked bracelet. White dial with Arabic numerals.
- *2.5cm x 2cm*
- **£495**   • The Swan

Bulova Gentleman's Wrist Watch ▲
- **1940**
A rectangular, gold-plated, curved gentleman's wrist watch by Bulova. With gold baton and black Arabic numerals on a white dial, with subsidiary seconds.
- *width 3.5cm*
- **£395**   • The Swan

Cine Alpha Wrist Watch ▲
- **1940**
A gold-plated gentleman's Cine Alpha wrist watch, with black Arabic numerals on an orange band within a white dial.
- *diameter 3.5cm*
- **£95**   • The Swan

145

Fob Watch ▲

- *circa 1890*
A small, silver, Swiss fob watch with enamel dial and red numerals and gold floral pattern to centre, with incised floral decoration to covers.
- £125 • Sugar

Expert Tips

Check that the case of a pocket watch labelled "gold" really is gold, particularly with American watches. Rolled gold – plating with gold fused to other metals – cases of excellent quality were produced in quantity and are not always easy to spot.

First World War Wristwatch ▲

- *circa 1916*
A very rare officer's First World War 'Hunting' cased wristwatch, with waterproof screw-back. The movement is signed by Rolex and the case is marked 'Rolex' with 'W&D', standing for Wilsdorf and Davis, the original founders of the Rolex company. The case is numbered 773185 and the enamel face shows luminous numerals and subsidiary seconds.
- £3,450 • Anthony Green

First World War Officer's Watch ▼

- *circa 1913*
Original, enamelled dial with Roman numerals and traditional red twelve. Subsidiary second dial and minute recording. Fabulous example of one of the very earliest wristwatch chronographs. Good condition and extremely attractive.
- £2,650 • Anthony Green

Double-Dialled Watch ▼

- *circa 1910*
A silver, keyless, lever double-dialled calendar watch with moon phases, time and subsidiaries on an enamel dial with Roman numerals on the obverse, and world time indications for seven cities on the reverse dial. The watch, which is unsigned, was made in Switzerland.
- £2,750 • Anthony Green

Pocket Chronometer ▲

- *circa 1895*
An 18ct. gold openface keyless fusée, free sprung pocket chronometer.
- *diameter 58mm*
- £9,500 • C. Frodsham

Gold and Enamel Watch ▲

- *1801*
A rare 18ct. gold and polychrome enamel watch, Peto-cross-detent escapement with scene of children feeding chickens. By Ilbery, London.
- *diameter 6cm*
- £42,500 • C. Frodsham

Art-Deco Wristwatch ▲

- *circa 1935*
Gentleman's high quality wristwatch of Art-Deco design. Case with hooded lugs and thick raised UB glass. The jewelled lever movement with original gilt dust cover.
- £775 • Anthony Green

Fob Watch ▲
- *1910*
Large gold fob watch by Vetex Revue, with black Roman numerals on a white face with a subsidiary seconds dial.
- *diameter 5cm*
- **£223** • **Bellum Antiques**

Gold Fob Watch ▲
- *1900*
9ct rose gold plated fob watch with Roman numerals and a subsidiary semi-concealed dial.
- *diameter 4.5cm*
- **£595** • **Bellum Antiques**

Expert Tips

Pocket watches date back to 1675. Engraved or hand-painted pictures of rural or hunting scenes add value, as do those of classical mythology, so keep a look out for these.

Gold Pocket Watch ▼
- *circa 1880*
Gold gentleman's pocket watch. Black Roman numerals, gold seconds on a white enamel face, with a foliate engraved design on the back of the case.
- *diameter 3cm*
- **£400** • **Bellum Antiques**

Half Hunter ▼
- *circa 18th century*
Half Hunter gold fob watch with blue Roman numerals on the outer casing of the watch surrounding an inset white dial.
- *diameter 4cm*
- **£975** • **Bellum Antiques**

Fly-Back Chronograph ▶
- *circa 1970*
A rare German air force issue aviator's 'Fly-Back' chronograph by Heuer in steel. The black dial with subsidiary seconds and minute recording dial 1 and red '3H' in circle, case #6445-12-146-3774 and stamped 'BUNDWEHR'.
- **£2,200** • **Anthony Green**

Gentleman's Pocket Watch ▲
- *circa 1870*
Austrian gentleman's pocket watch with a cover engraved with a cartouche depicting a parrot on a swing surrounded by a foliate design.
- *diameter 1.5cm*
- **£400** • **Bellum Antiques**

Omega Fob Watch ▲
- *circa 1900*
Gold Omega pocket watch with Arabic numerals on a white face, with gold hands and a subsidiary seconds dial. Swiss made.
- *diameter 1.5cm*
- **£345** • **Bellum Antiques**

Scientific Instruments

Prismatic Compass ▼

- *late 19th century*

A dry-card prismatic compass, with polished and lacquered brass case and leather outer case.

- *7cm x 9cm*
- **£299**   • **Langfords Marine**

Medicine Cabinet ▼

- *circa 1850*

A mahogany medicine cabinet with a full set of bottles, scales, pestle and mortar, and pill boxes.

- *height 22cm*
- **£1,375**   • **Gerald Mathias**

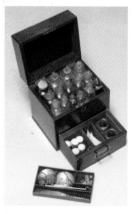

Drawing Instruments ▶

- *early 19th century*

A set of drawing instruments in a pocket case with the trade label, "T. Blunt Optician & Co., 22 Cornhill, London". Includes a signed ivory folding sector, an ivory scale, a brass semi-circular protractor and three assorted compasses all contained in a black fish skin case.

- *20cm x 8cm*
- **£649**   • **Langfords Marine**

Equinoctical Instrument ▼

- *circa 1830*

Newman & Co. of Calcutta compass with roman numeral dial.

- *diameter 14cm*
- **£1,605**   • **H. & H.**

Travelling Microscope ▼

- *circa 1890*

A predominantly brass monocular microscope, with original case by Henry Grouch of London.

- *height 35cm*
- **£750**   • **Finchley**

Brass Microscope ▶

- *circa 1910*

Monocular brass microscope, with lenses of two magnifications by W. Watson and Sons, 313 High Holborn, London.

- *height 34cm*
- **£650**   • **H. & H.**

Victorian Barometer ▲

- *1890*

A Victorian desk barometer with silvered dial signed "Halstaf and Hannaford, 228 Regent Street". The setting hand is adjusted by the ships wheel.

- *height 32cm*
- **£490**   • **Clock Clinic**

Stick Barometer ▲
- *circa 1830*
Mahogany bow-fronted stick barometer with swan neck pediment and silver-brass register. Operated by rack and pinion vernier with tortoiseshell knob.
- *length 1.02m*
- £6,350　　　　• Alan Walker

Astronomical Telescope ▲
- *circa 1848*
Equatorial three-inch astronomical telescope by Troughton & Simms, with mahogany turned handles.
- *length 1.39m*
- £12,000　　　　• Talbot

Ship's Compass ▼
- *circa 1830*
All-brass ship's compass, on gimbals, with black and white dial, in a mahogany box.
- *length 12cm*
- £150　　　　• H. & H.

Brass Pantograph ▼
- *circa 1950*
A brass pantograph instrument, consisting of pivoted levers for copying drawings etc, to scale. Complete with case.
- *length 87cm*
- £985　　　　• Hatchwell

Aquatic Microscope ▼
- *circa 1780*
An Ellis design, botanist's aquatic microscope. In brass, with original sharkskin fitted box.
- *height 16.5cm*
- £750　　　　• Talbot

Dispenser's Scales ▲
- *circa 1930*
Scales in chromed steel on a mahogany base.
- *height 31cm*
- £65　　　• Antique Warehouse

Wheel Barometer ▲
- *circa 1830*
Mahogany wheel barometer, with swan neck, in flame mahogany by John Messar, Gravesend.
- *height 1.03m*
- £1,050　　　• Alan Walker

Expert Tips

Fakes of early instruments do exist, but more frequently found are copies, which were honestly made for instructional purposes to demonstrate the principles.

149

Terrestrial Globe ▼

- **1824**

Eight-inch terrestrial globe by Delamarche and is supported on an ebonised beech stand which has four quadrants giving the names and latitudes of various different cities.
- *height 20cm*
- **£7,500**   • **T. Phillips**

Travelling Thermometer ▼

- *circa 1810*

Fisherman's or travelling thermometer in original wooden morocco case. Signed: Richardson, 1 Drury Lane, Holborn, London.
- *height 12cm*
- **£875**   • **T. Phillips**

Boxwood Nocturnal ▲

- *mid 18th century*

Fine boxwood nocturnal. The central volvelle marked for the Great Bear G and Little Bear L constellations, the centre scale marked with a calendar and hour scale. The reverse of the instrument is marked with the polar distance correction for the Pole star for both the Great and Little Bear constellations when finding the latitude marked Sam Bosswell Fecit on the fiducial arm and David Boswell on the handle.
- *height 25cm*
- **£10,750**   • **T. Phillips**

Pocket Globe ▼

- *mid 19th century*

Unsigned but probably German. Composed of 12 engraved, hand coloured gores with the continents outlined in primary colours. Housed in a blue card box, the lid marked: 'The Earth and its inhabitants'. The box contains a folded engraved and hand coloured illustration of 16 males from various parts of the world in their national costumes, labelled in English, French and German.
- *diameter 5cm*
- **£3,500**   • **T. Phillips**

Noon-Day Cannon Dial ▼

- *early 19th century*

Fine noon-day cannon dial by Boucar, 35 Q de L'Horloge, Paris. The marble base supports a brass cannon, adjustable magnifier and calendar scale. The sun dial graduated from 5 to 12 to 7, with brass gnomon correct for latitude 48.5 and 13 minutes.
- *height 26cm*
- **£5,750**   • **T. Phillips**

Map Measure ▼

- *early 19th century*

Map measure by W. & S.Jones, 30 Holborn, London. The gilt brass case incorporates an enamel dial graduated in Arabic numerals, housed in its original leather case.
- *height 8cm*
- **£3,750**   • **T. Phillips**

Expert Tips

The original finish is what gives a scientific item its value, so be careful, as many instruments have been ruined by the lavish use of metal polishes combined with the buffing wheel.

Aneroid Barometer ▼

- *circa 1840*
English aneroid barometer with exposed movement, silver dial and curved thermometer.
- *diameter 30cm*
- £420   • Alan Walker

Hour Glass ▼

- *mid 19th century*
Turned mahogany framed hour glass of hand-blown glass.
- *height 18cm*
- £750   • Talbot

Barometer ▲

- *late 19th century*
Unusual oak-cased 'Royal Polytechnic Barometer', in carved case with scalloped sunmount shell.
- *height 1.07m*
- £1,490   • Alan Walker

Explorer's Sextant ▲

- *circa 1800*
Gimballed explorer's sextant on stand, by Cary of London.
- *height 49cm*
- £4,000   • Talbot

Medicine Cabinet ▼

- *circa 1850*
A mahogany medicine cabinet with a full set of bottles, scales, pestle & mortar and pill boxes.
- *height 22cm*
- £1,375   • Mathias

Library Globe ▼

- *1821*
Library globe by Cary, supported on a mahogany stand. The tripod ledge is joined by a cross-stretcher supporting a compass, with a facsimile compass rose. The cartouche reads as follows: Cary's new terrestrial globe, Delineated from the best Authorities extant; Exhibiting the late Discoveries towards the North Pole, and every improvement in Geography to the present time London: Made & Sold by G & J Cary, 86 St. James's Street March15th 1821.
- *height 66cm*
- £14,750   • T. Phillips

Coins & Medals

Coins are probably the most collected antiques of all, existing in sufficient quantities to provide for both large and small collections.

Nothing traces the ascent of civilisation as accurately and as thoroughly as the coin. The study of coin development from its beginnings, in about 640 BC, to the present day is richly endowed with history. Ancient Greek and Roman coins are usually very expensive and Oriental coinage is best left to the expert, but general world coinage provides a fascinating field of study and is much more accessible to the new collector. Coins and medals of all types have the advantage of telling the collector exactly what they are – provided that he can read the relevant script or language. It is then a matter of historical knowledge and common sense to work out what may make an item a rarity. The value of coins is dependent on their design, legend, mintmark, date, current demand and condition, the latter graded from 'FDC' or fleur de coin, meaning 'in mint condition', to 'F', meaning 'fair', which indicates that, despite hard usage, the main features of the coin are still recognisable. Medals are divided between campaign medals and those awarded for individual bravery and depend for value on condition, rarity and the circumstance and individual involved – the action and the deed. The Napoleonic Wars, the Crimean War, the Indian Mutiny and other Victorian engagements are ones to look out for.

Zulu War Medal ◄
- **1879**
 A Zulu war medal, clasp inscribed "1879 to 889 Private J. Kiernan 2/3 foot".
- **£295** • Chelsea (OMRS)

Gulf War Medal ►
- **1991**
Gulf War medal with clasp, awarded to Steward I. McMillan of the Royal Fleet Auxiliary.
- **£135** • Chelsea (OMRS)

Boer War Medal Group ◄
- **1893–1902**
A Boer war medal group with four to a kafaking defender consists of a British South Africa Company medal "Matabeleland 1893", Queen South Africa medal with three clasps including "Defence of Making". Kings South Africa Medal with two clasps and South Africa Prison Services Long Service medal. Awarded to trooper A H Brady, South Africa Light Horse.
- **£1,800** • Chelsea (OMRS)

Third Reich Army Long Service Cross ▼

• *1935–45*
Gold Third Reich Army Long Service Cross awarded for 40 years service, with gilt eagle standard and oak leaves on ribbon. A very fine specimen.
• *diameter 4cm*
• £225 • Gordons Medals Ltd

Luftwaffe Combined Pilot/Observer's Badge ▼

• *1935–45*
Luftwaffe combined pilot / observer's badge. Two part gilt and silver, mid-war version, in super crisp condition. Makers marked: CEJ for Junckers.
• *diameter 4cm*
• £650 • Gordon's Medals

British War Medal ▼

• *1914–19*
1914-15 Star, British War medal, Victory medal, and Royal Naval Volunteer Reserve Long Service Good Conduct medal, as awarded to: 1/945. R. Ryandell. Sig. R.N.V.R. Bristol DIV.
• *diameter 4cm*
• £135 • C.F. Seidler

Third Reich Medal ▲

• *1935–45*
1939 Iron Cross 2nd Cl., Danzig Cross, 2nd Cl., the latter, one of only 254 awarded, maker's mark on reverse: B.V.A. Hulse-Berlin.
• *diameter 4cm*
• £365 • Gordon's Medals

Crimean War Medal ▲

• *1854–5*
Crimean War medal with 3 Clasps; Alma, Inkerman, Sebastopol, regimentally impressed naming: Serjt J McBlain Scots Fusilier Guards.
• *diameter 4cm*
• £425 • Gordon's Medals

Army of India Medal ▼

• *1799–1826*
Army of India medal, 1799-1826, with three clasps; Allighur, Battle of Delhi, Laswaree, as awarded to: Lieut Alexr Duncan, Brigade Major. Officially impressed naming Alexander Duncan who served during the Second Mahratta War of 1803-4 and later became a General. He retired in 1854 and died in 1859. This is a very rare medal, one of only 150 three clasp medals awarded, of which not many have survived, 28 were issued with clasp combination.
• *diameter 4cm*
• £6,950 • Gordon's Medals

German Imperial Group ▼

• *1900–18*
Iron Cross 2nd Cl., 1914; Prussia, German Service Cross 1900-1918; Officer's Long Service Cross for 25 yrs; Friedrich Wilhelm 3rd Civil Service medal, 2nd Cl., 1847-1918, in silver; Army Lower Ranks Long Service medal for 15 yrs; Wilhelm 1st Centenary medal 1897; Braunschwieg: Military Service Cross 2nd Cl., 1914-1918 and Service Cross 1st Cl., in gold. All mounted court style for wear.
• *diameter 18.5cm*
• £475 • Gordon's Medals

Boer War Medal ▼

● *1899–1900*

Queen's South Africa medal, 1899-1900 with six clasps; Relief of Kimberley, Paardeberg, Driefontein, Johannesburg, Diamond Hill, Wittebergen, as awarded to: 82180 Bomb: WHLR: H. BlissEett. 'P' BTY: R.H.A. This man was wounded during a Victoria Cross action at Nooitedacht on the 13th of December 1900.

● *diameter 4cm*

● £375   ● Gordon's Medals

Campaign Service Medal ▼

● *1970–82*

Campaign Service medal with one clasp; Northern Ireland, South Atlantic medal 1982, with rosette, UN Cyprus medal (UNFICYP), as awarded to: 24501637 Gunner J.C Howe Royal Artillery. Group mounted court style for wear.

● *diameter 12cm*

● £345   ● Gordon's Medals

Victorian Crown ▼

● *1887*

Mounted example of a Victorian crown with fine enamels.

● £95   ● James Vanstone

Air Force Cross ▲

● *1960–present*

US Airforce, Air Force cross.

● *diameter 5cm*

● £43   ● Gordon's Medals

Distinguished Service Medal ▲

● *1970–present*

US Defence Distinguished Service medal.

● *diameter 5cm*

● £43   ● Gordon's Medals

Victoria Half Crown ▲

● *1876*

Enamel half crown commemorating the reign of Queen Victoria with fine enamels.

● £250   ● James Vanstone

Five Mark ▼

● *1875*

Unusual five mark coin. Well-defined example centred with the Habsburg Eagle.

● £350   ● James Vanstone

George II Crown ▼

● *1743*

Rare example of George II crown with fine enamels representing England, Scotland and Ireland.

● £400   ● James Vanstone

British Medal ▼

● *1890–97*

British South Africa Company medal without clasp. Inscribed on the reverse: Rhodesia 1896. As awarded to: 93593 Shoeg.Smith W.Didoe. 10.B.Y.R.A. Died in South Africa on 26th May 1900.

● *diameter 4cm*

● £295   ● Gordon's Medals

Imperial Iron Cross

- *1914*

A World War I Imperial Iron
Cross, Second Class with crown,
'W' mark, dated and with
Friedrich Wilhelm crest.
- £20   • Gordon's Medals

Crimean Medal ▲

- *1854*

Crimean Medal with Sebastapol
bar. Officially impressed 'E. Moss
of the Coldstream Guards'. With
yellow and pale blue ribbon –
Prince Albert's colours.
- £145   • Gordon's Medals

Austrian Coin ▼

- *1936*

Gold Austrian 100-schilling coin
with Madonna on obverse and
Austrian shield on reverse.
- *diameter 32mm*
- £450   • Malcolm Bord

German Coin ▼

- *1698*

A gold German six-ducat
Nuremberg coin.
- *diameter 44mm*
- £6,000   • Malcolm Bord

Silver Penny ▲

- *circa 1025*

A short cross-type silver penny
from the court of King Cnut.
- *diameter 32mm*
- £100   • Malcolm Bord

Expert Tips

*Bars on Victorian medals,
indicating the actions within a
campaign, add to the value.*

George III Guinea Coin ▼

- *1813*

A gold George III guinea coin.
This coin is known as the
'Military Guinea'.
- *diameter 19mm*
- £800   • Malcolm Bord

George III Crown ◄

- *1750*

A silver George III crown coin,
with the early head portrait.
- *diameter 38mm*
- £750   • Malcolm Bord

155

Memorial Plaque

- *1914*

Great War memorial plaque
dedicated to Ernest George
Malyon of the 2nd/16th Battalion
London Regiment and inscribed
"He died for freedom and
honour".
- *diameter 12cm*
- £25 • Chelsea (OMRS)

Leopold II Medal ▲

- *1915*

Order of Leopold II 2nd Class
neck badge.
- £175 • Chelsea (OMRS)

Waterloo Medal ▼

- *1815*

A Waterloo medal, 1815,
awarded to Joseph Porch of the
11th Light Dragons, wounded in
action.
- £1,000 • Chelsea (OMRS)

Military Clasp ▲

- *1943*

World War II German Navy
U-boat Clasp for Bravery. Mid-
war zinc example by Peeuhaus.
- £575 • Chelsea (OMRS)

Cap Badge ▲

- *1939–45*

Royal Armoured Corps WWII
plastic cap badge.
- £25 • Chelsea (OMRS)

Air Force Medal ▼

- *1945*

A European Aircrew Star,
awarded to a serving member of
the Royal Air Force in World
War II.
- £105 • Chelsea (OMRS)

Military Medal Trio ▼

- *1918*

A trio of World War I medals,
including the Victory medal,
awarded to Private H. Codd of
the East Yorkshire Regiment.
- £35 • Chelsea (OMRS)

Knight Templar Collar ▲
- *1850*

Unusual Knight Templar's collar jewel with enamelled double cross in silver, gold, red, black and white .
- £100
- James Vanstone

Founder Jewel ▲
- *1940*

Hall marked silver Founder jewel with Masonic symbols painted on the enamel, set between two pillars
- £40
- James Vanstone

George IV Shilling ▲
- *1820*

Attractive example of the George IV shilling with enamel centre, with the Crown and Lion.
- £40
- James Vanstone

Victorian Shilling ▼
- *1897*

Victorian shilling with enamel standard and the date 1897.
- £25
- James Vanstone

Diamond Jubilee Medal ▼
- *1897*

Commemorative medal for the Diamond Jubilee of Queen Victoria decorated in silver, gilt and paste settings. The central cartouche of Queen Victoria is set within twenty-four paste diamonds within the angle and the divider.
- £60
- James Vanstone

Canada General Service Medal ▼
- *1866–70*

Canada General Service medal 1866-70, with one clasp; Fenian Raid 1866, as awarded to: 311 Pte. A. Carroll, 7th Bn. Royal Fusiliers.
- *diameter 4cm*
- £295
- Gordon's Medals

Gold Post Master Jewel ▲
- *1930*

9ct gold Post Master jewel representing the guild of Freeman Lodge, decorated with the City of London's coat of arms.
- £140
- James Vanstone

Burmese Rupee ▲
- *1920*

Burmese rupee centred with a peacock. Whilst of exceptionally high quality this example is one of the more common seen on the market.
- £120
- James Vanstone

Victorian Crown ▲
- *1897*

A Victorian crown with a strong depiction of George and the dragon highlighted in enamel. Reasonably common example.
- £60
- James Vanstone

Collector's Items

The important rule for the collector of 'collectables' is to take care of the ephemera of today – they may be the antiques of tomorrow.

Rarity and condition are the two factors that make collectable items collectable. The great advantages with collectables is that they do not need to be especially old and they do not need to cost a great deal of money. Take almost any disposable item commonly in use at the moment, and you can be certain that someone is building a collection of it and that, in a few years, it will be much in demand. The most collectable of these essentially ephemeral items are those that are in some way ground-breaking or

revolutionary. The first SLR cameras, for instance, or the first refillable fountain pens. It is not too difficult to spot the collectables of the future using this as a criterion – what about the first truly mobile phones, or lap-top computers? The important thing is that everything is collectable and that you have the opportunity to collect something that you really like and really know about – and discover that there are any number of other people interested in the same thing. Start gathering the antiques of tomorrow today!

Advertising & Packaging

Stilton Cheese Dish ▲
- *circa 1955*
A stilton cheese dish, designed by Gilroy to advertise Guinness.
- *height 16cm*
- £50 ● Huxtable's

Polish Box ▼
- *circa 1930*
A metal polish box with a secondary use as a string dispenser.
- *height 15cm*
- £35 ● Huxtable's

Expert Tips

Many tins were specifically designed to have secondary uses – presumably for reasons of product awareness – such as toffee tins designed to be used as kitchen containers.

Johnson's Wax Tin ▼
- *circa 1950*
A tin of Johnson's Wax polish.
- *diameter 10cm*
- £4.50 ● Magpies

Belgian Biscuit Tin ◀
- *circa 1939*
A Disney biscuit tin from Belgium, with cartoon characters.
- *length 32cm*
- £120 ● Huxtable's

Huntley & Palmers ▼
- *1930*
Yellow tin for Huntley & Palmers biscuits showing a young lady smiling with dark hair and eyes, wearing a blue scarf.
- *width 13.5cm*
- £24   • The Manic Antique

Gin Fizz Stocking Box ▼
- *circa 1956*
Cardboard box for stockings with a picture of a lady sitting cross legged on a stool at a bar holding a glass, and inscribed with, 'Gin Fizz Crestmont created in Italy' in red lettering on a white background.
- *18cm square*
- £18   • The Manic Antique

Art Deco Tin ▶
- *1920*
Art Deco tin showing a smiling lady in a white dress, holding a letter and seated on a large cushion. Beside her is a Pekinese wearing a pink bow,, a vase and a large pink lampshade on a red circular table.
- *width 23cm*
- £20   • The Manic Antique

India and China Tea ▲
- *1920*
White enamel sign for Indian and China tea in red writing, with heads of an Indian and a Chinese man.
- *width 71cm*
- £55   • Michael Laws

Duncan Chocolates ▲
- *1930*
Cardboard box for Duncan Edinburgh chocolates, showing a young girl wearing a yellow ruff holding a bunch of flowers, wearing a blue hat with yellow pom-poms.
- *height 5cm*
- £15   • The Manic Antique

Walter Palm Toffee Tin ▼
- *1950*
'Walter's Palm Toffee' tin with a lady in a red and white striped bikini with matching sunshade, towel and holding a bottle of orange juice on the beach.
- *24cm square*
- £25   • The Manic Antique

Huntley and Palmers ▼
- *circa 1950*
Circular biscuit tin with a pink and white striped sunshade above a garden chair and table with cocktail shaker and glasses and a tin of cocktail biscuits.
- *diameter 18cm*
- £15   • Michael Laws

Bottle of Broseden ▲
- *1930s*
A bottle of "Broseden" made in
Germany. A drink used to calm
the troops during lonely times.
- *height 9cm*
- £5   • Huxtable's

Bournvita Mug ▲
- *1950s*
A white Bournvita mug in the
shape of a face with a blue
nightcap and a red pom-pom.
With large handle.
- *height 14cm*
- £40   • Huxtable's

Toffee Tin ▲
- *20th century*
A Macintosh's toffee tin
commemorating the marriage
of George VI to Elizabeth
Bowes-Lyon.
- *diameter 14cm*
- £20   • Huxtable's

Brilliantine ◄
- *1930s*
A glass bottle of "Saturday Night
Lotion", men's hair styling gloss.
- *height 13cm*
- £12   • Huxtable's

Carton of Cigarettes ▲
- *1960s*
A carton of Senior Service
cigarettes. In original white paper
wrapping with navy blue
lettering, unopened.
- *13cm x 5cm*
- £40   • Huxtable's

Nib Boxes ◄
- *1920s*
An assortment of unopened
nib boxes.
- *width 7cm*
- £7   • Huxtable's

Book Mark ▼

- *circa 1910*

A book mark advertising give-a-ways. The one is for Wright's Coal Tar Soap. The Nursery Soap, inscribed with the words, 'The Seal of Health and Purity.'

- *length 15.4cm*
- £12   • Old Advertising

Player's Ash Tray ▼

- *1930*

Pottery Player's ashtray showing an interior scene with a man seated smoking a pipe, a lady in a green dress, a hound, and the words 'Player's Tobacco Country Life and cigarettes'.

- *width 11.5cm*
- £25   • Huxtable's

Golden Leaf Tobacco Tin ▲

- *circa 1912*

Golden leaf navy cut tobacco tin, manufactured by Louis Dobbelmann, Rotterdam. Showing an angel blowing a horn and flying on wings in the center of the tin, surrounded by flowers and the Dutch flag.

- *width 8cm*
- £60   • Old Advertising

Grimbles Brandy ◄

- *circa 1900*

Grimbles royal cognac brandy of Albany St, London. 3s per bottle. Set in a red shield with gold foliate design.

- *height 45cm*
- £30   • Michael Laws

Senior Service Tobacco ▲

- *1940*

Red plaque with the written inscription 'Senior Service Satisfy - Tobacco at its best'.

- *height 28cm*
- £15   • Michael Laws

Ceramic Coaster ▼

- *circa 1890s*

A white beer coaster advertising The Cannon Pale Ale, from the Cannon Brewery Co Ltd and bottled by Plowman & Co Ltd, London.

- *diameter 16cm*
- £175   • Old Advertising

Lux Soap Flakes ▲
- *circa 1960*
An unopened box of Lever Brothers' Lux soap flakes.
- *height 28cm*
- £10 • Huxtable's

McVitie Biscuit Box ▲
- *circa 1910*
A 'Billie Bird' biscuit box by McVitie.
- *height 32cm*
- £120 • Huxtable's

Toothpaste Lid ▼
- *circa 1900*
A Woods Areca Nut toothpaste lid by W. Woods, Plymouth.
- £20 • Magpies

Biscuit Tin ▼
- *circa 1910*
A biscuit tin in the shape of a book, made by Hoffman Suisse.
- *height 36cm*
- £90 • Huxtable's

Talcum Powder ▶
- *circa 1950*
A 'Jolly Baby' talcum powder container, with voluptuous cover.
- *height 15cm*
- £40 • Huxtable's

Horlicks Mixer ▲
- *circa 1950*
A Horlicks promotional glass jug with a metal mixer.
- *height 15cm*
- £10 • Magpies

Battery Advertisement ◀
- *circa 1960*
An Oldham Batteries metal advertising sign, incorporating the 'I told 'em – Oldham' slogan.
- *height 37cm*
- £28 • Magpies

My Guinness Tray ▼
- **1955**

Metal tray with a pelican balancing a mug of Guinness inscribed with the slogan, 'My Goodness My Guinness'.
- *diameter 27cm*
- **£55** • Huxtable's

Colman's Mustard ▼
- **1935**

Small red, yellow and black tin of Colman's mustard, with a red bull's head in the centre.
- *height 5cm*
- **£8** • Huxtable's

Player's Glass Ash Tray ▼
- **1950**

Glass ashtray depicting a man in naval uniform surrounded by a white life ring and inscribed with 'Player's Navy cut' in black writing.
- *width 15cm*
- **£20** • Huxtable's

Lyons Tea ▲
- **1925**

Set of four Lyon's tea tins, each one inscribed with a different slogan, -'Degrees Better', 'Lyons has stood the test of time', 'Mirror for reflection, Lyon's tea for perfection', 'All the year round drink Lyon's tea'.
- *height 14cm*
- **£200** • Huxtable's

Oxo Cube ▲
- **1950**

Dark blue painted red metal box with 'Oxo cube' in yellow writing and the slogan 'Invaluable for cooking'.
- *35cm square*
- **£40** • Huxtable's

Gramophone Needle Tins ▲
- **1910-1940**

Six gramophone needle tins. The National Band, Pathe, Salon-Tanz Nadeln. Sem Aeor-needles.
- *4cm square*
- **£30-100 each** • Huxtable's

A1 Salt ▲
- **1940**

Metal sign with two ladies, one cutting salt and the other opening a packet of 'A1 crushed lump salt.'
- *height 25cm*
- **£20** • Huxtable's

Coffee Packet ▲

- *circa 1920s*
A packet of 'delicious coffee', 'fresh roasted' by George Bowman of 84 Main Street, Cockermouth. 4oz nett weight.
- *24cm x 19cm*
- £5 • Old Advertising

Probyn's Sign ▲

- *circa 1930*
An enamel sign for Probyn's Guinness's Stout – the Harp label. From the Argus Brand showing a picture of two stout bottles.
- *65cm x 40cm*
- £400 • Old Advertising

Cherry Blossom Shoe Stand ▶

- *circa 1930*
A tin and wood shoe stand advertising Cherry Blossom shoe polish in dark tan, with printed transfer on its sides.
- *height 30cm*
- £150 • Old Advertising

McVities & Prices Digestive Biscuits ▼

- *1930*
Small red tin with a cream lid and a boy seated on a red tin of McVitie & Price's Digestive Biscuits.
- *diameter 8cm*
- £12 • Huxtable's

Redbreast Tobacco Tin ▼

- *1930*
Ogden's Redbreast Flake tobacco tin, made in Liverpool, decorated with a robin shown perched on a branch.
- *width 14cm*
- £12 • Old Advertising

Pot Lid ▲

- *circa 1890s*
Areca Nut toothpaste for 'Beautiful White Teeth' with black and white underglazing, made in London.
- *diameter 6cm*
- £85 • Old Advertising

Show Card ▲

- *circa 1890*
Greensmith's Derby dog biscuits showcard (chrono lithograph) showing a clown holding a hoop for a dalmatian to jump through.
- *45cm x 34cm*
- £200 • Old Advertising

Savings Bank Tin ▼

- *1930s*

A savings bank tin issued by
various banks of the 1930s.
- £15
- Huxtable's

Washing Powder ▼

- *1950s*

Original unused boxes of "Surf"
and "Tide" washing powder.
- *height 17cm*
- £12
- Huxtable's

Royal Busts ▼

- *1902*

Busts of Edward VII and Queen
Alexandra made by Britains.
- *height 5cm*
- £55
- Huxtable's

Cigarette Tin ◄

- *1910*

A green cigarette tin with the
painting of a lady in red wearing a
straw hat, with the lettering
"Muratt's young ladies cigarettes"
written on the tin.
- *14cm x 9cm*
- £120
- Huxtable's

Money Tin ▲

- *1934*

A Crawfords biscuit cum money
tin fairy house by Lucie Attwell.
- *height 21cm*
- £300
- Huxtable's

Match Holder ▲

- *1910*

An Apploinaris match holder
and striker.
- *height 8cm*
- £30
- Huxtable's

Gramophone Tins ◄

- *1910–50*

Assortment of gramophone
needle tins from around the
world.
- £15
- Huxtable's

Bottles

Opaque Bottle ▲
- *circa 1900*
Chinese opaque glass snuff bottle
decorated with emerald green
flowers and an oriental bird. With
a cornelian stopper set within a
silver rim.
- *height 7.5cm*
- £175 • Bellum Antiques

Blue Glass Bottle ▲
- *circa 1900*
Blue glass Chinese snuff bottle
with green stone stopper set in
silver.
- *height 6cm*
- £95 • Bellum Antiques

Porcelain Snuff Bottle ▼
- *circa 1900*
Chinese porcelain snuff bottle
with topaz stopper and silver rim.
- *height 7.5cm*
- £65 • Bellum Antiques

Snuff Bottle ▼
- *circa 1900*
Opaque glass Chinese snuff bottle
with a stylised sepia leopard
chasing its tail.
- *height 6cm*
- £145 • Bellum Antiques

Pagoda Snuff Bottle ▲
- *circa 1900*
Chinese white snuff bottle
decorated with crimson fish
underneath a pagoda roof. Green
stone stopper set in silver.
- *height 7cm*
- £175 • Bellum Antiques

Chinese Bottle ▲
- *circa 1900*
Chinese snuff bottle decorated
with a panda and palm trees with
a semi precious stone stopper set
in silver.
- *height 8cm*
- £95 • Bellum Antiques

Venetian Glass Bottle ▼
- *1860*

Blue and white scent bottle with silver top. The blue is created by a Venetian Latticina technique.
- *length 9cm*
- £228 • Trio

Scent Bottles with Portraits ▼
- *circa 1870*

Pair of Czechoslovakian opaque and clear glass scent bottles with oval portraits of young girls, circled with grey and gold to stopper base and rim.
- *height 20cm*
- £590 • Trio

Victorian Scent Bottle ▼
- *circa 1860*

Victorian double-ended ruby scent bottle in silver with gilt stoppers, with one side for perfume and the other for smelling salts.
- *length 10cm*
- £358 • Trio

Bohemian Scent Bottle ▼
- *1880*

Victorian ruby Bohemian scent bottle and circular gold stopper. Decorated with alternating white panels with flowers and a gold floral design.
- *height 26cm*
- £288 • Trio

Turquoise Scent Bottles ▶
- *1880*

Pair of nineteenth century turquoise scent bottles with gold banding and stoppers.
- *height 18cm*
- £368 • Trio

Red Glass Scent Bottle ▼
- *circa 1860*

Cranberry glass scent bottle with gilt flower decoration and chain for holding on finger.
- *length 6cm*
- £195 • Trio

Silver Scent Bottle ▼
- *circa 1886*

English, decorative silver scent bottle with scrolls and a cut-glass stopper.
- *height 5.5cm*
- £250 • John Clay

Wedgwood Bottle ▼

- *circa 1930*
Wedgwood blue bottle with silver plate stopper.
- *height 4cm*
- £85   ● Trio

Silver Bottle ▼

- *1893*
Small silver bottle ornately engraved with a floral design.
- *height 5cm*
- £158   ● Trio

Ruby Red Bottle ▶

- *1880*
Ruby red double ended perfume bottle with silver stoppers.
- *height 12.5cm*
- £188   ● Trio

Candy Stripe Bottle ▲

- *circa 1850*
Candy stripe pink glass perfume bottle with a rose gold stopper.
- *height 6cm*
- £288   ● Trio

Ruby Bottle ▶

- *1911*
Ruby red perfume bottle with a foliate design engraved in the silver stopper.
- *height 7cm*
- £98   ● Trio

Green Double Bottle ▲

- *1880*
Green perfume bottle with pinch back stoppers.
- *length 13cm*
- £168   ● Trio

Ruby Flashed Bottles
- *circa 1880*
A pair of ruby flashed Bohemian glass scent bottles with floral decoration.
- *height 12cm*
- £245 • Trio

Georgian Scent Bottle
- *1727–1820*
Scent bottle in purple glass with silver stopper.
- *length 6cm*
- £240 • Trio

Opaque Glass Bottle
- *19th century*
French scent bottle of opaque glass with a cameo of a lady on the top.
- *height 11cm*
- £238 • Trio

Oval Scent Bottle
- *1870*
A French green oval glass bottle. with an elaborate foliate and bird design and a gold stopper.
- *length 6cm*
- £230 • Trio

Bohemian Scent Bottles
- *circa 1880*
A pair of ruby Bohemian bottles with foliage design with cusp and angle rims.
- *height 18cm*
- £548 • Trio

Art Deco Scent Bottle
- *1920*
An Art Deco perfume bottle in turquoise and silver, with stopper. Decorated with geometric design and inscribed "R.M.S. Homeric".
- *height 6cm*
- £68 • Trio

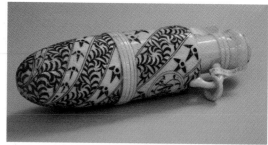

Japanese Perfume Bottle ▲

- *1890*

Japanese cylindrical perfume bottle made from bone decorated with a foliate design.
- *length 13cm*
- **£795**   • **Bellum Antiques**

Pump Action Perfume Bottle ▲

- *circa 1920*

Red glass perfume bottle with silver screw top lid with a pump action spray and a hand painted butterfly on one side.
- *height 13cm*
- **£250**   • **Bellum Antiques**

Victorian Scent Bottle ▲

- *circa 1890*

A Victorian, oval scent bottle in clear glass, decorated with gold flowers and fitted with a pinch-back gold chain.
- *height 6cm*
- **£199**   • **Trio**

Victorian Perfume Bottle ▼

- *1899*

Small cut glass perfume bottle with a silver stopper.
- *height 5cm*
- **£95**   • **Bellum Antiques**

Glass Perfume Bottle ▲

- *1880*

Circular glass bottle with silver top.
- *height 8cm*
- **£225**   • **Bellum Antiques**

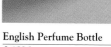

English Perfume Bottle ▲

- *1896*

Porcelain white perfume bottle with floral design and a silver top.
- *length 8cm*
- **£1,850**   • **Bellum Antiques**

Guerlain 'L'Heure Bleue' ▼

• *circa 1940*
Made by Baccarate perfume, with original box.
• £125   • Linda Bee

Conical Bottle ▼

• *circa 1866*
A mid-Victorian silver fluted perfume bottle, of conical form, with silver stopper.
• £210   • Trio

French Apothecary's Bottles ▶

• *circa 19th century*
Collection of nine apothecary's bottles including stoppers.
• £655 set   • Ranby Hall

Grossmith 'Old Cottage' Lavender Water ▲

• *circa 1930*
A bottle of English lavender water of etched glass.
• £95   • Linda Bee

Bohemian Glass Bottle ▲

• *circa 1860*
Floral perfume bottle, in Bohemian glass, with enamelling and large cut stopper.
• £300   • Trio

Nina Ricci 'Coeur-Joie' ▼

• *1946*
Lalique bottle with heart-shaped centre and floral decoration.
• £210   • Linda Bee

Unknown Heart-Shaped Perfume Bottle ▼

• *circa 1940*
With etched glass and bakelite base with dipper.
• £65   • Linda Bee

Cameo Bottle ▼

- 1860

Thomas Webb Cameo bottle in original box.

- *height 11cm*
- £2,750
- Lynda Brine

Perfume Bottle ▼

- 1870

Glass perfume bottle with a silver gilt stopper with amethyst stones inscribed M.S.V.

- *height 9cm*
- £425
- Lynda Brine

Heart Shaped Bottle ▶

- 1870

Silver heart-shaped bottle with scrolled design.

- *height 9cm*
- £520
- Lynda Brine

Twisted Glass Bottle ▲

- 1890

Twisted glass perfume bottle with an opal and diamond stopper.

- *length 6.5cm*
- £550
- Bellum Antiques

Blood Stone Bottle ▲

- *circa 19th century*

Blood stone snuff bottle and stopper from China.

- *7.5cm x 3.2cm*
- £220
- Ormonde

Silver Scent Bottle ▲

- 1760

Silver lozenge shaped perfume bottle with a foliate design.

- *height 11.5cm*
- £650
- Lynda Brine

Cranberry Perfume Bottle ▲

- 1870

Cranberry glass perfume bottle with moulded bubbles with a silver lid.

- *height 10cm*
- £400
- Lynda Brine

Bohemian Glass Bottle ▼

- *circa 1860*

Floral perfume bottle and large cut stopper in Bohemian glass, with enamelling.
- £300 • Trio

Red Glass Scent Bottle ▼

- *1920*

Art Deco perfume bottle in deep red glass, with a tassel and opaque glass stopper.
- *height 14cm*
- £168 • Trio

Jug-Shaped Scent Bottle ▶

- *1860*

A French ruby scent bottle in the shape of a stylised jug, with ruby stopper. Decorated with a gilt foliage design on the bottle and handle. The metal base carries a gilt foliage design.
- *height 12cm*
- £210 • Trio

Square Scent Bottle ▼

- *1930*

Square glass Art Deco perfume bottle, with a clear glass stopper and large grey silk tassel. Decorated with a black floral design.
- *height 10cm*
- £138 • Trio

Heart-Shaped Porcelain Bottle ▲

- *circa 1906*

A heart-shaped porcelain scent bottle, with a silver stopper. Decorated with a pair of eighteenth century figures.
- *diameter 4cm*
- £178 • Trio

Owl Perfume Bottle ▼

- *circa 1895*

A blue perfume bottle with silver owl's head shaped top with glass eyes, by Morden & Co, London.
- £1,700
- S. & A. Thompson

Lancome Tresor ▼

- *circa 1950*

Original Tresor with cut glass bottle stand.
- £195
- Linda Bee

Bourjois 'Evening in Paris' ▲

- *circa 1935*

A novelty perfume bottle in perspex wheelbarrow.
- £250
- Linda Bee

Perfume Set ▲

- *circa 1890*

A late 19th-century perfume set of vaseline and cranberry coloured glass bottles, having silver-plated stoppers with recessed corks, all in original leather case.
- £200
- Trio

Decanter Bottle ▼

- *circa 1920*

A decanter bottle with handle in original wicker coat.
- *height 23cm*
- £25
- Ranby Hall

Christian Dior 'Miss Dior' ▼

- *circa 1945*

A Christian Dior perfume bottle of obelisk shape.
- £450
- Linda Bee

Art Deco Set ◄

- *1920*

An Art Deco perfume bottle and powder box, cut and engraved, with enameling.
- £210
- Trio

Cameras

Rectaflex Camera ▼
- **1950s**

Rare Rota Rectaflex camera with three French-made Angenieux rotatable lenses. The lenses have three focal lengths: 50mm, 35mm and 135mm.
- *15cm x 9cm*
- **£3,000**   • Jessop Classic

Voigtlander Camera ▼
- **1958–60**

Rare Voigtlander Prominent II camera with an Ultron 50mm F2 lens. The camera has a 35mm rangefinder with interchangeable lenses and a clear viewfinder.
- *14cm x 8.5cm*
- **£699**   • Jessop Classic

Sakura Petal Camera ▲
- **1948**

Sakura Petal camera with film and case included. This is the world's smallest mass-produced camera.
- *2.5cm x 1.2cm*
- **£250**   • Jessop Classic

Kodak "Girl Guide" Camera ▲
- **1933**

Blue Kodak "Girl Guide" camera with an F6.3 Anistigmat lens. Supplied with blue case.
- *13cm x 7cm*
- **£200**   • Jessop Classic

Voigtlander Bessamatic SLR Camera ▲
- **circa 1950s**

Voigtlander Bessamatic SLR camera, with a 36–82mm F2.8 zoom lens. This was the first commercially produced zoom lens for a 35mm camera.
- *16cm x 10cm*
- **£149**   • Jessop Classic

Microtechnical Camera ◄
- **circa 1970s**

Microtechnical MK8 camera with a 150mm Symmar lens. Accompanied by a guide book.
- *18cm x 18cm*
- **£599**   • Jessop Classic

Bolex Super 8 ▲
- *circa 1970*
Bolex Super 8 480 Macrozoom.
- *height 19cm*
- £170   • Mac's Cameras

Miniature Mec 16 ▶
- *1950*
German miniature Mec 16 camera with an unusual pressed gold tin casing. With original leather case.
- *width 10cm*
- £99   • Jessop Classic

Kodak Eastman ▲
- *circa 1920*
No.2 Hawkette brown tortoiseshell effect bakelite folding camera by Kodak.
- *height 18cm*
- £69   • Jessop Classic

Wallace Heaton ▶
- *1925–35*
Wallace Heaton Zodel model folding camera with a 105mm F3.8. Zodellar lens and original leather case with handle.
- *height 14cm*
- £149   • Jessop Classic

Sputnik Camera ▼
- *1950*
Russian Sputnik camera and case with 75mm F4.5 Lomo lens.
- *height 8cm*
- £149   • Jessop Classic

Mick A Matic ▲
- *1971*
Mick A Matic American camera in the shape of Mickey Mouse made by Child Guidance Product Inc.
- *height 20cm*
- £49   • Jessop Classic

Balda Camera ▲
- *circa 1960*
Balda proximeter 2 and a quarter square camera with a range finder. 35mm lens including poxymetre.
- *height 9.5cm*
- £90   • Mac's Cameras

Expert Tips

Collecting cameras is not only fun but you also have the bonus that they are usable. SLR cameras are a good future investment, especially with the onset of the digital age.

Rollei 35 Camera ▼
- *1971*

Gold Rollei 35 camera, supplied with a brown leather case and a red felt-lined wooden box. Fitted with an F3.5 Tessar lens.
- *9.5cm x 6cm*
- £899   • Jessop Classic

Kodak Retina II F, 35mm Camera ▼
- *1963*

Kodak Retina II F, 35mm camera with an F2.8, 45mm Xenar lens. The built-in flash bulb holder is an unusual feature for this style of camera.
- *13cm x 8.5cm*
- £100   • Jessop Classic

Blair Stereo Weno with Case ▶
- *1902*

Blair stereo Weno camera with case (as seen underneath), made in Rochester, New York. Supplied with a pair of Plastigmat lenses. Uses 116 Kodak film which has now been discontinued.
- *26.5cm x 11.5cm*
- £299   • Jessop Classic

Rollei Camera ▲
- *1966–7*

Rollei 35 standard camera fitted with an F3.5 Tessar lens.
- *9.5cm x 6cm*
- £299   • Jessop Classic

Houghton Ticka Camera ▲
- *1905–14*

Houghton Ticka Spy camera. This is designed to look like a pocket watch with an engraved monogram on the cover. The camera is hidden underneath the winding mechanism.
- *6.5cm x 5cm*
- £249   • Jessop Classic

Canon IV Camera ▲
- *circa 1950s*

Canon IV range finder camera with detachable flash unit and a 50mm 1.9 Serenar lens. Supplied with a brown leather case. This model is based on a Leica design.
- *14cm x 7cm*
- £499   • Jessop Classic

Skeky Camera ▲
- *1947*

Subminiature Skeky camera with a tele-lens. The camera uses 16mm film and comes with a brown leather case.
- *2cm x 1cm*
- £299 • **Jessop Classic**

8mm Cine Camera ▲
- *1927*

Extremely compact 8mm Kodak cine camera. This was the first model to use standard 8 film.
- *15cm x 11.5cm*
- £120 • **Photo. Gallery**

Expert Tips

A complete camera set in its original box or case is very desirable and should prove to be a good investment.

Minox Camera ▼
- *circa 1950s*

Minox A camera which was used in the World War II as a spy camera. It takes 8 x 11mm negatives, has a brushed aluminium body and a Complan 15mm, 3.5 lens.
- *1cm x 10cm*
- £180 • **Photo. Gallery**

"Boy Scout" Camera ▼
- *1933*

Green Kodak "Boy Scout" camera, fitted with an F6.3 Anstigmat lens. The model is supplied with a brown leather case and uses 127 Kodak film.
- *12.5cm x 7cm*
- £150 • Jessop Classi

Midget Coronet Camera ◄
- *circa 1930s*

Art-Deco style, blue bakelite, Midget Coronet camera, fitted with a Taylor Hobson F10 lens. The colour is very rare.
- *2cm x 6cm*
- £325 • Jessop Classi

Leica Range Finder Camera ▲
- *circa 1930s*

Leica Range Finder camera fitted with a Summar 5cm F2 lens. This camera remains in production.
- *13cm x 7cm*
- £299 • Jessop Classi

Retina Kodak Camera ▲

- *circa 1960*
Retina -Xenar F2.8 45mm lens by
Kodak.
- *height 8cm*
- **£70**   • Mac's Cameras

Franke & Heidecke
Rolly Camera ▲

- *1921–40*
Frank & Heidecke Braunschweig,
Germany, Rolley Heidoscop three
lens stereo camera including its
own case. 7.5cm F4.5 Tessar
Lens.
- *height 17cm*
- **£699**   • Jessop Classic

Soligor Camera ▲

- *circa 1960*
Soligor 50mm lens Japanese made
auto lens.
- *height 7cm*
- **£74**   • Mac's Cameras

Robin Hood Camera ▼

- **1930**
Black marbelised bakelite Robin
Hood camera with a picture of
Robin Hood by Standard
Cameras of Birmingham. Takes
darkroom loaded single sheets of
45 x 107mm film. Originally
came with film, paper and
darkroom safelight. Sometimes
seen in England, but rarely seen
elsewhere.
- *height 5cm*
- **£69**   • Jessop Classic

Miniature Tessina ▼

- **1960**
Swiss made miniature Tessina
camera in the style of a watch,
with meter and strap. It took
exposure on 35mm film, which
was divided up in special
cartridges.
- *width 6.8cm*
- **£899**   • Jessop Classic

Mamiya ▲

- **1959**
Japanese Mamiya 16 camera.
- *width 11.5cm*
- **£49**   • Jessop Classic

Contina Zeiss Camer ▲

- *circa 1960*
Zeiss Contina camera with an
F2.8 45mm Novica lens.
- *height 7cm*
- **£30**   • Mac's Cameras

Chess Sets

Ivory Chess Set ◀

- *circa 1845*
A rare 19th-century French design ivory chess set.
- *height 10cm (king)*
- £8,500   • G.D. Coleman

Tortoiseshell & Ivory Chess Set ◀

- *circa 19th century*
Interlaced vine decoration on light mahogany base.
- *height 19cm*
- £650   • Shahdad

Boxwood and Ebony Staunton Chess Set ▲

- *late 19th century*
Mahogany green baize-lined lift-top box with Jacques of London green paper label to the inside lid.
- *height 19cm (king)*
- £950   • G.D. Coleman

Mythological Chess Set ▶

- *circa 1920*
Unusual French decorated lead chess set on a mythological classical theme.
- *height 13cm (king)*
- £1,800   • G.D. Coleman

Selenus Chess Set ▲

- *circa 1800*
German carved bone with red and white kings and queens topped by Maltese crosses.
- *height 12cm*
- £2,850   • G.D. Coleman

Painted Metal Chess Set ▼

- *circa 1920*
King and queen representing mythical gods. White figures show a mottled effect.
- £1,800   • G.D. Coleman

Portuguese European vs Chinese Chess Set ▲

- *circa 1865*
Fine carved ivory, from Macau.
- *height 10cm (king)*
- £1,850   • G.D. Coleman

American Chess Set ▼
- *1876*
American chess set in soft metal,
signed "Le Mon" and dated 1876.
Presented in its original box.
- *height 10cm/king*
- **£3,500**   • G.D. Coleman

Coromandel Games Compendium ▲
- *circa 1880*
Coromandel games box in wood,
containing chess, backgammon,
checkers, cribbage, dominoes
and draughts.
- *33cm x 20cm x 22cm*
- **£1,900**   • Langfords Marine

French Chess Set ▶
- *1800*
French chess set with pieces
carved from lion wood and
bone. Figures are black or red,
both colours decorated with
white edging.
- *height 8cm/king*
- **£1,650**   • G.D. Coleman

German Chess Set ▲
- *1795*
German chess set of Selenus
design, with black and white
pieces in ivory.
- *height 8cm*
- **£790**   • G.D. Coleman

Expert Tips

*The Victorian era
(1837–1901) saw a great
expansion in board games, and
chess was no exception, and
with the expansion of the British
Empire pieces can be found
from all over the world. The
most celebrated designer of chess
pieces is Jack Staunton whose
work is of the Victorian era, and
remains highly collectable.*

Military Chess Set ◀
- *1870*
Chinese export ivory chess
set based on the military theme
of the Emperor Napoleon versus
the Duke of Wellington.
- *height 10cm/king*
- **£2,450**   • G.D. Coleman

Chess Board ▶

- *circa 1910*
An English Edwardian inlaid
wood chess board.
- *42cm x 42cm*
- £180 • G.D. Coleman

Ivory Burmese Chess Set ▲

- *19th century*
White and red very ornate set.
Kings and queens have ornate
crowns and castles have waving
flags on their battlements.
- £1,850 • G.D. Coleman

Chinese Macau Ivory ▲

- *circa 1840*
Red and white pieces. Made for
European market, slightly
oriental features. Queen has
oriental headdress and the king
has a crown.
- £1,850 • G.D. Coleman

Ivory Bears Chess Set ▼

- *circa 1820*
Early 'Bears of Berne' chess set.
- £14,000 • G.D. Coleman

English Chess Set ▼

- *circa 1835*
An English ivory 'Lund'-style
chess set in red and white.
- *height 7.5cm*
- £620 • G.D. Coleman

German Chess Set ◀

- *circa 1880*
Rare German decorated wood,
plaster and metal large figural
chess set. Comes in original
two layer decorated card-
lidded box.
- *height 13.5cm*
- £5,850 • G.D. Coleman

Commemorative Ware

Bust of General ▼
• *circa 1900*
A terracotta pottery bust of a general wearing a hat.
• *height 18cm*
• £120   • P. Oosthuizen

Pottery Jug ▼
• *circa 1890*
Pottery jug modelled as a man with a top hat and a crown on the back of his head.
• *height 15cm*
• £195   • P. Oosthuizen

Doulton Jug ▶
• *circa 1900*
Doulton commemorative jug depicting a soldier with a rifle and the words 'The Handy Man' in the centre and Capt H. Lambton on one side and Capt. P. M. Scott.
• *height 21cm*
• £625   • P. Oosthuizen

Doulton Jug ▲
• *circa 1900*
Doulton jug with a cartouche of the Prime Minister of South Africa flanked by a kangaroo, beaver and ostrich.
• *height 20cm*
• £590   • P. Oosthuizen

Copeland Commemorative Cup ▲
• *circa 1899*
A Copeland commemorative three handled cup, with a cartouche depicting Queen Victoria with the words 'Victoria Queen and Empress comforter of the afflicted' with flags from the Transvaal War 1899. Imperial Federation around the rim, and 'Unity is strength' around the base.
• *height 13cm*
• £1250   • P. Oosthuizen

Soldier Figurine ▲
• *circa 1900*
A model of a soldier standing with a rifle on a circular base with the inscription 'A gentleman in khaki'.
• *height 15cm*
• £68   • P. Oosthuizen

Victorian Cypher ▼
- **1890**
Victorian English carved wooden gesso royal cypher.
- *90cm x 65cm*
- **£2,500**   • Lacquer Chest

Jubilee Mug ▼
- **1935**
Ceramic mug celebrating the silver jubilee of King George V and Queen Mary.
- *height 7cm*
- **£24**   • Magpies

Miners' Strike Plate ▲
- **1984**
Bone china plate to commemorate the great miners' strike of 1984–1985. Issued by the National Union of Mineworkers.
- *diameter 27cm*
- **£58**   • Hope & Glory

Loving Cup ▲
- **1987**
Bone china loving cup by Royal Crown Derby. Commemorating the third term in office of Margaret Thatcher. Limited edition of 650.
- *height 7.75cm*
- **£160**   • Hope & Glory

Engagement Mug ▲
- **1981**
China mug depicting Prince Charles's ear. Drawn by Marc Boxer, made at the engagement of Charles and Diana.
- **£5**   • Hope & Glory

Royal Visit Teapot ▼
- **1939**
Teapot issued in commemoration of a royal visit to Canada made by George VI and Queen Elizabeth II in 1939.
- *height 13cm*
- **£85**   • Hope & Glory

Expert Tips

The condition of any commemorative ware is just as important as the attractiveness of the item; even so, limited editions considerably enhance the desirability of a piece. Make sure that the transfers are bright and unscratched. In terms of subjects, opt for kings, queens or politicians who ruled for a short time.

Toby Jug ▲
- *circa 1939*

Small earthenware toby jug of
Neville Chamberlain, the handle
modelled as an umbrella.
Manufactured by Lancaster.
- *height 7.7cm*
- £65 • Hope & Glory

Child's Teapot and Jug ▲
- *1937*

Child's teapot and jug with
transfers showing Princess
Elizabeth and Princess Margaret
as children.
- *tea pot height 8.8cm*
- £70 • Hope & Glory

Princess Diana Mug ▼
- *1996*

Bone china by Chown. Limited
edition of 70 to commemorate
her 35th birthday and was her
last mug made before her death
and is rare.
- *height 9cm*
- £95 • Hope & Glory

Wedgwood Plaque ▼
- *1974*

Black basalt Wedgwood plaque to
commemorate the centenary of
the birth of Winston Churchill.
- *diameter 16.4cm*
- £65 • Hope & Glory

Bone China Mug ▲
- *1937*

Bone china mug by Hammersley
to commemorate the coronation
of King George VI and Queen
Elizabeth. Transfer with enamel
colours.
- *height 7.8cm*
- £75 • Hope & Glory

Ovaltine Jubilee Mug ▲
- *1977*

Ovaltine Jubilee mug inscribed
with the words, 'This was
presented to you by Ovaltine and
Woman's Own because you were
born in the week February 6th-
12th, 1977, The Silver Jubilee of
Queen Elizabeth II'.
- *height 10.7cm*
- £29 • Hope & Glory

Expert Tips

*The market for commemorative
items is driven by emotion.
They start off overprices and, as
the individual becomes less well
known, may lose value.*

Ainsley Plate ◄
- *1953*

An elaborate commemorative
plate by Ainsley in cobalt blue
with a gold border centred with a
portrait of the Queen.
- *diameter 26.4cm*
- £250 • Hope & Glory

Jubilee Jug ▼

- *1897*

Doulton commemorative jug of Queen Victoria's Diamond Jubilee with a silver rim and olive green cartouches showing Queen Victoria.
- *height 16cm*
- £240　　• Hope & Glory

Doulton Mug ▼

- *1901*

Doulton bone china mug depicting Queen Victoria in memoriam with purple decoration around the rim, and decorated with a prayer book, inscribed below with the words, "She wrought her people lasting good".
- *height 7.6cm*
- £475　　• Hope & Glory

Diamond Jubilee Beaker ▲

- *1897*

Goss white bone china beaker celebrating Queen Victoria's Diamond Jubilee.
- *height 9.7cm*
- £110　　• Hope & Glory

Royal Wintonia Mug ▲

- *1911*

Royal Wintonia earthenware mug for the Investiture of Edward Prince of Wales made for the City of Cardiff.
- *height 8cm*
- £90　　• Hope & Glory

Royal Doulton Beaker ▼

- *1902*

Royal Doulton earthenware Kings coronation beaker celebrating the coronation of Edward VII in rare purple.
- *height 9.8cm*
- £95　　• Hope & Glory

Princess Mary Mug ▼

- *1929*

Earthenware mug to commemorate the visit of Princess Mary Viscountess Laschelles to Castleford.
- *height 8.6cm*
- £175　　• Hope & Glory

Coronation Mug ▼

- *1911*

Green and white coronation mug of George V. Manufactured by Booths.
- *height 7.5cm*
- £70　　• Hope & Glory

Coronation Mug ▼
- *1911*

Coronation mug of King George V and Queen Mary.
- *height 7cm*
- £24   • **Magpies**

Loving Cup ▲
- *1937*

A bone china loving cup, by Shelly, to commemorate the proposed coronation of King Edward VIII.
- *height 11.5cm*
- £275   • **Hope & Glory**

Royal Horse Guard ▼
- *1915*

'The Blues' made by Copeland to commemorate the centenary of the Battle of Waterloo.
- *height 39cm*
- £1,700   • **The Armoury**

Musical Teapot ◄
- *circa 1953*

Teapot in the form of a coach, commemorating the coronation of Queen Elizabeth II. Plays the National Anthem.
- *height 13cm*
- £240   • **Hope & Glory**

Winston S. Churchill Toby Jug ▼
- *circa 1941*

With anchor handle, by Fieldings, representing Churchill's second appointment as First Lord.
- *height 15cm*
- £190   • **Hope & Glory**

Pottery Mug ▶
- *circa 1969*

A mug from the Portmerion pottery to commemorate the first landing of men on the moon by Apollo II.
- *height 10cm*
- £70   • **Hope & Glory**

Snuffbox ▶
- *1895*

Victorian silver table snuffbox, inscribed as presented by HRH Albert Edward of Wales.
- *length 14cm*
- £2,850 • **S. & A. Thompson**

Officer on Horseback ▼
- *circa 1910*
German. Napoleonic period.
Probaby Dresden.
- *height 38cm*
- £2,500   ● The Armoury

Pair of Perfume Flasks ▲
- *circa 1840*
Hand-decorated porcelain
perfume flasks by Jacob Petit,
commemorating the marriage of
Queen Victoria and Prince Albert.
- *height 31cm*
- £3,750   ● Hope & Glory

Ceramic Plaque ▲
- *circa 1911*
Plaque, by Ridgways, to
commemorate the coronation of
George VI and Queen Mary.
- *16cm x 21cm*
- £85   ● Hope & Glory

Coronation Mug ▼
- *1902*
Copeland mug commemorating
the coronation of King Edward
VII and Queen Alexandra. This
mug shows the correct date of
August 9th, 1902. Most
commemorative ware gives the
date as June 26th, from when the
event was postponed due to the
King's appendicitis.
- *height 7.5cm*
- £160   ● Hope & Glory

Wedgwood Mug ▼
- *circa 1937*
A Wedgwood mug
commemorating the coronation
of King George VI, designed by
Eric Ravilious.
- *height 11cm*
- £475   ● Hope & Glory

Children's Plate ▼
- *1847*
Showing the young Edward,
Prince of Wales, on a pony.
Entitled 'England's Hope'.
- *diameter 16.5cm*
- £340   ● Hope & Glory

Teapot ▶
- *circa 1897*
Commemorating the Diamond
Jubilee of Queen Victoria.
Copeland bone china with gold
decoration. Portrait of Victoria in
relief.
- *height 14cm*
- £525   ● Hope & Glory

Toby Jug ▼
- *1940*

A wartime Toby jug of Winston Churchill as first Sea Lord.
- *height 17cm*
- **£125**   • Hope & Glory

Diamond Jubilee Jug ▲
- *1897*

A set of three Copeland/Spode diamond jubilee jugs.
- *height 16cm/largest*
- **£650**   • Hope & Glory

Four Castles Plate ▼
- *1901*

Black transfer on earthenware plate to commemorate the death of Queen Victoria.
- *diameter 24.5cm*
- **£240**   • Hope & Glory

Coronation Mug ▼
- *1911*

Bone china mug commemorating the coronation of George V.
- *height 8.5cm*
- **£58**   • Hope & Glory

Minton Loving Cup ▼
- *1953*

Bone china loving cup by Minton. Coronation of Queen Elizabeth II, designed by John Wadsworth.
- *height 10.5cm*
- **£190**   • Hope & Glory

Musical Teapot ◀
- *circa 1953*

Teapot in the form of a coach, commemorating the coronation of Queen Elizabeth II. Plays the national anthem.
- *height 13cm*
- **£240**   • Hope & Glory

Ephemera

Wonder Woman ▼
- **2000**
Wonder Woman. An archive-volume No. 9. By William Mouton Marston & H.G. Peter.
- £38 • Gosh

Girl ▼
- **1951**
Girl . No.1. Published by Hulton Press.
- £25 • 30th Century Comics

Courage ▲
- **circa 1950**
Courage. Vol.1. No.1. Published by Miller & Son Ltd.
- £4 • 30th Century Comics

Look and Learn ◀
- **1962**
Look and Learn No.2, published by Odhams.
- £2 • 30th Century Comics

The Amazing Spiderman ▲
- **1963**
The Amazing Spiderman, 'The Enforcer' No.10, published by Marvel Comics.
- £140 • Gosh

Rupert Weekly ▲
- **1983**
Rupert Weekly published by Marvel Comics.
- £1.50 • 30th Century Comics

Fantastic Four ▲
• 1963
Fantastic Four - the Living Bomb-burst. Published by Marvel Blastaar.
• £22   • Gosh

The Eagle ▲
• 1951
The Eagle ,Vol.2 No.3. Published by Hulton Press.
• £6   • 30th Century Comics

Tales of Suspense ▼
• 1962
Tales of Suspense -The Teenager who ruled the World!
• £75   • Gosh

Sensation ◄
• 1949
Sensation Comics featuring Wonderwoman, 'The End of Paradise Island!' No.104.
• £68   • 30th Century Comics

The Comet ◄
• 1958
The Comet published by J.B. Allen No.57.
• £5   • 30th Century Comics

Countdown ▲
• 1971
Countdown Dr. Who. Published by Sun Printers.
• £11   • 30th Century Comics

Film Fun Annual ◄
• 1938
Film Fun Annual. Published by Amalgamated Press.
• £25   • 30th Century Comics

Batman Year One ▲
• 1988
Batman Year One by Frank Miller and David Mazzucchelli with Richmond Lewis. Published by D.C.
• £8.99   • Gosh

Original Cartoon ▼
- 1997

A drawing by Ed MacLachlan for NET magazine.
- £140   • Cartoon Gallery

Dope Fiend Funnies ▼
- 1974

Published by Cosmic Comics.
- £8   • Book & Comic

Daily Telegraph Cartoon ▼
- 1998

A cartoon for *The Daily Telegraph* by Matt.
- £100   • Cartoon Gallery

Film Directors ▲
- 1992

A set of 20 famous film directors, issued by Cecil Court Collectors Centre.
- £6   • Murray Cards

Sandman Comic ▲
- 1989

Issue no. 1 of Sandman Comic, from D.C. Comics.
- £20   • Book & Comic

'X Files' Series ▲
- 1996

Set of 72 spin-off cards, from the X Files TV series, by Topps Chewing Gum, USA.
- £12   • Murray Cards

Guardian Cartoon ▼
- 1999

A cartoon for *The Guardian* newspaper, by Steve Bell.
- £250   • Cartoon Gallery

American Indian Chiefs ▼
- 1888

Set of 50 cards, by Allen & Ginter of Virginia, USA. Illustration shows Sitting Bull.
- £1,500   • Murray Cards

New Statesman Cover ▼
- 1999

Cartoon by Chris Riddell, used on cover of *New Statesman*.
- £250   • Cartoon Gallery

Kabuki ▲
- *1999*

Kabuki published by Wizard
Entertainment.
- £7.50   • Gosh

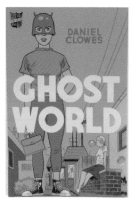

Ghost World ▲
- *2000*

Ghost World by Daniel Clowes -
published by Jonathan Cape
Random House Comic Books Inc.
- £6.99   • Gosh

Essential Avengers ▼
- *2001*

Essential Avengers Vol.1,
published by Marvel Comics.
- £11.50   • Gosh

The Beano Book ▼
- *1973*

The Beano Book. Published by
D.C. Thompson.
- £20   • 30th Century Comics

League of Extraordinary Gentlemen ▶
- *2000*

*The League of Extraordinary
Gentlemen* published by America's
Best Comics Vol.1.
- £18.99   • Gosh

Film Fun ◀
- *1958*

Film Fun published by
Amalgamated Press.
- £13   • 30th Century Comics

X-Men ▲
- *1986*

X-Men published by Marvel. 25th
Anniversary.
- £6   • Gosh

Batman Annual ▲
- *1964–5*

Batman Annual with Batman and
Robin also John Jones from Mars
and Congo Bill.
- £20   • 30th Century Comics

Bomp! ▲
- **1976–77**

Music magazine, *Bomp!*, featuring Brian Wilson.
- £5 • Book & Comic

Zeta ▲
- **1960s**

Issue No. 5, Volume 2, of erotic photography magazine, *Zeta*.
- £10 • Book & Comic

Rolling Stone ◄
- **1970**

October 1970 issue of US rock music magazine, *Rolling Stone*, featuring the life story of Janis Joplin.
- £6 • Book & Comic

Costume Prints ▼
- **1585**

A pair of prints by Nicolo Nicolai, depicting courtly figures in Ottoman costumes, displayed in handcrafted frames.
- 39cm x 29cm
- £800 • Chelsea Gallery

Gent ▼
- **1961**

Men's magazine, *Gent*, featuring interviews with Mark Russell and Klaus Rock.
- £8 • Book & Comic

Crawdaddy ▲
- **July 1973**

US music magazine, *Crawdaddy*, featuring Marvin Gaye.
- £4 • Book & Comic

Animated Cerebus Folder ▼

- *1990s*

Book of art for cancelled film project.

- £30 • Book & Comic

Sir! ▼

- *1962*

April 1962 issue of adult magazine, *Sir!*, featuring "Death of the Hoover" on the cover.

- £4 • Book & Comic

Les Rendez-Vous de Sevenoaks ▼

- *1994*

Hardback edition of *Les Rendez-Vous de Sevenoaks*, featuring the first appearance of Richard Hughes.

- £5 • Book & Comic

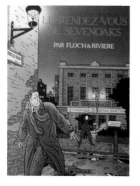

Men in Vogue ▼

- *1970*

One of the few issues of this magazine to appear, featuring B.A.L Newman on the cover. Contains features on men's fashion.

- £15 • Book & Comic

Town ◄

- *1963*

September 1963 issue of fashion and lifestyle magazine, *Town*.

- £10 • Book & Comic

Jamming ▲

- *1964*

Issue No. 12 of rock music magazine, *Jamming*.

- £1.50 • Book & Comic

Forbidden Worlds ▲

- *Sept–Oct 1951*
*Forbidden Worlds Exploring the
Supernatural*. A.C.G.
publications. Issue No.2.
- £120 • 30th Century Comics

Rangers Comics ▲

- *1944*
Rangers Comics featuring U.S.
Rangers in Raider of Red Dawn.
Fiction House Magazine No.17.
- £70 • 30th Century Comics

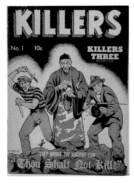

The Dandy ▼

- *1967*
The Dandy Book, published by
D.C. Thompson.
- £30 • 30th Century Comics

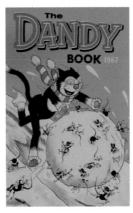

Our Army at War ▼

- *1959*
Our Army at War No.1 by D.C.
National Comics, including, 'The
Rock of Easy Co.!' and other
explosive Battle-Action Stories.
- £125 • 30th Century Comics

Sandman ▶

- *1988*
Sandman Master of Dreams
published by D.C.
- £10 • Gosh

The Killers ◀

- *1947*
The Killer No.1, 'Killers Three
Thou shalt not kill!', published
by Magazine Enterprises, cover
artist L.B. Cole.
- £200 • 30th Century Comics

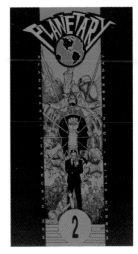

The Fourth Man ▲

- *2001*
Planetary - The Fourth Man.
Published by Wildstorm
Productions.
- £18.95 • Gosh

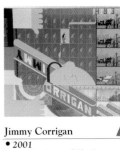

Jimmy Corrigan ▲

- *2001*
*Jimmy Corrigan and The Smartest
Kid on Earth*.
- £27.50 • Gosh

Aircraft of the Royal Air Force ▲

- **1938**
Set of 50 cigarette cards from Players. Illustration shows Hawker Hurricane.
- **£45** • **Murray Cards**

Sunday Times Cartoon ▲

- **1997**
A cartoon for *The Sunday Times* by Nick Newman.
- **£120** • **Cartoon Gallery**

Roses Series ▲

- **1912**
Set of 50 cigarette cards from Wills. Illustration shows a Mrs Cocker Rose.
- **£50** • **Murray Cards**

Akira Comic ▼

- **1988**
Akira issue no. 2, by Epic publishers. Signed by the translator Frank Yonco.
- **£10** • **Book & Comic**

Boys' Ranch ▼

- *June 1951*
Boys' Ranch issue no. 5 – *Great Pony Express Issue* – published by Home Comics.
- **£45** • **Gosh**

Noted Cats Series ▼

- **1930**
Set of 24 cards by Cowans Confectionery, Canada. Shows a Persian male cat.
- **£132** • **Murray Cards**

Notable MPs ▼

- **1929**
Series of 50 cigarette cards of politicians, from Carreras Ltd. Illustration shows caricature of David Lloyd George.
- **£45** • **Murray Cards**

Custard Drawing ▼

- **1999**
A drawing of the character Custard, by Bob Godfrey, taken from the TV series 'Roobarb'.
- **£130** • **Cartoon Gallery**

Children of Nations Series ▼

- *circa 1900*
Set of 12 cards by Huntley & Palmer biscuit manufacturers, for sale in France.
- **£66** • **Murray Cards**

Robotech ▶

- **1985**

The Macross Saga 7 issue, signed by the translator Frank Yonco with characteristic beard and glasses doodle. Published by Comico comics.

- **£8**
- Book & Comic

Mad Monsters ▼

- **1964**

Issue No. 7 of comic *Mad Monsters*.

- *height 30 cm*
- **£1.50**
- Book & Comic

Zig Zag ◀

- **1976**

Issue No. 65 of rock music magazine, *Zig Zag*, with feature on the Beach Boys.

- **£4**
- Book & Comic

The Beano ◀

- **1969**

Issue No. 1,405 of popular UK children's comic, *The Beano*.

- **£1**
- Book & Comic

The Dr Who Annual ▼

- **1979**

1979 annual based on the cult TV series *Dr Who*.

- **£5**
- Book & Comic

Continental Film Review ▼

- *August 1968*

August 1968 issue of adult film magazine.

- **£3**
- Book & Comic

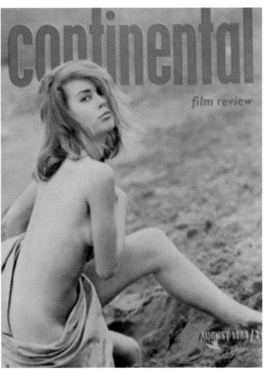

The Atom ◀

- *1962*

First issue of *The Atom* comic, published by DC Comics.

- £40　　　● Book & Comic

The Incredible Hulk ▼

- *1976*

Issue No. 202 of *The Incredible Hulk*, feautring the Origin of Cadavros. Published by Marvel Comics.

- £2　　　● Book & Comic

Bat Masterson ▶

- *1960*

Issue No. 3 of *Bat Masterston*, a comic published by Dell.

- £5　　　● Book & Comic

Fantastic Adventures ▲

- *1951*

March 1951 issue of US science-fantasy magazine, *Fantastic Adventures*.

- £5　　　● Book & Comic

Venus Moderne ▼

- *1950s*

Issue No. 1 of digest-sized nude photography magazine, *Venus Moderne*.

- £4　　　● Book & Comic

Psychotronic ▼

- *1992*

Issue No. 13 of US film magazine, *Psychotronic*.

- £4　　　● Book & Comic

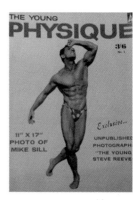

Young Physique ▲

- *1960s*

Issue No. 3 of the vintage muscle magazine, *The Young Physique*.

- £4　　　● Book & Comic

Boyfriend ▼

- *1964*

1964 annual of teenage pop magazine *Boyfriend* featuring Elvis Presley on the cover.

- £10　　　● Book & Comic

The Flash ▲
- *1961*
The Flash featuring Superman
C.C. National Comics featuring,
'Flash of two worlds!' No.123.
- £120 • 30th Century Comics

X-Men ▼
- *1966*
The X-Men – Holocaust.
Published by Marvel Comics
Group.
- £17.50 • Gosh

Blackhawk ◄
- *1956*
Blackhawk, The Delphian Menace.
A Quality Comic Publication.
- £35 • Gosh

Exciting Comics ▲
- *1947*
Exciting Comics featuring, The
Black Terror, Nemesis of Crime.
No.58, published by Better
Comics. Art Cover by Xela.
- £95 • 30th Century Comics

The Fantastic Four ▲
- *1961*
The Fantastic Four, featuring the
Fantastic-Car, and Fantastic
Four's skyscraper hide-out!
Published by Marvel Comics.
- £300 • 30th Century Comics

Iron Man & Captain America ▼
- *1965*
Tales of Suspense featuring Iron
Man and Captain America.
Published by Marvel.
- £65 • Gosh

Gentlemen's Accessories

Top Hat ▲

- *circa 1940*

Grey top hat by Army and Navy, London.

- *height 14cm*
- £45 • Julian Smith Antiques

Shaving Brush ▲

- *1903*

Gentlemen's travelling silver shaving brush.

- *length 14.5cm*
- £400 • Bentleys London

Set of Razors ▲

- *circa 1880*

Set of ivory handled straight razors in an original silver and ivory box.

- *width 18cm*
- £1,000 • Bentleys London

Bowler Hat ▼

- *circa 1930*

Black bowler hat with original box from James Lock & Co. Ltd., 6 St James Street, London SW1.

- *height 32cm*
- £45 • Julian Smith Antiques

Spirit Flasks ▼

- *1920*

Pair of silver-plated spirit flasks housed in original leather case.

- *height 15cm*
- £300 • Bentleys London

Ironing Kit ▼

- *circa 1900*

Campaign officer's batman's ironing kit in original leather case, complete with board and a paraffin flask, a lighter and bright nickel-plated steel.

- *width 24cm*
- £1,000 • Bentleys London

Grey Top Hat ▲

- *1930*

Grey top hat with original box by Herbert Johnson of New Bond St, London, W1.

- *height 16cm*
- £75 • Julian Smith Antiques

Travelling Cutlery Set ▲

- *1900*

Travelling cutlery set with ivory handles.

- *width 56cm*
- £550 • Bentleys London

Travelling Mirror ▲

- *1930*

Travelling mirror in original leather case with the letter H.R.B. inscribed on the lid.

- *diameter 23cm*
- £40 • Julian Smith Antiques

Handbags

American Felt Handbag ▼
- **1950**

A 1950s American handbag made out of felt. Features a poodle design fashioned from sequins with a gilt chain lead.
- *28cm x 28 cm*
- **£220**
- **Linda Bee**

American Handbag ▼
- **1960**

An American handbag made from black velvet with gold metal geometrical bands and shiny black perspex handle and lid.
- *20cm x 17cm*
- **£150**
- **Linda Bee**

Poodle Handbag ▶
- **1950**

A fun American handbag in laminated fabric with poodles on the front.
- *19cm x 28cm*
- **£125**
- **Linda Bee**

American Handbag ▲
- **1940**

An American fabric and bamboo handbag with scrolled design.
- *24cm x 28cm*
- **£150**
- **Linda Bee**

Crocodile Handbag ▼
- **1940**

A 1940s classically elegant Argentinian crocodile skin handbag with brass trim.
- *23cm x 28cm*
- **£195**
- **Linda Bee**

American Handbag ◀
- **1950**

An American 1950s handbag with a handle of pink velvet, hand-painted with pink flowers.
- *16cm x 24cm*
- **£150**
- **Linda Bee**

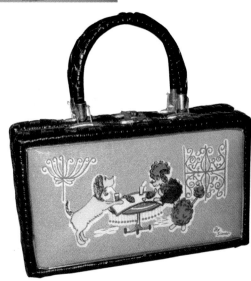

Clochette Evening Bag ▶

- *circa 1920*

Clochette shaped beaded evening bag, with rows of blue and pink with a black metal filigree clasp and silver and black handle.
- *height 18cm*
- **£395** • Beauty and the Beasts

Chain Link Bag ▼

- *1900*

Gilt chain link bag with an Art Nouveau lady on the rim inset with sprays of berries inset with red stones and foliate design.
- *height 14cm*
- **£395** • Beauty and the Beasts

Victorian Beaded Bag ▲

- *1890*

Cream Victorian fine beaded bag with pink and yellow roses, with a silver gilt frame and pink and green glass beaded tussles.
- *height 25cm*
- **£495** • Beauty and the Beasts

French Beaded Bag ▼

- *circa 1950*

French beaded bag decorated with pink roses and a gold and white beaded frame inset with enamel roses.
- *width 22cm*
- **£695** • Beauty and the Beasts

Ken Lane Handbag ▲

- *1960*

Ken Lane brown handbag with a dramatic coral circular diamante handle.
- *height 15cm*
- **£295** • Beauty and the Beasts

Velvet Bag ▼

- *circa 1860*

Victorian cream velvet evening bag with a silver filigree frame, and fine cut-steel looped fringing.
- *height 23cm*
- **£495** • Beauty and the Beasts

Floral Handbag ▲

- *circa 1940*

Petit point floral design bag with black enamel frame with gilt scalloped edge and gilt chain.
- *width 19cm*
- **£295** • Beauty and the Beasts

Silk Evening Bag ▲

- *circa 1920*

Black silk evening bag decorated with flowers in blue, red, and green with steel chips decoration.
- *height 18cm*
- **£295** • Lynda Brine Antiques

Black Beaded Bag ▼
• *1890*
Fine black beaded Victorian bag
with floral design of pink roses,
blue cornflowers and daisies, with
a filigree frame and paste jewels.
• *height 25cm*
• **£495** • **Beauty and the Beasts**

Clear Perspex Bag ▼
• *circa 1950*
Clear perspex American bag with
foliate design on the lid.
• *height 111cm*
• **£248** • **Lynda Brine Antiques**

Petit Point Handbag ▶
• *circa 1940*
A handbag with black petit point
background decorated with
flowers in a vase.
• *width 21cm*
• **£275** • **Beauty and the Beasts**

Moiré Silk Evening Bag ▲
• *circa 1940*
Brown moiré silk evening back
with a geometric gilt clasp by
Josef.
• *height 17cm*
• **£265** • **Beauty and the Beasts**

Wicker Bag ▼
• *1950*
Wicker bag made by Midas of
Miami, decorated with birds, and
green, orange and blue sequins.
• *width 37cm*
• **£135** • **Beauty and the Beasts**

Velvet Bag ▲
• *circa 1860*
Black velvet bag with cut steel
beading of a heraldic design.
With metal clasp and chain.
• *height 28cm*
• **£895** • **Beauty and the Beasts**

Red Plastic Bag ▲
• *1930*
Red plastic bag with a gold and
black geometrical design, with a
gilt chain handle.
• *width 19cm*
• **£395** • **Beauty and the Beasts**

Kitchenalia

Copper Kettle ▲
- *1860*

Victorian copper kettle with good patination.
- *height 22cm*
- £140　　　• R. Conquest

Chocolate Tin ▼
- *1890*

Dutch blue and orange chocolate tin from Weesp, the Netherlands.
- *height 19cm*
- £110　　　• R. Conquest

Tea Tins ▶
- *1920s*

Numbered and pre-painted tea tins, with oriental designs.
- *£950*　　　• North West 8

Tea Sample Tins ▼
- *circa 1880–1920*

Soldered tin containers, stamped and numbered. Originally used by tea merchants to store tea samples.
- *8cm x 5cm x 3cm*
- £550　　• After Noah (KR)

Dutch Milk Jug ▲
- *1840*

Dutch copper milk jug of baluster form and cover with handle.
- *height 45cm*
- £160　　　• R. Conquest

Coal Iron ▲
- *1880*

Dutch coal iron fitted with wooden handle.
- *height 22cm*
- £60　　　• R. Conquest

Enamelled Teapot ▲
- *1950s*

Blue-enamelled tin teapot.
- *height 23cm*
- £25　　• Kitchen Bygones

Flour Shaker ▲

- *circa 1940*

Green enamelled flour shaker
with the words 'Fine Flour' in
cream writing, decorated with
yellow banding.
- *height 12cm*
- £10 • Michael Laws Antiques

Green French Candleholder ▼

- *1890*

French green enamel
candleholder with white trim and
scrolled handle.
- *diameter 16cm*
- £15 • Rookery Farm Antiques

French Coffee Pot ▲

- *1890*

Orange enamel French coffee pot
decorated with a bunch of
cherries.
- *height 28cm*
- £85 • Rookery Farm Antiques

Rolling Pin ▼

- *1880*

Turned wood rolling pin made
from fruitwood.
- *length 30cm*
- £18 • Michael Laws Antiques

Brass Jelly Mould ▲

- *circa 1950*

Circular brass jelly mould with a
stepped pattern.
- *diameter 22cm*
- £15 • Michael Laws Antiques

Harlequin Cups ▲

- *1950*

Harlequin melamine set of six
plastic cups and saucers. Argosy
Ware made by Melmex.
- *height 3cm*
- £45 • The Manic Antiques

Art Deco Coffee Pot ▼

- *1920*

French enamel coffee pot with
angular design and variegated
brown and cream panels.
- *height 29cm*
- £60 • Rookery Farm Antiques

Rocket Ice Crusher ▶
- *1950*

American rocket ice crusher
made from aluminium with red
plastic handle and container.
Made by Fortuna.
- *height 32.5cm*
- £150 • The Manic Antique

Enamel Coffee Pot ▲
- *1890*

French corn flour blue enamelled
coffee pot with turned fruitwood
side-handle.
- *height 22cm*
- £70 • Rookery Farm Antiques

Scales ▲
- *1920*

European cast iron weighing
scales with copper pans and iron
weights.
- *height 32cm*
- £45 • Michael Laws Antiques

Café and Chicorée Pots ▲
- *1920*

Café and chicorée, brown
enamelled pots with white
writing and banding.
- *height 20cm*
- £45 • Rookery Farm Antiques

Enamel Funnel ▶
- *1890*

French blue and white enamel
funnel.
- *height 12cm*
- £12 • Rookery Farm Antiques

Wood Butter Pat ▲
- *1910*

Wood butter pat moulded one
side with a handle.
- *length 19.5cm*
- £10 • Rookery Farm Antiques

Small Metal Mould ▲
- *1890*

Small metal mould in the shape
of a fish.
- *length 9.5cm*
- £12 • Rookery Farm Antiques

French Storage Jar ▼
- *1920*

French hanging storage jar with a
wood lid with red and white
panels and the word 'Sel' in
black.
- *height 27cm*
- £65 • Rookery Farm Antiques

Horlick's Mixer ◀

- *1940*

A Horlick's mixer jug and whisk with transfer detail.
- *height 20cm*
- £19   ● Kitchen Bygones

Flour Jar ▼

- *1950s*

Circular enamelled flour jar in tin with twin handles.
- *height 40cm*
- £25   ● Kitchen Bygones

Flour Shaker ◀

- *1940*

Cornish Ware flour shaker.
- *height 12cm*
- £58   ● Magpies

Cast-Iron Skillet ▲

- *1910*

Edwardian cast-iron skillet semi-circular handle.
- *diameter 28cm*
- £40   ● Kitchen Bygones

Muffin Maker ▲

- *1920*

Cast-iron muffin maker.
- *diameter 25cm*
- £25   ● Kitchen Bygones

Dessert Set ▲

- *1950s*

Pyrex dessert set comprising five pieces.
- *diameter 24cm*
- £30   ● Kitchen Bygones

Jam Maker ◀

- *1920*

A brass jam-making pan with carrying handle.
- *diameter 30cm*
- £65   ● Kitchen Bygones

Kitchen Dolly ▲

- *1920*

A dolly made by Simplex with wooden shaft and turned handle.
- *height 25cm*
- £25   ● Kitchen Bygones

English Sugar Jar ▲
• 1950

English white porcelain sugar jar
with a circular wood lid with a
royal blue geometric design with
the words 'Sugar' in black.
• height 17cm
• £28 • Rookery Farm Antiques

Porcelain Wall Box ▲
• 1950

Porcelain wall box with wooden
lid and decorated with fruit and
blue banding with "Allumettes"
in gold writing.
• height 15.5cm
• £45 • Rookery Farm Antiques

Bread Bin ▲
• 1890

French enamel red and white
marbling bread bin with handles
each side and a handle on the
cover.
• height 23cm
• £50 • Rookery Farm Antiques

Metal Salad Sieve ▲
• 1920

Metal salad sieve with handles
and two feet.
• height 24cm
• £15 • Rookery Farm Antiques

Ham Stand ▼
• 1910

English white pottery ham stand.
• height 20cm
• £45 • Rookery Farm Antiques

Enamel Utensil Rack ◄
• 1880

French Royal and light blue
enamel wall hanging utensil rack,
with two ladles.
• height 52cm
• £75 • Rookery Farm Antiques

Copper Kettle ▼
• 1850

Large English rose copper kettle
with original patina.
• height 30cm
• £125
• Rookery Farm Antiques

Bread Bin ▼
- *1930*
White-enamelled bread bin with green lettering.
- *height 40cm*
- £44   • Magpies

Hen-Shaped Dish ▼
- *1970*
Ceramic hen dish produced by Susan Wilkans Ellis, Portmeirion.
- *height 13cm*
- £25   • Magpies

Metal Candlestick ▼
- *1930*
Metal candlestick with green and black enamelling.
- *height 6cm*
- £12   • Magpies

Enamelled Kettle ▼
- *1950s*
Blue enamelled kettle.
- *height 25cm*
- £25   • Kitchen Bygones

Herb Storage Jar ▼
- *1950*
Herb jar and cover with red banding and the word "Marjoram" on the body. Produced by Kleen Kitchenware.
- *height 10cm*
- £5.50   • Magpies

Household Iron ▲
- *1940*
Small iron by J & J Siddons, West Bromwich.
- *height 8cm*
- £14.50   • Magpies

Expert Tips

Where would the prop finder be on period costume dramas without the collector of these everyday objects? Kitchenware items have proved to be good investments, but be careful not to pay over the odds for them as the margins for error are small. When examining items, look out for split seams, bad repairs or over-thinning of the brass or copper as this affects their collectability.

Pie Crust Funnel ▼
- *1940*
Ceramic pie crust funnel formed as a blackbird.
- *height 13cm*
- £9.50   • Magpies

Enamel Coffee Pot ▼
● 1890
White enamel coffee pot in two
sections with purple flowers and
red banding.
● *height 33cm*
● **£70** ● **Rookery Farm Antiques**

Enamel Utensil Rack ▼
● 1890
Enamel French utensil rack
painted red and black with a
shaped top and white tray.
● *height 54cm*
● **£65** ● **Rookery Farm Antiques**

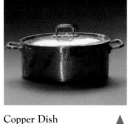

Metal Weighing Scales ▲
● 1890
Metal kitchen weighing scales
with metal base and copper scoop
and weights, inscribed 'To weigh
2lbs'.
● *height 22cm*
● **£98** ● **Rookery Farm Antiques**

Worcester Ware
Cake Tin ▲
● 1950
Worcester Ware cake tin with a
red lid and 'Cakes' in red letters
on the front and Worcester Ware
made in England on the base.
● *diameter 22cm*
● **£28** ● **Rookery Farm Antiques**

Copper Dish ▲
● 1920
Medium size copper dish with
cover with brass handles.
● *9cm x 22cm*
● **£58** ● **Rookery Farm Antiques**

Small Iron ▲
● *circa 1920*
Small iron with a moulded base
made by W. Cross and Son.
● *length 12cm*
● **£18** ● **Michael Laws Antiques**

Sucre and Café Pots ◄
● 1920
French enamel blue and white
marbled pots printed in black
with the words 'sucre' and 'café'.
● *height 23cm*
● **£45** ● **Rookery Farm Antiques**

Enamel Jug ▲
- *1880*

French enamel jug with a large group of irises with terracotta banding around the lip.
- *height 36cm*
- £68 • Rookery Farm Antiques

Bread Knife ▶
- *1920*

Bread knife with a wooden handle inscribed 'Hovis'.
- *length 30cm*
- £22 • Rookery Farm Antiques

Metal Weighting Scales ▼
- *1880*

Kitchen weighing scale with 'OK' and 'domestic use only' written on the base, four weights and a copper weighing scoop.
- *height 21cm*
- £88 • Rookery Farm Antiques

French Red Pot ▲
- *1920*

French red coffee pot with variegated panels of red and white and red handle and spout.
- *height 27cm*
- £78 • Rookery Farm Antiques

Copper Ice Bucket ▲
- *1940*

Copper ice bucket with foliate design.
- *height 13.5cm*
- £15 • Rookery Farm Antiques

French Utensil Rack ◀
- *1880*

French white enamel utensil rack with shaped top and a red and white check design to the centre with two ladles with red handles.
- *height 54cm*
- £75 • Rookery Farm Antiques

Storage Jar ▼
- *circa 1940*
Cornish Ware jar with characteristic blue and white banding.
- *height 22cm*
- £11 • Magpies

Metal Funnel ▼
- *1940*
Blue enamelled metal funnel with handle.
- *height 17cm*
- £8.50 • Magpies

Baker's Paddle ▼
- *1920*
A baker's folding paddle with spatulate head.
- *length 185cm*
- £45 • Kitchen Bygones

Bean Slice ▼
- *1920*
Iron bean slice with a brass handle, produced by Alexander Ware.
- £12 • Magpies

Copper Jelly Moulds ◄
- *circa 1900*
Set of three copper jelly moulds in the shape of oven-ready chickens. Used for making savoury jellies and pates.
- £14 • Magpies

Ceramic Rolling Pin ▲
- *1950*
Ceramic white rolling pin with green handles, inscribed "Nutbrowne".
- *length 41cm*
- £25 • Magpies

Food Storage Flask ►
- *1930s*
A vacuum flask for food storage. with eagle clasping the world.
- *height 38cm*
- £40 • Kitchen Bygones

Potato Cutter ▼

- *1940*

The New "Villa" French fried potato cutter supplied in its original box.
- *26cm x 12cm x 12cm*
- £14 • Radio Days

Glass Creamer ▼

- *1940*

Jubilee model glass hand-creamer with primrose yellow plastic cup and handle designed by Bel.
- *height 22cm*
- £16 • After Noah (KR)

Mini-Sweeper ▲

- *1940*

Mini-sweeper presented in its original box.
- *20cm x 14cm*
- £12 • Radio Days

Enamelled Bread Bin ▲

- *1940s*

English enamelled bread bin with the letters in stylised font.
- *height 50cm*
- £25 • Kitchen Bygones

Cream Maker ▼

- *1950s*

Bakelite and glass cream maker with alloy handle.
- *height 21cm*
- £15 • Kitchen Bygones

Cornish Ware Mug ▼

- *1940*

Cornish ware mug decorated with blue and white hoops.
- *height 8cm*
- £10.50 • Magpies

Luggage

English Leather Suitcase ▼
- *circa 1900*

English leather suitcase, with brass fittings and leather handle.
- *70cm x 40cm x 20cm*
- **£180**   • Henry Gregory

Travelling Case   ▼
- *circa 1900*

English leather suitcase with brass fittings and leather straps.
- *95cm x 56cm x 30cm*
- **£280**   • Henry Gregory

Picnic Case for Two   ▼
- *circa 1910*

English leather picnic case, fully fitted with custom-made accoutrements.
- *width 28cm*
- **£550**   • Mia Cartwright

Gladstone Bag   ▲
- *circa 1860*

Victorian crocodile Gladstone bag with leather handle and brass fittings.
- *40cm x 26cm x 15cm*
- **£70**   • Henry Gregory

Leather Suitcase   ▼
- *circa 1900*

All-leather suitcase with brass fixtures.
- *70cm x 40cm x 25cm*
- **£240**   • Henry Gregory

Leather-Handled Suitcase ▼
- *circa 1900*

A small leather suitcase with brass fittings and leather handle.
- *64cm x 38cm x 15cm*
- **£110**   • Henry Gregory

Gladstone Travelling Bag

- *circa 1870*
All leather Gladstone bag with brass attachments, two straps and double handles.
- *length 69cm*
- £480 • Henry Gregory

Cartridge Case

- *circa 1910–20*
Army and Navy case used for carrying cartridges. Hide leather, brass fittings and blue felt interior.
- *height 13cm*
- £650 • Mia Cartwright

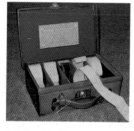

Leather Hat Box

- *circa 1890*
Hide leather. Initials 'P. C.' inlaid on lid. Hat included in the red silk quilted interior. Beautiful condition.
- *width 82cm*
- £350 • Mia Cartwright

Leather Suitcase

- *circa 1910*
Square leather travelling case with brass fittings.
- *depth 40cm*
- £110 • Henry Gregory

Official Mail Bag

- *circa 1920*
English leather mail bag.
- *length 45cm*
- £155 • A.P. Mathews

Travelling Wardrobe

- *circa 1900*
Leather and brass trunk with canvas drawers and interior fittings. French.
- *length 1.2m*
- £900 • Henry Gregory

Square Travelling Case

- *circa 1910*
Leather and canvas square case with brass fittings, with inner tray and ticking lined.
- *height 40cm*
- £110 • Henry Gregory

Military Boot Trunk

- *circa 1870–80*
Late Victorian English boot trunk, all in leather with fitted and compartmentalised interior and carrying handles on the front and both ends. Made by Peel & Co, Victoria, for Captain A. Pepys, whose name is inscribed. Possibly for the Crimea.
- *length 66cm*
- £875 • Mia Cartwright

Jewellery Case ▲
- *circa 1915*
Crocodile skin jewel case, with velvet and silk lining, with gilded brass fittings.
- *width 20cm*
- £950 • Bentleys

Gladstone Bag ▶
- *1960*
Gladstone python skin bag with brass fittings double bolt straps with stitched leather handle, in good condition.
- *width 42cm*
- £395 • Beauty

Wicker Picnic Case ▲
- *circa 1925*
Wicker motoring hamper. Well fitted with two white enamel sandwich boxes, and one large chrome sandwich box. A circular jam pot with leather strap, two wicker bottles and six glass holders, salt and pepper shakers, with place settings for six persons.
- *29cm x 57cm*
- £3,000 • Bentleys

Picnic Set ▲
- *circa 1925*
A leather cased picnic set with nickel-plated fittings and a setting for four people.
- *width 47cm*
- £1,800 • Bentleys

Louis Vuitton Trunk ▲
- *1905*
Louise Vuitton patterned trunk with beech wood rails leather binding solid brass fittings and handles each side.
- *54cm x 110cm*
- £7,200 • Bentleys

Louis Vuitton Trunk ◀
- *1920*
Rare leather covered Louis Vuitton trunk with brass fittings, copper rivets and leather handles.
- *70cm x 110cm*
- £9,000 • Bentleys

Crocodile Hat Box ▶

- *circa 1920*
Crocodile skin hat box with gilt over brass locks, with brown Moiré silk lining.
- *26cm x 41cm*
- **£4,000** • Bentleys

Crocodile Case ▲

- *circa 1900*
Small crocodile case with handle and nickle fittings, with the letters L.T. on the lid.
- *width 35cm*
- **£650** • Bentleys

Attaché Case ▲

- *circa 1900*
Rare moulded Norfolk hide attaché case with original brass fittings, a leather handle, and a green leather interior.
- *10cm x 47cm x 32cm*
- **£1,000** • Bentleys

Goyard Hat Case ▶

- *1920*
Goyard canvas hat case with a painted chevron pattern and a tan leather trim with small brass nails, leather handle and brass fittings.
- *25cm x 49cm*
- **£1,500** • Bentleys

Lady's Travelling Case ▶

- *circa 1930*
Lady's green leather travelling case in two separate sections, fitted with a silk interior incorporating a turquoise enamel brush set, boxes with silver gilt lids and a travelling clock.
- *width 32cm*
- **£600** • Julian Smith

Gladstone Bag ◀

- *1890*
Small leather Gladstone bag with brass fittings and leather handle.
- *24cm x 34cm*
- **£500** • Bentleys

Mechanical Music

Rock-Ola Princess ▲

- *1946*

American Rock-Ola Princess No.1422, manufactured in 1946, plays 20, 78 R.P.M. records. In good original condition with pheonilic pilasters, and a central panel with decorative metal scrolling.
- *149cm x 54cm*
- **£5,200**   • Juke Box Services

Eight Air Musical Box ▲

- *circa 2885*

Swiss eight air music box with five bells and drum by Paillard, in an inlaid rosewood case with brass handles each side standing on square ebonised feet.
- *23cm x 68cm*
- **£4,000**   • Vincent Freeman

Singing Bird Autometer ▼

- *circa 1880*

Rare French singing bird autometer in a brass and gilded cage with moving chicks and singing bird. The cage with foliate design and gilded panelling around the base. Coin operated and in perfect working order.
- *58cm x 21cm*
- **£6,800**   • Vincent Freeman

Heart Musical Box ▼

- *1950*

Heart shaped musical manicure box, lined with pink silk, with a circular mirror on the inside of the lid and a couple in evening dress dancing. Fitted with pink manicure set and two small circular metal boxes.
- *diameter 23cm*
- **£48**   • The Manic Antique

Ami Continental ▲

- *1961*

American Ami Continental juke box, which has push button electric selection and plays both sides. In good working condition and fully restored.
- *170cm x 70cm*
- **£6,500**   • Juke Box Services

Seeburg HF100R ▲

- *1954*

Seeburg H.F. 100R. Holds 60 records with push button electric selection. Plays both sides. Considered by many to be the best design of a series of jukeboxes made by Seeburg in the 50s and 60. Made in the U.S.A.
- *158cm x 87cm*
- **£7,000**   • Juke Box Services

219

Bal-Ami S100 ▲
- **1960**

The Bal-Ami Jukebox, made in Britain by Balfoure. Engineering, using *High Tech* parts manufactured in the U.S.A by Ami, to overcome import ban on luxury goods after the Second World War.
- *147cm x 80cm*
- **£3,500** • **Juke Box Services**

Key-Wind Musical Box ▲
- **1858**

Nicole Frères key-wind musical box playing six operatic airs by Bellini, in an inlaid rosewood case. No.37625.
- *11cm x 56cm*
- **£2,600** • **Vincent Freeman**

Liepee Music Box ▲
- *circa 1880*

6 bell music box by Liépee, playing 8 operatic airs contained in an inlaid rosewood case.
- *22cm x 58cm*
- **£4,000** • **Vincent Freeman**

Ami J 200 ▼
- **1959**

Ami J.200. Holds 100 records. With pink plastic push-button electric selection, playing both sides. Made in U.S.A. Fully restored.
- *152cm x 83cm*
- **£5,800** • **Juke Box Services**

Birdcage Autometer ▼
- **1870**

French birdcage with two singing birds in rustic setting with roses, standing on a circular gilded base with a leaf design and circular feet. In perfect working order.
- *height 61cm*
- **£5,600** • **Vincent Freeman**

German Symphonion ▲
- **1895**

German symphonion in a rococo walnut case carved with cherubs and a courting couple on the lid, with carved foliate design. Standing on bracket feet.
- *height 30cm*
- **£6,000** • **Vincent Freeman**

Musical Jewellery Box ▲
- **1960**

Red plastic musical jewellery box in the form of a radiogram with turn-table that rotates when music plays, Blue interior, red drawers and a gold fleur de lys.
- *height 11cm*
- **£55** • **The Manic Antique**

Music Box ▲
- *circa 1875*

Music box by Nicole Frères playing 8 operatic airs.
- *12cm x 58cm*
- **£2,500** • **Vincent Freeman**

English Organette
• *circa 1910*
By J.M. Draper, England.
Fourteen notes, with three stops,
flute, expression and principal
which operate flaps over the reed
box to control the tone.
• £950 • Keith Harding

Phonograph Cylinders ▲
• *circa 1900*
Three phonograph cylinders, two
from Edison and one from Bell, in
their original packaging.
• £25–£45 • Talk. Mach.

Polyphon Table Model ▲
• *circa 1890*
Rare, style 48, with two combs.
Sublime Harmony accompanied
by Twelve Saucer Bells. Supplied
with eight discs in a walnut case.
• £5,800 • Keith Harding

Concert Roller Organ ▲
• *circa 1900*
Twenty-key organette by
Autophone Company, N.Y.
Played by 'cobs' or barrels. Ten
cobs supplied.
• £1,750 • Keith Harding

Faventia Spanish Street Piano ▼
• *circa 1900*
Two barrels, each playing six
tunes. With red-grained finish, on
original green and yellow cart.
• £1,495 • Keith Harding

English Gramophone ◄
• *circa 1915*
An English gramophone by
HMV, 'His Master's Voice Junior
Monarch'.
• *height 36cm*
• £3,500 • Keith Harding

Expert Tips

*The Edison Gem and Edison
Standard phonographs were
produced in vast quantities.
Condition needs to be very good
to excite the collector.*

Dog Model Gramophone ◄
• *circa 1900*
By the Gramophone and
Typewriter company. Model
number 3. With original brass
horn and concert soundbox.
Completely overhauled.
• £1,950 • Keith Harding

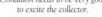

Musical Mandolin Player ▲

• *circa 1890*
Two-air musical automaton by
Lambert in the form of a white-
faced Pierrot playing a mandolin,
swaying from side to side and
plucking the strings, in original
costume and hat. Key pierced
"LB". Porcelain head marked
"TBJ, 222, Paris". Plays
"Valencia" and "On the Riviera".
• *height 50cm*
• £3,900   • Keith Harding

Carillon Musical Box ▲

• *circa 1900*
Carillon musical box by L'Epée,
the nine individually played bells
surmounted with doves. Eight
listed airs are pinned on a 33cm
cylinder. Rosewood inlaid lid
with marquetry design of pipes,
harp and flute.
• *22.5cm x 56.25cm*
• £4,900   • Keith Harding

Spanish Dancer ▼

• *circa 1890*
A Spanish dancer musical
automaton, probably by Lambert,
Paris. Porcelain head by Simon &
Halbig, mould no. 1039. She
turns her head from side to side,
flicks her tambourine and stamps
her foot in time to the music.
With red plush base and original
shoes and stockings.
• *height 52.5cm*
• £2,800   • Keith Harding

Six-Air Musical Box ▶

• *1870*
Six-air Swiss musical box in
marquetry rosewood with 22cm
cylinder, by Ami Rivenc,
Geneva.
• *13.75cm x 43.75cm*
• £2,900   • Keith Harding

Key-Wound Musical Box ◀

• *1830*
Swiss rosewood musical box with
end flap over the controls, key
wind and 20cm cylinder. Plays
four airs, by Henriot.
• *10.75cm x 36cm x 15cm*
• £2,900   • Keith Harding

Seeburg Wall-O-Matic ▲

• *1955*
Chrome Seeburg Wall-O-Matic,
also known as an American Diner
Box. Type 3WA, with 200
selections. It has a hide-away
player and is wall mounted.
• *38cm x 31cm*
• £1,200   • Juke Box Services

Expert Tips

*Automatons are expensive items
to buy and much depends on their
working order and condition.
Genuine examples are proving
increasingly difficult to find.*

Disc Table Polyphon ◀

• *1900*
Rare German 50cm disc table
Polyphon with two combs, 118
notes. Carved mouldings to the
case, shaped figured walnut
panels and marquetry panel on
the lid. Comes with original table
with four turned legs at the
corners supporting shelves for the
discs.
• *112.5cm x 68.5cm*
• £8,500   • Keith Harding

Miscellaneous

Royal Doulton Mug ▶
- *20th century*

A Royal Doulton mug
naturalistically moulded as an
R.A.F. pilot from World War II.
- *height 15cm*
- **£65** • London Antique

Soda Siphons ▲
- *1960*

An English soda siphon with an
emerald green metallic plastic
body and a black plastic lid.
- *height 30cm*
- **£10** • Radio Days

Tortoiseshell Comb ▲
- *1880*

Large tortoiseshell comb
for hair.
- *height 16cm*
- **£95** • Abacus Antiques

Tortoiseshell Letter Opener ▶
- *1911*

Tortoiseshell letter opener with
coins inserted.
- *length 20.5cm*
- **£85** • Abacus Antiques

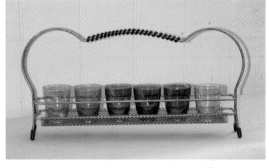

Harlequin Glass Cocktail Set ▲
- *1950*

Harlequin glass cocktail set with
brass holder, plastic feet and
roped handle.
- *18cm x 35cm*
- **£25** • Radio Days

Victorian Opera Glasses ▼
- *Victorian*

A pair of blue enamelled and
gilded brass opera glasses with
taupe leather carrying case.
- *9cm x 4cm*
- **£99** • Langfords Marine

223

Detachable Heels ◀
- *1920*

A pair of French black plastic detachable heels decorated with rhinestones.
- *height 5cm*
- £45   • Linda Bee

Card Case ◀
- *1880*

A pink mother-of-pearl card case decorated with birds.
- *height 9cm*
- £155   • Japanese Gallery

Beehive ▲
- *1890*

A most unusual English beehive, with original basket work with wooden finial.
- *height 70cm*
- £120   • Myriad

Pack of Cigarettes ▼
- *1940*

Original 1940s cigarettes branded "Dandy, Special Virginia".
- £20   • Linda Bee

Pair of Hair Brushes ▼
- *1921*

A pair of tortoiseshell and silver hair brushes with a silver hallmark.
- *length 27cm*
- £55   • Aurum

English Lady's Powder Compact ▲
- *1940*

An English lady's powder compact with plastic dice made by Wadsworth.
- *diameter 7cm*
- £195   • Linda Bee

French Lady's Compact ◀
- *1920*

A French Art Deco circular lady's powder compact with a picture of a young girl with auburn hair in a romantic pose.
- *diameter 7cm*
- £65   • Linda Bee

Magazine Rack ▼

- *1960*

Brown plastic magazine rack.
Giotto stopping for Kartell.

- *39cm x 40cm*
- £75　　　• **Retro Home**

Card Case ▼

- *1870*

Attractive, small crocodile skin
card case.

- £125　　　• **The Reel Thing**

Set of Six Glasses and Tray ▼

- *1960*

A black and gold metal tray with
the inscription "Benedictine
Cherry Brandy" in bright red
lettering and six clear glasses with
gold banding.

- *20cm x 14cm*
- £6　　　• **Radio Days**

Victorian Cigar Case ▶

- *circa 1900*

A Victorian crocodile skin cigar
case with silver trim.

- *length 15cm*
- £495　　　• **The Reel Thing**

Bonny Scotsman Caricature ▲

- *1986*

A ceramic caricature of a bonny
Scotsman entitled "Jock" by
Legend Productions.

- *height 15cm*
- £35　　　• **London Antique**

Soda Siphon ▲

- *circa 1960*

An English 1960s reflective silver
plastic soda siphon, with a green
plastic cup to handle.

- *height 31cm*
- £10　　　• **Radio Days**

Paperweights

Baccarat Mushroom ▲

- *circa 1850*

Baccarat Millefioni paperweight mushroom with blue tonsade and stonecut base.
- *diameter 7cm*
- £950   • G.D. Coleman

Baccarat Garland Posy ▼

- *circa 1850*

Baccarat paperweight inset with a red pansy and leaves, with stonecut base.
- *diameter 6cm*
- £1,850   • G.D. Coleman

Expert Tips

When choosing paperweights, look out for bold colours and pleasing designs, as well as items with a touch of the unusual.

St Louis Sanam-Holed ▼

- *circa 1850*

St Louis Sanam-holed, faceted paperweight with pastel jumbled cones.
- *diameter 7cm*
- £995   • G.D. Coleman

St Louis Crown Weight ◀

- *circa 1850*

St Louis Crown weight with a multicoloured canes design.
- *diameter 5.5cm*
- £1,350   • G.D. Coleman

St Louis Miniature ▲

- *circa 1855*

St Louis miniature paperweight with pink floral design.
- *diameter 4.5cm*
- £385   • G.D. Coleman

White Friars ▼

- *circa 1880*

White Friars paperweight with concentric canes.
- *diameter 8.5cm*
- £290   • G.D. Coleman

St Louis Magnum ▼
- *circa 1850*
Rare, magnum sized glass
paperweight, decorated with a
bouquet on a cigar background.
Unrecorded, so probably a one-off
design and size.
- *diameter 10cm*
- £5,560 ● G.D. Coleman

Clichy Swirl ▼
- *circa 1850*
Clichy swirl paperweight in green
with central flower.
- *diameter 6cm*
- £1,200 ● G.D. Coleman

French Suphide ▶
- *1840*
Paperweight commemorating the
interment of Napoleon at Les
Invalides, Paris. The sulphide
with various Napoleonic
emblems, inscription and date.
- *diameter 8cm*
- £250 ● G.D. Coleman

Baccarat Millefiore ▼
- *1847*
Closepack. Signed 'B 1847'.
- *diameter 6cm*
- £1,500 ● G.D. Coleman

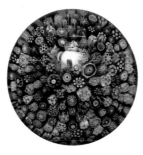

Baccarat Millefiori ▶
- *circa 1850*
Millefiori closepack designed
paperweight with various
coloured and patterned canes.
- *diameter 6cm*
- £1,500 ● G.D. Coleman

Rainbow Hand Coolers ◀
- *late 19th century*
Two rare hollow blown St Louis
rainbow striped hand coolers.
- *length 6cm*
- £780 ● G.D. Coleman

Clichy Green Swirl ▲
- *circa 1850*
Clichy paperweight with green
and white swirls and central pink
and white canes.
- *diameter 7cm*
- £1,350 ● G.D. Coleman

Whitefriars Paperweight ▲
- **1977**
Whitefriars paperweight from a
limited edition to commemorate
the Silver Jubilee of Her Majesty
Queen Elizabeth 1952-1977
No.418/1000.
- *diameter 8cm*
- **£135** • London Antique

Multi coloured
Paperweight ▲
- *circa 1950*
Closepack designed paperweight
with emerald green, red, cobalt
blue and turquoise canes.
- *diameter 7cm*
- **£40** • London Antique

Jubilee Moonflower
Paperweight ▼
- **1977**
Jubilee moonflower using abstract
techniques. Echoes the glitter and
ceremony of the Silver Jubilee.
Engraved on the base with the
Royal Cipher, designed by Colin
Terris No.2846.
- *diameter 7.5cm*
- **£85** • London Antique

Paperweight ▼
- **1977**
Crystal paperweight by Baccarat
commissioned by Spinks. Limited
edition of 500 to commemorate
the Silver Jubilee of Queen
Elizabeth II.
- *diameter 8.5cm*
- **£245** • Hope & Glory

Purple Paperweight ▶
- *circa 1970*
Purple faceted paperweight with a
central flower.
- *diameter 8cm*
- **£55** • London Antique

Whitefriars Paperweight ◀
- **1976**
English Whitefriars hexagonal
faceted paperweight, with puce
composite canes divided by six
gauze tubes around a central
turquoise cluster of canes.
- *diameter 7cm*
- **£195** • London Antique

Faceted Baccarat ▲
- **1976**
Baccarat sulphite paperweight in
facetop form. Faceted with six
lozenge cuts printed with a bust
of Prince Charles.
- *diameter 7cm*
- **£2,670** • London Antique

Whitefriars Paperweight ▲
- **1970**
Faceted paperweight by
Whitefriars of London, cut with
five roundels and moulded
turquoise purple and white canes.
- *diameter 7.5cm*
- **£195** • London Antique

Photographs

Take It ▼

- *September 1970*
Painter Salvador Dali (1904 - 1989) in a characteristic pose with his trademark walking stick, with some of his works at Port Ligat, Costa Brava, Spain. Colour Lambda photograph. Limited edition: one of only 4 signed by the photographer Slim Aaron.
- *50.8cm x pro*
- **£2,400**   ● **Hulton Getty**

Film Makers ▲

- *1960*
Three Italian neo-realist filmmakers, from l to r; Vittorio de Sica (1901-1974), Roberto Rossellini (1906-1977) and Federico Fellini (1920-1993) on the set of de Sica's film, 'Generale delle Rovere'. Black and white fibre, silver gelatin photograph. Limited edition: one of only 4 signed by the photographer Slim Aarons. Printed from original negative in Hulton Getty darkrooms.
- *length 25.4cm*
- **£1,500**   ● **Hulton Getty**

Groucho Marx ▼

- *circa 1954*
American comic Julius 'Groucho' Marx (1895 - 1977), member of the Marx brothers, in bed with a joke cigar in Beverly Hills, California. Black and white, fibre silver gelatin photograph, from a limited edition: one of only 4 signed by the photographer Slim Aarons. Printed from original negative in Hulton Getty darkrooms.
- *length 61cm*
- **£1,500**   ● **Hulton Getty**

Capucine ▲

- *1957*
French actress Capucine, (Germaine Lefebvre) (1933 - 90) fanning herself at a New Years Eve party held at Romanoffs in Beverly Hills. By Photographer Slim Aarons. Black and white fibre, silver gelatin photograph. Limited edition: one of only 4 signed by the photographer. Printed from original negative in Hulton Getty darkrooms.
- *length 50.8cm*
- **£1,500**   ● **Hulton Getty**

Expert Tips

If you are considering collecting photographs, an image by a well known photographer can greatly enhance value, along with a limited print run and the signature of the photographer.

Bacall and Bogart ▶

- *24th December 1951*
American actor Humphrey Bogart (1899 - 1957) with his wife Lauren Bacall and their son Stephen at their home in Beverly Hills in California on Christmas Eve. Black and white fibre, silver gelatin photograph from a limited edition: one of only 4 signed by the photographer Slim Aarons. Printed from original negative in Hulton Getty darkrooms.
- *length 61cm*
- **£1,500**   ● **Hulton Getty**

Kings of Hollywood ▲

- *31st December 1957*
Film stars (left to right) Clark Gable (1901 - 1960), Van Heflin (1910 - 1971), Gary Cooper (1901 - 1961) and James Stewart (1908 - 1997) enjoy a joke at a New Year's party held at Romanoff's in Beverly Hills. A black and white, fibre silver gelatin photograph. Limited edition: one of only 250 signed by the photographer.
- *length 50.8cm*
- **£2,000**   ● **Hulton Getty**

Coronation Photograph ◄
- *1949*

Framed family group photograph of King George VI, Queen Elizabeth and Princess Margaret, with autographed letter by Princess Margaret.
- £300   • The Armoury

Signed C-Type ▲
- *20th century*

Untitled photograph by Nigel Shafran, from 'Ruthbook', featuring blue hippo on radiator sill with green ground. Signed limited edition of 20.
- *length 40cm*
- £450   • Photo. Gallery

C-Type Print ▲
- *1996*

'Making the Bed', c-type print, by Elinor Carrucci. Limited edition of 15.
- *length 50cm*
- £750   • Photo. Gallery

Audrey Hepburn ▼
- *1953*

Audrey Hepburn on Paramount Lot. Signed modern silver-gelatin print by Bob Willoughby.
- *length 30cm*
- £400   • Photo. Gallery

Expert Tips

Pictures of famous subjects are collectable, but the price should reflect the quantity of prints in circulation and the age of the print; new prints from old negatives command less interest.

Signed C-Type ▼
- *1999*

'Corridor of Hydrotherapy Treatment Rooms, Mishkov Sanatorium' by Jason Oddy.
- *length 50cm*
- £775   • Photo. Gallery

Silver Gelatin Print ▲
- *1965*

'March Climax, Trafalgar Square' London photograph by John 'Hoppy' Hopkins.
- *length 40cm*
- £350   • Photo. Gallery

Signed Print ▲
- *1955*

'Dreaming of Home' by Thurston Hopkins. Signed, modern silver-gelatin print.
- £800   • Photo. Gallery

John Hopkins Print ▲
- *1964*

"Thelonius Monk" taken in 1964 by John 'Hoppy' Hopkins. Silver gelatin print, signed recto.
- *30.5cm x 40cm*
- £350   • Photo. Gallery

Cornel Lucas Print ▼
- *1948*

"Yvonne de Carlo as Salome" by Cornel Lucas. A silver gelatin print, signed recto and titled verso.
- *30.5cm x 40cm*
- £400   • Photo. Gallery

Silver Gelatin Print ◀
- *1948*

"Movie cameraman in the South Pacific, 1948" by Cornel Lucas. Silver gelatin print, signed recto.
- *30.5cm x 40cm*
- £400   • Photo. Gallery

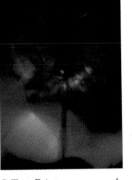

C-Type Print ▲
- *2000*

"Hot Dandelion, 2000" by photographer Delilah Dyson. C-type print, signed verso.
- *30.5cm x 40cm*
- £250   • Photo. Gallery

Humphrey Spender Print ▲
- *1937*

"Bolton, 1937" by Humphrey Spender. For mass observation. Silver gelatin print, signed and titled recto.
- *30.5cm x 40cm*
- £300   • Photo. Gallery

Signed Print ▼
- *2000*

"Snow Drops, 2000" by Delilah Dyson. C-type print, signed verso.
- *30.5cm x 40cm*
- £300   • Photo. Gallery

Silver Gelatin Print ◀
- *1955*

"The Popes and the last passenger steam train, 1955" taken by O. Winston Link.
Silver gelatin print, signed verso by the photographer.
- *30.5 x 40cm*
- £1,750   • Photo. Gallery

Fair Fun ▲
- **8th October 1938**

Two young women enjoying themselves on a roller coaster at Southend Fair, England by the photographer Kurt Hutton, Picture Post. Modern black and white, fibre silver gelatin archival photograph, printed in Hulton Getty Darkrooms. Limited edition: 300.
- *length 50.8cm*
- **£225**   ● Hulton Getty

Bright Lights ▲
- **1970**

Aerial view of the Manhattan skyline at night, looking southeast down Fifth Avenue, from the RCA Building Rockefeller Center, New York City by photographer Lawrence Thornton. Modern black and white, fibre silver gelatin archival photograph, printed in Hulton Getty Darkrooms. Limited edition: 300.
- *length 50.8cm*
- **£225**   ● Hulton Getty

Snow in the Park ▼
- **1947**

A man trudging through Central Park West, New York City, in a blizzard by photographer: Nat Fein/ Courtesy of Nat Fein's Estate. Exclusive. Black and white, fibre silver gelatin archival photograph, printed from original negative in Hulton Getty darkrooms.
- *length 50.8cm*
- **£485**   ● Hulton Getty

Fonda in Town ▼
- **1951**

Film star Henry Fonda (1905-1982) on a balcony overlooking a street in New York by photographer Slim Aarons. Black and white, fibre silver gelatin photograph, printed from original negative in Hulton Getty darkrooms. Limited edition: 300.
- *paper: 40.7cm x 30.5cm image: 30.5cm x 30.5cm*
- **£185**   ● Hulton Getty

Jazz Scooter ▶
- **1949**

Lucille Brown takes control of the Vespa scooter as her husband Louis Armstrong (1898 - 1971) displays his musical appreciation of the ancient Coliseum in Rome. Black and white fibre, silver gelatin photograph, from a limited edition of 300 by photographer Slim Aarons. Printed from original negative in Hulton Getty darkrooms.
- *length 50.8cm*
- **£225**   ● Hulton Getty

Walking in the Rain ▲
- *circa 1955*

A man and his dog walking in the rain in Central Park, New York City by photographer: Nat Fein/Courtesy Of Nat Fein's Estate. Black and white, fibre silver gelatin archival photograph, printed from original negative in Hulton Getty darkrooms. Exclusive.
- *length 40.7cm*
- **£415**   ● Hulton Getty

Guggenheim Window ▲
- *circa 1955*

The Guggenheim Museum of Modern and Contemporary Art in New York. Photographer: Sherman, Three Lions Collection. Black and white fibre, silver gelatin photograph, printed from original negative in Hulton Getty darkrooms. Limited edition: 300.
- *length 61cm*
- **£250**   ● Hulton Getty

Signed Print ▶

- *1964*

Beatles on the way to Teddington studios, 1964, by John 'Hoppy' Hopkins. Silver gelatin print, signed verso.
- *51cm x 61cm*
- £500 • Photo. Gallery

Bob Willoughby Print ▲

- *1967*

Silver gelatin print by Bob Willoughby of Katherine Hepburn walking in the Wicklow mountains in Ireland in 1967 during the filming of "The Lion in Winter". Signed recto.
- *30.5cm x 40cm*
- £600 • Photo. Gallery

Silver Gelatin Print ▶

- *1964*

"Martin Luther King at Oxford peace conference, 1964" by John 'Hoppy' Hopkins. Signed verso.
- *25.5 x 20cm*
- £200 • Photo. Gallery

John Hopkins Print ▼

- *circa 1964*

"The Rolling Stones, studio group" by John 'Hoppy' Hopkins. Silver gelatin print, signed verso.
- *35.5cm x 51cm*
- £350 • Photo. Gallery

Silver Gelatin Print ▼

- *1997*

"Le Grande Arche, Paris, 1997" by Marcus Davies. With photographer's signature verso.
- *16cm x 20cm*
- £400 • Photo. Gallery

Willoughby Signed Print ◀

- *1950*

"Louis Armstrong with All Stars, 1950" by Bob Willoughby. A silver gelatin print, signed verso.
- *30.5cm x 35.5cm*
- £600 • Photo. Gallery

233

Silver Gelatin Print ▲
- 1934
'Cafe Soho, London' by Wolfgang
Suschitzky. Signed verso.
- *length 40cm*
- £300   • Photo. Gallery

Silver Gelatin Print ▲
- 1966
A pair of portraits, this showing
Queen Elizabeth II, the other of
Prince Philip.
- £950   • Jim Hanson

Silver Gelatin Print ▼
- 1991
'Kazaksthan', signed print by
Sebastiao Salgado.
- *length 35cm*
- £2,500   • Photo. Gallery

Expert Tips

*Portrait albums appear
frequently for sale, and family
and military albums from the
1850s, compiled by aristocratic
amateurs, are very popular
with collectors.*

Solarised Portrait ▶
- circa 1935
One of an edition of 50 prints of
'Dorothy Hill, Solarised Portrait,
New York 1935' by Lee Miller,
estate stamped verso.
- £300   • Photo. Gallery

Signed Modern Print ◀
- 1938
'Good Reputation Sleeping' by
Manuel Alvarez Bravo.
- *length 20cm*
- £1,250   • Photo. Gallery

Signed Gelatin Print ▲
- 1957
'US 6th Fleet in the
Mediterranean' by Bert Hardy.
- *length 50cm*
- £400   • Photo. Gallery

Silver Gelatin Print ▲
- 1967
'Manchester' by Shirley Baker.
- *length 30cm*
- £200   • Photo. Gallery

Chrysler Building ▲
- **3rd May 1957**
The Chrysler Building in New York by Photographer: Phil Burcham, Fox Photos. Modern black and white, fibre silver gelatin archival photograph, printed in Hulton Getty darkrooms. Limited edition: 300.
- *length 50.8cm*
- **£225**   • Hulton Getty

Taylor Reclines ▲
- **1954**
American actress Elizabeth Taylor reclining in bed by the photographer Baron. Modern black and white, fibre silver gelatin archival photograph, printed in Hulton Getty darkrooms. Limited edition: 300.
- *length 50.8cm*
- **£225**   • Hulton Getty

John Lennon Profile ▼
- **26th June 1967**
John Lennon (1940 - 1980), singer, songwriter and guitarist with pop group 'The Beatles' by photographer Peter King, Fox Photos. Modern black and white, fibre silver gelatin archival photograph, printed in Hulton Getty darkrooms. Limited edition: 300.
- *length 50.8cm*
- **£225**   • Hulton Getty

Ali In Training ▼
- **August 1966**
American heavyweight boxer Muhammad Ali in training in London for his fight against Brian London. Photographer: R.McPhedran, Express Collection. Modern black and white, fibre silver gelatin archival photograph, printed in Hulton Getty darkrooms. Limited edition: 300.
- *length 50.8cm*
- **£225**   • Hulton Getty

Commissionaire's Dog ◄
- **22nd October 1938**
A hotel commissionaire talking to a small dog in London. Photographer: Kurt Hutton, Picture Post. Modern black and white, fibre silver gelatin archival photograph, printed in Hulton Getty darkrooms. Limited edition: 300.
- *length 40.7cm*
- **£185**   • Hulton Getty

The Beatles ▲
- **10th January 1964**
Paul McCartney, Ringo Starr, John Lennon (1940 - 1980) and George Harrison of British pop group, 'The Beatles'. Photographer: Terry Disney, Express Collection. Modern black and white, fibre silver gelatin archival photograph, printed in Hulton Getty darkrooms. Limited edition: 300.
- *length 50.8cm*
- **£225**   • Hulton Getty

Gorbals Boys ▲
- **31st January 1948**
Two boys in the Gorbals area of Glasgow. The Gorbals tenements were built quickly and cheaply in the 1840s. Conditions were appalling; overcrowding was standard and sewage and water facilities inadequate. The tenements housed about 40,000 people with up to eight family members sharing a single room, 30 residents sharing a toilet and 40 sharing a tap. By the time this photograph was taken 850 tenements had been demolished since 1920. Photographer: Bert Hardy, Picture Post. Modern black and white, fibre silver gelatin archival photograph, printed in Hulton Getty darkrooms. Limited edition: 300.
- *length 40.7cm*
- **£185**   • Hulton Getty

235

Shirley Baker Print ▼
- *1964*

"Salford, 1964" by Shirley Baker. A silver gelatin print, signed verso.
- *30.5cm x 35.5cm*
- **£200**
- **Photo. Gallery**

Silver Gelatin Print ▼
- *1955*

James Dean on the set of "Rebel Without a Cause" by photographer Bob Willoughby. Silver gelatin print, signed verso.
- *30.5cm x 40cm*
- **£400**
- **Photo. Gallery**

Matthew Murray Print ▼
- *1999*

"Morris Dancers, 1999" by Matthew Murray. C-Type print, signed verso.
- *30.5cm x 35.5cm*
- **£200**
- **Photo. Gallery**

Signed Willoughby Print ▷
- *1962*

"Billie Holliday, Tiffany Club, 1962" by Bob Willoughby. A silver gelatin print, signed verso.
- *30.5cm x 35.5cm*
- **£400**
- **Photo. Gallery**

Signed C-Type Print ▲
- *1952*

Marilyn Monroe photographed in 1952 by Bob Willoughby. C-Type print, signed verso.
- *30.5cm x 40cm*
- **£600**
- **Photo. Gallery**

Lartique Print ▼
- *1931*

"Cours automobile à Monthery, 1931" by Jacques-Henri Lartique. A silver gelatin print, signed verso.
- *30.5cm x 35.5cm*
- **£2,800**
- **Photo. Gallery**

Bob Willoughby Print ◀
- *1962*

"Audrey Hepburn, 1962" by Bob Willoughby. A silver gelatin print, signed verso.
- *25.5cm x 30.5cm*
- **£600**
- **Photo. Gallery**

Expert Tips

Look out for prints that capture a freak or unusual moment, or that portray a familiar subject in surroundings that are out of context. Some photographs are now ranked alongside art so it is worth concentrating on the work of a favourite up-and-coming photographer.

Posters

Jungle Book Poster ▲

- *circa 1967*
Released by Buena Vista with credits to voice talents.
- *length 1m, width 69cm*
- £300 • Reel Poster Gallery

Andy Warhol's 'Bad' ▲

- *circa 1977*
Artwork by John Van Hamersveld. With caption.
- *length 1m, width 69cm*
- £325 • Reel Poster Gallery

Expert Tips

Posters are a very good way to start collecting as they are fun, vibrant and are usually reasonably priced. Posters of great movies and their stars should be at the top of the list.

2001: A Space Odyssey ▼

- *circa 1968*
Entitled 'The Ultimate Trip' and signed by Kaplan.
- *length 1m, width 69cm*
- £3,000 • Reel Poster Gallery

Coca-Cola Card Sign ▼

- *circa 1940*
A Coca-Cola card sign with caption 'Have a Coke'.
- *height 65cm*
- £115 • Dodo

Stand-Up Card Sign ▶

- *circa 1940*
A Hartley's three-dimensional stand-up card sign.
- *height 53cm*
- £160 • Dodo

Goldfinger Poster ▲

- *circa 1964*
Original French poster by Jeism Mascii. Released by United Artists. Captions in French.
- *length 79cm, width 61cm*
- £500 • Reel Poster Gallery

Anatomy of Murder ▲

- *circa 1959*
Graphic artist style by Saul Bass. Photographs by Sam Leavitt.
- *length 1m, width 76cm*
- £850 • Reel Poster Gallery

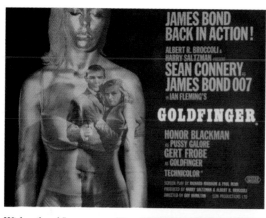

Goldfinger

- 1964

"Goldfinger" poster with Sean Connery as James Bond and Honor Blackman as Pussy Galore.

- 76cm x 101cm
- £2,800   • Cine Art Gallery

Withnail and I ▼

- 1987

"Withnail and I" starring Richard E. Grant and Paul McGann.

- *height 103cm*
- £400   • Cine Art Gallery

The Godfather ▲

- 1972

"The Godfather" and "Italian Photobusta".

- 45cm x 65cm
- £350   • Cine Art Gallery

Alfie ▲

- 1966

"Alfie", with Michael Caine.

- 28cm x 36cm
- £95   • Cine Art Gallery

Brigitte Bardot ▲

- 1963

"Le Mepris", with Brigitte Bardot.

- *height 158cm*
- £1,500   • Cine Art Gallery

Goldfinger ▼

- 1967

"Goldfinger" with Sean Connery.

- 56cm x 102cm
- £1,200   • Cine Art Gallery

High Society ▼

- 1956

"High Society" with Frank Sinatra, Gene Kelly and Bing Crosby.

- 28cm x 36cm
- £120   • Cine Art Gallery

Cena Strachu/ The Wages of Fear ▲
- 1953
Original Polish poster, paper backed, with artwork by Jan Lenica.
- 84cm x 58cm
- £500 • Reel Poster Gallery

La Mort Aux Trousses/ North by Northwest ▼
- 1959
Original French poster, paper backed, for the Hitchcock film "North by Northwest".
- 79cm x 61cm
- £225 • Reel Poster Gallery

Diamonds Are Forever ▶
- 1971
Original Japanese poster, paper backed, style B.
- 76cm x 51cm
- £350 • Reel Poster Gallery

Apocalypse Now ▲
- 1979
Original Italian poster, linen backed, style B, for the film "Apocalypse Now".
- 201cm x 140cm
- £600 • Reel Poster Gallery

Ascenseur pour l'Echafaud/ Lift to the Scaffold ▼
- 1957
Original French poster, linen backed, style B.
- 160cm x 119cm
- £750 • Reel Poster Gallery

Zawrot Glowy/Vertigo ▼
- 1958
Original Polish poster, linen backed, with artowrk by Roman Cieslewicz.
- 84cm x 58cm
- £1,200 • Reel Poster Gallery

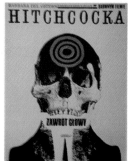

239

Psycho ▲
- 1962
"Psycho" 2962 re-issue US sheet.
- *width 29cm*
- £600   • Cine Art Gallery

Gilda ▲
- 1946
"Gilda". U.S Insert.
- *92cm x 35cm*
- £1,600   • Cine Art Gallery

Love is My Profession ▼
- 1959
"Love is My Profession", starring
Brigitte Bardot.
- *83cm x 60.5cm*
- £350   • Cine Art Gallery

Breakfast at Tiffany's ▼
- 1961
"Breakfast at Tiffany's", starring
Audrey Hepburn.
- *28cm x 36cm*
- £475   • Cine Art Gallery

Manhattan ▼
- 1979
"Manhattan" Lobby Carl.
- *28cm x 36cm*
- £95   • Cine Art Gallery

Revenge of the Creature ▲
- 1955
"Revenge of the Creature" U.K.
Quad John Agar Laurie Nelson.
- *102cm x 60.5cm*
- £850   • Cine Art Gallery

My Fair Lady ▲
- 1965
"My Fair Lady" with Audrey
Hepburn and Rex Harrison.
- *75cm x 137cm*
- £450   • Cine Art Gallery

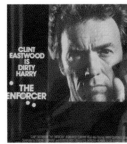

The Enforcer ▲
- 1977
"The Enforcer" with Clint
Eastwood as Dirty Harry.
- *28cm x 36cm*
- £95   • Cine Art Gallery

F for Fake ▼
- 1973

Original US poster, linen backed, designed by Donn Trethewey.
- 104cm x 69cm
- £500 • Reel Poster Gallery

The Graduate ▼
- 1967

Original US poster, linen backed, designed by United Artists Corporation.
- 206cm x 104cm
- £2,250 • Reel Poster Gallery

Turtle Diary ▶
- 1985

Original British poster, paper backed, featuring artwork by Andy Warhol, for the film "Turtle Diary".
- 76cm x 102cm
- £225 • Reel Poster Gallery

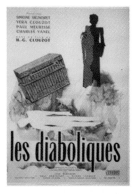

Les Diaboliques ▲
- 1955

Original French poster, linen backed, style A, with artwork by Raymondgid.
- 160cm x 119cm
- £1,500 • Reel Poster Gallery

La Donna Che Visse due Volte/Vertigo ▲
- 1958

Original Italian poster featuring art by Sandro Simeoni, for the Hitchcock film, "Vertigo".
- 140cm x 99cm
- £1500 • Reel Poster Gallery

Expert Tips

The condition and rarity of a poster enhance its value, so focus on these factors. Film posters distributed and printed in small countries have become rare and are a good investment.

Sueurs Froides/ Cold Sweat ◀
- 1958

Original French poster, paper backed, art by Claude Venin.
- 79cm x 61cm
- £425 • Reel Poster Gallery

Apocalypse Now ◄

- *1979*
"Apocalypse Now" with Marlon Brando. German double panel.
- *85cm x 118cm*
- **£1,300** • **Cine Art Gallery**

Way out West ▼

- *1937*
"Way out West" with Laurel and Hardy.
- *28cm x36cm*
- **£650** • **Cine Art Gallery**

Ice Cold in Alex ▼

- *1958*
"Ice Cold in Alex" with John Mills and Sylvia Syms. Directed by Bruce Robinson.
- *height 102cm*
- **£350** • **Cine Art Gallery**

The Untouchables ▲

- *1987*
"The Untouchables", with Kevin Costner, Sean Connery and Robert De Niro.
- *28cm x 36cm*
- **£75** • **Cine Art Gallery**

Bladerunner ▲

- *1982*
"Bladerunner" with Harrison Ford.
- *104cm x 58cm*
- **£400** • **Cine Art Gallery**

Sherlock Holmes Faces Death ▲

- *1951*
"Sherlock Holmes faces Death". Spanish one sheet.
- *104cm x 29cm*
- **£450** • **Cine Art Gallery**

The Birds ▲

- *1963*
"The Birds" by Alfred Hitchcock, with Tippi Hedren and Rod Taylor.
- *102cm x 79cm*
- **£500** • **Cine Art Gallery**

Goldfinger ▲

"Golfinger" starring Sean Connery.
- *28cm x 36cm*
- **£325** • **Cine Art Gallery**

Radio, TV & Sound Equipment

Bendix Model 526C ▼

- *1946*

Black Bakelite American radio
with the inscription "Strong
Machine Age".
- *28cm x 35cm*
- £750   • Decodence

Fada Streamliner ▲

- *1940*

American onyx and amber
streamlined Catalin radio, with
large oval dial on the right.
- *height 19cm*
- £1,000   • Decodence

GEC Radio ▼

- *circa 1950*

GEC radio with Bakelite handles.
- *32cm x 44cm x 17cm*
- £55   • Radio Days

Intercom Speaker ◄

- *1940s*

English Art Deco-style red
intercom system speaker, tube
operated.
- *height 28cm*
- £100   • Decodence

Sonorette ▲

- *1940s*

French brown radio in bakelite,
with a bulbous form and grille-
design speaker.
- *height 34cm*
- £500   • Decodence

Emersa Radio ▲

- *1932*

American Art Deco Bakelite
radio with a central fan design.
- *40cm x 50cm*
- £300   • Decodence

Pye Record Player ▲

- *1955*

Pye record player in a bow fronted teak case with cream turntable. Holds ten records on stack.

- *height 26cm*
- £100 • The Manic Antique

Radio and T. V. Diary 1957 ▲

- *1957*

Radio and T. V. Diary for 1957 with photographs on each page of actors and musicians. Showing a photograph of David Attenborough.

- *height 12cm*
- £10 • The Manic Antique

P.Y. E. Record Player ▼

- *1955*

P. Y. E. record player in a grey with white polka dot case, with unusual curved sides, white plastic carrying handles and a black and gold sparkling grill.

- *height 25cm*
- £75 • The Manic Antique

Perdio Transistor ▶

- *1962*

Perdio Super Seven Transistor radio, inscribed with 'Real Morocco leather made in England', on the back, with a dial for an aerial and phone or tape, and a large brass dial and gold writing.

- *height 12.5cm*
- £38 • The Manic Antique

E.A.R. Triple Four ◀

- *1958*

E. A. R. Triple four record player in a blue and grey Rexine case with cream piping and handles.

- *height 27cm*
- £80 • The Manic Antique

Hacker ▲

- *1964*

Hacker record player in a black and grey case with metal fittings.

- *height 27cm*
- £50 • The Manic Antique

Roberts Radio ▲

- *1958*

Roberts radio in original condition with red Rexine case and handle and brass dials and fittings.

- *height 15cm*
- £68 • The Manic Antique

Rock & Pop

Beatles Album ▲
- *circa 1966*
'The Beatles Yesterday and Today'. Original USA stereo with 'Butcher' cover.
- £825 • More Than Music

Andy Warhol Magazine ▲
- *December 1966*
Set of postcards and flip-book magazine incorporating Velvet Underground flexidisc.
- £950 • Music & Video

Expert Tips

The transient nature of the pop world means that there is a great deal of material around, much of it by forgotten bands. The quality of the act does reflect in the value of the souvenir.

Collage Postcard ▶
- *9th November 1978*
'Que serait la vie sans les soirs?', signed by Genesis P. Orridge and dedicated to Mark Penny.
- £950 • Music & Video

'The Beautiful Freaks' ▼
- *circa 1969*
Oz magazine issue no. 24, with cover by Robert Crumb.
- £30 • Book & Comic

Beatles First No. 1 ▼
- *circa 1963*
A copy of the 'Red A' label demo 45rpm recording of 'From Me to You' and 'Thank You Girl' – The Beatles first No. 1.
- £695 • More Than Music

Powder Compact ▲
- *circa 1963*
A circular powder compact featuring a Dezo Hoffman black and white shot of The Beatles.
- £475 • More Than Music

Rolling Stones Album ▲
- *1975*
Japanese five-LP, 62-track promo of 'The great History of The Rolling Stones'. Box comes with large book and OBI.
- £347 • Music & Video

Bob Dylan
● *1961*
Bob Dylan's first recording
produced by John Hammond.
● £735   ● Music & Video

Instant Karma
Lennon ▲
● *1971*
John Ono Lennon "Instant
Karma" produced by Phil Spector.
● £117   ● Music & Video

Equinoxe 4 ▼
● *1979*
"Equinoxe 4", an album by Jean
Michel Jarre, with a signed
autograph in black biro on front
cover.
● £60   ● Music & Video

Yellow Submarine ▼
● *1960s*
The Beatles - "Yellow Submarine
and Eleanor Rigby".
● £72   ● Music & Video

Time Will Pass ▲
● *1977*
"Time Will Pass" by the Spriguns.
Distributed by The Decca Record
Company Limited, London.
● £175   ● Music & Video

Status Quo ▲
● *1970*
"In my Chair / Gerdundula"
Status Quo.
● £72   ● Music & Video

Agogo ▲
● *1963*
"Agogo", with Ray Charles, The
Supremes, Petula Clark, and The
Everly brothers.
● £35   ● Music & Video

The Monkees ▲
● *1968*
The Monkees. Original motion
picture sound track "Head".
● £95   ● Music & Video

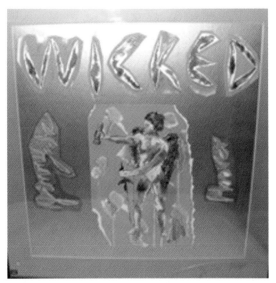

Album Artwork ◀
- **1984**
Unused album artwork for
Jimmy the Hoover by Jamie Reid,
with glass broken and damaged
intentionally for the "Leaving the
21st Century" series held at the
Mayfair gallery.
- *50cm x 50cm*
- **£200**   • **Music & Video**

4AD Calendar ▼
- **1993**
Collector's item calendar
issued by record company,
4AD, and designed
by 23 Envelope.
- *35cm x 55cm*
- **£25**   • **Music & Video**

Brute Force Album
featuring John Lennon ▼
- **1970**
"Extemporaneous" album
by Brute Force featuring John
Lennon.
- *£395*   • **Music & Video**

Withdrawn Single ▼
- **1981**
"Ha ha I'm drowning" single by
The Teardrop Explodes.
Withdrawn issue.
- *18cm x 18cm*
- **£60**   • **Music & Video**

Wing's Record Sleeve ▼
- **1975**
Record sleeve for Wing's "Listen
to what the man said" and "King
Alfred's Rubbish", autographed
by Paul and Linda McCartney.
- **£675**   • **More Than Music**

Rolling Stones Album ▼
- **1971**
Copy of the Rolling Stones album
"Sticky Fingers".
- *30cm x 30cm*
- **£240**   • **Music & Video**

Portrait by Joe Meek ▲
- *circa 1966*
'Pat as I see Him' – pen and ink on envelope by producer Joe Meek of his boyfriend.
- £5,950   • Music & Video

John's Children ▲
- *circa 1967*
Copy of 'Desdemona' by John's Children, featuring Marc Bolam and banned by the BBC.
- £100   • Music & Video

Iron Maiden Disc ▼
- *circa 1983*
A picture disc of Iron Maiden's 'Peace of Mind' album, illustrated on both sides.
- £40   • Music & Video

The Verve ▼
- *circa 1992*
Mint condition copy of 'Voyager 1', recorded live in New York, by The Verve.
- £65   • Music & Video

Mojo ▲
- *circa 1995*
Mojo issue no. 24 showing The Beatles. Published with three different covers, this one with a blue background.
- £20   • Book & Comic

Expert Tips

Brian Epstein, The Beatles' manager, was famously dismissive of the value of merchandising. As a result, 'official' souvenirs proliferate and prices are unpredictable.

Beatles Sketch ▼
- *circa 1967*
An original sketch of Paul McCartney from The Beatles' film 'Yellow Submarine'.
- £300   • Music & Video

Elvis 68 ◄
- *circa 1988*
A copy of the NBC TV 'Comeback Special' commemorative Elvis Presley promotional album.
- £125   • Music & Video

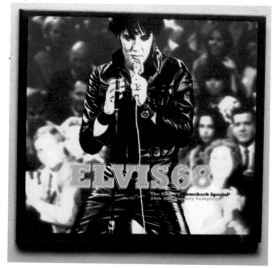

Beatles' Scarf ▲
- 1960

Sourvenir scarf decorated with pictures of each of The Beatles.
- 50cm x 50cm
- £55   • **Radio Days**

Presentation Disc for U.F. Orb ◄
- 1992

Presentation silver disc awarded by the British Phonograph Industry to the "U.F. Orb" LP. The award was presented to a member of the band.
- 40cm x 50cm
- £290   • **Music & Video**

John Lennon Signature Watch ▲
- 1991

Sample watch with John Lennon's signature on its face, produced for Toshiba, Japan. Given to visiting signees circa 1991 after the estate refused a production license.
- £200   • **Music & Video**

Mirrorball ▼
- 1997

U2 pop mirrorball that opens up. Contains a video, poster and pen.
- 40cm x 40cm
- N/A   • **Music & Video**

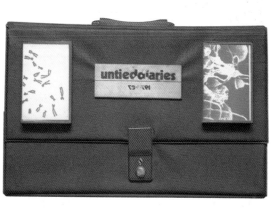

Untied Diaries Box Set ▲
- 1988

Untied Diaries edition No. 30, with 32 cassettes individually recorded and packaged. This is different from the vinyl version.
- £900   • **Music & Video**

Beatles Dolls ◄
- 1966

Set of four NEMS/King Features syndicate inflatable cartoon dolls of the Beatles.
- 35cm x 15cm
- £120   • **Music & Video**

The Police Box ▼
- **1997–87**

"The Police Box" The Police (Sting. Stewart Copeland. Andy Summers) from 1977 to 1987.
- **£150**   • **Music & Video**

Elvis ▼
- **1971**

"You'll Never Walk Alone" by Elvis. Manufactured and Distributed by RCA Limited.
- **£1,800**   • **Music & Video**

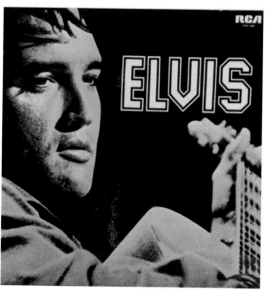

H. M. S. Donovan ▲
- **1971**

"H.M.S. Donovan" produced by Donovan Engineered by Mike Bobak at Morgan Studios London. All paintings by Patrick.
- **£130**   • **Music & Video**

Sticky Fingers: Rolling Stones ▲
- **1972**

"Sticky Fingers", an album by The Rolling Stones.
- **£220**   • **Music & Video**

Whitehouse Present Total Sex ▼
- **circa 1980**

Whitehouse present "Total Sex".
- **£125**   • **Music & Video**

The Velvet Underground ▼
- **circa 1967**

Andy Warhol presents the The Velvet Underground and Nico, original German Issue with Erice Emmerson Sleeve (No Banana).
- **£248**   • **Music & Video**

Roy Harper Sophisticated ▼
- **1966**

Roy Harper "Sophisticated Beggar" Strike JHL 105. Test pressing. W/Proff Sleeve in excellent condition.
- **£550**   • **Music & Video**

Scripophily & Paper Money

New Orleans Note ▲

- *circa 1860*

New Orleans $20 note issued by Canal Bank.
- **£12.50**   • **C. Narbeth**

Military Payment Note ▼

- **1970**

Military payment certificate to the value of 10 cents.
- **£6**   • **C. Narbeth**

Colonial Note ▶

- **1773**

Colonial 15 shillings note issued in Pennsylvania. Numbered and signed by hand.
- **£48**   • **C. Narbeth**

American Note ▲

- **1995**

American note in the amount of $2.
- **£3**   • **C. Narbeth**

Confederate States Note ▼

- **1864**

Confederate States $10 note issued in the US Civil War.
- **£28**   • **C. Narbeth**

National Currency $20 Dollar Note ▼

- **1900**

$20 dollar note issued by the Citizen's Bank of Eureka, Kansas, during the Battle of Lexington.
- **£595**   • **C. Narbeth**

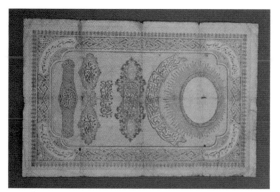

Quebec Railway Company Bonds ▼

● *1907*
The Atlantic Quebec and Western Railway Company. Five per cent. First mortgage debenture bonds for 9,050,000 dollars.
● £45   ● Yasha Beresiner

Mexican Bond ▼

● *1921*
Mexican Bond Minas Pedrazzini. Gold and Silver Mining Co.
● £20   ● Yasha Beresiner

Turkish Note ▲

● *1854*
Turkish note '10 Kurush, Ordu Kaimesi 6th Issue.
● £300   ● Yasha Beresiner

Mexican Bond ▼

● *1921*
Mina Pedrazzini Gold and Silver Mining Co.
● £20   ● Yasha Beresiner

Bank Note ▼

● *1800*
Peruvian bond that circulated as currency, 207 Pesos, Casa de Moneda.
● £210   ● Yasha Beresiner

Gold Mining Share Certificate ▼

● *1900*
The road block Gold Mining Company of India Limited share certificate.
● £28   ● Yasha Beresiner

White English Note ▼

● *1944*
Bank of England white five pound note.
● £70   ● Yasha Beresiner

Egyptian Bank Note

- circa 1960

Note of 10 pounds' value with a cartouche of King Tutankhamen. Uncirculated.

- £22   • C. Narbeth

American Bank Note ▼

- 1850

Five dollar bank note from an obsolete US bank – the Citizens' Bank of Louisiana. Extremely fine bank note.

- £14   • C. Narbeth

Mafeking 10 Shilling Note ▼

- 1900

Issued during the siege of Mafeking, January–March 1900 by Baden-Powell. In extremely fine condition.

- £250   • C. Narbeth

Expert Tips

The Scandinavians are avid collectors of banknotes. The first European banknotes were produced in Sweden in 1661.

Five Pound Note ▼

- circa 1838

From Newcastle-upon-Tyne, with a nautical cartouche, and in fine condition.

- £38   • C. Narbeth

American 15 Shilling Note ▶

- circa 1773

A colonial 15 shilling note, from Pennsylvania, with a prominent signature.

- £48   • C. Narbeth

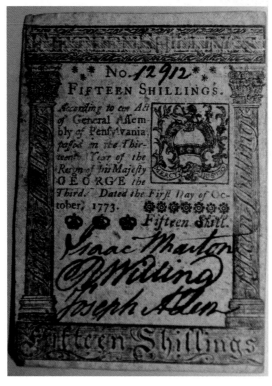

English Share Note ▼

- *circa 1850*

Share note issued by The Hornsey Freehold Estate Tontine Company.

- £10
- C. Narbeth

South African Note ▼

- *1864*

£25 note issued by Durban Bank, a private bank in South Africa.

- £350
- C. Narbeth

Republic Note ▶

- *1872*

£1 noted issued by the South African Republic.

- £325
- C. Narbeth

Railway Bond ▲

- *1909*

Armavir Touapse Railway Company bond in the amount of 189 roubles.

- £4
- C. Narbeth

Railroad Bond ▲

- *1866*

Bond issued by the Boston Hartford Erie Rail Road Co.

- £85
- C. Narbeth

Russian Bond ▲

- *1914*

Russian South Eastern bond to the value of 945 roubles.

- £7
- C. Narbeth

English Share Note ◀

- *1866*

Note in respect of one £20 share issued by Charles Lafitte & Co. .

- £4
- C. Narbeth

Scottish Banknote ▼

- *1915*

£1 note issued by The National Bank of Scotland

- £85
- C. Narbeth

Sewing Items

Sewing Table ▼
- *circa 1840*
A lyre-ended chinoiserie sewing
table of the 19th century.
- *height 65cm*
- £750   ● North West 8

Needle Case ▼
- *circa 1890*
Ivory and mother-of-pearl needle
case with hinged lid and silver
cornucopia.
- *length 7.5cm*
- £149   ● Fulton

Regency Table Cabinet ▲
- *circa 1815*
Shaped late-Regency table
cabinet in rosewood, with
mother of pearl inlay and fitted
sewing tray.
- *width 32.5cm*
- £1,800   ● Hygra

Tunbridge Ware ▲
- *circa 1800*
A turned and painted early
Tunbridge-ware sewing
companion.
- *height 6cm*
- £450   ● Hygra

Small Sewing Machine ▼
- *circa 1900*
An American 'Little Comfort',
handle-driven sewing machine.
- *height 17.5cm*
- £350   ● Talk. Mach.

Work Table ▼
- *circa 1850*
Scandinavian birchwood work
table. With turned, adjustable
central column.
- *height 1.1m*
- £995   ● Old Cinema

Compartmentalised
Thread Box ◄
- *circa 1810*
A straw-work thread box.
- *width 44cm*
- £180   ● Hygra

Expert Tips

When buying sewing machines try to look out for the smaller versions, for example a miniature Singer or the "Little Comfort", an American-made sewing machine, as these tend to be more expensive then their larger counterparts. For those who would like to collect smaller items the necessaires and thimbles, especially from the Elizabethan period are very expensive, although anything pre-eighteenth century will still command a good price.

Silver Thimbles ▲
- **mid 19th century**
A selection of three silver thimbles with intricate silver skirts set with coloured stones.
- *height 2.6cm*
- **£90 each**   • Thimble Society

Hardwood Sewing Box ◄
- *circa 1775*
An eighteenth century sewing box with native and imported hardwoods juxtaposed and a neo-classical central motif.
- *width 29cm*
- **£720**   • Hygra

Kingwood Sewing Box ▲
- **1830**
Kingwood sewing box inlaid with ivory in a diamond pattern, enclosing silver gilt needlework tools.
- *length 10cm*
- **£490**   • Thimble Society

Sycamore Sewing Box ▼
- *circa 1810*
A shaped sycamore fitted sewing box with a hand-painted design of a basket with overflowing flowers.
- *width 27cm*
- **£1,800**   • Hygra

Rosewood Sewing Box ▲
- *circa 1835*
Fully fitted rosewood and mother-of-pearl sewing box labelled "George Johnston Glasgow".
- *width 31cm*
- **£1,800**   • Hygra

Inlaid Sewing Box ▼
- **1820**
Very fine early nineteenth century anglo-Indian ivory and sadeli mosaic fitted sewing box.
- *width 32cm*
- **£950**   • Hygra

Regency Sewing Box ▼
- **1835**
Regency rosewood sewing box of sarcophagus form with pewter stringing, gadroon bordering, and lozenge feet. The interior with original red velvet and silk lining. The box contains a letter dated 1843, probably from the original owner.
- *16cm x 33cm x 26cm*
- **£995**   • J. & T. Stone

Mouse Tape Measure ◀

- **1900**
Silver mouse tape measure, with
tail used to wind the tape back
into the mouse.
- *length 7cm*
- **£175**   • Arca

Pink Enamel Case ▼

- **1920**
Black ebonised case with pink
enamel lid with a gold shield on
the lid, and two silver line
borders, complete with sewing
items.
- *length 13cm*
- **£180**   • Arca

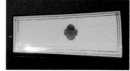

Bakelite Tape ▼

- *circa 1900*
Bakelite figure of a girl smiling
and holding a red apple, on her
right side is a tape measure.
- *height 5.5cm*
- **£225**   • Arca

Porcelain Thimble ▼

- *circa 1900*
Porcelain thimble with a painted
robin and roses and gold banding.
- *height 2cm*
- **£210**   • Arca

Gold Thimble ▼

- *circa 1770*
Fine engraved gold thimble.
- *height 3cm*
- **£450**   • Arca

Ivory Sewing Case ▲

- *circa 1890*
Ivory sewing case inscribed with
the name Enid on the top of the
lid, complete with gold sewing
implements.
- *length 7.5cm*
- **£495**   • Arca

Japanese Sewing Case ▲

- *circa 1880*
Japanese ivory sewing case with
raised gilt foliate and bird design
with mother of pearl
chrysanthemums, complete with
silver scissors and thimble.
- *length 9cm*
- **£695**   • Arca

Silver Needle Case ▼

- *circa 1880*
Oblong silver needle case with
decorative flower design.
- *length 6cm*
- **£125**   • Arca

Silver Boot Pincushion ▼

- *circa 1870*
Silver boot pincushion.
- *height 5cm*
- £280 • Arca

Silver Wool Winder ▼

- *circa 1780*
Silver wool winder in the shape of a ball made of fine foliate filigree, with small flowers on each leaf.
- *circumference 18cm*
- £850 • Arca

Gold Chatelaine ▶

- *circa 1780*
French gold five piece sewing chatelaine, with heavily engraved design of flowers in baskets, ribboning, and scrolling joined by linked chains to a central foliate scrolled hook.
- *length 18cm*
- £1,350 • Arca

Silver Scissors ◀

- *circa 1880*
Victorian silver case with scissors.
- *length 9.5cm*
- £260 • Arca

Gothic Chair Pincushion ▲

- *circa 1900*
Gothic silver metal chair the red velvet seat being a pincushion.
- *height 6.5cm*
- £135 • Arca

Walnut Sewing Case ▶

- *circa 1840*
French walnut sewing case in the form of a nut, lined with red satin and containing small scissors, thimble, needle case and pick.
- *width 5cm*
- £690 • Arca

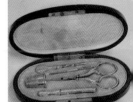

French Etui ▲

- *circa 1880*
French ebonised etui with silver gilt fitting.
- *length 12cm*
- £550 • Arca

Snuff Boxes & Smoking Equipment

Cigarette Case

- *circa 1900*

Silver cigarette case with an enamel lady reclining with a large fan at her side.
- *length 9cm*
- £1,550 • Arca

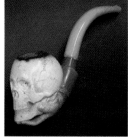

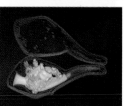

Novelty Lighter

- 1980

Novelty cigarette lighter, modelled as a roll of film with a picture of a model wearing Formula One overalls.
- *height 5cm*
- £10 • Jessops Classic

Skull Meerschaum

- *circa 1880*

Meerschaum pipe in the shape of a skull, with amber stem.
- *length 15cm*
- £300 • Arca

Lady's Meerschaum

- circa 1880

Lady's meerschaum holder for cigar or cigarettes, with a lady standing beside a horse.
- *length 14cm*
- £235 • Arca

Ladies' Cigar Holder

- *circa 1860*

Ladies' meerschaum cigar holder, with a reclining lady holding a spray of flowers.
- *length 13cm*
- £260 • Arca

Greyhound Meerschaum

- *circa 1880*

Meerschaum holder in the form of a head of a greyhound.
- *length 22cm*
- £650 • Arca

Chieftain Meerschaum

- *circa 1880*

Meerschaum in the form of a chieftain with a large headdress, and plume.
- *length 19cm*
- £360 • Arca

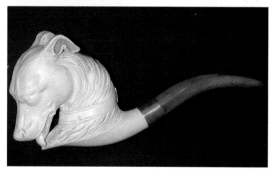

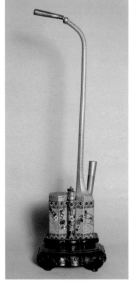

Cigarette Display Case ▲
• *circa late 19th century*
Shop counter cigarette display
box. Box contains four sections
for single cigarette sales.
• *width 27.5cm*
• £80   • Ian Spencer

Cloisonné Opium Pipe ▲
• *circa 1900*
Brass body with floral enamelling
on a carved wooden base.
• £265   • Finchley

Mr Punch Cigarette Lighter ▼
• *circa 1920*
Silverplated with registered
design mark on base. Lighter
is underneath character's hat. Of
English make.
• *height 16.5cm*
• £290   • Barham

Miners Snuff Box ▼
• *mid 19th century*
Lead-lined. Half-hinged lid
shaped for the back pocket.
• £60   • Ocean Leisure

Regimental Humidor ◄
• *circa 1930*
Unusual oak and brass-bound
regimental humidor with brass
emblem and motto. Original
partitioned interior with plated
presentation plaque. By Edward
& Sons, London.
• *length 15cm*
• £900   • Henry Gregory

Monkey Snuff Box ▲
• *circa 1800*
Finely carved coquilla nut snuff
box representing a monkey.
French.
• £895   • A. & E. Foster

Mastiff Snuff Box ▲
• *late 19th century*
Continental coloured bisque
snuff box in the shape of a
mastiff, with pewter fittings
and a hinged flap.
• *height 8cm*
• £630   • Elizabeth Bradwin

Expert Tips
*Solid rolls of tobacco were
carried by early snuff-takers,
together with snuff rasps for
making the powder. Rasps
became decorative and elaborate
during the eighteenth century.*

Cigar Box ▶
- *1920*

Unusual burr walnut cigar and cigarette box with gilded handle and decoration. Two lighter drawers with match strikers.
- *width 24cm*
- **£495**   • J. & T. Stone

Continental Vesta Case ▲
- *circa 1900*

A continental vesta case decorated with an enamel chestnut horse's head.
- *3cm*
- **£450**   • N. Shaw

George IV Snuff Box ▼
- *1822–3*

A George IV snuff box made in Birmingham by Joseph Willmore.
- *length 4cm*
- **£450**   • N. Shaw

Victorian Snuff Box ▼
- *1840*

A silver Victorian snuff box with an oak leaf pattern, presented to Mr William McKelvic of Redruth.
- *length 3.5cm*
- **£2,750**   • N. Shaw

Silver Taper ◀
- *1880*

A Victorian, silver vesta/ taper lighter made in London by Louis Dee.
- *length 11cm*
- **£650**   • N. Shaw

Expert Tips

Cigarette boxes are extremely collectable, especially the examples from the Art Deco period. Their value also increases if they are made from gold or silver and carry a hallmark. When purchasing these items it is important that one bears in mind the craftsmanship and style of the piece. Early cigar cutters will always command a high price, and any snuff box with a zoographical theme is always worth buying.

Double Snuff Box ▶
- *1858*

A George IV double Regi Mari snuff box inscribed, "London 1827, Tria Juncta In Uno. Presented by Lieut Col Caulfield and the Married Officers of the mess of the 33rd Roscommon Regiment, 17 March 1858". Engraved with a four-leaf clover.
- *length 6cm*
- **£3,950**   • N. Shaw

Telephones

English Telephone ▶
- *circa 1900s*

An English telephone with a wooden base, chrome bell and metal handset by Electric and Ordnance Accessories Ltd.
- *22.5cm x 20cm*
- £295   • Telephone Lines

Desk Telephone ▼
- *1908*

A desk phone with magneto handle, raised on a wooden base by Thomson-Houston, France.
- *33cm x 18cm*
- £385   • Telephone Lines

Burgunder Telephone ◀
- *1912*

A Candlestick telephone by A. Burgunder, made in Paris, France.
- *height 32cm*
- £285   • Telephone Lines

Western Electric Telephone ▼
- *1930*

An American candlestick telephone with original ringer box by Western Electric.
- *height 29cm*
- £345   • Telephone Lines

Candlestick Telephone ▼
- *1880*

French candlestick telephone with a chrome clip.
- *height 25cm*
- £350   • Telephone Lines

Expert Tips

Coloured telephones fetch higher prices, especially the 1930s pyramid telephones. Look out for the Belgium telephones – they have a delightful ring and are not necessarily very expensive.

Queen's Silver Jubilee ◀
- *circa 1977*
Very rare and limited edition,
unused with type 64d bell set.
Introduced to commemorate the
25th year of Elizabeth II's reign.
- £150 • Old Telephone Co.

Ericofon Telephone ◀
- *circa 1955*
Designed in 1953 by Ralph Lysell
and Hugo Blomberg. In white
and red with dial underneath.
- £70 • Telephone Lines

Bakelite Pyramid Phone ▲
- *circa 1930*
Series 200 with chrome rotary
dial, cloth flex and address drawer.
- £295 • After Noah

Model 1000 ▲
- *circa 1962*
Made by GEC of Coventry and
was intended as a replacement
for the 300 series but not
adopted.
- £160 • Old Telephone Co.

300 Series Telephone ▼
- *circa 1957*
A rare 328 telephone made by
Plessey, Ilford, Essex. With bell-
on and bell-off push buttons.
- £650 • Old Telephone Co.

Candlestick Telephone ▲
- *circa 1927*
Type 150, in bakelite, featuring a
replacement microphone. Made
by Ibex Telephones.
- £460 • Old Telephone Co.

Expert Tips

*Telephones do not have to work
in order to be collectable. Very
early ones are intrinsically
valuable as are some of the
antiques of the future – early
mobiles and car-phones.*

Genie Telephone ▶
- *circa 1978*
BT special range, a much sought-
after designer telephone in white
with metal dial.
- £39 • Telephone Lines

Ivory Telephone ▼

- *circa 1950*
Ivory bakelite telephone with
drawer and ringing bell.
- *14cm x 25cm*
- £225 • H. Duffield

GPO Pyramid Telephone ▲

- *circa 1930*
British Ivory bakelite GPO
Pyramid telephone with ringing
bell.
- *15cm x 24cm*
- £295 • H. Duffield

British Telephone ▶

- *circa 1970*
British GPO plastic telephone
with Warble ringing and
adjustable volume.
- *12cm x 10cm*
- £48 • Geri

Black Bakelite Telephone ◀

- *circa 1950*
Black bakelite British GPO
telephone with drawer and
ringing bell.
- *16cm x 24cm*
- £135 • H. Duffield

Lysell & Bloomberg Telephone ▲

- *circa 1957*
The first ever one piece
telephone designed by Ralph
Lysell & Hugo Bloomberg in
cream with rotary dial
underneath.
- *height 23.5cm*
- £100 • Old Cinema

GPO Telephone ▶

- *circa 1946*
Black bakelite British GPO
telephone with function on/off
switch for ringing.
- *16cm x 24cm*
- £175 • H. Duffield

Walking Sticks

Wooden Cane

- *circa 1890*
Gargoyle head on a gnarled wooden cane.
- *92cm x 6cm x 3cm*
- £240 • Henry Gregory

Snakewood Walking Cane ▲

- *circa 1900*
An elegant, rare snakewood cane with gold collar and looped handle.
- *length 89cm*
- £550 • Michael German

Whalebone Cane ▼

- *circa 1840*
A fine whalebone cane with full barley twist shaft. The whale handle loop carved with a serpent's head.
- *length 70cm*
- £1,600 • Michael German

City Walking Cane ▼

- *circa 1900*
Ebonised cane with gioche enamel ball, gold band and Austrian mark.
- *length 55cm*
- £750 • Michael German

Hoof Walking Stick ▲

- *circa 1880*
Carved horn hoof handle mounted on unusual segmented shaft formed from paper washers.
- *length 100cm/handle*
- £650 • Michael German

Japanese Walking Cane ▲

- *circa 1900*
Japanese bamboo cane inset with ivory face and silver collar.
- *length 20cm*
- £680 • Michael German

Parrot Cane ▼
- **1870**

Oversized head of a parrot carved from fruitwood, with fine detail, mounted on a hardwood shaft, with ornate gilt collar.
- **£850**   • Michael German

English Walking Stick ▼
- **1870**

Country walking stick with a carved wood handle, modelled as a hare with large glass eyes and silver collar, mounted on a briar wood shaft.
- **£580**   • Michael German

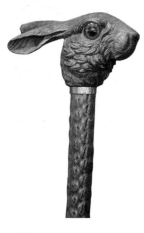

Ebony Cane ▲
- **1840**

Ebony cane with the handle carved as the head of a Negro with ivory teeth and boxwood hat and collar, mounted on a rosewood shaft.
- **£480**   • Michael German

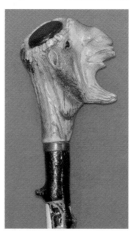

Stag Horn Cane ▲
- **1860**

Country walking stick carved as a grotesque with a beard and glass eyes, mounted on a knotted wood shaft, with a silver collar and an antler handle.
- **£390**   • Michael German

Victorian Cane ▼
- **1860**

Elegant Victorian cane with a well carved handle depicting a hunting dog with a bird, mounted on a partidge wood shaft, with a gilt collar.
- **£1,100**   • Michael German

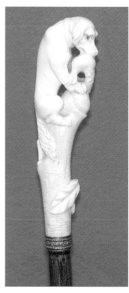

Hussar Head Cane ▼
- **1860**

A painted and carved wood cane with the handle modelled as a Continental hussar, with a plumed helmet.
- **£950**   • Michael German

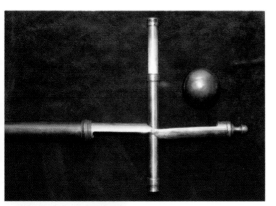

Rare Victorian Telescope Cane

- *1870*

Rare Victorian telescope cane with pullout laquered brass pivot and scope. For use by naturalists (birdspotting). Upper section of cane in lacquered brass, rest of shaft in ebony. Of English make.
- £1,400   • Michael German

Steel- and Gold-Handled Stick ▼

- *circa 1870*

Steel crook-handle walking stick. Inlaid with gold floral and geometric designs. Of Spanish, Toledo make. The shaft is of snake wood.
- £750   • Michael German

Ladies Cane ▲

- *1880*

Small silver club-shaped handle with bands of enamel blue flowers. Ebony shaft. Sterling marked. Made in USA.
- £550   • Michael German

Victorian Silver ▲

- *1895*

Late 19th-century Victorian silver parrot-head walking stick. Showing glass eyes on an ebonised shaft. Silver hallmark with finely chased feather relief.
- £420   • Michael German

Snake- and Hand-Headed Stick ▼

- *1850*

Mid 19th-century walking stick with folk art cane shaft. It is decorated with two snakes entwining themselves along the shaft with a hand clutching the snake heads at the top.
- £550   • Michael German

Porcelain-Handled Stick ▲

- *circa 19th century*

Porcelain-handled stick portraying a woman's head. Decorated with flowers and insects on a white background. Probably continental malacca shaft. Made in the early 19th century.
- £1,200   • Michael German

Sailor's Walking Stick ▲

- *circa 1800*

English walking stick. Used by early 19th-century sailors. Decorated with a characteristic Turk's head knot.
- £950   • A. & E. Foster

Ivory Tau Cane ▲
● *1880*
Ivory tau shaped handled cane with a carved grotesque, mounted on a lacquered shaft.
● £800　　● **Michael German**

Victorian Walking Stick ▲
● *1870*
A Victorian cane with a finely carved ivory handle depicting an amusing dog seated with a hat and holding a stick, mounted on an ebony shaft, with a silver collar.
● £1,800　　● **Michael German**

Japanese Stick ▼
● *1880*
Fine Japanese ebonised cane fitted with a silver handle, with trailing foliate designs.
● £900　　● **Michael German**

Victorian Greyhound Cane ▼
● *1870*
Finely carved ivory Victorian greyhound with an engraved silver collar and ebonised shaft.
● £1,500　　● **Michael German**

Russian Enamelled Cane ▲
● *1890*
Russian cane with enamelled handle with floral designs and jewelling on an ebonised shaft.
● £1100　　● **Michael German**

Mother of Pearl Cane ▲
● *1880*
Elegant mother of pearl inlay handled cane, with delicate scrolling floral designs in gilt, mounted on a ebonised shaft.
● £480　　● **Michael German**

Decorative Arts

The market for decorative arts has consolidated and expanded over the last 20 years and shows no sign of easing up.

The term decorative arts is ambiguous but it can generally be ascribed to an object that has no practical application other than as a thing to be admired and discussed. The decorative arts – or the applied arts – although difficult to define, have undergone a collecting revolution over the past two decades. Originally, activity largely centred around artefacts of European Art Nouveau and Art Deco but has since expanded across the Atlantic. There is now intense interest in European decorative arts in Japan, which has helped the values

considerably, particularly in the case of works by Gallé, Daume and Lalique. Riding on the same wave of collecting enthusiasm are the English potters, with Clarice Cliff in the van and Susie Cooper, William Moorcroft and the Poole Pottery lagging not far behind. The metal artefacts of Dr Christopher Dresser find an excellent market if you happen upon one at anything less than an astronomical price. This is an area that is shifting and expanding all the time. There are no rules, but as long as you like what you buy, you won't be the loser.

Figures & Busts

Figure of Young Egyptian ▼
- *1890*
Austrian terracotta group of Egyptian youth playing a stringed instrument. Gold Schneider signature on back.
- *height 5.5cm*
- £2,650   • Gavin Douglas

Cherub Group ▶
- *circa 1870*
English Victorian plaster figures on a painted pine plinth.
- *width 205cm*
- £1,800   • Tredantiques

Bust of Marie Antoinette ◀
- *late 18th century*
A terracotta bust of Marie Antoinette, her head inclined to dexter, raised on a splayed pedestal base.
- *65cm x 44.5cm*
- £950   • Westland & Co.

Terracotta Bust ▼
- *20th century*
An Italian terracotta bust of David after Michelangelo.
- *56cm x 14cm*
- £850   • Westland & Co.

Terracotta Bust ▼

- *circa 1890*

Bust of Marie Antoinette with head inclined to sinister. Raised on a spreading square plinth.

- *height 65cm*
- £950 • Westland & Co.

French Statue ▼

- *circa 1890*

A statuary marble and alabaster statue of La Poete de la Danse.

- *height 57cm*
- £2,500 • Westland & Co.

Terracotta Roundel ▲

- *circa 1890*

A French terracotta roundel of a horse's head. Dated ' '92'.

- *diameter 99cm*
- £3,500 • Westland & Co.

Stone Torso ▲

- *circa 1880*

A classical reconstructed stone torso of a woman, with loincloth and shell fastening.

- *height 86cm*
- £950 • Westland & Co.

Bust of Bacchus ▼

- *20th century*

A plaster bust of Bacchus, with head inclined to dexter.

- *height 67cm*
- £950 • Westland & Co.

Statue of Neptune ▼

- *circa 1765*

A finely carved stone figure of the god Neptune in traditional pose, with broken hand.

- *height 205cm*
- £4,850 • Drummond

Marble Bust ◄

- *circa 1800*

Large marble bust of Lorenzo di Medici, patron of Michelangelo.

- *height 62cm*
- £9,500 • Westland & Co

Carved Oak Saint ▲
- *circa 1880*

Large carved oak ecclesiastical figure standing with hands in a praying position, mounted on a wood base.
- *height 163cm*
- £2,800 • John Clay

Marble Head ▲
- *circa 1900*

A French statuary marble head of a woman after Rodin.
- *36cm x 30cm*
- £1,250 • Westland & Co.

Bronze Dog ▲
- *circa 1880*

Fine bronze dog front signed by G. Fontaine.
- *height 11.5cm*
- £475 • Gavin Douglas

Ajax ▼
- *1893*

Fine bronze mounted onyx table thermometer surmounted by a figure of Ajax, signed and dated by Barnel.
- *height 36cm*
- £1,150 • Gavin Douglas

Bronze Venus ▼
- *circa 1860*

Good patinated Italian bronze of the kneeling Venus after the antique. Set on a fine moulding.
- *height 56cm*
- £3,500 • Gavin Douglas

Italian Bust ▲
- *circa 1800*

Good early 19th century Italian bust of a young woman with her hair tied high on her head in the classical style.
- *height 56cm*
- £3,450 • Gavin Douglas

Marble Bust of Boy ▲
- *circa 1811*

Fine marble bust of a young boy standing on a grey marble base with gilt bronze frieze.
- *height 48cm*
- £1,850 • Hatchwell

Italian Marble Figure ◄
- *circa 1890*

An Italian marble figure showing a slave girl sitting on a rug. Signed by Branlony.
- *height 60cm*
- £3,850 • Gavin Douglas

Venus ▲

- *circa 1860*

A Victorian re-constituted stone figure of Venus by the Farnley Co. Standing by a pillar in flowing chiffon, her hair dressed in a chignon, on a rectangular plinth.

- *134cm x 55cm*
- £750 • Westland & Co.

Alabaster Wrestling Pair ▲

- *1840*

White alabaster statue of figures wrestling.

- *52cm x 59cm*
- £4,200 • J. Fox

Expert Tips

There are no rules for the buyer of decorative objects, it is solely up to the individual and how he or she sees the world and how this can be expressed in the privacy of one's own living space.

Marble Statue ▶

- *circa 1890*

An attractive Italian marble statue of a young girl leaning against a fountain playing a set of 'panpipes'. Signed 'Pittaluga'.

- *height 80cm*
- £8,750 • Gavin Douglas

Stone Roundels ▼

- *circa 1850*

A pair of Italian carved stone roundels in the Renaissance manner, each with a carved head, one depicting Benvenuto Cellini (1500-1571), Florentine sculptor, goldsmith and amorist. The other depicts Giulio Romano (1499-1546), painter and architect, one of the creators of mannerism, and chief assistant of Raphael.

- *diameter 102cm*
- £12,000 • Westland & Co.

Pair of Maidens ▶

- *circa 1730*

A pair of white marble busts of maidens in the antique manner, attributed to Michael Rysbrach (1694-1770). With finely carved robes pinned at the shoulder with a brooch, the hair flowing loosely over one shoulder, supported on later Portoro marble socles.

- *76cm x 36cm*
- £33,000 • Anthony Outred

Marble Bust ▲

- *circa 1840*

A carved statuary marble bust of a lady in the eighteenth century manner, the head slightly turned to dexter with a full wig and two tresses of hair curling around her shoulders and drapery swathed across her dress.

- *58.5cm x 34cm*
- £3,850 • Westland & Co.

Grand Tour Bronze ▼

- *circa 1860*

Unusual and small Italian grand tour bronze of a man about to use a sling.

- *height 12cm*
- £425 • Gavin Douglas

Lighting

Italian Candelabra ▼

- *circa 1900*

A metal hour-glass base, with wire and enamel flower decoration with pierced finial of acanthus and trellis design.
- *height 106cm*
- £950
- R. Conquest

Ormolu Chandelier ▲

- *circa 1790*

A fine late 18th-century Baltic glass and ormolu chandelier, with suspended pendants and swags linking six curved branches. Converted to electricity.
- *height 102cm*
- £40,000
- Norman Adams

Expert Tips

Always check that lamps converted to electricity adhere to current safety standards. Some of them were converted a long time ago.

Pewter Candelabra ▼

- *1885*

A candelabra of English pewter with a shaft of pierced, organic form on a square, splayed base. The branches with cup sconces.
- *height 28cm*
- £2,500
- Kieron

Puppy Oil Lamp ▲

- *circa 1910*

A continental oil lamp mounted on the ceramic model of a begging puppy, with glass eyes, on a moulded, circular base. New shade and frame.
- *height 32cm*
- £650
- Elizabeth Bradwin

Pair of Candelabra ▼

- *circa 1825*

Pair of Regency, cut glass and ormolu, two-branch candelabra with long faceted drops.
- *height 36cm*
- £9,000
- Norman Adams

Elephant Oil Lamps ▼

- *circa 1900*

Pair of continental, miniature oil lamps mounted on porcelain, elephant bodies with all original fittings and leather covers.
- *height 22cm*
- £670
- Elizabeth Bradwin

Bronze Lamps ▼

- *circa 1830*

Pair of bronze lamps with acanthus-leaf decoration.
- *height 51cm*
- £1,850
- Lynda Franklin

Victorian Chandelier ▲

- *circa 1870*

Victorian glass 10-branch chandelier with heavily cut and faceted crystal dishes and droplets.
- *height 80cm*
- £1,600   • Sign of the Times

Crystal Chandelier ▼

- *1870*

French gilt bronze chandelier consisting of 16 arms with cut crystal glass droplets.
- *92.5cm x 50cm*
- £3,400   • Guinevere

Four-Armed Chandelier ▼

- *1890*

Small giltwood and bronzed effect chandelier with four arms.
- *84cm x 70cm*
- £3,500   • O.F. Wilson

Wall Sconces ▲

- *1890*

Pair of Art and Crafts wall sconces with enamel plaques. Designed and executed by John Fleetwood Varley.
- *19cm x 16cm*
- £1,800   • Gooday Gallery

Expert Tips

It is important to consider damage and incomplete objects as these tend to be unique and therefore expensive to repair.

Baccarrat Chandelier ▼

- *19th century*

A French glass, twelve-branch chandelier signed "Baccarrat".
- *75cm x 62cm*
- £6,900   • M. Luther

Ormolu Candelabra ▲

- *1840*

Pair of four-branch ormolu candelabra with acanthus leaf detail.
- *height 60cm*
- £3,850   • O.F. Wilson

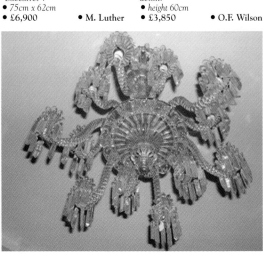

'Go To Bed' Candlestick ▲
- *circa 1850*

'Go to bed' Victorian Tunbridge Ware and rosewood candlestick, and taper holder. The lid rises to reveal storage for candles and tapers.
- *height 11cm*
- £365 • Period Pieces

Italian Gilded Candlesticks ▲
- *circa 1880*

A pair of Italian gilded bronze candlesticks, with three foliate scrolled branches.
- *height 74cm*
- £2,950 • Poppets

Victorian Table Lamp ▼
- *1880*

Victorian brass pedestal lamp with a pink and glass shade with a cherry blossom painted design.
- *height 49cm*
- £895 • Turn On Lighting

French Student Lamp ▼
- *circa 1899*

French highly decorative adjustable library lamp with a frosted glass shade, standing on a reeded Corinthian column with laurel leaf decoration, standing on a rouge royale marble base.
- *height 65cm*
- £1,200 • Turn On Lighting

French Chandelier ◄
- *circa 1880*

French ormolu and cut glass bag and waterfall eight branch chandelier.
- £2,400 • Mora Upham

Victorian Bijou Lamp ▲
- *1880*

Victorian adjustable reading lamp with a pink glass tulip shade, metal rim and a curved brass stand, on a circular wooden base.
- *height 24cm*
- £700 • Turn On Lighting

Silver Plated Table Lamp ▲
- *circa 1895*

Late Victorian silver-plated table lamp, fitted with feathered white glass lampshade, standing on a moulded silver column and base.
- *height 36cm*
- £895 • Turn On Lighting

Ecclestastical Candelabra ▼

- *circa 1900*

An ecclesiastical candelabra of
two sections, the upper half
forming a triangular section with
five candle-spikes.

- *height 165cm*
- £295   • Youll's Antiques

French Candelabra ▼

- *circa 1880*

A pair of French table candelabra
with brass fittings and stand,
profusely decorated in hanging,
faceted crystals.

- *height 50cm*
- £750   • Rainbow

Expert Tips

*Cleaning candlesticks of excess
wax is best achieved by
immersing them in boiling
water, which is more efficient
and less damaging than using a
sharp tool. Ensure, however,
that you put the plug in the sink,
as otherwise the wax will solidify
in the drain.*

Stoneware Lamps ▲

- *circa 1850*

A pair of mid 19th-century
continental stoneware,
urn-shaped lamps, with double
handles on square base.

- *height 75cm*
- £3,500   • Norman Adams

Gothic Candlesticks ▲

- *circa 1860*

A fine pair of 19th-century
bronze, Gothic candlesticks with
architectural and Gothic tracery
with hexagonal bases on
matching, white marble
hexagonal plinths.

- *height 58cm*
- £1,200   • Lynda Franklin

Art Nouveau Table Lamp ▼

- *circa 1895*

A silver oxidised cast brass lamp
fitted with an overlay glass shade.

- *height 32cm*
- £1,600   • Turn On Lighting

French Chandelier ▼

- *circa 1880*

A double tier French chandelier
with twelve branches, faceted
crystals and rewired bronze.

- *diameter 70cm*
- £1,650   • Rainbow

French Wall Lights ▼

- *circa 1880*

A set of four French wall lights
with bronze fittings and crystals.

- *height 30cm*
- £1,200   • Rainbow

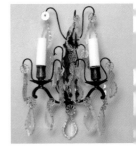

Edwardian Ceiling Lights ◀

- *circa 1901*
Pair of Edwardian cast brass flash ceiling lights fitted with frosted glass covers.
- *height 20cm*
- **£1,600**   • **Turn On Lighting**

Victorian Table Lamp ▼

- *circa 1890*
A highly decorative Victorian, cast brass table lamp fitted with acid edged glass lampshade, standing on a tripod base.
- *height 44cm*
- **£895**   • **Turn On Lighting**

English Electric Wall Lamp ▼

- *circa 1890s*
One of a pair decorative cast brass electric wall lamps fitted with hobnail glass shades.
- *27cm*
- **£1,500**   • **Turn On Lighting**

Ceiling Pendant ▼

- *circa 1895*
Late Victorian three branch ceiling pendant in brass, fitted with three green vaseline shades.
- *height 42cm*
- **£1,200**   • **Turn On Lighting**

French Candelabra ▼

- *circa 1830*
Pair of large gilt ormolu candelabra, with four gilt scrolling branches and a gilt finial, on a central reeded column standing on three bent goat legs with cloven hooves.
- *height 66cm*
- **£4,500**   • **O.F. Wilson**

'Palmer & Co.' Lamp ▼

- *circa 1850*
Victorian 'Palmer & Co' lamp with original glass shade and an emerald green column with gilt foliate design.
- *height 78cm*
- **£2,200**   • **O.F. Wilson**

Bronzed Gas Wall Light ▼

- *circa 1865*
An important English bronzed gas wall light fitted with opal glass gas shade with decorative motives.
- *height 45cm*
- £1,200   • Turn On Lighting

French Chandeliers ▼

- *circa 1890*
A pair of gilt brass French Gothic revival chandeliers.
- *62cm x 91cm*
- £3,500   • Westland & Co.

Three Light Ceiling Pendant ▶

- *circa 1899*
Edwardian three light ceiling pendant in brass, fitted with acid edged cranberry glass shades.
- *height 43cm*
- £1,500   • Turn On Lighting

Wall Appliques ▲

- *circa 1860*
A pair of gilt brass Neo-Classical wall appliqués.
- *length 81cm*
- £1,500   • Westland & Co.

Brass Wall Lamp ▲

- *circa 1880*
One of a pair of English decorative gas brass wall lamps fitted with cut and acid edged glass shades.
- *height 20cm*
- £995   • Turn On Lighting

French Candelabra ▼

- *circa 1840*
One of a pair of French four branch ormolu candelabra with a snake circling a tapered column, with scrolled acanthus leaf and shell decoration and a flame finial, the whole on a solid platform base.
- *height 60cm*
- £3,850   • O.F. Wilson

Italian Chandelier ▼
- *circa 1880*
Empire-style chandelier.
- £695 • Rainbow

Wooden Chandelier ▼
- *circa 1900*
An unusual wooden chandelier with a nautical theme, incorporating capston, sails, ships wheel, rigging and masts.
- *115cm x 140cm*
- £14,000 • Hatchwell

Italian Candlesticks ◀
- *early 19th century*
A pair of Italian gilt ormolu candlesticks with three arms on urn shaped bases.
- *61.5cm x 20cm*
- £2,850 • O.F. Wilson

Painted Lamps ▲
- *1880*
Pair of painted toile Boullotte lamps with pierced metal lamp shades.
- *51cm x 35cm*
- £2,900 • O.F. Wilson

Gothic Candlesticks ▲
- *19th century*
A pair of gothic candlesticks in brass with ecclesiastical designs.
- *height 55cm*
- £875 • N.E. McAuliffe

Sculpted Group ▲
- *late 19th century*
An Italian sculpted alabaster group. The partially draped figure shown resting against a pedestal with plinth modelled as an elephant, supporting a column to the bowl fitting. The plinth is inscribed, "Domte Zoi, Firenze".
- *height 144.8cm*
- £25,000 • Emanouel

Boullotte Lamps ▲
- *1850*
Boullotte brass table lamp with three branches on an oval base.
- *height 56cm*
- £1,500 • O.F. Wilson

279

Metalware

Bronze Carp ◀
- *19th century*

A Japanese signed gilt and shakudo bronze model of a carp, naturalistically formed.
- *length 36cm*
- **£5,800** • Gregg Baker

Japanese Rooster ▶
- *18th century*

An iron suzuribako with a rooster and poem, signed by Myochin.
- *height 22cm*
- **£1,950** • Gregg Baker

Helen of Troy on Horse ▲
- *circa 1900*

French, Art Nouveau, patinated bronze, ormolu and ivory model, showing Helen of Troy mounted on a horse. Anonymous artist.
- *height 41cm*
- **£5,250** • Gavin Douglas

Bronze Flower Vessel ▼
- *17th century*

Rikka-form vase cast with a central band of geometric design with 'arrow vase'-style handles. Edo period, Japan.
- *height 21cm*
- **£6,000** • Gregg Baker

Cherub Candelabra ▲
- *circa 1785*

A pair of Louis XVI bronze and ormolu cherub candelabra on marble bases.
- *height 60cm*
- **£25,000** • Norman Adams

Alloy Bowl ▲
- *12th century*

Bell metal-alloy bowl of the Ghaznavid period, with circular geometric designs to the exterior.
- *diameter 27.5cm*
- **£600** • Oasis

Expert Tips

Beware of polishing bronzes. They have a patina which, when they are overcleaned, disappears to become a brassy colour. This will halve or quarter the value, particularly of a good bronze.

Iron Wall Plaque ▶
- *circa 1890*

A burnished cast-iron belle epoque wall plaque of extravagant foliate design.
- *height 56cm*
- **£1,250** • Westland & Co.

Bronze Figures ▲

- 1880

A fine pair of bronze portrait figures of Albrecht Durer and Paul Romaine, each signed Solmson.
- *height 25.25cm*
- £2,450 • Gavin Douglas

Ethiopian Cross ▲

- *circa 1800*

An Ethiopian processional copper cross.
- *36cm x 25cm*
- £1,450 • Iconastas

Brass Tripod Incense Burner ▼

- 1860

Unusual Renaissance-style brass tripod incense burner.
- *height 40cm*
- £575 • Gavin Douglas

Prix de Rome Group ▲

- 1860

A superb patinated bronze group of Paul and Virginia by Charles Cumberworth. He was awarded the Prix de Rome for this piece in 1849. Susse Frès foundry on marble base.
- *height 37cm*
- £4,750 • Gavin Douglas

Decorated Tazzas ▼

- 1880

Pair of late nineteenth century leaf decorated tazzas.
- *height 28cm*
- £875 • Gavin Douglas

Pharmacy Sign ▶

- *18th century*

A French bronze pharmacy sign in the shape of a coiled serpent around a chalice.
- *height 70cm*
- £1,300 • Solaris

Tribute to Flight ▼

- 1915

A fine bronze which celebrated the flight of the Wright brothers. Entitled "Inspiration Humaine" by Kolakowski. It was reduced by the F. Barbedienne foundry.
- *height 19.5cm*
- £1,250 • Gavin Douglas

Singer Bronze ◀

- 1898

Superb bronze of a naked kneeling woman entitled "Helgn" signed and dated Albert Toft 29/3/98. Cast at the Singer factor as were many English bronzes. This was owned by the Singer family until 2001.
- *41cm x 39cm*
- £6,750 • Gavin Douglas

Gilt Bronze Vase ▲
- *1898*
Gilt bronze vase, signed and dated by Moreau. The ceramic is by Gurin & Keller, Belgium.
- *height 31cm*
- **£1,800**   • **Succession**

Figurine ▲
- *1895*
"Nature revealing herself to science" signed Barriass.
- *height 58cm*
- **£8,500**   • **Succession**

Chinese Figure ▲
- *1875*
Chinese figure of a man riding a mythical beast.
- *height 26cm*
- **£1,025**   • **Sign of the Times**

Bronze Retriever ▲
- *circa 1880s*
A bronze, naturalistically styled retriever, on a figured marble base.
- *23cm x 23cm*
- **£1,250**   • **Sign of the Times**

Bust of Napoleon ▲
- *1885*
A bronze bust of Napoleon with an eagle, by R Colombo, 1885.
- *height 25cm.*
- **£3,800**   • **David Brower**

Bronze Figure ▲
- *1868–1912*
A bronze figure of a Japanese girl carrying a harvest basket.
- *height 40cm*
- **£1,100**   • **David Brower**

Bronze Urn ▲
- *circa 1860s*
One of a pair of bronze Chinese vases with shaped dragon handles.
- *height 28cm*
- **£1,600**   • **Sign of the Times**

French Empire Candlesticks ▼

● *circa 1815*
A fine pair of patinated bronze and original ormolu French Empire candlesticks. In the form of a classically draped vestal standing holding an oil lamp in her arms, with a very well formed candleholder on her head, with round ormolu socle.
● *height 38cm*
● £3,950　　● Gavin Douglas

Bronze Young Girl ▼

● *circa 1880*
Bronze classical figure of a young girl semi-clad, holding her robe in one hand.
● *height 52cm*
● £1,320　　● John Clay

Reclining Nude Plaque ▲

● *circa 1880*
Reclining nude with her head resting on her hand and an angel at her feet.
● *width 51cm*
● £275　　● John Clay

Boy Water Carrier ▲

● *circa 1870*
Gilt on bronze boy carrying two ewers on a yoke, standing on a circular bronze base and signed Moreau.
● *height 23cm*
● £1,250　　● John Clay

Orient ▶

● *circa 1900*
A good quality early 20th century French bronze bust of a woman inscribed 'ORIENT', and stamped: E VILLANIS.
● *51cm x 34cm*
● £2,750　　● John Riordan

Bronze Figures ▲

● *circa 1870*
Very attractive pair of patinated bronze figures of negro slaves carrying produce. Produced and signed by Susse Frères from models by Charles Cumberworth an American born artist working in Paris. On reeded onyx bases.
● *height 50cm*
● £4,750　　● Gavin Douglas

Bronze Figures ▲

- *circa 1850*
A patinated bronze group of
Baccanalian revellers, on red
marble base, by Marc Chal.
- *height 41cm*
- **£2,450**　　● Gavin Douglas

Chinese Bronze Censer ▲

- *circa 1800*
Censer with dog of Fo, pierced
floral decoration to lid and body,
with dragon-head handles.
- *height 33cm*
- **£500**　　● Namdar

French Vases ▼

- *circa 1795*
A pair of French directoire
patinated bronze and ormolu
vases, with scrolled handles.
- *height 35cm*
- **£8,250**　　● Gavin Douglas

Islamic Incense Burner ▼

- *13th century*
Bronze incense burner in the
form of a bird with a hinged beak.
- *height 6cm*
- **£2,200**　　● Shiraz

Chinese Canton ▲

- *18th century*
A metal brazier decorated with
flowers and foliage on turquoise
enamel ground. Qianlong period.
- *height 43cm*
- **£3,800**　　● Guest & Gray

Fleur De Lys ▲

- *circa 1850*
One of a set of burnished fleur de
lys with star-shaped piercing.
- *height 54.4cm*
- **£750**　　● Westland & Co.

Expert Tips

*Bronzes are notoriously easy
to fake. Only experience in
handling will make you sure
of the piece you are buying.*

Bronze Hounds ◄

- *circa 1880*
A French bronze by J. Moigniez; a
rare model of two hounds tugging
at a hare.
- *height 14cm*
- **£1,320**　　● Elizabeth Bradwin

Bronze Horse ▲
- *circa 1880*
19th-century French bronze
figure of a stallion. Signed Vidal.
- *32cm x 39cm*
- £1,995   • John Riordan

Bronze Vase ▲
- *1868–1912*
A Japanese bronze metal vase
with silver, gold and shakadu
decoration, from the Meiji
period.
- *height 35cm*
- £2,900   • David Brower

Bronze Samurais ▲
- *1868–1912*
A pair of Japanese bronze
Samurai warriors with gold inlay
on a wooden base, signed Koichi.
- *height 38.5cm*
- £13,750   • David Brower

Bronze Figure ▼
- *1868–1912*
A Japanese bronze figure of Hotei
shown holding a staff, from
the Meiji period.
- *height 30cm*
- £950 • David Brower

Bronze Vase ◄
- *circa 1880s*
Bronze vase of ovoid form with a
splayed fluted neck, decorated
with a coiled dragon.
- *height 46cm*
- £1,850   • Sign of the Times

Bronze Eagle ▲
- *1930*
A bronze eagle with spread wings
on a figured marble base
- *height 34cm*
- £1,200   • Westland & Co.

Incense Burner ▲
- *1850*
Bronze incense burner with
splayed lip and moulded
decoration around the body, with
ear shaped handles.
- *height 9cm*
- £550   • Sign of the Times

Bronze Dolphins

- **1880**

A pair of English stylized bronze dolphins with mounted seashells resting on their tails, on a rectangular marble base.
- *height 16cm*
- £1,650
- Heytesbury

Bronze Lady

- *circa 1880*

Bronze lady with a pensive expression, one arm over a chair and the other at her spinette.
- *height 53cm*
- £720
- John Clay

Gothic Revival Splint Holders ▲

- *circa 1850*

An attractive pair of gothic revival splint holders in the style of Pugin. With fine original ormolu in superb condition. Probably French.
- *height 20.5cm*
- £1,750
- Gavin Douglas

Bronze Girl with Dragonfly ▲

- *circa 1880*

Painted spelter figure of a young laughing girl with a bow in her hair, one arm outstretched and the other holding a bowl with a dragonfly. Standing on a foliate rustic mound and circular wood base.
- *height 49cm*
- £220
- John Clay

Ormolu Ewers ▲

- *circa 1795*

A pair of French Directoire period patinated bronze and finest original ormolu ewers. Of slender ovoid form, the sinuous lip continuing to an SOR-scroll arm with finely chased griffin and satyrs mask terminal, on a circular base with stiff leaf and engine turned decoration, resting on a square plinth.
- *height 38cm*
- £11,250
- Gavin Douglas

Ormolu Tazza ▼

- *circa 1815*

A fine quality fire gilded ormolu tazza or dish set on a porphry base. Almost certainly Swedish from early 19th century. With fine quality work to tazza and original ormolu.
- *25cm x 25cm.*
- £2,250
- Gavin Douglas

Expert Tips

Get to know your metals! Can you tell the difference between spelter and bronze, or ormolu and brass? If you can't, this could be an expensive gap in your knowledge.

Furniture

The market for antique furniture goes from strength to strength and is spreading across the world.

The most used antiques of them all and, obviously, a vast field of study, antique furniture varies considerably in style depending on the period and the country in which it was made. Most collectors tend to concentrate on one area or one period, bookcases and cabinets, for instance, or Victorian furniture. Fakes, reproductions and updated pieces abound in this field more than any other, and it is important to be able to tell when a piece is 'right'. A methodical approach to examination is important to be able to judge whether there has been any restoration – or whether distressing is evident in a place that would not have been distressed during the course of natural usage or wear. There is no substitute for experience. The more used you are to handling and examining the real thing, the more likely you are to identify the 'wrong' one. The best reason for buying a piece of furniture is a genuine liking for it, so there is some satisfaction and pleasure in the possession in any event. However, the better informed you are about the main buying criteria – style, materials, method of construction, period, manufacturer – the more likely you are to make a wise purchase and the more you will enjoy the experience of owning it.

Beds

Walnut Bed ▶
- **1860**
Walnut Louis XV style bed, with elaborately carved and scrolled head and footboard, standing on scrolled splayed feet.
- *width 1.8cm*
- **£6,250** • Sleeping Beauty

French Walnut Bedhead ▲
- **1860**
French walnut, Louise Phillipe bedhead, with carved moulded arched headboard, foliate design and panelling, on bun feet.
- *width 1.5m*
- **£5,750** • Sleeping Beauty

Italian Inlaid Bedheads ▼
- **circa 1880**
Pair of unusual Italian hand-painted iron bedheads, inlaid with mother of pearl, standing on tapered legs.
- *width 90cm*
- **£4,500** • Sleeping Beauty

Louis XV Daybed ◀
- **1870**
Louise XV-style daybed with painted and parcel-gilt frame and shell and leaf carving, on scrolled cabriole legs.
- *length 2.42m*
- **£6,500** • O.F. Wilson

Oak Bed ▶

- *19th century*

Oak bed with carved rosettes and finial decoration on tapered fluted legs.
- £980   • Drummonds

French Renaissance Bed ▲

- *circa 1860*

A heavily carved solid walnut Renaissance bed with finials and turned and fluted posts.
- *length 2m*
- £4,500   • Sleeping Beauty

Spanish Bedstead ▲

- *circa 1860*

A Spanish hand-forged iron bedstead with large ornate cast-brass ornamentation.
- £1,695   • Sleeping Beauty

Pair of Marquetry Beds ▲

- *circa 1870*

Italian, fine-quality beds with oval figurative panels and floral borders in the manner of Maggiolina.
- *height 1.33m*
- £9,500   • Brown's

Expert Tips

The side irons of metal beds are essential, providing a frame on which to fit the base and mattress. Duplicates are almost impossible to find, so do not buy a bed where the irons are missing or don't fit properly.

French Brass Bedstead ◀

- *circa 1885*

French all-brass bedstead with beautiful cast ornamentation and finials.
- £2,500   • Sleeping Beauty

Victorian Bedsteads ▼

- *circa 1880*

A pair of Victorian brass and cast-iron bedsteads.
- *length 1.95m*
- £1,295   • Sleeping Beauty

Louis XVI Bed ▼

- *circa 1890*

A French mahogany bow-fronted bed with inlaid panels, adorned with ormolu mounts.
- £4,200   • Sleeping Beauty

Carved Bedroom Suite ▼
- **1785**

Directoire-style bedroom suite, comprising bed, armoire, bedside table, washstand, chest of drawers, mirror and three chairs.
- *length 2.42m*
- **£25,000** • **Sleeping Beauty**

Pair of Single Beds ▼
- **1885**

Pair of single divan beds with carved headboards and swept front, standing on cabriole legs.
- *width 1m*
- **£4,500** • **Sleeping Beauty**

Carved Throne Bed ▶
- **18th century**

A very rare carved throne bed used by the tribal elder or chief, from the Pakistani border.
- *length 2.46m*
- **£4,200** • **Gordon Reece**

Expert Tips
With wooden bed heads, check that the feet are in good repair and that the supporting frames are intact and show no signs of worm infestation. It is unwise to retain the original mattress.

Empire Bed ▲
- **1860**

French Second Empire heavily carved and ebonised four-poster bed, with scrolled broken pediment and turned posts.
- *width 1.5m*
- **£8,500** • **Sleeping Beauty**

Victorian Brass Bedstead ▲
- **1890**

An English Victorian brass and iron bedstead with dipped rail.
- *width 1.5m extending to 1.8m*
- **£2,450** • **Sleeping Beauty**

Louis XVI-Style Bed ▼
- **1880**

A French painted Louis XVI-style bed with fluted posts and finials.
- *width 1.5m*
- **£5,250** • **Sleeping Beauty**

Panatière Bedhead ▼
- **1860**

A French ornately carved fruitwood bedhead with baluster decoration and carved scrolled apron front, on bulbous legs.
- *length 1.1m*
- **£1,650** • **Tredantiques**

French Empire Bedstead ▼

- *circa 1870*

French empire flame mahogany bedstead with pilaster moulding, cross banded and inlaid designs with ormolu mounts.

- *width 153cm*
- £6,500 • Sleeping Beauty

French Mahogany Bedstead ▼

- *circa 1880*

French mahogany Louis XVI bed with a moulded headboard with a gilt torchière in the centre with two cherubs below, and gilt finials.

- *length 178cm*
- £5,500 • Sleeping Beauty

Mahogany French Bedstead ▶

- *circa 1860*

Flame mahogany Louis XV bedstead with highly decorative floral and ribbon ormolu mounts.

- *width 137cm*
- £6,000 • Sleeping Beauty

French Louis XV Bedstead ▲

- *circa 1880*

French Louis XV solid walnut single bed with moulded and carved headboard and footboard.

- *length 184cm*
- £4,200 • Sleeping Beauty

Bow Fronted Bedstead ▼

- *19th century*

Upholstered bow fronted and padded Louis XV bedstead with original green paintwork.

- *148cm*
- £1,295 • Sleeping Beauty

Walnut Louis XVI Bedstead ◀

- *circa 1880*

Large French solid walnut Louis XVI bed with a carved ribboning on the headboard, and floral swags footboard, with fluted posts.

- *length 179cm*
- £6,750 • Sleeping Beauty

Bonheurs du Jour

Bonheur du Jour ▼
- *circa 1890*
Bonheur du jour with pierced brass rail and two small drawers, flanked by cupboards with circular inlay panels and a gallery single drawer, standing on slender tapering legs.
- *104cm x 73cm*
- **£1,150** • **The Swan**

Victorian Dressing Table ▼
- *circa 1870*
Fine quality Victorian burr walnut dressing table and mirror supported by scrolled carving.
- *height 174cm*
- **£2,800** • **Hill Farm**

George IV Bonheur du Jour ▲
- *circa 1825*
George IV rosewood writing table in solid and veneered rosewood. With pierced gallery drawers and moving writing slide supported by twist columns.
- *height 122cm*
- **£7,800** • **Gerald Brodie**

Sheraton Bonheur du Jour ▲
- *circa 1790*
Fine Sheraton period bonheur du jour, with harewood inlay fold-over tops, enclosing a rising nest of drawers and pigeonholes.
- *89cm x 114cm*
- **£22,500** • **John Bly**

Victorian Dressing Table ▲
- *circa 1880*
Victorian mahogany dressing table with central mirror and drawer, flanked by eight small drawers.
- *height 167cm*
- **£2,350** • **C. Preston**

Bonheur du Jour ▼
- *circa 1890*
Late Victorian mahogany bonheur du jour with satinwood stringing, a roll top cover, the interior fitted with five pigeonholes and a central small drawer, above a pull out writing slope and two drawers, the whole on straight legs.
- *103cm x 72cm*
- **£1,500** • **Macnaughton-Smith**

Chippendale Style Bonheur du Jour ▼
- *circa 19th century*
Chippendale style bonheur du jour in the style of Angelica Kauffman, decorated with floral designs and classical scenes in the finest satin wood. Shield style bevelled glazed mirror with urn finial, standing on delicate turned legs.
- *165cm x 107cm*
- **£24,500** • **J. & T. Stone**

Expert Tips
Never stand an antique directly in front of a radiator or fire, as dramatic changes in temperature can cause shrinkage and warping, especially to drawers. Dryness can be regulated by a humidifier.

Louis XV-Style Bonheur du Jour ▲

- *late 19th century*
Kingwood and crossbanded bonheur du jour in the Louis XV-style, applied with gilt metal mounts and Sèvres-style porcelain plaques. The stepped superstructure with a three-quarter gallery and marble top above a panelled door inset with a plaque depicting courtly lovers, and four short drawers. The rectangular galleried top above a frieze drawer with similar applied decoration, on slender cabriole legs and scroll feet with sabots.
- *117cm x 92cm x 51cm*
- £15,000   • Emanouel

Rosewood Bonheur du Jour ▼

- *circa 1820*
Regency rosewood bonheur du jour, with satinwood inlay and mirrored back panel, flanked by cupboards with oval satinwood panels, standing on straight square tapering legs.
- *105cm x 90cm x 46cm*
- £2,995   • Harpur Deardren

Satinwood Bijouterie ▼

- *circa 1870*
Satinwood bijouterie with fine floral design, standing on slender tapered legs, with scrolled stretcher.
- *height 84cm*
- £6,500   • Butchoff

Coromandel Lady's Necessaire ◀

- *1920–30*
A coromandel lady's necessaire with fitted interior containing original bottles and pull-out flaps, and a stretcher below. Standing on squared tapered legs on splayed feet.
- *72cm x 25cm*
- £3,450   • Great Grooms

Mahogany and Satinwood Bonheur du Jour ▼

- *1850*
Mahogany and satinwood bonheur du jour with a raised pierced gallery, with four small drawers and a leather writing top, with two small drawers below, raised on reeded tapered legs.
- *95cm x 81cm x 48cm*
- £5,950   • Ashcombe

English Regency Bonheur du Jour ▼

- *1815*
Outstanding and rare Regency coromandel bonheur du jour. This is a fine and elegant example of English Regency furniture.
- *119cm x 70cm x 67cm/extended*
- £14,500   • Freshfords

Bookcases

George IV Mahogany Bookcase ▲

- *circa 1825*

A George IV cream-painted and parcel-gilt mahogany bookcase in the manner of William Kent. The rectangular moulded cornice above an egg and dart dentilled lower cornice above a foliate swagged frieze centred by a female mask and flanked by shells, with four glazed panelled doors below between Ionic pilasters. The base section with four panelled doors between plain panelled uprights, each enclosing an adjustable shelf.

- *308cm x 210cm*
- £48,000 • Anthony Outred

Mahogany Bookcase ▲

- *circa 1840*

Fine flame mahogany secretaire bookcase with two glazed doors and fitted interior and two cupboards below on a square base.

- *236cm x 104cm*
- £10,500 • Butchoff

Mahogany Bookcase ▼

- *1880*

Unusually large breakfront bookcase with mahogany and satinwood cross-banded decoration, swan neck pediment, galleried and moulded designs, raised on a plinth base.

- *233cm x 313cm*
- £28,000 • Butchoff

Glazed Bookcase Cabinet ▼

- *circa 1760*

An early George III mahogany glazed bookcase cabinet. With a broken, moulded dentil work pediment, each door composed of two astragal glazed octagonal panels with glazing bars connecting to the door frames, the interior lined and fitted with glass shelves. The cabinet with figured timber, the doors each with a shaped fielded panel defined by ribbon and flower-head moulding. The cabinet fitted with a moulded lip at the base above.

- *232.5cm x 117cm*
- £24,500 • Anthony Outred

Victorian Walnut Bookcase ▲

- *circa 1880*

Victorian walnut bookcase with moulded flat top pediment, glazed doors enclosing five shelves, two deep drawers above two moulded doors, standing on moulded bracket feet.

- *height 251cm*
- £2,850 • Hill Farm

Secretaire Bookcase ▲

- *circa 1820*

Regency secretaire bookcase with Gothic glazed upper section, the fall opens to reveal a well fitted interior above matched flame veneer doors, the whole raised on splayed feet with shaped apron.

- *262cm x 120cm*
- £18,750 • Serendipity

Biedermeier Bookcase ▼

- *circa 1910*
Swedish birchwood bookcase in
the style of Biedermeier, with
ebonised pillars and details, plus
a moulded top.
- *201cm x 165cm x 40cm*
- **£9,800**   • R. Cavendish

Pair of Bookcases ▼

- *circa 1900*
Pair of mahogany Victorian open
bookcases with boxwood
stringing on a plinth base.
- *110cm*
- **£5,500**   • Brown

Victorian Ebonised Bookcase ▶

- *circa 1870*
Ebonised Victorian bookcase
with moulded pediment, two
glazed doors enclosing two
shelves, floral swag decoration
and blue Wedgwood plaques
applied to the cupboards,
standing on a plinth base.
- *230cm x 137cm x 52cm*
- **£2,800**   • Tredantiques

Bombe Bookcase ▲

- *1720*
A walnut Dutch bombe bookcase
with arched moulded cornice,
inlaid with box foliate designs
above three long drawers fitted
with brass handles. raised on lion
paw feet.
- *230cm x 184cm*
- **£18,000**   • J. Fox

Victorian Mahogany Bookcase ▲

- *circa 1870*
Victorian mahogany bookcase,
with cavetto style moulding with
two glazed doors, two longs
drawers above two cupboards, by
Mawer & Stevenson of London.
- *228cm x 138cm x 46cm*
- **£1,850**   • Tredantiques

Oak Bookcase ▼

- *19th century*

Light oak bookcase with glazed doors above two drawers and two doors, all with original mounts.
- *height 2.25m*
- £1,295   • Old Cinema

Walnut Bookcase ▼

- *19th century*

Three-tiered bookcase with Gothic bars and two drawers.
- *height 1.96m*
- £850   • Tower Bridge

Breakfront Bookcase ▶

- *circa 1825*

A George IV figured mahogany breakfront bookcase.
- *height 2.52m*
- £100,000   • Norman Adams

Open Bookcase ▼

- *circa 1820*

Simulated rosewood bookcase with two shelves on turned feet and brass castors.
- *height 1.3m*
- £1,650   • M.J. Bowdery

Breakfront Bookcase ▶

- *circa 1830*

A 19th-century English Gothic country house burr elm and amboyna breakfront bookcase with cabinet.
- *height 1.17m*
- £9,800   • M. Luther

Globe Werniker ▲

- *circa 1915*

Six-stack, oak Globe Werniker bookcase with lifting glass panels.
- *height 2m*
- £950   • Oola Boola

Chinese Lacquer Bureau Bookcase ▼

- *circa 1770*

Chinese lacquer bureau bookcase with broken arched pediment featuring an elaborate chinoiserie design, standing on bracket feet.
- *232cm x 91cm x 55cm*
- £90,000
- O.F. Wilson

Victorian Ebonised Bookcase ▼

- *circa 1870*

An ebonised Victorian bookcase with moulded pediment, two glazed doors enclosing two shelves, floral swag decoration and blue Wedgwood plaques applied to the cupboards, standing on a plinth base.
- *230cm x 137cm x 52cm*
- £2,800
- Tredantiques

Oak Bookcase ◄

- *19th century*

Victorian oak bookcase with two glazed doors featuring tilt top enclosing small drawers and pigeon holes, with two cupboards below, standing on a plinth base.
- *160cm x 140cm*
- £2,420
- Old Cinema

Japanned Bookcase ▲

- *1860*

A Chippendale period black and red japanned bookcase/display cabinet with swelled frieze, with gold chinoiserie designs and three panelled cupboards below.
- *232cm x 174cm x 44cm*
- £12,500
- Ranby Hall

Secretaire Bookcase ▲

- *1830–7*

A William IV mahogany secretaire bookcase with ogée moulded frieze above two glazed doors, fall front with turned handles, raised on a plinth base.
- *230cm x 110cm x 52cm*
- £4,800
- Ranby Hall

Boxes

Tortoiseshell Box ◀

- *circa 1810*

Tortoiseshell cylindrical box with silver gilt trim.
- *height 12cm*
- **£178** • **Abacus**

Regency Tea Caddy ▲

- **1835**

Late Regency walnut-based chevron strung tea caddy with two compartments.
- *12cm x 9cm x 13cm*
- **£395** • **J. & T. Stone**

South German Table Cabinet ▲

- *circa 1700*

South German cabinet in European hardwoods. The characteristic inlay style can be seen on a portative organ at the Victoria and Albert Museum in London. The shading was created using hot sand.
- *width 36cm*
- **£2,400** • **Hygra**

Penwork Box ▲

- **1830**

Octagonal penwork box with floral designs around a central eight-sided star with silver escutcheon plate.
- *11cm x 26.5cm x 20.5cm*
- **£1,250** • **O.F. Wilson**

William IV Tea Caddy ▼

- **1835**

Very unusual William IV rosewood sarcophagus-shaped double tea caddy, with extensive brass inlaid patterns and glass sugar bowl.
- *23cm x 37cm*
- **£995** • **J. & T. Stone**

Medical Box ▲

- *circa 1790*

A fully fitted eighteenth century mahogany medical box with bottles, funnel, balance and weights.
- *width 15cm*
- **£1,700** • **Hygra**

American Tea Chest ▲

- **1730**

Rare early American eighteenth century walnut tea chest with unusual brass decoration.
- *14.5cm x 24cm x 14cm*
- **£4,950** • **J. & T. Stone**

George III Tea Caddies ▼

- *circa 1790*
Pair of square George III tea caddies with canted corners, in quartered mahogany veneers, with boxwood rosewood and ebony line inlays and box and hare-wood pattern to front and cover. It is unusual to find a matching pair.
- *height 11.5cm*
- £5,860 • Period Pieces

Voting Box ▼

- *circa 1880*
Victorian oak voting box inscribed with the brass letters 'Y' and 'N', with two small drawers and a central hole with emerald green satin.
- *28cm x 25cm*
- £495 • A.I.G.

Tortoiseshell Tea Caddy ▲

- *circa 1820*
Very rare Regency pressed tortoiseshell tea caddy with ribbed and bowed front panel, dome top, silver stringing, insignia plate, escutcheon and top ball finial.
- *height 22cm*
- £9,450 • J. & T. Stone

Pen Work Tea Caddy ▲

- *circa 1825*
Regency pen work double tea caddy with extensive Chinoiserie scenes of a festive parade. The whole standing on brass lion's paw feet, with matching side ring handles.
- *12cm x 14cm*
- £4,750 • J.& T. Stone

Victorian Coromandel Wood Box ▲

- *circa 1870*
Unusual Victorian coromandel wood jewel box with gilded ormolu decoration and hand painted ivory miniature of an Eastern Princess on the lid.
- *6cm x 9cm*
- £995 • J. & T. Stone

Pear Shaped Tea Caddy ▶

- *circa 1800*
Fine pear shaped George III tea caddy made from fruitwood, comprising two sections with brass fitting and stem.
- *height 19cm*
- £5,350 • Period Pieces

Regency Tea Caddy ▼

- *circa 1820*
Tortoiseshell tea caddy with twin compartments, chamfered corners, a Pagoda cover and mother of pearl inlay depicting thistles and roses, standing on silver plated ball feet.
- *height 14cm*
- £4,980 • Period Pieces

Travelling Dressing Case ◀

- *circa 1934*

An early 20th-century, fine-quality, Art Deco, crocodile-skin, gentleman's travelling dressing case. Made by Cartier of London. Hallmarked silver, inscribed 'Sir W. Rollo'.
- **£3,995**   • J. & T. Stone

Expert Tips

It is important when purchasing a tea caddy that the container has its original liner. In general, tea caddies that are styled in the form of a fruit are extremely rare. The most affordable boxes tend to be those made from wood or papier mâché.

Russian Hatbox ▼

- *circa 1900*

An early 20th-century Russian hatbox made of birchwood, with a leather strap.
- *diameter 36.9cm*
- *height 22.5cm*
- **£490**   • R. Cavendish

Sewing Box ▲

- *1832*

Exceptional, tortoise-shell sewing-box with extensive mother-of-pearl floral inlay. With pull-out lower drawer and a note from the original owner.
- *height 14cm*
- **£4,950**   • J. & T. Stone

Gold Japanese Kogo ▲

- *circa 19th century*

Japanese, gold lacquered 19th-century kogo (box) in the form of a very unusual piebald puppy. The box is a container for incense.
- *height 6cm*
- **£1,650**   • Gregg Baker

Tortoiseshell and Silver Perfume Box ▼

- *circa 1918*

Original and complete. The box contains an inset of floral panel decorations. Made in England.
- *height 7.5cm*
- **£1,270** • S. & A. Thompson

English Tortoiseshell Tea Caddy ▲

- *circa 1850*

Mid 19th-century English bow-front tortoiseshell tea caddy. Contains a mother-of-pearl floral inlay to the front panel. A fine quality piece.
- *height 33cm*
- **£2,875**   • J. de Haan

Tunbridgeware Tea Caddy ▲

- *circa 1860*

Mid 19th-century, rectangular tea caddy. A view of Eridge Castle is shown on the lid. The box is made from rosewood with a keyhole in the panel of the box.
- *height 12cm*
- **£625**   • J. de Haan

299

Mahjong Set ▲

- 1920

Impressive and imposing Mahjong set of the highest quality in a solid oak case with extensive brass work decoration to the sides and top. With solid brass handle and sliding front panel revealing five similarly decorated drawers containing solid ivory tiles, game sticks and dice. Provenance: The Right Honourable The Viscount Leverhulme, K. G. of Thornton Manor.

- *29cm x 32cm*
- **£5,950** • **J. & T. Stone**

Apothecary Box ▲

- *circa 1830*

Georgian mahogany apothecary box with an almost complete set of original bottles, some with original contents. With lower drawer with original scales, weights, mortar, pestle and key.

- *13cm x 19cm*
- **£1,950** • **J. & T. Stone**

Tortoiseshell Tea Caddy ▶

- *circa 1775*

Exceptional red tortoiseshell tea chest with ivory stringing, silver ball feet and top handle; the interior with three original glass canisters with silver plate lids and original key.

- *height 14cm*
- **£29,500** • **J. & T. Stone**

Jewellery Case ▼

- *circa 1880*

Black lacquered jewellery box with a red interior and polychrome paintings of flora and fauna. Inside the lid is a folding mirror. Ex Fuzhou.

- *20cm x 24cm*
- **£390** • **Eastern Interiors**

Regency Chinoiserie Box ▼

- *circa 1820*

English Regency penwork box with trailing floral designs around a central panel depicting a group of hand painted Chinese figures.

- *height 16cm*
- **£1,650** • **O.F. Wilson**

Scholar's Parchment Box ▲

- *19th century*

Scholar's leather parchment box embossed with the design of the Buddhist swastika, the cover designed with the character of 'long life'. Ex-Shanghai.

- *18cm x 28cm*
- **£465** • **Eastern Interiors**

Tea Tins ▲

- 1880

Set of six cylindrical tea tins with covers and a central cartouche of a classical ruin surrounded by a foliate design, each with a gilt shield and numerals.

- *height 48cm*
- **£2,500** • **Goodison Paraskeva**

Chinese Lacquer Tea Caddy

- *circa 1850*

Shaped Chinese lacquer tea caddy with boldly defined gold decoration and pewter lines, standing on claw feet.

- *width 19cm*
- £650 • Hygra

Tortoiseshell Box

- *1760*

Anglo-Dutch box with ivory stringing and silver mounts on silver bun feet.

- *16cm x 28cm x 20cm*
- £3,000 • O.F. Wilson

Sycamore Box

- *circa 1900*

A small sycamore box with oval pictures depicting Western Road, Littlehampton.

- *8.5cm x 7cm*
- £34 • John Clay

Gilt Casket

- *late 19th century*

A porcelain and gilt-bronze casket, depicting romantic couples in pastoral settings with putti at each corner.

- *36cm x 27cm*
- £12,000 • Emanouel

Circular Robe Box

- *1830*

A Japanese black lacquered robe box of circular form with gilded floral decoration to both body and lid.

- *46cm x 39cm*
- £800 • O.F. Wilson

Etched Sycamore Box

- *circa 1900*

A sycamore box with etched scenes depicting the Isle of Wight.

- *6cm x 17cm*
- £55 • John Clay

Tunbridge Ware Box

- *circa 1850*

Decorative Tunbridge ware box attributable to Alfred Talbot who worked from 1843–58.

- *width 22cm*
- £310 • Hygra

Miniature Postbox ▼

- **1900**
Late Victorian oak miniature
postbox with original inset rate
card, brass plate inscribed
'"Letters", and carved leaf top.
- *height 38cm*
- **£2,950**   • J. & T. Stone

Small Lacquer Chest ▼

- *late 18th century*
A Chinese small lacquer chest
with three tiers of drawers behind
two doors painted with extensive
chinoiserie designs.
- *height 24cm*
- **£2,250**   • O.F. Wilson

Chinese Tea Caddy ▼

- *circa 1840*
Shaped and lacquered Chinese
tea caddy with gold decoration,
on carved dragon feet.
- *width 21cm*
- **£850**   • Hygra

French Domed Box ▼

- **19th century**
Box with domed lid decorated
with faux tortoiseshell design.
- *length 30cm*
- **£950**   • O.F. Wilson

Oblong Tea Caddy ▼

- *circa 1770*
Fine eighteenth century tea
caddy of oblong form in native
and imported hardwoods, with
mother of pearl accents, having a
brass handle and paw feet.
- *width 22cm*
- **£950**   • Hygra

Amboyna Tea Caddy ▼

- *circa 1830*
A George IV amboyna tea
caddy of sarcophagus form with
side handles, mother of pearl
roundels, pewter stringing, and
an interior with twin
compartments.
- *length 30cm*
- **£1,200**   • O.F. Wilson

Games Compendium ▲

- **1880**
Late Victorian dome-topped
and front opening coromandel
wood games compendium with
a comprehensive assortment of
games including chess, dominoes,
backgammon, tiddlywinks and
numerous set of playing cards
and counters all housed in a front
compartment and two lift out
trays.
- *18cm x 33.5cm x 23cm*
- **£4,950**   • J. & T. Stone

Chinese Canton Enamel Panelled Box ▲

- **18th century**
A fine canton enamel-panelled
huanghuali box and cover of
rectangular form and regular
construction with floating panels,
mitred corners and hidden
dovetails, set with two bail
handles at the sides and a wood
lock plate.
- *18.1cm x 31.7cm*
- **£6,000**   • Gerard Hawthorn

Tea Tin ▲
- 1880

One of a set of four black metal tea tins with a central cartouche of two birds perched on a cherry blossom branch.
- *height 44cm*
- £1,500 • Goodison Paraskeva

Games Compendium ▲
- *circa 1860*

Victorian walnut games compendium comprising: solid board for chess and backgammon, ivory cribbage and score board, ivory hand counters, lower drawer containing; playing cards, shakers and tiddlywinks and counters.
- *width 23cm*
- £5,950 • J. & T. Stone

Jewel Casket ▶
- *circa 1860*

French lustre tortoiseshell jewel casket with bowed panels, extensive ormolu decorative mounts and original silk lined interior.
- *height 25cm*
- £9,500 • J. & T. Stone

Oak Box ▲
- *circa 1880*

Oak box with silver-plated mounts of cherubs holding a plaque, with mermaids each side of the escutcheon plate.
- *10cm x 25cm*
- £350 • A.I.G.

Teapot Holder ▲
- *circa 1890s*

Ex-Fukien teapot holder. The lid secured with finely carved inverted scroll handles and dragons heads under clouds.
- *height 22cm*
- £260 • Eastern Interiors

Japanese Travelling Box ▲
- *circa 1880*

A small Japanese Kiri-sugi wood, tansu storage box for travelling salesmen, from the Meiji period.
- *30cm x 52cm*
- £995 • Gordon Reece

Regency Tea Caddy ▲
- *circa 1820*

Regency rosewood tea caddy of sarcophagus form with brass bun feet and double ring handles hanging from lion mask mounts.
- *30cm x 25cm*
- £295 • A.I.G.

Bureaux

Queen Anne Bureau ▼

- *circa 1710*

Queen Anne Irish walnut bureau bookcase with double domed top, the drawer and door fronts with elm herringbone cross banding.

- *width 88cm*
- £110,00
- John Bly

Burr-Walnut Secretaire ▼

- *circa 1880*

French burr walnut fall front secretaire with central pillared cupboard flanked by five drawers and two below.

- *height 142cm*
- £2,950
- The Swan

Biedermeier Bureau ▲

- *circa 1830*

Swedish birch Biedermeier bureau commode.

- *100cm x 106cm*
- £5,900
- R. Cavendish

William & Mary Bureau ▲

- *circa 1700*

A transitional William and Mary English writing bureau in well figured veneered walnut, the top fall and drawer fronts strung with double feather banding, with a fully fitted interior with drawers and well pelmeted pigeonholes, the whole on bracket feet.

- *99cm x 97cm x 51cm*
- £17,000
- Wakelin Linfield

English Elm Bureau ▶

- *circa 1700*

English veneered bureau in well figured elm with good patination, the fall with good stepped interior above two short and two long drawers, the whole raised on turned bun feet.

- *106cm x 92cm x 53cm*
- £16,500
- Wakelin Linfield

George III Bureau ▼

- *circa 1800*

A fine George III mahogany cylinder bureau with fitted interior, eight pigeonholes and three small drawers with ivory handles, the whole on slender tapered legs on brass castors.

- *142cm x 123cm*
- £10,500
- Westland & Co.

George III Mahogany Bureau ▼

- *circa 1810*

George III figured mahogany bureau with boxwood stringing, having four graduated drawers raised on splayed bracket feet.

- *height 104cm*
- £3,650
- Ranby Hall

Walnut Bureau ▼

- *1740*

A small walnut bureau with stepped interior. Boxwood and ebony line inlay on bracket feet.
- *100cm x 81cm*
- **£14,500**   • Midwinter

Fiddle-Back Bureau ▼

- *circa 1900*

Edwardian fiddle-back mahogany roll-top bureau bookcase having three shelves, original glass, boxwood inlay, leather top writing desk with three drawers below.
- *207cm x 91cm x 48cm*
- **£3,950**   • Hatchwell

Oak Bureau ◀

- *circa 1800*

Oak bureau with well-fitted interior and swan neck handles on moulded bracket feet.
- *104cm x 91cm x 51cm*
- **£2,250**   • Rod Wilson

English Walnut Chest Escritoire ▲

- *1690*

Fine English walnut William and Mary fall front escritoire with heavily moulded cornice over a cushion-moulded plan drawer. The interior having a secret drawer, with leathered writing surface. The whole on chest of two short and two long herring bone strung drawers. Raised on feet.
- *171cm x 54cm x 103cm*
- **£22,500**   • Wakelin Linfield

Marble-Topped Secretaire ▼

- *circa 1840*

A flame mahogany Second Empire secretaire biblioteque with marble, two panelled doors, with turned columns and ormolu mounts, above two cupboards on a plinth base.
- *143cm x 83cm x 50cm*
- **£6,450**   • Ranby Hall

Cedarwood Bureau ▼

- *circa 1790*

An eighteenth century cedarwood bureau with superb colour and patination, the fall with fitted interior above graduated drawers the whole raised on moulded bracket feet.
- *102cm x 91cm x 48cm*
- **£3,950**   • Rod Wilson

George III Bureau ◄

- *early 19th century*
Mahogany bureau with sloping
lid enclosing fitted interior.
- *height 1.06m*
- £5,500 • Old Cinema

George II Escritoire ▼

- *circa 1785*
George II kingwood and
marquetry escritoire on stand.
- *height 1.21m*
- £20,000 • Norman Adams

Bureau Bookcase ▲

- *circa 1730*
George II burr oak bureau with
walnut crossbanding. Fitted
interior with drawers below.
- *height 2.06m*
- £14,500 • Red Lion

Bureau Bookcase ▲

- *circa 1800*
Oak and mahogany crossbanded
bureau bookcase on plinth feet.
- *height 2.14m*
- £4,950 • Red Lion

Bookcase Bureau ▶

- *circa 1810*
A Regency secretaire bookcase,
in mahogany.
- *height 2.21m*
- £4,950 • Old Cinema

Secretaire/Bureau ◄

- *circa 1825*
North European elm-wood
secretaire commode. Pull-out
first drawer over two other
drawers.
- *height 94cm*
- £950 • M. Constantini

Cabinets

Goncalo Alvez Wood Chiffonier

- *circa 1820*

Regency period Goncalo Alvez wood chiffonier. The use of ionic capitals on this piece is both rare and appealing. With a finely figured rectangular top above a moulded lip. Two doors each with a pleated green moire silk panel, columns with ionic capitals and turned bases.

- *93cm x 130cm*
- **£9,500**   • **Anthony Outred**

Rosewood Specimen Cabinet

- *circa 1850*

An unusual rosewood specimen cabinet with panelled doors fitted with wire grilles and pleated silk. Each corner fitted with cantered brass cornering, with pigeonholes in the interior above a fall front satinwood drawer leading to rosewood and satinwood panelled doors enclosing ten graduated drawers with a further fourteen of various sizes. The whole raised on a stand with barley twist supports and stretchers.

- *137cm x 78cm*
- **£3,750**   • **Anthony Outred**

Japanese Lacquer Cabinet ▼

- *circa 1705*

Queen Anne period black lacquer and gilt Japanese cabinet on English base. Decorated with a relief landscape on the exterior, the pair of doors revealing an arrangement of eight drawers. Raised on a stand with cabriole legs and pad feet.

- *135cm x 76cm*
- **£8,500**   • **Anthony Outred**

Dutch Display Cabinet ▼

- *circa 1830*

Dutch marquetry display cabinet with serpentine moulded cornice, centred with a crisply carved finial, above two glazed doors with shelving. The base consisting of three tiers of drawers, raised on scrolled feet.

- *239cm x 168cm*
- **£22,000**   • **Butchoff**

Ebony and Tortoiseshell Cabinet ▲

- *circa 1680*

Fine 17th century ebony and tortoiseshell cabinet on later stand with architectural designs and gilt ormolu mounts.

- *142cm x 107cm*
- **£12,500**   • **Butchoff**

Display Cabinet ▲

- *circa 1900*

One of a pair of fine mahogany Chippendale style display cabinets of cylindrical form, with gallery cornice above glazed doors, with a heavily carved and molded base concealing two double doors.

- *203cm x 81cm*
- **£15,000**   • **Butchoff**

Regency Cabinet ▶

- *1830*

A Regency flame mahogany
bedside cabinet, with black
marble top, the door with
moulded foliate designs on a
gadrooned square plinth base.
- *79cm x 47cm*
- £2,800   • John Clay

Spoon Rack ▲

- *1770*

A fine George III oak spoon rack
with lidded box drawer, dentil
course and shaped apron.
- *74cm x 35cm x 15cm*
- £2,750   • Paul Hopwell

Fruitwood Cupboard ▲

- *18th century*

A late eighteenth century
fruitwood corner cupboard with
shaped shelves.
- *92cm x 67cm*
- £1,100   • Great Grooms

Mahogany Cabinet ▼

- *circa 1900*

A mahogany cabinet with twelve
panelled doors, standing on a
square moulded base.
- *214cm x 135cm x 61cm*
- £3,000   • John Nicholas

Hanging Cupboard ▼

- *1620*

Oak hanging cupboard, the
panels with geometric carving.
- *68cm x 63cm x 35cm*
- £6,750   • Peter Bunting

Tibetan Carved Cabinet ▼

- *18th century*

A Tibetan cabinet with carved
and painted decoration showing
deer in a woodland setting.
- *105cm x 106cm*
- £2,250   • Great Grooms

Walnut Cabinet ▼

- *circa 1860*

A fine light walnut cabinet with
porcelain cartouches depicting
romantic scenes, standing on a
plinth base decorated with floral
ormolu design.
- *95cm x 120cm*
- £16,500   • Butchoff

Mahogany Side Cabinets ▼
- *circa 1880*
Matched pair of mahogany side
cabinets with marble tops.
- *height 84cm*
- **£1,150**   • **Ranby Hall**

Corner Cabinet ▶
- *circa 1910*
One of a pair of Edwardian
mahogany cabinets with glazed
upper part and a cupboard base.
- *height 2.16m*
- **£750**   • **Canonbury**

Oak Corner Cabinet ▲
- *circa 1780*
A full standing cupboard with
patina and original mounts.
- *height 2.09m*
- **£3,975**   • **Red Lion**

Italian Walnut Cabinet ▲
- *circa 1880*
A cabinet in the Bambocci
manner, decorated with figural
uprights and panelled doors.
- *height 91.5cm*
- **£2,400**   • **Westland & Co.**

French Pearwood Cabinet ▼
- *circa 1830*
Carved pearwood cabinet from
Normandy. Good colour with
diamond-shaped panels and
chamfered columns on both sides.
- *height 1.23m*
- **£2,750**   • **Town & Country**

Corner Cupboard ▼
- *circa 1780*
A rare George III, chinoiserie-
patterned, Japanned, standing
corner cupboard.
- *height 2.03m*
- **£40,000**   • **Norman Adams**

Secretaire/Cabinet ▼
- *19th century*
A boulle-work ebonised secretaire
with rosewood interior and
various compartments.
- *height 1.36m*
- **£2,750**   • **Ranby Hall**

Shrine Cabinet ▲
- *1830*

A rare Chinese black lacquer and hardwood shrine cabinet decorated in gold, red and black, with inlaid mother of pearl. With fitted interior in the shape of a pagoda and decorated panelled doors, on straight square legs.
- *183cm x 177cm x 44cm*
- **£38,000**   • **Ranby Hall**

Lacquer Cabinet ▼
- *circa 1880*

Black and red lacquer cabinet with brass fittings, standing on plain straight legs, from Yangtze, China .
- *78cm x 60cm x 36cm*
- **£1,850**   • **Ranby Hall**

Indian Cabinet ▼
- *circa 1880*

A fine quality Indian cabinet in the Dutch style with two bottom drawers at bottom, and a top and bottom cupboard with single shelf.
- *195cm x 122cm x 52cm*
- **£3,950**   • **Simon Hatchwell**

Pair of Pine Cabinets ▶
- *1900s*

A pair of English pine cabinets with one drawer and one panelled cupboard below, standing on bun feet.
- *75cm x 45cm*
- **£250**   • **Old School**

Hanging Cupboard ▲
- *circa 1750*

A good quality mid-eughteenth century hanging oak corner cupboard with a moulded oak panel door.
- *100cm x 70cm*
- **£1,150**   • **Rod Wilson**

Bijouterie Display Cabinet ▲
- *1837*

Louis Phillipe mahogany brass inlaid bijouterie display cabinet, with pierced brass gallery and banding, on tapered legs.
- *131 x 82cm x 47cm*
- **£2,650**   • **Ranby Hall**

Giltwood Vitrine ▲
- *circa 1860*

Giltwood chinoiserie vitrine with chamfered corners on cabriole legs with a carved x-frame stretcher.
- *104cm x 86cm x 45cm*
- **£5,650**   • **Ranby Hall**

Dutch Walnut Display Cabinet ▲

- *circa 1780s*
A slim Dutch walnut display cabinet profusely decorated with floral and foliate motifs in marquetry, the shaped cornice above shaped glazed doors and canted corners to the upper section. The lower section of bombe form, the whole on turned and ebonised bun feet.
- *236.5cm x 170cm*
- £22,500 • Wakelin Linfield

Dutch Display Cabinet ▲

- *circa 1780*
Dutch walnut display cabinet with foliate inlay with glass panels to front and doors.
- *height 85cm*
- £4,850 • Paul Hopwell

Japanese Lacquer Cabinet ▶

- *circa 1880*
Japanese lacquer cabinet with two doors decorated with mother of pearl floral inlay, two small drawers and one long drawer inlaid with boxwood.
- *39cm x 29cm*
- £450 • Younger Antiques

Mahogany Chiffonier ▼

- *circa 1840*
Flame mahogany chiffonier with single long drawer, above two gilt brass grills with doors silks, flanked by turned pilasters, raised on turned feet.
- *93cm x 91.5cm x 41cm*
- £3200 • O.F. Wilson

Two Part Kortan Cabinet ▼

- *circa 1800*
A kortan cabinet of two parts made from elm, with four drawers above two cupboard doors with brass mounts.
- *145cm x 105cm*
- £2,950 • Wakelin Linfield

George IV Display Cabinet ▲

- *circa 1825*
George IV mahogany display cabinet, the top section with two glazed doors, above a lower section with four octagonal tapering legs decorated with stylised palmetto.
- *191cm x 94cm*
- £8,750 • Wakelin Linfield

Swedish Mahogany Cupboard ▲

- *circa 1890s*
Swedish Louis XVI style mahogany cupboard with two doors, above one long single drawer, with moulded apron with gilt ormulu mounts, on tapering slender legs.
- *106cm x 59cm*
- £1,950 • R. Cavendish

Camphor Wood Cabinet ▼

- *circa 1900*

Late Qing Dynasty Chinese black lacquer camphor wood cabinet, in three parts with gilded carvings, and a couplet in Chinese characters. Man celebrates four seasons with festivals and self-attainment for all in quiet meditation.

- *75cm x 28cm*
- £1,680
- Younger

Georgian Corner Cupboard ▲

- *circa 1780*

Georgian pine corner cupboard with astragal glazed doors and two moulded panel doors below with porcelain handles.

- *204cm x 105cm*
- £1,250
- Drummonds

Florentine Cabinet ◄

- *circa 1580*

Florentine ebony and rosewood cabinet with ivory and geometric inlay to the sides. Contains nine small and two long drawers, and one small cupboard with ivory stringing.

- *28cm x 62cm*
- £2,350
- W. John Griffiths

William IV Cabinet ▲

- *circa 1830*

William IV mahogany cabinet with eight glazed pillared doors and a single drawer, standing on moulded legs.

- *197cm x 78cm*
- £11,500
- Fred E Anderson

Empire Secretaire ▲

- *circa 1820*

Swedish mahogany empire secretaire with central foliate ormulu mount flanked by lion's head ring handles, with a fall front with fitted interior and three long drawers, with a shaped base.

- *141cm x 126cm*
- £9,500
- Rupert Cavendish

Regency Sideboard ◄

- *circa 1815*

An important English Regency mahogany and ebony inlaid sideboard, attributed to Gillow of Lancaster. The cabinet work is of the highest order, as one would expect with Gillow furniture making.

- *134.5cm x 74.5cm*
- £16,500
- Freshfords

Japanese Chest-Cupboard ▼

- *circa 1830*

A late Edo period Japanese chest-cupboard with three zelkova drawers above slatted cupboard fronts and two larger drawers below, all in an elm frame.

- *height 91cm*
- £2,800 • Gordon Reece

Satinwood Cupboard ▶

- *circa 1785*

An English, satinwood, bedside cabinet for storing the chamber pot, with inlaid detailing to the front and top, the whole on square, tapered legs.

- *height 77cm*
- £1,850 • O.F. Wilson

George II Escritoire ▲

- *circa 1750*

A kingwood and marquetry writing cabinet on stand.

- *height 1.21m*
- £120,000 • Norman Adams

Japanese Chest ▲

- *circa 1830*

An Edo chest with looking cabinet. The whole in Paulownia wood with original fittings.

- *height 59cm*
- £1,900 • Gordon Reece

Victorian Display Cabinet ▼

- *19th century*

A black ebonised and amboyna display cabinet.

- *height 1.06m*
- £1,100 • Old Cinema

Edwardian Vitrine ▼

- *circa 1890*

Mahogany, Sheriton-style vitrine with floral marquetry.

- *height 1.8m*
- £5,200 • Judy Fox

Display Cabinet ▼

- *circa 1905*

An unusually small, English Edwardian, mahogany, inlaid, bow-fronted cabinet, well proportioned with solid wood stretcher and tapered legs on spade feet.

- *height 1.66m*
- £2,950 • S. & A. Thompson

Expert Tips

Some cabinets have been cut down to suit modern size preferences. Look carefully at the underside of the bases and top surfaces, and check for joins that should not be there.

Victorian Credenza ▲

- *circa 1860*

A Victorian ebonised credenza with oval painted porcelain panels with gilt mounts and banding .
- *110cm x 178cm x 37cm*
- £3,250   • Ranby Hall

Empire-Style Cabinets ▲

- 1880

One of a pair of Empire-style satinwood side cabinets, the central panelled cupboard with a lyre shaped ormolu mount, on tapered legs.
- *75cm x 42cm x 40cm*
- £1,385   • Ranby Hall

Japanese Cabinet ▲

- *Edo period*

A mizuya dansu, or cabinet, from the late Edo period in cryptomeria. The drawer fronts in Zelkdva.
- *175cm x 170cm*
- £7,000   • Gordon Reece

Biedermier Cabinet ▲

- 1920

A Biedermier light mahogany cabinet inlaid with figurative and floral designs.
- *height 130cm*
- £3,850   • Ranby Hall

Lacquered Corner Cabinet ▲

- 1750

A George III black lacquered corner cabinet, decorated with a chinoiserie style relief .
- *58cm x 90cm x 38cm*
- £2,950   • Mac Humble

Tibetan Chest ▲

- *circa 1890*

A Tibetan chest with carved and painted decoration depicting long life symbols.
- *94cm x 107cm*
- £2,300   • Great Grooms

Medicine Cabinet ▲

- *circa 1890*

Stripped and polished nickel plated bathroom cabinet.
- *45cm x 30cm x 15cm*
- £245   • After Noah (KR)

Canterburies

Mahogany Canterbury

- *circa 1870*

Victorian mahogany canterbury with three compartments. The side drawer with turned knob handles, finials and supports, with original porcelain castors.
- *height 62cm*
- £995 • A.I.G.

Mahogany Canterbury ▶

- *circa 1830s*

Early Victorian mahogany galleried and tiered dumb waiter, with turned supports and single drawer with turned handles, the whole standing on bulbous turned legs with brass castors.
- *100cm x 38cm*
- £2,200 • Old Cinema

Rosewood Canterbury ▼

- *circa 1790*

Mahogany canterbury comprising four sections with a single side drawer with circular ring handle, raised on square tapered legs with original brass casters.
- *height 39cm*
- £1,950 • John Clay

Victorian Canterbury ▲

- *circa 1880*

Victorian walnut canterbury of four sections, with pierced scrolled decoration above a lower shelf, on upturned scrolled legs.
- *height 55cm*
- £1,195 • The Swan

Walnut Canterbury ▶

- *circa 1880*

Victorian walnut canterbury with four sections with heavily carved and pierced floral designs, turned handles, and a single side drawer, the whole raised on turned legs with brass castors.
- *height 54cm*
- £1,295 • The Swan

Three-Compartment Canterbury
- *1880*

A Victorian walnut canterbury with three compartments and drawer to front. With pierced frieze to the sides and turned legs on brass castors.
- *44cm x 59cm x 38cm*
- £1,250
- Judy Fox

Sheraton Canterbury
- *1860*

A Sheraton mahogany, four-division canterbury with a half shaped carrying handle, removable division slides, and a single drawer to the base, with turned legs on brass castors.
- *66cm x 49cm x 43cm*
- £4,850
- Wakelin Linfield

Victorian Canterbury with Writing Slide
- *1880*

A Victorian walnut canterbury with writing slide and drawer on the base, with turned bun feet.
- *79cm x 61cm x 48cm*
- £2,500
- Judy Fox

George III Canterbury
- *1810*

George III mahogany canterbury with single drawer, standing on turned baluster feet on brass castors.
- *height 65cm*
- £2,850
- Mac Humble

Regency Canterbury
- *circa 1820*

A Regency mahogany canterbury with one drawer and four compartments and carved wreath decoration, on brass castors.
- *34cm x 65cm*
- £2,450
- C.H. Major

Chairs

Tapestry Armchair ▼
- *circa 1680*
A rare French hardwood armchair with tapestry cover.
- *height 1.21m*
- **£6,500** • **Raffety Walwyn**

Grotto Harp Stool ▼
- *circa 1850*
A grotto stool with scallop shell seat on acanthus cabriole legs and claw feet. The whole in gilt.
- *height 65cm*
- **£1,600** • **Lynda Franklin**

Regency Bergère ▶
- *circa 1810*
A very good, large Regency bergère chair.
- *height 96cm*
- **£6,200** • **C. Preston**

Biedermeier-Style Chair ▲
- *circa 1915*
A pair of Swedish masur birch chairs in cream ultra-suede.
- *height 93cm*
- **£4,900** • **R. Cavendish**

Sheraton Chair ▲
- *circa 1780*
An English green-painted chair decorated with floral designs.
- *height 90cm*
- **£4,600** • **O.F. Wilson**

Bamboo Chair ▼
- *circa 1830*
A Regency single chair painted to simulate bamboo.
- *height 87cm*
- **£175** • **O.F. Wilson**

Hall Chair ▼
- *circa 1850*
An English mahogany mid 19th-century hall chair, with scrolled arms and an extensively turned frame, the whole resting on bun feet. The chair is in perfect condition, and reupholstered, with a red and gold Gothic pattern.
- *height 98cm*
- **£1,800** • **Gabrielle de Giles**

Spindle-Back Nursing Chair ▼

- *circa 1820*
Lancashire spindle back nursing chair, with rush seat on turned legs.
- *134cm x 54cm x 54cm*
- £295　　　• Rod Wilson

Oak Corner Chair ▼

- *circa 1750*
Oak corner chair in the Chippendale style.
- *124cm x 70cm*
- £1,250　　　• Rod Wilson

Regency Dining Chairs ▲

- *1820*
A set of six regency chairs and two carvers, with curved back and sabre legs.
- *height 81cm*
- £12,500　　　• C.H. Major

Queen Anne Chair ▲

- *circa 1700*
Queen Anne oak transitional chair with good colour and patination.
- *146cm x 60cm x 51cm*
- £3,450　　　• Rod Wilson

Oak Country Chairs ▶

- *1840*
One of four oak country chairs, with carved top rail, pierced splayed splat, and solid seat, on square moulded legs.
- *94cm x 48cm x 41cm*
- £1,800　　　• Lacquer Chest

Nursing Chair ▲

- *1890*
Victorian nursing chair upholstered in calico with mahogany turned legs and original porcelain castors.
- *117cm x 70cm*
- £420　　　• Myriad

Expert Tips

You need to maintain the patina of a chair through regular waxing with a good quality beeswax that is non-staining. Constant polishing with a stained wax will darken the patina and compromise the attraction of the furniture.

Painted Fauteuils ▼
• *circa 1880*
One of a pair of fauteuils with
painted decoration to the entire
frame work of the chair, with
carved and turned decoration to
the arm supports and front legs.
• *height 86cm*
• £3,750   • O.F. Wilson

Walnut and Beech Fauteuils ▼
• *circa 1760*
One of a pair of walnut and beech
fauteuils, with finely carved floral
designs, scrolled arm supports and
serpentine moulded apron front,
Stamped 'ROVAMAION'.
• *height 110cm*
• £25,000   • O.F. Wilson

Louis XVI Chairs ▶
• *circa 1780*
One of a pair of lyre backed,
Louis XVI chairs, with a carved
oval seat rail and pale green
paint, raised on turned legs .
• *height 92cm*
• £8,500   • O.F. Wilson

Hepplewhite Armchair ▲
• *circa 1780*
Ebonised hepplewhite armchair
with shield back, curved arm
supports and straight tapered legs
with hand painted designs of
trailing foliage and ribboning.
• *height 96.5cm*
• £4,450   • O.F. Wilson

Louis XV Style Bergères ▲
• *circa 1880*
One of a pair of large Louis XV
style bergères, with a high arched
back and moulded decoration,
centred with a carved and gilded
floral design.
• *99cm x 71cm*
• £5,250   • O.F. Wilson

French Fauteuils ▼
• *circa 1870*
One of a pair of Louis XV
fauteuils stamped 'BOVD', with
carved top rail and front rail,
scrolled arm supports and hand
painted decoration, raised on
cabriole legs,.
• *height 89cm*
• £5,500   • O.F. Wilson

Walnut Master's Chair ▼
• *circa 1835*
A walnut master's chair with
carved foliate, scrolled and
scalloped crest surmounted by a
recumbent lion. The arms
composed of a series of S-scrolls
and C-scrolls headed by imposing
carved lion heads, these
surrounded by a carved mane
above a scallop motif. Standing
on shaped front legs with paw
feet and substantial rear legs on
brass castors.
• *150cm x 84cm*
• £18,500   • Anthony Outred

Recumbent Easy Chair

- *circa 1830*

One of a pair of rare matched English Regency 'Daws' patent 'Recumbent Easy Chairs', both bear the maker's stamp, with one chair bearing an original label for 'Bantings of Pall Mall'.

- *height 79cm*
- £18,500 • Freshfords

Small Swedish Chair

- *1780*

Small Swedish pine nursing chair in original condition with moulded oval back, standing on turned legs.

- *height 92cm*
- £850 • Augustus Brandt

Oak Hall Chair

- *1870*

Victorian oak hall chair with an architecturally carved back, raised on turned legs with good patina.

- *height 84cm*
- £375 • Elyot Tett

French Fauteuils

- *circa 1870*

One of a pair of fine French fauteuils, with a high padded back and wings, with carved and gilded foliate decoration to the back and arms, raised on turned legs.

- *height 149cm*
- £1,850 • Elyot Tett

Regency Mahogany Bergères

- *circa 1820*

A fine pair of Regency mahogany bergères decorated with ebony mouldings and turnings, with later cane and hide coverings.

- *width 66cm*
- £21,500 • Freshfords

Windsor Side Chairs ▼

- *circa 1810*
A pair of comb-back windsor side chairs with turned legs.
- *height 87cm*
- £145   • Castlegate

Invalid's Chair ▼

- *circa 1910*
An invalid's chair with original green upholstery.
- *height 1.36m*
- £190   • Lacquer Chest

George I Oak Chairs ▶

- *circa 1720*
A solid pair of George I oak chairs with good colour.
- *height 99cm*
- £595   • Red Lion

Louis XVI Bergère ▲

- *19th century*
A Louis XVI-style bergère with gold leaf on tapered, reeded legs.
- *height 1.06m*
- £1,395   • Red Lion

Simulated Bamboo Chairs ▲

- *circa 1820*
Set of six Regency simulated and painted bamboo chairs.
- *height 84cm*
- £1,200   • North West 8

French Dining Chairs ▼

- *circa 1885*
A set of eight French Empire-style dining chairs.
- *height 91cm*
- £4,500   • North West 8

Expert Tips

Large sets of chairs have often been broken up, and carvers manufactured from them. Check the wood match on the arms of the carver and, particularly, the size of the seat. The carver should be at least two inches wider than the other chairs.

Mahogany Hall Chair ▲

- *circa 1820*
English Regency period, of unusual shape, with sabre legs.
- *height 80cm*
- £4,650   • O.F. Wilson

Arts & Crafts Chair ▼
- **1890**
Arts and Crafts chair with curved arms and turned legs, with pressed brass inlay back.
- *height 115cm*
- **£550**　　　● Old Cinema

Rosewood Chair ▼
- **1860**
One of a pair of Victorian Rosewood chairs with shaped carved top rail.
- *height 82cm*
- **£795**　　　● Old Cinema

Expert Tips

If the chair is Queen Anne or George I, the condition is not so important. Later chairs should be in perfect condition.

Library Chairs ▲
- **1880**
One of a pair of library chairs with a hooped back, ten shaped spindles, circular seat, horseshoe stretcher base and fluted legs.
- *height 76cm.*
- **£725**　　　● Old Cinema

Berger Chair ▲
- **1880**
One of a pair of French chairs with a shaped tall cane back with padded shaped seat, and gilt shells carved at the top of the legs, standing on a pad foot.
- *height 108cm*
- **£725**　　　● Old Cinema

Oak Country Chair ▼
- **1810**
One of a pair of oak ladder-back chairs with a rush seat, standing on turned legs and pad feet.
- *height 104cm*
- **£495**　　　● Old Cinema

Chippendale Style Carver ▼
- **1880**
One of a set of Chippendale style mahogany chairs with swept arms, carved back splat and ball feet, with six dining chairs and two carvers.
- *height 105cm*
- **£6,500**　　　● Old Cinema

Windsor Chair

- *1820*

An early nineteenth century Windsor made from yew wood, with turned legs and arm rests.
- *height 88cm*
- £695 • Red Lion

French Mahogany Chair

- *1830*

French mahogany chair featuring a carved back with scrolled top rail, on turned legs with pad feet.
- *91cm x 49cm*
- £560 • John Clay

George II Library Chair

- *1760*

George 11 carved mahogany open library chair with back swept arms, on cabriole legs and scroll feet.
- *94cm x 72cm*
- £30,000 • Pimlico

Mahogany Chair

- *Early 19th century*

An English mahogany chair with carved top rail and pierced back splat with curved arms.
- *92.5cm x 45cm*
- £1,800 • C.H. Major

Nursing Chair

- *circa 1830*

Rosewood nursing chair with original rose decorated upholstery, on turned legs with castors.
- *89cm x 52cm*
- £950 • John Clay

Ladder Back Chairs

- *1820*

One of a set of six ladder back chairs with turned decoration on hoof feet, the carvers with splayed arms.
- *99cm x 57cm*
- £375 • Red Lion

Spindle Back Chair

- *1820*

One of a pair of spindle back chairs with rush seats and turned arm supports.
- *height 90cm*
- £1,820 • Red Lion

Laburnham Wood Chairs ▲
- *circa 1840*
One of a pair of laburnham wood ladder back chairs with concave seats, raised on straight square legs.
- *96cm x 51cm*
- **£780**   • Lacquer Chest

Giltwood Chair ▲
- *circa 1890*
Small giltwood French chair, delicately carved with roses and torchiere motifs, with original upholstered padded seat.
- *height 75cm*
- **£595**   • A.I.G.

Library Chair ▼
- **1870**
Light oak library chair with circular back scrolled arms and turned legs, with a circular padded green leather seat.
- *height 78cm*
- **£1,695**   • A.I.G.

William IV Chair ▼
- **1830**
One of a pair of William IV mahogany hall chairs, with circular turned back with scrolled supports, raised on turned front legs.
- *height 81cm*
- **£975**   • A.I.G.

Rococo Chair ◀
- **1730–1760**
One of a set of six Rococo chairs, of simple design, with carved back splat, raised on cabriole legs with scrolled decoration and hoof feet.
- *height 103cm*
- **£9,500**   • Augustus Brandt

Victorian Rosewood Chair ▲
- *circa 1860*
Victorian rosewood spoon back armchair, finely carved with floral designs and raised on scrolled legs fitted with casters..
- *height 96cm*
- **£1,895**   • A.I.G.

William IV Chairs ▲
- **1830**
One of a set of six mahogany William IV dining chairs, with shaped top rail and carved stretcher, raised on turned front legs.
- *height 85cm*
- **£2,995**   • A.I.G.

Pair of Fauteuils ▶

- *circa 1820*
A pair of early 19th-century French mahogany fauteuils with original tapestry.
- £1,900 • Sieff

Chinese Chairs ▲

- *circa 1820*
A rare pair of tall-backed Chinese hardwood chairs.
- *height 82cm*
- £680 • P.L. James

Chippendale Chair ▲

- *circa 1780*
With a pierced vase-shaped splat, solid seat and square chamfered legs with stretchers.
- *height 95cm*
- £1,450 • M.J. Bowdery

George III Elbow Chair ▲

- *circa 1800*
In mahogany, with lyre-shaped centre splat and turned supports.
- *height 85cm*
- £795 • M.J. Bowdery

Victorian Low Chair ▲

- *19th century*
A walnut low chair with carved decoration and turned legs terminating in casters.
- *height 76cm*
- £695 • Old Cinema

Mahogany Library Chair ▼

- *circa 1810*
An English library armchair with turned front legs.
- *height 94cm*
- £2,750 • Riverbank

Elbow Chair ▼

- *circa 1800*
An elbow chair in elm with remains of the original paint.
- *height 97cm*
- £850 • Lacquer Chest

325

Papier-Mâché Chair ▼
- *early 19th century*
An early nineteenth century lacquered papier-mâché chair with scrolled back, painted and heavily inlaid with mother of pearl, on cabriole legs.
- *132cm x 49cm x 42cm*
- £1,250 • S. Duggan

Convertible Library Chair ▲
- *19th century*
An unusual oak library chair that converts into a step ladder, with carved back and hinge within the seat.
- *87cm x 37cm*
- £1,200 • New Century

Tuscan Chair ▲
- *16th century*
A late sixteenth century Tuscan walnut country chair with leafy corbel finials and carved panels of entwined branches.
- *107cm x 49cm*
- £2,200 • Sign of the Times

Mahogany Wing Chair ▼
- *late 19th century*
George I-style mahogany wing chair with carved legs on claw and ball feet.
- *127cm x 94cm x 81cm*
- £3,350 • Harpur Deardren

William IV Library Chair ▲
- *1830–7*
A William IV carved walnut library chair with button back, turned decoration and heavily carved griffins.
- *89cm x 66cm*
- £4,950 • Pimlico

Satinwood Bergère Chair ▲
- *circa 1890*
A satinwood bergère chair with carved cane back and seat with scrolled top, standing on turned legs painted with a floral design.
- *height 73cm*
- £2,800 • Butchoff

Expert Tips

With winged chairs it is important to make sure that the arms and the wings of the chair are in firm condition as any movement will indicate damage.

Irish Hall Chairs ▶
- *1830*
One of a pair of fine mahogany hall chairs with the crest of McGarrel-Hog, County Antrim Ireland.
- *90cm x 43cm x 41cm*
- £2,700 • Lacquer Chest

Set of Dining Chairs ◀

- *circa 1835*

A set of eight William IV period mahogany dining chairs. Stamped: J. Porter, Cabinet Chairs & Sofa Manufacturer, Upholsterer, 166 High Street Camden Town. Each consisting of a panelled klismos tablet back, supported by shaped uprights which are in the form of stylised ionic columns with leaf motifs to capitals. With turned reeded legs and saber back legs.
- *89.4cm x 44cm*
- £16,500   • Anthony Outred

George I Dining Chairs ▲

- *circa 1720*

Set of walnut George I dining chairs, with shaped top rail, vase shaped back splat and moulded seat and rail, raised on cabriole legs, with turned cross rails.
- *97cm x 47cm*
- £14,000   • Wakelin Linfield

George IV Hall Chairs ▼

- *circa 1825*

A pair of George IV, mahogany hall chairs, with original painted armorials to the shaped and reeded backs, raised on reeded front legs with outswept rear legs.
- *85cm x 42.5cm*
- £4,950   • Wakelin Linfield

English Regency Chair ▲

- *circa 1830*

English Regency mahogany chair, with a shield back and a 'klismos' shaped seat, with carved and reeded designs.
- £3,500   • Mora Upham

William IV Library Chair ▲

- *circa 1835*

Outstanding William IV gentleman's library chair. The massive mahogany frame heavily carved with C scrolls and acanthus leaf designs. Supported on large brass castors.
- *102cm x 98cm*
- £7,950   • Wakelin Linfield

Tub/Desk Chair ▶

- *circa 1880*

French flame mahogany clysmos shaped tub/desk chair, the downswept arms decorated with gilt ormolu palmettos and supported by winged swans, raised on square tapered legs.
- *109cm x 68cm*
- £4,500   • Wakelin Linfield

Victorian Curved Back Ship's Chair ▼

- *circa 1880*
A Victorian walnut ship's chair, with curved back, circular padded seat on a cast iron base.
- *130cm x 57cm*
- £400 • Tredantiques

Biedermeier Armchairs ▼

- *circa 1900*
Pair of Biedermeier-style birchwood armchairs, with inlays of mother of pearl, satinwood and rosewood.
- *149cm x 60cm x 52cm*
- £5,900 • R. Cavendish

Oriental Elm Chairs ▼

- *18th century*
A pair of eighteenth century Southern Chinese elm chairs with cane seats.
- *104cm x 56cm x 48cm*
- £3,500 • Gerard Hawthorn

Child's Correction Chair ▲

- *1820*
A child's correction chair with turned ladder back and needlework seat, standing on splayed legs.
- *96cm x 33cm x 25cm*
- £1,100 • Mac Humble

Gripsholm Armchairs ▲

- *circa 1930*
Pair of Swedish Gripsholm armchairs with original paint on ball feet.
- *height78cm*
- £2,900 • R. Cavendish

Hepplewhite-Style Dining Chairs ▲

- *circa 1890*
A set of mahogany Hepplewhite-style dining chairs which include eight single chairs and two arm chairs. With splayed back, square moulded legs .
- *height 11ocm*
- £9,500 • Butchoff

William IV Nursing Chair ◄

- *1830–1837*
A William IV mahogany framed nursing chair with deeply scrolled arms and arched legs.
- *100cm x 60cm*
- £2,200 • John Clay

Chinese Armchairs

- *circa 1850s.*
One of a pair of Chinese arm chairs in padouk wood with original seats, from the Meiji period.
- *height 90cm*
- £3,950 • Wakelin Linfield

Ladder Back Chair

- *circa 1780*
Well proportioned 18th century ladder back chair made from elm with rush seat and good patina.
- *106cm x 57cm*
- £1,750 • Wakelin Linfield

Yew-wood Rocking Chair ▼

- *circa 1820s*
Yew-wood early 19th century rocking chair, with carved and turned decoration.
- *105cm x 49cm*
- £1,750 • Wakelin Linfield

Blade & Gilt Dining Chair

- *circa 1840*
One of a set of eight Harlequin blade and gilt japanned dining/salon chairs, with shaped seat rails, turned baluster legs, the black ground with pil work depicting flowers, foilage and birds.
- *90cm x 46cm*
- £5,800 • Wakelin Linfield

English Elbow Chairs

- *circa 1900*
Stylish pair of English elbow chairs in an Egyptian style, with carved heads and paw feet and hand worked signed tapestry upholstery in the Regency manner.
- *95cm x 62cm*
- £4,500 • Wakelin Linfield

Country Armchair ▶

- *circa 1700*
A rare traditional English country arm chair, the back with two vase shaped splats, with down swept arms on two turned supports, solid seat and turned front legs.
- *120cm x 55cm*
- £7,850 • Wakelin Linfield

Hepplewhite Chair

- *1785*
Hepplewhite mahogany chair. The shield back with pierced decoration above a concave leather upholstered seat, raised on square tapered legs.
- *98cm x 57cm*
- £26,000 • Wakelin Linfield

Italian Chair

- *circa 1870*
One of a pair of Italian walnut
chairs, heavily carved with
depictions of Pan, ram's heads,
and griffins, raised on claw feet.
- *height 154cm*
- **£18,000** • **Hatchwell**

Ladder Back Chair

- *circa 1820*
One of a pair George IV ash and
elm ladder back chairs, with
domed top rail above four
graduated ladders, on turned legs
standing on pad feet.
- *height 94cm*
- **£1,075** • **Great Grooms**

Court Chairs

- *circa 1810*
Pair of Chinese court chairs of
simple elegant form
- *100cm x 61cm*
- **£3,100** • **Gordon Reece**

Horseshoe Shaped Chair

- *circa 1800*
A single low horseshoe shaped
back rail chair. Originally low in
construction
- *82cm x 57cm*
- **£1,480** • **Gordon Reece**

Syrian Folding Chair

- *circa 1890*
Attractive and decorative,
folding, Syrian chair with inlaid
ivory stars, profusely carved with
scrolled, foliate designs
throughout.
- *height 105cm*
- **£485** • **Elyot Tett**

Regency Dining Chairs

- *circa 1820*
One of a set of eight Regency
mahogany dining chairs, with
pierced back splats, raised on
turned legs.
- *height 84cm*
- **£12,000** • **Barry Cotton**

Writing Chair ▲
- *circa 1840*

A fine 19th-century Portuguese carved rosewood writing chair.
- *height 98cm*
- £20,000 • Norman Adams

Provincial Fauteuil ▲
- *circa 1820*

An oversized French provincial walnut open armchair, with escargot feet, covered in moleskin.
- *width 1.15m*
- £1,950 • French Country

Red Walnut Chairs ▼
- *circa 1730*

A fine pair of red walnut chairs with cabriole legs.
- *height 96cm*
- £9,500 • Raffety Walwyn

Victorian Chairs ▼
- *circa 1885*

Set of four rosewood chairs with cabriole legs and pierced leaf decoration.
- *height 85cm*
- £950 • Castlegate

French Bergère ◄
- *19th century*

A pair of French bergères painted with scroll and shell motifs on scrolled feet.
- *height 1.03m*
- £2,550 • Lynda Franklin

Bedroom Chair ▲
- *circa 1880*

A French gold bedroom chair with original upholstery.
- *height 90cm*
- £190 • Lacquer Chest

Piano Chair ▲
- *circa 1860*

A mahogany balloon back revolving piano chair.
- *height 80cm*
- £550 • North West 8

Expert Tips
Beware overstuffed drop-in seats. If these have been pushed hard onto the frame, they may have put pressure on the rail joints, causing them to split.

Lamp Hanger Armchairs ◀

- *1830*
Pair of Chinese high backed lamp hanger armchairs with carved central slat.
- *110cm x 72cm*
- £1,450   • Gordon Reece

Walnut Armchairs ▼

- *circa 1880*
One of a pair of French armchairs in walnut with carved decoration depicting gothic cruettes and medieval masks.
- *150cm x 70cm*
- £7,800   • Wakelin Linfield

Wing Chair ▼

- *circa 1899*
19th century William & Mary style wingchair, with generous scrolled arm rests, raised on turned legs.
- *125cm x 105cm*
- £5,950   • Wakelin Linfield

Rope Back Oxford Chairs ▼

- *circa 1880*
One of a pair of rope back Oxford chairs, with turned legs and shaped seat.
- *height 88cm*
- £170   • John Clay

Georgian Armchair ▲

- *circa 1750*
Georgian armchair with shaped top rail and unusually carved willow tree splat, standing on square straight legs, and single bar stretcher.
- *96cm x 52cm*
- £1,500   • John Clay

Mahogany Armchair ▼

- *circa 1840*
Mahogany Chippendale armchair and three singles, with unusual pierced back splat.
- *height 96cm*
- £1,500   • John Clay

Swedish Rococo Armchairs ◀

- *1780*
One of a pair of Swedish Rococo armchairs with moulded frame, out turned arms, cabriole legs and padded seat. In original condition.
- *height 96cm*
- £8,000   • Heytesbury

Button Back Chair ▼

- *1830*

A William IV mahogany button back armchair, with padded scroll arms, standing on cabriole legs on brass castors.

- *160cm x 70cm x 90cm*
- £2,350 • Harpur Deardren

Chinese Export Chair ▼

- *circa 1860*

A rare Chinese chair made for the European market with balloon back and apron, heavily carved, raised on cabriole legs.

- *147cm x 56cm x 40cm*
- £975 • Fay Orton

Carved Oak Chairs ▲

- *1870*

A set of six nineteenth century English carved oak chairs, with heavily carved back splat, padded leather seat, and turned legs, in the Flemish style.

- *160cm x 44cm*
- £850 • Tredantiques

Panelled Oak Chair ▲

- *1640*

An oak arm chair with a carved panelled back and scrolled decoration on turned legs.

- *108cm x 61cm*
- £4,950 • Peter Bunting

Open Fronted Giltwood Chairs ▲

- *1850*

A pair of giltwood open fronted bergères with carved decoration, on cabriole and knurled feet.

- *67cm x 68cm*
- £6,500 • Ranby Hall

Empire-Style Armchairs ▲

- *circa 1890*

Pair of Empire style Swedish mahogany armchairs with ormolu mounts.

- *height 83cm*
- £6,500 • R. Cavendish

Rosewood Dining Chairs ▲

- *1820*

A Regency rosewood dining chair, one of a set of six, the concave top rail with fruitwood inlay, heavily gadrooned, on turned legs.

- *48cm x 47cm*
- £3,995 • Harpur Deardren

Painted Fauteuils ▼

- *circa 1760*

One of a pair of beechwood fauteuils with oval backs and gilt foliate designs over cream paint. Stamped 'Premy'.
- *height 83cm*
- £7,800   • O.F. Wilson

Regency Chairs ▼

- *circa 1820*

One of a pair of Regency faux rosewood chairs, with turned and gilded designs, raised on sabre legs.
- *height 82cm*
- £2,750   • O.F. Wilson

Ebonised Beechwood Chairs ▲

- *circa 1880*

One of a pair of ebonised beechwood chairs with rush seats, influenced by William Morris.
- *height 84cm*
- £220   • O.F. Wilson

French Louis XV Fauteuils ▲

- *circa 1760*

Pair of Louis XV fauteuils with curved top rail, inverted arm supports and serpentine front rail, raised on cabriole legs.
- *height 84cm*
- £5,250   • O.F. Wilson

Mahogany Armchair ◄

- *1880*

One of a pair of mahogany Chippendale style armchairs, with a heavily carved serpentine top rail and pierced back splat, raised on carved cabriole legs.
- *height 95cm*
- £8,800   • Butchoff

Directoire Armchair ▼

- *circa 1795*

Fine directoire mahogany armchair, with scrolled top rail, pierced back splat, and turned arm supports.
- *height 86cm*
- £2,500   • O.F. Wilson

Empire Bergère ▼

- *circa 1815*

Mahogany Empire bergère, with turned top rail and curved, padded arms.
- *height 94cm*
- £2,8501   • O.F. Wilson

Expert Tips

The more chairs in a set, the greater the value. A pair will be worth more than twice the value of a single chair, and a set of eight perhaps 20 times as much.

Hepplewhite Armchairs ▼
- *circa 1770*
A pair of shield-back Hepplewhite armchairs with the decoration restored as new.
- *height 83cm*
- £3,850   • P.L. James

Gothic Painted Chairs ▼
- *19th century*
A pair of Victorian Gothic red-painted chairs with turned legs, Gothic tracery and a pierced backrest with finials.
- *height 89cm*
- £640   • Myriad

Gilt Wood Chair ▲
- *19th century*
George I-style chair in carved gilt wood with green upholstery.
- *height 85cm*
- £4,000   • Browns

Gothic Armchairs ▲
- *19th century*
Pair of Gothic armchairs with fine tracery.
- *height 1.1m*
- £4,850   • C. Preston

Expert Tips

The Victorians introduced suites of sofas, armchairs, chairs without arms and, sometimes, footstools. It is rare to find these pieces together; even pairs of armchairs are uncommon.

Arts and Crafts Chair ▼
- *circa 1860*
An early arts and crafts English chair in the style of Pugin.
- *height 83cm*
- £1,500   • Riverbank

French Empire Chairs ▼
- *circa 1830*
One of a set of six mahogany chairs with scrolled arms.
- *height 72cm*
- £5,950   • O.F. Wilson

French Leather Armchair ▼
- *circa 1880*
A French button leather armchair with turned legs.
- *height 69cm*
- £975   • Youll's

Chaises Longues & Day Beds

Cuban Chaise Longue ▲
- **1880**
A Cuban mahogany bergère longue with serpentine back and padded seat, on claw feet.
- *91cm x 193cm x 94cm*
- **£5,750**   • Old Cinema

Mahogany Chaise Longue ▲
- **19th century**
Victorian mahogany chaise longue with scrolled padded back and seat, raised on turned baluster legs.
- *43cm x 197cm x 76cm*
- **£1,995**   • Old Cinema

German Chaise Longue ▲
- *circa 1820*
German Biedermeier chaise longue, the birchwood frame with scrolled back, arms and legs.
- *95cm x 183cm x 70cm*
- **£9,800**   • R. Cavendish

Louis XVI Chaise Longue ▼
- *circa 1890*
Double-ended chaise longue in Louise XVI style.
- *length 1.7m*
- **£2,700**   • North West 8

French Chaise Longue ▼
- *circa 1900*
Mahogany walnut Louis XVI style meridienne.
- *length 84cm*
- **£1,650**   • French Room

Victorian Chaise Longue ▲
- *circa 1870*
Recently upholstered chaise longue dating from the Victorian period. Presented with original marble castors and brass fittings.
- *length 2.13m*
- **£1,900**   • Gabrielle de Giles

Expert Tips

Chaise longues should be elegant and have great style, and can be a focal point of any room. They can be employed in a multitude of ways: at the foot of a bed, in a hall or as a daybed. Swept feet, although attractive, are prone to splitting or breaking so check them carefully before making a purchase.

Mahogany Chest of Drawers ▲

- *circa 1890s*
Louis XVI style Swedish mahogany chest of four long drawers with tapered legs and ormulu mounts and a marble top.
- *83cm x 77cm*
- £2,900   • R. Cavendish

Miniature Chest of Drawers ▲

- *circa 1890*
Miniature rustic oak chest, with six small drawers and original turned wooden handles.
- *30cm x 38cm*
- £160   • Lacquer Chest

William & Mary Chest of Drawers ▲

- *circa 1690*
Excellent and rare William & Mary chest of drawers with two short and three long drawers, the top, sides and drawer fronts decorated with reserves of floral marquetry on well figured walnut.
- *93cm x 96cm x 59cm*
- £48,000   • Wakelin Linfield

Plum Chest of Drawers ◄

- *circa 1840*
Unusual plum chest of four deep drawers with a fan holly-wood inlay to each corner turned handles, standing on turned legs.
- *height 120cm*
- £5,850   • Denzil Grant

Victorian Mahogany Chest ▲

- *circa 1880*
Victorian mahogany chest of drawers. The upper section with six small drawers above three long drawers, with turned wooden handles, standing on a straight base, with small raised feet.
- *118cm x 110cm*
- £1,250   • Old Cinema

Chest of Drawers ◄

- *circa 1890*
One of a pair of burr walnut veneered pedestal chest of four drawers.
- *height 89cm*
- £1,750   • The Swan

Dutch Chest of Drawers ▲
- *mid 18th century*
Dutch mahogany chest of drawers, of serpentine form with oval brass mounts.
- *78cm x 75cm x 47cm*
- **£7,800**   • **M. Luther**

Louis XVI Commode ▲
- *1790*
Louis XVI commode with brass moulding and gallery on a white marble top.
- *88cm x 110cm x 55cm*
- **£10,000**   • **O. F. Wilson**

Figured Mahogany Chest ▲
- *19th century*
Figured mahogany and pine chest with banding and graduated drawers, raised on bun feet.
- *120cm x 120cm*
- **£770**   • **Drummonds**

William and Mary Chest ▲
- *1690*
Rare William and Mary chest of drawers in walnut. The top, sides and drawer front decorated with reserves of floral marquetry. Raised on original bun feet.
- *94cm x 96cm x 60cm*
- **£48,000**   • **M.W. & H.L.**

Campaign Chest ▼
- *early 19th century*
A colonial rosewood chest consisting of two sections with four drawers on bracket feet.
- *93cm x 77cm x 35.5cm*
- **£3,200**   • **M. Luther**

Victorian Chest ▲
- *19th century*
Victorian mahogany chest of drawers with turned handles and four drawers resting on bun feet.
- *130cm x 120cm*
- **£825**   • **Drummonds**

George III Chest of Drawers ▲
- *circa 1760*
Rare English George III oak chest of drawers with oval brass mounts, on shaped bracket feet.
- *77cm x 76cm x 44cm*
- **£4,450**   • **M. Luther**

Dutch Chest of Drawers ▶

• *circa 1725*
An excellent early 18th century
Dutch chest of drawers of
serpentine form, with four
graduated long drawers. The top
quarter veneered and walnut
strung. This is an exceptionally
small example of this type of
furniture.
• *75cm x 79cm*
• **£18,750**   • Wakelin Linfield

Collector's Chest ▲

• *circa 1880*
Mahogany collector's chest of
eight small drawers with wooden
bar with lock and key.
• *28cm x 33cm*
• **£170**   • Lacquer Chest

Louis XV Style Commode ▲

• *circa 1880*
Louis XV style bombe commode,
with violet marble top with three
long drawers, veneered in
rosewood and mahogany with
marquetry panels, profusely gilded
with foliate bronze ormolu
mounts.
• *102cm x 115cm*
• **£5,500**   • Hatchwell

George III Oak Chest of Drawers ▶

• *circa 1817*
George III chest of drawers with
two short and three long drawers,
with boxwood banding and brass
handles, standing on shaped
bracket feet.
• *90cm x 88cm*
• **£1,425**   • Rushlight

English Mahogany Chest of Drawers ▼

• *circa 1780*
Fine English Mahogany chest of
two small and three long drawers
standing on plain bracket feet.
• *height 106cm*
• **£2,550**   • C. Preston

Oak Coffer ▲

• *circa 1780*
George III oak chest with carving
to the front standing on square
straight legs.
• *height 56cm*
• **£6,850**   • Paul Hopwell

Mahogany Chest of Drawers ▲

• *circa 1880*
Georgian mahogany chest of
drawers, consisting of three deep
drawers with original brass swan
neck handles, on low bracket
feet.
• *85cm x 115cm*
• **£1,500**   • Drummonds

Oak Chest of Drawers ◀

- *circa 1680*
A 17th-century oak chest of drawers, with moulded decoration and brass mounts.
- *height 90cm*
- £2,500   • Angel

Georgian Chest ▼

- *circa 1790*
With pierced, latticed brass mounts, on bracket feet.
- *height 78cm*
- £950   • Albany

Flame Mahogany Chest ▼

- *circa 1885*
Round-cornered chest of drawers with bun feet.
- *height 86cm*
- £650   • Fulham

Sword Chest ▶

- *circa 1620*
A continental sabre or sword chest on shaped legs.
- *length 1.44m*
- £3,650   • Red Lion

Georgian Tallboy ▲

- *circa 1820*
A late Georgian mahogany, seven-drawer tallboy with oval brass handles and replacement pediment, on shaped, bracket feet.
- *height 2.09m*
- £2,850   • Old Cinema

Oak Chest on Stand ▲

- *circa 1740*
Chest with four tiers of drawers above stand with hoof foot.
- *height 1.36m*
- £4,975   • Red Lion

French Commode ▲

- *circa 1890*
A French commode chest with range marble top, ormolu mounts and floral inlay designs.
- *height 89cm*
- £1,480   • Ranby Hall

Kusuri Dansu ▼

- *circa 1890s*

A Japanese Kusuri Dansu (storage chest) with small drawers, from the Meiji period.

- *50cm x 43cm*
- £1,495   • Gordon Reece

Burr Walnut Tall Boy ▶

- *circa 1740*

A good George II period burr-walnut tall-boy with original metalwork. The top surmounted with a canted concave cornice above three short drawers and three graduated long drawers, all drawers having herringbone inlay and cross banded with panels of distinctively figured walnut and fitted with open brass plate handles, with fluted canted corners terminating in an ogee point. The lower section with moulded lip above three long graduated drawers flanked by canted fluted corners headed and terminating in ogee points.

- *191cm x 109cm*
- £25,500   •Anthony Outred

Mahogany Chest of Drawers ◀

- *circa 1890*

One of a pair of small Victorian mahogany chest of four drawers.

- *height 93cm*
- £1,380   • The Swan

Bombe Commode ▲

- *circa 1890*

Swedish serpentine fronted, walnut bombe commode, with cross banded designs and gilt brass mounts raised on splayed legs.

- *82cm x 92cm x 20cm*
- £2,250   • Hatchwell

Biedermeier Tallboy ▲

- *1842-1843*

Biedermeier birchwood tallboy with a gentleman's chest interior signed and dated: Carl Christian Hoff, Trondhjem, Norway.

- *140cm x 118cm*
- £8,800   • R. Cavendish

Lacquer Commode ▶

- *circa 1860*
English bombé commode,
chinoiserie painted and lacquered.
- *height 92cm*
- £8,000 • David Ford

Italian Commode ▲

- *circa 1895*
Venetian amboyna commode on
splayed legs with scrolled feet.
- *height 92cm*
- £4,850 • Lamberty

Large Chest of Drawers ▲

- *circa 1800*
A George III chest of drawers
with original brass handles on
splayed, bracket feet.
- *height 1.2m*
- £1,100 • Castlegate

Bombé Commode ▲

- *circa 1876*
An Italian, bombé serpentine
commode in figured burr walnut
and mounted on cabriole legs.
- *height 83cm*
- £4,250
- M.Wakelin & H. Linfield

Italian Commode ▲

- *circa 1785*
A double bow-fronted Italian
commode, made in the 18th
century and painted in the early
19th, with découpage decoration.
(Découpage is the art of using
paper cutouts to decorate
furniture and accessories such as
boxes and trays, after they have
been sanded and painted. The
finished object which has been so
decorated looks and feels, after
the application of a protective
sealant, like fine enamel).
- *height 78cm*
- £5,850 • Browns

Chest on Chest ▼

- *circa 1760*
Figured mahogany chest on chest
with original brass handles.
- *height 2.1m*
- £10,400 • Chambers

Expert Tips

*Furniture with a wax finish
should be polished no more
frequently than every few weeks
or so. To be properly protective,
the surface needs time to harden
between polishes.*

Miniature Chest ◀

- *circa 1880*
A Cuban mahogany miniature
chest of drawers with rounded
corners and plinth base.
- *height 75cm*
- £1,650 • Walpole

Spanish Oak Coffer ▼

- *circa 1680–1700*
Spanish coffer with elaborate geometric carving, standing on a square base.
- *59cm x 137cm x 52cm*
- **£2,750**   • Rod Wilson

Margot Fonteyn's Chest of Drawers ▼

- *1820*
An unusual decorated chest of drawers. Provenance: the Prima Ballerina, Margot Fonteyn.
- *97cm x 103cm*
- **£5,250**   • Pimlico Antiques

Small Carved Coffer ▲

- *circa 1680*
A well-carved late seventeenth century oak coffer in good original condition.
- *53cm x 108cm x 46cm*
- **£1,400**   • Rod Wilson

Heavily Carved Coffer ▲

- *circa 1680*
Oak coffer with bold carving and superb colouring and patination.
- *195cm x 144cm x 47cm*
- **£1,650**   • Rod Wilson

Mahogany Chest of Drawers ▼

- *circa 1800*
Mahogany chest of drawers with five long drawers with brass fittings, standing on bracket feet.
- *118cm x 107cm x 56cm*
- **£1,975**   • Rod Wilson

Oak Coffer ▼

- *circa 1670*
An oak coffer carved with a central rose and foliate designs. Standing on straight square legs.
- *45cm x 105cm x 75cm*
- **£1,295**   • Rod Wilson

Large Mahogany Chest of Drawers ▲

- *circa 1760*
A rare oversized mahogany chest of drawers with exceptional colour and patination, raised on feet.
- *119cm x 94cm x 52cm*
- **£2,450**   • Rod Wilson

Wellington Chest ▼

- *circa 1835*

Unusually tall rosewood Wellington chest and with finely figured rosewood, the rectangular top with moulded lip, with eight drawers with wooden pulls, with hinged and locking stile, the whole raised on a plinth.
- *56.5cm x 53cm*
- **£5,500** • **Anthony Outred**

William & Mary Chest of Drawers ▲

- *circa 1690*

William & Mary chest of two short and three long drawers on turned bun feet, the whole in oyster laburnum with broad cross banding to the side, top and drawer fronts.
- *84cm x 94cm x 26cm*
- **£24,500** • **Wakelin Linfield**

Mahogany Chest of Drawers ▲

- *circa 1860*

Flame mahogany, marble topped, chest of drawers with good colour and patination, one long single drawer above three deep drawers, standing on scrolled bracket feet.
- *92cm x 74cm*
- **£1,850** • **Drummonds**

Himalayan Kist ▶

- *circa 17th century*

Fine Himalayan pine chip slab Kist (chest) with deeply carved designs, from the Indian state of Himachal Pradesh.
- *56cm x 130cm*
- **£780** • **Gordon Reece**

French Commode ▲

- *1880*

French marquetry commode of small proportions, with serpentine top and fine gilt ormolu mounts.
- *79cm x 74cm*
- **£5,500** • **Butchoff**

Biedermeier Tallboy ▶

- *1820-1830*

A rare narrow Swedish mahogany Biedermeier tallboy with one narrow and five wider drawers with ormulu mounts, standing on gilt paw feet.
- *136cm x 67cm*
- **£4,500** • **Rupert Cavendish**

William IV Chest of Drawers ▲

- *1830–1837*

William IV mahogany chest with carved pilasters and turned wooden handles on bun feet
- *120cm x 110cm*
- £1,350　　• Old Cinema

Tibetan Scripture Table ▲

- *circa 1890*

A red lacquered Tibetan scripture table with gilding and painted floral decoration.
- *54cm x 80cm x 28cm*
- £1,000　　• Great Grooms

Miniature Wellington Chest ▲

- *19th century*

Miniature Wellington chest of drawers made from mahogany with turned wooden handles on a plinth base.
- *40cm x 36cm x 25cm*
- £975　　• Ashcombe House

Victorian Mahogany Chest ▼

- *1890*

A flame mahogany chest of drawers with two short drawers above four long drawers, with turned handles on bun feet.
- *128cm x 118cm*
- £1,250　　• Old Cinema

Victorian Chest of Drawers ▼

- *19th century*

Georgian bow fronted, mahogany chest of drawers, with four drawers and turned handles, raised on bun feet.
- *140cm x 118cm*
- £1,075　　• Drummonds

Graduated Chest of Drawers ▶

- *1765*

A good flame mahogany Irish chest of drawers with two short drawers above six graduated drawers with brass mounts on shaped bracket feet.
- *165cm x 83cm x 44cm*
- £12,500　　• Wakelin Linfield

George II Chest ◀

- *circa 1755*

George II mahogany chest of drawers with four tiers of drawers on shaped bracket feet.
- *70cm x 68cm*
- £8,750　　• C.H. Major

Carved Chest-on-Chest ▲

- *circa 1770*

A George III mahogany chest-on-chest with a carved dental course, canted and fretted corners with original brass handles on bracket feet.
- *170cm x 150cm*
- £6,500　　• C.H. Major

Satinwood Commode ▶

- *circa 1899*
A pair of satinwood marquetry demi lune George III style commodes, with exceptional marquetry inlay.
- *94cm x 149cm*
- £30,000
- Butchoff

Georgian Chest of Drawers ▲

- *circa 1780*
Georgian chest of drawers with two small and three long graduated drawers, with brass ring handles, supported on bracket feet.
- *95cm x 95cm x 51cm*
- £1,450
- Vale Antiques

Choba Dansu ▶

- *19th century*
A Japanese Meiji period Choba Dansu (document chest), made from kiri wood with good markings and original metalwork.
- *93cm x 76cm*
- £2,995
- Gordon Reece

Mahogany Chest of Drawers ▲

- *circa 1890*
Mahogany chest of four drawers with small turned handles, on splayed bracket feet.
- *108cm x 105cm*
- £1,650
- C. Preston

Scandinavian Chest of Drawers ▼

- *circa 1880*
Scandinavian serpentine fronted chest of drawers with moulded top and three long drawers with large foliate brass handles and lockplates. With original lilac paint, standing on bracket feet.
- *height 83cm*
- £6,800
- Augustus Brandt

Miniature Chest of Drawers ▼

- *circa 1880*
Victorian mahogany miniature chest of drawers.
- *24cm x 21cm*
- £295
- Amandini

Davenports

Victorian Davenport ▶
- *circa 1870*
An unusual Victorian burr walnut rising top davenport, enclosing a fitted interior and pull out ratcheted writing slope.
- *90cm x 60cm*
- **£4,350**   • **Amandini**

English Regency Davenport ▲
- *circa 1820*
Regency rosewood davenport stamped "Johnstone & Jeans, New Bond Street, London", with pierced gallery and leather writing slope.
- *80cm x 57cm*
- **£4,500**   • **C.H. Major**

Walnut Davenport ▲
- *circa 1860*
Fine Walnut Victorian davenport with original leather, inlaid with satinwood, with four side drawers, pierced brass rail and maple interior.
- *height 88cm*
- **£1,950**   • **Old Cinema**

Burr Walnut Davenport ▼
- *circa 1860*
Burr walnut davenport with piano lid, central cupboard flanked by eight small side drawers with turned wood handles.
- *98cm x 62cm*
- **£3,750**   • **The Swan**

Rosewood Davenport ▼
- *circa 1820*
Small Regency rosewood davenport, with pierced brass gallery and pen drawer to the side of a writing slope with unusual side action.
- *88cm x 34cm*
- **£3,995**   • **W. John Griffiths**

Expert Tips

The name davenport came from an entry in the book of Captain Davenport in the 1790s. Look out for the following:

fine vaneer in walnut
panelled back
original inkwells
pen trays
mother of pearl escutcheons
secret drawers

Up to 1840 their style was quite plain, but after 1840 davenports tended to be more feminine, with scrolled supports.

Walnut Davenport ◀
- *circa 1840*
An English figured walnut davenport with stunning matched sunburst veneers. The sliding top is fitted with a hinged pen and inkwell drawer raised above four graduated drawers and four dummy panel drawers supported on a shaped plinth base.
- *79cm x 46cm*
- **£7,500**   • **Freshfords**

Chinese Davenport ▼

- *circa 1830*

An exported small Chinese davenport with chinoise decoration. On bun feet.
- *height 92cm*
- £5,500   ● Martin-Taylor

Ebony Davenport ▲

- *circa 1830*

With maple-wood fitted interior and new black-leather top.
- *height 92cm*
- £7,500   ● R. Hamilton

Victorian Davenport ▼

- *19th century*

Davenport with inkwells, geometric inlay designs and side drawers with ceramic handles.
- *height 79cm*
- £1,280   ● Castlegate

Piano Pop-up Davenport ◄

- *circa 1860*

Burr walnut with fitted interior and sliding writing surface with red leather inlay. Has carved supports on bun feet.
- *height 90cm*
- £4,250   ● Judy Fox

Expert Tips

Small and desirable, the davenport is often found in poor condition because these attractive pieces of furniture tended to be neglected.

Rosewood Davenport ▼

- *19th century*

Original leather insert with well turned side columns.
- *height 84cm*
- £2,850   ● Ranby Hall

Walnut Davenport ▶

- *19th century*

With lockable pen and pencil compartment and walnut gallery.
- *height 81cm*
- £1,550   ● Old Cinema

Desks

Pedestal Desk ▶

- *circa 1850*

A superb example of a mid 19th-century burr walnut pedestal desk with all original brass handles, raised on bun feet.
- *height 75cm*
- **£5,750** • **Brown's**

Satinwood Desk ▲

- *circa 1890*

Sheraton revival high quality Victorian inlaid satin wood pedestal desk with two side compartments. The base containing single drawer, stamped 'Maple & Co.
- *124cm x 104cm*
- **£12,500** • **J. & T. Stone**

Expert Tips

There are many kneehole desks in circulation which did not start out in life in that role. Some have been converted from chests of drawers; to establish this check that the drawers look complete and that the veneers match. Desks with kneeholes but drawers on only one side should be avoided. It is most probable that they are converted from washstands.

Partners' Desk ▶

- *circa 1745*

Victorian partners' desk in mahogany. Pedestals can be reversed. Smaller than usual.
- *length 1.51m*
- **£4,250** • **Antique Warehouse**

Pedestal Desk ▲

- *circa 1930*

A continental art deco pedestal desk made in birch with two panelled cupboards with four sliding shelves and three drawers with locks and keys.
- **£1,600** • **C. Newland**

Walnut Secretaire ▼

- *circa 1870*

A rare, open-fronted secretaire with walnut birch and ebony stringing. With lockable cabinet.
- **£3,250** • **C. Newland**

Victorian Partners' Desk ◀

- *circa 1880*

A 19th-century mahogany desk with reversible full hide leather pedestals.
- *length 1.76m*
- **£4,950** • **Antique Warehouse**

Louis XVI Desk ▲

- *circa 1800*
Louis XVI Swedish Gustavian desk, with long drawer with, plain gilt ring handle, raised on slender tapered legs.
- *75cm x 80cm*
- **£1,950**   • R. Cavendish

Mahogany Partner's Desk ▲

- *circa 1825*
A historically important George IV mahogany partner's desk by Robert Lawson for Gillows of Lancaster. With a central drawer above the kneehole flanked by a bank of four drawers.
- *79cm x 183cm*
- **£95,000**   • Anthony Outred

Satinwood Writing Table ▼

- *1870*
Satinwood and ormolu writing table. The top with egg and dart moulded rim, above two side drawers, by Wright & Mansfield.
- *74cm x 110cm*
- **£10,500**   • Butchoff

Edwardian Desk ▼

- *1908*
Edwardian rosewood writing desk with inlaid foliate designs on the drawers, standing on tapered legs with brass castors.
- *73cm x 107cm x 57cm*
- **£3,800**   • Judy Fox

George II Partner's Desk ▲

- *circa 1755*
George II ebony-inlaid mahogany partners pedestal desk with a rich, untouched patina. Raised on a plinth base.
- *80.5cm x 139.5cm*
- **£68,000**   • Anthony Outred

Birchwood Desk ▲

- *circa 1890s*
Swedish free standing veneered Biedermeier style birchwood desk. The top with leather insert and three drawers, above two pedestals with panelled doors.
- *76cm x 143cm*
- **£5,900**   • R. Cavendish

Georgian Mahogany Desk ▲

- *circa 1820s*
Georgian kneehole mahogany desk with leather top, two long and two small drawers, original laurel wreath brass handles.
- *79cm x 101cm*
- **£1,350**   • Old Cinema

Figured Walnut Desk ▶
- *1837–1901*

Continental figured walnut desk with ebonised mouldings and architectural columns with eight drawers either side of the kneehole.
- *80cm x 166cm x 85cm*
- **£6,975** • Old Cinema

Louis XVI Bureau Plat ▲
- *circa 1780*

A Louis XVI bureau plat cross banded and veneered, in the manner of Reisener with leather lined top. The panelled frieze with three drawers, on square tapering fluted legs, mounted with chandelles.
- *98cm x 110cm*
- **£6,500** • Butchoff

Mahogany Partner's Desk ▼
- *circa 1810*

A large George III partner's desk in figured light mahogany. Provenance: the American author Sydney Sheldon.
- *162cm x 89cm*
- **£20,000** • Pimlico

Satinwood Desk ▼
- *1870*

A lady's satinwood writing desk wiith leather writing top on tapered legs with brass castors.
- *81cm x 72cm x 58cm*
- **£2,800** • Judy Fox

Carlton House Desk ▼
- *1890*

Mahogany Carlton House desk with a brass gallery and a horseshoe arrangement of drawers, including a raised writing slide, on tapered legs.
- *143cm x 76cm*
- **£9,000** • Judy Fox

Louis XV Bureau Plat ▲
- *circa 1900*

Fine French Louis XV style mahogany bureau plat with gilt bronze mounts.
- *80cm x 145cm x 76cm*
- **£9,500** • Hatchwell

The small lady's writing desk, also known as an escritoire, if well proportioned, delicate and featuring good veneers, will always be desirable and achieve a high value. The Carlton House desk is also in demand among collectors, especially if it is in satinwood and has applied painted decoration. When purchasing this type of desk, keep a keen eye on the elegance, lightness and quality of the overall concept of the design, taking special note of the legs.

Lady's Writing Desk ▼
- 1825
Rare lady's writing desk in burr ash. Stamped "Gillows of Lancaster".
- 93cm x 73cm x 53cm
- £14,500   • Ashcombe House

Walnut Kneehole Desk ▲
- 1870
A walnut desk with four small drawers each side of the kneehole, and one central drawer and cupboard, with leather writing top, standing on bracket feet and moulded base.
- 78cm x 107cm x 66cm
- £2,400   • Old Cinema

Victorian Oak Desk ◀
- 1880
An unusual oak desk with four drawers to the left of the kneehole, and a unusual filing frame with cupboard and leather writing top.
- 77cm x 153cm x 82cm
- £1,995   • Old Cinema

Chinese Lacquered Desk ▲
- 1870
A red lacquer Chinese desk with three drawers above ornately carved kneehole.
- height 95cm
- £1,585   • Ranby Hall

Satinwood Writing Table ▼
- 1870
A nineteenth century satinwood bow-fronted writing table with three drawers and curved apron front and brass fittings on straight legs with brass castors.
- 79cm x 114 cm x 55cm
- £1,350   • Great Grooms

Mahogany Dining Table ▶
- *circa 1860s*

A mid-Victorian mahogany circular dining table. The moulded top in two halves, on a large ring-turned shaft with gadrooned stem, on an X-frame base with scrolled feet and countersunk brass castors. Provenance: by repute, William Hesketh Lever, 1st Viscount Leverhulme (d.1925).
- *75cm x 274.5cm*
- £80,000 • Anthony Outred

English Dining Table ▼
- *circa 1880*

Mahogany circular dining table. With finely figured mahogany tilt top, cross-banded, with a gadrooned edge above a cross-banded frieze, raised on a tri-form, panelled pedestal, with large scrolled feet.
- *height 75cm*
- £32,000 • Anthony Outred

Regency Dining Table ▼
- *circa 1825*

A late regency mahogany dining table with excellent figuring. The top with rounded corners and a reeded moulded edge, incorporating five identically sized leaves. The top supported on a mahogany concertina bearer mechanism, on eight slender reeded legs.
- *length 364cm*
- £28,500 • Anthony Outred

Mahogany Extending Dining Table ◀
- *circa 1820*

Regency mahogany extending dining table by Thomas Wilkinson of London. The scissor-action, 'lazy-tongs' mechanism for extending the table was covered by the King's patent.
- *length 379cm*
- £32,000 • Freshfords

Mahogany Table ▶

- *19th century*
A mahogany extending dining table with two inserts standing on turned legs.
- *height 225cm*
- £4,600 • Drummonds

Two-Leaved Dining Table ▲

- *1830*
Early nineteenth century two-leaf mahogany draw-leaf dining table raised on turned and carved legs with original castors.
- *width 130cm*
- £16,500 • Midwinter

Cuban Mahogany Table ▼

- *19th century*
A Victorian Cuban mahogany three-leaf dining table of wide proportions with heavily carved and turned legs on brass castors.
- *300cm x 105cm*
- £4,950 • Old Cinema

Circular Dining Table ▼

- *early 19th century*
Irish-made circular mahogany table with three leaves, on carved and turned legs with original castors.
- *114 cm x 180cm*
- £5,200 • Drummonds

Swedish Dining Table ▲

- *circa 1920*
Swedish Biedermeier-style dining table made from birchwood, with masur birch banding on a square pedestal base.
- *136cm x 196cm*
- £10,500 • R. Cavendish

Extending Table ▼

- *circa 1840*
Cuban mahogany-top extending table, with tapered legs and brass tips. Supplied complete with original mahogany chairs.
- *width 180cm*
- £3,750 • Abbey Green

Doors

Metal-Studded Door ▼
• *circa 1885*
Substantial Gothic oak, metal-studded door, with six panels and Gothic tracery.
• £2,450   • Drummonds

Teardrop Loft Door ▼
• *circa 1870*
Game-larder or loft door of possible French origin.
• *height 2.34m*
• £1,475   • Annette Puttnam

Pine Overdoor ▲
• *circa 1890*
Carved pine overdoor in the George I style.
• *height 77.5cm*
• £450   • Westland & Co.

Double Doors ▲
• *circa 1910*
A pair of six-panelled mahogany doors with brass furniture.
• *height 2.8m*
• £3,500   • Ian Spencer

Italian Double Doors ▼
• *circa 1790*
A pair of giltwood and ivory painted double doors, centred by jasper panels.
• *height 2.95m*
• £15,000   • Westland & Co.

Carved Oak Doorway ▼
• *circa 1850*
A finely carved oak doorway in the Venetian renaissance manner.
• *height 2.49m*
• £3,200   • Westland & Co.

Baroque-Style Overdoor ◄
• *circa 1890*
A carved wood overdoor in the baroque manner.
• *height 1m*
• £1,600   • Westland & Co.

355

Gothic Oak Door ▲
- *1880*

Gothic oak paneled door and surround with a glazed panel with gothic mouldings, with iron letter box and handle.
- *280cm x 87cm*
- **£875**   • **Drummonds**

Oriental Door Frame ▼
- *circa 1860*

Oriental door within a deep surround with a panel set over the door, carved with amorphous designs.
- *200cm x 104cm*
- **£2,100**   • **Drummonds**

Stone Door Surround ▼
- *1880*

Victorian door with stone surround, incorporating a gothic arch with stone coining, housing a grey painted door with cast iron fittings.
- *211cm x 105cm*
- **£4,250**   • **Drummonds**

Set of Twelve Mahogany Doors ◄
- *circa 1900*

Set of twelve flame mahogany five panelled doors with brass door furniture.
- *221cm x 91cm*
- **£3,300 each**   • **Drummonds**

Queen Anne Doorcase ▲
- *circa 1710*

A rare Queen Anne carved pine Baroque doorcase with a projecting canopy on scrolled brackets. The central frieze carved with the attributes of war flanked by fluted Tuscan pilasters.
- *308cm x 189cm*
- **£14,500**   • **Westland & Co.**

Georgian Style Door ▲
- *1870*

Georgian style oak door and surround. The arch with wood mouldings and the surround with lead glazing bars.
- *300cm x 124cm*
- **£1,580**   • **Drummonds**

Victorian Mahogany Door ▲
- *circa 1840s*

Early Victorian mahogany four-panelled door with original brass fittings.
- *200cm x 75cm*
- £2,100   • Drummonds

Gothic Oak Doors ▲
- *Late 19th century*

Oak-panelled doors with gothic tracery, original brass fittings and stained glass windows.
- *101cm x 226cm*
- £850   • Drummonds

Linen Fold Door ▼
- *18th century*

Light oak linen fold panelled door.
- *300cm x 120cm*
- £1,350   • Drummonds

Indian Panelled Doors ▼
- *18th century*

Antique panelled door with elaborate strapwork and floral decorated brass.
- *192cm x 120cm*
- £1,250   • Gordon Reece

Victorian Slatted Doors ▲
- *19th century*

A pair of Victorian oak-slatted doors with original scrolled iron hinges and fittings.
- *165cm x 219cm*
- £1,475   • Drummonds

Panelled Mahogany Door ▲
- *19th century*

Mahogany six panelled door, with no fittings and the original "PRIVATE" sign on the front.
- *200cm x 90cm*
- £875   • Drummonds

Expert Tips

Church doors with their elaborate iron hinges are sought after by garden designers for use within a garden scheme

Dressers

Maplewood Chiffonier ▼
- **1885**

An early Victorian maplewood chiffonier with open shelf and back board and two glazed cupboard doors flanked by turned barley twist columns.
- *138cm x 107cm x 40cm*
- **£2,950**   • S. Duggan

Dresser Base ▼
- **18th century**

A provincial eighteenth century oak dresser base with three drawers with original swan neck handles on turned legs.
- *83cm x 210cm x 49.5cm*
- **£4,995**   • Great Grooms

Regency Sideboard ▲
- *circa 1825*

A Regency mahogany breakfront sideboard with ebony stringing on turned and fluted tapered legs.
- *95cm x 152cm x 72cm*
- **£3,800**   • Tredantiques

Oak Court Cupboard ▲
- **1740**

A Welsh oak court cupboard with three moulded cupboards above three drawers and two panelled cupboards on moulded bracket feet.
- *191cm x 146cm x 52cm*
- **£7,500**   • Peter Bunting

Painted Pine Dresser ▶
- *circa 1790*

An pine Welsh dresser with painted grain effect.
- *211cm x 159cm x 52cm*
- **£5,500**   • Rod Wilson

Altar Dresser ▲
- **1775**

Antique Chinese altar dresser with four drawers with a humped back stretcher beneath cylindrical legs with two cross numbers.
- *83cm x 46cm x 22cm*
- **£4,500**   • Gordon Reece

Breakfront Sideboard ▲

- *circa 1800*

Mahogany Breakfront D Shaped sideboard, one cellaret drawer and a shallow centre drawer over a linen drawer. Raised on four front finely reeded legs and two turned back legs.
- *94.5cm x 168cm x 66.5cm*
- **£16,500** • **Wakelin Linfield**

George III Oak Rack ▲

- *circa 1790*

George III oak wall mounted dresser with moulded and shaped cornice and three shelves flanked either side with additional shelving.
- *height 97cm*
- **£3,250** • **Paul Hopwell**

Oak Dresser Base ▲

- *circa 1786*

George III oak dresser base. Carved drawers with geometric designs, with brass drop handles, the whole raised on turned front legs.
- *height 97cm*
- **£22,500** • **Paul Hopwell**

Pine Glazed Dresser ▲

- *circa 1840*

Pine dresser with three glazed doors enclosing three shelves, with two long drawers and cupboards below with brass knob handles.
- *235cm x 170cm*
- **£1,600** • **Drummonds**

Pine Dressers ▶

- *circa 1820*

One of a pair unusual narrow pine dressers or bookcases with panelled backs and adjustable shelves.
- *width 67cm*
- **£3,350** • **C. Preston**

Miniature Dresser ◀

- *circa 1890*

Miniature English oak dresser with moulded gallery, turned supports all above carved panel doors and turned bun feet.
- *height 47cm*
- **£225** • **Great Grooms**

Oversized Dresser ▲

- *circa 1840*

Large pine dresser painted pea green, with moulded pediment and two central cupboards flanked by four deep long drawers with brass handles, standing on a straight base.
- *height 425m*
- **£3,650** • **Drummonds**

359

Welsh Dresser ▲

- *circa 1740*
A Welsh oak dresser with three shelves flanked by spice panelled cupboards, standing on bracket feet and brass fittings.
- *186cm x 136cm x 49cm*
- £9,500 • Rod Wilson

Welsh Deuddiarw ▲

- *circa 1740*
An original eighteenth century Welsh deuddiarw. The upper section with cornice above panelled cupboards.
- *177cm x 104cm x 52cm*
- £5,950 • Rod Wilson

Victorian Mahogany Chiffonier ▶

- 1850
Victorian mahogany chiffonier with long drawer above two panelled cupboards, standing on small bun feet.
- *91cm x 42cm x 104cm*
- £590 • Tredantiques

Court Cupboard ▼

- 1691
A Westmoreland oak court cupboard, with overhanging cornice and turned decoration with turned wood handles and good patina.
- *160cm x 133cm x 56cm*
- £7,950 • Peter Bunting

French Mahogany Dresser ▼

- 1860
A fine Victorian figured mahogany dresser with two shelves, the back having a scallop design, with two drawers and panelled cupboards below, standing on bun feet.
- *169cm x 123cm x 46cm*
- £1,800 • Tredantiques

English Oak Dresser ◀

- *circa 1760*
An oak dresser with carved frieze above three shelves with a solid back, the dresser base with three tiers of drawers flanked by two moulded cupboard doors.
- *191cm x 181cm x 59cm*
- £5,500 • Rod Wilson

Dumb Waiters & Whatnots

Three-Tier Stand ▼
- 1890

A three-tier mahogany cake stand with fruitwood banding
- *height 89cm*
- £195   • Great Grooms

Victorian Cake Stand ▼
- 1890

A Victorian mahogany three-tiered cake stand with fruitwood banding.
- *height 95cm*
- £280   • John Clay

Butler's Tray ▲
- 1850–70

A Victorian mahogany butler's tray resting on a Georgian-style stand.
- *54cm x 65.5cm*
- £795   • Great Grooms

Rosewood Cake Stand ▲
- *circa 1880*

Rosewood circular cake stand with a turned base.
- *height 19cm*
- £400   • Sign of the Times

Mahogany Buffet ▼
- 1870

A flame mahogany buffet with two shelves, one single long drawer and two shelves below, standing on turned legs.
- *152cm x 113cm x 44cm*
- £2,375   • Harpur Deardren

Rosewood Whatnot ▼
- 1825

A rosewood four-tier whatnot with small baluster turnings. Single drawer to the lower shelf, on original brass castors.
- *125cm x 46cm x 41cm*
- £5,250   • Wakelin Linfield

Wall Shelves ◀
- *circa 1840*

A hanging wall shelf with ormolu decorative mounts made from kingswood.
- *59cm x 39cm x 15cm*
- £1,650   • Butchoff

Mahogany Washstand ▲

- *circa 1860*

Mahogany washstand inset with a circular pink marble top and two shelves, supported by pillared turned legs on a triangular base, raised on shallow bun feet.

- *85cm x 32cm*
- **£980** • **Lacquer Chest**

Mahogany Plant Stand ▲

- *circa 1870s*

Fine Victorian mahogany plant stand, with a slender baluster column on three curved legs with drop turned finial.

- *90cm x 29cm*
- **£495** • **Old Cinema**

Walnut Whatnot ▼

- *circa 1870s*

Victorian walnut whatnot, the scrolled gallery with turned finials, above four graduated triangular tiers, with carved apron and turned supports.

- *130cm x 57cm*
- **£550** • **Old Cinema**

Teak Whatnot ▼

- *1890*

Victorian corner whatnot made from teak with scrolled gallery, above four graduated tiers, supported by turned Solomonaic columns.

- *height 127cm*
- **£450** • **Salem Antiques**

Regency Rosewood Whatnot ▲

- *circa 1825*

English Regency rosewood whatnot of small proportions with three well-figured tiers, raised on finely turned supports, the middle tier having a fitted drawer with small brass circular handles.

- *102cm x 38cm*
- **£4,650** • **Freshfords**

French Etagère ▲

- *1890*

French etagère with pierced brass gallery, single narrow drawer with brass handle and two shelves below, on ebonised shaped legs.

- *height 94cm*
- **£675** • **Vale Antiques**

Lowboys

Dutch Lowboy ▼
- *18th century*
Dutch marquetry walnut with lobed top above three drawers on slender cabriole legs on pad feet.
- *75cm x 86cm x 55cm*
- **£9,500** • **S. Duggan**

Plank Top Lowboy ▼
- *18th century*
An early eighteenth century lowboy, with serpentine plank top, above three drawers, with herring bone stringing. Mounted on four cabriole legs.
- *71cm x 86cm x 51cm*
- **£14,500** • **Wakelin Linfield**

Regency Lowboy ◄
- *circa 1820*
An English 19th-century lowboy, in walnut, with three drawers and brass mounts, the whole on cabriole legs.
- *height 72cm*
- **£2,700** • **Mora Upham**

Expert Tips

Lowboys were sometimes made in solid wood, particularly oak, and sometimes with straight legs. The most sought after, however, are those that are veneered and on cabriole legs.

George I Lowboy ▲
- *1720*
A George I walnut lowboy, three drawers with moulded apron front, standing on cabriole legs with a pad foot.
- *92cm x 62cm*
- **£3,480** • **Dial Post House**

Dutch Lowboy ▲
- *circa 1750*
A fine, Dutch lowboy, with serpentine front and quarter drawers each side of the two main drawers. Original handles and fine marquetry decoration.
- *height 77cm*
- **£8,250**
- **Ronald G. Chambers**

Mahogany Lowboy ▼
- *circa 1740*
A Chippendale period, well-figured mahogany lowboy with three drawers, two small below one large, with original brass mounts, the whole raised on cabriole legs with pad feet. The piece has an unusually shaped kneehole and apron, reflecting its original purpose as a dressing-table.
- *height 71cm*
- **£3,500** • **L. & E. Kreckovic**

Mirrors

Brass Mirror ▼
- *1800*

A brass circular mirror with
foliate designs and two
candlestick holders attached to a
pierced metal back.
- *26cm x 42cm*
- £350   • New Century

Gilded Overmantle Mirror ▲
- *circa 1860s*

A Victorian overmantle mirror
with serpentine arch and a gilded,
moulded edge
- *130cm x 64cm*
- £850   • Old Cinema

Overmantle Mirrors ▲
- *circa 1850s*

One of a pair of Victorian
moulded giltwood overmantle
mirrors.
- *128cm x 65cm*
- £1,950   • Old Cinema

Oak-Framed Mirror ▲
- *19th century*

An English carved oak mirror,
with ogée moulding above a
dental course and carved frieze,
the mirror flanked by turned
pillars.
- *120cm x 90cm*
- £480   • Old Cinema

Queen Anne Mirror ▲
- *circa 1710*

Rare black lacquer Queen Anne
table mirror of large proportions,
retaining the original glass with
bureaux front on turned bun feet.
- *95cm x 48cm*
- £4,900   • Ashcombe House

Expert Tips

*The dressing table or table
mirror reached its zenith in the
Queen Anne period.*

Mahogany Table Mirror ▲
- *1780*

George III mahogany serpentine
fronted mirror on ogée moulded
feet with original patination.
- *height 58cm*
- £1,550   • Ashcombe House

William IV Giltwood Mirror ▲

- *circa 1835*

William IV period giltwood and gesso convex mirror with a carved frame depicting acorns and foliage, surmounted by a crest in the form of a seated deer upon a rocky ground, the mirror fitted with sconces in the form of serpents.

- *112cm x 76cm*
- £7,500 • Anthony Outred

Irish Mirror ▶

- *circa 1850s*

Irish oval mirror with a blue and gold strip border on the mirror.

- *71cm x 46cm*
- £2,500 • Looking Glass

Venetian Giltwood Mirror ▲

- *circa 1780*

Venetian giltwood mirror with lion, armorial crest and trophies, with trailing foliate designs to the rim, with original plate glass.

- *84cm x 47cm*
- £3,800 • O.F. Wilson

Italian Giltwood Mirror ▼

- *circa 1780*

Italian giltwood swept mirror with carved scrolling, decorated with trailing ivy and small pink roses.

- *49cm x 44cm*
- £650 • Augustus Brandt

Venetian Mercury Plate Mirror ▼

- *circa 1850s*

Small mid 19th century Venetian blue oval glass mirror, etched with floral sprays, with original mercury plate mirror.

- *56cm x 43cm*
- £2,250 • Looking Glass

Regency Girandole Mirror ▲

- *circa 1820s*

Regency giltwood convex mirror, with ebonised slip surrounded by ropework design, surmounted by a giltwood deer and grapevines, at the base stylised leaf designs flanked by two scrolled candle holders of candle holders.

- *104cm x 56cm*
- £4,250 • Looking Glass

Victorian Mirrors ▲

- *circa 1870s*

One of a pair of rectangular giltwood mirror with arched top surmounted by a stylised acanthus leaf, flanked by giltwood urn finials, and a carved border with foliate swag decoration.

- *94cm x 53cm*
- £3,250 • Looking Glass

Regency Mirror ▲
- *1830*
A Regency wall mirror with a carved frieze depicting shepherds and their flock within architectural details .
- *height 57cm*
- **£2,350** • **Ashcombe House**

Oval Gilt Mirror ▼
- *1895*
Victorian oval gilt mirror with a carved moulded border.
- *height 125cm*
- **£1,400** • **Looking Glass**

Swedish Mirror ▲
- *circa 1860*
Ninteenth century giltwood and painted overmantle mirror with original finish, after a neo-classical style.
- *178cm x 170cm*
- **£6,900** • **M. Luther**

Regency Mirror ▲
- *1820*
Regency convex gilt mirror surmounted with an eagle and decorated with carved acanthus leaf and beading.
- *117cm x 64cm*
- **£3,680** • **Looking Glass**

George III Mirror ▶
- *1800*
A George III carved wood mirror with water gilding in a chinoiserie style.
- *134cm x 82cm*
- **£3,300** • **Looking Glass**

Victorian Mirror ▲
- *1880*
Victorian oval gilt mirror in the Adam style with applied floral swag and ribbon detail.
- *87cm x 82cm*
- **£1,350** • **Looking Glass**

Wall Mirror ▲
- *Early 18th century*
An unusual early eighteenth century wall mirror.
- *100cm x 80cm*
- **£4,800** • **M. Luther**

Regency Mirrors ▲
- *circa 1820s*

One of a pair of Regency pagoda mirrors surmounted by a pineapple, flanked by Corinthian columns.
- *109cm x 37cm*
- £4,200 • Looking Glass

Regency Mirror ▲
- *circa 1820s*

Fine Regency giltwood mirror with central ivory plaque of a bird with flowers, with reeded columns, on a straight base.
- *82.5cm x 51cm*
- £2,250 • Looking Glass

Queen Anne Mirror ▶
- *circa 1710*

Small Queen Anne maroon lacquered mirror with original plate.
- *60cm x 29cm*
- £1,500 • O.F. Wilson

Venetian Mirror ▼
- *circa 1610*

Venetian Moorish style mirror, flanked by two elongated narrow mirrors, within a carved wood frame with spires, finials, and a raised floral carving.
- *height 117cm*
- £5,800 • Augustus Brandt

Pier Mirrors ▶

- *circa 1860*
Graduated pair of French
giltwood pier mirrors with vines
and grapes carved into the frame.
- *160cm x 96cm*
- £18,500 • Guinevere

Dressing Table Mirror ▲

- *1780*
George III mahogany dressing
table mirror with shield back glass
and shaped drawer front with
satinwood banding.
- *height 70cm*
- £1,780 • Ashcombe House

Walnut Table Mirror ▲

- *1714–27*
A George I walnut toilet mirror
with single concave drawer to
base on bracket feet.
- *25.5cm x 17.7cm*
- £795 • Great Grooms

Venetian Mirror ▲

- *1780*
Venetian giltwood mirror with
lion and armorial cresting.
Original condition and plate.
- *84cm x 53cm*
- £3,800 • O.F. Wilson

Florentine Mirror ▶

- *circa 1750*
A Florentine silvered and
giltwood mirror with a carved
stylised acanthus leaf frame.
- *130cm x 75cm*
- £6,500 • Guinevere

Rococo Mirrors ▲

- *circa 1760*
One of a pair of Venetian rococo
giltwood shield mirrors with
asymmetric carved decoration.
- *65cm x 65cm*
- £11,000 • Guinevere

Regency Mirror ▶

- *circa 1830*

A Regency gilt mirror, decorated with balls, vine eglomise and with Corinthian columns.

- *height 82.5cm*
- £1,350   • Looking Glass

Chippendale Mirror ▲

- *circa 1760*

A fine Chippendale-period gilded, carved-wood mirror.

- *height 2.32m*
- £125,000 • Norman Adams

George II Wall Mirror ▲

- *circa 1760*

A walnut, fret-cut mirror with gilded motif and inner slip.

- *height 91.5cm*
- £875   • J. Collins

English Mirror ▼

- *circa 1890*

An English carved giltwood mandalin and flute top mirror.

- *height 72.5cm*
- £650   • Looking Glass

Regency Dressing Mirror ▼

- *circa 1820*

A mahogany dressing mirror with three drawers outlined with boxwood stringing.

- *height 65cm*
- £950   • J. Collins

George III Mirror ▼

- *circa 1770*

A good, oval Chippendale mirror.

- *height 1.33m*
- £16,500   • P.L. James

Console and Mirror ▼

- *circa 1830*

A mahogany console and mirror, with architectural pillars supporting the pediment.

- *height 250cm*
- £4,850   • Ranby Hall

369

Italian Giltwood Mirror ▲
- *circa 1820s*
Italian giltwood mirror with carved and moulded frame and trailing floral designs.
- *43cm x 35.5cm*
- **£475**   • **Looking Glass**

Victorian Bow Mirror ▲
- *circa 1890s*
Victorian oval giltwood mirror with a trailing foliate design terminating in a bow.
- *142.4cm x 94cm*
- **£5,600**   • **Looking Glass**

Georgian Mirror ▼
- *circa 1800*
Georgian mahogany dressing mirror with three drawers and ebony stringing, standing on bracket feet.
- *52cm x 51cm*
- **£440**   • **Salem Antiques**

Seahorse Mirror ▼
- *1860*
Circular bevelled plate mirror, within an architectural frame. The pediment gilded with a gilt lyre flanked by seahorses, with gilt ormolu butterfly mounts.
- *107cm x 87.3cm*
- **£2,800**   • **Looking Glass**

Giltwood Oval Mirror ◄
- *circa 1890*
Giltwood oval mirror with two candle holders with scrolled floral decoration, raised on splayed legs.
- *height 87cm*
- **£895**   • **Drummonds**

Watergilt Mirror ▲
- *circa 1850s*
Oval watergilt mirror with four corner acanthus scrolls.
- *73.6cm x 58.4cm*
- **£1,850**   • **Looking Glass**

Victorian Giltwood Mirror ▲
- *circa 1870s*
Victorian gilded oval mirror with foliate carving and flowers, with scrolling and crest above.
- *135cm x 82.5cm*
- **£4,230**   • **Looking Glass**

Expert Tips

The condition and thickness of the plate glass provide a useful guide for distinguishing a genuine period mirror from a fake. Look out for pitted rust and dampness. The colour of old plate is greyer than colourless modern glass and gives a softer reflection.

Miscellaneous

Blackamoor Torchères ▼
- *mid 19th century*
Fruitwood torchères with serpentine tops, figures and acanthus-leaf body on tripod base.
- *height 91cm*
- £2,850   • Lesley Bragge

Library Steps ▼
- *circa 1900*
Oak library steps with carved decoration to the sides.
- *height 47cm*
- £500   • Lacquer Chest

Painted Jardinère ▲
- *late 19th century*
Painted steel body with floral scrolled handles.
- *height 21cm*
- £90   • Riverbank

Corner Washstand ▲
- *circa 1800*
Mahogany, two-drawer washstand, the top with a rounded splashback.
- *height 86.5cm*
- £1,250   • J. Collins

Cane Jardinière ▼
- *late 19th century*
Gilt, cane top with leaf decoration and cloven feet.
- *height 101cm*
- £550   • Youll's

Birdcage ▼
- *circa 1940*
A 20th-century birdcage of rectangular shape with covered back and sides.
- *height 31cm*
- £22   • Curios

Regency Bookcarrier ◄
- *circa 1810*
A fine Regency bookcarrier in the bullock style with a drawer below.
- *width 43cm*
- £2,350   • P.L. James

Birdcage ▲
- *circa 1850s*
Mid 19th century French
birdcage, modelled on the Notre
Dame of Paris.
- *210cm x 110cm*
- £6,950 • Wakelin Linfield

Cast Iron Trivet ▲
- *circa 1830s*
Early Victorian cast iron trivet
with a scrolled design within a
lattice border.
- *26cm x 42cm*
- £295 • Old Cinema

French Plant Holder ▲
- *1880*
Dark green French circular tôle
plant holder, standing on gilt paw
feet with a laurel wreath design
around the lip, and a cartouche of
a hand painted classical scene.
- *height 49cm*
- £495 • Goodison Paraskeva

Georgian Tray ▼
- *circa 1820*
Georgian oval tray, with
fruitwood inlay around the rim,
brass handles and a central shell
design.
- *length 54cm*
- £275 • Salem Antiques

Mahogany Piano Stool ▼
- *circa 1880s*
An ornate Victorian mahogany
piano stool with a music
compartment under seat with
turned and scrolled decoration.
- *56cm x 51cm*
- £550 • Old Cinema

Luggage Rack ▼
- *circa 1870*
Yew-wood luggage rack, standing
on four tapered square legs with
shaped apron.
- *45cm x 72cm*
- £1,250 • John Clay

Rosewood Music Stand ▲
- *circa 1820s*
Early 19th century rosewood
music stand with candle holders,
supported by a turned column on
a tripod base with scrolled feet.
- *height 150cm*
- £2,200 • Old Cinema

Torchère Stand ▲
- *circa 1890*
A Regency style torchère stand
decorated with three female
busts, with stylized acanthus
leaf designs, surmounted by a black
marble top on a tripod base
standing with gilt paw feet.
- *height 114cm*
- £450 • Vale Antiques

French Basin Stand ▼

- *19th century*

A French mahogany basin stand with carved lyre-shaped supports.

- *height 77cm*
- £495   ● Rod Wilson

Mahogany Tray ◄

- *19th century*

A mahogany campaign butler's tray on a mahogany trestle stand.

- *70cm x 47cm*
- £2,250   ● S. Duggan

Mahogany Basin Stand ▲

- *circa 1740*

Eighteenth century oak basin stand on turned supports, the draw within the stretcher, on splayed legs.

- *height 86cm*
- £1,250   ● Rod Wilson

George III Bucket ►

- *circa 1790*

A mahogany brass-bound bucket of navette shape.

- *height 33cm*
- £2,350   ● J. de Haan

Bamboo Umbrella Stand ▲

- *1920*

A provincial bamboo painted umbrella and stick stand with original metal liner.

- *height 80cm*
- £340   ● Myriad

Expert Tips

Umbrella stands, mainly from the Victorian era, can be made in a variety of materials, including cast iron, brass and mahogany. They are attractive items to decorate the entrance to any home. All should have their original zinc liners, which are used to prevent rot from wet umbrellas and walking sticks.

Empire Birdcage ◄

- *circa 1820*

French Second Empire mahogany birdcage with pierced front and architectural pillars with gilt mounts.

- *35cm x 60cm*
- £1,500   ● C.H. Major

Butler's Tray ◀

- *circa 1810*
A mahogany butler's tray and reading stand with turned and tapered legs.
- *height 32cm*
- £480   • P.L. James

English Washstand ▼

- *circa 1820*
In mahogany with inlay, three drawers and brass handles.
- *height 1.25m*
- £850   • Youll's

Turquoise Jardinière ▲

- *circa 1875*
A jardinière on stand in a turquoise glaze. Probably French.
- *height 116cm*
- £1,950   • Kenneth Harvey

Gothic Stand ▲

- *late 19th century*
A stand of pentagonal form with gothic tracery.
- *height 110cm*
- £450   • Youll's

Papier Maché Tray ▼

- *circa 1800*
A red lacquered papier maché tray showing Oriental decoration.
- £2,850   • P.L. James

Edwardian Gong ▲

- *circa 1913*
An oak and horn gong with baton and trophy plaque.
- *height 34cm*
- £165   • Castlegate

Victorian Hall Stand ▲

- *circa 1890*
Oak hall stand with ceramic tiles and marble-topped drawer.
- *height 206cm*
- £950   • Old Cinema

Screens

Paper Screen ◀

- *19th century*

A pair of two-fold paper screens painted in ink on a gold ground.

- *length 53.3cm*
- **£4,800** • **Gregg Baker**

Silk Screen ▼

- *circa 1850*

Silk screen on a brass stand and crossbar with a gilt wood base.

- *height 1.41m*
- **£750** • **Castlegate**

Japanese Screen ▶

- *18th century*

Lacquer border, textile surround, painted pagodas and figures.

- *length 3.63m*
- **£1,600** • **Lynda Franklin**

Japanese Fold Screen ◀

- *19th century*

One of a pair of six-fold screens with a Chinese poem in Japanese calligraphy, on buff ground.

- *1.72m x 3.78m*
- **£11,000 (pair)** • **Gregg Baker**

Silk Screen ▲

- *early 20th century*

Two-fold silk screen painted in ink with birds flying above rose mallow on which are a praying mantis and a cricket.

- *1.81m x 1.17m*
- **£6,800** • **Gregg Baker**

Chinoiserie Screen ▲

- *mid 18th century*

An adjustable screen that changes to a side table. On a bronze tripod base.

- *height 1.06m*
- **£2,200** • **Riverbank**

Expert Tips

Oriental screens are becoming more collectable all the time, but the best markets are still in Japan and the USA.

Two-Fold Paper Screen ▲

- *20th century*

A Taisho period screen painted in ink and colour with hydrangea, peony and poppy.

- *1.81m x 1.62m*
- **£8,600** • **Gregg Baker**

Chinese Fire Screen ▲

- *circa 1860*
Chinese fire screen embroidered with peonies, chrysanthemums, butterflies and birds, in silk with gold threads. Supported by a mahogany stand.
- *78cm x 62cm*
- £385   • Younger Antiques

Dutch Leather Screen ▲

- *circa 1720*
Dutch leather panel screen, with a Japanese influenced painting showing birds, bamboo, water lilies and pink chrysanthemums.
- *153cm x 200cm*
- £5,800   • Anthony Sharpe

Soolmaker Screen ▲

- *1690*
Dutch six fold screen by Soolmaker, with a painted romantic landscape of an impression of Italy.
- *126cm x 244cm*
- £3,800   • Butchoff

Louis XV Screen ▼

- *circa 1760*
Louis XV period six fold painted canvas screen, showing children playing the game of leapfrog, hoops and flying kites, within a pastoral setting.
- *length 198cm*
- £8,500   • O.F. Wilson

Victorian Beadwork Screens ▼

- *circa 1840*
One of a pair of excellent Victorian pole screens in walnut carved frames containing fine examples of beadwork of the period.
- *height 140cm*
- £4,500   • Wakelin Linfield

Victorian Screen ▲

- *1870*
A good size painted leather four fold screen in the 18th century style, painted with floral arrangements.
- *160cm x 153cm*
- £4,200   • Butchoff

Regency Rosewood Screen ▲

- *circa 1820*
Regency rosewood pole screen with floral tapestry panel, on a turned pedestal and tri-partite platform base.
- *height 143cm*
- £545   • R. & S. Antiques

Settees & Sofas

Carved Canapy Sofa ▲
- *circa 1870*
A Louis XV style sofa with painted, moulded wooden frame carved with flowers, a curved back and padded seat with small padded arm-rests, above a carved apron, on fluted cabriole legs.
- *104cm x 154cm x 60cm*
- **£2,350** • **Ranby Hall**

Giltwood Settee ▲
- *circa 1860*
A French Louis XVI-style giltwood sofa, with carved oval padded back and seat, serpentine-fronted, elaborately carved apron, standing on cabriole legs.
- *102cm x 187cm x 65cm*
- **£2,850** • **Ranby Hall**

Expert Tips

The settee was a direct descendant of the wooden settle, which was the earliest form of furniture to accommodate two or more people. Sofa is a later term and has come to mean 'a well-unholstered settee'.

Empire Sofa ▼
- *1805*
Empire sofa attributed to Ephraim Stahl, with fluted legs and painted and gilded decoration.
- *91cm x 197cm x 74cm*
- **£8,800** • **R. Cavendish**

Regency Settee ▲
- *1830*
A Regency mahogany classical style settee with a serpentine apron front with curved back and scroll ends, and curved cornucopaiae style legs terminating in foliate castors.
- *78cm x 200cm x 67cm*
- **£3,650** • **Ranby Hall**

French Canapy Sofa ▲
- *circa 1860*
A French giltwood canapy with padded carved oval back and seat. With profusely carved serpentine apron, on carved cabriole legs.
- *119cm x 174cm x 62cm*
- **£2,850** • **Ranby Hall**

Gustavian Suite ▶

- *circa 1880*
Suite of Gustavian-style furniture
including a sofa, pair of armchairs
and four chairs.
- £5,600 • R. Cavendish

Chesterfield Sofa ▲

- *circa 1900*
A two-seater chesterfield with
mahogany bun feet and brass
castors, covered in hessian.
- *width 1.72m*
- £1,250 • Annette Puttnam

Leather Sofa ▶

- *circa 1840*
A 19th-century, two-seater
upholstered sofa, in original black
leather, with brass castors and
mahogany legs.
- *width 2.06m*
- £3,600 • D. Martin-Taylor

Three-Seater Sofa ◀

- *19th century*
Upholstery and cushions in good
condition.
- *width 1.92m*
- £1,850 • Ranby Hall

Silk Sofa ◀

- *circa 1860*
A beige and gold silk-covered
sofa with gilt decoration.
- *width 1.2m*
- £2,200 • Mora Upham

Sofa & Two Chairs ▲

- *circa 1860*
A red silk sofa with two chairs. •
width 1.62m (sofa)
- *width 64cm (chairs)*
- £1,200 • Mora Upham

'Dolphin' Sofa ▶

- *circa 1820*
North German birchwood and
masur birch sofa covered in
calico. With noticeable tunnel
armrests with dolphin designs.
The whole resting on scrolled
feet.
- *width 2.1m*
- £7,500 • R. Cavendish

Regency Sofa ▲

- *circa 1810*

Regency beech wood faux rosewood sofa with double scroll arms and a carved moulded back with scrolling, inlaid with brass decoration.
- *93cm x 195cm*
- **£5,250** • **R. & S. Antiques**

Walnut Sofa ▶

- *circa 1890s*

Small late Victorian sofa with arched padded button back and carved walnut frame with small scrolled arms, the whole on slender turned legs.
- *94cm x 133cm*
- **£1,200** • **John Riordan**

High Button Back Sofa ▲

- *circa 1860*

Victorian rosewood button back sofa with moulded top rail, sides and arms, curved apron and four cabriole legs below, and four splayed legs to the rear.
- *length 156cm*
- **£2,400** • **Drummonds**

Chesterfield Sofa ▼

- *circa 1860*

Victorian Chesterfield sofa upholstered in Venetian damask, with padded moulded back and seat, standing on turned legs.
- *length 197cm*
- **£1,950** • **The Swan**

French Louis XVIII Sofa ▲

- *circa 1780*

French Louis XVIII sofa with painted and moulded carved wooden frame, curved back and a padded seat and small padded arm rests, above a carved apron of fluted cariole legs, by D. Julienne.
- *82cm x 191cm*
- **£6,200** • **Augustus Brandt**

Italian Hallbench ▶

- *circa 1790*

Italian pine hall bench with a straight back swept arms, heavily carved apron and short cabriole legs.
- *82cm x 193cm*
- **£4,700** • **Anthony Sharpe**

Stools

Gothic Gallery Seats

- *circa 1860*

A pair of American carved polychrome and gilded Gothic gallery seats, labelled Ketcham & Rothschild Inc, Makers Chicago, USA. With scroll arms to each end, the frames polychrome and parcel gilt, carved along the apron with rope twist moulding and trefoil arcading interspersed with stylised leaves in the spandrels. The ends carved with heavy rope twist moulding and acanthus leaves.
- *84cm x 168cm*
- £33,000   • Anthony Outred

Miniature Stool   ▼

- *circa 1820s*

Early 19th century fruit wood miniature stool with turned stretcher and legs.
- *19cm x 18cm*
- £395   •Wakelin Linfield

Empire Style Window Seats   ▲

- *circa 1880*

Pair of mahogany Empire style window seats with scrolled arms and gilded dolphin supports, raised on swept feet.
- *height 70cm*
- £2,800   • Mora Upham

Wicker Seated Stool   ▲

- *circa 1880*

Louis XVI style stool with cane seat with turned and fluted legs, with X frame stretcher.
- *height 49cm*
- £485   • The Swan

French Giltwood Stool   ▶

- *circa 1840*

French giltwood stool, the legs carved with a rope twist design terminating on tassel feet.
- *height 42cm*
- £4,000   • Augustus Brandt

Expert Tips

When examining a stool check for hessian under the seat as it was never used before 1840 and is often used to conceal an alteration.

French Stool
- *circa 1750*
French stool in the Louis XV style with gilded wooden legs.
- *height 46cm*
- £2,000 • O.F. Wilson

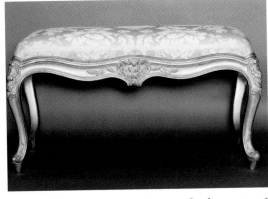

Victorian Walnut Stool
- *circa 1870*
A serpentine-fronted, upholstered walnut stool or window seat, seating two, with original ceramic castors. Recovered.
- *height 44cm*
- £3,200 • Judy Fox

Victorian Stool
- *circa 1840*
Early Victorian carved stool in gilt with cabriole legs and salmon velvet upholstery.
- *height 18cm*
- £265 • Castlegate

Carved Oak Stool
- *mid 19th century*
Victorian oak stool with contemporary needlework to cover, cabriole legs and original ceramic castors.
- *height 42cm*
- £16,000 • Norman Adams

Giltwood Stool
- *circa 1720*
An early 18th-century giltwood stool on ornate 'H' frame with reeded legs.
- *height 90cm*
- £950 • Fulham

Savanarola Stool
- *circa 1880*
One of a pair of Savanarola stools, of 'X' frame form.
- *height 59cm*
- £1,200 • Riverbank

Rosewood Footstools
- *late 19th century*
A pair of Victorian stools with serpentine-shaped cabriole legs.
- *height 22cm*
- £880 • Lesley Bragge

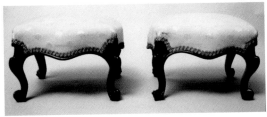

Queen Anne Stool ▶

- **1710**

A rare Queen Anne period stool in walnut circular top mounted on four carved cabriole legs with turned stretcher.
- *height 47cm*
- **£15,500** • Wakelin Linfield

Chippendale-Style Stool ▲

- **Victorian**

Late Victorian stool in the Chippendale style on ball and claw feet.
- *40cm x 47cm x 34cm*
- **£425** • Fay Orton

Louis XV Stool ▶

- *circa 1760*

A Louis XV walnut stool with a circular buttoned top, the seat rail scrolled to meet the cabriole legs standing on a whirl foot with a scrolled stretcher.
- *height 75cm*
- **£1,650** • Butchoff

Painted Tabourets ▼

- **1790**

Pair of late eighteenth century tabourets with painted decoration. Fluted tapered legs and carved frieze.
- *16cm x 31cm x 25cm*
- **£2,600** • O.F. Wilson

French Giltwood Stool ◀

- *circa 1811*

A Louis XVI giltwood stool with moulded frame and floral carving standing on cabriole legs.
- *46cm x 38cm x 86cm*
- **£2,200** • O.F. Wilson

Expert Tips

A set of two or more stools is rare and can considerably enhance the price.

George I Walnut Stool ◀
- *circa 1720*
George I walnut stool with cabriole legs, carved at each knee with a carved shell.
- *height 54cm*
- £22,500   • John Bly

Mahogany Stool ▶
- *circa 1890*
Miniature mahogany stool fashioned as a small table.
- *22cm x 33cm*
- £89   • The Swan

Piano Stool ▲
- *circa 1880*
Walnut revolving piano tool with circular padded seat on cabriole legs with claw feet.
- *height 49cm*
- £500   • Nicholas Mitchell

Piano Stool ▲
- *circa 1830s*
William IV piano stool on adjustable reeded and carved column, on a platform base with scroll end feet and original tapestry seat.
- *height 54cm*
- £495   • The Swan

Ebonised Stool ◀
- *circa 1860*
Ebonised stool with a rush seat, with faux bamboo designs and gilding with curved rails connected by gilded balls.
- *42cm x 40cm*
- £220   • Lacquer Chest

Gustavian Bench ▲
- *circa 1800*
Louis XVI Swedish Gustavian pine bench seat painted white with carved arms, raised on turned feet.
- *37cm x 109cm*
- £2,900   • R. Cavendish

Tables

Huan Huali Sofa Table ▲

- *circa 1810*

Rare Anglo-Chinese Huan Huali sofa table with a rectangular solid huan-huali wood top flanked by drop leaves with rounded corners, above a frieze with two short drawers flanking one long drawer, each decorated with ebony stringing and fitted with macassar ebony knobs, having dummy drawers to the reverse. Raised on trestle-end supports with ebony stringing terminating in brass sabots and castors.

- *74cm x 148cm*
- **£16,500** • **Anthony Outred**

Victorian Writing Table ▲

- *circa 1870*

Victorian writing table/workbox, standing on cabriole legs and stretcher base.

- *84cm x 70cm*
- **£5.500** • **The Swan**

Dutch Lowboy ▼

- **1740**

Dutch walnut lowboy with a serpentine front with foliate inlaid marquetry, moulded shaped apron standing on slender cabriole legs, with ball and claw feet.

- *71cm x 72cm*
- **£7,500** • **Butchoff**

Regency Tables ▼

- **1820**

Regency set of four tables, attributed to Gillow, with ebonised stringing. The well figured mahogany top with side flaps above two short drawers with turned knob handles. The whole raised on carved supports with reeded, splayed legs.

- *76cm x 56cm*
- **£14,000** • **Butchoff**

Regency Library Table ◄

- *circa 1815*

Regency library table in veneered rosewood with shaped top over a frieze supported on shaped end standards quarter beaded plinth, supported on rosettes and acanthus carved scrolled feet.

- *74cm x 140cm x 74cm*
- **£10,800** • **Wakelin Linfield**

French Games Table ▲

- *circa 1890s*

French Provincial walnut games table with four counter corners and two drawers standing on cabriole legs with small hoof foot.

- *height 72.5cm*
- **£3,400** • **Augustus Brandt**

Sheraton Card Table ▲

- *circa 1790*

Sheraton mahogany demi-lune card table with boxwood stringing, raised on square tapered legs.

- *72cm x 92cm*
- **£2,950** • **Barry Cotton**

Games Table ▲

- **1880**

Victorian rosewood games table with inlaid chess

- *height 78cm*
- **£695** • **A.I.G.**

Hall Table and Chairs ▼
- *1850*

An oak hall suite comprising of a table on turned legs with carved back, and two hall chairs. Rigin style, marked "SP".
- *width 94cm (table)*
- **£3,350**   • Mac Humble

Ebonised Table ▼
- *circa 1890*

Hexagonal ebonised table with green leather top, standing on four turned legs with a hoof pad foot.
- *60cm x 58cm*
- **£800**   • New Century

Regency Table ▼
- *1812–1830*

Regency mahogany table on an ebonised, X-framed stretcher base.
- *71cm x 107cm*
- **£3,350**   • The Old Cinema

Satinwood Table ▲
- *1815*

Satinwood table banded in rosewood, on a single pedestal on a tripod base with scrolled feet.
- *74cm x 52cm*
- **£5,900**   • Dial Post House

Standing Tray ▲
- *1780*

A satinwood tray on stand, with detachable tray with brass fittings and reeded legs.
- *48cm x 58cm*
- **£1,795**   • Great Grooms

Demi-Lune Card Table ▲
- *1837-1901*

Victorian burr walnut demi-lune card table with scrolled carved legs and feet.
- *74cm x 35cm x 43cm*
- **£1,995**   • Old Cinema

Edwardian Occasional Tables ▼
- *1910*

A nest of three Edwardian occasional tables with boxwood inlay and banding and tapered straight legs.
- *55cm x 50cm*
- **£495**   • Great Grooms

Inlaid Card Table ▼
- *circa 1900*

A mahogany card table with inlaid marquetry banding and medallions, on straight tapered legs.
- *72cm x 45cm*
- **£2,550**   • Great Grooms

Expert Tips

Occasional tables are always of interest as they have such a useful function in everyday living. They can obtain high prices, especially the ones made in rare woods and with high quality inlay.

Inlaid Regency Tables ▼

- *circa 1810*
A pair of Regency polescreens
converted into tables.
- *height 80cm*
- £3,250   • P.L. James

French Side Table ▼

- *circa 1880*
Painted French side table with
marble top and rosette decoration
on turned and fluted legs.
- *height 79cm*
- £350   • Youll's

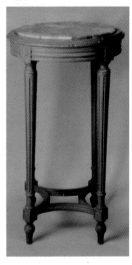

Dining Table ▶

- *circa 1810*
Mahogany D -ended Regency
dining table, cross-banded in
kingwood with boxwood stringing.
- *length (fully extended) 195cm*
- £8,750   • J. Collins

Table de Chevet ▲

- *circa 1790*
Table de chevet in cherrywood
with marble shelves.
- *height 72cm*
- £2,200   • O.F. Wilson

Supper Table ▲

- *circa 1780*
Georgian mahogany tambor-
fronted gentleman's supper table
on square legs with side flaps.
- *height 70cm*
- £4,000   • Castlegate

Painted Side Table ▼

- *circa 1860*
Painted side table of oval form
with inset marble top, set on
turned, fluted legs. Oval cupboard
at base with oval cane panel.
- *height 75cm*
- £650   • Youll's

Gueridon Table ▼

- *circa 1830*
A very good gueridon French
table, with an unusual marble top
and acanthus scroll legs.
- *height 71cm*
- £6,750   • C. Preston

Mahogany Side Table

- *circa 1870s*

Victorian mahogany table with leather writing top and one long single drawer on tapered turned legs with original brass castors.
- *height 70cm*
- £595　　　• Old Cinema

Victorian Chess Table ▼

- *1860*

A Victorian mother-of-pearl chess table by Jenning and Betteridge, with pierced fan shaped decoration to top, single turned pedestal on circular base with upturned tripod feet.
- *73cm x 49cm*
- £1,250　　　• Tredantiques

Italian Console Table ▶

- *1830*

A Venetian giltwood console table, with pink and white marble top, serpentine carved front, with profusely carved legs and stretcher.
- *90cm x 140cm x 46cm*
- £1,950　　　• Tredantiques

Expert Tips

Period chess tables are always of great interest to the collector as the game of chess has a timeless appeal.

Cricket Table ▲

- *1750*

An oak oval cricket table, on a tripod base with square, straight legs.
- *62cm x 57cm*
- £3,600　　　• Paul Hopwell

Boulle Table ▲

- *1880*

A magnificent circular green ebonised boulle circular table with brass inlaid decoration.
- *77cm x 138cm*
- £8,500　　　• Old Cinema

French Circular Table ▼

- *circa 1900*

A French circular satinwood and fruitwood table standing on square tapering legs.
- *72cm x 50cm*
- £900　　　• Tredantiques

Spider-legged Work Table ▼

- *1800*

Mahogany work table with unusual spider legs.
- *72cm x 53cm x 40cm*
- £4,200　　　• O.F. Wilson

Circular Side Table ▲
- *1890*
Small circular table on tripod base, inlaid with satinwood, box and rosewood with an inlaid knight on horseback.
- *height 74cm*
- £1,400   • Judy Fox

Welsh Oak Table ▲
- *circa 1740*
A Welsh country-made eighteenth century oak three drawer side table with original handles.
- *74cm x 83cm x 47cm*
- £1,850   • Rod Wilson

French Marquetry Table ▲
- *circa 1890*
A French centre table with shaped top with marquetry inlay and ormolu mounts on cabriole legs.
- *77cm x 152cm x 95cm*
- £8,500   • Tredantiques

Chinese Lacquered Table ▼
- *1800*
A pair of eighteenth century Chinese lacquer panels inset into more recent brass frames.
- *65cm x 55cm*
- £1,750   • C.H. Major

Marquetry Table ▼
- *circa 1875*
French marquetry table with hinged table top with fitted interior and carved and gilded legs.
- *74cm x 81cm*
- £2,750   • C.H. Major

Oval Hall Tables ▲
- *1860*
Victorian small oval top table with a basket base on cabriole legs with ceramic castors.
- *72cm x 116cm x 142cm*
- £4,500   • Judy Fox

Mahogany Drinks Table ▲
- *1880*
A mahogany side table by Maples with silver-plated mounts and original decanters on silver plated castors.
- *97cm x 118cm x 56cm*
- £3,800   • Judy Fox

Carved Writing Table ▲
- *1825*
A fine Regency rosewood table. Writing on side table attributed to Gillows of Lancaster. Made in 1825. The well figured veneers to the top are complimented by exquisite gadrooned carving to the edge and is fitted with two frieze drawers. The design for this table is included amid Gillows estimate drawerings and costings book for 1826, nos 3480 & 3496.
- *75cm x 106cm x 60cm*
- £8,950   • Freshfords

Mahogany Console Table ▼
- *circa 1810*

A console table with a
rectangular top with an ebonised
moulded edge over a frieze inlaid
with repeated brass sunburst
motifs on an ebonised
background, raised on a pair of
columns joined to the panelled
back with an arcaded profile. The
whole raised on a concave plinth
base leading to gilt paw feet, the
front two facing forward, the back
two to the side.
- *89cm x 95cm*
- **£9,800**   • **Anthony Outred**

George III Table ▼
- *circa 1800*

George III small mahogany
birdcage table, with well shaped
baluster tri-pod support on
splayed legs.
- *height 79cm*
- **£2,500**   • **Great Grooms**

Victorian Table ▶
- *circa 1870*

Victorian walnut and marquetry
table on a pedestal base with
carved gadrooned decoration and
carved splat legs, by Taylor &
Son, Dover St, London.
- *height 137cm*
- **£9,800**   • **Butchoff**

Peachwood Centre Table ▲
- *circa 1820*

A rare peachwood centre table
with turned legs and bamboo
skirting.
- *81cm x 175cm*
- **£8,200**   • **Gordon Reece**

Oval Table ▲
- *circa 1800s*

Small oval table with a George
III tray with a scalloped edge on
four splayed legs joined by a X
frame sretcher.
- *height 56cm*
- **£695**   • **Old Cinema**

Rosewood Table ▲
- *circa 1835*

William IV rosewood
sewing/games table with trestle
supports and bun feet.
- *73cm x 61cm*
- **£2,600**   • **Salem Antiques**

Victorian Dressing Table ▲
- *circa 1885*

Victorian mahogany dressing
table with an oval mirror with
heavily carved decoration, above
fitted drawers and turned front
legs.
- *height 1.3m*
- **£4,500**   • **Sleeping Beauty**

Victorian Games Table ▲
- *circa 1850*

Victorian mahogany inlaid
walnut games table with inlaid
chessboard and heavily turned
column, standing on a tripod base
with carved legs.
- *height 82cm*
- **£875**   • **Hill Farm**

Expert Tips

*During the middle of the 18th
century the tea gardens around
London were regarded as
vulgar, and it therefore became
fashionable to invite friends to
drink tea at home. Cabinet
makers turned their attention to
designing suitable ornamental
tables for the occasion.*

Side Tables ▼
- *circa 1860*
Pair of French, walnut side
cabinets with gilt-metal mounts
and inset marble tops.
- *height 72cm*
- £1,485   • Ranby Hall

Card Table ▼
- *circa 1830*
Regency rosewood, brass inlaid
card table on square base, with
gilt claw casters.
- *height 74cm*
- £2,300   • Castlegate

Console Table ▲
- *circa 1890*
Late 19th-century carved walnut
console table in George I style,
with cabriole legs.
- *height 85cm*
- £2,450   • Brown's

Bentwood Table ▲
- *19th century*
Round table with bentwood legs,
slightly splayed, from ball
decoration.
- *height 54cm*
- £225   • North West 8

Tripod Table ▼
- *circa 1760*
A Chippendale period mahogany
table with piecrust top.
- *height 70.5cm*
- £20,000   • Norman Adams

Tile Table ▼
- *circa 1890*
Table of bamboo construction,
with legs and stretchers pale and
top darker, with inlaid tile to top.
- *height 47cm*
- £120   • North West 8

Art Deco Coffee Table ◄
- *circa 1925*
Masur birch and rosewood coffee
table with inlays of satinwood
and cross-banding in 'tiger' birch.
- *length 99cm*
- £2,700   • R. Cavendish

Victorian Washstand ▼

- *circa 1840*

Victorian mahogany washstand with two drawers with turned handles and side table, in excellent original condition.
- *width 98cm*
- **£595**　　　● **The Swan**

Side Table ▼

- *circa 1880*

Mahogany table with moulded serpentine top supported by two turned columns, joined by a turned stretcher above heavily carved legs with leaf designs.
- *height 89cm*
- **£695**　● **Macnaughton-Smith**

Mahogany Serving Table ▶

- *circa 1795*

English serving table, of breakfront D-shaped form, surmounted by the original brass gallery, the frieze fitted with a long oak lined drawer, with a finely flamed mahogany front. The rounded corner panels and side panels of the frieze finished in a similar manner each panel flanked by finely carved urns heading the six elegant fluted tapering legs.
- *82cm x 290cm*
- **£28,000**　● **Anthony Outred**

Sewing Table ▲

- *1870*

Victorian rosewood sewing table with single drawer standing on a pedestal base with turned feet.
- *88cm x 84cm*
- **£1,995**　● **Flower Antique**

Mahogany Jardinière ▲

- *1830*

Rare William IV mahogany occasional table stamped Freemans on a carved and turned column raised on a tripod base, resting on bun feet.
- *76cm x 44cm*
- **£4,500**　　● **Butchoff**

Victorian Tilt Top Table ▼

- *circa 1880*

Victorian mahogany tilt top table with turned baluster pedestal base, raised on splayed legs.
- *height 74cm*
- **£580**　● **Nicholas Mitchell**

Mahogany Side Table ▼

- *circa 1830*

Mahogany side table with square top single long drawer with brass handle, standing on four straight square legs.
- *height 82cm*
- **£475**　　　● **John Clay**

George III Tripod Table ▲
- **1760**
George III small circular mahogany tripod table.
- **£2,950**   • Ashcombe House

Rosewood Table ▲
- **1860**
A rosewood occasional table, with central long drawer, two side extensions, standing on a turned stretcher with twin scrolled supports.
- *74cm x 119cm x 65cm*
- **£3,250**   • Old Cinema

Austrian Work Table ▼
- **early 19th century**
An early nineteenth century olive wood work table made in Austria on stretcher base.
- *47cm x 63cm x 77cm*
- **£1,150**   • N.E. McAuliffe

Biedermeier Sofa Table ▶
- **circa 1820**
Swedish birchwood, Biedermeier sofa table with ebonised and gilt decoration on lion paw feet.
- *77cm x 120cm x 64cm*
- **£4,500**   • R. Cavendish

Italian Rosewood Table ▼
- **1900**
Italian inlaid rosewood octagonal occasional table, with circular satinwood inlay standing on eight square tapering legs.
- *72cm x 60cm*
- **£900**   • Tredantiques

Rosewood Games Table ◀
- **1810–1820**
A Regency rosewood games table with Moroccan leather top and brass inlay and ormolu mounts.
- *height 95cm*
- **£8,500**   • C.H. Major

Regency Writing Table ▲
- **1810**
An excellent Regency mahogany standard end writing table on turned stretcher base.
- *height 53cm*
- **£14,500**   • Ashcombe House

Victorian Drinks Table ▼
- **1880**
A Victorian drinks table with an Eastern influence in light oak with ebony finials on unusual legs.
- *76cm x 58cm x 43cm*
- **£460**   • Myriad

Expert Tips

Snap-top or tripod tables should have good firm bases and the table top should be constructed out of a single piece of wood.

Drum Table ▲

- **1810**

Regency mahogany drum table with fitted short drawers on a turned pedestal base with splayed legs.

- *75cm x 87cm*
- **£13,500**   • Butchoff

Regency Table ▲

- *circa 1820*

Regency mahogany fold over tea table, with U support and platform with brass beading, and flared legs standing on brass claw feet and castors.

- *height 83cm*
- **£3,350**   • Vale Antiques

Demi-Lune Table ▼

- *circa 1810*

Demi-lune mahogany table

- *height 87cm*
- **£950**   • Old Cinema

Sutherland Table ▼

- **1870**

Satin birchwood Sutherland table with two folding flaps and a stretcher base, on porcelain castors.

- *height 71cm*
- **£1,100**   • Old Cinema

Louis XV Rafraichissoir ▲

- *circa 1760*

Louis XV rafraichissoir fitted with rouge royale marble top, brass handles and savots with copper fitting for ice/bottles.

- *65.5cm x 44.5cm x 28.5cm*
- **£4,000**   • O. F. Wilson

Mahogany Card Table ▼

- *circa 1870*

Unusual Victorian mahogany card table, on a turned pedestal column, scroll feet and swivel top (re-baized).

- *84cm x 83cm*
- **£850**   • The Swan

George I Lowboy ◄

- *circa 1720*

Very pretty and exceptionally small George I lowboy, the top with quartered veneers in well figured walnut, herringbone stringing and cross banding. With shaped frieze, one shallow and two deep drawers.

- *69cm x 68cm*
- **£17,500**   • Wakelin Linfield

Tilt Table ▼

- *circa 1830*

A Regency lacquered tripod table in chinoiserie style, showing scenes of pagodas and kite flying.
- *height 117cm*
- £2,450 • O.F. Wilson

Satinwood Table ▼

- *circa 1920*

Two-tier, Edwardian satinwood table on square, splayed legs.
- *height 70cm*
- £2,100 • T. Morse

Centre Table ▶

- *circa 1845*

Rosewood centre table with figural top with gadrooned edge. Carved centre column.
- *height 71cm*
- £3,850 • M.J. Bowdery

Queen Anne Side Table ▲

- *circa 1695*

18th-century walnut side table with single drawer with brass fittings, turned legs on bun feet and turned stretchers.
- *height 67cm*
- £1,750 • C. Preston

Work Table ▲

- *circa 1880*

An octagonal work table with games top on an eight-sided, fluted base, tapering to base with three legs.
- *height 79cm*
- £950 • Castlegate

Pair of Console Tables ▼

- *circa 1805*

A rare pair of Swedish neoclassical Empire console tables, by Jonas Frisk, Stockholm.
- *height 86cm*
- £16,500 • R. Cavendish

Mahogany Night Table ▼

- *circa 1780*

George III night table with dipped front edge and surrounding gallery.
- *height 78.5cm*
- £2,250 • J. Collins

Wardrobes

Walnut Cupboard ▼
- *early 18th century*
A fine English walnut hall cupboard with unusual carved inlays and designs on bracket feet.
- *188cm x 121cm*
- **£12,500** • M. Luther

Mahogany Linen Press ▶
- *early 19th century*
English mahogany linen press in the manner of Gillows.
- *215cm x 159cm*
- **£7,800** • M. Luther

Expert Tips
When purchasing a cupboard with brass inlay look carefully for any missing or broken pieces in the design, as it is expensive to restore.

Combination Wardrobe ▼
- *19th century*
A good quality combination wardrobe with flame mahogany panelled doors, fitted interior with sliding drawers.
- *220cm x 185cm*
- **£3,395** • Old Cinema

Boulle Cupboard ▲
- *19th century*
A French ebony and ebonised boulle cupboard with brass inlay raised on interlaced cross stretcher and carved legs.
- *154cm x 85cm x 43cm*
- **£4,400** • M. Luther

Walnut Wardrobe ▼
- *18th century*
French walnut wardrobe with a moulded arch cornice above two shaped cupboard doors, with a serpentine apron on shaped bracket feet.
- *height 169cm*
- **£1,906** • Drummonds

Mahogany Compactona ▼
- *circa 1880*
An Edwardian mahogany compactona with satinwood banding, chequered stringing, with marquetry panels and cornice.
- *170cm x 160cm*
- **£2,900** • Old Cinema

Victorian Wardrobe ◀
- *circa 1890s*
A late Victorian single-door mahogany wardrobe with central mirror, flanked by circular carved panels with ribbon decoration.
- *170cm x 90cm*
- **£925** • Old Cinema

Louis XVI Cupboard

- *1800–1810*

Swedish Louis XVI Gustavian cupboard in two sections, with architecturally styled pediment and doors to top chest, and the lower chest with two panelled door, the whole standing on small bracket feet.

- *188cm x 113cm*
- £2,700   • R. Cavendish

Mahogany Linen Press

- *circa 1780*

Mahogany linen press with moulded dentil course and two doors with inlaid oval panels concealing original trays. The lower section with two short and two long drawers.

- *212cm x 122cm x 58cm*
- £10,950   • Wakelin Linfield

Indian Linen Press ▼

- *circa 1880*

Indian linen press, with panelled doors carved with central pleated medallions and corner spandrels, above two long drawers raised on bracket feet.

- *height 175cm*
- £2,500   • Hatchwell

French Provincial Cupboard ▼

- *circa 1780*

French painted Provincial cupboard in three parts, with heavily panelled doors on the top cupboard fitted with two serpentine shelves, and elongated hinges.

- *223cm x 172cm*
- £4,300   • Anthony Sharpe

Black Lacquer Cupboard ▶

- *1880*

Small Chinese black lacquer cabinet, with fitted interior of one long and seven other drawers. With brass fittings at each corner with curved edges. Flanked by brass carrying handles.

- *37cm x 40cm x 28.5cm*
- £2,250   • O.F. Wilson

Mahogany Wardrobe ▲

- *circa 1880*

Fine Victorian figured mahogany moulded two-door wardrobe, with scrolled moulding below a moulded pediment. Standing on a straight base.

- *height 206cm*
- £1,850   • Hill Farm

George III Commode ▲

- *circa 1790*

George III mahogany tambour door commode with square tapering legs.

- *79cm x 53cm x 49cm*
- £3,450   • Serendipity

Fruitwood Armoire ▼
- *circa early 19th century*
French fruitwood armoire with carved doors with rosettes and fluted centre panel above carved apron, the whole on scrolled feet.
- *height 2.09m*
- £2,495   • Old Cinema

Gillows Press ▼
- *circa 1805*
A linen press, stamped 'Gillows of Lancaster', retaining its original patina and with all original handles and interior, with sliding trays.
- *height 2.3m*
- £14,500
- Ronald G. Chambers

Ash Wardrobe ▶
- *circa 19th century*
Hungarian wardrobe with four doors above two deep drawers.
- *height 2.8m*
- £5,995   • Old Cinema

Victorian Linen Press ▲
- *circa 1840*
A linen press with secret drawer and Gothic moulded doors.
- *height 2.35m*
- £6,800   • T. Morse

Venetian Armoire ▲
- *circa late 17th century*
Venetian armoire with painted panel doors with dental course and cast-bronze cherub handles.
- *height 1.95m*
- £7,500   • Paul Andrews

French Oak Armoire ▼
- *1844*
Armoire with shaped apron with date, profuse leaf carving, beading and scale motif.
- *height 2.2m*
- £7,400   • Paul Andrews

First Empire Linen Press ▼
- *circa 1810*
In flamed mahogany with two doors above four tiers of drawers, the columns with fine gilt mounts.
- *height 2.25m*
- £13,000   • Pillows

Glass

Glass forms some of the most beautiful artefacts with which to create a collection – and its inherent fragility ensures ongoing rarity value.

It is only relatively recently that glass has become a popular field for collectors. The probable reasons for this were the fragility of the items in question and the fact that there are considerable difficulties in authentication and attribution. Drinking glasses were made in large numbers throughout the eighteenth century and are very popular with collectors. Value depends on the rarity of the decoration as well as the shape of the bowl, stem and foot. Colourful glass of the nineteenth century is increasingly popular with collectors. Many new glassmaking techniques and more varied colours were introduced during this period, and services of glass were introduced in numbers for the first time. Continental glass is an enormous field, from medieval German and early Venetian to the beautiful colour of Bohemian glass of the nineteenth century, which can fetch staggering prices. On the other hand, unmarked glass of the nineteenth century is still an excellent buy and can often be less expensive than its modern equivalent.

Georgian Rummer ◀
- 1810
A Georgian rummer slightly waisted bowl with unusual triple banding, on a plain conical foot.
- *height 16.5cm*
- £110   • Jasmin Cameron

Engraved Rummer ◀
- 1820
A George III Sunderland Bridge rummer engraved with pastoral scenes.
- *height 15cm*
- £850   • Templar

French Urns ▲
- 1880
A pair of turquoise French urns with gilt mounts and a central plaque showing romantic figures.
- *height 26cm*
- £680   • Mousa

Bohemian Goblet ◀
- 1880
A Bohemian goblet in red glass with crenellated rim, white enamelled panels and gilding.
- *height 27cm*
- £760   • Mousa

Expert Tips

Bohemian glass can suffer from chips to the enamel and worn gilding which can be extremely expensive to repair.

Amethyst Spirit Bottles ▲
• *circa 1839*
A fine pair of amethyst coloured
spirit bottles, with silver mounts
and stoppers with elaborate
chasing of bunches of grapes.
• *height 36cm*
• £980   • Somervale

Tall Bohemian Vase ▲
• *circa 1890*
Tall elegant Bohemian dark red
vase with a conical neck and
splayed lip, engraved with trailing
bunches of vine and fruit,
supported on a splayed foot.
• *height 51cm*
• £750   • Mousa

Green Drinking Glass ▼
• *1840*
Dark green drinking glass, with a
plain ring stem on a splayed foot.
• *height 12cm*
• £65   • Somervale

Victorian Silver Tantalus ▼
• *circa 1860*
Victorian silver plated tantalus
with three decanters.
• *height 32cm*
• £650   • Barry Cotton

Blue Spirit Bottle ▲
• *1890*
Blue tapering spirit bottle with
flute cutting and a cut spire
stopper.
• *height 34cm*
• £480   • Somervale

Bohemian Glass Dish ▲
- *1880*

Bohemian glass dish on a stand, with white enamelled panels, stylised leaf design and gilding.
- *height 24cm*
- **£540**   • Mousa

Cock Fighting Trophy ▲
- *1860*

Large goblet-shaped bowl standing on a knobbed pedestal stem. The body skillfully engraved with scene of fighting cocks.
- *height 22cm*
- **£550**   • Templar

Toddy Lifter ▼
- *1825*

Exceedingly rare toddy lifter from the early ninteenth century.
- *height 18cm*
- **£350**   • Jasmin Cameron

Bohemian Bottles ▲
- *1880*

Blue Bohemian faceted glass bottles with gilded decoration and lozenge-shaped stoppers.
- *height 15cm*
- **£350**   • Mousa

Glass Decanter ▼
- *1880*

Rose coloured glass decanter with clear glass ribbon handle and stopper.
- *height 23cm*
- **£110**   • Mousa

Jug and Two Beakers ◀
- *1890*

Green Bohemian glass jug and two beakers with white enamelling and gilding.
- *height 18cm*
- **£126**   • Mousa

Expert Tips

On decanters, check that the stopper is original and has not been ground down to fit.

Glass Twisted Canes ▼

- *circa 1830*

Three assorted glass barley twist canes.

- *length 110cm*
- £150
- Somervale

Green Spirit Decanters ▼

- *1790*

Pair of green spirit decanters of ovoid form inscribed 'Rum' and 'Brandy' within gilt cartouches in the shape of a label, supported by gilt ribboning around the neck.

- *height 22cm*
- £1,200
- Somervale

Amber Vase ▲

- *circa 1850*

Amber vase with cover, engraved with stags and deer running through a forest and a trailing foliate design around the cover, with an octagonal base.

- *height 57cm*
- £5,800
- Mousa

Irish Oval Fruit Bowl ▼

- *circa 1790*

Fine Irish oval fruit bowl with panels of raised diamond design, knopped stem and radial moulded dual scalloped foot.

- *height 22cm*
- £2,600
- Somervale

Cut Glass Goblet ▼

- *circa 1810*

Large goblet engraved with the words 'London to Bath' and a scene showing a horse and carriage, with knop to stem and a square heavily cut base.

- *height 17cm*
- £1,500
- Somervale

Pink and Amber Goblet ▼

- *circa 1880*

Bohemian raspberry-coloured goblet with gilt trophy cartouche within a foliate border, raised on a topaz leaf-shaped base.

- *height 18cm*
- £460
- Mousa

Port Glass ▲

- *circa 1810*
An early 19th-century port glass with knops to stem.
- *height 10cm*
- £110 • Jasmin Cameron

Bohemian Green Glass ▲

- *19th century*
Pot and cover on a base with gilding and enamelling.
- *height 12cm*
- £1,200 • Sinai

Bohemian Vases ▼

- *19th century*
With cherubs, enamel flowers and gilding on an ormolu base.
- *height 27cm*
- £2,600 • Sinai

Venetian Vase ▼

- *18th century*
A Venetian marbelised small vase on a pedestal foot.
- *height 17cm*
- £800 • Shahdad

Mammoth Wine Glass ▼

- *circa 1850*
With gilded rim and marked JH on the base. Scale cutting to leg.
- *height 28cm*
- £300 • Jasmin Cameron

Strawberry Cut Jug ▼

- *circa 1825*
An Irish jug with prismatic stars, radial base and fluted handle.
- *height 17cm*
- £180 • Jasmin Cameron

Venetian Vases ◄

- *19th century*
Two mille fiore double handled vases in perfect condition.
- £400, £500 • Shahdad

Mead Glass ▽

- *circa 1840*

A beaker-shaped green Bristol mead glass.
- *height 11cm*
- **£75**   • Jasmin Cameron

Port Glasses ▽

- *1820*

A pair of Regency port glasses engraved with the monogram "Lac".
- *height 14cm*
- **£135**   • Jasmin Cameron

Expert Tips

Scent bottle stoppers should be of the same quality and design as the bottle. If the neck of the scent bottle has a silver mount this should be firmly fitted and should have a hallmark. Dressing table sets and travelling sets should be matching and complete.

Coloured Wine Glass ▽

- *1890*

Cranberry coloured wine glass with long stem on a domed foot.
- *height 11cm*
- **£65**   • Jasmin Cameron

Scent Bottle ▶

- *1901*

Small rose glass perfume bottle, diamond cut and faceted with clear stopper.
- *height 3.5cm*
- **£55**   • Mousa

Victorian Glass Epergne ◀

- *1860*

Victorian vaseline glass épergne with four hanging flutes stemming from a central trumpet.
- *height 52cm*
- **£690**   • Templar

Bohemian Covered Vase ▲

- *1890*

A large Bohemian vase and cover, the cylindrical body tapering from a lobed base, the whole engraved with romantic designs.
- *height 64cm*
- **£1,680**   • Mousa

French Vase

- *circa 1880*

French white porcelain vase of baluster form, with a gilt cartouche of pale pink roses, poppies and cornflowers, surrounded by trailing pink wild roses, possibly by Baccarat.
- *height 44cm*
- £1,050   • Mousa

Baluster Wine Glass ▼

- *circa 1720*

Wine glass with bell shape bowl on an angular and true inverted baluster stem, with air twists and folded conical foot.
- *height 16cm*
- £1,100   • Somervale

Glass Rolling Pin ▼

- *1860*

Amethyst glass rolling pin with gilt inscription 'Forget me not', a gift from a soldier going to war.
- *length 41cm*
- £160   • Somervale

Blue Spirit Decanters ▲

- *1800*

Pair of blue octagonal spirit decanters, inscribed 'Brandy' and 'Rum' within gilt labels, with faceted stoppers and fluted rims.
- *height 20cm*
- £800   • Somervale

Bristol Blue Spirit Decanters ▲

- *1790*

A pair of blue spirit decanters with the gilt inscriptions 'Hollands' and 'Brandy' hanging from gilt ribbons around the neck, within a silver stand with handle.
- *height 28cm*
- £700   • Somervale

Bohemian Glass Bottle ▲

- *circa 1860*

Opaque bohemian bottle chased in gilt with butterflies, birds and pale pink and blue flowers.
- *height 20.5cm*
- £750   • Mousa

Bohemian Vase ▼
- *19th century*

With cut and engraved scenes of
deer among woodland.
- *height 44cm*
- £2,600
- Sinai

Pickle Preserve Jar ▼
- *circa 1825*

With an octagonal body, star base
and star stopper.
- *height 18cm*
- £85
- Jasmin Cameron

Dessert Service ▶
- *circa 1890*

20-piece enamelled dessert
service with gilded vine and fruit
decoration.
- £4,200
- Sinai

Port Glass ▲
- *19th century*

A 19th-century port glass with
base knop.
- *height 11cm*
- £65
- Jasmin Cameron

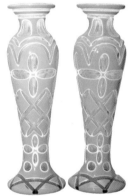

Bohemian Vases ▲
- *circa 1895*

A pair of green overlay vases with
strong geometric patterns.
- *height 27cm*
- £480
- Mousa

German Vase ▼
- *circa 1880*

A German vase with scrolling. In
a 17th-century style.
- *height 28cm*
- £200
- Mousa

Hookah Base ▼
- *circa 1880*

Made for the Middle-Eastern
market. Heavily cut and gilded
with painted enamel flowers.
- *height 26cm*
- £680
- Mousa

405

Plain Bucket Rummer ▲
- *1890*

Plain bucket rummer signed "Val
St Lambert". This maker was on a
par with Baccarate & St. Louis.
- *height 21cm*
- £330 • Jasmin Cameron

Pair of Victorian Goblets ▶
- *1880*

Extremely fine pair of matching
Victorian goblets of super quality.
The tall funnel bowls engraved
with a fern pattern on barley
twist stems by W. & J. Bailey E.
Lerche.
- *height 20cm*
- £380 • Jasmin Cameron

Celery Glass ▼
- *1820*

Large engraved celery glass with
acid etching around the bowl, on
a pedestal base.
- *height 24cm*
- £300 • Jasmin Cameron

Amber Glass Decanters ◀
- *1825*

Rare George III amber glass
dessert decanters with moulded,
cut and faceted designs.
- *height 22cm*
- £740 • Jasmin Cameron

Brandy Glasses ▶
- *1800*

Called "Joeys" after Joseph Hume,
an eighteenth century politician
from the English West Country.
- *height 5cm*
- £180 • Jasmin Cameron

Bristol Decanter ▲
- *1810*

Blue Bristol decanter with faceted
stopper and gilt oval plaque with
the inscription "Brandy".
- *height 27cm*
- £320 • Jasmin Cameron

Expert Tips

*Engraved glasses should be looked
at closely, and the age and style
of the glass should be taken into
account when examining the
style of the engraving, as it is
often the case that the original
plain glasses were actually
engraved at a later date.*

Large Green Goblet ▲

- *circa 1800*

Large dark green goblet with cup shaped bowl.

- *height 19cm*
- £1,200 • Somervale

Set of Spirit Bottles ▲

- *1840*

A fine set of spirit bottles in amethyst, blue and green glass, with silver foliate bands around the neck and grape finials, resting in a pierced silver stand on three leaf shaped feet.

- *height 36cm*
- £980 • Somervale

Bohemian Bottles ▼

- *circa 1880*

Pair of Bohemian bottles with a white bulbous body with pink roses and blue cornflowers, orange flowers painted over red glass, with a slender fluted neck with a red lozenge-shape stopper and gilding.

- *height 22cm*
- £780 • Mousa

Bristol Blue Oil Bottle ▼

- *1840*

Bristol blue bottle inscribed with 'Oil' in gilt lettering within a gilt foliate cartouche, with a painted chain around the neck.

- *height 12cm*
- £200 • Somervale

Bohemian Lustres ▲

- *circa 1880*

One of a pair of Bohemian green lustres with white overlay with gilt borders, decorated with clear, cut glass hanging pendants.

- *height 30cm*
- £1,000 • Mousa

William III Glass ▲

- *circa 1780*

Irish wine glass with a cigar shaped stem and engraved with the figure of King William on horseback with the inscription 'The Glorious Memories of William III'.

- *height 15.5cm*
- £4,000 • Somervale

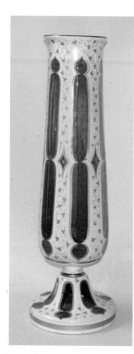

Cylinder Spirit Decanter ▶

- *1840*

Clear glass cylinder spirit decanter with mushroom stopper.
- *height 23cm*
- £185　　• Jasmin Cameron

Turkish Hooka ▼

- *1880*

Turkish hooka used for smoking, the faceted and enamelled glass reservoir with brass apparatus.
- *height 123cm*
- £130　　• Mousa

Bohemian Vase ◀

- *1880*

A large Bohemian glass vase, with white enamelled designs and gilt banding on a splayed foot.
- *height 42cm*
- £350　　• Mousa

Pair of Lithayalin Beakers ▲

- *1880*

A pair of white Bohemian Lithayalin beakers, of waisted form in translucent glass, the outer surface cut with broad facets, with gilding.
- *height 12cm*
- £380　　• Mousa

Coin Glass Goblet ▶

- *1864*

Very rare coin glass goblet, with threepenny silver piece inserted in leg.
- *height 18cm*
- £400　　• Jasmin Cameron

Irish Decanter ▲

- *circa 1770*

Irish ribbed decanter in clear glass with a lozenge stopper.
- *height 21cm*
- £330　　• Jasmin Cameron

Pair of Enamelled Vases ▲

- *1880*

A pair of translucent blue Bohemian vases of baluster form, enamelled with birds and foliage.
- *height 28cm*
- £550　　• Mousa

Glass Twisted Cane ▼

- *circa 1810*
Turquoise twisted glass walking stick.
- *length 100cm*
- £150 • Somervale

Glass Barrel Decanters ▼

- *1820*
Set of three Bristol blue glass barrel decanters inscribed with 'Rum', 'Whiskey' and 'Brandy' in gilt lettering within gilt banding. Each decanter has a gilt ball stopper.
- *height 20cm*
- £1,400 • Somervale

Bristol Rum Decanter ▼

- *1800*
Rum decanter inscribed with 'Rum' in gilt lettering on the body and 'R' on the lozenge shape stopper.
- *height 28cm*
- £280 • Somervale

Victorian Epergné ▲

- *circa 1890*
One of a pair of Victorian epergnés, with a central flute flanked by matching hanging baskets, suspended on spiral branches.
- *height 48cm*
- £2,200 • Sinai

French Opaline Vase ▲

- *circa 1880*
Opaline pink glass vase with jewelled beading and gilt decoration with an eastern inspiration.
- *height 48cm*
- £850 • Sinai

Jacob Sang Wine Glass ▼

- *circa 1759*
Composite air twist stem wine glass, engraved with a scene showing the Customs House in Amsterdam and cargo being unloaded, marked 'Jacob Sang 1759', on the foot.
- *height 23.5cm*
- £8,000 • Somervale

Ale Glass ▼

- *circa 1760*
Ale glass with a round funnel bowl engraved with hops and barley and a double series twist stem, standing on a plain foot.
- *height 21cm*
- £580 • Somervale

Green Wine Glasses ▲

- *circa 1830*
One of a set of twelve green wine glasses, with conical shaped bowls, bladed knob stems and a circular base.
- *height 11cm*
- £896   • Somervale

Bohemian Vases for Candles ▲

- *circa 1880*
One of a pair of dark green Bohemian candle holders with white overlay panels, painted with pink roses within gilt borders, raised on a conical stem and circular base.
- *height 34cm*
- £980   • Mousa

Posset Pot ▼

- *circa 1740*
Posset pot with a trumpet bowl with a carved spout flanked by two scroll handles, on a plain conical foot.
- *height 7cm*
- £995   • Somervale

Nailsea Container ▼

- *circa 1860*
Nailsea double container of clear glass with white pull up decoration, with emerald green rims.
- *height 21cm*
- £160   • Somervale

Mallet Shaped Decanter ▲

- *circa 1780*
Mallet-shaped decanter engraved with 'Port' within an oval cartouche, flanked by trailing vine and grapes.
- *height 31cm*
- £1,000   • Somervale

Amber Glass Cane ▼

- *circa 1810*
Amber glass barley twist cane with knob.
- *length 100cm*
- £150   • Somervale

Emile Gallé Dish ▶

- *late 19th century*
With fine floral enamelling and
figuration scenes in the panels.
The whole with profuse gilding.
- £8,500 ● Sinai

Ewer and Goblets ▲

- *19th century*
Bohemian ewer and two goblets
with panels of flowers and profuse
floral gilding.
- £3,200 ● Sinai

Cameo Scent Bottle ▶

- *circa 1860*
An English cameo scent bottle
engraved with flowers and leaves.
- *height 8cm*
- £260 ● Mousa

Port Glass ▲

- *19th century*
A 19th-century port glass with
knop and domed base.
- *height 11cm*
- £65 ● Jasmin Cameron

German Glass Beaker ▲

- *circa 1880*
A German green glass beaker
with a coat of arms and coronet.
- *height 10cm*
- £85 ● Mousa

Red Bohemian Vase ▼

- *circa 1870*
A red vase with a painted flower
frieze and gilded floral decoration.
- *height 31cm*
- £380 ● Mousa

Monteith or Bonnet Glasses ◀

- *circa 1750*
Mid 18th-century glasses.
- *height 8cm*
- £220 ● Jasmin Cameron

Jewellery

An incredible amount of jewellery changes hands every day in auction rooms, dealers' shops, market stalls and boot fairs. Look for quality first.

The manufacture of jewellery may well be the second oldest profession and, some might argue, in some ways not unrelated to the oldest. One of the most outstanding features of the jewellery market is the simply enormous quantity of it out there and changing hands. A glance at any local paper will reveal the number of antiques fairs, markets and car-boot sales taking place on any given weekend throughout the year and, when one considers that this is going on throughout the country, it boggles the mind as to how much jewellery is being placed before the public quite literally all the time. There is an enormous diversity of jewellery being collected, from early plastic items through such relatively inexpensive materials as marcasite sets in silver and stained horn, up to the highly prized and precious items that usually dignify the name. While demand for jewellery is strong in nearly all areas, from Victorian silver to diamond tiaras, the one requirement throughout is for quality. Good design and delicate workmanship can count for a lot more than a bucket-full of poor-quality diamonds.

American Watch Bracelet ▼
- 1940

Gold-plated American watch bracelet, similar to one worn by Gloria Swanson.
- £250   • Linda Bee

Cameo Brooch ◄
- 1820

Italian cameo head of young girl with English mount.
- *height 4cm*
- £750   • RBR Group

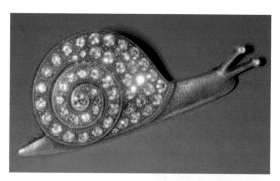

Snail Brooch ▲
- 1930

A snail brooch in paste and silver.
- £65   • Linda Bee

Christian Dior Brooch ◄
- 1960

Circus horse brooch by Christian Dior.
- £295   • Linda Bee

Expert Tips

A poor setting normally reflects a poor stone and cheap manufacture. Moreover, poor settings increase the likelihood of stone loss.

Sapphire and Diamond ▶

• *circa 1910*
Sapphire and diamond earrings
set in a flower head design of
platinum and gold.
• *length 3cm*
• £4,850 • Wimpole Antiques

Diamond Earrings ▲

• *1920*
Pair of diamond earrings with
oval, circular and rectangular
diamonds within gold settings.
• *length 2.5cm*
• £4,400 • N. Bloom

Gold Victorian Earrings ▲

• *circa 1875*
Victorian Etruscan revival 15ct
gold earrings with a central wheel
motif.
• *width 1cm*
• £875 • Wimpole Antiques

Diamond Leaf Earrings ▼

• *circa 1925*
Mille grain set in platinum
diamond earrings in the form of a
leaf.
• *length 2cm*
• £3,475 • Wimpole Antiques

Victorian 15ct Earrings ▲

• *circa 1880*
15ct gold Victorian articulated
lozenge shaped earrings.
• *length 5cm*
• £1,295 • Wimpole Antiques

Expert Tips

*Bear in mind that the majority
of items of jewellery are second
hand and will have been subject
to some wear and tear.*

Silver Gilt Brooch ▼

• *1940s*
American large silver gilt and cut
glass sapphire floral brooch.
• *7cm x 6cm*
• £95 • Linda Bee

French Pearl and Diamond Earrings ▼

• *circa 1875*
French enamel, gold and
platinum earrings set with
diamonds and natural pearls.
• *length 3cm*
• £2,650 • Wimpole Antiques

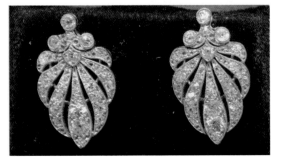

Enamel Brooch ◀

- *circa 1840*
Victorian enamel brooch with a painted panel of Lake Geneva, within a blue oval frame with gold mounts.
- *length 5cm*
- £1,150　　• RBR Group

Rose Diamond Pendant ▼

- *circa 1880*
Victorian 18ct. gold pendant with enamel flowers set with rose diamonds within scrolled borders.
- *length 4cm*
- £750　　• RBR Group

Victorian Gold Earrings ▲

- *circa 1880*
Victorian 18ct. gold hoop earrings with pierced floral decoration.
- *diameter 3cm*
- £1,050　　• RBR Group

Victorian Pendant ▲

- *circa 1890*
Victorian pendant set in 15ct. gold with a peridot to the centre, surrounded by pearls.
- *height 4cm*
- £950　　• RBR Group

Mosaic Brooch ▼

- *circa 1860*
Italian floral mosaic brooch within a stylised 18ct. gold star setting.
- *length 4cm*
- £950　　• RBR Group

Regency Brooch ▲

- *1800–30*
Regency 18ct. gold filigree garnet and turquoise brooch.
- *length 5cm*
- £650　　• RBR Group

Garnet Earrings ◀

- *1820*
Drop earrings in 18ct. gold with garnets within a flower shaped setting.
- *length 6cm*
- £1,450　　• RBR Group

Berlin Necklace ▲

- 1870
Berlin 'iron-work' necklace with 8 plaques.
- *length 3cm*
- £3,750   • N. Bloom

Night and Day Pin ▲

- 1950
Gold metal flower 'night and day' brooch made by Warner, USA.
- *6cm x 4cm*
- £85   • Linda Bee

Bakelite Brooch ▶

- 1930s
French bakelite black and white brooch, with an incised feather design.
- *8cm x 4cm*
- £65   • Linda Bee

Navajo Bull Bracelet ▼

- 1960
Navajo silver sand-cast bracelet with two large silver bull's heads on a scrolling border, flanked by turquoise stones.
- *height 6cm*
- £499   • Wilde Ones

Navajo Bracelet ▲

- 1950
Navajo coral and turquoise set on a circular engraved base, signed P.M.
- *diameter 6cm*
- £499   • Wilde Ones

Mic-Mak Indian Belt ▲

- 1920
Glass Mic-mak 'Morning Star' Indian belt made from glass beads with butterflies and geometric blue and black design with a cream background, lined with antique pink material with floral design.
- *length 87cm*
- £399   • Wilde Ones

Gold Collar ▲

- *circa 1875*
Victorian 15ct. gold collar engraved linkages.
- £3,750   • Wimpole Antiques

Navajo Shadow Box Bracelet ◀

- 1960
Navajo silver shadow box bracelet set with five large coral pieces stamped by the artist P. Benally.
- *length 17cm*
- £699   • Wilde Ones

Brooch ▼

- *circa 1965*

A 'KJL' brooch, by Kenneth J.
Lane. The brooch is of a
flamboyant, baroque design,
formed as a four-pointed star with
rounded ends, set with a central,
square cut faux cabochon ruby,
and French lapis lazuli.

- *height 8cm*
- £150   • Hilary Conqy

Turquoise Beads ▼

- *circa 1930*

Antique spider web turquoise
beads, from New Mexico, which
have been restrung with new
clasp on a silver chain.

- *length 60cm*
- £499   • Wilde Ones

Brooch/Pendant ▶

- *1880*

A French cameo, all carved out of
one piece of sardonyx, showing a
Greek mythological figure in
profile, surrounded by twelve
natural sea pearls with a half-
pearl leaf design surround.

- *height 10cm*
- £1,750   • Emmy Abé

Dragonfly Brooch ▲

- *circa 1880*

Victorian gold dragonfly brooch,
inset with rubies and diamonds
surrounding a natural pearl, all in
gold settings.

- *length 6cm*
- £14,500   • Sandra Cronan

Necklace ▲

- *circa 1940*

A continental necklace of the
Art Deco period, fashioned with
interlinked chrome rings hung
with green bakelite discs.

- £75   • Hilary Conqy

Crystal Beads ▼

- *circa 1940*

A necklace of crystal glass, amber,
faceted beads with the principal
pendant an extremely large,
cushion-cut stone in a pierced,
filigree mounting.

- £35   • Sugar

Hairslides ▼

- *circa 1910*

Set of three tortoiseshell
hairslides with 9ct. gold
mountings with a solitaire
amethyst and two small pearls to
each piece.

- *11cm x 7.5cm (one slide)*
- *10cm x 5cm (two slides)*
- £900   • Arwas

Expert Tips

*To tell shell cameos
from hardstone, scratch
the back of the piece. With
shell, the scratch will be
apparent; it will have no
effect on hardstone.*

Gold Earrings ▲
- *1840*

A pair of William IV gold and foil backed earrings with aquamarine settings and gold tassels.
- *height 4cm*
- £750 ● Michele Rowan

Pearl Ring ▲
- *circa 1890*

Victorian lozenge-shaped gold ring set with a diamond surrounded by pearls.
- *length 4cm*
- £750 ● Michele Rowan

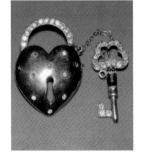

Masonic Gold Locket ▲
- *1900*

Masonic gold locket formed as a ten-page book with various engravings.
- *height 2cm*
- £500 ● Michele Rowan

Padlock Brooch ◄
- *1940*

An American heart-shaped brooch in the shape of a padlock connected to a key, with paste diamonds. Designed by Castlecliff and set in sterling silver.
- *diameter 2cm*
- £120 ● Linda Bee

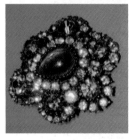

Green Lozenge-Shape Brooch ▲
- *1950*

Czechoslovakian brooch set with a dark green lozenge stone surrounded by bright green, faceted stones.
- *diameter 5cm*
- £55 ● Linda Bee

Navajo Ring ◄
- *circa 1970s*

Silver Navajo ring with two oval turquoise stones set within a feather design.
- *length 4cm*
- £169 ● Wilde Ones

Expert Tips

Prior to the Victorian age the rose cut was the most popular technique used for cutting gems and stones. It was replaced by the brilliant cut, which increases the sparkle and desirability of the stone.

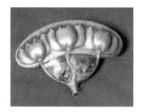

Art Nouveau Brooch ▲
- *circa 1900*
Art Nouveau brooch with silver tulips with orange and green enamel settings, designed by Liberty & Co.
- *length 3cm*
- £350　　　• Gooday Gallery

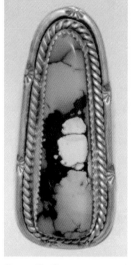

Zuni Ring ▲
- *circa 2000*
Zuni silver ring with a central sun symbol inset with jet and turquoise stones, surrounded by a feather design.
- *length 3.5cm*
- £169　　　• Wilde Ones

Navajo Ring ▼
- *circa 1930s*
A Navajo silver ring with a lozenge-shaped and elongated Kingman turquoise stone.
- *length 5.6cm*
- £299　　　• Wilde Ones

Cannetille Cross ◀
- *1820*
A gold Cannetille cross designed as a pendant.
- £550　　　• Michele Rowan

Gold Earrings ▼
- *1870*
Gold and coral Etruscan revival hooped earrings.
- £650　　　• Michele Rowan

American Indian Bracelet ▲
- *circa 1980s*
Gentleman's channel-work silver bracelet inset with chrysocolla and azurite stones.
- *diameter 23.2cm*
- £299　　　• Wilde Ones

Turquoise Pendant ▲
- *circa 1970*
Zuni silver and beaded pendant set with four lozenge-shaped turquoise stones surmounted by a sun symbol with red coral insert.
- *length 6cm*
- £399　　　• Wilde Ones

Deco Lapiz Bracelet ▶

- 1950

Art Deco bracelet with circular lapis lazulai discs with gold links and rectangular enamels with dragon designs.
- *length 19cm*
- £4,500 • N. Bloom

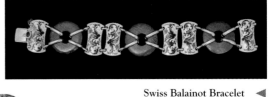

Swiss Balainot Bracelet ◀

- 1960

Swiss gold bracelet by Balainot from the 'Sheet Range'.
- *height 6cm*
- £3,950 • N. Bloom

Snake Bracelet ▼

- 1930

Gilt bracelet styled as a coiled serpent with a spiralled chain link, body and scale design to the head and tail.
- *8cm x 8cm*
- £85 • Linda Bee

Coral and Diamond Earrings ▼

- *circa 1910*

Carved coral ball and lozenge shape earrings set in platinum and 18ct gold with a diamond bow linking the upper and lower sections.
- *length 5.5cm*
- £2,475 • Wimpole Antiques

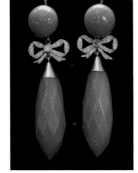

Bear Claw Belt Buckle ▲

- 1950

Bear claw set in silver foliate design with two flowers with coral and turquoise. Stamped E. King and found on an Apache reservation.
- *diameter 7cm*
- £699 • Wilde Ones

Jade Earrings ▼

- 1930

Carved flower jade earrings set in 14ct gold.
- *width 2.5cm*
- £1,150 • N. Bloom

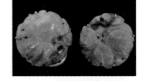

Expert Tips

It is advisable to test all joints in bracelets and necklaces for play, and brooch clasps for security, while ring shanks should not be too thin as they can snap.

French Jade Brooch ▶

- 1940

French jade carved dragon bar brooch set in gold with gold scrolling.
- *length 9cm* **
- £2,400 • N. Bloom

Ruby and Emerald Pendant ▶

- **1950**
French ruby and emerald flower pendant with diamonds and pearls.
- *length 9.5cm*
- **£19,500**   • N. Bloom

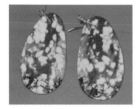

Santa Domingo Earrings ▲

- **1960**
Oval Santa Domingo rare turquoise and black earrings from Arizona.
- *length 4cm*
- **£129**   • Wilde Ones

Navajo Green Bracelet ▲

- **1930**
Navajo silver bracelet with two rosettes each side of a large green stone.
- *length of stone 6cm*
- **£459**   • Wilde Ones

Metal Enamel Pin ▲

- **circa 1930**
English metal enamel pin by Dismal Desmond, with a seated black dog with a purple bow around its neck.
- *7.5cm x 2.5cm*
- **£75**   • Linda Bee

Ruby Heart Locket ▼

- **1850**
Ruby enamelled heart shaped locket with central gold star with diamonds and a single pearl in the centre, surrounded by scrolling set with diamonds with gold ring clasps on a velvet neck ribbon.
- *width 2.5cm*
- **£8,950**   • N. Bloom

Zuni Ceremonial Ring ▲

- **1920**
Lady's Zuni traditional ceremonial ring set with 17 turquoise stones in a flower design.
- *diameter 5cm*
- **£269**   • Wilde Ones

Expert Tips

Recently, with the return of retro design in both fashion and furniture, jewellery from the 1960s and 1970s has become popular.

Art Deco Brooch ▲
- *circa 1925*
An unusual brooch of the Art Deco period, made in the form of an undulating diamond and onyx scroll, with carved emerald terminals, mounted in platinum. By Boucheron of Paris.
- *length 5.5cm*
- £75,000   • Sandra Cronan

Pendant and Earrings ▼
- *circa 1880*
A matching set of pendant and earrings, pendant showing enamel figure inside ornate, gold flower and petal surround. The earrings (not shown) are of two cherubs with pearls and flowers.
- £2,500   • Emmy Abé

Amethyst Collar ▼
- *circa 1870*
Victorian gold and brilliant-cut faceted amethyst collar. Made in England, in original case.
- £950   • Michelle Rowan

Tab Necklace ▲
- *circa 1936*
Santa Domingo Pueblo tab necklace of red coral, spiny oyster shell and natural matrix turquoise, strung on double-strand original cord.
- *length 46cm*
- £499   • Wilde Ones

Earrings ▲
- *circa 1895*
A pair of late Victorian cultivated pearl and diamond set earrings, formed as flower-head clusters, with twelve diamonds set about a pearl. English.
- £14,500   • Sandra Cronan

Headdress ◄
- *circa 1970*
Turkmen harem-style metal headdress with chain and plate pendant adornments and plated band with metal teardrop to centre with turquoise inset. Made in Afghanistan.
- £83   • Oriental Rug

Art Deco Brooch ▲
- *circa 1925*
An Art Deco brooch of two highly naturalistic parrots, wings spread, fighting over a perch. With diamonds and calibré, buff-topped emeralds, sapphires, rubies and onyx. Mounted on platinum. Made in England.
- £36,500   • Sandra Cronan

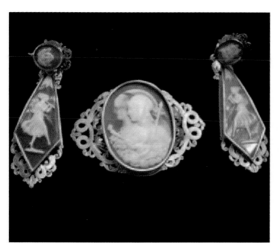

Victorian Cameo Brooch ▼
- *1875*

A cameo of a pre-Raphaelite lady looking to dexter, in classical dress.
- *height 6cm*
- £950   • RBR Group

French Cameo Brooch ▲
- *1870*

French cameo of lady's head set in 18ct. gold encrusted with diamonds and pearls.
- *diameter 4cm*
- £3,250   • RBR Group

Shell Cameo Earrings and Brooch ◄
- *1840*

Shell cameo set with a mythological tone, in 18ct. gold with scrolled borders.
- £2,500   • RBR Group

Italian Cameo Brooch ▲
- *1885*

An Italian shell cameo showing a bust of a lady set in an English 18ct. gold base.
- *length 7cm*
- £1,950   • RBR Group

Medusa Cameo Ring ▲
- *1880*

Ring in 18ct. gold with a cameo of Medusa.
- *diameter 1cm*
- £750   • RBR Group

Angel Cameo Brooch ◄
- *1860*

Cameo of an angel with a dove, set within a 15ct. gold base with gadrooned border.
- *height 4cm*
- £850   • RBR Group

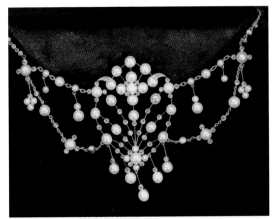

Pearl and Diamond Necklace

- *circa 1905*

Edwardian pearl and diamond necklace with droplets and swag designs.

- *length 6cm*
- £3,950 • Wimpole Antiques

Victorian Gold Bracelet

- *circa 1880*

Victorian gold bracelet in the Etruscan revival style with architectural designs, set with pearls.

- £2,250 • Wimpole Antiques

Gold Brooch/Pendant

- *circa 1875*

Victorian 15ct gold brooch/pendant with natural pearls and floral enamel designs.

- *length 8cm*
- £1,275 • Wimpole Antiques

Pearl Necklace

- *circa 1900*

15ct gold necklace with half pearls and a second row of swagged pearls between floral droplets.

- *length 4cm*
- £2,955 • Wimpole Antiques

Art Deco and Diamond Clasp

- *1920*

Art Deco jade and diamond clasp together with a re-strung twisted cultured pearl necklace.

- *clasp 4cm*
- £3,950   • N. Bloom

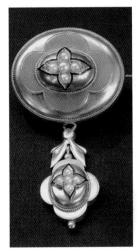

American Gold Bracelet

- *1950*

American heavy textured gold link bracelet with geometric engraving on some of the links.

- *4cm (link size)*
- £3,300   • N. Bloom

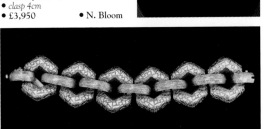

Dress Buttons ▶

- *circa 1880*

A set of gold dress buttons, enamelled in blue, by Fabergé, contained in their original box.
- *length 14cm*
- £8,500   • Sandra Cronan

Spray Brooch ▼

- *circa 1890*

A French 'tremblant' mounted diamond and emerald flower-spray brooch.
- *height 8cm*
- £16,500   • Sandra Cronan

Masonic Jewel ◀

- *circa 1855*

An engraved masonic treasurer's collar jewel, engraved as a money bag with three interlocking keys and pierced ribbon decoration.
- *height 12cm*
- £350   • Guest & Gray

Pearl and Diamond Necklace ▲

- *circa 1875*

An articulated French pearl and diamond necklace, mounted in silver and gold.
- £56,000   • Sandra Cronan

Enamelled Brooch ▲

- *circa 1620*

A fine polychrome enamelled plaque brooch depicting the Annunciation to the Blessed Virgin Mary. In a gold frame of later date.
- £8,500   • Sandra Cronan

Mourning Brooch ▲

- *circa 1870*

A Victorian pinchbeck mourning brooch or scarf pin, with hair arrangement in the pattern of a flower, behind glass
- *diameter 4.5cm*
- £75   • Sugar

Bracelet ▶

- *circa 1910*

A French platinum bracelet mounted with sapphires, diamonds and carved jade and moonstone.
- *length 16cm*
- £6,800   • Sandra Cronan

Amethyst Necklace ▶

- **1950**
Amethyst necklace consisting of
25 lozenge amethysts of varying
sizes set in gold with a nine-stone
amethyst flower design pendant.
- *size of pendant 6cm*
- £2,750 • N. Bloom

Czechoslovakian Brooch ▼

- **1930s**
Czechoslovakian shield brooch
with numerous cut glass stones
within gilt metal settings.
- *7.5cm x 5cm*
- £85 • Linda Bee

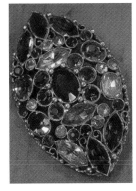

Pig Earrings ▶

- **1930s**
English mother of pearl earrings
styled as little pigs.
- *2.5cm x 2cm*
- £95 • Linda Bee

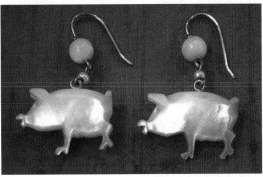

Silver Necklace ▼

- **1960s**
Silver heart necklace with a
bridle link chain.
- *length 30cm*
- £65 • Linda Bee

Spider Brooch ◀

- **1940s**
Gilt metal spider brooch with two
cut glass amethysts.
- *5cm x 5cm*
- £45 • Linda Bee

Marine Items

Marine antiques, apart from being very well made, appeal to the romantic souls of an island race.

Not surprisingly, the sea is a particular obsession with the British. Chronometers and timekeepers, sextants, compasses and barometers always find a ready market. This is not only for sentimental reasons. All these instruments were and, to a lesser extent, still are essential to the lives of sailors. You cannot navigate without being able accurately to tell the time and the importance of being able to gauge the barometric pressure is paramount. As a result, no economies were made on these instruments. If money needed to be saved, it came

off the ship's biscuits, not the clock. These item were made of brass and generally boxed in brass bound mahogany. They tend to have been very we cared for. Life aboard a sailing ship has bee described as 'lon periods of boredor interspersed by brie moments of terror', an it was during the lon periods that many mode of ships, scrimshaw on whalebone an tusk, shellwork pictures and the like were create Modern ecological thinking has steadied the pric of items made from whale over recent years.

Two Day Chronometer ▼
- *circa 1950*

A fine presentation condition chronometer by Hamilton, USA. In mahogany brass-bound case.
- **£3,900** • Langfords Marine

'Prisoner of War' Model ▲
- *circa 1800*

Napoleonic 'Prisoner of War' model. Made of beef bone. All relevant deck detail with standing and running rigging. Warrior figurehead. Contained within a glass dome.
- *30cm x 32cm*
- **£8,800** • Langfords Marine

Marine Mug ▼
- *circa 1930*

A rare marine store-dealer mug by Royal Doulton. Dickensware, showing Mr Micawber from *David Copperfield*, a novel with strong nautical associations.
- *height 13cm*
- **£239** • Ocean Leisure

Model of Life Boat ▶
- *circa 1860*

Clinker-built Pakefield lifeboat. With copper and brass fittings.
- *length 1.4m*
- **£4,800** • Langfords Marine

Chinese Dish from the Ship Diana ▼

- *circa 1817*

Chinese porcelain blue and white dish from the ship 'Diana' which sank near Malacca on 4 March 1817.
- *diameter 28cm*
- £185 • Langfords Marine

Sextant by Whitbread ▲

- *circa 1850*

Sextant by G. Whitbread, in original oak box with brass fittings.
- *width 27cm*
- £1,650 • Langfords Marine

Weichert Chronometer ▼

- *circa 1860*

Two-day chronometer by Weichert, in a coromandel box with brass inlay and handles.
- *height 20cm*
- £4,300 • Langfords Marine

Celestial Globe ▲

- *circa 1950*

Celestial globe with brass fittings, and original oak box carrying handle.
- *height 28cm*
- £1,280 • Langfords Marine

Marine Chronometer ▲

- *circa 1840*

Fine 2-day marine chronometer by Parkinson & Frodsham, Change Alley, London 1705. Housed in a mahogany double-tier case.
- *height 16cm*
- £7,000 • T. Phillips

Steam Yacht ▼

- *circa 1910*

Model steam yacht complete with planked hull, working steam engine, brass funnel prop and lights, and eight portholes.
- *length 100cm*
- £8,000 • Langfords Marine

Octagonal Telescope ▲

- *circa 1780*

Fine octagonal fruitwood telescope with brass single draw and lens housing.
- *length of case 31cm*
- £800 • Langfords Marine

Porthole ▼

- *1901–1910*

Polished porthole made of brass with hinge and locking nut and six bevelled screw holes.
- *diameter 17cm*
- £69 • Ocean Leisure

Model Ship ▼

- *circa 1860*

A model of a four-masted clipper, with long bowsprit, including all rigging, deck fitments and figures. Housed in a glass case.
- *height 42cm*
- £175 • Mark Sullivan

Expert Tips

Marine barometers are always aneroid barometers, which are less precise but less delicate than mercury barometers.

Globe ▲

- *20th century*

A reproduction of a 12-inch diameter, 19th-century globe on a mahogany stand. The original by Nerzbach & Falk, published in 1881.
- *height 43cm*
- £680 • Langfords Marine

Barometer ▲

- *circa 1910*

A rare, Edwardian brass-cased aneroid barometer with scale and weather indications around the circumference of the dial.
- *diameter 24cm*
- £880 • Langfords Marine

Telegraph ▼

- *circa 1880*

A brass model of the engine-room terminal of a ship's telegraph, with bone handle.
- *height 16cm*
- £90 • Mark Sullivan

Porthole ▼

- *circa 1930*

A brass porthole with hinge, but missing locking screw, with six bevelled screw holes.
- *diameter 29cm*
- £45 • Briggs

Ship's Wheel ◄

- *circa 1890*

A small, teak, eight-spoked ship's wheel, with turned spokes and brass hub and banding.
- *diameter 62cm*
- £590 • Langfords Marine

Napoleonic Model Ship ▲
- *1810*
Napoleonic prisoner-of-war ship
Defender on a stand, made of
bone. Very fine detail, good
rigging, good provenance.
- *52cm x 53cm*
- **£85,000** • **Langfords Marine**

Russian Chronometer ▲
- *1880*
Brass Russian chronometer with a
two-day movement in a rosewood
box with brass fittings.
- *19cm x 19cm*
- **£1,400** • **Langfords Marine**

Ivory Box ▲
- *circa 1840*
An unusual and charming ivory
box, possibly originally a
toothpick holder, the hinged lid
with a compass inset, the base
with rose gold fastener.
- *7cm x 3cm*
- **£239** • **Langfords Marine**

Ship's Bell ▶
- *early 20th century*
Ship's brass bell made for the
"Grangeburn".
- *height 31cm*
- **£780** • **Langfords Marine**

Cylindrical Rule ▲
- *1929*
A very rare cranberry glass
cylindrical rule with silver
mounts.
- *length 30cm*
- **£399** • **Langfords Marine**

Oak-Barrelled Telescope ▲
- *19th century*
Polished brass telescope, with a
lacquered oak barrel, signed on
the single drawer "George Leone,
Liverpool".
- *85cm x 7cm*
- **£349** • **Langfords Marine**

Magnifying Glass ◀
- *1837–1901*
Victorian magnifying glass
with ivory handle and silver
decoration.
- *length 19cm*
- **£69** • **Langfords Marine**

Model Yacht ◄

- *circa 1910*

Model yacht inscribed, 'Marine d'autrefois Gildas de Kerdrel, 80 Avenue des Ternes, Paris'.
- *height 27cm*
- £750　　• Langfords Marine

Ebony Octant ▼

- *circa 1840*

Ebony and brass octant in original oak box with label and the inscription, 'W. Hughes, Instrument Maker, 40 Fenchurch Street, London'.
- *width 28cm*
- £785　　• Langfords Marine

Nautical Chandelier ▼

- *circa 1900*

Unusual German oak nautical chandelier. The corona in the form of a ship's wheel, each arm decorated with an iron anchor, with further chains linked to three finely carved life-boats, each with a carved watchman holding a lantern over the bow of the boat. The chandelier centred by a carved lighthouse with a pendant light fitting.
- *height 81.5cm*
- £3,400　　• Anthony Outred

Chinese Porcelain Cup and Bowl ▼

- *circa 1817*

Blue and white Chinese cup and bowl salvaged from the ship 'Diana', a trading ship working the India-China route, which sank near Malacca on 4 March 1817. Found in December 1993.
- *diameter of bowl 17cm*
- £250　　• Langfords Marine

Expert Tips

Early compasses can be found in fitted mahogany boxes. Signatures are important but not mandatory. It is best to avoid the temptation to purchase an instrument that has been over-zealously polished.

Mary Tin ◀

- **1914**

A polished and embossed brass Mary Tin, presented by Princess Mary, aged 17, to all those wearing the King's uniform at Christmas, 1914.
- *width 13cm*
- £79 • Langfords Marine

Ship in a Bottle ▼

- **1885**

Square-rigged ship in a bottle on a mahogany stand.
- *length 28cm*
- £320 • Langfords Marine

Large Brass Compass ▲

- **1880**

Brass compass with original leather case.
- *diameter 440cm*
- £440 • Langfords Marine

Dry Card Compass ▲

- **1870**

Victorian brass dry card compass encased in glass.
- *diameter 16.5cm*
- £680 • Langfords Marine

Bronze Porthole ▼

- **19th century**

A replica polished bronze or gunmetal porthole, with hinged glass port.
- *diameter 35cm*
- £119 • Langfords Marine

Pocket Sextant ◀

- **1895**

Victorian brass pocket drum sextant.
- *diameter 8cm*
- £650 • Langfords Marine

Mahogany Whaling Boat ▼

- **1800**

Rare mahogany model of a whaling boat with brass fittings on original stand.
- *100cm x 16cm*
- £5,600 • Langfords Marine

Musical Instruments

Some musical instruments are also beautiful pieces of furniture; some have been played by the famous. Only the musically excellent are worth real money.

In the field of collecting musical instruments, as in no other, it can be very expensive not to know what you are buying. Violins and cellos by Stradivari fetch astronomical sums of money, as everyone knows; on the other hand, it is quite possible to find an early nineteenth-century violin for no more than a couple of hundred pounds – and then find that it isn't even worth that. Quality of materials, craftsmanship and, crucially, musical quality are all important. There is no way of mass-producing musical instruments, so every one is an individual. Whether they will last depends on the quality of the materials and the manufacture. Stradivari used materials that made his instruments improve with age; many people did not. Because of their individuality and hand-made quality, even very new instruments are highly collectable. Guitars, for instance, can fetch stratospheric prices. The Gibson flying Vee, listed here, was made in 1958, one of a total of 98 produced, and is worth a staggering £55,000. Modern musical instruments are subject to the memento trade – famous players signing their instruments for charity sales. Remember, no two instruments are alike, and it is unlikely that they will be giving away their best.

Sphere Speaker ▼
- 1970

Metal sphere enclosing 12 speakers, with a chrome stand, by Grundig of Germany.
- *height 87.5cm*
- £900   • Zoom

Casino Guitar ▲
- 1967

Epiphone Casino guitar in sunburst.
- *110cm x 41cm*
- £2,500   • Vintage Guitars

Gibson Guitar ▼
- 1963

Custom-made Gibson guitar in sunburst with block markers and ebony fingerboard (left handed), serial no. ES335.
- £8,500   • Vintage Guitars

Gretsch Guitar ▼
• *1957*
Gretsch guitar. Mode: 6120, with
original white cowboy case.
S/N:22080
• *height 105cm*
• **£5,545**   • **Vintage Guitars**

Gibson Guitar ▼
• *1953*
Gibson Model SJ200. Sunburst
finish. S/N A17263.
• *height 105cm*
• **£5,850**   • **Vintage Guitars**

Gibson Guitar ▲
• *1960*
Gibson. Model: ES330. Sunburst
finish. Dot neck. Factory order #
R29523.
• *height 99cm*
• **£2,850**   • **Vintage Guitars**

Gibson Flying Vee ▲
• *1958*
Korina wood Gibson Flying Vee,
the Holy Grail of vintage solid
body guitars. Only 100 were ever
made.
• **£55,000**   • **Vintage Guitars**

Fender Guitar ▼
• *1959*
Fender. Model: Esquire. Blond
finish. S/N 40511.
• *height 95cm*
• **£5,500**   • **Vintage Guitars**

Fender Guitar ▼
• *1959*
Fender. Model: Jazzmaster.
Sunburst finish. Original tweed
case. S/N 31596
• *height 104cm*
• **£2,095**   • **Vintage Guitars**

Ampeg Guitar ▲

- *1962*
AEB-1 scroll base Ampeg guitar in cherry with white pick-guard.
- £1,580 • Vintage Guitars

Lead Amplifier ▼

- *circa 1970s*
A British Park 100-watt lead amplifier.
- £950 • Vintage Guitars

Expert Tips

Amplifiers and speakers are increasing in interest and value as the musician strives for an authentic sound that can only be truly heard or expressed by using vintage equipment of the rock era. This market still has great potential for growth.

Epiphone Frontier ▼

- *1960*
Epiphone Frontier guitar in sunburst finish.
- £2,500 • Vintage Guitars

Music Box ▲

- *1820*
A French oval maplewood music box, finely painted with birds and flowers.
- *diameter 16cm*
- £1,200 • John Clay

Gibson Trini Lopez ▲

- *1967*
Gibson Trini Lopez in cherry red finish with diamond inlay and sound holes.
- £2,500 • Vintage Guitars

Precision Bass ◄

- *1963*
Fender Precision bass in metallic turquoise with rosewood fingerboard, custom ordered.
- £3,995 • Vintage Guitars

Gibson Les Paul ▲
- *1959*

With faded flame top, serial no. 91258. The '59, between the chubbier '58 and the flat '60, was regarded as the players' favourite.
- £35,000 • Vintage Guitars

Epiphone Riviera ▲
- *circa 1967*

Riviera, in sunburst, with a Frequentata tailpiece, mini-humbuckers and 'f' holes. Favoured by The Beatles.
- £1,800 • Vintage Guitars

Silver Sparkle ▼
- *circa 1955*

A Gretsch Duo Jet with Bigsby tremelo and block inlays. Serial no. 17177.
- £5,000 • Vintage Guitars

Grecian Harp ▼
- *circa 1821*

Grecian harp by S. & P. Erard of Paris, with 43 strings. Painted black with gold decoration to the pillar.
- £9,575 • Clive Morley

Grand Piano ▶
- *circa 1939*

Steinway model M grand piano, fully rebuilt by Steinway, in high-polished mahogany.
- *length 1.7m*
- £27,500 • Steinway

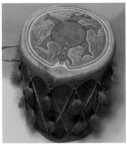

Drum ▲
- *circa 1970*

Native American drum made of wood and skin and decorated with bone and feathers, with a green turtle on the skin.
- *height 65cm*
- £400 • Wilde Ones

Gothic Harp ▲
- *circa 1850*

Gothic, 46-string harp in maple and gold, with decorated pillar. Made in Paris, in the mid-19th-century, by Erard.
- £15,000 • Clive Morley

435

Mahogany Cased Organ ▼
- 1805
Rare organ by Broderip &
Wilkinson, London, in full
working order, complete with six
barrels each with up to eight
different tunes.
- *height 226cm*
- **£24,500**   • Anthony Outred

Rosewood Satin Piano ▼
- 1906
Model K. rosewood satin piano
with inlay veneer. Fully rebuilt by
Steinway & Sons. Made in
Hamburg.
- *height 135cm*
- **£21,500**   • Steinway

Square Piano ▼
- *circa 1790*
Richyardus Horfburgh mahogany
square piano, made in Edinburgh.
- *width 1.58m*
- **£5,775**   • Clive Morley

Steinway Grand Piano ▼
- *circa 1960*
Mahogany, model B grand piano,
rebuilt by Steinway.
- *length 2.1m*
- **£40,000**   • Steinway

Console Piano ▲
- *circa 1840*
A Pape console piano in
rosewood, with bracket-type legs.
- *height 99cm*
- **£2,500**   • Riverbank

Art Deco Piano ▲
- *circa 1930*
An Art Deco, mahogany baby
grand piano, by Monnington &
Western, with German
mechanism, resting on square,
tapered legs.
- *length 1.26m*
- **£3,400**   • Oola Boola

Square Piano ▲
- *circa 1787*
Thomas Haxby square piano,
made in York, with mahogany
case with inlaid banding and
decorative nameboard.
- **£5,360**   • Clive Morley

Silver & Pewter

Cream jugs, sugar bowls, salt cellars and tea pots are a sensible place to start collecting silver. Utility is always worth its price.

Smaller and less spectacular items in silver and pewter tend to be valued more highly if they are useful. Large, important pieces by well-known makers are expensive because there is always a demand at the top of the market, but, at the lower end of the market, it is utility that holds sway. Silver collectors have the advantage over the collectors of other types of antiques, in that most items carry hallmarks, which give information on the date and place of manufacture and the maker. Pewter too carries makers' marks, known as 'touch marks', which were registered with Pewterers' Hall in London until 1824. In theory, therefore, a collector equipped with a comprehensive key to all the codes should need to know very little else, but the practice, fortunately, is not so simple. Hallmarks, like most things, can be faked and the serious collector will be more concerned to identify a piece stylistically and by other characteristics – such as weight and general 'feel' – and will only consult the hallmark for confirmation.

Liberty Silver Vase
- *circa 1900*
English silver Tudric Liberty bomb vase.
- *height 19cm*
- £800   ● Arwas

Barmaid's Measure ▶
- *circa 1860*
English pewter barmaid's half-pint measure tankard with waisted body, ear shaped handle and banded design.
- *11cm x 8cm*
- £55   ● Jane Stewart

Silver Condiment Set ▲
- *1964*
Silver condiment set consisting of a salt, mustard and pepper pot. Made in Sheffield, England.
- *height 8cm*
- £400   ● Stephen Kalms

Liberty Bulb Vase ▲
- *circa 1900*
Tudric pewter Liberty bulb vase with a hammered finish and five conical necks.
- *height 22cm*
- £480   ● Arwas

Dublin Dish Ring ▼

- **1913**

A Irish dish ring, made in Dublin, highly decorated with gadrooned borders, and pierced floral designs centered with oval cartouches.
- *10cm x 19cm*
- **£3,500**   • **B. Silverman**

Dessert Suite ▼

- **1862**

A Victorian solid silver épergne dessert suite, highly decorated with embossed foliate designs, raised on a serpentine base.
- *height 54cm*
- **£16,000**   • **B. Silverman**

Wine Coaster ▼

- **1845**

A finely detailed wine coaster, with pierced designs depicting flowers and birds, surmounted by a serpentine rim.
- *diameter 14cm*
- **£1,800**   • **B. Silverman**

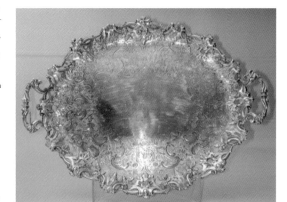

Silver Serving Tray ▲

- **1836**

A fine William IV silver serving tray, with lavish foliate and shell design to the rim and handle, made by Robert Garrard.
- *59cm x 44cm*
- **£9,000**   • **B. Silverman**

Knife Set ▲

- *circa 1800*

Twelve pairs of George III knives with mother-of-pearl handles with unmarked silver terminals.
- *length 19cm*
- **£1,500**   • **B. Silverman**

Silver Dessert Set ▲

- **1800**

Silver dessert set, designed by Pitts & Preedy, consisting of five pieces with solid silver bases and cut glass bowls.
- *diameter 18cm (largest)*
- **£15,000**   • **B. Silverman**

Cream Pail ▼

- **1764**

A finely detailed George III silver cream pail with hinged lattice handle.
- *diameter 8cm*
- **£850**   • **B. Silverman**

Adam Style Teapot ◀
- *circa 1860*
English Adam style pewter teapot with floral and swag decoration, surmounted by ivory finial.
- *16cm x 25cm*
- £65　　　　　• Jane Stewart

Silver Perfume Spray ▼
- *circa 1910*
Silver perfume spray on a faceted glass circular bottle.
- *height 17cm*
- £175　　　　　• Barrett Towning

Glass Sugar Shaker ▼
- *circa 1906*
Glass sugar castor of baluster form, with a pierced silver cover, engraved floral designs and ball finial.
- *height 16.5cm*
- £225　　　　• Barrett Towning

English Pewter Ladle ▼
- *circa 1820*
English pewter ladle with a wide circular bowl.
- *33cm*
- £50　　　　　• Jane Stewart

Pepper Caster ▲
- *circa 1800*
English pewter pepper caster of baluster form with acorn finial.
- *12cm*
- £30　　　　　• Jane Stewart

Georgian Silver Candlesticks ◀
- *1782*
A superb set of four Georgian silver candlesticks, fully hallmarked by John Parsons, Sheffield, England.
- *height 34cm*
- £10,750　　　　• Percy's Ltd

Silver Ash Tray ▶
- **1900**
Silver ashtray made in London
with five recesses within the
border.
- *8cm x 8cm*
- **£1,900** • Henry Gregory

Silver Art Nouveau Vase ▼
- **1850**
Silver Art Nouveau vase with
green glass lining and profuse
pierced decoration.
- *height 34cm*
- **£1,850** • Tagor

Silver Soap Box ▲
- *circa 1888*
Victorian silver soap box of plain
design with curved corners.
- *width 8cm*
- **£225** • Barrett Towning

Four Silver Salts ▼
- *circa 1808*
Set of four urn-shaped silver salts
with gadrooned and fluted
decoration, made in London.
- *height 6cm*
- **£475** • Barrett Towning

Claret Jug ▲
- *circa 1880*
Victorian claret jug with silver
spout and collar with scrolled
decoration, made in London.
- *height 21cm*
- **£1,350** • Tagor

Cream Jug ▼
- *1802*

George III cream jug with ornate flower and scallop tooling and a ribbon handle.
- *height 12cm*
- £220 • Vivienne Carroll

Coffee Pot ▼
- *1762*

Large George III coffee pot of exceptional weight, with 'C' scroll spout, gadrooned border and armorial cartouche. By Smith & Sharp, London.
- *height 31cm*
- £4,750 • Percy's Ltd

Candlesticks ▲
- *1713*

Fine pair of Queen Anne candlesticks on octagonal bases. Made by William Twell.
- *height 19cm*
- £22,500 • Marks Antiques

Set of Napkin Rings ▲
- *1895*

Originally boxed set of four napkin rings with cartouches and heavy floral decoration and serpentine borders. By George Jackson, London.
- £700 • Stephen Kalms

Baluster Tankard ▼
- *1765*

Solid silver tankard marked inside lid and base with 'C' scroll handle. By John and William Bold, London.
- *height 20.5cm*
- £1,800 • J. First

Centrepiece ▼
- *1890*

Showing a romantic figure holding aloft a cornucopia and etched glass dish, on heavily engraved base and lion feet.
- *height 50cm*
- £5,750 • Stephen Kalms

Wine Coolers ◄
- *1825*

Pair of Sheffield plate wine coolers, camana-shaped. Original condition with original liners, leaf, shell and gadroon decoration with let-in shield.
- *height 23cm*
- £3,650 • Langfords

441

Victorian Silver Cruet ◀

- **1867**
A fine solid silver cruet comprising ten items, with pierced scrolled sides and scrolled central handle, by G Angel, London.
- *25cm x 30cm*
- **£3,750** • **Percy's Ltd**

Art Nouveau Frame ▲

- *circa 1900*
Silver and enamel Art Nouveau picture frame by William Connell.
- *height 23cm*
- **£2,800** • **Arwas**

Silver Teapot with Bee ▶

- *circa 1900*
Silver teapot with unusual foliate and insect design with a bee finial, and stylised bamboo spout and handle.
- *height 16cm*
- **£1,500** • **Tagor**

Continental Pewter Plate ▼

- *circa 1790s*
Continental pewter plate with a rifle stamp on the border with a single reeded rim.
- *diameter 25.5cm*
- **£70** • **Jane Stewart**

Tudric Jug ▲

- *circa 1900*
Tudric Liberty pewter 'fish and the sea' jug with brass handle, and the inscription U. C. C.
- *height 19cm*
- **£680** • **Arwas**

Liberty Biscuit Tin ▲

- *circa 1900*
Pewter tudric box by Archibald Knox with floral design.
- *height 12.5cm*
- **£1,200** • **Arwas**

Expert Tips

On most coasters one must look out for hallmark on the lower rim, which overlaps the wooden base.

Silver Planter ▼

● **1892**
A Victorian silver planter made in Sheffield with scrolled designs on a lattice ground.
● *height 11cm*
● **£650**   ● **Stephen Kalms**

Boxed Dish Set ▼

● *circa 1900*
A fitted oak case with three dishes made by Elkington & Co. of Birmingham.
● *length 60cm*
● **£2,400**   ● **Stephen Kalms**

Covered Serving Dish ▶

● **1900**
A silver covered serving dish with gadrooned borders and asymmetric scrolled designs made by Hatkins of Sheffield.
● *diameter 22cm*
● **£1,200**   ● **Stephen Kalms**

Scallop-Shaped Dishes ▲

● **1884**
A pair of Victorian silver dishes, naturalistically formed as scallop shells.
● *width 12cm*
● **£325**   ● **Stephen Kalms**

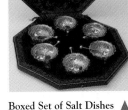

Double-Handled Trophy Cup ▲

● **1861**
A silver urn-shaped cup and cover with C-scrolled handles on fluted pedestal base, made by H. Wilkinson of Sheffield.
● *height 29cm*
● **£1,950**   ● **Stephen Kalms**

Boxed Set of Salt Dishes ▲

● **1880**
A set of small, fine salt dishes in a fitted box made in London.
● *diameter 6cm*
● **£1,100**   ● **Stephen Kalms**

Three-Handled Cup ▲

● **1914**
A silver cup on a raised splayed foot with three ribbon handles, made in Birmingham.
● *height 15cm*
● **£700**   ● **Stephen Kalms**

Gilded Fruit Bowl ◀

- *1910*

Silver-plated fruit bowl with gilded interior and a glass liner on a pedestal foot with geometric designs and gadrooned border, engraved "W.M.F".

- *12cm x 24cm*
- £650 • Gooday Gallery

Silver Wine Funnel ▲

- *1834*

A detailed silver wine funnel made by Joseph & Albert of London.

- *height 14cm*
- £1,750 • B. Silverman

George III Candlesticks ▼

- *1760*

A pair of fine George III loaded candlesticks in the style of a Corinthian column, handcrafted by Dennis Wilks.

- *height 32cm*
- £6,500 • B. Silverman

Straight-Sided Tankard ▲

- *1850*

A silver and pewter half-pint tankard of straight-sided form, with banded decoration to the base.

- *height 10cm*
- £40 • Jane Stewart

George III Wine Funnel ▲

- *1804*

A fine George III silver wine funnel by R & D Flennell.

- *height 15cm*
- £1,500 • B. Silverman

Victorian Blotter ▼

- *1899*

A fine silver blotter made in Birmingham with engraved floral designs on the back with thistle-shaped handle.

- *width 9cm*
- £375 • Stephen Kalms

French Pewter Plate ◀

- *1900*

A French pewter plate from Orleans with embossed designs to the rim and centre.

- *diameter 24cm*
- £65 • Jane Stewart

Expert Tips

The earliest silver table candlesticks date back to the first half of the seventeenth century, during the reign of Charles I, and are now very rare. American candlesticks of this period are also extremely rare.

Soup Ladle ▶
- *1790*

George III soup ladle, old English pattern. By Hester Bateman.
- *length 32cm*
- £1,050　　　• **Langfords**

Vesta ▲
- *1887*

Very fine silver and enamel vesta with hunting scene of three riders and hounds at water's edge.
- *length 6cm*
- £3,400　• **S. & A. Thompson**

Expert Tips

Decorations involving a sport or a recognisable place are popular with collectors.

Menorah ▼
- *1925*

Jewish menorah candle holder in solid silver.
- *height 32cm*
- £850　　　　　• **J. First**

Bonbon Dish ▶
- *19th century*

Continental silver bonbon dish embossed with a central panel showing musicians in a wooded glade, with pierced surround.
- *length 13.5cm*
- £160　　　　• **John Clay**

Goblet ▼
- *1792*

Embossed with floral and leaf decoration, with cartouche (possible later application). Made in London.
- *height 15cm*
- £850　　• **Stephen Kalms**

Chinese Silver Tray ▶
- *circa 1860*

Tray with pierced trellis and floral border. Centre of tray with engraved floral spray decoration. Bamboo form handles and four ball feet. By Luen Wo.
- *length 55cm*
- £900　　　　　• **J. First**

Wine Coolers ▲
- *circa 1850*

A pair of silver-plated wine coolers with heavy vine and fruit decoration and profuse beading to lip and base. By Elkington & Co.
- *height 31cm*
- £7,250　　• **Percy's Ltd**

Art Nouveau Sauce Boat ▶

- *circa 1900*
German Art Nouveau pewter
sauce-boat with fixed base
designed by Orovit.
- *height 12cm*
- £300   • Arwas

Salts with Shell Feet ▲

- *1913*
Pair of silver circular salts with
a serpentine scalloped rim,
standing on three scalloped
feet.
- *diameter 7.5cm*
- £395   • Barrett Towning

Scrolled Silver Box ▼

- *1840*
Oblong silver box with embossed
scrolling and floral designs and a
cartouche inscribed with the
name 'Hilda'.
- *length 13cm*
- £175   • Barrett Towning

Silver Pepper Caster ▲

- *circa 1860*
Silver pepper caster of baluster
form with a pierced and engraved
cover surmounted by a finial lid.
- *height 19cm*
- £325   • Barrett Towning

Silver Milk Jug ▶

- *circa 1940*
Silver milk jug with a lobbed
body, engraved and embossed
decoration and a reeded handle.
- *height 11cm*
- £300   • Barrett Towning

Silver Tea Set ◀

- *circa 1851*
Three piece silver tea set with
large scrolled handle standing on
small paw feet.
- *height 17cm (teapot)*
- £540   • Henry Gregory

Silver Champagne Cup ▼

- *1902*

A silver champagne cup with saucer-shaped bowl, made by William Adams Ltd, Birmingham.

- *height 14cm*
- £1,160 • Linden & Co.

Edwardian Centrepiece ▼

- *1902*

A silver centrepiece with pierced and moulded floral designs on a raised foot, made by C.S. Morris of London.

- *14cm x 23cm*
- £990 • Stephen Kalms

Coffee Pot ▲

- *1767*

A fine silver coffee pot of simple design with high domed lid and finial, and reeded scroll handle, by T. Jones of London.

- *height 26cm*
- £1,750 • Stephen Kalms

George III Argyle ▲

- *1783*

A fine George III argyle with finial lid, thumb piece, reeded side handle and gadrooned base, made in London.

- *height 11cm*
- £6,250 • Stephen Kalms

Victorian Centrepiece ▼

- *circa 1850*

An ornate silver-plated centrepiece with four branches set with engraved cut glass bowls, surmounted by a large fifth bowl to the centre.

- *height 65cm*
- £6,500 • Butchoff

Sheffield Caster ▼

- *1911*

A fine caster of conical form with fluted designs, finial top and serpentine moulded base. Made in Sheffield.

- *height 13cm*
- £600 • Stephen Kalms

[image of caster]

Pierced Silver Dish ◄

- *1893*

A Victorian silver dish with a wide pierced border on scrolled feet, made by W. Hutton of London.

- *width 19cm*
- £450 • Stephen Kalms

447

Set of Four Dishes ▲

- *1736*
An unusual set of four George II silver chalice-shaped dishes, by John Le Sage.
- *5cm x 9cm*
- £11,500   • B. Silverman

Biscuit Box ▲

- *1896*
A Victorian silver biscuit box with scrolled designs centered with cartouches, the cover with ivory finial, made in Birmingham.
- *18cm x 23cm*
- £3,950   • Stephen Kalms

Sheffield Coffee Pot ▲

- *1898*
A coffee pot of baluster form with domed lid and scrolled bone handle made by Mappin & Webb of Sheffield.
- *height 25cm*
- £1,475   • Stephen Kalms

Chalice-Shaped Dishes ▼

- *1862*
A Victorian pair of silver dishes with fluted design made in Birmingham by Elkington.
- *16cm x 22cm*
- £4,350   • Stephen Kalms

Silver-Mounted Claret Jug ▼

- *1879*
A fine silver-mounted glass claret jug with engraved stars on the glass. Made by Jenner & Knewstub of London.
- *height 32cm*
- £2,900   • Stephen Kalms

Silver Ink Stand ▼

- *1997*
A silver ink tray with reservoir of simple design, made in Birmingham.
- *width 24cm*
- £490   • Stephen Kalms

Goldsmiths Vases ▼

- *1912*
A set of three vases made by Goldsmiths of London with tapered conical necks on a splayed foot.
- £1,450   • Stephen Kalms

Spoons and Fruit Scissors ▶

- *circa 1860*

Fruit scissors with a fleur de lys on the join and a pair of silver plated fruit spoons, with the initials J. E., complete with the original presentation box.
- *length 23cm*
- £425 • Barrett Towning

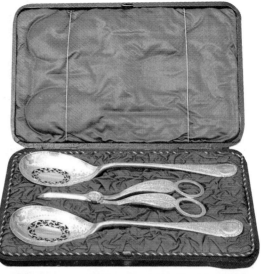

Slim Cigarette Case ▲

- *circa 1920*

Slim silver cigarette case with a diamond pattern design within banded borders.
- *length 11cm*
- £68 • Henry Gregory

Silver Sugar Spoon ▲

- *1816*

Silver sugar spoon, the bowl embossed with fruit, the letters J.R. on the handle and engraved lattice designs.
- *length 18cm*
- £165 • Barrett Towning

Expert Tips

When deciding to purchase a silver box always check the hinges as they are are almost impossible to repair.

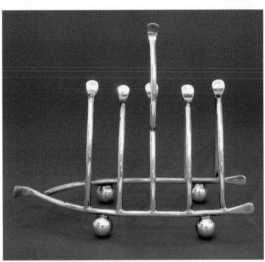

Wish Bone Toast Rack ▲

- *circa 1880*

Silver toast rack incorporating a wish bone design, standing on four ball feet.
- *height 13cm*
- £155 • Barrett Towning

Silver Cigar Case ◀

- *circa 1920*

Silver bullet shaped cigar case with three compartments.
- *length 11cm*
- £160 • Henry Gregory

Condiment Set ▶
- *1935*

Six-piece condiment set comprising two salt, two pepper and two mustard pots of rectangular form with champfered corners. Art Deco by Mappin & Webb of London.
- £600
- Linden & Co.

Liberty Cup ▲
- *1900*

Liberty cup of beaten pewter with traditional tree pattern typical of Art Nouveau period.
- *height 20cm*
- £600
- Arwas

Candlesticks ▲
- *1770*

Pair of George III cast silver candlesticks on gadrooned bases. By John Carter, London.
- *height 25cm*
- £6,250
- Marks Antiques

Fruit Stands ▲
- *1795*

Set of three fruit stands with solid silver bases and cut-glass bowls. By William Pitts and William Preedy, London.
- £5,700
- J. First

Urn ▲
- *circa 1790*

Silver-plated urn with scalloped rim and lion-mask handles on ball foot pedestal base.
- *height 49cm*
- £1,250
- Langfords

Candelabra ▼
- *1901*

An unusual pair of silver candelabra of woven stem and branches with leaf motif. On gadrooned square bases. By Charles Stuart Harris, London.
- *height 42cm*
- £6,750
- Percy's Ltd

Neff ▼
- *1902*

A four-wheeled neff in the shape of a schooner, with several figures, cannon, pennants, anchors and all exaggerated detail. By B. Müller.
- *height 41cm*
- £6,000
- Stephen Kalms

Victorian Silver Basket

- 1897

A silver cake basket with pierced designs and ribbon handle on shaped feet, made in Sheffield.

- 7cm x 30cm
- £900   • Stephen Kalms

Edwardian Silver Card Box ▼

- 1900

A silver card box profusely engraved with floral meanderings, including two original sets of cards from Vienna. Made in Birmingham.

- height 6cm
- £475   • Stephen Kalms

Double-Handled Chalice ▼

- 1937

A simply designed silver bowl with double scrolled handles and moulded rim on a splayed shaped foot, made in Birmingham.

- 8cm x 21cm
- £1,100   • Stephen Kalms

Silver Bell with Ivory Handle ▲

- 1884

A small silver tea-bell with an ivory handle made by C. & T. Fox.

- height 10cm
- £1,250   • B. Silverman

Silver Oval Basket ▼

- 1918

An oval silver basket with a pierced diamond lattice design and plain splayed rim, made in London.

- length 33cm
- £600   • Stephen Kalms

Victorian Silver Dish ▼

- 1896

A silver dish of oval form with leaf and scroll design and serpentine border, made in London.

- length 30cm
- £495   • Stephen Kalms

Cutlery Set ◄

- 1840–1905

A silver cutlery set of shell and fiddle design comprising 173 pieces including: table spoons, table knives and forks, dessert spoons, forks and knives, teaspoons, one butter knife, two stuffing spoons and two sauce ladles.

- £21,000   • B. Silverman

Sheffield Silver Basket ▶
- *1916*
A silver basket with shaped
borders hand crafted by J.
Dickson of Sheffield.
- *14cm x 39cm x 29cm*
- **£6,000**   • **Stephen Kalms**

Christening Mug ▼
- *1878*
A fine silver christening mug
with gilded interior and floral
engraving, made in Sheffield.
- *height 10cm*
- **£350**   • **Stephen Kalms**

Silver Pierced Basket ▼
- *1907*
A pierced silver basket with floral
designs, gadrooned borders and
cartouche on four ball feet. Made
by C.S. Hennell of London.
- *14cm x 27cm*
- **£2,450**   • **Stephen Kalms**

Condiment and Caster Set ▼
- *1895*
A fine boxed set incorporating
salt, pepper, sugar and mustard
condiments highly decorated
with scrolled meanderings. Made
in Birmingham.
- *height 20cm*
- **£1,200**   • **Stephen Kalms**

Raised Silver Dish ▶
- *1932*
A silver shallow dish on a raised
splayed foot with scrolled border,
made by Walker & Hall of
Sheffield.
- *10cm x 23cm*
- **£525**   • **Stephen Kalms**

Goldsmiths Scent Bottle ▲
- *1902*
A silver and glass scent bottle
with profuse foliate designs to the
body and stopper, made by
Goldsmiths of London.
- *height 14cm*
- **£1,275**   • **Stephen Kalms**

Expert Tips

*When cleaning pierced silver
frames or mounts with a leather
or velvet backing, it is possible
to remove the silver, as they are
generally pinned in place.*

Edwardian Monteith ▶
- *1906*
A fine silver bowl in the style of
an eighteenth century monteith
with scalloped collar and floral
designs on a raised foot. Made in
Birmingham.
- *20cm x 37cm*
- **£2,450**   • **Stephen Kalms**

Liberty & Co. Tea Set ◄

• 1903

Pewter tudric tea set with turquoise enamel mounts, and tray designed by Archibald Knox for Liberty & Co.
• *length 42cm*
• £4,500   • Liberty plc

Silver Pierced Dish ▼

• 1950

Silver dish with pierced border, supported on a pedestal base with banded decoration.
• *height 15cm*
• £175   • Stephen Kalms

Silver Gilt Heron Cigarette Box ▲

• *circa 1909*

Silver gilt heron standing on a silver box, the mechanism opens the cover for the heron to bend and pick out a cigarette. Made by W. H. Sparrow of Birmingham.
• *height 30cm*
• £4,250   • Stephen Kalms

Set of Salts ▶

• 1880

Set of six silver gilt salts with individual spoons with original presentation box.
• *width 24cm*
• £1,100   • Stephen Kalms

Polar Bear Inkwell ◄

• *circa 1900*

Continental silver polar bear inkwell and tray, with a pair of silver candlesticks, together with silver letter opener.
• *18cm x 29cm*
• £2,250   • Stephen Kalms

453

French Silver Bowl ◀

- *circa 1890*

Silver punch bowl/wine cooler with elaborate chasing and foliate designs, four scrolled handles, acanthus leaf swags and ribboning.
- *height 47cm*
- £32,500   • Stephen Kalms

Silver and Glass Jar ▶

- *1945*

Glass cosmetic container with a silver cover and a bone moon shaped thumb piece, made in London.
- *height 9cm*
- £150   • Evonne Antiques

Silver Bon-Bon Dish ▼

- *1901*

Liberty & Co. cymric silver bon-bon dish designed by Oliver Baker. Hallmarked 'Birmingham 1901'.
- *9cm x 10.5cm*
- £1,500   • Liberty plc

Art Nouveau Mirror ▲

- *circa 1930*

Art Nouveau silver mirror with elaborate scrolling and a young lady holding a light in the shape of a lily.
- *height 59cm*
- £4,500   • Stephen Kalms

Condiment Set ▲

- *1911*

Condiment set comprised of two glass bottles with faceted stoppers, on a silver stand with extended ring handle, supported on silver ball feet.
- *height 21cm*
- £240   • Evonne Antiques

Flatware ▶

• 1876–82
A full set of cutlery for twelve settings, double-struck bead pattern. Made in England by George Adams.
• £8,500 **• Langfords**

Dinner Service ▲

• circa 1900
Russian silver-gilt and enamel plique-à-jour dinner service with twelve settings, comprising plates, sorbet cups, saucers and spoons in varying colours.
• £200,000 **• Marks Antiques**

Assorted Pewter ▲

• 19th century
Flagon, two chalices and two plates in English pewter. Quart capacity flagon banded with domed lid and moulded base.
• £425 **• Castlegate**

Cruet ▼

• 1832
Cruet comprising seven pieces, with shell and leaf moulding and interlaced floral designs to the handle. By Emes & Barnard.
• height 26cm
• £2,750 **• Percy's Ltd**

Claret Jugs ◀

• 1875
Pair of French silver claret jugs with cut and engraved glass with leaf designs and pierced lattice panels, the whole on a moulded foot. Made in Paris.
• height 30cm
• £5,750 **• Percy's Ltd**

Candlesticks ▼

• 1781
Set of four George III candlesticks with fluted stems on a fluted, twisted base with beading. John Winter, Sheffield.
• height 30cm
• £11,505 **• Percy's Ltd**

Sauce Tureens ◀

• 1793
Pair of George III sauce tureens, with fluted lids and half bases, by Cornelius Bland of London.
• length 24cm
• £5,500 **• Marks Antiques**

Silver Egg Cruet ▼

- *1788*

A George III silver egg cruet by Matthew Boulton, with six silver egg cups within a lightly designed base and finial handle.

- *width 21cm*
- £1,500   • B. Silverman

Silver Cream Jug ▼

- *1897*

A silver jug by Wakely & Wheeler, with a scrolled handle, wide splayed lip, raised on three lion paw feet from lion mask decoration.

- *height 20cm*
- £1,800   • B. Silverman

George III Goblets ▲

- *1810*

A pair of George III urn-shaped goblets with half-fluted bodies engraved with grape and vine designs, raised on pedestal bases, by J.X. Story & W.M. Elliot.

- *height 17cm*
- £6,000   • B. Silverman

Four Silver Salts ▼

- *1841–56*

A set of four silver salts with blue glass liners, pierced decoration and gadrooned rim, raised on three pad feet.

- *5cm x 8cm*
- £1,900   • B. Silverman

Pair of Sauce Boats ▲

- *1771*

A fine pair of George III silver sauce boats with splayed lip and scrolled handles, on three splayed feet, made by John Irvine.

- *17cm x 6cm*
- £2,900   • B. Silverman

Early Georgian Salts ▲

- *1744*

A pair of circular silver salts with gilt interiors made in London, raised on animal feet from mask decoration.

- *diameter 7cm*
- £475   • Percy's Ltd

Victorian Montieth ▲

- *1900*

Victorian montieth by Goldsmith & Silversmith, based on a seventeenth century design with shaped collar and ring handles from mask decoration.

- *26cm x 41cm*
- £9,000   • B. Silverman

Vignelli Carafe ▶

- **1970**
Christofle and Venini silver
carafe and six shots, designed by
Vignelli. Stamped Christofle,
Italy.
- *height of carafe 22.5cm*
- **£2,000** • **Themes**

Silver Photograph Frame ▲

- **1935**
Silver photograph frame with a
concave design.
- *height 26cm*
- **£350** • **Evonne Antiques**

Pair of Decanters ▶

- **1910**
Pair of glass decanters with silver
mounts and handle, made by
Walker and Hall.
- *height 23cm*
- **£3,900** • **Stephen Kalms**

Twenties Toast Rack ▼

- *circa 1929*
Silver Art Deco toast rack with
six bays, canted corners and a
pieced apron.
- *height 6cm*
- **£190** • **Barrett Towning**

Archibald Knox Barrel ◀

- **1902**
Tudric pewter biscuit barrel
designed by Archibald Knox,
with blue and green enamelling.
- *15cm x 13cm*
- **£1,500** • **Liberty plc**

Sauce Boat

- *circa 1860*

Mid-Victorian sauce boat in Britannia metal (high-grade pewter), with pear-shaped body on three claw feet with scrolled, curved handle and moulded rim.
- *height 10cm*
- £50 • Jane Stewart

Georgian Charger

- *circa 1750*

English George II charger, with single reeded rim in polished pewter, by Richard King.
- *diameter 42cm*
- £275 • Jane Stewart

English Tankard

- *circa 1850*

English, Victorian pewter half-pint tankard, with banded and double-banded decoration around body and curved handle with moulded leaf decoration. By Yates & Birch of Sheffield.
- *height 9cm*
- £45 • Jane Stewart

Church Flagon

- *circa 1840*

A Victorian, spouted ecclesiastical wine flagon, in pewter, by Walker & Hall of Sheffield, with scrolled handle and acorn thumb-piece.
- *height 30cm*
- £150 • Jane Stewart

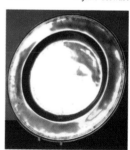

Stuart Charger

- *circa 1680*

Touchmarked Stuart charger, triple-reeded with ownership initials – P.M.W.
- *diameter 51cm*
- £650 • Jane Stewart

Pewter Spoon

- *circa 1750*

Dutch pewter spoon, recovered from the River Thames with 'Nature's Gilding'.
- *length 15.5cm*
- £75 • Jane Stewart

Teapot

- *circa 1850*

Pewter teapot, by Shaw & Fischer of Sheffield, with fluted spout and acanthus-leaf handle.
- *height 16cm*
- £65 • Jane Stewart

Victorian Sauce Boat ▼
- 1850
A pewter sauce boat with large splayed lip and curved handle, on three claw feet.
- length 12cm
- £30   • Jane Stewart

Silver Casters ▼
- 1759
A set of George II silver casters with decorative piercing and engraving, on a tall foot with good unrestored finial.
- height 19cm
- £2,900   • B. Silverman

Engraved Teapot ▲
- 1850
An Adam-style pewter teapot, finely engraved with floral decoration.
- height 12cm
- £55   • Jane Stewart

Pewter Fruit Bowl ▲
- 1905
Art Nouveau pewter fruit bowl with green glass liner and pewter mounts incorporating organic designs, by Orivit.
- 11cm x 16.5cm
- £380   • Gooday Gallery

Knox Pewter Dish ▼
- 1903
Art Nouveau pewter fruit bowl with green glass liner raised on three legs reserved on a circular base, designed by Archibald Knox for Liberty & Co.
- 13cm x 13cm
- £650   • Gooday Gallery

Tobacco Box ▼
- 19th century
A pewter oriental-style tobacco box with engraved floral designs.
- height 8cm
- £55   • Jane Stewart

Set of Pewter Goblets ◄
- 20th century
A set of five, half-pint capacity, pewter goblets of typical form, in fine condition on a circular base. Handcrafted by Aquineas Locke of London.
- height 15cm
- £100   • Jane Stewart

459

Sporting Items

The constantly ascending value of sporting artefacts and memorabilia provides a fascinating study – and an object lesson in not throwing anything away.

The area of sporting antiques is one in which the urban myth of 'finding a fortune in the attic' may actually come true. Old golf clubs, for instance, and old golf balls have fetched staggering sums of money – but they do have to be significantly old. The prices of sporting artefacts have been helped by the fact that they are nostalgically attractive. They adorn the walls of many a pub, wine bar and private house. Some items start off with a built-in advantage, if they are signed, can be proven to have belonged to a well-known sportsman or are of a generally commemorative nature, although these latter do not gain value as fast as the others, in view of the thousands that are produced – and the fact that no-one throws them away. The most sought after items relate to the most popular pastimes, so golf, football, tennis, cricket, rugby and skiing memorabilia are avidly collected, together with related ceramic and printed ephemera. The most popular participant sport of them all is fishing and this is a particularly fascinating and rewarding field for the enthusiastic collector.

General

Black Rugby Boots ▶
- 1930
Pair of black leather rugby boots with white laces and leather studs.
- *length 29cm*
- **£165**   • Sean Arnold

Riding Boots ▼
- *circa 1900*
Brown leather riding boots together with wooden trees and brass trim.
- *height 54cm*
- **£225**   • Sean Arnold

Football Player ▲
- *circa 1930*
Spelter figure of a football player poised and about to kick a ball.
- *height 25cm*
- **£425**   • Sean Arnold

Hotspur Football Boots ▼
- 1920
Pair of brown leather football boots with leather studs and cream laces, from a Hotspur footballer.
- *length 30cm*
- **£225**   • Sean Arnold

Child's Skis ▼

- *1920s*
Child's wooden skis with
matching poles and bindings.
- *105cm x 8cm*
- **£120**   • **Henry Gregory**

Travelling Primus Stove ▲

- *circa 1890*
Travelling primus in a circular
leather case with leather strap.
- *diameter 13cm*
- **£155**   • **Sporting Times**

French Boules ▼

- *circa 1900*
Pair of French boules with
original leather carrying strap.
- *diameter 20cm*
- **£32**   • **Sporting Times**

B. C. F. C. Cap ▼

- *1933*
B. C. F. C. velvet blue and
maroon football cap with silver
braiding and tassel on the inside
'English manufactured Christys,
London, Horton Stephens, Ltd.,
The Shops Brighton College and
Ward 1933–45.
- *diameter 20cm*
- **£45**   • **Sporting Times**

Riding Whip ▶

- *circa 1900*
Leather riding whip, with silver
collar.
- *length 170cm*
- **£140**   • **Henry Gregory**

Cribbage Board ▼

- *circa 1900*
Marchline tartan ware cribbage
board box.
- *26cm x 10cm*
- **£310**   • **Henry Gregory**

Travelling Sandwich Tin ▲

- *circa 1890*
Travelling leather case, the
interior enclosing a sandwich tin
and flask.
- *15cm x 15cm*
- **£155**   • **Sporting Times**

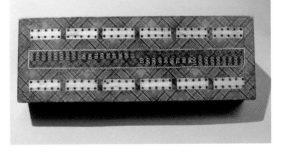

Signed Chelsea Football Shirt ▼

- *2000*

Chelsea football shirt from the 2000 season. Shirt is signed by the team, including Zola, Vialli and De Goey.

- £350   • **Star Signings**

Signed Fiorentina Photograph ▼

- *1999–2000*

Fiorentina squad photograph, 1999–2000 season. Signed at Wembley stadium at a game against Arsenal.

- £350   • **Star Signings**

Ping Pong Bats ▲

- *circa 1880*

Pair of 19th-century ping pong bats. Head of bats made from vellum. Handles are tapered and made of mahogany. In good condition.

- *length 40cm*
- £125   • **Sean Arnold**

Football Tobacco Box ▲

- *1905*

Silver tobacco box styled as a rugby ball. Hinged flap. Made in Birmingham.

- *length 8cm*
- £525   • **S. & A. Thompson**

Expert Tips

Modern signed artefacts are mementos worth a great deal to a limited number of people. It should be remembered that the prices of these have been loaded from the outset.

Signed Liverpool Football ▼

- *1999–2000*

Liverpool team ball from the 1999–2000 season. Signatures from the team include players such as Owen, Redknapp, Fowler and Berger.

- £150   • **Star Signings**

Shooting Stick ▼

- *circa 1900*

Early 20th-century shooting stick with bamboo and cane seat. Stick made from mallacca. Brass fittings.

- *height 68cm*
- £215   • **Sean Arnold**

Tennis Rackets ◄

- *circa 1895–1910*

Tennis rackets with convex and concave wedges. The rackets are made from beech and ash. Gut strings and wooden handles. Stamped with maker's name. In good condition.

- £145 each   • **Sean Arnold**

Wall Billiard Scorer ▲
• *circa 1910*
Mahogany and brass billiard scorer, with a slate panel in the centre.
• *60cm x 105cm*
• £700   • Henry Gregory

Silver Football Tropy ▼
• *1928*
Silver footballer trophy presented to the Alexanders Welfare Football League for the Annual Competition London.
• *45cm x 22cm*
• £680   • Henry Gregory

Brass Binoculars ▶
• *circa 1880*
Silver-plated brass binoculars engraved with hunting scenes.
• *5.5cm x 9cm*
• £120   • Henry Gregory

Swiss Army Ice Pick ▲
• *1940s*
Wooden ice pick with steel head and spike made for the Swiss Army.
• *90cm*
• £70   • Henry Gregory

Tennis Press ▼
• *circa 1920*
Mahogany tennis press in excellent condition with brass fittings.
• *diameter 27cm*
• £155   • Sporting Times

Rugby Ball ▼
• *1950s*
Brown leather rugby ball with original stitching.
• *33cm x 18cm*
• £85   • Henry Gregory

Leather Punchball ◀
- **1920**
Leather punchball with leather strap used to suspend from the ceiling.
- *diameter 30cm*
- **£185**   • Sean Arnold

Expert Tips

Skis, tennis rackets and cricket bats are becoming popular for decorating sporting clubs.

Rugby Ball ▼
- **circa 1900**
Original hand-stitched, four panel leather rugby ball with laces.
- *length 30cm*
- **£680**   • Sean Arnold

Brass Dinner Gong ▼
- **circa 1930**
Brass dinner gong flanked by two brass tennis racquets, supported on an oval mahogany stand.
- *30cm x 24cm*
- **£695**   • Sean Arnold

Football Trophy ▼
- **1900**
Continental red football trophy with silver metal finial and circular base.
- *height 44cm*
- **£645**   • Sean Arnold

Boxing Gloves ▲
- **1920**
Pair of large leather boxing gloves stuffed with horsehair.
- *length 30cm*
- **large boxing gloves £145, small gloves £95**
- • Sean Arnold

Shuttlecock Racquets ▲
- **1895**
Three Victorian shuttlecock and ping pong racquets, made of vellum with leather-bound handles.
- **£5**   • Sean Arnold

Bowling Balls ▼
- **circa 1910**
Lignum Vitie bowling balls with bone monogram panels.
- *diameter 16cm*
- **£60**   • Henry Gregory

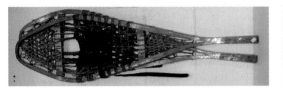

Snow Shoes ▲
- *circa 1900*
Canadian snow shoes made from wood with leather mesh base and fasteners.
- *length 103cm*
- **£95** • **Sporting Times**

Bamboo Shooting Stick ▶
- *circa 1920*
Bamboo shooting stick with a folding rattan seat, with metal spike and brass fittings.
- *length 75cm*
- **£195** • **Sporting Times**

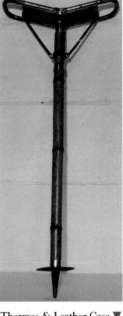

Thermos & Leather Case ▼
- *circa 1900*
Brass thermos with original leather case with the inscription 'B. R.' and a long leather carrying handle with leather buckle.
- *height 38cm*
- **£125** • **Sporting Times**

Leather Football Boots ▼
- *1930*
Leather football boots in excellent condition appointed by Stanley Matthews.
- *length 30cm*
- **£125** • **Sporting Times**

Goggles ▲
- *1940*
Goggles with brass and metal rim on a leather backing with adjustable rubber straps.
- *width 18cm*
- **£28** • **Sporting Times**

Billiard Scorer ◀
- *circa 1910*
Wall-mounted mahogany billiard scorer, with brass numerals and sliding markers.
- *92cm x 35cm*
- **£280** • **Henry Gregory**

Victorian Hip Flask ▶

- *1880*

A Victorian, clear glass hip flask with silver top and case.
- *height 16cm*
- **£375**　　● The Reel Thing

Leather Sandwich Case ▲

- *1910*

Leather sandwich case with brass clasp and a leather shoulder strap, inscribed: "J.S.W".
- *19cm x 19cm*
- **£295**　　● The Reel Thing

Sporting Magazines ▲

- *1930*

Two tennis magazines signed by Fred Perry and a selection of lawn tennis books.
- *30cm x 25cm*
- **£125-145**　　● Sean Arnold

Crocodile Hip Flask ◀

- *circa 1900*

Crocodile hip flask with hinged silver top and case.
- *height 16cm*
- **£275**　　● The Reel Thing

Riding Boots ▼

- *circa 1915*

Gentleman's leather riding boots, with wooden trees with brass handles.
- *height 58cm*
- **£200**　　● Henry Gregory

Hunting Crop ▶

- *1940*

Hunting whip with braided leather strap, ivory handle and brass collar.
- *length 120cm*
- **£145**　　● The Reel Thing

Silver-Topped Flask ▲

- *1890*

Crocodile skin hip flask, with a hinged silver top and case.
- *height 15cm*
- **£345**　　● The Reel Thing

Expert Tips

Sporting magazines and signed photographs of sports personalities should all be in good condition and come with a certificate of authenticity. Sporting programmes should also be in fine condition as damaged or dog-eared examples have little value.

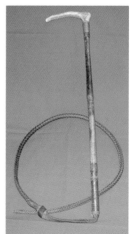

Fishing

Devon Bait Lure
• *circa 1930*
Artificial bait lure, with four triple hooks, manufactured by Devon. With original case.
• £40   • The Reel Thing

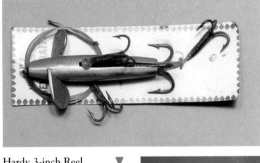

Small Creel
• *circa 1940*
Mid 20th-century small child's creel. Made from wicker.
• £95   • The Reel Thing

Hardy 3-inch Reel
• *circa 1903*
A Hardy Perfect 3-inch metal body with ivory handle.
• £475   • The Reel Thing

Three Fishing Reels
• *circa 1900–1930*
Selection of fishing reels. The reels are made, from left to right, of walnut and brass, brass and steel.
• £45–£65   • Sean Arnold

Bamboo Rod Holder
• *circa 1920*
Hardy Brothers bamboo rod holder. String-bound with leather carrying handle and cover.
• £145   • The Reel Thing

Hardy Reel Case
• *circa 1930*
Well-preserved Hardy reel case. For 4 inch reel. Made from leather and lined in red velvet.
• £125   • The Reel Thing

Split-Cane Rods
• *circa 1900–1930*
Assortment of split-cane trout and salmon rods. Various makers; cork handles, brass or alloy fittings. All in excellent condition.
• £65–£220   • Sean Arnold

Fly Rod ◀
- *circa 1880*

Green heart trout rod of three sections, with brass reel and ivory handle.
- *length 280cm*
- £190
- Henry Gregory

Fly Box ▼
- *circa 1915*

Leather lined box with twelve glass and alloy containers for flies, with original tweezers and pocket.
- *13cm x 10cm*
- £90
- Henry Gregory

Small Fishing Reel ◀
- *circa 1920–40*

Small wood fishing reel with a brass plate and turned decoration.
- *diameter 7cm*
- £25
- Sporting Times

Fishing Reel ▼
- *circa 1920–40*

Wood fishing reel with brass handles and plate with turned decoration.
- *diameter 10cm*
- £45
- Sporting Times

Leather Fly Wallet ▼
- *circa 1920–40*

Leather fly wallet with eight compartments.
- *width 16cm*
- £28
- Sporting Times

Wood Fishing Reel ▼
- *circa 1920–40*

Wood fishing reel with banded decoration, brass fittings and ebonised double handles.
- *diameter 8cm*
- £35
- Sporting Times

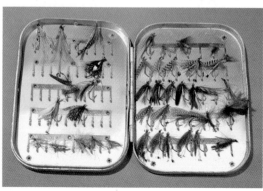

Hardy Fly Box ◀
- *circa 1920*

Hardy alloy fly box, includes collection of trout flies.
- *13cm x 10cm*
- £110
- Henry Gregory

Scottish Reel ▲

- *circa 1900*

Brass salmon reel, with ivory handle, by Turnbull Princess of Edinburgh.
- *diameter 11cm*
- £275 • The Reel Thing

Leather Fly Wallet ▲

- *circa 1900*

Hardy leather fly wallet with a good fly selection, and leather strap.
- *length 17cm*
- £275 • The Reel Thing

Fishing Gaff ▶

- *1890*

A Hardy fishing gaff with leather handle and steel and brass hook.
- *length 45cm*
- £295 • The Reel Thing

Salmon Reel ▼

- *1890*

A Scottish, solid brass salmon reel, made by Anderson & Son, with bone handle.
- *diameter 10cm*
- £145 • The Reel Thing

Brass Fishing Reel ◀

- *circa 1900*

A Hardy brass fishing reel in original condition, with ivory handle.
- *diameter 11cm*
- £895 • The Reel Thing

Spinning Reel ▲

- *circa 1800*

Brass Mallock spinning reel.
- *diameter 10cm*
- £245 • The Reel Thing

English Line Dry ▼

- *1990*

An English mahogany Line Dry with bone handle.
- *height 32cm*
- £288 • The Reel Thing

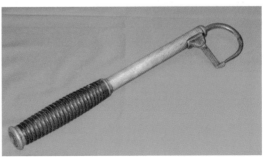

Shooting

Leather Gun Case ▼

- *circa 1890*

Leather leg of mutton gun case with leather shoulder strap and carrying handle.
- *length 79cm*
- £125　　● **Sporting Times**

Holland & Holland Rifle ▼

- *2001*

Holland & Holland 375 H&H. New bolt-action magazine rifle.
- *length 119cm*
- £15,615　　● **H. & H.**

Cartridge Case ▶

- *circa 1890*

Gannochy loader canvas cartridge case with holders for 30 rounds of ammunition.
- *26cm x 13cm*
- £1,500　　● **H. & H.**

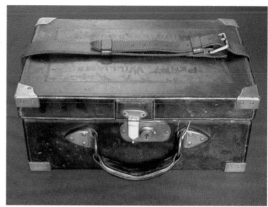

Magazine Case ▲

- *circa 1920*

Ammunition case with brass fittings and leather straps by Penry Williams, Middlesbrough.
- *41cm x 16cm*
- £950　　● **H. & H.**

Pistol ▲

- *circa 1840*

Flintlock percussion double-barrel pistol with back-action locks, engraved lockplates and trigger guards.
- *25cm x 10cm*
- £430　　● **H. & H.**

Magazine Box ▲

- *circa 1890*

Leather magazine box by James MacNaughton, Edinburgh.
- *23cm x 24cm*
- £650　　● **H. & H.**

Brass Powder Flask ▲

- *circa 1875*

Brass black powder flask with embossed decoration.
- *10cm x 19cm*
- £48　　● **H. & H.**

Hunter's Display Case ▼

- *circa 1923*

Display case showing tusks
and moths of India.
- *32cm x 30cm*
- **£420**
- **H. & H.**

Paradox Gun ▼

- *date 1890*

10-bore paradox gun. Decorated
with a fading leaf design along
the grip. 27-inch barrels. Gun of
excellent condition.
- *length 65cm*
- **£7,500**
- **H. & H.**

Gun Cases ▼

- *circa 1900*

Two leg of mutton gun cases in
fine condition.
- *length 30cm (top)*
- *length 31cm (bottom)*
- **£445 top, £390 bottom**
- **Sean Arnold**

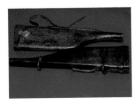

Leather Gun Case ▶

- *circa 1900*

Early 20th-century gun case.
Made from black leather and
oak. The case has brass mounts to
protect corners and two leather
straps. Inside there are various
compartments.
- **£2,200**
- **H. & H.**

Shotgun Belt ▼

- *circa 1930*

Leather shotgun belt. Twenty-five
cartridge compartments and a
brass buckle.
- **£55**
- **The Reel Thing**

Cap Remover ▲

- *circa 1890*

16-bore all brass cap remover
with wooden handle.
- **£195**
- **The Reel Thing**

.375 (2½ inch) Calibre Rifle ▲

- *date 1901*

.375 calibre Royal rifle. Folding
leaf sights, double trigger; 26-inch
barrels.
- **£21,000**
- **H. & H.**

Expert Tips

*It is not advisable
to shoot modern smokeless
powder in a damascus barrel.
Apart from giving due
deference to the age of such
barrels and to the method of
their construction, smokeless
powder burns more slowly,
lowering the pressure at
the breech end, but considerably
raising it further down the
barrel to a level such
barrels were rarely
designed to handle.*

Duck Decoy ▼

- *circa 1890*

Vintage duck decoy. Painted in
natural colourings.
- **£295**
- **The Reel Thing**

Cartridge Bag ▲
- *1930*

Leather cartridge bag with webbing shoulder strap and the monogram "M.G.F." on the buckle.
- *length 38cm*
- **£145** • **The Reel Thing**

Double Barrel Hunting Rifle ▼
- *1949*

A 300 calibre Flanged Dominion double barrel hunting rifle, made by Holland and Holland
- *length 71cm*
- **£19,750** • **H. & H.**

Magazine Rifle ▲
- *1975*

Excellent quality Holland & Holland 7mm calibre magazine rifle, with telescopic sight.
- *length 64cm*
- **£7,000** • **H. & H.**

Oak Gun Case ▼
- *circa 1929*

Holland & Holland oak and leather fitted gun case, with red base lining.
- *length 70cm*
- **£2,200** • **H. & H.**

Double Barrel Rifle ◄
- *1945*

A 300 calibre Holland & Holland Royal, double barrelled rifle, belted and rimless.
- *length 61cm*
- **£32,000** • **H. & H.**

Canochy Loader ▼
- *circa 1930*

Leather canochy loader, with carrying strap.
- *diameter 15cm*
- **£2,250** • **H. & H.**

Shooting Stick ◄
- *1940s*

Leather-bound shooting stick, with metal spike.
- *length 90cm*
- **£144** • **Henry Gregory**

Expert Tips

Without doubt, shotguns, rifles or handguns that retain their original boxes or travelling cases and are intact command the best prices and attract the serious collector.

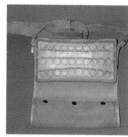

Taxidermy

The demand for taxidermy has fallen off a little since the Victorian period, when no drawing room was complete without the glassy stare of a furry mammal.

The word 'Taxidermy' is derived from an amalgamation of the Greek words meaning 'arrangement' and 'skin', which may have led to a little confusion around the fleshpots of Athens, but proves that taxidermy is an ancient craft. Taxidermy is a complex art. It requires a knowledge of anatomy, natural history, drawing, sculpture, mechanics, tanning and dyeing. It is also quite a laborious process, from the careful removal of the skin and its treating with a preservative, through the preliminary drawings of an animal's anatomy, with all its muscles, bones and

depressions, to making a model from wood, metal and clay, followed by a hollow casting in plaster, papier-mâché, burlap and wire mesh and the replacement of skin, addition of features, mounting and presentation. It takes time and patience. Which makes it all the sadder that, as a collecting area, taxidermy is not enjoying a golden age at the moment. Victorian stuffed fish do well, but our furry friends seem to be, well, too furry for today's tastes. Which, given the notorious mood swings of the collecting public, might make it exactly the time to start buying.

Albino Cobra ▼
- **20th century**

Albino cobra shown in an aggressive pose.
- **60cm x 28cm**
- **£195**   • Get Stuffed

Mallard ▲
- **20th century**

Two male mallards, one shown standing and the other recumbent.
- **40cm x 64cm**
- **£295**   • Get Stuffed

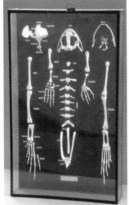

Hooded Crow ▼
- **20th century**

Hooded crow shown perched on a branch and mounted on a plinth base.
- **57cm x 28cm**
- **£125**   • Get Stuffed

Bullfrog ◄
- **20th century**

Bullfrog skeleton in sections with documentation.
- **30cm x 40cm**
- **£140**   • Get Stuffed

Tawny Owl ▼

- *20th century*
Tawny owl naturalistically posed and mounted on a circular base, with original glass dome.
- *55cm x 27cm*
- **£395**
- **Get Stuffed**

Eagle Owl ▼

- *20th century*
Eagle owl in fine condition with a good expression mounted on a circular base.
- *65cm x 35cm*
- **£550**
- **Get Stuffed**

Sparrowhawk ▼

- *20th century*
Sparrowhawk with wings pinned back.
- *27cm x 35cm*
- **£190**
- **Get Stuffed**

Yorkshire Terrier ▲

- *20th century*
Yorkshire terrier seated with a curious expression and a red ribbon.
- *30cm x 20cm*
- **£245**
- **Get Stuffed**

Tropical Birds ▲

- *circa 1880*
Victorian glass dome containing various tropical birds.
- *54cm x 36cm*
- **£650**
- **Get Stuffed**

Roach ▼

- *1996*
Roach in a bow fronted case with natural grasses and weeds, with gilt lettering documenting the catch.
- *32cm x 50cm*
- **£385**
- **Get Stuffed**

Barn Owl ▼

- *20th century*
Barn owl with wings outstretched at the point of take off, mounted on a branch.
- *70cm x 70cm*
- **£275**
- **Get Stuffed**

Red Fox ▼

- *20th century*
Red fox vixen shown recumbent with head slightly raised.
- *35cm x 57cm*
- **£200**
- **Get Stuffed**

Asiatic Jungle Cat ◀

- *20th century*
Asiatic jungle cat shown on a branch set upon a polished wood base.
- *height 105cm*
- **£475**　　● **Get Stuffed**

Carnelian ▶

- *20th century*
African carnelian shown with its tail coiled around a branch, on an oval wood base.
- *height 33cm*
- **£175**　　● **Get Stuffed**

Capuchin ▼

- *20th century*
A capuchin naturalistically posed on branches, on a circular wood base.
- *height 60cm*
- **£250**　　● **Get Stuffed**

Expert Tips

When inspecting any example of taxidermy, it is important to establish its condition. It should be complete and free from damage, and not be threadbare or worn.

Hedgehog ▲

- *20th century*
Adult hedgehog on all fours, mounted on oval wooden base.
- *23cm x 15cm*
- **£175**　　● **Get Stuffed**

Woodcock ▼

- *20th century*
Naturalistically posed woodcock, on a branch with an oval wood base.
- *height 28cm*
- **£145**　　● **Get Stuffed**

Baboon ▼

- *20th century*
Baboon shown on all fours baring his teeth in an aggressive stance.
- *71cm x 81cm*
- **£450**　　● **Get Stuffed**

Bull's Skull ▲

- *20th century*
Finely preserved skull of a bull.
- *length 55cm*
- **£225**　　● **Get Stuffed**

Textiles & Fans

Often no longer useful for their original purpose, textiles are frequently hung on the wall, a practice that has maintained their value.

Age and condition are fundamental to the value of collectable textiles. Sewing was, until recently, regarded as an important skill and pastime for a lady, and a great deal of embroidery has resulted. In general, the finer the stitching and the brighter the colours the more desirable. Silk is more valuable than wool, naturally enough, but 19th-century examples of both are freely available, with the brightest colours coming from the Middle East, China, Japan and India. Samplers – needlework pictures incorporating different stitching, in wool or silk and often carrying a religious message – are also very collectable. The earliest example known was made in 1598, but most of those on the market tend to be 19th century. Fans were much collected in the 19th century, when some great collections were built up. Most of those on the market date from the 18th and 19th centuries, although late 17th-century ones can be found. Some of those from the 1920s, either advertising or made of extravagant ostrich feathers, are highly sought after.

French Louis XIV Needlepoint ▶

- *circa 1670*
French Louis XIV needlepoint panel showing a mythological scene with Neptune, romantic figures and animals in an Arcadian setting.
- *32cm x 30cm*
- £4,000 • Marilyn Garrow

Needlepoint Panel ◀

- *18th century*
French needlepoint panel showing a romantic couple on horseback within a heraldic border of blue, red and cream.
- *50cm x 46cm*
- £9,500 • Marilyn Garrow

Royal Feather Fan ▼

- *circa 1900*
Feather fan with tortoiseshell sticks applied with the gold Royal cypher of Princess Marie Maximilianova of Lechtenberg (1841–1911).
- £850 • Zakheim

Feather Fan ◀

- *circa 1900*
Pink ostrich feather fan with tortoiseshell sticks. Provenance: Princess Marie Maximilianova of Lechtenberg (1841–1911).
- £750 • Zakheim

Mother of Pearl Fan ▲
- *circa 1910*

Cream silk lace fan covered with cream floral lace and a mother of pearl handle.
- *length 29cm*
- £275   • Sheila Cook

Red Lady's Hat ▲
- *circa 1920*

Red lady's soft silk mesh hat by Pauline Louy's, decorated with red felt flowers.
- *medium*
- £145   • Sheila Cook

Russian-Style Cape and Hat ▲
- *circa 1950*

Dramatic red Russian-style cape with black embroidery and white fur lining, with matching hat.
- *medium*
- £695   • Sheila Cook

Ivory Fan ▼
- *circa 1904*

Cream silk fan with a trailing design of pink and yellow apple blossom mounted on carved ivory spines.
- *length 35cm*
- £125   • Sheila Cook

Lady's Parasol ▲
- *circa 1920*

Lady's parasol with a black floral design and a handle with a black and beige geometric pattern.
- *length 53cm*
- £95   • Sheila Cook

Child's Shoes ◀
- 1870

Child's leather shoes with black studs and metal fittings.
- *length 13cm*
- £65   • Sheila Cook

Italian Allegorical Panels ▼
- 1763

Rare set of Italian silk-work allegorical panels signed Gaetano Pati, Rome. Part of a set of eight panels composed of fine silk threads, arranged and pressed into wax. The facial and body detailing is hand painted onto finely woven silk. The tonal detailing and intricacy is very fine.
- *34cm x 27cm*
- £32,000   • Anthony Outred

Crewel-Work Waistcoat ▲

- *18th century*
Fine crewel-work waistcoat, embroidered with red, yellow and blue flowers with green foliate designs.
- *95cm x 67cm*
- **£4,600** • **Marilyn Garrow**

French Screen ▼

- *18th century*
French nineteenth century giltwood Chasurrables screen, with eighteenth century embroidered panels.
- *168cm x 70cm*
- **£4,800** • **Marilyn Garrow**

Chinese Embroidery ▶

- *18th century*
Chinese silk panel embroidered with birds and foliate design on a cream background.
- *52cm x 45cm*
- **£1,800** • **Marilyn Garrow**

Jacobean Curtains ◀

- *circa 1680*
One of a pair of Jacobean curtains in beautiful condition, with a trailing foliate design of blue and red flowers, on a cream background.
- *200cm x 120cm*
- **£14,500** • **Marilyn Garrow**

Needlework Casket ▼

- *circa 1680*
Superb Restoration period needlework casket worked in colonized silks depicting Paris and Aphrodite, with fitted interior and original glass bottles with pewter lids.
- *22cm x 28cm*
- **£10,500** • **Midwinter**

Velvet Appliqué ◀

- *1680*
French velvet embroidered appliqué wall hanging, with fine silver thread woven throughout.
- *170cm x 65cm*
- **£6,800** • **Marilyn Garrow**

Stump Work ▼

- *circa 1630*
Stump work fragments of a rural scene, with Charles I and Henrietta Maria in the foreground and a figure in a striped tent.
- *35cm x 50cm*
- **£4,500** • **Marilyn Garrow**

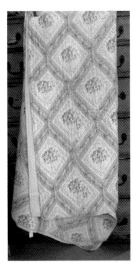

Welsh Patchwork Quilt ▲

- *circa 1880*
Welsh patchwork quilt with a
white and lilac diamond design
centered with lilac floral sprays.
- *80cm x 80cm*
- **£650**　　　● Sheila Cook

Smoking Hat ▲

- *circa 1880*
Black velvet smoking hat with
white embroidered floral design, a
central yellow silk button, pink
gold and white tassel, with
original box in good original
condition.
- *size 7*
- **£165**　　　● Sheila Cook

Cut Pile Cushion Cover ▼

- *circa 1880*
Cut pile Victorian cushion cover
with a red, green and pink
geometric design.
- *42cm x 30cm*
- **£95**　　　● Sheila Cook

Hanging Fragment ▼

- **17th century**
A fragment of a hanging –
Portuguese or Italian – with
canvas work on silk, showing
oversized birds and flowers.
- **£4,000**　　　● Marilyn Garrow

Slipper Pattern ▼

- *circa 1850*
Fine continental unused beaded
slipper 'cut out' pattern, with a
turquoise background, pink and
yellow flowers and two deer by a
river.
- *length 22cm*
- **£225**　　　● Sheila Cook

Purple Silk Kimono ▲

- *circa 1900*
Purple silk kimono with trailing
pink apple blossom design.
- *medium*
- **£295**　　　● Sheila Cook

Gentleman's Smoking Hat ▲

- *circa 1880*
Black velvet gentleman's smoking
hat with trailing foliate designs of
pink and blue flowers,
surmounted by a red satin-
covered button on the top with a
trailing green, white and red
tassel.
- *size 6*
- **£110**　　　● Sheila Cook

Beaded Pelmet ◄

- *circa 1880*
Beaded cream pelmet with red
tassel design below a gold and red
diamond design.
- *length 320cm*
- **£495**　　　● Sheila Cook

Tools

**The only rule in collecting tools is that there are no rules.
This most arcane of all fields baffles the layman.**

Collectable tools are invariably joiner's or cabinet maker's tools, the works of art which were used to construct works of art. Tool collecting is a particularly arcane subject, with, to the layman, not a lot of logic in it. In general terms, the tools which are most collected fall into three categories, smoothing tools, grooving tools and boring tools. Smoothing tools are basically planes, which vary in value according to the maker, how limited the edition may have been and any unusual features, even if not very efficacious. A joiner would have had about 30 of these, so they are not hard to come by. Planes could also be used as grooving tools, but more collectable are ploughs, which were the most expensive tools in a joiner's kit and which could make several different widths and depths of groove. A joiner would have owned only one of these, and so they are rarer as well as intrinsically more valuable. The best braces, for boring, were usually made in brass or steel and filled with rosewood, beech, boxwood or ebony but, as with all tools, the most expensively made do not necessarily hold the highest value.

Plated Brace ▲
- *1880*
Victorian Robert Marples beech-registered plated brace in good condition.
- *length 37.5cm*
- £55 • Tool Shop Auctions

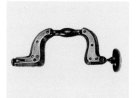

Bow Drill ▲
- *circa 1870*
A pianomaker's rosewood and brass bow drill with original bow.
- *length 25cm*
- £195 • Tool Shop Auctions

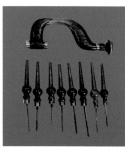

Rosewood Wedge ▲
- *1890*
Victorian gunmetal bullnose rosewood wedge.
- *length 10cm*
- £100 • Tool Shop Auctions

Dutch Pod ◄
- *circa 1850*
A Dutch pod brace made of ash with brass chuck and eight pods.
- *length 37cm*
- £155 • Tool Shop Auctions

Expert Tips

Tools should be stored in a dry and well-ventilated place and kept lightly oiled, and wiped with a soft dry cloth.

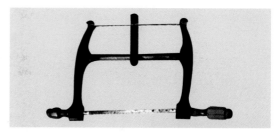

Moulding Plane ▲
- *1880*

A Scottish four-iron gothic sash moulding plane by Wilson, Glasgow.
- *length 24cm*
- **£270** • **Tool Shop Auctions**

Beech Bow Saw ▲
- *1860*

An unusually small beech bow saw with octagonal boxwood handles by Buck, with six-inch blade.
- **£50** • **Tool Shop Auctions**

Victorian Level ▲
- *1860*

Victorian rare waisted rosewood and brass level.
- **£445** • **Tool Shop Auctions**

Spirit Level ▲
- *1880*

Victorian Mathieson 14C highly decorative rosewood and brass spirit level.
- **£165** • **Tool Shop Auctions**

Pitchmeter ◄
- *1885*

Rare W. Tates Pitchmeter made by J. Robson of Newcastle upon Tyne. With German silver mounts, graduated protractor arm and adjustable spirit level. Scales calculate diameter in feet versus pitch in feet.
- **£620** • **Tool Shop Auctions**

Rule and Measuring Stick ▲
- *1875*

Rare French Fisheries Officer's boxwood rule and iron measuring stick. The rule measures the denier of the nets to see if they comply with regulations. It has different scales on each face depending on the species being caught. The length of the fish is checked against the fish rule.
- *length 15cm*
- **£200** • **Tool Shop Auctions**

Stanley 45E ◄
- *1923*

An immaculate Stanley 45E, a presentation piece in 1923. Type 15 Sweetheart, in a tin box, complete with instructions and original screwdriver.
- *length 25cm*
- **£130** • **Tool Shop Auctions**

Bedrock Jointer plane ▲
- *circa 1920*
A rare plane by the US company, Stanley, with greatly extended base plate for the precision smoothing of larger wooden surfaces. With mahogany grips and original cutter plate.
- *length 62cm*
- £175   • Old Tool Chest

Pair of Garden Tools ▲
- *early 20th century*
Tools for aid in the growing of asparagus. A hoe for the amassing of soil over and round the 'head', and a cutter for harvesting the plant by cutting it off under the soil.
- *height 139cm*
- £48 each   • Myriad

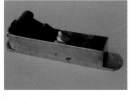

Mitre Plane ▲
- *circa 1790*
An 18th-century plane, by John Green, used for bevelling wood, after it had been cut to size, into corresponding angles for the creation of a mitred corner.
- *length 31cm*
- £850   • Old Tool Chest

Soil Sifter ▲
- *circa 1940*
Made of bentwood, cut and steamed to be moulded into shape, with a steel grill for catching stones when sifting.
- *diameter 45cm*
- £20   • Curios

Expert Tips

An upsurge in the prices of second-hand gardening tools – many still in production – has been caused by peoples' desire to 'theme' pubs.

Bridle Plane ▼
- *circa 1890*
Scottish plough, by well-known maker, Mathieson of Glasgow. With adjustable fence.
- *length 27cm*
- £165   • Old Tool Chest

Topping Tool ▼
- *circa 19th century*
Used for trimming the profiles of watch-wheel teeth. With separate box and cutters. A precision instrument, constructed of brass and steel and standing on a wooden base.
- *height 30cm*
- £1,000
- **Aubrey Brocklehurst**

Watering Cans ▼
- *circa 1920s*
A selection of galvanised watering cans, one with an unusually large spout emanating from the top.
- **from £24**   • S. Brunswick

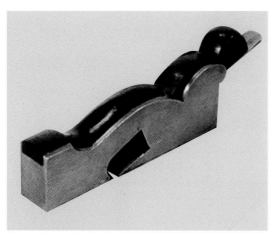

Victorian Shoulder Plane ◀

- *1890*

Victorian steel-soled gunmetal shoulder plane with mahogany infill and wide mouth.

- *length 23cm*
- **£55**   • **Tool Shop Auctions**

Scottish Plane ▼

- *1870*

Victorian gunmetal Scottish smoothing plane with overstuffed rosewood infill.

- *length 23cm*
- **£220**   • **Tool Shop Auctions**

Mathieson Plane ▲

- *circa 1920s*

A Mathieson dovetailed parallel-sided smoothing plane with rosewood infill made as a special order for a man with large hands.

- *length 26.3cm*
- **£575**   • **Tool Shop Auctions**

Boxwood Planes ▼

- *1880*

A pair of rare, miniature boxwood planes by Preston, with a radiussed rebate and a compassed rebate.

- *length 7.5cm*
- **£210**   • **Tool Shop Auctions**

Scottish Smoothing Plane ▲

- *1860*

Stylish Scottish iron smoothing plane with walnut overstuffing, cove front and moulded infill at the rear.

- *length 22cm*
- **£280**   • **Tool Shop Auctions**

Cutting Gauge ▲

- *1895*

A Victorian fine quality ebony and brass cutting gauge by Frost.

- *length 25cm*
- **£110**   • **Tool Shop Auctions**

Expert Tips

Box planes should be avoided if severely damaged, or if they are infested with woodworm.

Cooper's Joiner Plane ▶

- *circa 18th century*
An Austrian construction plane for use in the manufacture of barrels.
- *length 112cm*
- £375   • Old Tool Chest

Garden Shears ▼

- *circa 1930*
A pair of tempered steel-bladed garden shears with turned ash handles. In working order.
- £25   • Curios

Bulb Planter ▲

- *circa 1900*
A Kentish bulb-planting tool with turned ash handle and cross-piece for exerting foot pressure. For use in planting bulbs in lawns and replacing turf plug.
- £75   • S. Brunswick

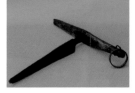

Bow Saw ▲

- *circa 19th century*
An English carpenter's bow saw of mahogany construction, with original blade and tension stay.
- *length 63cm*
- £28   • Old Tool Chest

Lawn Edger ◀

- *circa 1940*
A well-worn half-moon lawn edger with rustic shaft of hornbeam construction and rusted steel blade. For sale as decorative artefact.
- *height 94cm*
- £15   • Curios

Wheelwright's Hub Borer ▲

- *circa 18th century*
An English wheelwright's hub tool with turned double handle and tapered, concave blade.
- *height 76cm*
- £350   • Old Tool Chest

Expert Tips

Carpenters' tools by known makers are the most valuable. Many tools were made by the carpenters themselves and may become valuable when the provenance becomes known.

French Watering Can ◀

- *circa 1930*
Enamelled French watering can of drum construction and screw-on lid, for indoor use.
- *height 38cm*
- £110   • Myriad

Plumb Bob ▲
• *1850*
Victorian steel-tipped brass
plumb bob with brass reel.
• *length 8.8cm*
• **£60**   • **Tool Shop Auctions**

Norris Smoothing Plane ▲
• *1920*
A Norris 20R gunmetal
smoothing plane in its original
box.
• *length 22cm*
• **£700**   • **Tool Shop Auctions**

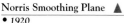

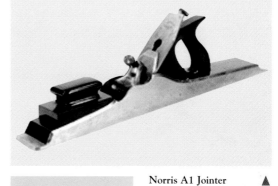

A1 Panel Plane ▲
• *1930*
A Norris A1 panel plane with
dovetailed and rosewood infill.
• *length 44cm*
• **£2,050** • **Tool Shop Auction**

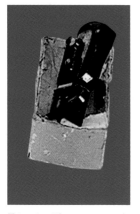

Norris A1 Jointer ▲
• *1925*
A Norris A1 jointer with
rosewood infill and dovetailed
body in excellent condition.
• *length 56cm*
• **£4,100** • **Tool Shop Auctions**

Victorian Plumb and Square ▲
• *1850*
A fine Victorian brass plumb and
square with original patina.
• *length 27.5cm*
• **£195**   • **Tool Shop Auctions**

Plumb Board and Bob ▼
• *1830*
George IV decorative mahogany
plumb board and bronze plumb
bob in classical style with simple
carved ornamentation.
• *width 45cm*
• **£470**   • **Tool Shop Auctions**

Trimming Plane ▲
• *1880*
Victorian Stanley 95 edge
trimming plane in the original
box.
• *length 15cm*
• **£125**   • **Tool Shop Auctions**

Toys, Games & Dolls

Toys need to have been depressingly well cared for to appeal to the collector.

It always appears that the toys which are worth a lot of money have been the ones that were least loved. A toy car which has been properly played with, with chipped paint and three wheels missing, is never going to excite a collector. Whereas a pristine model which has never enjoyed the wind in its headlights prior to smacking into the skirting board can be worth a fortune. If it has got its original box, of course. Most valuable toys are not strictly antiques, generally having been produced in the half century 1890-1940, when factory production was taking over from craftsman manufacture. Surprisingly, most collectable toys were produced in factories, rather than studios or workshops, and most often in Germany, where specialist toy manufacturers existed on a large scale. As result of this, many toys included mass-produced factory parts which can be difficult to reproduce, and are thus hard to restore. Dolls and teddy bears are more individual, made with artistry and by revered manufacturers and are not dependent on packaging – but it is important that they, too, have not been overloved.

Gold Cadillac ▲
- *circa 1950*
American gold cadillac with red interior and chromed fittings, made by Bandiai, Japan.
- *length 29cm*
- £150   • P. McAskie

Fred Flintstone ▼
- 1960
Tin plate 'Fred Flintstone' sitting astride his dinosaur 'Dino', made by Louis Marks in Japan.
- *length 2cm*
- £265   • P. McAskie

Smiley of the Seven Dwarfs ▲
- *circa 1930*
Padded soft toy of 'Smiley', one of the dwarfs from the children's story, 'Snow White and the Seven Dwarfs'.
- *height 27cm*
- £160   • Glenda Dolls

Huntley & Palmers Van ◄
- *circa 1920*
Brown toy van with a hinged lid and the gilt inscription, 'Huntley & Palmers Ltd, Reading Biscuits' and a Royal Crest above.
- *19cm x 25cm*
- £875   • P. McAskie

Dumper Truck ▼

- *circa 1950*

English, all wood dumper truck. The moving wheels activate the tipping action. In original painted livery of red and green.

- *length 67cm*
- £75
- After Noah

Mickey Mouse Toy ▼

- *1930s*

Cardboard Mickey Mouse 'rolly' toy with bakelite round base. Made from cardboard. Chad Valley, USA.

- *height 23cm*
- £180
- P. McAskie

Thunderbirds Doll ▲

- *circa 1966*

A 'Brains' doll from the Gerry and Sylvia Anderson TV programme, 'Thunderbirds', complete with original clothing, plastic spectacles, spanner and pliers.

- *height 30cm*
- £200
- Dolly Land

Miss Piggy ▲

- *1979*

The Muppet Show's Miss Piggy shown in pink sports car in famous waving pose.

- *length 11cm*
- £10
- Retro Exchange

Dutch Rocking Horse ▲

- *circa 1900*

Dutch wooden rocking horse with two semi circular side panels. All originally painted with horsehair tail.

- *height 63cm*
- £425
- R. Conquest

Ford Zodiac Model ▲

- *circa 1960*

Model of a Ford Zodiac convertable. Matchbox toy number 39. Pink bodywork with a white and green interior and green towbar. Original box.

- *length 9cm*
- £45
- P. McAskie

Expert Tips

After 1939, the mark 'Walt Disney Productions' appears on their toys. Prior to that you will find 'Walter E. Disney' or 'Walt Disney Enterprises' on German or American toys, and 'Walt Disney Mickey Mouse Ltd.' on British ones.

11th Hussars Models ◄

- *1949*

Britains lead soldiers set 182, with huzzars dismounted with officer and horses. Original Fred Whisstock hand-painted box. Immaculate condition.

- *length 60 cm*
- £200
- Stephen Naegel

Dumper Truck ▲
- **1950s**
Yellow and red dumper truck, made in Japan by Haji for the American market.
- *length 23cm*
- **£60** • Dr Colin B. Baddiel

Mickey Mouse
Driving a Car ▲
- **1961**
Mickey Mouse driving a blue open car, with yellow spoked wheels.
- *length 12cm*
- **£60** • Dr Colin B. Baddiel

Horse Box ▲
- **1950**
Yellow and orange horse box, with original packaging.
- *length 21cm*
- **£69** • Dr Colin B. Baddiel

Clockwork Windmill ▼
- **1900**
English clockwork metal windmill with orange sails.
- *height 4cm*
- **£90** • Dr Colin B. Baddiel

Clockwork Clown ▲
- **1950**
Clockwork clown with red jacket and yellow and black hat, riding a bike, with original key.
- *height 7cm*
- **£155** • Dr Colin B. Baddiel

Clown on Stilts ▶
- *circa 1950s*
Clown on stilts with red and white striped trousers, red top and green hat, playing a violin, with original box and key.
- *height 20cm*
- **£100** • Dr Colin B. Baddiel

Clockwork Steamboat ▶
- *circa 1925*
Clockwork white steamboat boat with yellow funnels and red wheels and trim.
- *length 12cm*
- **£238** • Dr Colin B. Baddiel

German Fire Engine
- *1950*

Red German fire engine with fireman, manufactured by Gamma.
- *length 43cm*
- £110   • P. McAskie

Mummy Bear ▼
- *circa 1930*

Padded jointed bear with glass eyes and cloth paws.
- *height 39cm*
- £85   • Glenda Dolls

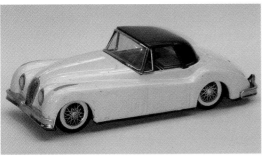

XK Yellow Jaguar ▲
- *circa 1950*

XK yellow Jaguar with a bottle green top, with a chromed bumper, made by Hoku.
- *length 25cm*
- £225   • P. McAskie

Ovaltine Van ▶
- *circa 1950*

Blue Dinky Bedford 10cwt Ovaltine van, inscribed 'Ovaltine' and 'Ovaltine Biscuits' on the side, with original box.
- *length 8cm*
- £65   • P. McAskie

Mickey Mouse ▲
- *1950*

Mickey Mouse puppet carved from wood with yellow composition feet, by Pelham.
- *height 29cm*
- £75   • P. McAskie

Tri-ang Blue Van ▶
- *1950*

Tri-ang Mimic navy-blue London and North Eastern Railway van.
- *length 18cm*
- £225   • P. McAskie

Woodbine Dominoes

- *circa 1930*

A box of dominoes in original green box with cream lettering with the words, "Wills Woodbine Dominoes" inscribed on the front of the tin.
- *length 27cm*
- £36 • After Noah (KR)

Black Train

- *1930*

Black metal train with red and gold trim. The maker's name is Maerklin.
- *length 42cm*
- £2,500 • Dolly Land

Delivery Van

- *1950*

Green delivery van made by Dinky with its original cardboard yellow box.
- *length 8cm*
- £67 • Dr Colin B. Baddiel

Curatt Car

- *20th century*

Red motor car with black roof and a brass radiator and side lamp, red running boards, and a man driving, made by Curatt.
- *length 44cm*
- £2,350 • Dolly Land

Steiff Bear

- *circa 1991*

A Steiff bear, one of a limited edition of 300 which were made only for the UK market in 1991. This is a replica of a Steiff bear salvaged from the Titanic and sold for £94,400.
- *height 48cm*
- £450 • Dolly Land

Barbie Doll

- *1960*

Plastic flexible Barbie doll with long blonde hair, a pink hairband and pink pumps, by Matel.
- *height 30cm*
- £75 • Zoom

Expert Tips

Although toy electric locomotives made in the 1960s are currently cheap to buy, their value will increase over the years, making them a good potential purchase for the new collector.

Tudor Doll's House

- *1930s*

Mock Tudor doll's house with white walls and black beams, circa 1930.
- *height 87cm*
- £125 • Dolly Land

Terrafish ◀
- **1960**

Green Terrafish with yellow spots and large white eyes, from the Gerry Anderson TV show, by Lakeside Toys, Japan.
- *length 23cm*
- **£275**   • P. McAskie

Shoe-Shine Panda ▼
- *circa 1960*

Shoe-shine soft panda, battery-operated, sitting with a pipe in its mouth and a brush in each paw, wearing red dungarees.
- *height 25cm*
- **£80**   • P. McAskie

American Racing Car ▲
- **1930**

Red and silver racing car and driver, made from an interesting combination of metals, die cast and cast iron, probably by Hubbly American. No. 22 on the side.
- *length 25cm*
- **£67**   • P. McAskie

Bobby Bear ▶
- **1950**

Padded 'Bobby Bear' made by Pedigree, in good overall condition.
- *height 44cm*
- **£89**   • Glenda Dolls

Yellow Milk Float ▼
- *circa 1960*

Rare yellow Dinky promotional milk float, with 'Jobs Dairy' inscribed on the front and rear, with red interior and hubs.
- *length 7cm*
- **£145**   • P. McAskie

Orober Fire Engine ◀
- **1920**

Fire engine set of two vehicles with a driver on a pumper, and three figures on the fire engine carrier, complete with red garage, made by Orober in Germany.
- *19cm x 33cm*
- **£650**   • P. McAskie

491

Figure with Drum ▶
- *1940*

German clockwork figure with drum and cymbal.
- *height 10cm*
- £130 ● Dr Colin B. Baddiel

Green Flying Scotsman ▼
- *1950*

Green Flying Scotsman by Bassett, coke O-gauge.
- *length 28cm*
- £1,950 ● Jeff Williams

Alfa Romeo ▼
- *1978*

Red Alfa Romeo Dinky racing car with red wheels and a figure of a racing driver at the wheel in white, with original box.
- *length 14cm*
- £78 ● Dr Colin B. Baddiel

Green Centurion Tank ◀
- *1954–60*

English green centurion tank.
- *length 12cm*
- £50 ● Dr Colin B. Baddiel

Green MG ◀
- *1950*

Green MG TF sports car made by Band Japan for the USA market.
- *length 22cm*
- £60 ● Dr Colin B. Baddiel

Royal Mail Van ▼
- *1950*

Red Royal Mail van made by Dinky, with the original yellow box and picture.
- *height 9cm*
- 120 ● Dr Colin B. Baddiel

Tin Motorcyclist ▼
- *1950*

German tin model of a clockwork motorcyclist with an expression of speed.
- *length 16cm*
- £225 ● Dr Colin B. Baddiel

Clockwork Cat ▼
- *1950*

German clockwork tabby cat, playing with yellow and green striped ball.
- *length 5cm*
- £45 ● Dr Colin B. Baddiel

Model Train ◀

- *circa 1947*

Lionel GG1 model train. Rare USA train '0' gauge. Black cast metal. 'Pennsylvania' written on the side. This is one of the first models produced by the company.
- *length 36cm*
- £450 • Wheels of Steel

Battery-Operated Robot ▼

- *late 1970's*

Robot with preset animated programme with moving head and illuminating eyes.
- *height 11cm*
- £18 • Retro Exchange

Roly Poly ▼

- *circa 1860–1870*

Roly Poly papier maché with weighted balance in the figure of a large boy wearing tunic of blue and red with yellow buttons.
- *height 14cm*
- £350 • Judith Lassalle

Selection of Marbles ▲

- *late 19th century*

Selection of marbles on solitaire board. Most are onion skins of various colours. The marbles alone are extremely collectable.
- £300 • Judith Lassalle

Formula 1 Car ▼

- *circa 1950*

Lancia Formula 1 by Mercury of Italy. Unusual with petrol tanks on the side. With original box.
- *length 9cm*
- £78 • P. McAskie

Timpo Models ▼

- *1970*

Clay County Jail Wagon and horse with seven cowboys in different poses. Still boxed.
- £80 • Stephen Naegel

Rock and Roll Flower ▶

- *1988*

Sound-activated, dancing 'rock and roll' flower shown with painted face upside-down glasses and yellow trumpet, in white flower pot.
- *height 35cm*
- £18 • Retro Exchange

493

Catterfelda Doll ▶

- *circa 1870*
A German hand-painted porcelain doll made by Catterfelda, wearing the original lace dress.
- *height 66cm*
- **£480** ● Dolly Land

Expert Tips

The 'teddy' bear originates from 1902, when a cartoon depicting President Theodore 'Teddy' Roosevelt, a keen hunter, showed him refusing to shoot a bear cub. At this time toy bears were being imported from Germany and Roosevelt's followers named them 'teddy'.

Brown Steiff Bear ▼

- *1993*
Brown Steiff bear. Limited edition of 3,000.
- *height 61cm*
- **£375** ● Dolly Land

Cheeky ◀

- *1995*
'Cheeky', the Merrythought Bear. Limited edition to 250.
- *height 65cm*
- **£225** ● Dolly Land

Limited Edition Doll ▶

- *1994*
Annabette Himstedt doll, one of a limited edition.
- *height 75cm*
- **£750** ● Dolly Land

Annabette Himstedt Doll ▲

- *1993–4*
Limited edition of an Annabette Himstedt doll. Hand painted with long blonde hair and original white dress.
- *height 68cm*
- **£650** ● Dolly Land

Steiff Bear Watches ▲

- *1992*
Steiff bear watch collection.
- *height 51cm*
- **£350** ● Dolly Land

Porcelain Doll ▼

- *circa 1940*
A Burggrub-Princess Elizabeth Pozellanlabrik porcelain doll with blonde hair and a white organza dress.
- *height 38cm*
- **£1,200** ● Dolly Land

Simon & Halbig Doll ▼

- *circa 1880*

Jointed porcelain girl doll with blue eyes, long dark hair and a painted face, wearing a floral dress and green leather shoes, by Simon & Halbig.
- *height 52cm*
- £648 • Glenda Dolls

Snow White ▼

- *circa 1930*

French padded doll of Snow White with composition face and hands.
- *height 44cm*
- £368 • Glenda Dolls

Norah Wellings Admiral ▲

- *circa 1880*

Soft toy of an admiral by Norah Wellings, wearing a brown velvet uniform with silver metal buttons, and a blue hat with gold trimmings.
- *height 28cm*
- £90 • Glenda Dolls

Steiff Pekinese ▲

- *circa 1940*

Velvet padded pekinese by Steiff, with glass eyes.
- *height 10cm*
- £48 • Glenda Dolls

Red Fiat ▼

- *1960*

Red Fiat 600 made in Japan, in excellent condition, with working spring-back sunshine roof.
- *length 22cm*
- £180 • P. McAskie

Black Seal ▼

- *circa 1950*

Black seal balancing a striped ball, manufactured in Japan.
- *height 16cm*
- £90 • P. McAskie

Expert Tips

Steiff teddy bears and other animals, such as pekinese dogs, deer and owls, are steadily climbing upwards in value and are worth looking out for.

Round the World Space Toy ◄

- *circa 1950*

Round the World space toy made by Technofix, Germany.
- *length 60cm*
- £265 • P. McAskie

495

Treen

Treen means 'made from trees'; anything wooden qualifies. Artefacts vary from the highly decorated to the basically carved, and all have their own charm.

Treen has become valuable in recent years partly by default. Previous generations discarded it as valueless; as a result, the scarcity of early treen today can lead to extremely high prices. It is peasant, provincial art – household items and ornaments fashioned from wood. You would have to be very lucky to find sixteenth-century treen outside a museum – usually items such as standing cups and platters. Objects from the seventeenth century occasionally turn up, the more workaday in hardwoods such as sycamore and holly, the more important fashioned from lignum vitae, which had to be imported. Most treen consists of domestic and practical items of which interesting and pleasing collections can be made for a relatively small investment – but quite a large expenditure in time spent tracking them down. Among the most expensive is Scandinavia treen. Long nights and an abundance of wood led the Scandinavians to carve and decorate their handiwork to an extent seldom found elsewhere. Many treen artefacts were originally carved as love tokens, and these are among the most charming.

Rosewood Box ▼
- *circa 1825*
Small rosewood box with a silver plaque with the letters E. M.
- *4cm x 7cm*
- £225   • **Rupert Gentle**

Pressed Wood Box ▼
- *circa 1840*
Pressed circular wood box with a carving of a boy and sword beside a dog jumping.
- *diameter 6cm*
- £550   • **Rupert Gentle**

Fruitwood Box ▲
- *1830*
Small fruitwood box with gold foliate banding between bands of gold leaves on a black background.
- *2cm x 8cm*
- £275   • **Rupert Gentle**

Tunbridge Ware Box ▲
- *circa 1850*
Tunbridge Ware box by Burrows. From Tunbridge Wells.
- *8cm x 8cm*
- £140   • **Jasmin Cameron**

Carved Deer Heads ▼
- *circa 1860*
One of a pair of Continental carved reindeer with red paint and genuine horns.
- *height 64cm*
- £1,800   • **Anthony Sharpe**

Figure of a Friar ▲
- 1860

A figure of a friar with a beard and habit, standing with clasped hands.
- *height 10cm*
- £725   • Bill Chapman

Walnut Carving ▲
- *18th century*

A fine eighteenth century Venetian carving in walnut showing the bust of a young boy in a scallop shell border with a hunting motif at the base.
- *height 15cm*
- £895   • Dial Post House

Pair of Swags ▶
- *18th century*

Pair of painted swags with fruit.
- *40cm x 88cm x 14cm*
- £3,250   • O.F. Wilson

Sycamore Container ▶
- 1900

Container with a view of the Windsor Castle round tower.
- *height 9cm*
- £45   • John Clay

Carved Eagles ▲
- 1810

Pair of French First Empire carved giltwood eagles.
- *height 25cm*
- £2,200   • O.F. Wilson

Fruitwood Match Holder ▲
- 1870

Fruitwood match holder in the shape of a boot.
- *height 6cm*
- £170   • Bill Chapman

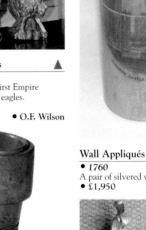

Wall Appliqués ▼
- 1760

A pair of silvered wall appliqués.
- £1,950   • O.F. Wilson

Tribal Art

The proliferation of fakes from Africa and the Far East makes Tribal Art a perilous, but nonetheless rewarding, area for the collector.

Tribal art is characterized by strong images and shapes and has become increasingly popular in recent years. The problem concomitant with this popularity is that the fakes market has proliferated and that these fakes are very difficult for the amateur to identify. It is important, therefore, to buy from a reputable source who can guarantee authenticity. African masks are a particularly popular collecting area, especially desirable if they have been used in some form of ritual and carry some spiritual significance. Like all wooden items, they tend to be adversely affected by the extremes of climate and examples predating the twentieth century are rare. Because of this natural deterioration, a worn patina on wooden objects tends rather to add to the value than detract from it. Tribal art usually finds its best market in countries with which it has an association. Thus, Native American and Hawaiian artefacts fetch high prices in the USA and Indonesian artefacts are very popular in Holland, which has a colonial history in the East Indies. The most popular areas in the UK are, generally, Africa and the Pacific Islands.

Zuni Pot ▲
- *circa 2000*
Zuni ceramic seed pot with two painted frogs, by A. Peynetsa.
- *height 6cm*
- **£89.99**   • **Wilde Ones**

Garuda Mask ▶
- *19th century*
Deeply carved mask of Garuda Bhutan (code HYM9233).
- *26cm x 32cm*
- **£495**   • **Gordon Reece**

African Wall Hanging ▶
- *early 20th century*
An unusual ceremonial dance skirt with black abstract patterns on a light brown background, from the Neongo tribe, Zaire.
- *76cm x 40cm*
- **£2,800**   • **Gordon Reece**

Native American Pot ◀
- *circa 2000*
Native American ceramic pot with a painted black and red geometric pattern, signed "P Beneto".
- *height 24cm*
- **£129**   • **Wilde Ones**

Expert Tips

When considering purchasing tribal masks or shields, the natural patina is of the utmost importance. These may have been used in fetishism, which can involve the sprinkling of blood, used for exercising their religious rituals.

Indian Gloves ▲
- **1950**
Pair of Indian gloves with a glass beadwork woodland design and fringing. Lined with pink silk and worn in Wild West Shows.
- *length 28cm*
- **£299** • **Wilde Ones**

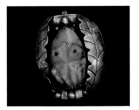

Zuni Fetish Frog ▲
- **1930**
Large circular silver pendant with a central turquoise styled frog flanked by silver leaves.
- *length 4.5cm*
- **£59** • **Wilde Ones**

Ivory Coast Mask ▼
- *circa 1910*
Heavily encrusted Dan mask from the Ivory Coast, Africa.
- *height 24cm*
- **£680** • **Gordon Reece**

Heavily Patinated Mask ▼
- *circa 1910*
Heavily patinated tribal mask.
- *height 26cm*
- **£740** • **Gordon Reece**

Naga Figure ◀
- *circa 1910*
Carved wood Naga figure depicting a standing male with hands clasped.
- *height 64cm*
- **£950 the pair** • **Gordon Reece**

Baule Tribe ▲
- *circa 1910*
Well formulated naturalistic human face with a delicate pouting mouth, finely shaped nose, almond eyes painted white, crossbanded hair and surmounted by a white crescent moon, in excellent condition, from the west coast of Africa.
- *height 48cm*
- **£3,200** • **Gordon Reece**

Calabar Mask ▲
- *circa 1910*
Calabar mask from Benue River, Nigeria, with a strong Cameroon influence.
- *height 29cm*
- **£720** • **Gordon Reece**

Hopi Indian Pot ▲
- *circa 1999*
Hopi Indian ceramic pot with black painted geometric design signed "ACC".
- *height 5cm*
- £39.99 • Wilde Ones

Gable Mask ▲
- *early 20th century*
A Gable mask from Papua New Guinea decorated with cowrie shells and pig tusks.
- *height 90cm*
- £550 • Gooday Gallery

Expert Tips

Beware of the modern copy as these are in abundance due to the influx of tourism into many tribal areas. The local carvers often produce much cruder and simpler objects for the mass market.

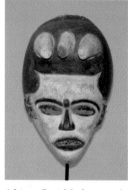

African Ogni Mask ▲
- *early 20th century*
African Ogni mask.
- *26cm x 14cm*
- £350 • Gooday Gallery

Yoruban Mask ▼
- *circa 1900*
Nigerian Yoruban helmet mask.
- *50cm x 24cm*
- £400 • Gooday Gallery

Lega Mask ▼
- *circa 1900*
Lega mask from Zaire.
- *width 34cm*
- £425 • Gooday Gallery

Native American Ceramic Pot ◄
- *circa 1998*
Native American pot with black incised design painted with porcupine quills, inscribed, "ACOCMA NM KSC".
- *height 7cm*
- £149.99 • Wilde Ones

Embroidered Panel ▶

- *circa 1935*

A Shoowa tribe velvet knotted and embroidered panel, with geometric, repeated diamond patterns. From Zaire, formerly the Belgian Congo.

- *1.3cm x 1.3cm*
- £330 • **Gordon Reece**

Mask ▲

- *circa 1900*

A fine example of a mask from the Punli of Gabon Society, originally in a Paris collection and with excellent provenance.

- *height 28cm*
- £3,800 • **Gordon Reece**

Tree of Life Carving ▲

- *circa 1990*

A carved ebony statue showing a small tree of life with ancestral characters about a central figure.

- *height 31cm*
- £48 • **Something Different**

Painted Drum ▼

- *circa 1980*

A wooden painted drum with calfskin drumskin, pegged for tension, the body decorated with masks and geometric patterns.

- *height 58cm*
- £48 • **Something Different**

Table ▼

- *circa 1990*

An ebony table, with interlocking carved support and top carved with rhino pattern and elephant pattern on reverse.

- *height 42cm*
- £30 • **Something Different**

Bambara Mask ▼

- *circa 1900*

A fine example of a mask of the Bambara tribe of Mali, stylised with hair standing on end. From a continental collector.

- *height 35cm*
- £3,200 • **Gordon Reece**

Weapon ▼

- *circa 1910*

Ngombe Doko-Mbudja double-edged cutting weapon from Zaire, formerly the Belgian Congo.

- *height 40cm*
- £220 • **Gordon Reece**

Buffalo Helmet Mask ◄
- *circa 1920*
Kanos buffalo carved wood mask
from the Ivory coast of Africa.
- *height 38cm*
- £1,400   • Gordon Reece

M'Bun Currency ▼
- *unknown*
M'Bun status currency in
throwing knife form.
- 48cm x 39cm
- £720   • Gordon Reece

Guardian of the Spirits ▼
- *circa 1820*
West Nepalese bronze figure of a
village guardian of the spirits.
- *height 22cm*
- £720   • Gordon Reece

Pulley Goure Bete ▲
- *circa 1890*
Figure of a Pulley Goure Bete.
- *height 19cm*
- £490   • Gordon Reece

Man Betu Gabon ▼
- *circa 1890*
A cephalomorphic ceramic from
the Man Betu, Gabon, used only
in court art.
- *height 42cm*
- £630   • Gordon Reece

Igbo Tribe Figures ▲
- *circa 1910*
One of a pair of figures from the
Igbo tribe. A terracotta seated
ancestorial couple, displaying
typical central crested headdress
and multiple anklets, bracelets
and necklaces symbolising
wealth.
- *height 54cm*
- £6,500   • Gordon Reece

Bhutan Nepal Mask ◄
- *circa 1700*
Early mask of dynamic primitive
form relying on simplicity, from
Bhutan on the Nepalese border.
Very rare and in excellent
condition.
- *height 33cm*
- £1,380   • Gordon Reece

Twentieth-Century Design

The twentieth century was rich in innovatory design and revolutionary manufacture. What were 'the antiques of tomorrow' are rapidly becoming the antiques of today.

Each succeeding century is more artistically innovative and revolutionary than its predecessor, due to improved methods, new materials, better communication and, we hope, an increase in wisdom. Currently, the twentieth century is the standard-bearer of this tradition, with not only those advances, but a series of the bloodiest wars in history to enhance the imagination. As recently as the 1960s, Victoriana was mercilessly lampooned by antique dealers and critics alike, before gaining respectability and massive price increases. Any criticism levelled at Victoriana was as nothing compared with the critics' merciless reaction to the Art Nouveau style that emerged at the start of the twentieth century. Now that style has a fantastic following, combining, at its best, quality, originality and, if you're lucky, affordability. Antiques from the Art Deco period, evocative of the giddy 1920s and '30s, with their high quality craftsmanship and inventive shapes, is also greatly in demand. It is not only nostalgia that fuels the collector's demand for twentieth-century artefacts, it is appreciation of genuine craftsmanship and imagination. Get collecting.

Ceramics

Glass Jug ▶
- *20th century*
Finely crafted glass gourd-shaped jug with abstract designs, made by Muller Croismare.
- *height 15cm*
- £2,200   • **Bizarre**

Porcelain Teapot ◀
- *circa 1990s*
English porcelain teapot, with hand-painted ribbon decoration, by Graham Clarke.
- *height 27.5cm*
- £75   • **Richard Dennis**

Bee Vase ◀
- *late 1990s*
Dennis China Works ceramic vase of baluster form, decorated with a repeated honeycomb pattern with bees in the foreground.
- *height 11.25cm*
- £300   • **Richard Dennis**

Toucan Vase ▲
- *late 20th century*
English vase decorated with a toucan on a black ground, by Dennis China Works.
- *height 30cm*
- £470   • **Richard Dennis**

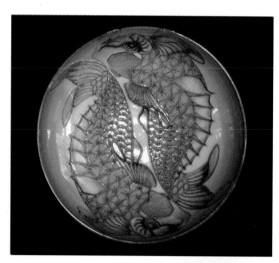

Carp Charger ▲

- *circa 2000*
Pottery charger with a design of
two carp on a green background,
by Dennis China Works.
- *diameter 36cm*
- £540   • Richard Dennis

Ocelot Design Vase ▶

- *2000*
Dennis China Works pottery vase
of a leopard on a leopard spot
background, painted by
Catherine Mellor.
- *height 24cm*
- £411   • Richard Dennis

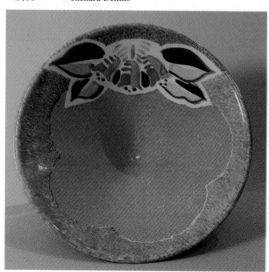

Shelley Bon-Bon Dish ▼

- *1927*
Bon-bon dish with a serpentine
rim, orange centre and four black
trees.
- *diameter 11cm*
- £65   • Susie Cooper

Shelley Cake Plate ▼

- *1927*
Shelley cake plate with a
scalloped border and bold black
trees within an orange border.
- *diameter 24cm*
- £65   • Susie Cooper

Bulb Vase ▼

- *1936*
Clarice Cliff bulb vase with metal
rim from the 'Citrus Delicier'
collection.
- *diameter 20cm*
- £350   • Susie Cooper

Nuage by Clarice Cliff ◀

- *1935*
'Nuage' bowl by Clarice Cliff,
with hand painted flowers and
leaves with an orange centre on a
green ground.
- *diameter 19cm*
- £950   • Susie Cooper

Ceramics

Danish Ceramic Vase ▶
- **1950s**

Danish ceramic vase of
asymmetric form with a white
elongated diamond-shaped
pattern on a black ground, by
Soholm Bornholm.
- *height 57cm*
- **£400** • Vincenzo Caffarella

Italian Ceramic Vase ▲
- **1950s**

Italian bottle-shaped ceramic
vase by GTA, decorated with
stylised faces.
- *height 48cm*
- **£250** • Vincenzo Caffarella

Expert Tips

*The Italian ceramic designs
from the 1950s are elegant and
highly decorative. Look for a
clear elegant shape with
uncluttered strong lines.*

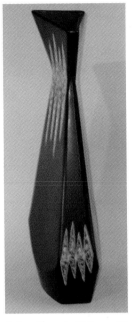

Italian Ceramic Dish ▼
- **1950s**

Italian black and white ceramic
dish of ovoid form on three
conical feet by Antonia Campi.
- *8cm x 29cm x 9cm*
- **£200** • Vincenzo Caffarella

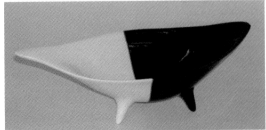

Enamel Ashtray ◀
- **1960**

Square enamel ashtray with two
figures outlined in white on a
purple base with a raised black
rim.
- *16cm x 16cm*
- **£120** • Vincenzo Caffarella

Ceramic Painted Figure ▲
- **1925**

French ceramic painted figure
modelled as a female reclining on
a plain base, by Parvillee.
- *24cm x 60cm*
- **£1,800** • Gooday Gallery

Bosch Frères Vase ▼
- **1920**

Bosch Frères vase of oval form
with splayed lip incorporating a
geometric design in orange, black
and cochineal glaze on a white
ground.
- *height 26cm*
- **£280** • Gooday Gallery

Ribbed Italian Jug ▼

- *1950*

Brown Italian jug of conical form with small neck and ear-shaped handle with a ribbed incised design.
- *height 19cm*
- £45
- Ventesimo

Highland Pottery Vase ▼

- *circa 1974*

Highland Stoneware Pottery baluster-shaped vase, hand painted with a coastal scene.
- *height 25cm*
- £150
- Richard Dennis

Sèvres Group ▶

- *1920*

'Les Pecheurs', a Sèvres group showing two ladies and two children. One of the ladies holds a fishing net beside a basket of fish, the whole on a rustic base.
- *height 27cm*
- £1,500
- Stockspring

Alan Caiger Smith Jug ▲

- *circa 1978*

Large white pottery water jug with green and blue design by Alan Caiger Smith.
- *height 38cm*
- £400
- Richard Dennis

Zebra Vase ▶

- *1999*

Dennis China Works vase with a zebra design on a zebra pattern background, designed by Sally Tuffin and painted by Heidi Warr.
- *height 23cm*
- £298
- Richard Dennis

Parrot Plate ▼

- *2000*

Parrot designed by Sally Tuffin and painted by Tania Pike for Dennis China Works.
- *diameter 16cm*
- £70
- Richard Dennis

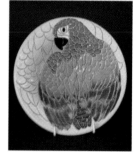

Terracotta Poole Vase ▲

- *circa 1929–34*

A well-proportioned Poole pottery vase. The vase is in terracotta with white glaze overpainted with greens, blues and purples, depicting summer scenes of swallows, passion flowers and buddleia.
- *height 18cm*
- £350   • Richard Dennis

Poole Vase ▲

- 1950

Poole vase with printed Poole mark. The vase is of a conical shape with a hand-painted basket pattern in purple and yellow.
- *height 19cm*
- £400   • Richard Dennis

Expert Tips

Highland Stoneware produces a limited quantity of freehand painted tableware. The shapes are repeated but no two pieces are identical – thus very collectable.

Eggshell Porcelain Pot ▼

- 1902

Mocca pot with lid by H.G.A. Huyvenaar, from Rozenburg of the Hague, in the finest eggshell porcelain. Painted with purple floral decoration and in perfect condition.
- *height 25.5cm*
- £10,000   • P. Oosthuizen

Poole Studio Plate ▼

- 1999

Showing a scene of a sunset with seagull, predominantly in black, orange and blue glaze. By Tony Morris, with Poole dolphin mark.
- *diameter 40cm*
- £450   • Richard Dennis

Highland Dish ▶

- 1999

A Highland Stoneware painted salmon dish. The dish has a representation of a Salmon in blue and purple glazes with a yellow underbelly.
- *height 42cm*
- £52.50   • Richard Dennis

Swedish Sculpture ▲

- 1953

Swedish abstract sculpture in avante garde style, of interwoven, architectural designs forming an assymetrical whole and painted in black and white. The shape and the colour combine to create a complex play on light and form.
- *height 25.5cm*
- £1,500   • Kieron

Bernam Smith Owl ▲

- 1999

A David Bernam Smith owl, laboriously hand-painted in intricate detail with a matt glaze. Highly collectable. The owl is signed and dated D.B.S.
- *height 19cm*
- £600   • Richard Dennis

Dennis Jar and Cover ▲

- *late 1990s*
Jar painted with a polar bear and cub in an arctic setting, with a polar bear finial, by Dennis China Works.
- *height 10cm*
- **£305** • Richard Dennis

Poole Ceramic Plate ▲

- *20th century*
Poole pottery plate with a one-off abstract pattern, designed by Tony Morris.
- *diameter 40cm*
- **£450** • Richard Dennis

Expert Tips

Pottery is prone to chipping and in some cases the glaze can flake. Pottery can be a good starting point for a collection as many pieces can still be bought at reasonable prices.

Kaffe Fasset Vase ▶

- *late 20th century*
Scottish Highland stoneware baluster vase, hand painted with leaf and fruit designs by Kaffe Fasset.
- *height 36.25cm*
- **£600** • Richard Dennis

Highland Stoneware Bowl ▶

- *1990–9*
Highland stoneware bowl decorated with a repeated scene of gold fish within blue borders, with ear-shape handles.
- *diameter 16.25cm*
- **£95** • Richard Dennis

English Abstract Dish ▲

- *circa 1950s*
An English ovoid dish with an abstract geometric pattern on a black ground with a white rim.
- *32cm x 23cm*
- **£75** • Vincenzo Caffarella

Lawrence McGowan Vase ◀

- *late 20th century*
Lawrence McGowan vase decorated with a foliate design, with scrolled handles.
- *height 28.75cm*
- **£140** • Richard Dennis

Poole Owl Plate ▼

- *late 1990s*
Poole pottery plate painted with an black owl, with a sunset in the background, by Tony Morris.
- *diameter 40cm*
- **£450** • Richard Dennis

Butter Container ▼

- *circa 1940*

Cream ceramic butter dish with a lattice and apple blossom design in relief.
- *12cm x 18cm*
- £30   ● Old School

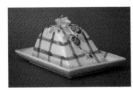

William de Morgan ▼

- *circa 1900*

William de Morgan designed pottery, decorated with a yellow bird with a trailing cornflower design on a turquoise border, painted by Charles Passenger.
- *diameter 20cm*
- £200   ● Richard Dennis

Ovoid Vase ▲

- *circa 1920*

Italian bottle-shaped vase with yellow, green and brown abstract design.
- *height 29cm*
- £250   ● Iconastas

English Cup and Saucer ▲

- *circa 1920*

English cup, saucer and plate with a cartouche of a painted bird within gilt borders, surrounded by pink roses and cornflowers.
- *height 7.5cm*
- £38   ● A. Piotrowski

Cigarette Holder ▼

- 1950

Circular cigarette holder with push-action lid to extinguish the cigarettes.
- *height 21cm*
- £38   ● Ventesimo

Janice Tchlenko Vase ▼

- *circa 1999*

Poole pottery vase of baluster form with a vibrant cany strip design by Janice Tchalenko.
- *height 37cm*
- £200   ● Richard Dennis

Dutch Jar ◀

- *circa 1923*

Dutch jar with cover by Corona Gouda, designed by W. P. Harispring.
- *height 11cm*
- £280   ● P. Oosthuizen

Foxglove Bottle ▼
- *late 1990s*
Foxglove ceramic bottle-shaped vase painted with foxgloves on a blue ground, by Dennis China Works.
- *height 37.5cm*
- £517   • Richard Dennis

Sicart Ashtray ▼
- *circa 1970s*
Italian circular ceramic ashtray with metal insert by Sicart.
- *6cm x 21cm*
- £185   • Paolo Bonino

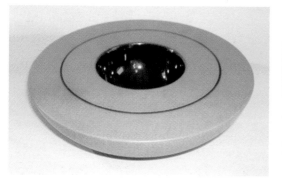

Bisque Rabbit ▲
- *20th century*
Bisque porcelain model of a rabbit with ears erect and head turned to the side.
- *height 30cm*
- £340   • North West 8

Highland Dish ▲
- *late 1990s*
Octagonal Highland stoneware dish, hand painted with a floral design of lillies on a lustre ground.
- *46.25cm x 40cm*
- £189   • Richard Dennis

Cockran Bowl ▲
- *1990–9*
British ceramic deep bowl decorated with a blue octopus, by Roger Cockran.
- *15cm x 21.25cm*
- £130   • Richard Dennis

Cream-Glazed Vase ▲
- *circa 1930*
French ceramic vase of ovoid proportions with a cream glaze and a rusticated finish.
- *height 20cm*
- £150   • Bizarre

Asymmetric Vase ▲
- *1950s*
Italian ceramic vase of asymmetric form with a green and white design on a black ground.
- *height 30cm*
- £40   • Goya

Moorcroft Vase ▲

- 1995

Lisa Moorcroft urn-shaped
vase or planter with a raised
design of mushrooms in red
on a tobacco background.
- *height 60cm*
- **£175**   • **Richard Dennis**

Floral Poole Vase ▲

- *circa 1929–34*

Poole pottery vase with stamp
mark decorated with crocuses and
daffodils with a leaf design and
interlacing floral pattern.
- *height 25cm*
- **£600**   • **Richard Dennis**

Expert Tips

*Hand-thrown pieces have
irregular ribbing on the inside
and a less clinical appearance
than moulded wares. However,
all hand-thrown pieces are not
necessarily desirable!*

Moorland Vase ▼

- 1999

Moorland conical vase with a
repeated pyramid pattern in
white, black and grey. Metalic
banding running around neck.
- *height 19cm*
- **£40**   • **Richard Dennis**

Baxter Plate ▼

- 1999

Glen Baxter plate created for the
Poole pottery showing cartoon
printed on the face, wording
around the edge of the rim and
Glen Baxter's signature.
- *diameter 22cm*
- **£18**   • **Richard Dennis**

Gouda Deep Dish ▶

- 1928

Early 20th-century. Zuid-Holland
factory. Gouda deep dish on
stand. Dish designed by
Rembrandt Pottery.
- **£600**   • **P. Oosthuizen**

Dennis Pot ▲

- 1999

Dennis Chinaworks pot and
cover decorated in a cobweb
pattern in black and brown
glaze with cobweb and leaf
indentation. A spider is painted
on the inside of the lid.
- *height 10cm*
- **£180**   • **Richard Dennis**

Pantomime Vase ▲

- 1997

Vase decorated with pantomime
buttons and the ugly sisters.
Showing three faces with
different expressions, detailed
painting inside and out with
enamelling. By David Burnham
Smith.
- *height 10cm*
- **£950**   • **Richard Dennis**

Eagle Vase ▼
- *circa 2000*

Large vase of baluster form with a
design of an eagle with wings
folded and head turned to one
side.
- *height 41cm*
- £611   • Richard Dennis

Ceramic Jar ▶
- *circa 1940s*

Pale green ceramic biscuit jar and
cover, with a raised Chinoiserie
cherry blossom design and basket-
style handle.
- *13cm x 10cm*
- £65   • Old School

Cake Server ▲
- *circa 1930*

Cream ceramic cake stand with
orange and yellow flowers and
folia, and a geometric metal
handle.
- *13cm x 23cm*
- £30   • Old School

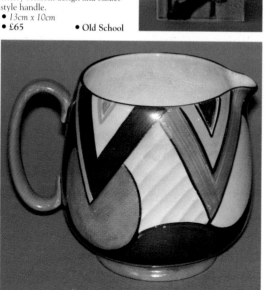

Alfred Read ▼
- *circa 1953-4*

Poole pottery vase No. YHP,
designed by Alfred Read.
- *height 25cm*
- £175   • Richard Dennis

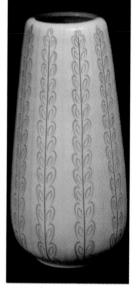

Eduardo Paolozzi Plate ▼
- *circa 1950*

Wedgwood bone china plate
made in England by Eduardo
Paolozzi with a red, black and
gold geometric design.
- *diameter 27cm*
- £150   • Richard Dennis

Susie Cooper Jug ◀
- *circa 1930*

Crown Devon yellow, black,
orange and aubergine geometric
design jug by Fieldings of
England.
- *height 14cm*
- £240   • Arwas

Glazed Candlesticks ▶

- **1917–34**

Pair of candlesticks by Minton Hollins Astraware, with a distinct variegated blue green glaze.
- *height 21cm*
- **£200**   • **A.D. Antiques**

French Vase ▲

- **20th century**

French green vase, on a bronze tripod base by Daum Majorelle.
- *height 15cm*
- **£1,200**   • **Bizarre**

Read Water Jug ◀

- *circa 1920*

Blue water jug with a floral trellis pattern by Frederick Read.
- *height 17.5cm*
- **£295**   • **A.D. Antiques**

Burmantoft ◀

- **early 20th century**

An amber glazed Burmantoft of amphori form with two elongated handles.
- *height 20cm*
- **£235**   • **A.D. Antiques**

Royal Lancastrian Vase ▲

- *circa 1920*

Green Royal Lancastrian vase of organic form in matt green glaze.
- *height 18cm*
- **£195**   • **A.D. Antiques**

Expert Tips

There are many different types of glazes for ceramics, and certain potters become renowned for the types of glazes that they favour.

Moorcroft Vase ◀

- **1913–7**

Early Moorcroft pomegranate vase by William Moorcroft.
- *height 19cm*
- **£575**   • **A.D. Antiques**

Holyrood Pottery Vase ▼

- **1917–27**

Holyrood pottery bulbous vase with crazing to base.
- *height 34cm*
- **£95**   • **A.D. Antiques**

Moon & Mountain ▲
• **1928**
'Moon and Mountain' plate with a hand-painted abstract design by Susie Cooper.
• *length 26cm*
• £325   • Susie Cooper

Spring Vase ▶
• **1936**
'Spring' vase of ovoid form with a hand-painted design of crocuses by Clarice Cliff.
• *height 15cm*
• £465   • Susie Cooper

Susie Cooper Tea Set ◀
• **1929**
Seventeen piece Susie Cooper tea set consisting of five cups and saucers, a milk jug and a sugar bowl, with a black, yellow, orange and grey geometric design.
• *height of cup 9cm*
• £2,600   • Susie Cooper

Grays Pottery Jug ▼
• **1929**
Water jug with an abstract pattern and gilding designed by Susie Cooper for Gray's pottery.
• *height 35cm*
• £300   • Susie Cooper

Arts Stable Jug ▼
• **circa 1930**
Arts stable jug with geometric design by Poole Pottery.
• *height 17cm*
• £400   • Arwas

Susie Cooper Tea Trio ◀
• **1929**
Susie Cooper tea trio cup and saucer and plate with a yellow, green, black and yellow 'lightning' pattern.
• *height 9cm*
• £450   • Susie Cooper

Durtington Plate ▲
- 1999

A Durtington plate ovate in shape with flower decorations and high-fired reduction glaze.
- *length 43cm*
- £65 • Richard Dennis

Gouda Vase ▲
- 1926

Zuid-Holland, Gouda vase, of baluster form with flamboyant repeated organic pattern in blue, white and gold on a green ground. Made by C.A. Prins.
- *height 21.5cm*
- £225 • P. Oosthuizen

Leopard Vase ▼
- 1999

Dennis Chinaworks vase showing leopards on a leopard pattern background in shades of brown and black glazes.
- *height 24cm*
- £330 • Richard Dennis

Poole Pottery Vase ▼
- *circa 1950*

A hand-painted and hand-decorated Poole pottery vase, decorated in blue and yellow with a vertical alternating pattern.
- *height 18cm*
- £250 • Richard Dennis

Poole Plate ◀
- *circa 1999*

A Poole pottery plate showing a traditional shipping scene with artistic representation of the sun and wind. The reverse is signed and dated. The ship was drawn by Arthur Broadby and painted by Eileen Hunt.
- *height 41cm*
- £1,000 • Richard Dennis

Jersey Cow ▲
- *circa 1950*

A Royal Worcester Jersey cow, standing on a wooden plinth. Part of a limited edition, all modelled on champion stock by Doris Lindner.
- *height 19cm*
- £490 • R.A. Barnes

Monkey With Baby ▲
- 1920s

Royal Copenhagen model of a monkey with baby. Signed and dated. Matt stone finish with grey and blue glaze.
- *height 17cm*
- £750 • Cameo Gallery

Expert Tips

The most important firm operating from the Poole Pottery at the beginning of the 20th century was Carter, Stabler and Adams. The bases of their pieces are imprinted with their name or initials. If the base is unmarked, then it is not Poole.

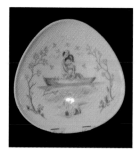

Rosenthal Pottery ▲
- *circa 1950*
Peynet design plate of ovoid
form, depicting a hand-painted
design of a couple in a boat with
birds circling.
- *diameter 20cm*
- £100   • **Richard Dennis**

Clarice Cliff Cup and Saucer ▲
- *1934*
Clarice Cliff cup and saucer with
a 'tulip' pattern and wedge-
shaped handle, the saucer with
pink and blue banding.
- *height 8cm*
- £350   • **Susie Cooper**

Susie Cooper Jug ▲
- *1929*
'Cubist' collection cream jug by
Susie Cooper for Grays Pottery.
- *height 13cm*
- £350   • **Susie Cooper**

Fantasque by Clarice Cliff ▼
- *1936*
Plate by Clarice Cliff from the
Fantasque collection centred with
a hand-painted design of a
country setting within black and
orange borders.
- *diameter 18cm*
- £450   • **Susie Cooper**

Tea Cup and Saucer ▲
- *1936*
Clarice Cliff 'Spring' cup and
saucer hand painted with
crocuses with gilt banding and
pale green borders.
- *height 7cm*
- £110   • **Susie Cooper**

Clarice Cliff Pallet Plate ▲
- *circa 1900*
Clarice Cliff palette plate by
Wilkinson with a lady in the
wind, her scarf blowing, and a
ship in turbulent seas.
- *diameter 24cm*
- £400   • **Victor Arwas**

Balinese Dancer ▶

- *20th century*

A ceramic figure of a Balinese
dancer by Royal Copenhagen.
- *height 14cm*
- £120 • Bizarre

German Ceramic Vase ▲

- *1960*

A German ceramic vase
decorated with a romantic scene,
with a chinoiserie influence, from
the Lover's collection by
Raymond Peynet.
- *height 20cm*
- £700 • Richard Dennis

Italian Ceramic Vase ▶

- *circa 1950s*

Italian three-sided bottle-shaped
vase with abstract cartouches on
a green ground, by Cossa.
- *height 12cm*
- £150 • Vincenzo Caffarella

Porcelain Plate ◀

- *late 1990s*

Porcelain plate hand painted
with a Norfolk scene in a blue
glaze, by Graham Clarke.
- *diameter 40cm*
- £450 • Richard Dennis

Poole Pottery Pot ▶

- *1970*

Green Poole Pottery pot
decorated with large lime green
and darker green scrolls, by
Caroge Holdan.
- *height 45cm*
- £580 • Gooday Gallery

Egg-Shaped Vase ▲

- *1960–70*

German ceramic vase of ovoid
form decorated with an
embracing couple on a bench, by
Raymond Peynet.
- *height 21.25cm*
- £300 • Richard Dennis

Ceramic Cat ▼

- *20th century*

Cat in red living glaze, a type of
glaze pioneered by Poole Pottery.
- *height 28.75cm*
- £27.50 • Richard Dennis

Furniture

Cone Chair ▼

- **1958**
A Danish Verner Panton cone chair, with red wool upholstery and cushioned seat and backrest.
- *height 84.5cm*
- **£850**　　　　• Zoom

French Occasional Table ▼

- *circa 1950*
A French occasional table, with painted pierced metal apron on a tripod base.
- *70cm x 55cm*
- **£680**　　　　• Myriad

Expert Tips

Modern furniture by designers such as Philippe Starck is increasingly in demand, not just as a collector's item, but also for use in the house. Indeed, much of this furniture is being copied by leading stores.

Italian Sofa ▲

- *circa 1950s*
Italian sofa with shaped back and buttoned upholstery, by Gio Ponti.
- *100cm x 192.5cm*
- **£5,500**　　　• Themes

Scandinavian Art Deco Hall Stand ▲

- *circa 1928*
Scandinavian Art Deco hall stand, with large oval central mirror and stainless steel and light elmwood side panels, with three central drawers with large stainless steel and plastic handles.
- *184cm x 139cm x 28cm*
- **£1,700**　　　• Judy Fox

Steamer Chair ▶

- *circa 1900*
Aesthetic Movement ebonized steamer chair, with folding mechanism and cane seat with bobbin turned uprights, after designs by E.W. Godwin.
- *67.5cm x 37.5cm*
- **£1,200**　　　• Liberty plc

Egg Chair ▲

- **1958**
Egg chair in black leather on a metal base, by Arne Jacobsen, Denmark.
- *105cm x 85cm*
- **£4,000**　　　• Themes

Art Nouveau Sideboard ▼

- *early 20th century*
Oak sideboard with organic designs and copper handles.
- *height 1.87m*
- £1,250   • Old Cinema

White Table ▼

- *circa 1965*
Small, Italian white 'Tulip' occasional table.
- *height 1.25m*
- £300   • Whitford

Diner Stools ▲

- *circa 1940*
A set of four round American diner stools with chromed steel base and red leather-covered seats. Very typical of the Art Deco, American café style.
- *height 51cm*
- £350   • After Noah

Shelving Unit ▲

- *circa 1930*
An Art Deco shelving unit, in bent ply, walnut-veneered, designed by Finnish architect Alvar Aalto.
- *height 55cm*
- £4,000   • Libra Designs

Commode Serpentine ◀

- *circa 1920*
Italian Venetian painted and gilded commode serpentine on cabriole legs with scrolled feet.
- *length 2.06m*
- £2,200   • The French Room

English Table ▲

- *circa 1930*
Tubular aluminium base, on three legs with cast bakelite top.
- *height 52cm*
- £250   • After Noah

Expert Tips

Collectable office furniture must be of high quality and of a functional, usually simple design.

Arts and Crafts Chairs ▼

- *circa 1900*
Set of six chairs, four side and two carvers. With heart motif.
- *height 1.15m*
- £2,500   • After Noah

Writing Desk ▶

• *circa 1900s*
An Edwardian ladies writing
desk/dressing table with mirrored
writing surface above three
drawers and brass lattice panels,
all above straight tapered legs.
• *88cm x 121cm*
• **£1,250**   • **John Riordan**

Italian Red S Chair ▲

• *circa 1960*
One of a pair of Italian red
padded soft man-made fabric S-
bend chairs with tubular metal
base.
• *height 80cm x 46cm*
• **£600**   • **Vincenzo Caffarella**

Franco Albini Chairs ▲

• *circa 1950*
One of a pair of Italian walnut
chairs with green upholstered
padded seats and back, by Franco
Albini.
• *height 78cm*
• **£1,200**   • **Francesca Martire**

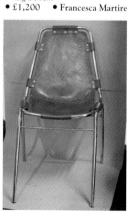

Oak Corner Cupboard ▲

• *circa 1900*
Substantial oak Arts and Crafts
corner cabinet/hall cupboard with
tracerie copper overlay in the Art
Nouveau manner. Made by
Shapland & Petter, England.
• *205cm x 115cm*
• **£3,500**   • **Liberty plc**

Arts and Crafts Dining Chairs ▼

• *circa 1910*
One of a set of six light oak
English Arts and Crafts single
dining chairs and two carvers.
• *104cm x 38cm*
• **£2,995**   • **Liberty plc**

Charles Perriand Chairs ◀

• *circa 1973*
Set of four chairs with brown
leather upholstery, stitching and
metal studs looped to moulded
tubular chrome, designed by
Charles Perriand.
• *height 84cm*
• **£950**   • **Francesca Martire**

Sacco Beanbag ▼
- 1960
Red leather and vinyl beanbag of teardrop shape, by Gatti-Paolini-Teodori of Italy.
- *height 82.5cm*
- £800   • Zoom

Seagull Chairs ▲
- *circa 1990s*
A pair of seagull chairs by Arne Jacobsen of Denmark, for Fritz Hansen.
- *height 75cm*
- £980   • Themes

X-Chair ▲
- 1958
An X-chair in wood and cane, by Huidt and Nielson, Denmark.
- *height 82cm*
- £1,600   • Themes

Dressing Chest ▲
- *circa 1910*
An Arts and Crafts dressing chest with two large and three smaller drawers, original brass handles, and a swing mirror.
- *167cm x 107cm x 53cm*
- £600   • Old Cinema

Orkney Chair ▼
- *circa 1905*
Child's stained oak Orkney chair with carved arms and legs. Original Liberty & Co London enamel label on underside of chair.
- *height 82.5cm*
- £475   • Liberty plc

Storm Oak Chairs ◄
- 1987–88
One of a pair of oak chairs, part of a set which includes a sofa. The oak is a relic of the great storm in 1987.
- *106cm x 94cm*
- £2,750   • Zakheim

Expert Tips

Chromium or tubular-framed furniture can become dented and rusty. The best examples are often made of bronze, aluminium or stainless steel. When choosing twentieth-century furniture it is important to look for high-quality materials, as these will help to maintain the durability of the piece in years to come.

Folding Chair ▼
• *circa 1930*
Eastern European painted green
metal folding chair.
• *90cm x 44cm*
• **£35**   • **Old School**

School Cupboard ▶
• *circa 1940*
European pine cupboard with
panelled cupboards below and
above, standing on a straight
square base.
• *227cm x 167cm*
• **£1,100**   • **Old School**

Green Chair for
Kandya Ltd ◀
• *circa 1950*
One of a set of six lime-green
chairs by Carl Jacobs for Kandya
Ltd., with teak legs.
• *72cm x 51cm*
• **£485**   • **The Country Seat**

Oak Wardrobe ▼
• *circa 1890*
Aesthetic movement oak
wardrobe with mirror panelled
door flanked by two tongue-and-
groove panel doors with brass
hinges.
• *205cm x 183cm*
• **£1,750**   • **Old Cinema**

Teak Bedroom Suite ▼
• *circa 1930s*
Teak Art Deco bedroom suite.
• *175cm x 95cm*
• **£1,650**   • **Old Cinema**

Antelope Chairs ◀
• *circa 1950*
One of a set of six 'Antelope'
painted metal chairs, with Ernest
Rays, London, England on the
base of the seat. Made for the
Festival of Britain.
• *83cm x 55cm*
• **£1,050**   • **The Country Seat**

Kitchen Dresser ▼

- *circa 1920*

Oak kitchen dresser with original jars and various compartments.
- *height 1.88m*
- £850   • Old Cinema

Toleware Vase ▼

- *circa 1935*

A Toleware vase with tortoiseshell finish.
- *height 43cm*
- £295   • Butchoff Interiors

'Wave' Sofa ▶

- *circa 1968*

A sofa designed by the French designer Pierre Paulin and entitled 'The Wave'.
- *length 1.67m*
- £2,750   • Whitford

Wall Panels ▲

- *circa 1970*

Four decorative Verner Panton wall panels, in red perspex plastic, of bulbous design.
- *height 1.2m*
- £480   • Planet Bazaar

Art Deco Armchairs ▲

- *circa 1930*

A pair of English-made Art Deco armchairs, upholstered in leather with walnut sides.
- *height 84cm*
- £1,200   • Libra Designs

Ministry Locker ▼

- *circa 1950*

A steel Air Ministry locker with four doors, vents and label holders. In government grey.
- *height 1.65m*
- £175   • Metro Retro

Expert Tips

Laminated wood was first employed in the Art Deco period. The wood tends to chip, flake and bubble and, consequently, furniture has not survived in great quantities.

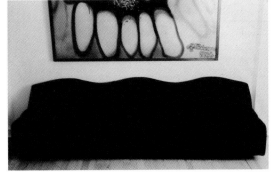

Art Nouveau Settee ▼
- *circa 1900*

Art Nouveau two-seater walnut settee. The curved upper rail with scrolled terminals above a turned back rail, with shaped arms above turned legs and square legs at back.
- *120cm x 120cm*
- **£1,995** • Liberty plc

Victorian Stick Stand ▼
- *1900*

Victorian stick stand with pierced back rail with a repeated heart motif, and ebony and boxwood inlay.
- *70cm x 85cm*
- **£475** • Liberty plc

Oak Sideboard ▲
- *circa 1910*

Medium oak Arts and Crafts sideboard, with mushroom bracket supports on upper shelf, above an arched recess between two panelled doors.
- *127.5cm x 147.5cm*
- **£2,250** • Liberty plc

Anglo-Japanese Walnut Fire Screen ▼
- *circa 1900*

Highly unusual Anglo-Japanese walnut fire screen with yellow glass panels enclosed within flat banding, with an ebonized button at the intersection of each. The whole supported on tapered legs.
- *height 82.5cm*
- **£1,950** • Liberty plc

Child's Chair ◀
- *circa 1990s*

Swedish child's chair in shaped wood with black and white cowhide upholstery, by Caroline Schlyter.
- *height 57.5cm*
- **£980** • Themes

Sofa Table ▲
- *circa 1900*

Arts and Crafts oak sofa table in the manner of C.F.A. Voysey. The plank top supported on tapered legs, with an undertier with a storage area for papers, with stylised heart motifs either side.
- *47.5cm x 72.5cm*
- **£1,250** • Liberty plc

Limed Oak Desk with Art Deco Chairs ▲
- *20th century*

A limed oak partner's desk with drinks bar concealed behind curved panel doors, with two Art Deco chairs.
- *77cm x 140cm x 80cm*
- **£4,500** • Bizarre

Chair by Carl Jacobs ▼

- *circa 1950*
One of a set of six red chairs by Carl Jacobs for Kandya Ltd., with teak legs.
- *72cm x 51cm*
- **£485** • **The Country Seat**

Walnut and Chrome Table ▼

- *circa 1980*
Small circular walnut table with metal circular ashtray standing on a teak pedestal and circular base with metal turned legs.
- *height 58cm*
- **£365** • **The Country Seat**

Kasthole Armchair ▶

- *circa 1970*
One of a pair of leather and bent rosewood armchairs with metal and leather arms by Fabricius and Kastholme.
- *82cm x 72cm*
- **£1,950** • **The Country Seat**

Brass Brolly Stand ▲

- *circa 1910*
Art Nouveau brass brolly stand with hand-beaten finish and embossed tulip design.
- *height 63cm*
- **£375** • **Old Cinema**

Edwardian Plant Stand ▼

- *circa 1910*
Oak plant stand with copper banded decoration, raised on three carved supports with tripod stretcher.
- *88cm x 28cm*
- **£145** • **Old Cinema**

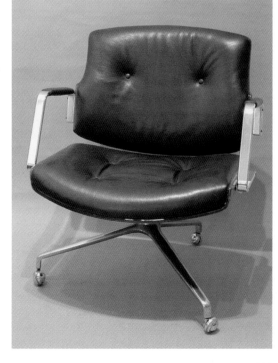

Octagonal Tables ▲
- *circa 1900*
Pair of Islamic-Egyptian octagonal tables, with bone and abalone inlay.
- *height 51cm*
- £680   ● North West 8

The 'Joe' Sofa ▲
- *circa 1970*
Inspired by the American baseball legend, 'Joltin' Joe DiMaggio. Designed by J.de Pas, D. D'Urbino and P. Lomazzi and produced Poltronova, Italy. the design is that of a surreal, giant baseball glove in brown leather.
- *width 1.05m*
- £2,750   ● Whitford

German Fan ▼
- *circa 1940*
German bakelite fan designed by Dieter Rams.
- *height 27cm*
- £400   ● Decodence

School Desk ▼
- *circa 1940*
English elm school desk with child-size chair. Good patination.
- *height 84cm*
- £175   ● After Noah

Armchair ▲
- *1932*
An Alvar Aalto cantilever armchair. Model no. 31
- *height 77cm*
- £2,000   ● Libra Designs

Arts and Crafts Chairs ▲
- *circa 1910*
Set of six oak chairs with rexine seats.
- *height 92cm*
- £1,800 (six)   ● Riverbank

Danish Bench Seat ◄
- *circa 1950*
Special commission for a bank with button-cushion leather.
- *height 87cm*
- £1,650   ● Themes

French Chinese-Style Chair ▼

circa 1920
One of a pair of French oak chairs with a strong Chinese influence and a distressed paint effect, standing on straight square legs.
● *height 74cm*
● £1,250 ● Anthony Sharpe

Art Deco Cabinet ▼

circa 1930
Art deco figured mahogany walnut cocktail cabinet of circular design with pull-out mixing surface.
● *161cm x 85cm*
● £995 ● Old Cinema

Art Deco Three-Piece Suite ▶

circa 1930
A very rare and unusual Art Deco upholstered leather three-piece suite.
● *86cm x 95cm*
● £5,330 ● Old Cinema

Red Stereophonic Chair ▼

circa 1960s
Red moulded fibreglass egg chair on a circular metal base, with grey and white wool-padded upholstery and leather-padded seat cover and back rest, with fitted stereo and matching ottoman, designed by the Lee Co. of California for a commission.
● *129cm x 86cm*
● £4,200 ● The Country Seat

Dressing table ◀

circa 1950
Modernist oak dressing table with two columns of graduated drawers and single drawer above knee hole.
● *165cm x 122cm*
● £225 ● Old Cinema

Liberty Oak Stand ▲

circa 1900
Liberty's oak stand with three moulded shelves, slated side panels and shaped carrying handle.
● *80cm x 30cm*
● £190 ● Old Cinema

Walnut Bureau ▲

circa 1940
A very good early 20th century figured walnut bureau in the George II style.
● *104cm x 84cm*
● £1,895 ● John Riordan

English Oak Stools ▲
- *1910–15*
One of a pair of Art Nouveau oak
English stools on tapered square
legs, with metal ringed stretcher.
- *height 82cm*
- £500   • Solaris

French Art Deco Stools ▲
- *1820–30*
One of a pair of French Art Deco
metal and upholstered stools on
scrolled cabriole legs.
- *height 40cm*
- £1,400   • Solaris

Charles Eames Chair ◄
- *1960*
Charles Eames swivel office chair
with a chrome tripod stand.
- *height 91cm*
- £1,960   • Zoom

French Mirror ◄
- *20th century*
French wrought-iron mirror
designed by Raymond Subes.
- *120cm x 95cm*
- £2,800   • Bizarre

Finnish Leather
Armchairs ▲
- *1970*
One of a pair of tan leather
moulded armchairs with a metal
circular base, by Wryo
Kukkapuro, Finland.
- *height 80cm*
- £1,500   • Themes

Leopard Chest ◄
- *circa 1990s*
A chest of drawers decorated with
leopards in a jungle setting, by
Formasetti, Italy.
- *82.5cm x 100cm*
- £6,400   • Themes

Pair of Eames Armchairs ▲

- *circa 1975*
A pair of Eames padded brown
armchairs with aluminium arms
and base.
- *height 101cm*
- £1,450   • The Country Seat

Leather Rotating Chair ▲

- *1970*
Tan leather rotating and
adjustable desk chair with padded
seat and back, and metal legs on
wheels.
- *height 74cm*
- £495   • The Country Seat

Walnut Buffet ▶

- *1930*
Art Deco breakfront walnut
buffet with solid supports and
moulded decoration.
- 84cm x 106cm
- £650   • Old Cinema

Black Leather Armchair ▼

- *circa 1960*
Black leather armchair with
padded seat and back, with metal
and leather arms, standing on a
rotating star-shaped metal base.
- *height 89cm*
- £750   • The Country Seat

Edwardian Chest of Drawers ▼

- *circa 1905*
Edwardian chest of two small and
two long drawers, with metal
foliate handles standing on
straight legs.
- *82cm x 108cm*
- £240   • Old School

Butterfly Chair ▲

- *circa 1950*
One of a pair of plastic mock
snakeskin butterfly chairs on a
early tubular frame, manufactured
by Knoll.
- *height 100cm*
- £550   • The Country Seat

White Folding Bench ▲

- *circa 1920*
Continental pine folding bench,
painted white, on metal legs and
arms.
- *90cm x 125cm*
- £220   • Old School

Table ◄
● *circa 1950s*
Oak circular coffee table with turned supports and circular moulded stretcher, raised on bun feet.
● *51cm x 100cm*
● £495 ● Old Cinema

Reclining Armchair ▼
● *1920s*
Oak reclining armchair with carved and turned decoration with slated side panels.
● *100cm x 65cm*
● £395 ● Old Cinema

Butterfly Stool ▼
● *circa 1950*
Butterfly stool designed by Son Yanagi for Tendo Mokko.
● *height 46cm*
● £985 ● The Country Seat

Charles and Ray Eames Chair ▶
● *circa 1950*
Bent birchwood chair by Charles and Ray Eames, for Evans.
● *height 84cm*
● £1,150 ● The Country Seat

Expert Tips

In the 1960s and '70s the influence of pop art led to a series of outlandish designs such as the Blow, an inflatable chair.

Art Deco Chest ▲
● *circa 1930s*
A very good quality Art Deco chest in solid oak with wonderful early plastic handles.
● *83cm x 94cm*
● £450 ● Old Cinema

Pair of Armchairs ▲
- *circa 1925*

One of a pair of French-made armchairs in their original salmon pink fabric with carved gilt wood.
- *height 86cm*
- £3,200 • Bizarre

Swan Chairs ▼
- *circa 1950*

Arne Jacobsen Danish swan chairs with all-leather upholstery.
- *height 74cm*
- £2,200 • Themes

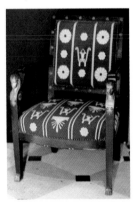

Egyptian Chairs ▼
- *circa 1920*

A pair of elbow chairs with Egyptian-design tapestry covers.
- *height 94cm*
- £3,950 • Wakelin Linfield

Bathroom Cabinet ▲
- *circa 1930*

An Art Deco tin bathroom cabinet with mirrored door and one shelf.
- *height 36cm*
- £55 • Metro Retro

'Up' Chair ▲
- *1969*

From the 'Up' series designed in 1969. Beige and red striped stretch fabric over moulded polyurethane foam.
- *height 65cm*
- £4,500 • Whitford

Red Chairs ▲
- *20th century*

Pair of red 'Champagne' chairs, in plastic, on central metal column and circular base.
- *height 77cm*
- £2,500 • Whitford

Expert Tips

Classic designs of the 1960s are organic to the point of eroticism, with 'lip' sofas, 'egg' chairs and 'mushroom' stools – in hot colours – all now avidly sought.

Steel Desk ◀
- *circa 1950*

Twin pedestal with black rubber top, central locking mechanism and seven chrome handles.
- *height 76cm*
- £475 • Metro Retro

Glass

Mazzega Murano Glass ▼
- *circa 1960*
Italian circular clear and dark blue glass object, designed by Mazzega, with the option of being wall-mounted.
- *diameter 40cm*
- £400 • Vincenzo Caffarella

Barovier and Toso ▲
- *circa 1970*
Italian Murano vase of globular form by Barovier and Toso with black, green and red geometric design.
- *height 35cm x 19cm*
- £950 • Vincenzo Caffarella

Expert Tips

In the early post-war years designers created a fresh start with a feel good factor through a 'new look' based on curves and natural organic shapes.

Cenedese Ash Tray ▼
- *circa 1970*
Lime-green ash tray in the form of a halved lime, by S. Cenedes.
- *width 35cm*
- £185 • Vincenzo Caffarella

Nichetti Vase ▼
- *circa 1990*
Hand-blown orange vase with a gold and grey abstract geometric design and a moulded rim, by Nichetti for Murano.
- *height 28cm*
- £380 • Francesca Martire

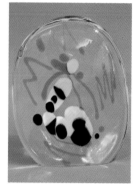

Spanish Abstract ▲
- *circa 1960s*
Spanish hand-blown abstract glass object, with yellow, black and blue design. Signed Vinas.
- *height 27cm*
- £850 • Francesca Martire

Pale Pink Jug ▲
- *1960*
Pale pink Murano jug with slender neck, pinched lip and clear strap handle.
- *height 49cm*
- £85 • Francesca Martire

Danish Indigo Vase ▼
- *early 1970s*
Danish indigo blue glass vase of
bottle shape form with splayed lip
by Holmegaard.
- *14.5cm x 7cm*
- £125　　• Paolo Bonino

Venetian Vase ▲
- *circa 1950s*
Italian vase with air bubbles and
aquatic scenes of fish and organic
forms.
- *38cm x 18cm*
- £1,250　　• Zakheim

Murano Glass Ashtray ▼
- *1950s*
Italian, Murano glass basket-
shaped ashtray, with sea green
and black design within the glass.
- *diameter 13cm*
- £35　　• Goya

Art Deco Glass Bowl ▲
- *1920*
Art Deco French aubergine glass
bowl, decorated with silver plated
bands, signed "Fains".
- *28cm x 30cm*
- £350　　• Gooday Gallery

French Vase ▶
- *1950*
A French pink and clear vase of
ovoid form.
- *35cm x 25cm*
- £65　　• Goya

Circular Bowl ▼
- *1969*
Round glass bowl with orange
design by Tagliapietra.
- *diameter 21cm*
- £450　　• Vincenzo Caffarella

English Vase ▼
- *1960*
Indigo and turquoise blue English
vase with pinched lip by
Whitefriars.
- *24cm x 9cm*
- £45　　• Paolo Bonino

533

Loetz Vase ▼

- *circa 1905*

A Loetz vase, decorated with orange free-form pattern. Gold iridescent medallion splashes.

- *height 27cm*
- **£5,500** • **French Glasshouse**

Blue Bowl ▼

- *circa 1960*

A blue bowl with white enamelled rim, probably from Scandinavia.

- *height 12cm*
- **£75** • **Circa**

Two Vases ▼

- *circa 1988*

Two, teardrop-shaped vases by Peter Layton, with blue swirled patterns within the predominantly white glass.

- *height 32cm (left)*
- *height 35cm (right)*
- **£250 each** • **Circa**

Dragonfly Box and Cover ▲

- *circa 1900*

A Daum box and cover, with applied dragonfly over water lilies, in shades of green.

- *9cm x 15cm*
- **£8,000** • **French Glasshouse**

Daum Lampstand and Shade ▶

- *circa 1900–1910*

A toadstool-shaped lampstand and shade with purple overlay showing an evening scene with a lake setting and trees.

- *height 32cm*
- **£4,000** • **French Glasshouse**

Bubbled Vase ▼

- *circa 1980*

A bubbled vase by Arvid Bakkene, made for Hadeland.

- *height 17cm*
- **£75** • **Circa**

Daum Vase ◀

- *circa 1900*

A mauve Daum vase, with overlay of bats in an evening sky.

- *height 23cm*
- **£4,800** • **French Glasshouse**

Overlay Gallé Vase ▲

- *circa 1900*

Gallé red overlay vase with red foliate design over amber.
- *height 17cm*
- £1,700 • French Glasshouse

Amber Glass ▲

- *circa 1940*

Amber glass jelly mould by William Wilson of globular design. No 9250.
- *17cm x 20cm*
- £140 • The Country Seat

Modernist Lalique Vase ▲

- *1920*

Rare 'Modernist' Lalique vase with raised geometric structural design.
- *height 15cm*
- £1,400 • Susie Cooper

Raison by Lalique ▼

- *1920*

'Raison' design vase by Lalique, with a raised floral design.
- *height 16cm*
- £1,200 • Susie Cooper

French Opaline Goblets ▼

- *circa 1900*

A pair of French opaline goblets with gilt and floral enamel decoration.
- *height 36cm*
- £2,300 • Sinai

Ruby Red Bubble Vase ▲

- *1965*

Ruby red bubble vase Whitefriars Studio range, by Harry Dyer.
- *height 18cm*
- £130 • The Country Seat

Expert Tips

Glass was the ideal medium for the expression of the new look that emerged in the 1950s – plastic and malleable, it could be free or mould blown.

Venini Glass Bowl ▶

- *1962*

Glass bowl with bright red
trailing design signed Venini
Italia and designed by Ludovioc
di Santilliana.
- *diameter 25cm*
- £2,000 • Themes

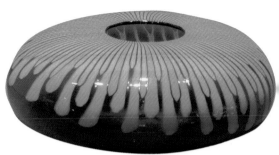

Whitefriars Drunken Bricklayer ▲

- *circa 1969*

Large tangerine 'Drunken
Bricklayer'object by Baxter.
- *height 33.5cm*
- £650 • The Country Seat

Vase for Venini ▲

- *1965*

Blue vase for Venini designed by
T. Zucheri.
- *height 31cm*
- £1,200 • Themes

Bubble Vase by Baxter ▼

- *circa 1957*

Whitefriars strawberry bubble
glass vase by Baxter of organic
form with a blue recess.
- *19.5cm x 16cm*
- £115 • The Country Seat

Whitefriars Red Lamps ▼

- *1964*

A pair of Whitefriars 'Studio
Range' red glass candle holders of
globular form by Harry Dyer.
- *height 24cm*
- £125 • The Country Seat

Sunburst Mirror ▲

- *1950*

One of a pair of sunburst mirrors.
- *diameter 63cm*
- £285 • Goya

Tangerine Oblong Vase ▲

- *1969*

Tangerine Whitefriars rectangular
vase with twelve globular
inclusions, resembling a mobile
phone, by Baxter.
- *height 16.5cm*
- £95 • The Country Seat

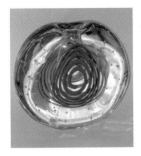

Cenede Vase ▲
- *circa 1980s*
Glass vase of ovoid form with red and blue spiral design and tears, by Cenede.
- *height 28cm*
- **£850** • **Vincenzo Caffarella**

Signed Lalique Cat ▲
- *1970*
Lalique cat shown sitting with tail curled, with signature etched on the base.
- *height 21cm*
- **£750** • **Jasmin Cameron**

René Lalique Bowl ▲
- *1920*
René Lalique bowl, with four clam shells at the base.
- *diameter 18.2cm*
- **£600** • **Jasmin Cameron**

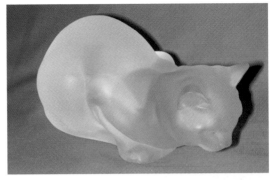

Crouching Lalique Cat ▲
- *1970*
Lalique cat in a crouching position.
- *length 23cm*
- **£750** • **Jasmin Cameron**

Gallé Vase with Bluebells ▲
- *1900*
Gallé vase, with bluebells and a variegated translucent blue and white background, signed.
- *height 32cm*
- **£2,800** • **French Glasshouse**

Expert Tips

When choosing Lalique pieces, especially the frosted ware, inspect it very carefully, as re-grinding and re-application of the frosted effect by acid is often used in the case of damaged pieces.

Ice Relief Vase ▲
- *circa 1960s*
An amorphous glass vase with moulded ice relief by Mazzuccato.
- *height 41cm*
- **£400** • **Vincenzo Caffarella**

René Lalique Ash Tray ▲
- *1920*
Cendrier ashtray incorporating a celtic design on the border, signed "Gao' René Lalique".
- *diameter 9cm*
- **£450** • **Jasmin Cameron**

Three Whitefriars Vases ◀

- *circa 1960–70*
A selection of Geoffrey Baxter-designed, Whitefriars kingfisher blue vases in textured glass.
- **£33, £48 & £45** • Circa

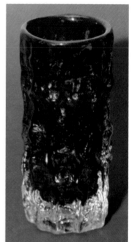

Iceberg Vase ▼

- *circa 1950*
A Finnish vase by Tapio Wirkkala. Signed.
- *height 21cm*
- **£1,200** • Themes

Textured Vase ▲

- *circa 1960–70*
A vase in bark-textured, ruby-coloured glass.
- *height 13cm*
- **£22** • Circa

Two Red 'Gul' Vases ▲

- *circa 1960*
Two 'Gul' vases, designed by Otto Braver for Holmegaard, in cased red over white glaze.
- *height 26cm (left)*
- *height 30cm (right)*
- **£50, £70 resp.** • Circa

Whitefriars Glass Bowl ▼

- *circa 1940*
An English glass bowl, by Whitefriars, of circular form with ribbon-trailed decoration.
- *height 24cm*
- **£180** • Circa

Impressionist Daum Vase ▲

- *circa 1900*
A small, beaker-shaped vase with coloured glass overlay showing trees and grass.
- *height 9cm*
- **£2,900** • French Glasshouse

Murano Beakers ▲

- *circa 1960*
A pair of Aureliano Toso Murano glass beakers.
- *height 14cm*
- **£120** • Vincenzo Caffarella

Spanish Abstract by Vinas ◀

- *circa 1990*

Spanish hand-blown lozenge-shaped glass with yellow, black and turquoise abstract circles and geometric design. Signed.
- *width 28cm*
- £780   ● Francesca Martire

Mazzega Murano Glass ▼

- *circa 1960*

Italian glass object with a red and white glass dome within a circular clear glass halo, has the option of being wall-mounted, designed by Mazzega.
- *diameter 40cm*
- £400   ● Vincenzo Caffarella

Orange Striped Vase by Venini ▼

- *1960*

Venini Murano glass vase with an orange and white striped design within the glass and a moulded, pinched rim.
- *height 34cm*
- £650   ● Vincenzo Caffarella

Murano Glass Duck ▶

- *1950*

Murano glass duck with silver and gold iridescence.
- *length 34cm*
- £590   ● Castello Antiques

Antonio Da Ros ▼

- *circa 1960*

Clear Murano glass with dark blue teardrop and secondary droplet, by Antonio Da Ros, designed for Cenedese.
- *height 29cm*
- £600   ● Vincenzo Caffarella

Green Vase ▲

- *1960*

Green Murano bottle-shaped vase with long slender neck and black and white banding around the rim.
- *height 49cm*
- £65   ● Francesca Martire

Mosaic Murrina Vase ▼

- *1998*

Mosaic vase of baluster form, with blue and yellow organic design by 'Murrina'.

- *height 29cm*
- £1,500 • Francesca Martire

Amber Bowl ▼

- *circa 1970*

Amber glass bowl on a clear stand by Cevedex.

- *height 23cm*
- £500 • Themes

Fish in Glass by Cenedese ▲

- *1950*

Glass object with a seascape design including a tropical fish with underwater plants, by Cenedese for Murano.

- *width 14cm*
- £225 • Francesca Martire

Green Vase with Cactus ▲

- *circa 1950s*

Green 'Cactus' vase by Recardo Licata for Murano.

- *height 44cm*
- £1,200 • Francesca Martire

Hutton Vase ▼

- *circa 1920*

Clear glass vase by Oroffords and etched by John Hetton.

- *height 33cm*
- £1,000 • Arwas

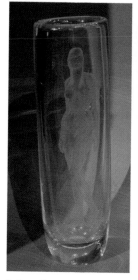

Italian Glass Fish ▼

- *1960*

Italian glass object fashioned as a stylised coiled fish.

- *height 24cm*
- £285 • Ventesimo

Small Daum Jug ◄

- *circa 1900*

Small Daum variegated amber to pink jug with 'Bleeding Heart' floral overlay.

- *6cm x 12cm*
- £2,200 • French Glasshouse

Cenedese Glass Vase ▼

- *circa 1980s*

Italian amorphous glass vase with orange Murrina design by Cenedese.
- *height 38cm*
- **£950** • Vincenzo Caffarella

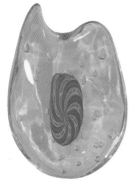

Purple Perfume Bottle ▼

- *circa 1960s*

Purple glass perfume bottle of bulbous form, with an oversized stopper by Cenedese, Italy.
- *height 45cm*
- **£650** • Vincenzo Caffarella

Italian Ashtray ▲

- *circa 1950s*

Italian amber coloured, shell-shaped, glass ashtray with Venturina design by Barovier.
- *21cm x 16cm*
- **£200** • Vincenzo Caffarella

Italian Oval Dish ▲

- *circa 1970s*

Italian emerald glass oval dish, by Cenedese.
- *34cm x 15cm*
- **£250** • Vincenzo Caffarella

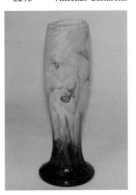

Daum Art Nouveau Vase ▲

- 1900

Daum Art Nouveau vase with translucent blue and white ground, decorated with flowers, butterflies and insects.
- *height 27cm*
- **£2,500** • French Glasshouse

Bottle-Shaped Vase ▲

- 1900

Galle bottle-shaped vase with a long tapering neck, decorated with a pastoral scene with purple trees on a soft green background.
- *height 18cm*
- **£1,500** • French Glasshouse

French Gallé Vase ▲

- 1900

A red and yellow Gallé vase decorated with pink apple blossom.
- *height 14cm*
- **£2,000** • French Glasshouse

Daum Vase ▼
- **1900**

A slightly waisted green Daum vase with a forest pattern, on a moulded foot.
- *height 16cm*
- **£2,600** • **French Glasshouse**

Maltese Medina Glass ▼
- **1978**

Maltese Medina glass with an abstract marine design on an aqua green ground.
- *7.5cm x 5cm*
- **£65** • **Paolo Bonino**

Italian Teardrop Vase ▼
- *circa 1950s*

A glass vase of teardrop form with gold leaf set within the glass, by Seguso.
- *height 30cm*
- **£400** • **Vincenzo Caffarella**

Cenedese Glass Vase ◄
- *circa 1980s*

An amorphous Cenedese glass vase sculpture, with blue and amber designs within the glass.
- *height 31cm*
- **£850** • **Vincenzo Caffarella**

Gallé Vase with Prunus Design ◄
- **1900**

Gallé vase with a prunus design on an amber ground with black rim and base.
- *height 30cm*
- **£2,400** • **French Glasshouse**

Cherry Blossom Vase ▲
- **1900**

Signed Galle vase of oval form with trailing red cherry blossom.
- *height 21cm*
- **£2,400** • **French Glasshouse**

Gallé Cameo Vase ▲
- **1900**

Gallé cameo glass vase with white and orange floral design.
- *height 31cm*
- **£900** • **French Glasshouse**

Lighting

Ceiling Lamps ▲
- *circa 1950s*
Three perspex and metal ceiling lamps in aqua green, red and white.
- *diameter 45cm*
- **£800**   • Zoom

Italian Chrome Lamp ▲
- **1970**
Italian heavy chrome lamp of oval form with brass fittings.
- *diameter 35cm*
- **£350**   • Zoom

Table Lamp ▲
- **1968**
English table lamp designed for British Home Stores, with a green glass base, chrome neck and pale green perspex shade.
- *height 40cm*
- **£150**   • Zoom

Glass Table Lamp ◄
- *circa 1970*
Plum and black glass table lamp.
- *height 38cm*
- **£30**   • **Retro Home**

Italian Desk Lamp ▼
- *circa 1970s*
Fully adjustable desk lamp with variable strength switch by Arteluce of Italy.
- *height 37.5cm*
- **£175**   • Zoom

Cloth Lamp Covers ▼
- **1952**
Pair of English, moulded and stretched cloth wall lamp covers by George Nelson.
- *length 30cm*
- **£100**   • Zoom

Expert Tips

It may seem obvious, but always inspect the wiring and the light fittings themselves, as faulty connections and fittings can create fires and be a hazard to small children.

Table Lamp ▲

- *circa 1930*
Chrome and plastic table light
with glass shade.
- *height 46cm*
- £150   • Henry Hay

Art Deco Lamp ▲

- *circa 1930*
Acrylic base fitted with enclosed
frosted and clear glass shade.
- *height 38cm*
- £450   • Turn On Lighting

American Desk Lamp ▼

- *circa 1910*
An Edwardian American desk
lamp in brass with a bell-shaped
shade and circular plinth.
- *height 43cm*
- £875   • Turn On Lighting

Table Lamp ▼

- *circa 1960*
A very rare lamp with chromed
metal, various shaped glass
spheres and a 'U' section support.
- *height 31cm*
- £1,250 • Vincenzo Caffarella

Italian Metal Chandelier ▼

- *circa 1930*
An Italian metal chandelier with
six lights and brightly coloured
floral motifs.
- *height 70cm*
- £525   • Rainbow

Venetian Wall Lights ▲

- *circa 1920*
A pair of Venetian gilt and glass
wall lights with a mirror and five
hanging crystals.
- *height 30cm*
- £250   • Rainbow

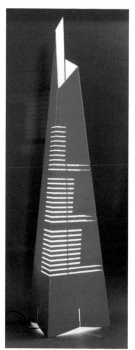

Prism Light ▲

- *circa 1960*
A red plastic triangular prism
light with vertical cuts. Designed
by Magistratti and produced
by Francesconi.
- *height 1.37m*
- £950   • Themes

Perspex Lamp ▼
- **1970**
Italian U shaped perspex lamp on a metal base by Stilnovo.
- *38cm x 32cm*
- **£1,200**   • **Themes**

Brancusi Standing Light ▼
- **1990**
Brancusi standing light made from Japanese paper with a metal base, by Tom Dixon.
- *height 280cm*
- **£1,600**   • **Themes**

Art Deco Lamp ▲
- *circa 1930*
Art deco lamp with a twisted metal stand and a white glass lampshade with a grey geometric pattern.
- *height 47cm*
- **£75**   • **Old School**

Italian Light ▲
- *circa 1950*
Italian light with a white conical shade supported on a black circular base.
- *height 40cm*
- **£280**   • **Francesca Martire**

Wall Lights by Vemini ▼
- *circa 1950*
One of a pair of abstract Italian glass wall lights with a design of assorted squares with amber, tobacco and clear glass, by Vemini.
- *31cm x 31cm*
- **£1,280**   • **Francesca Martire**

Cube Floor Light ▼
- **1970**
Free-standing floor light made from three white and yellow glass cubes, connected by metal bands with a circular metal top and handle.
- *height 115cm*
- **£1,100**   • **Themes**

Italian Chandelier ▼
- *1900*

Italian brass chandelier with splayed leaves and blue drop crystals.
- *width 45cm*
- £175　　　　　● Rainbow

Free-Standing Lamp ▲
- *1960*

Large orange and brown free-standing lamp, with double handles.
- *height 60cm*
- £80　　　　　● Retro Home

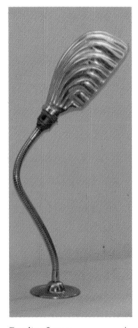

Reading Lamp ▲
- *1970*

Brass reading lamp on a flexible stand and circular base.
- *height 52cm*
- £55　　　　　● Radio Days

Hour-Glass Candelabra ▼
- *1920*

Italian candelabra with a metal hour-glass base and wire and green glass flower decoration.
- *60cm x 40cm*
- £475　　　　　● Rainbow

Perspex Lamp ▶
- *1960*

Free-standing lamp with an amber perspex base and fine raffia shade.
- *height 36cm*
- £40　　　　　● Retro Home

Brass Desk Lamp ▲
- *circa 1930s*

Brass cylinder-shape lamp on a stand with circular base.
- *height 32cm*
- £250　　　　　● North West 8

Crystal Chandelier ▲
- *1920s*

Italian chandelier with a gilt metal foliate designed base, and crystal and red glass pendants.
- *65cm x 60cm*
- £395　　　　　● Rainbow

Metalware

Cigar Holder ▼
- *circa 1900*
Brass stand incorporating
openings to hold cigars.
- *height 30cm*
- £250   • Henry Gregory

Stacking Ash Trays ▼
- *1970*
Set of ten brass stacking ash trays.
- *diameter 11cm*
- £130   • Ventesimo

Bronze Nude ▲
- *circa 1900*
English bronze figure of a nude
lady standing on a plinth by
March.
- *height 36cm*
- £1,500   • Arwas

Arts and Crafts Bowl ▼
- *circa 1900*
Arts and Crafts pot pourri copper
bowl with two handles, standing
on four legs.
- *13cm x 26cm*
- £280   • Arwas

Bronze by C Vorton ▼
- *circa 1900*
French bronze study of a cat in a
crouching position chewing a fish
by Charles Virion.
- *height 8cm*
- £1,600   • Arwas

Pontiac Car Mascot ▼
- *circa 1920*
American chrome car mascot for
a Pontiac of a nude lady with
outstretched body and her chin
resting on her hands, by Petty.
- *length 30cm*
- £500   • Arwas

A. Clergel Inkpot ◄
- *circa 1900*
Gilt bronze figure of a young girl
entwined by leaves and a large
poppy inkpot, signed by A.
Clerget.
- *width 24cm*
- £3,000   • Arwas

547

Bronze Vase ▲
- *1930s*
Dinoderie bronze vase designed by Grange.
- *height 27cm*
- £1,500　　　　　• Bizarre

Art Deco Figure ▲
- *1930*
French Art Deco silvered bronze figure of a dancer, by Henri Molins.
- *height 47cm*
- £1,400　　　　• Succession

Dalou Bronze ▲
- *circa 1905*
Bronze figure of a man digging, by Aime Joule Dalou. Pupil of Carpeaux and Duret his debut was at the Salon in Paris in 1867, signed with the Swiss French Foundry mark.
- *height 9cm*
- £1,650　　　• Gavin Douglas

Hussman Bronze Figure ▲
- *circa 1920*
Erotic bronze of a nude man on horseback, Signed on the base "Hussman".
- *height 35.5cm*
- £2,750　　　• Gavin Douglas

Bronze Dancer ▲
- *20th century*
Bronze figure of a female dancer by Rena Rosenthal.
- *height 20cm*
- £300　　　　　• Bizarre

German Silver Tray ◄
- *1905*
German silver Art Nouveau tray decorated with red poppies and head of a girl with long red hair.
- *32cm x 40cm*
- £7,000　　　　• Succession

Vegetable Dishes ▶

- *circa 1930*

A pair of silver-plated vegetable dishes with octagonal lids with wooden finials.
- *diameter 22cm*
- £360 • **Bizarre**

Bronze Flower Vessel ▲

- *20th century*

Japanese vessel with carp in low relief from the Taisho period.
- *height 34cm*
- £5,000 • **Gregg Baker**

Bronze Prawn ▲

- *20th century*

A large, model of a prawn in mother-of-pearl with verdigris bronze, in naturalistic pose.
- *length 27.5cm*
- £170 • **Butchoff**

Metal Milk Churn ▶

- *circa 1920*

A large domestic milk churn.
- *height 51cm*
- £45 • **Lacquer Chest**

Floor Standing Light ▲

- *20th century*

A decorative floor-standing light with wind-proof glass bowl.
- *height 116cm*
- £425 • **Butchoff**

'Ziglical' Column ▼

- *1966*

Stainless steel with stove enamelling. By Joe Tilson.
- *height 81cm*
- £4,500 • **Whitford**

Pair of Brass Planters ◀

- *circa 1900*

Embossed with oranges and blossoms. Standing on ball feet with original zinc liners.
- *height 21cm*
- £1,100 • **David Pickup**

549

Bronze Vase ▼
- *circa 1900*

Two-colour patinated gilt bronze with cats' heads around the rim and field mice, wheat and poppies encircling the body, signed by Leopold Savine, L. Colin and Cie. With Paris founder's mark.
- *height 27cm*
- £6,500   • Victor Arwas

Italian Seal ▼
- *1950*

Italian silver torpedo-shaped seal stamp with base by Murini.
- *height 18cm*
- £120   • Ventesimo

Fugare Spelter Figure ▲
- *circa 1893*

Gilded spelter figure of winged Mercury engraved 'A. Recompense by Fugare' and exhibited in Paris in 1893.
- *height 34cm*
- £430   • Hayman

Bronze Lady ▲
- *1911*

Gilt bronze figure of a lady with a parasol by H. Varenne.
- *height 20cm*
- £2,500   • Victor Arwas

Letter Rack ▼
- *circa 1950*

Black wire cat letter rack, the body in the form of a spring with plastic eyes and rotating eye balls.
- *height 14cm*
- £45   • Francesca Martire

Italian Chrome Teapot ▼
- *circa 1950*

Round chrome teapot with cork stopper for the spout.
- *height 19cm*
- £65   • Castello

Chrome Coffee Pot ▼
- *circa 1950*

Italian circular chrome coffee pot.
- *height 24cm*
- £50   • Castello

Bronze Figure ▼
● *1921*
Bronze figure entitled "Wind",
signed and dated 1921. Exhibited
by the Royal Academy.
● *height 24cm*
● **£1,100** ● Succession

Bronze Ibex ▲
● *1925*
Fine bronze of a leaping Ibex on a
pink marble plinth, by Fayral.
● *21cm x 28cm*
● **£750** ● Succession

Metal Lighter ▶
● *1970*
Metal lighter with clear piezo
perspex fluid container by Kogen-
Kingsway.
● *height 15cm*
● **£70** ● Zoom

Chrome Lighter ▼
● *1970*
Chrome globe lighter raised on a
circular base.
● *height 10cm*
● **£35** ● Zoom

Spelter Figure ▲
● *20th century*
Bronze spelter bust of the dancer
Isadora Duncan, of a
phantasmagorical theme.
● *height 42cm*
● **£4,500** ● Bizarre

Wall Sconces ▶
● *1940*
One of a pair of French metal
wall sconces with enamelled leaf
and flower design.
● *height 40cm*
● **£480** ● Solaris

Expert Tips

*Bronze figures and objects
should retain their original
patina and show no signs of
over cleaning. Spelter as a
material should be avoided
as it is so easily broken
and is extremely rare.*

Wine-Related Items

From corkscrews to taste vins, labels to wine coolers, coasters to trolleys, funnels to claret jugs, wine antiques are not just a good investment, but great to use.

Increasing affluence leads to the spread of enthusiasm for fine wines, which, in turn, builds the market for wine-related artefacts and curios. It is much nicer to open your bottle with an antique corkscrew and to fill your guest's glass from a silver-mounted claret jug than to unscrew the bottle top and tip it out! Greater interest in wine over a wider public has re-engendered an interest not just in these familiar items, but in more arcane and, seemingly, dated objects such as wine funnels, decanting cradles, champagne taps, toddy ladles and wine labels or 'bottle tickets'.

Increasing interest in all things vinous comes from America, where not only the above, but even more obscure and less intrinsically valuable items, such as pottery bin labels and seventeenth- and eighteenth-century sealed glass bottles, find a ready market. The most conventionally attractive pieces are generally the most valuable and, if you are going to use them as you should, buying the items that most appeal to you is always the best way to go – Victorian novelty animal claret jugs are highly collected, but do you really want to use them for your prized Haut Medoc?

Decanter Labels ▼
- **1798**
Thread design silver labels by Joseph Taylor of Birmingham.
- *7cm x 4cm*
- **£250**   ● Linden & Co.

Silver Wine Goblet ▼
- **1870**
Silver wine goblet by Cooke & Kelvey of Calcutta, India.
- *height 16cm*
- **£275**   ● Linden & Co.

Silver Champagne Flute ◄
- **1910**
Silver champagne flute made by Aspreys of London, dated 1910.
- *height 15cm*
- **£300**   ● Linden & Co.

Silver Decanter Labels ▼
- **19th century**
Silver George IV claret label made in London by Charles Rawlings, and a Silver George IV Madeira label by John Robins.
- *7cm x 4cm*
- **£120**   ● Linden & Co.

Oak Ice Bucket ▼

- **1880–1900**

Oak barrel ice bucket with silver plate banding and lid.
- *15cm x 13cm x 16cm*
- **£75**   • Henry Gregory

Three Barrel Cask ▶

- *circa 1880*

Unusual English oak three-barrel spirit cask with ivory stoppers.
- *35cm x 40cm x 20cm*
- **£1,300**   • Henry Gregory

Expert Tips

Hand-made decanters always have a number scratched into the stopper with a corresponding number scratched into the rim. This was to ensure that perfect pairings did not become separated.

Mahogany Wine Cooler ▲

- **1815**

Superb Regency mahogany and ebony inlaid wine cooler of sarcophagus form with canted corners. The wine cooler retains its original finely cast brass lion mask handles. Raised on swept sabre legs.
- **£1,100**   • Freshfords

King Screw ▶

- **1870**

Four-pillar king screw with bone handled brush and nickel base.
- *height 19cm*
- **£600**   • Emerson

Beer Tankards ◀

- *circa 1880*

Pair of English beer tankards made of oak, with silver banding and shields.
- *height 18cm*
- **£280**   • Henry Gregory

Horn Beakers ▲

- *circa 1906*

Pair of English horn beakers with a silver rim and shield cartouche.
- *12cm x 8cm x 7cm*
- **£150**   • Henry Gregory

Victorian Claret Jug ▼
- *1888*

A rare claret jug, the body cut with an unusual design, by Barnards, London.
- *height 40cm*
- **£4,750**　　　● **Percy's Ltd**

Magnum Claret Jug ▼
- *1872*

An extremely rare Victorian magnum claret jug with beautiful engraving, the cast silver mount with dragon handle, by Stephen Smith, London.
- *height 40cm*
- **£8,750**　　　● **Percy's Ltd**

Queen Anne Shilling Ladle ▲
- *circa 1777*

18th century punch ladle with whalebone handle and a Queen Anne shilling incorporated in the base of the bowl.
- *length 33cm*
- **£150**　　　● **Jasmin Cameron**

Rosewood Corkscrew ▲
- *circa 1850–80*

Rosewood corkscrew with grip shank and brush.
- *length 13cm*
- **£120**　　　● **Jasmin Cameron**

Rosewood Corkscrew ▼
- *circa 1850*

Rosewood gripshank corkscrew.
- *length 12cm*
- **£180**　　　● **Jasmin Cameron**

Small Silver Coaster ▼
- *circa 1820*

Old Sheffield silver-plated wine coaster with lattice work decoration.
- *diameter 10cm*
- **£95**　　　● **Jasmin Cameron**

Staghorn Corkscrew ▼
- *circa 1890*

Staghorn corkscrew with brush.
- *length 15cm*
- **£120**　　　● **Jasmin Cameron**

Silver Wine Funnel

- *1785*

George III silver and glass wine funnel with beaded edging, by Robert Hennell. Assayed in London.
- *height 13cm*
- £850 • Linden & Co.

Silver Wine Coaster

- *1811*

George III silver wine coaster with gadroon edge, on a wooden base by Rebecca Eames and Edward Barnard of London, England.
- *diameter 9cm*
- £900 • Linden & Co.

French Wine Taster

- *circa 1880*

Parisian silver wine taster with circular body with domed centre, with embossed design.
- *diameter 5cm*
- £350 • Linden & Co.

Wine Bottle Pourer

- *1880*

Silver wine bottle holder and pourer made by William Hutton & Sons of Sheffield, England.
- *height 24cm*
- £195 • Linden & Co.

George III Cellaret

- *1800*

George III mahogany hexagonal brass-bound cellaret, with carrying handles on the sides.
- *67cm x 49cm*
- £2,750 • Great Grooms

Chinese Wine Cooler

- *circa 1770*

Chinese export wine cooler with applied handles of European silver form, decorated with flowers within elaborate borders.
- *height 29cm*
- £3,100 • Cohen & Cohen

Brass Bar Corkscrew

- *circa 1900*

Rapid brass bar corkscrew with steel clamp, made in England.
- *57cm x 29cm x 6cm*
- £400 • Henry Gregory

Champagne Bucket ▼

- *circa 1910*
A silver-plated Edwardian champagne bucket on open tripod stand. Made by Mappin & Webb, Sheffield.
- *height 61cm*
- £350   • Barham

Barrel Tap ▼

- *circa 1890*
A steel barrel tap by Farrow & Jackson, with oval, open tap and square striking head.
- *height 16cm*
- £50   • Emerson

Steel Corkscrews ▶

- *circa 1880*
Three steel corkscrews, two identical with folding handles and one with handgrip doubling as bottle opener.
- £18–22 each
- Henry Gregory

English Decanter ▲

- *circa 1920*
A lead crystal handcut decanter of unusual shape.
- *height 32cm*
- £85   • Barham

Silver-Plated Fruit Press ▲

- *19th century*
A fruit press by Kirby & Beard & Co. With beaten organic-shaped stem and maker's name plaque.
- *height 32cm*
- £440   • Lesley Bragge

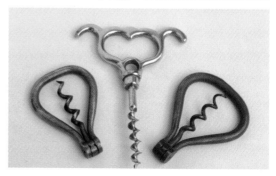

Double Lever Corkscrew ▼

- *circa 1888*
An English Heeley double lever corkscrew. Patent number 6606.
- *height 19.5cm*
- £90   • Emerson

Expert Tips

There is a Scottish version of the English tasting cup, or the French taste vin, also a shallow vessel with two handles and known as a 'quaich'. This was not an arcane wine vessel, however, but was, at one time, the most common drinking vessel in Scotland. Originally these were made of hollowed-out wood, but later from stone, horn, silver, pewter, brass or bell-metal. The most collectable quaiches are those made of hallmarked silver, with the Celtic symbol, from Aberdeen, Inverness or Edinburgh.

Spirit Decanter ▲

- **1930**

Spirit decanter with moulded body and lozenge shape stopper with foliate and bird engraving.
- *height 27cm*
- £320 • Jasmin Cameron

Horn Corkscrew ▲

- *circa 1910*

Corkscrew with a horn handle and metal screw.
- *length 12cm*
- £44 • Henry Gregory

Silver Coaster ▶

- *circa 1920*

Silver-plated circular coaster, one of a pair with scrolled rim and a teak base.
- *diameter 17cm*
- £160 • Henry Gregory

Claret Jug ▼

- **1850**

Deeply faceted claret jug, electroplated lip and cover, twisted rope handle and an acorn finial.
- *height 20cm*
- £440 • Jasmin Cameron

Lion Handles Coaster ▼

- *circa 1900*

Silver circular coaster with scrolling to the rim and lion ring handles to the side.
- *height 16cm*
- £70 • Henry Gregory

Bone Handle Corkscrew ▲

- *circa 1900*

Bone handle corkscrew with brass end and metal screw.
- *length 14cm*
- £70 • Henry Gregory

Wine Coaster ▲

- *circa 1900*

Silver-plate wine coaster with scrolled handles and pierced floral and geometric design.
- *height 57cm*
- £72 • Henry Gregory

◀

Silver Beer Mugs

- *circa 1940*

Silver beer mugs with glass bottoms and bamboo decoration.
- *height 13cm*
- £130 the pair
- Henry Gregory

Cocktail Shaker ▼

- *1920*

Silver-plate cocktail shaker.
- *height 20cm*
- £68 • Henry Gregory

Claret Jug ▼

- *circa 1880*

Continental elegant claret jug with fine engraving around the body and a silver geometric band around the neck, standing on a plain silver circular base.
- *height 29cm*
- £335 • Henry Gregory

Pair of Glass Decanters ▲

- *circa 1890*

Pair of glass decanters with diamond pattern on the body and stopper.
- *height 27cm*
- £150 • Henry Gregory

Spirit Barrels ▼

- *circa 1880*

Three oak spirit barrels with silver banding and taps, on an oak stand with silver banding.
- *36cm x 37cm*
- £1,080 • Henry Gregory

Oak Water Jug ▶

- *circa 1880*

Oak cordial jug with silver lid, ball finial and spout with a shield below, standing on three ball feet.
- *height 29cm*
- £330 • Henry Gregory

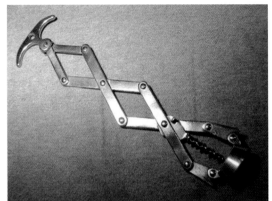

Metal Corkscrew ◀

- *circa 1910*

Expanding polished metal corkscrew.

- *length 14cm*
- £50   • Henry Gregory

Expanding Corkscrew ▼

- *circa 1902*

English expanding corkscrew by Armstrong.

- *27cm x 16cm*
- £120   • Henry Gregory

Dachshund Corkscrew ▲

- *1930*

Dachshund novelty corkscrew, with brass corkscrew tail.

- *length 8cm*
- £45   • Emerson

Italian Corkscrew ▼

- *1880*

Italian boxwood and steel club corkscrew.

- *height 22cm*
- £325   • Emerson

Champagne Corkscrew ▲

- *1880*

Holborn champagne nickel plated corkscrew with wood handle.

- *height 17cm*
- £260   • Emerson

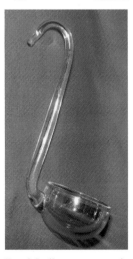

Punch Ladle ▲

- *1820*

Regency glass punch ladle.

- *length 22cm*
- £220   • Jasmin Cameron

Corkscrew with Blade ▲

- *1870*

Simple corkscrew with blade with brass and rosewood handle with a brush.

- *height 13cm*
- £180   • Emerson

Works of Art & Sculpture

Collecting ancient sculptures and works of art presents the most compelling insight into early civilisations, but is not without its difficulties.

This most fascinating area is fraught with problems for the collector. The most immediate and obvious of these being that there is no way of knowing exactly what quantities of artefacts were made and have been preserved. The Chinese were the great wanderers of the Orient, and tombs are constantly being found revealing more, better and earlier treasures than had hitherto been suspected. Faking is thus a problem. Although it is possible to have a piece thermo-luminescence tested to establish its age to within 300 years or so, the process is not really designed to prevent fraud and is not impossible for the determined criminal to circumvent. Then there is exportation and importation and the documentation required for both. All antiques and works of art can be imported into the UK, as long as the correct paperwork is completed, but it is not necessarily as easy to export from a country of origin. Of course, all these problems become exacerbated in direct ratio to the value of the artefact purchased, and great pleasure can be derived with little red-tape and risk if your requirements are fairly modest.

Asian/Oriental

White Marble Buddha ▼
- *circa 549–577 AD*
Finely carved marble Buddha, from the Northern Qi Dynasty.
- *height 49cm*
- **£10,000** • **Malcolm Rushton**

Food Vessel ▲
- *1650–1027 BC*
Bronze Chinese food vessel "ding" with "thread relief" frieze of animal masks to the body and similar decoration to the legs, from the Shang Dynasty.
- *46cm x 34cm*
- **£9,000** • **Malcolm Rushton**

Sumo Wrestlers ▼
- *1868–1912*
A carved wood and dry lacquered model of two fighting Sumo wrestlers.
- **£10,000** • **Augustus Brandt**

Lacquer Case ◄
- *circa 1850*
Japanese lacquer case in three parts decorated in gold and inlaid with butterflies and birds.
- *length 12cm*
- **£5,550** • **Japanese Gallery**

Bronze Figure ▼

- *18th century*

Indian bronze six-armed deity with three heads, on a figured marble plinth base.
- *19cm x 24cm*
- £4,000   • Arthur Millner

Bidri Huqqa ▼

- *circa 1800*

Silver Bidri huqqa inlaid alloy huqqa with engraved floral decoration.
- *18cm x 17cm*
- £800   • Arthur Millner

Expert Tips

Bronze figures of deities are hugely collectable. However, care must be taken as forgeries are abundant – many of these are of such a high quality that it is difficult to distinguish them from the genuine article.

Brass Ewer ▲

- *18th century*

Brass Indian ewer with bulbous form with incised floral decoration with scrolled handle and finial.
- *28cm x 36cm*
- £1,500   • Arthur Millner

Sri Lankan Figure ▲

- *circa 1800*

Female ivory figure from Sri Lanka, standing wearing pleated costume and necklace, with arms by her side.
- *10.7cm x 4cm*
- £200   • Arthur Millner

Portrait of a Raja ▲

- *circa 1770*

Portrait of Raja Surimal of Nurpur dressed in a white turban and an orange tunic holding a falcon in right hand.
- *19cm x 13cm*
- £1,500   • Arthur Millner

Figure of a Female ▼

- *circa 1850*

Carved and painted alabaster figure in front of an orange shrine.
- *31cm x 14cm*
- £350   • Arthur Millner

Ivory Figure ▼

- *circa 1880*

Carved ivory Indian woman holding a water jug.
- *22cm x 6cm*
- £600   • Arthur Millner

Terracotta Horse ▲
- *206 BC–220 AD*
Horse and groom standing with hand extended, from the Han Dynasty.
- *height of horse 29cm, height of groom 26cm*
- £1,200   • Ormonde

Lacquer Figure ▲
- *206 BC–220 AD*
Wooden figure of a lady with arms folded, wearing a dress with red and black lacquer details, from the Han Dynasty.
- *height 51cm*
- £1,200   • Ormonde

Reclining Lion ▲
- *circa 17th century*
Grey selegon jade lion shown in a reclining position. Ming Dynasty.
- *height 8cm*
- £850   • Ormonde

Burmese Table ▼
- *circa 1900*
Carved wood circular table top with carved legs in the style of an elephant's head and trunk.
- *70cm x 100cm*
- £1,200   • Sharif

Chinese Burial Object ▼
- *206 BC–220 AD*
Burial object of a well-modelled horse's head, with strong traces of pigment, highlighting a red bridle, from the Han Dynasty.
- *height 15cm*
- £300   • Ormonde

Banshan Pottery Jug ▼
- *mid 3rd millennium BC*
Banshan-type painted pottery jug from the Gansu or Qinghai province of Majiayao culture.
- *height 35cm*
- £1,250   • Ormonde

Group of Soldiers ▲
- *206 BC–220 AD*
Group of five soldiers standing, from the Han Dynasty.
- *height 47cm*
- £750   • Ormonde

Dinosaur Egg ▲
- *60–70 million years old*
Dinosaur egg from outer Mongolia.
- *height 13cm*
- £300   • Ormonde

Expert Tips

Ivories from the Ming dynasty are usually distinguishable by extensive surface cracking caused by oils within the ivory evaporating over time.

European

Classical Relief of a Centaur ▲

- *circa 1820*
A plaster relief showing the classical scene of the centaur Nessus carrying off Delamra.
- *134cm x 133cm*
- £5,500 • Westland & Co.

Bronze Gymnast ▲

- *1976*
English bronze of a female gymnast on the vault, with a marble plinth, signed by Kelsey.
- *height 35cm*
- £1,850 • Zakheim

Bronze Sculpture ▼

- *20th century*
Amorphous French polished bronze sculpture after Jean Arp.
- *width 23cm*
- £4,450 • Zakheim

Figure of a Knight ▲

- *late 18th century*
French knight carved from pine in a gothic revival manner showing the period armour of the time.
- *183cm x 64cm*
- £4,500 • Westland & Co.

Bronze Gymnast ▶

- *1979*
English bronze of a female gymnast on the bar, with a rectangular marble plinth, signed "K.Carter 1979 2/4".
- *height 42cm*
- £1,850 • Zakheim

Limestone Head ▲

- *circa 1970*
English head of a girl carved from limestone, on a square wooden base, by Mike Grevatte.
- *height 70cm*
- £2,850 • Zakheim

Royal Vienna Vase ▼

- *circa 1870*
A Royal Vienna vase and cover with gold relief, featuring six Greek mythical scenes from the Palace of Athena.
- *140cm x 50cm*
- £25,000 • Emanouel

Italian Marble Figure ▼

- *circa 1890*
An Italian marble figure of Virtue after Tino Camaino, possibly by Alceo Dossena.
- *105cm x 32cm x 20cm*
- £4,488 • Westland & Co.

French Statue ▲
- *circa 1890*
French statuary marble and
alabaster statue of Le Poete de la
Danse. Belle epoque.
- *height 57cm*
- £2,500 • Westland & Co.

Marble Bust ▲
- *circa 1840*
Carved statuary bust of a lady
with head turned slightly to
dexter and wearing a full wig.
- *height 58.5m*
- £3,850 • Westland & Co.

Torso ▼
- *circa 1920*
Modernist Jiri Strada torso of a
woman cropped at top of head
and thighs.
- *height 1.5m*
- £5,300 • Drummonds

Terracotta Model ▼
- *late 19th century*
French model of a river god. The
god crowned with a bullrush and
wearing drapery around waist.
- *height 59cm*
- £3,500 • Westland & Co.

Chimneypiece ▲
- *circa 1890*
Catalonian Art Nouveau
modernista chimneypiece,
decorated with mosaics.
- *height 3.48m*
- £150,000 • Westland & Co.

Carved Figure ▲
- *circa 1860*
Finely carved pine figure of a
Medieval knight. In the Gothic
revival manner.
- *height 1.93m*
- £4,500 • Westland & Co.

Milo of Croton ▼

- *circa 19th century*

Bronze figure of Milo of Croton, the legendary athlete renowned for his strength who lived at Croton, a Greek settlement in the 6th century BC.
- *height 84cm*
- **£14,500**   • Crowthers

Young Bacchus ▼

- *circa 1860*

Marble figure of the young Bacchus clad in only a crumpled tunic and carrying a bunch of grapes in his left hand, whilst clutching another bunch in the crook of his elbow.
- *height 102cm*
- **£15,700**   • Crowthers

Expert Tips

Be aware of chips and cracks when purchasing a sculpture as this can seriously devalue the item.

Bust of Niobe ▲

- *circa 18th century*

Larger than life size statuary marble classical bust of Niobe, attributed to the 18th-century sculptor, F. Harwood.
- *height 96cm*
- **£15,000**   • Crowthers

Putto Astride a Dolphin ▲

- *circa 1890*

A contemporary bronze replica of a late nineteenth century Doulton Stoneware fountain figure of a putto astride a dolphin.
- *height 70cm*
- **£4,950**   • Crowthers

John Locke ▶

- *circa 1650*

Marble bust of John Locke, who was once secretary to the Earl of Shaftesbury.
- *height 71cm*
- **£5,500**   • Crowthers

Marble Figure of Ceres ▼

- *circa 17th century*

Rare 17th-century marble figure of Ceres, the goddess of summer carved with flying drapery in the Baroque manner. She stands contraposto, clasping a sheaf of corn to her side.
- *height 95cm*
- **£5,500**   • Crowthers

Islamic

Persian Vases ▼
- *circa 1930*
A pair of fluted Persian blue and
turquoise floral pattern vases with
two handles on circular bases.
- *height 56cm*
- £200 • Sharif

Algerian Brass Jug ▼
- *circa 1930*
Brass inlay teapot on a tall brass
stand with circular base.
- *length 172cm*
- £650 • Sharif

Mother-of-Pearl Chair ▲
- *circa 1930*
Mother-of-pearl and bone inlay
chair, with carved top rail and
scrolled arms.
- *93cm x 64cm*
- £500 • Sharif

Mother-of-Pearl Table ▲
- *circa 1920*
Mother–of-pearl and bone inlay
in geometric patterns with
architecturally carved legs.
- *64cm x 44cm*
- £400 • Sharif

Crystal Chess Piece ◄
- *8th–7th century BC*
Clear lozenge-shape crystal chess
piece.
- *height 4cm*
- £1,000 • Pars

Qajar Gold Pendant ▼

- *19th century*

A Qajar gold pendant incised with a gazelle and wolf motif surrounded with prolific foliate decoration.

- *diameter 7cm*
- £1,250 • Yazdani

Inlaid Wooden Box ▼

- *circa 1915*

Turkish wooden box with mother-of-pearl inlay to the front panel and rim of the lid.

- *height 50cm*
- £400 • Sharif

Islamic Chandelier ◄

- *circa 1870*

An Islamic bronze chandelier of bulbous form with pierced foliate decoration, and blue enamel design.

- *height 77cm*
- £1,200 • Emanouel

Egyptian Brass Kursi ▲

- *19th century*

An Egyptian brass kursi in the Mamluk style with extensive silver inlay, the hexagonal top with a radiating part open-work design involving panels of inscriptions and knot work roundels around a central kufic roundel with gilt centre inscribed Muhammed. The six sides divided into panels, with arches below rising from turned feet.

- *height 81cm*
- £22,000 • Emanouel

Syrian Damascus Table ▲

- *circa 1915*

Damascus table with geometric bone and ivory inlay and architecturally carved legs.

- *62.5cm x 42.5cm*
- £400 • Sharif

Turkish Mosaic Table ▲

- *circa 1870*

A mosaic wood table with applied mother-of-pearl, tortoiseshell and bone inlay, alternating geometric radiating bands surrounded by a raised border, the base decorated with chequered square design raised on ten chamfered legs separated by scrolling brackets.

- *height 70cm*
- £5,000 • Emanouel

Moroccan Chair ◄

- *1910*

A Moroccan cedar chair inlaid with a floral and star pattern, in bone and boxwood. With a moulded seat and shaped legs.

- *height 103cm*
- £350 • John Clay

Cylindrical Flask ▶
- *7th century BC*
Islamic cylindrical flask with
brown, cream and blue marbling.
- *height 13cm*
- £1,200 ● Pars

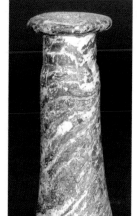

Syrian Table ▲
- *circa 1920*
Hexagonal mother-of-pearl and
bone inlay table with pierced
masharabi panels on turned legs.
- *49cm x 35cm*
- £200 ● Sharif

Syrian Tea Table ▲
- *circa 1910*
A tea table from Damascus with a
brass circular top.
- *47cm x 59cm*
- £150 ● Sharif

Vase Bowl and Saucer ▲
- *circa 1910*
Matching blue and turquoise
floral pattern vase bowl and
saucer.
- *height 37cm*
- £300 ● Sharif

Persian Copper Vase ▼
- *circa 1950*
A Persian copper and brass vase.
- *height 75cm*
- £250 ● Sharif

Islamic Chess Pieces ▼
- *9th century BC*
Islamic wooden chess pieces.
- *height 5cm*
- £3,000 ● Pars

Russian

Silver Bowl ▲
- *mid 19th century*
Silver-marked Russian silver bowl
from Georgia, showing seven
panels of beasts and forestry
scenes, with central roundel.
- *diameter 20cm*
- £1,200   • Shahdad

Virgin of Vladimir ▲
- *19th century*
Orthodox iconic depiction of the
Virgin of Vladimir, showing
Virgin Mary with Child.
- *34.5cm x 30cm*
- £860   • Temple Gallery

Paperweight ▼
- *circa 1940*
Obsidian and onyx paperweight
with intaglio of Lenin in profile,
looking to sinister.
- *height 15cm*
- £490   • Zakheim

Commemorative Vase ▼
- *circa 1940*
Baluster-shaped vase, showing
Lenin, in red glaze with gilded
lettering and floral decoration.
- *height 37cm*
- £750   • Zakheim

Archangel Michael ◄
- *19th century*
Archangel Michael Voyevada in
iconic form, shown on wood
panel and depicted on horseback.
- *34.8cm x 30.4cm*
- £1,650   • Temple Gallery

Virgin of Kazan ▲
- *19th century*
Icon of the Virgin of Kazan,
capital of Tartarstan.
- *37.7 x 31.5cm*
- £650   • Temple Gallery

Presentation Vase ▲
- *circa 1950*
Made for the anniversary of the
birth of Lenin. Cut and applied
decoration of social realism.
- *height 59cm*
- £6,500   • Zakheim

Expert Tips

*The biggest market for artefacts
from the old Soviet Union is
reported to be among rock
stars and bankers!*

Icon of Jesus ▲

- *17th century*
Russian icon showing Jesus
entering a temple in Jerusalem on
a donkey.
- *77cm x 59cm*
- **£7,500**   ● Iconastas

Icon of Virgin and Child ▲

- *17th century*
Icon depicting the Virgin and
Child, entitled "Hodegetria",
(Pointer of the Way).
- *31cm x 20cm*
- **£5,950**   ● Iconastas

Russian Icon ▲

- *17th century*
Russian icon depicting a saint
painted on a wood panel.
- *31cm x 26cm*
- **£2,950**   ● Iconastas

Expert Tips

*Pre-1950s Russian ballet figures
are becoming increasingly
scarce, along with books
relating to Russian ballet
from the same period.*

Bronze Ballerina ▼

- *circa 1950s*
Russian bronze Ballerina shown
standing on a stone base.
- *height 61cm*
- **£5,250**   ● Zakheim

Iron Statue ▲

- *circa 1950*
Iron statue of Ivan the Terrible in
armour on horseback.
- *height 15cm*
- **£50**   ● Zakheim

Bronze Seated Ballerina ▶

- *circa 1950s*
Bronze showing a ballerina seated
on a stool, on a square base.
- *height 29cm*
- **£3,950**   ● Zakheim

Cloisonné Cigarette Case ▶

- *circa 1900s*

Russian cloisonné cigarette case with blue, red, white and turquoise floral decoration.
- *height 9cm*
- £1,350 • Iconastas

Russian Pendant ▲

- *18th century*

Russian bronze cross inlaid with turquoise and blue enamel.
- *3cm x 3cm*
- £220 • Iconastas

Russian Icon ◀

- *18th century*

Russian enamel on copper icon depicting the Saints Zossima, Savarti, Phillip and Roman.
- *height 21cm*
- £1,350 • Iconastas

Imperial Cigarette Case ◀

- *circa 1900s*

Silver Russian cigarette case repoussé with Adam and Eve, with a dedication to Tsar Nicholas II on the reverse, and a gold coin, Imperial flags, crown and coat of arms.
- *10cm x 8cm*
- £1,950 • Iconastas

Russian Tray ▼

- *circa 1900*

Russian silver tray with blue, turquoise and gold enamel floral decoration. Engraved cypher on reverse, by Gustav Klingert.
- *length 25cm*
- £2,450 • Iconastas

Enamelled Case ◀

- *circa 1900s*

Russian cigarette case with an enamelled geometric and foliate design.
- *10cm x 8cm*
- £1,250 • Iconastas

Expert Tips

Beware of European gold and silver cigarette cases bearing heavily impressed Faberge marks, as these are always fakes. It is especially popular to use the Samorodok cases.

Russian Kovsh ▶

- *circa 1900*

Russian enamel kovs, highly decorated with blue turquoise foliate design by Lubwin.
- *length 19cm*
- £1,200
- Iconastas

Soviet Tea Holder ▼

- *1967*

Soviet silver propaganda tea glass holder with a scene showing a man in the foreground with a harvest and a rocket flying into space and the sun in the background.
- *height 10cm*
- £80
- Iconastas

Arts and Crafts Spoon ▲

- *circa 1900*

Arts and crafts silver spoon by Knox, with a handle fashioned as a peacock and the bowl as a leaf.
- *length 16cm*
- £800
- Iconastas

Silver Gilt Spoon ▼

- *circa 1900*

Silver gilt spoon with blue flowers on a cream background with a green and orange foliate design.
- *length 17cm*
- £750
- Iconastas

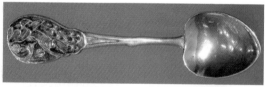

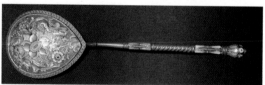

Enamel Russian Spoon ▲

- *circa 1900*

Russian silver spoon enamelled with blue and pink floral design on gold with a turquoise circular border design.
- *length 20cm*
- £600
- Iconastas

Silver Gilt Tea Set ▼

- *circa 1875*

Silver gilt tea pot, water jug and milk jug, with foliate scrolling and a central cartouche of a palace, by Ovchinnikov.
- *height 15cm*
- £2,500
- Iconastas

Silver Gilt Engraved Goblet ▲

- *1839*

Silver fluted gilt goblet from Moscow with foliate design.
- *height 20cm*
- £1,200
- Iconastas

Russian Enamel Spoon ▲

- *circa 1900*

Silver Russian spoon with gilt
bowl, and pink, blue and green
enamelling.

- *length 18cm*
- £850   ● Iconastas

Silver Enamel Spoon ▼

- *circa 1900*

Silver gilt small spoon with
enamel blue foliate and gold
design.

- *length 11cm*
- £180   ● Iconastas

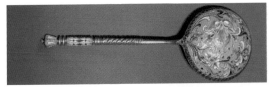

Six Russian Spoons ▼

- *circa 1900*

Six small Russian silver gilt
teaspoons, with pink flowers with
a turquoise and blue background.

- *length 10cm*
- £650   ● Iconastas

Russian Revolutionary Plate ▲

- *circa 1920*

Soviet Russian large porcelain
revolutionary plate decorated
with a fantasy architectural scene
of Rome by Vladimir Mosyagin,
painted by Vasilii Timorev
(1870–1942).

- *diameter 31cm*
- £2,750   ● Iconastas

Plate by Freze ▼

- *circa 1921*

Soviet plate decorated with a
vase and flowers by Varvara Freze
(1883–1970).

- *diameter 22.5cm*
- £1,200   ● Iconastas

Fabergé Belt Buckle ▼

- *circa 1880*

Fabergé silver belt buckle with a
fine leaf design with five large
rubies.

- *8cm x 5cm*
- £2,000   ● Iconastas

Fan with Imperial Cypher ▼

- *circa 1900*

Fine amber fan with diamond
scrolled initials 'A. M.', belonging
to the Grand Duchesse
Alexandra Mickolevich with the
Imperial cipher.

- *length 36cm*
- £1,500   ● Iconastas

Tea Spoons ◄

- *circa 1900*

Set of six silver gilt spoons with
enamel blue and cream foliate
design with scrolled handle.

- *length 10cm*
- £650   ● Iconastas

Bronze High-Jumper ▲

- *circa 1960*
Cast bronze high-jumper
naturalistically styled in the act of
landing on a stone landing mat.
- *height 94cm*
- **£4,500**   • Zakheim

'The Partisan' ▲

- *circa 1979*
Painting entitled 'The Partisan'
by M. S. Prokopyuk, in charcoal
and watercolour.
- *86cm x 61cm*
- **£850**   • Zakheim

Expert Tips

*Always look for the age of the
panel on which the icon is
painted. Old panels may have
older icons painted underneath.*

Saint Basil

- *late 18th century*
An iconic depiction of Saint
Basil the Great, the leader of the
Christian Church in the East and
promoter of monasticism.
- *31.5cm x 26.6cm*
- **£1,500**   • Temple Gallery

Mould of Lenin ▼

- *circa 1950*
A Plaster mould of Lenin made
for the production of bronze casts.
- *height 71cm*
- **£400**   • Zakheim

Annunciation ▶

- *19th century*
Good example of the revival of
late 15th-century style. Depicting
various saints.
- *35.6cm x 31.1cm*
- **£3,500**   • Temple Gallery

Commemorative Plaque ▲

- *circa 1971*
Gilt bronze with red glass inserts,
and central enamelled plaque
showing a nuclear power station
within a wreath.
- *diameter 30cm*
- **£750**   • Zakheim

Saint Nicholas ▲

- *16th century*
Icon of Saint Nicholas the
Wonderworker, from the Pskov
school. Tempera and gold on a
gesso and wood panel.
- *76cm x 55.3cm*
- **£68,000**   • Temple Gallery

Bishop's Cross ▲

- *1854*
Russian silver-gilt bishop's cross
with Christ at the centre,
decorated in garnets, inscribed by
Vilno.
- *height 23cm*
- **£1,650**   • Iconastas

Bishop's Silver Gilt Cross ▲

- *1890*
Bishop's silver gilt and blue
enamel cross depicting the head
of Christ surrounded by paste
diamonds and rubies. The clasp is
shaped as an Imperial crown,
with a linked silver chain.
- *17cm x 10cm*
- **£1,450**   • Iconastas

Lenin Figure ▶

- *circa 1925*
Porcelain figure of Lenin shown
standing on a circular base.
- *height 66cm*
- **£1,250**   • Zakheim

Dancing Scene ▲

- *1860*
Russian painted lacquer box
depicting dancers in colourful
costumes linking hands in a
woodland setting.
- *15cm x 8cm*
- **£1,250**   • Iconastas

Bronze Partisan ▶

- *circa 1940*
Revolutionary bronze Russian
partisan shown holding a gun
above his head, on a rectangular
plinth.
- *height 100cm*
- **£3,750**   • Zakheim

Football Trophy ◀

- *1960*
Russian football trophy painted
under glass, decorated with a
cartouche showing footballers.
- *height 38cm*
- **£250**   • Zakheim

Commemorative Vase ◀

- *circa 1950s*
Russian commemorative vase
showing Stalin in military
costume on a red glazed ground.
- *height 49cm*
- **£1,250**   • Zakheim

Writing Equipment

Pens, pencils, portable desks and all the paraphernalia of hand-written communication are the most personal of collectables.

In terms of the categories within this book, fountain pens and propelling pencils fall somewhere between Collector's Items and Scientific Instruments, but they and other artefacts connected with writing are so avidly collected these days that they deserve a slot of their own. When seeking to buy a pen, perfect condition is of the utmost importance, with no scratches or marks, no fading to the colour and with original fittings. Originally, pens were made of hardened rubber. Although

manufacture was very expensive, it was not until the 1920s that manufacturers turned to plastic – despite the fact that plastic in a useable form had been available for nearly a century. Individual pen-makers gave different names, such as Vulcanite and Raclite, to the hardened rubber composition. These are worth looking out for. In general, it is better to spend a lot of money on a pen, with a reputable dealer, and ensure that you have a good one then risk buying one that may have been adapted.

Gold Waterman Pen ▲
- **1920**
Gold Waterman fountain pen with basketweave pattern, No.55521/2, with original glass ink dropper.
- *length 14cm*
- **£600** • Jasmin Cameron

Glass Ink Pot ▼
- **1870**
Victorian glass ink pot with faceted glass stopper and brass collar.
- *height 9cm*
- **£135** • Jasmin Cameron

Pen Wipe and Pen ▶
- **1911**
Silver pen wipe with plain oval dip pen, made in London by S. Mordan.
- *height 7cm*
- **£165** • Jasmin Cameron

Brass Blotter ▲
- **1880–1912**
Arts and Crafts brass blotter, stamped "Gesci 9121.2463/10%", from estate of the late Alison Gibbons.
- *length 15cm*
- **£275** • Jasmin Cameron

Travelling Writing Box ▼
- *1850*

Wood and brass engraved
travelling writing box. Includes
inkwell, quill box, pen, pencil
and rolling blotter.
- *13cm x 8cm*
- £485   • Jasmin Cameron

French Writing Box ▲
- *1860*

French writing slope and
stationery box of outstanding
quality and design. Extensively
decorated with boulle style brass,
ivory and silver on a rosewood
base. Original matching inkwells
and recovered purple velvet
writing tablet. Original key.
- *40cm x 27cm*
- £3,950   • J. & T. Stone

Mr Punch Paperweight ▼
- *19th century*

English silver-plated Mr Punch
globe paperweight inscribed
"The Punch always on top",
by J. R. Gaunt.
- *height 12cm*
- £430   • Jasmin Cameron

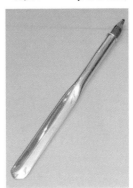

Pencil and Paper Knife ▲
- *1903*

Edwardian combination pencil
and silver paper knife, made
in Birmingham by Perry &
Company.
- *length 15cm*
- £185   • Jasmin Cameron

Silver Paper Knife ▲
- *1923*

English rat-tail silver paper knife
with cedar pencil, by Sampson
Mordan.
- *length 18cm*
- £220   • Jasmin Cameron

Ink Blotter ◀
- *circa 1880*

English Victorian brass ink
blotter with brass foliate
decoration.
- *height 23cm*
- £485   • Barham

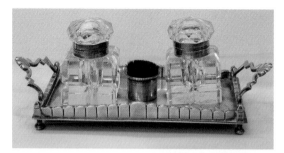

Cut-Glass Inkwell ▼

- *circa 1900*
Cut-glass inkwell with a hinged
silver cover.
- *height 10cm*
- £260　　　• Henry Gregory

Non-Spill Ink Pot ▲

- *circa 1900*
Non-spill vaseline glass ink pot of
ovoid form with a central tear
drop reservoir.
- *height 6cm*
- £24　　　　　• Hayman

Wood Blotter ▲

- *circa 1860*
Wood ink blotter with brass inlay.
- *length 19cm*
- £160　　　　• Hayman

Old Sheffield Ink Stand ▶

- *circa 1840*
Old Sheffield silver ink stand
with serpentine border decorated
with floral and leaf design, two
faceted glass inkwells and a
central silver sander.
- *width 27cm*
- £300　　　• Jasmin Cameron

Brass Ink Stand ◀

- *1830*
Double-handled brass ink stand
with scalloped design, holding
two glass inkpots with faceted lids
and brass rims, and a brush in a
brass container.
- *length 21cm*
- £340　　　• Jasmin Cameron

Silver Inkwell ▲

- *1930*
Small silver circular inkwell with
hinged lid.
- *diameter 9cm*
- £60　　　　• Henry Gregory

Satin Glass Ink Pot ▲

- *circa 1870*
Satin glass turquoise ink pot with
a white flower and hinged lid.
- *height 11cm*
- £220　　　　• Hayman

Writing Box ▼

- *circa 1860*

Indian brass inlaid writing box with folding writing slope and compartments inside, the exterior profusely decorated with scrolling foliage.

- *19cm x 30cm x 45cm*
- £800 • Arthur Millner

Waterman Pen ▼

- *1931–8*

Black and grey marbled Waterman Ideal fountain pen, No 32.

- *length 10cm*
- £270 • Jasmin Cameron

French Ink Stand ▲

- *circa 1840*

French boulle ink stand with brass and tortoiseshell inlay, resting on gilt bracket feet.

- *30cm x 11cm*
- £950 • Barham

Georgian Writing Box ▲

- *1830*

Georgian mahogany writing box with double opening and military brass fixtures.

- *46cm x 28cm x 18cm*
- £650 • Barham

Regency Boulle Inkstand ▲

- *1840*

Regency boulle inkstand in brass and inlaid with tortoiseshell, was formerly owned by David Garrick of the Garrick Theatre.

- *30cm x 14cm*
- £750 • Barham

Propelling Pencil ▲

- *1900s*

Ivory propelling pencil, decorated with painted enamel flowers, and silver mounts.

- *length 9cm*
- £79 • Langfords Marine

American Eversharp Pen ▲

- *1930*

American Eversharp black and red desk pen with gold banding, with a penholder on a square base.

- *length 22cm*
- £320 • Jasmin Cameron

Silver Swan ▲
- *circa 1910*

Silver swan gravity-fed, eye-dropper pen with 14-carat gold nib.
- *length 15cm*
- £130　　　　● Sugar

Swan Quills ▼
- *19th century*

French swan quills originally from Hudson Bay.
- *length 20cm*
- £30 each　　● Jasmin Cameron

Writing Box ▶
- *late 18th century*

Indo-Portuguese writing box with gold-backed tortoiseshell, inlaid with ivory.
- *length 30cm*
- £1,200　　　　● Shahdad

Inkwell ▼
- *19th century*

A bronzed seated cat with concealed inkwell. Its head lifts to reveal an ink reservoir.
- *height 7cm*
- £950　　● Elizabeth Bradwin

Painted Writing Slope ▼
- *circa 1720*

An English writing slope decorated with oriental figures within floral borders.
- *height 28cm*
- £1,850　　● O.F. Wilson

Glass Ink Pot ▲
- *circa 1930*

Multi-sided glass amethyst colour American inkpot with sliding glass lid.
- *height 5.5cm*
- £260　　● Jasmin Cameron

Stationery Case ▲
- *circa 1930*

Green crocodile case with various compartments and lined with green satin.
- £435　　　　● H. & H.

Quill Knife

- *1820*
Mother of pearl quill knife.
- *length 10cm*
- £125 • Jasmin Cameron

Circular Inkwell

- *circa 1930*
Large silver circular inkwell with a hinged lid.
- *diameter 11.5cm*
- £190 • Henry Gregory

Art Deco Ink Pot

- *circa 1920*
Moulded brass art deco inkwell with cover and porcelain bowl.
- *width 13cm*
- £68 • Hayman

Conway Stewart Dinkie Pen

- *circa 1935*
Conway Stewart dinkie pen with a blue and amber marbling effect.
- *length 12cm*
- £220 • Jasmin Cameron

Silver Ink Stand

- *February 1852*
Electroplated silver ink stand with pierced frieze of cherubs and vines, by Elkington Mason & Co.
- *width 14cm*
- £520 • Jasmin Cameron

Enamel Pen Tray

- *circa 1860*
Enamel chinoiserie pen tray with a nightingale in flight and pink and yellow flowers, with brass dragon handles, scrolled feet and a brass rim.
- *length 33cm*
- £168 • Hayman

Lady's Writing Box ▲
- **1875**
Victorian papier mâché lady's writing slope with extensive gilded mother-of-pearl decoration. Original silver topped inkwells and new internal gilded navy velvet covering.
- *10cm x 40cm x 29cm*
- **£1,575**   • **J. & T. Stone**

Edwardian Ink Stand ▲
- **1904**
Highly decorative ink tray with pierced gallery, two crystal glass reservoirs, and moulded apron raised on shaped feet. Made in London.
- *26cm x 15cm*
- **£2,350**   • **Stephen Kalms**

Inkwell and Bottles ▲
- *circa 1900*
Adrian Dalpayraat green and brown leaf design inkstand, with two glass ink bottles designed for La Maison Moderne.
- *22cm x 25cm*
- **£1,600**   • **Succession**

Stationery Box ▲
- *circa 1840*
Shaped papier mâché stationery box, the decoration depicting buildings in a landscape highlighted with mother of pearl.
- *width 22cm*
- **£450**   • **Hygra**

Glass Ink Stand ▲
- *circa 1925*
Art Nouveau green glass ink bottle resting on a brass stand.
- *height 8cm*
- **£180**   • **Barham**

Letter Scale ▼
- *circa 1870*
Victorian letter weighing brass scales for a post office, standing on a mahogany base.
- *height 8cm*
- **£285**   • **Barham**

Parker Pen ▲
- **1942**
Parker Victory fountain pen in black and green laminated plastic.
- *length 12.5cm*
- **£380**   • **Jasmin Cameron**

Glass Inkwell ▶

- *circa 1901*
Glass inkwell with faceted base
and silver hinged lid.
- *height 9cm*
- £290 • Henry Gregory

Green Malachite Blotter ▼

- *circa 1860*
Green malachite blotter with
knob handle.
- *length 19cm*
- £160 • Hayman

Victorian Writing Tray ◀

- *circa 1870*
Victorian double-handled brass
writing tray with two inkwells
and a central sander, decorated
with c-scrolling and raised on
four paw feet.
- *width 27cm*
- £175 • Hayman

Glass Square Ink Pot ▲

- *circa 1860*
Square glass ink pot with faceted
stopper and moulded shoulders.
- *height 9cm*
- £85 • Jasmin Cameron

Paper Weight Ink Pot ▼

- *1890*
Victorian circular paperweight
inkwell with brass lid.
- *diameter 11cm*
- £48 • Hayman

Butterfly Letter Rack ◀

- *circa 189*
Brass butterfly letter rack
standing on a rustic base.
- *height 10cm*
- £238 • Hayman

Ivory Writing Slope ▼
- *19th century*
Anglo-Indian ivory writing slope
with sadeli mosaic and opening to
reveal writing surface.
- *length 29cm*
- £1,200 • Hygra

Triple Writing Box ▼
- *circa 1810*
In traditional campaign style of
solid mahogany with brass strap
corners and countersunk handles.
- *length 50cm*
- £1,400 • Hygra

Silver Inkwell ▶
- *circa 1931*
Capstan silver inkwell with glass
reservoir and large spayed base.
Made in Birmingham.
- *diameter 20cm*
- £500 • Stephen Kalms

Waterman 512V Set ▲
- *circa 1930*
Pen and propelling pencil in
laminated plastic jet and mother-
of-pearl.
- *length 14cm*
- £275 • Jasmin Cameron

Parker 51 ◀
- *circa 1950*
A Parker 51 Special classic,
commemorating 51 years in the
business, with burgundy body,
rolled gold cap and pearlescent
hooded nib.
- *length 15cm*
- £250 • Jasmin Cameron

Inkwell ▲
- *circa 1920*
Decorative inkwell with metal
eagle figure on marble base.
- *length 30cm*
- £85 • Mark Sullivan

Draftsman's Pen ▲
- *late 19th century*
Brass draftsman's pen.
- *length 16cm*
- £18 • Mark Sullivan

Brass Blotter ◄

- *circa 1912*

Arts and crafts brass boat blotter period. Marked GESCi 9121.
- *length 15cm*
- £260   • Jasmin Cameron

Silver Capstan Inkpot ▼

- *1913*

Capstan silver inkwell with hinged lid and large splayed base. Made in Birmingham by H. Greaves Ltd.
- *diameter 14cm*
- £640   • Jasmin Cameron

Travelling Ink Set ▼

- *circa 1850*

Travelling ink set in original burgundy leather box fashioned as a trunk, with brass interior, two bottles with brass lids and a bone quill.
- *4cm x 9cm*
- £185   • Jasmin Cameron

Amber and Clear Glass Dip Pens ▼

- *1850*

Very rare amber and clear glass dip pens, in excellent condition.
- *length 20cm*
- £130   • Jasmin Cameron

Oak Desk Stand ▼

- *circa 1890*

Oak desk stand with single drawer and two inkwells with brass lids and handles, standing on bun feet.
- *11cm x 38cm*
- £85   • Sporting Times

Art Nouveau Inkwell ►

- *circa 1900*

French art nouveau pewter ink well of a lady with long hair.
- *width 12cm*
- £1,200   • Arwas

Main Chinese Periods

SHANG DYNASTY	c. 1523 – 1027 BC
CHOW DYNASTY	1027 – 221 BC
WARRING STATES PERIOD	481 – 221 BC
CH'IN DYNASTY	221 – 206 BC
HAN DYNASTY	206 BC – 220 AD
THREE KINGDOMS	220 – 280
SIX DYNASTIES	280 – 589
NORTHERN WEI	385 – 535
EASTERN WEI	535 – 550
WESTERN WEI	535 – 557
NORTHERN CH'I	550 – 577
NORTHERN CHOW	557 – 581
LIU SUNG (SOUTH)	420 – 478
SOUTHERN CH'I	479 – 501
LIANG	502 – 557
CH'EN	557 – 588
SUI DYNASTY	589 – 618
T'ANG	618 – 906
FIVE DYNASTIES	907 – 959
SUNG DYNASTIES	960 – 1280
YUAN DYNASTIES	1280 – 1368
MING DYNASTIES	1368 – 1643
CH'ING DYNASTIES	1644 – 1912

Ming Period

HUNG WY	1368 – 1398
CHIEN WIEN	1399 – 1402
YUNG LO	1403 – 1424
HUNG HSI	1425 – 1425
HSUAN TE	1426 – 1435
CHENG T'UNG	1436 – 1449
CHING T'AI	1450 – 1457
T'IEN SHUN	1457 – 1464
CH'ENG HUA	1465 – 1487
HUNG–CHIH	1488 – 1505
CHENG TE	1506 – 1521
CHIA CHING	1522 – 1566
LUNG CH'ING	1567 – 1572
WAN LI	1573 – 1619

Ch'ing Period

SHUNG CHIH	1644 – 1661
K'ANG HSI	1662 – 1722
YUNG CHENG	1723 – 1735
CH'IENG LUNG	1736 – 1795
CHIA CH'ING	1796 – 1820
TAO KUANG	1821 – 1850
HSIEN FENG	1851 – 1861
T'UNG CHIH	1862 – 1873
KUANG HSU	1874 – 1908
HSUAN T'UNG	1909 – 1912

Korean Periods

LO LANG	106 BC – 313 AD
PAEKCHE	18 BC – 663 AD
KOGURYO	37 BC – 668 AD
SILLA	57 BC – 668 AD
GREAT SILLA	668 – 936
KORYO	918 – 1392
YI	1392 – 1910

Japanese Periods

JOMON PERIOD	1000 BC – 200 BC
YAYOI PERIOD	200 BC – 500 AD
TUMULUS PERIOD	300 – 700
ASUKA PERIOD	552 – 645
EARLY NARA PERIOD	645 – 710
NARA PERIOD	710 – 794
EARLY HEIAN PERIOD	794 – 897
HEIAN OR FUJIWARA PERIOD	897 – 1185
KAMAKURA PERIOD	1185 – 1392
ASHIKAGA PERIOD	1392 – 1573
MOMOYAMA PERIOD	1573 – 1615
TOKUGAWA PERIOD	1615 – 1868

French General Periods

FRANÇOIS–PREMIER	1515 – 1547	Reign of Francis I
HENRI–DEUX	1547 – 1559	Reign of Henri II
	1559 – 1560	Reign of Francis II
	1560 – 1574	Reign of Charles IX
	1574 – 1589	Reign of Henri III
HENRI–QUATRE	1589 – 1610	Reign of Henri IV
LOUIS–TREIZE	1610 – 1643	Reign of Louis XIII
LOUIS–QUATORZE	1643 – 1715	Reign of Louis XIV
LOUIS–QUINZE	1715 – 1774	Reign of Louis XV
LOUIS–SEIZE	1774 – 1793	Reign of Louis XVI
EMPIRE	1799 – 1814	Reign of Napoleon

English General Periods

TUDOR	1485 – 1558	Reigns of Henry VII
		Henry VIII
		Edward VI
		Mary
ELIZABETHAN	1558 – 1603	Reign of Elizabeth I
JACOBEAN	1603 – 1649	Reigns of James I
		Charles I
COMMONWEALTH	1649 – 1660	Protectorship of Cromwell
CAROLEAN / LATE STUART	1660 – 1689	Reigns of Charles II
		James II
WILLIAM AND MARY	1689 – 1702	Reign of William and Mary
QUEEN ANNE	1702 – 1727	Reigns of Anne
		George I
GEORGIAN	1727 – 1820	Reigns of George II
		George III
REGENCY	1800 – 1830	Reigns of George III
		George IV
WILLIAM IV	1830 – 1837	Reign of William IV
VICTORIAN	1837 – 1901	Reign of Victoria
EDWARDIAN	1901 – 1910	Reign of Edward VII

English Monarchs since 1066

WILLIAM I	1066 – 1087
WILLIAM II	1087 – 1100
HENRY I	1100 – 1135
STEPHEN	1135 – 1154
HENRY II	1154 – 1189
RICHARD I	1189 – 1199
JOHN	1199 – 1216
HENRY III	1216 – 1272
EDWARD I	1272 – 1307
EDWARD II	1307 – 1327
EDWARD III	1327 – 1377
RICHARD II	1377 – 1399
HENRY IV	1399 – 1413
HENRY V	1413 – 1422
HENRY VI	1422 – 1461
EDWARD IV	1461 – 1470
HENRY VI	1470 – 1471
EDWARD IV	1471 – 1483
EDWARD V	1483 – 1483
RICHARD III	1484 – 1485
HENRY VII	1485 – 1509
HENRY VIII	1509 – 1547
EDWARD VI	1547 – 1553
MARY	1553 – 1558
ELIZABETH	1558 – 1603
JAMES I	1603 – 1625
CHARLES I	1625 – 1649
COMMONWEALTH	1649 – 1660
CHARLES II	1660 – 1685
JAMES II	1685 – 1688
WILLIAM AND MARY	1688 – 1694
WILLIAM III	1694 – 1702
ANNE	1702 – 1714
GEORGE I	1714 – 1727
GEORGE II	1727 – 1760
GEORGE III	1760 – 1820
GEORGE IV	1820 – 1830
WILLIAM IV	1830 – 1837
VICTORIA	1837 – 1901
EDWARD VII	1901 – 1910
GEORGE V	1910 – 1936
EDWARD VIII	1936 – 1936
GEORGE VI	1936 – 1952
ELIZABETH II	1952 –

Glossary

Not all of the terms that follow appear in this volume, but they may all prove useful in the future.

abadeh Highly-coloured Persian rug.

acacia Dull yellow hardwood with darker markings used for inlay and bandings towards the end of the eighteenth century.

acanthus A leaf motif used in carved and inlaid decoration.

Act of Parliament clock Eighteenth-century English clock, wall mounted and driven by weights, with a large, unglazed dial and a trunk for weights. These clocks often hung in taverns and public places and were relied on by the populace after the Act of Parliament of 1797, which introduced taxation on timepieces.

air-beaded Glass with air bubbles resembling beads.

air-twist Spiral pattern enclosed in a glass stem with air bubbles.

albarello Waisted ceramic drug jar.

alder Wood used for country-style furniture in the eighteenth century.

ale glass Eighteenth-century glass drinking vessel with long stem and tall, thin bowl.

amboyna West Indian wood used for veneers, marquetry and inlays. Light brown with speckled grain.

anchor escapement Late seventeenth-century English invented clock movement, named after the anchor shape of the linkage which moves the escape wheel.

angle barometer Also known as signpost barometers. Barometers where the movement of mercury is shown almost on the horizontal.

andiron Iron support for burning logs.

annulated Ringed (of glass).

apostle spoon Spoon with the figure of an apostle as the finial.

applied Attached or added, rather than modelled or carved as part of the body.

apron The decorative panel of wood between the front legs of a chair or cabinet.

arbor The axle on which the wheel of a clock's mechanism is mounted.

arch (clockmaking) The arch above the dial of a post-1700 longcase clock.

argyle Double-skinned metal pouring jugs and tea and coffee pots.

armoire French wardrobe, linen press or large cupboard.

ash Hardwood used for making country furniture and for its white veneer.

astragal Small semi-circular moulding, particularly used as glazing bar in furniture.

automaton clock A clock where the strike is performed by mechanically operated figures.

backboard The unseen back of wall furniture.

backplate The rear plate supporting the movement of a clock, often the repository of engraved information relating to its manufacture.

baff Knot in rug-making.

balance Device counteracting the force of the mainspring in a clock's movement.

balloon-back chair Popular, rounded-backed Victorian dining or salon chair.

baluster (adj.) Having a dominant convex swell at the base, culminating in a smaller, concave one at the neck. (noun) One of a set of upright posts supporting a balustrade.

banjo barometer Wheel barometer dating from circa 1775-1900, with shape resembling a banjo.

barley-sugar twist Spiral-turned legs and rails popular in the seventeenth century. Colloquial.

bat printed Transfer printed (of ceramics).

beech Hardwood used in the manufacture of country furniture and, when stained, as a substitute for mahogany.

bellarmine Stoneware flagon made in Germany from the sixteenth century.

bergère French for an armchair, used in English to describe a chair with caned back and sides.

bevel Decorative, shaved edge of glass, particularly mirror.

bezel The metal rim of a glass cover or jewel.

bird-cage Support mechanism at the top of the pedestal of some eighteenth-century tilt-top tables.

birch Hardwood used principally for carcassing; occasionally for low-quality veneer.

bird's eye maple Wood of the sugar maple with distinctive figure caused by aborted buds. Used in veneering.

biscuit (bisque) Ceramics fired but unglazed, originating in France in the eighteenth century.

blind fretwork Fretwork carving on a solid background.

block front Front shaped from thick boards allowing for a recessed centre section.

blue-dash Blue dabs around the rim of a delftware plate.

bob The weight at the bottom of a pendulum.

bobbin Turned furniture element, resembling a row of connected spheres.

bocage Foliage, bushes and shrubs supporting, surrounding or standing behind porcelain or pottery figures.

bombé Having an outswelling front.

bone china Clay with bone ash in the formula, almost entirely porcelanous. First produced at the end of the eighteenth century.

bonheur du jour Small, lady's writing desk with a cabinet and drawers above. Originally French, from the mid eighteenth century.

bottle glass Low quality coloured glass for bottles, jars etc.

boulle An eighteenth-century marquetry style employing brass and tortoiseshell.

boxlock Flintlock gun with the mechanism enclosed in the breach.

boxwood Pale yellow, close-grained hardwood used for carving and turning and for inlay and pattern veneers.

bow front Convex curve on the front of chests of drawers.

bracket clock Domestic clock so called because of the necessity of standing it on a bracket to allow its weights to hang down, the term later applied to domestic clocks of the eighteenth and nineteenth centuries regardless of their motive force.

bracket foot Plain foot carved into the rail or stretcher to form an ornamental bracket.

brandy saucepan Miniature, bulbous or baluster shaped saucepan with long handle at right angles to the spout.

breakfront Describing a piece of furniture with a central section which projects forward.

breech Rear end of the barrel of a gun.

breech-loading Gun loaded through an opening in the breech.

bright cut Late eighteenth-century silver engraving technique, making the design brilliant in relief.

Bristol glass Eighteenth century coloured (often blue) glass produced in Bristol.

Britannia metal Form of refined pewter used as a silver substitute in the early nineteenth century.

British plate Silver substitute from the nineteenth century, immediately preceding the introduction of EPNS.

broken arch Arch above the dial of a long-case clock which is less than a semi-circle, indicating an early Georgian date.

broken pediment Pediment with a symmetrical break in the centre, often accommodating an urn or some such motif.

bun foot Flattened spherical foot often found on later seventeenth-century furniture.

bureau Desk with a fall front enclosing a fitted interior, with drawers below.

bureau bookcase Bureau with glazed bookcase above.

burr Veneer used in furniture making, with a decorative pattern caused by some abnormality of growth or knotting in the tree. Usually taken from the base of the tree.

cabriole leg Leg of a piece of furniture that curves out at the foot and in at the top.

Introduced in the seventeenth century.

caddy Tea caddy.

caddy spoon Short-handled, large bowled spoon for extracting tea from the caddy.

calendar / date aperture Window in the dial of a clock displaying day, month or date.

canted corner Decoratively angled corner.

canterbury An eighteenth-century container for sheet music.

carcase/carcass The inner frame of a piece of furniture, usually made of inferior wood for veneering.

card case Case for visiting cards, usually silver, nineteenth century.

carriage clock Portable timepiece, invented in nineteenth-century France, with handle above.

cartel clock Eighteenth-century French wall clock with profusely decorated case.

case furniture Furniture intended as a receptical, e.g. chest of drawers.

caster / castor 1. Sprinkling vessel for e.g. sugar. 2. Pivoted wheel attached to foot.

Castleford ware Shiny white stoneware made in Castleford and elsewhere from circa 1790.

caudle cup Covered cup, often in silver.

cellaret A wine cooler or container, usually eighteenth century.

centrepiece Ornament designed to sit in the centre of a dining table. Often in silver.

chafing dish Serving dish, often in silver, with stand incorporating a spirit lamp to retain heat.

chain fusée The fusée of a clock from which a chain unwinds on to the barrel of the mainspring.

chamfer A flattened angle; a corner that has been bevelled or planed.

chapter ring The ring on a clock dial on which the numbers of the hours are inscribed.

Chesterfield Deep-buttoned, upholstered settee from the nineteenth century.

chest on chest Tallboy having two chests fitting together, the lower with bracket feet, the upper with pediment. From the seventeenth and eighteenth centuries.

chest on stand Known as a tallboy or highboy, a chest of drawers on a stand.

cheval mirror Tall mirror supported by two uprights on swivels.

chiffonnier Side cupboard, originally, in the eighteenth century, with solid doors, but latterly with latticed or glazed doors.

chinoiserie Oriental-style decoration on lacquered furniture or artefacts.

chronometer Precision timepiece, often for navigation.

circular movement Clock movement of circular plates.

cistern Chamber containing mercury at the base of the tube of a barometer.

claw-and-ball foot Foot modelled as a ball clutched in a claw, frequently used to terminate a cabriole leg.

clock garniture Mantelpiece ornamentation with a clock as centrepiece.

close helmet Helmet covering the whole head and neck.

coaster Small, circular tray, often in silver, for holding a bottle.

cockbeading Bead moulding applied to the edges of drawers.

cock bracket Bracket supporting a watch mainspring.

coin glass Early eighteenth-century English drinking glass with a coin moulded into the knop of the stem.

commode High quality, highly decorated chest of drawers or cabinet, with applied mounts.

compensated pendulum Pendulum with mercury reservoir, the mercury rising and falling to compensate for the effects on the pendulum of changes of temperature.

composition Putty-like substance for moulding and applying to e.g. mirror frames, for gilding.

console table Often semi-circular table intended to stand against a wall on the pier between two windows (hence also pier table). Usually with matching mirror above.

cordial glass Glass originating in the seventeenth century, with a small bowl for strong drinks.

corner chair Chair with back splats on two sides and a bowed top rail, designed to fit into a corner.

cornice Horizontal top part of a piece of furniture; a decorative band of metal or wood used to conceal curtain fixtures

coromandel Wood from India's Coromandel coast, used for banding and inlay.

counter-well The small oval wooden dishes inset into early Georgian card tables for holding chips or cash, hence also guinea-well.

country furniture Functional furniture made outside the principal cities. Also provincial furniture.

countwheel strike Clock mechanism determining the number of strikes per hour.

cow creamer Silver or china cream jug modelled as a cow.

crazing Fine cracks in glaze.

creamware Earthenware glazed in a cream colour giving a porcelain effect, in a widely used technique originally devised by Wedgwood in the 1760s.

credence table Late seventeenth-century oak or walnut table with folding top.

credenza Long Victorian side cabinet with glazed or solid doors.

crenellated Crinkly, wavy.

crested china Ware decorated with heraldic crests; originally by Goss, but subsequently by many Staffordshire and German potteries.

crinoline stretcher Crescent-shaped stretcher supporting the legs of some Windsor chairs.

cross-banding Decorative edging with cross-grained veneer.

cruet Frame for holding condiment containers.

crutch The arm connecting a clock's pendulum to the pallet arbor.

cuirass Breastplate (of armour).

cup and cover Round turning with a distinctly separate top, common on legs until circa 1650.

damascene Inlay of precious metal onto a body of other metal for decorative purposes.

davenport Small English desk, reputedly originally produced by Gillow for a Captain Davenport in 1834. A day-bed or sofa in the USA.

deadbeat escapement Version of the anchor escapement that eliminates recoil and improves accuracy.

deal Sawn pine wood.

delftware Seventeenth- and eighteenth-century tin-glazed earthenware, often decorated in the style of Chinese blue and white porcelain or after Dutch seventeenth-century painting, after the style pioneered by the Delft pottery.

Delft ware Items of delftware which actually emanate from Delft.

dentil Small, block-shaped moulding found under a furniture cornice.

dialplate Frontplate of a clock.

diamond cut (of glass) Cut in diamond shape.

dinanderie Fifteenth-century brass artefact from the factories of Dinant, Belgium.

dished table top Hollowed-out, solid top, particularly of a pie-crust, tripod table.

distressed Artificially aged.

dovetails Interlocking joints used in drawers.

double-action A gun which may be cocked or self-cocking.

douter Scissor-like implement for extinguishing a candle.

dowel Peg holding together wooden joint.

dram glass Small, short-stemmed glass with rounded bowl.

drop-in seat Framed, upholstered seat which sits in the framework of a chair.

drop handle Pear-shaped brass furniture handle of the late seventeenth and early eighteenth centuries.

drop-leaf table Table with a fixed central section and hinged flaps.

drum table Circular writing table on a central pedestal with frieze drawers.

dry-edge With unglazed edges.

dummy drawer False drawer with handle.

Dutch strike Clock chime which strikes the next hour on the half hour.

ebonise To stain a wood to the dark colour of ebony.

ebony Much imitated exotic black hardwood, used as veneer in Europe from the seventeenth century, generally for very high quality pieces.

écuelle Two-handled French soup bowl with cover and stand, often Sèvres.

electroplate The technique of covering one metal with the thin layer of another.

elm Hardwood used in the manufacture of chair seats, country furniture and coffins.

embossing Relief decoration.

enamel Second, coloured glaze fired over first glaze.

endstone In a clock mechanism, jewel on which an arbor pivots.

English dial Nineteenth-century English wall clock with large painted dial, previously a fixture in railway stations.

Engshalskrüge Large German tin-glaze jug with cylindrical neck.

épergne Centrepiece of one central bowl surrounded by smaller ones.

escritoire Cabinet with a fall-front which forms a writing surface. With a fitted interior.

escutcheon Brass plate surrounding the edges of a keyhole.

étuis Small, metal oddments box.

everted Outward turned, flaring (e.g. of a lip).

facet-cut (of glass) Cut criss-cross into straight-edged planes.

faience Tin-glazed earthenware.

fairings Porcelain figures, especially German, made in the nineteenth and twentieth centuries in the mould. Usually comical and carrying descriptive captions.

fall front Flap of a bureau or secretaire that pulls out to provide a writing surface.

famille rose Predominantly pink-coloured Oriental porcelain.

famille verte Predominantly green-coloured Oriental porcelain.

fauteuil Open-sided, upholstered armchair with padded elbows.

feather banding Two bands of veneer laid at opposite diagonals.

field Area of a carpet within its decorated borders.

fielded panel Raised panel with chamfered edge fitting into a framework.

figure Natural pattern created by the grain through the wood.

finial Decorative, turned knob.

flamed veneer Veneer cut at an angle to enhance the figuring.

flatware Plates, knives and forks.

flintlock Gun mechanism whereby the priming in the pan is ignited by a spark created by a flint.

flute glass Glass with tall, slender bowl.

fluting Decorative parallel grooving.

foliate carving Carved flower and leaf motifs.

foliot Primitive form of balance for clock mechanisms.

fretwork Fine pierced decoration.

frieze Long ornamental strip.

frit The flux from which glass is made. An ingredient of soft-paste porcelain.

frizzen The metal which a flint strikes to create a spark in a flintlock mechanism.

fruitwood Generally the wood of apple, cherry and pear trees, used for ebonising and gilding, commonly in picture frames.

fusee The conical, grooved spool from which a line or chain unwinds as it is pulled by the mainspring of a clock movement.

gadroon Carved edge or moulded decoration consisting of a series of grooves, ending in a curved lip, with ridges between them.

Gainsborough chair Deep, upholstered armchair with padded, open arms and carved decoration.

galleried Having a wood or metal border around the top edge.

garniture Set of ornamental pieces of porcelain.

gateleg Leg that pivots to support a drop leaf.

gesso Plaster-like substance applied to carved furniture before gilding or moulded and applied as a substitute for carving.

gilt-tooled decoration Gold leaf impressed into the edges of leather on desk-tops.

gimbal Mounting which keeps a ship's barometer level at all times.

girandole Wall-mounted candle holder with a mirrored back.

gorget Item of armour for protecting the throat.

Goss china Range of porcelain, particularly heraldic, produced in Stoke-on-Trent from 1858.

greave Armour protecting lower leg.

Greek key Ancient key-shaped decoration often repeated in fretwork on furniture.

gridiron pendulum Clock pendulum consisting of rods of a mix of metals positioned in such a way that the dynamics of their behaviour when subjected to heat or cold keep the pendulum swing uniform.

halberd Double-headed axe weapon with projecting spike.

half hunter Watch with an opening front cover with glass to the centre and a chapter ring, giving protection to the glass over the dial.

hallmark The mark by which silver can be identified by standard, place of assay and date.

hard-paste porcelain Porcelain made with kaolin and petuntse in the Chinese fashion, pioneered in Europe at Meissen in the early eighteenth century.

hunter Watch with a hinged, opening front cover in solid metal.

husk Formalised leaf motif.

ice glass Glass with uneven, rippling surface.

Imari Japanese porcelain made in and around Arita from the early eighteenth century and shipped to Europe from the port of Imari. Blue, red and gold coloured.

improved A pejorative term implying that a piece has been altered in order dishonestly to enhance its value.

inlay The decorative setting of one material into a contrasting one.

intaglio Incised design.

ironstone Stoneware patented by Mason in 1813, in which slag from iron furnaces was mixed with the clay to toughen the ware.

istoriato Of some Italian majolica, meaning 'with a story on it'.

japanned Painted and varnished in imitation of Oriental style lacquer work.

jardinière An ornamental pot or vase for plants.

jasper ware Variety of coloured stoneware developed by the Wedgwood factory.

joined Manufactured with the use of mortice and tenon joints and dowels, but without glue.

kabuto Japanese Samurai helmet.

kingwood Exotic, purplish hardwood used in veneer.

kneehole desk Desk with a recessed cupboard beneath the frieze drawer.

knop Rounded projection or bulge in the stem of a glass.

lacquer Resinous substance which, when coloured, provides a ground for chinoiserie and gilding.

ladder-back Chair with a series of horizontal back rails.

lantern clock Clocks made in England from the sixteenth century, driven entirely by weights and marking only the hours. Similar in appearance to a lantern.

lappit Carved flap at the top of a leg with a pad foot.

latten Archaic term for brass.

lead crystal Particularly clear, brilliant glass including lead in the process.

lead-glazed the earliest glaze for Western pottery, derived from glass making.

lever escapement Modification of the anchor escapement for carriage clocks and, particularly, watches.

lion's paw foot Foot carved as a lion's paw. Commonly eighteenth century and Regency.

lock Firing mechanism of a gun.

lockplate Base holding firing mechanism on a gun barrel.

loo table Large Victorian card or games table.

longcase clock The 'grandfather' clock, housed in a tall wooden case containing the weights and pendulum.

loper Pull-out arm that supports the hinged fall of a bureau.

lowboy Small side table with cabriole legs, from the seventeenth century.

lustre ware Ceramic ware decorated with a metallic coating which changes colour when fired.

mahogany The hardwood most used in the production of furniture in England in the eighteenth and nineteenth centuries. Used as a solid wood until the nineteenth century, when its rarity led to its being used for veneer.

majolica Originally tin-glazed earthenware produced in Renaissance Italy, subsequently all nineteenth century wares using the same technique.

mantel clock Clock with feet designed to stand on a mantelpiece.

maple North American hardwood used for its variety of veneers.

marine chronometer Precision clock for use in navigation at sea.

marquetry The use of wooden and other inlays to form decorative patterns.

married Pejorative term applied to a piece of furniture which is made up of more than one piece of the same period.

matchlock Firing mechanism of a gun achieved by lowering a slow match into the priming pan.

mazarine Metal strainer fitting over a dish.

mercury twist Air-twist in glass of a silver colour.

millefiori Multi-coloured or mosaic glass.

moonwork Clock mechanism which computes and displays the phases of the moon.

moquette Heavy imitation velvet used for upholstery.

morion Helmet with upturned front peak.

mortice Slot element of a mortice and tenon joint.

moulding decorative, shaped band around an object or a panel.

mount Invariably metal mounting fitted to a piece of furniture.

mule chest Coffer with a single row of drawers to the base.

musical clock Clock with a cylinder which strikes bells to play a tune.

Nailsea Late eighteenth-century, boldly coloured, opaque glass from Nailsea, near Bristol.

nest of tables Set of three or four occasional tables which slot into each other when not in use.

oak Hardwood which darkens with age, predominant in English furniture manufacture until the middle of the seventeenth century.

obverse The front side of a coin or medal.

ogee An S-shaped curve.

ogee arch Two S-shaped curves coming together to form an arch.

oignon Onion-shaped French watch of the eighteenth century.

ormolu From French *dorure d'or moulu*: 'gilding with gold paste', gold-coloured alloy of copper, zinc, and sometimes tin, in various proportions but usually containing at least 50% copper. Ormolu is used in mounts (ornaments on borders, edges, and as angle guards) for furniture, especially eighteenth-century furniture.

orrery Astronomical clock which shows the position of heavenly bodies. Named after Charles Boyle, fourth Earl of Orrery.

overglaze See **enamel**.

overmantel mirror Mirror designed to hang over a mantelpiece.

ovolo A rounded, convex moulding, making an outward curve across a right angle.

oyster veneer Veneer resembling an open oyster shell, an effect achieved by slanting the cut across the grain of a branch.

pad foot Rounded foot on a circular base, used as termination for cabriole legs.

pair-case A double case for a watch, the inner for protection of the movement, the outer for decoration.

pallet Lever that engages in a clock's escapement wheel in orderb to arrest it.

papier mâché Moulded and lacquered pulped paper used to make small items of furniture and other artefacts.

parian Typically uncoloured, biscuit-style porcelain developed in the nineteenth century by Copeland and named after Parian white marble.

parquetry Veneered pattern using small pieces of veneer, often from different woods, in a geometrical design.

patera Circular ornament made of wood, metal or composition.

patina The layers of polish, dirt, grease and general handling marks that build up on a wooden piece of furniture over the years and give it its individual signs of age, varying from wood to wood.

pearlware White, shiny earthenware, often print decorated.

pedestal desk A flat desk with a leathered top standing on two banks of drawers.

pediment Architectural, triangular gable crowning a piece of furniture or a classical building.

pegged furniture Early furniture constructed with the use of mortice and tenon joints and pegged together with dowels.

pembroke table Small, two-flapped table standing on four legs or a pedestal.

pepperette Vessel, often in silver, for sprinkling pepper.

petuntse Chinese name for the feldspathic rock, an essential element of porcelain, which produces a glaze.

pewter Alloy of tin, lead and often various other metals.

pie-crust Expression used to describe the decorative edge of a dished-top tripod table.

pier glass Tall mirror for hanging on a pier between windows.

pietra dura Composition of semi-precious stones applied to panels of – usually Italian – furniture.

pillar (watchmaking) A rod connecting the dial-plate and backplate of a movement.

pillar rug Chinese rug made to be arranged around a pillar.

pine Softwood used for carcassing furniture.

platform base Flat base supporting a central pedestal and table-top above and standing on three or four scrolled or paw feet.

plinth base Solid base not raised on feet.

pole screen Adjustable fire screen.

pommel Knob at the end of the handle of a dagger.

pontil mark Mark made by the pontil, or blowpipe, on the base of hand-blown glass.

porcellanous Having most of the ingredients or characteristics of porcelain.

porringer Large, two-handled cup with cover.

potboard Bottom shelf of a dresser, often just above the floor.

pounce box A sprinkler for pounce, a powder for drying ink.

Prattware Staffordshire earthenware of the late eighteenth and early nineteenth centuries, decorated in distinctive colours on a buff ground.

print decoration Mass-produced decoration. Not hand painting.

provincial furniture See **country furniture**.

punch bowl Large bowl for the retention and dispensation of punch.

quartered top Flat surface covered with four pieces of matching veneer.

quartetto tables Nest of four occasional tables.

quillon Cross-piece of a sword.

rail A horizontal member running between the outer uprights of a piece of furniture.

rating nut Nut under the bob of a clock's pendulum by which the rate of swing may be adjusted.

redware Primitive eighteenth-century American ware made from a clay which turns red when fired.

reeding Parallel strips of convex fluting.

re-entrant corner Shaped indentation at each corner of a table.

register plate Plate on a barometer with inscriptions to be read against the level of mercury.

regulator Precision timepiece of the eighteenth century.

relief Proud of the surface.

repeating work Mechanism by which the pull of a cord or the press of a button operates the striking mechanism of a clock or watch to the last hour.

repoussé An embossed design which has been refined by chasing.

rosewood Named after its smell when newly cut, rather than its flower or colour, a dark-brown hardwood with an attractive stripe or ripple, used for veneering.

rule joint Hinge on furniture which fits so well that, when open, no join can be detected between two hinged parts.

runners Strips of wood, fitted to furniture, on which drawers slide.

sabre leg Chair leg in the shape of a sabre, typical of the Regency period.

saltglaze Stoneware in which salt is added to the recipe creating a porcellanous, glassy surface. Dates back to the early eighteenth century.

salver A large metal dish or tray for transporting smaller dishes.

satinwood A light golden-coloured, close-grained hardwood used for veneer, panelling and turning from the mid-eighteenth century onwards.

scagiola Composite material resembling marble.

scalloped Having a series of circular edges in the shape of a scallop shell.

scalloped leaf Serpentine flap on some pembroke tables.

sconce 1. Cup-shaped candle holder. 2. Metal plate fixed to the wall, supporting candle holder or light.

scratch blue Eighteenth-century saltglaze decoration where the body is incised and the incisions painted blue.

scroll, scrolling Carving or moulding of a curled design.

seat rail Horizontal framework below the chair seat uniting the legs.

secretaire Writing desk with false drawer front which lets down to reveal a writing surface and fitted interior.

secretaire bookcase Secretaire with bookcase fitted above.

serpent The arm holding the match or flint by which the priming of a gun was ignited.

serpentine Of undulating shape.

settee Upholstered settle.

settle Hard bench seat with back. The earliest form of seating for two or more people.

Sheffield plate Rolled sheet silver placed either side of a layer of copper and fused. Recognised by the Sheffield assay office in 1784, but made elsewhere, notably Birmingham, as well.

shoe piece Projection on the back rail of a chair into which the splat fits.

side chair Chair without arms designed to stand against the wall.

side table Any table designed to stand against the wall.

skeleton clock Clock with the workings exposed.

slipware Earthenware to which mixed clay and water has been added as decoration.

sofa Well-upholstered chair providing seating for two or more people.

sofa table Rectangular table with hinged flaps designed to stand behind a sofa.

soft-paste porcelain Porcelain using frit or soapstone instead of the petuntse of hard-paste porcelain. English, from the eighteenth century.

spade foot Square, tapered foot.

spandrel Pierced, decorative corner bracket found at the tops of legs.

sparrow-beak jug Jug with a triangular spout.

spill vase Container for lighting-tapers.

spindle Thoroughly turned piece of wood. The upright bars of a spindle-back chair.

splat The central upright of a chair back.

sprig Applied or relief ornamentation of any kind on a ceramic artefact.

squab Detachable cushion or upholstered seat of a chair or bench.

standish Inkstand, often in silver.

stick barometer Barometer with a straight, vertical register plate running alongside the mercury tube.

stiles Archaic term for the vertical parts of the framework of a piece of furniture.

stoneware Earthenware that is not porous after firing.

stretcher Rail joining the legs of a table or chair.

strike / silent ring Dial to disengage or re-engage the striking of a clock.

stringing Fine inlaid lines around a piece of furniture.

stirrup cup Cup used for alcoholic refreshment prior to hunting, usually shaped in the head of a fox or, less usually, a hound.

stuff-over seat Chair that is upholstered over the seat rail.

subsidiary dial Small dial, usually showing seconds, within the main dial of a clock or watch. Hence **subsidiary seconds**.

swagged With applied strips formed in a mould (of metal).

swan-neck pediment Pediment with two broken curves.

swan-neck handle Curved handle typical of the eighteenth century.

sycamore Hardwood of the maple family, light yellow in colour, used for veneering.

tang The end of the blade of a sword, covered by the hilt.

tankard Large beer-mug with a hinged lid and thumb-piece.

tazza Italian plate, cup, basin or wide-bowled glass.

teapoy Small piece of furniture designed for holding tea leaves. Usually Anglo-Indian.

tenons The tongues in mortice and tenon joints.

thumb moulding Decorative concave moulding.

thumb-piece Projection attached to a hinged lid which will open the lid when pressure is applied by the thumb.

tine Prong of a fork.

tin-glazed Lead-glazed earthenware to which tin is added, e.g. majolica.

toilet mirror Small dressing mirror with a box base and drawers.

touch mark Individual mark of the maker of a piece of early English pewter.

transfer Ceramic print decoration using colours held in oil.

trefid spoon A seventeenth-century spoon with the handle terminating in the shape of a bud, usually cleft or grooved into two lobes.

trefoil Having three lobes.

trembleuse Cup-stand with feet.

tripod table Small, round-topped table on three-legged base.

tulipwood Pinkish, naturally patterned hardwood used in veneer.

turnery Any wood turned on a lathe.

tureen Large bowl in porcelain or metal, usually with a lid and two handles.

turret clock Clock of any size driven by a weight suspended by a rope wrapped round a drum.

underglaze Colour or design painted below the glaze of a ceramic artefact.

uniface Medal or coin with modelling on one side only.

urn table Eighteenth-century table designed to hold an urn.

veneer A thin sheet of wood laid across a cheaper carcase or used as inlay decoration.

verge escapement Mechanism for regulating a clock movement before the anchor escapement.

Vesta case Match box for Vesta matches, often in silver, from circa 1850.

vinaigrette Small, eighteenth-century box, often silver, to hold a sponge soaked in vinegar to ward off germs and the unpleasant odours of the day.

wainscot chair Joined chair with open arms and a panelled back.

walnut The hardwood used in England for the manufacture of furniture from the Restoration, originally in solid form but mostly as veneer, particularly burr walnut, after the beginning of the eighteenth century.

well Interior of a plate or bowl.

Wemyss ware Late nineteenth-century lead-glazed earthenware originally from Fife, Scotland.

whatnot Mobile stand with open shelves.

wheel-back chair Originally late eighteenth-century chair with circular back with radiating spokes.

windsor chair Wooden chair with spindle back.

yew Tough, close-grained hardwood used for turning, particularly in chair legs, and in veneer.

There follows a list of antique dealers, many of whom have provided items in the main body of the book and all of whom will be happy to assist within their areas of expertise.

Aaron Gallery
(ref: Aaron)
34 Bruton Street,
London W1X 7DD
Tel: 020 7499 9434
Fax: 020 7499 0072
www.AaronGallery.com
Islamic and ancient art; New Eastern, Greek, Roman and Egyptian antiquities.

Abacus Antiques
Grays Antiques Market,
58 Davies Street,
London W1Y 2LP
Tel: 020 7629 9681
Antiques.

Abbey Green Antiques
(ref: Abbey Green)
Mariaplatts 45,
Utrecht 3511 LL
The Netherlands
Tel: 030 232 8065

Emmy Abé
Stand 33, Bond Street
Antiques Centre,
124 New Bond Street,
London W1X 9AE
Tel: 020 7629 1826
Fax: 020 7491 9400
Exclusively selected antique and modern jewellery.

Aberg Antiques
(ref: Aberg)
42 The Little Boltons,
London SW10 9LN
Tel: 020 7370 7253
Fax: 020 7370 7253
Furniture.

Norman Adams Ltd
(ref: Norman Adams)
8–10 Hans Road,
London SW3 1RX
Tel: 020 7589 5266
Fax: 020 7589 1968
www.normanadams.com
Eighteenth-century fine English furniture, works of art, mirrors, paintings and chandeliers.

A.D. Antiques
The Swan at Tetsworth,
High Street,
Tetsworth, Thame,
Oxfordshire, OX9 7AB
Tel: 07939 508171
www.adantiques.com
Decorative arts.

After Noah
121 Upper Street,
London N1 8ED
Tel: 020 7359 4281
Fax: 020 7359 4281
www.afternoah.com
Antique furniture, linen and postcards.

After Noah (Kings Road)
(ref: After Noah (KR))
261 Kings Road,
London SW3 5EL
Tel: 020 7351 2610
Fax: 020 7351 2610
www.afternoah.com
Antique furniture, linen and postcards.

Albany Antiques
(ref: Albany)
8–10 London Road, Hindhead,
Surrey GU26 6AF
Tel: 01428 605 528
Fax: 01428 605 528
Georgian furniture, eighteenth-century brass, Victorian antiques, porcelain and statuary.

AM-PM
V35 Antiquarias Antiques
Market,
135 Kings Road,
London SW3
Tel: 020 7351 5654
Antique and modern watches.

Fred Anderson Antiques
(ref: Fred Anderson)
5/6 Hight Street
Welshpool
Powys SY2 1JF
Tel: 01938 553340
Mob: 07773 795931
Fine antique furniture.

Paul Andrews Antiques
(ref: Paul Andrews)
The Furniture Court,
553 Kings Road,
London SW10 0TZ
Tel: 020 7352 4584
Fax: 020 7351 7815
www.paulandrewsantiques.co.uk
Eclectic furniture, sculpture, tapestries, paintings and works of art.

Angel Antiques
Church Street, Petworth,
West Sussex GU28 0AD
Tel: 01798 343 306
Fax: 01798 342 665
Oak, country furniture.

Antique and Interiors Group Ltd., The
(ref: A.I.G.)
The Old Cinema
160 Chiswick High Road
London W4 1PR
Tel: 020 8742 8080
Fax: 020 8878 0184
Antiques in general.

Antiques Pavilion
175 Bermondsey Street,
London SE1 3LW
Tel: 020 7394 7856
Furniture from the Georgian period to the 1930s; also restorations.

Antique Warehouse
9–14 Dentford Broadway,
London SE8 4PA
Tel: 020 8691 3062
Fax: 020 8691 3062
www.antiquewarehouse.co.uk
Decorative antiques.

Arca
R & E Innocenti
Stand 351
Grays Antique Centre
Davies Street
London W1 2LP
Tel: 020 7692 729
e-mail:Innocenti@
arcaantiques.freeserve co.uk
Sewing and smoking items.

Armoury of St James, The
(ref: The Armoury)
17 Piccadilly Arcade,
London SW1Y 6NH
Tel: 020 7493 5083
Fax: 020 7499 4422
www.armoury.co.uk/home
Royal memorabilia and model soldiers.

Sean Arnold Sporting Antiques
(ref: Sean Arnold)
1 Pembridge Villas,
London W2 4XE
Tel: 020 7221 2267
Fax: 020 7221 5464
Sporting antiques.

Victor Arwas Gallery
(ref: Arwas)
3 Clifford Street,
London W1X 1RA
Tel: 020 7734 3944
Fax: 020 7437 1859
www.victorarwas.com
Art Nouveau and Art Deco, glass, ceramics, bronzes, sculpture, furniture, jewellery, silver, pewter, books and posters, from 1880–1940. Paintings, watercolours and drawings, 1880 to date. Original graphics, lithographs, etchings and woodcuts from 1890 to date.

Ashcombe House
Ashcombe Coach House,
Brighton Road, Lewes,
East Sussex BN7 3JR
Tel: 01273 474794
Fax: 01273 705959
Eighteenth and nineteenth-century furniture and decorative objects.

Ash Rare Books
(ref: Ash Books)
153 Fenchurch Street,
London EC3M 6BB
Tel: 020 7626 2665
Fax: 020 7626 2665
www.ashrare.com
Books, maps and prints.

Garry Atkins
107 Kensington Church Street,
London W8 7LN
Tel: 020 7727 8737
Fax: 020 7792 9010
www.englishpottery.com
English and continental pottery from the eighteenth century and earlier.

Aurum
Grays Antiques Market,
58 Davies Street,
London W1K 5LP
Tel: 020 7409 0215
www.aurum.uk.com
Antique and period jewellery, and Shelly china.

Axia Art Consultants Ltd
(ref: Axia)
21 Ledbury Road,
London W11 2AQ
Tel: 020 7727 9724
Fax: 020 7229 1272
Islamic and Byzantine works of art, textiles, metalwork, woodwork, ceramics and icons.

Dr Colin B. Baddiel
B24 Grays Antiques Market,
Davies Mews,
London W1
Tel: 020 7408 1239
Fax: 020 74939344
Die-cast and tin toys.

David Baker
Grays Mews Antique Market,
1–7 Davies Mews,
London W1Y 2LP
Tel: 020 8346 1387
Fax: 020 8346 1387
Oriental art.

**Gregg Baker Oriental Art
(ref: Gregg Baker)**
132 Kensington Church Street,
London W8 4BH
Tel: 020 7221 3533
Fax: 020 7221 4410
www.greggbaker.com
*Japanese and Chinese works
of art.*

B. & T. Antiques
79–81 Ledbury Road,
London W11 2AG
Tel: 020 7229 7001
Fax: 020 7229 2033
*Eighteenth-century Art Deco
English and continental furniture,
and objets d'art.*

Barham Antiques
83 Portobello Road,
London W11 2QB
Tel: 020 7727 3845
Fax: 020 7727 3845
*Victorian walnut and inlaid
continental furniture, writing
boxes, tea caddies, inkwells and
inkstands, glass épergnes, silver
plate, clocks and paintings.*

**R.A. Barnes Antiques
(ref: R.A. Barnes)**
26 Lower Richmond Road,
London SW15 1JP
Tel: 020 8789 3371
Fax: 020 8780 3195
*Continental glass, English and
continental porcelain, Art
Nouveau, small furniture,
paintings, English metalware,
eighteenth and nineteenth-century
brass, Belleed and Wedgwood.*

**Les Barrett & Ian Towning
(ref: Barrett Towning)**
Bourbon-Hanby Antiques
Centre
151 Sydney Street
London SW3 6NT
Tel: 020 7352 2106
Fax: 020 7565 0003
www.antiques-u.co.uk/bourbon-
hanby
*English ceramics, silver, writing
equipment and antique jewellery.*

Don Bayney
Grays Mews Antiques Market,
1–7 Davies Mews,
London W1Y 2LP
Tel: 020 7629 3644
Fax: 020 8578 4701
Japanese works of art.

**Bazaart 51 Antiques
(ref: Bazaart)**
51 Ledbury Road,
London W11 2AA
Tel: 020 7615 3472
Fax: 020 7615 472
*Italian ceramics and Venetian
glass from 1500–1900.*

**Beauty and the Beasts
(ref: Beauty)**
Antiquarius Antique Centre
Q9-10
141 King's Road
London SW3 4PW
Tel: 020 7351 5149
Antique handbags.

**Frederick Beck Ltd.
(ref: F. Beck)**
22–26 Camden Passage,
Islington, London N1 8ED
Tel: 020 7226 3403
Fax: 020 7288 1305
General antiques.

Linda Bee
Grays in the Mews Antiques
Market,
1–7 Davies Mews,
London W1Y 1AR
Tel: 020 7629 5921
Fax: 020 7629 5921
*Vintage costume jewellery and
fashion accessories.*

Bellum Antiques
Bourbon-Hanby Antiques
Centre
151 Sydney Street
London SW3 6NT
Tel: 020 7352 2106
Fax: 020 7565 0003
www.antiques-uk.co.uk/
bourbon-hanby
English ceramics.

Julia Bennet (Antiques)
Flemings Hill Farm,
Great Easton, Dunmow,
Essex CM6 2ER
Tel: 01279 850279
*Eighteenth and early nineteenth-
century furniture.*

**Bentleys
204 Walton Street**
London SW3 2JL
Tel: 020 7584 7770
Fax: 020 7584 8182
e-mail: lf@bentleyslondon.com
www.bentleyslondon.com
*Antique luggage and gentlemen's
accessories.*

Yasha Beresiner
Gallery at 114 Islington
High Street
(Inside the Camden Passage)
London N1 8EG
020 7354 2599
Fax: 020 8346 9539
Mob: 07468 292 066
www.intercol.co.uk
Scripophily and paper money.

Beverley
30 Church Street,
Marylebone,
London NW8 8EP
Tel: 020 7262 1576
Fax: 020 7262 1576
English ceramics, glass, metal,
wood, pottery, collectables and
decorative items from
1850–1950.

Andrew Bewick Antiques
287 Lillie Road,
London SW6 7LL
Tel: 020 7385 9025
Fax: 020 7385 9025
Decorative antiques.

Big Baby & Little Baby
Antiques
(ref: Big Baby Little Baby)
Grays Antiques Market,
Davies Mews,
London W1
Tel: 020 8367 2441
Fax: 020 8366 5811
Dolls, teddies, prams and related
collectables.

Bike Park
63 New Kings Road,
London SW3
Tel: 020 7565 0777
Bikes, rentals, repairs and
clothing.

Bizarre
24 Church Street,
London NW8 8EP
Tel: 020 7724 1305
Fax: 020 7724 1316
www.antiques-uk/bazarre
Art Deco, continental furniture,
wrought iron, glass, and
ceramics.

Oonagh Black Antiques
(ref: Oonagh Black)
Lower Farm House,
Coln Rogers,
Gloucestershire GL54 3LA
Tel: 01285 720717
Fax: 01285 720910
French and English furniture and
French science and textiles.

David Black Oriental Carpets
(ref: David Black)
96 Portland Road
London W11 4LN
Tel: 020 7727 2566
Fax: 020 7229 4599
Antique carpets and rugs.

N. Bloom & Son Ltd.
(ref: N. Bloom)
Antique Jewellery
124 Bond Street Antique
Centre
124 New Bond Street
London WI8 IDX
Tel: 020 7629 5060
Fax: 020 7493 2528
e-mail: nbloom@nbloom.com
www.nbloom.com
Antique jewellery.

John Bly
27 Bury Street,
London SW1Y 6AL
Tel: 020 7930 1292
Fax: 020 7839 4775
www.johnbly.com
Eighteenth and nineteenth-
century English furniture, works
of art, paintings, silver, glass,
porcelain and tapestries.

Paolo Bonino
Stand S001, Alfie's Antique
Market,
13–25 Church Street,
London NW8 8DT
Tel: 020 7723 6066
European twentieth-century glass
and ceramics.

Book and Comic Exchange
(ref: Book & Comic)
14 Pembridge Road,
London W11 3HL
Tel: 020 7229 8420
www.buy-sell-trade.co.uk
Modern first editions, cult books
and comics.

Malcolm Bord Gold Coin
Exchange
(ref: Malcolm Bord)
16 Charing Cross Road,
London WC2 0HR
Tel: 020 7836 0631/
020 7240 0479/020 7240 1920
Dealing in all types of coin, medal
and bank note.

Julia Boston
2 Michael Road,
London SW6 2AD
Tel: 020 7610 6783
Fax: 020 7610 6784
www.juliaboston.co.uk
Tapestry cartoons, engravings and
eighteenth and nineteenth-century
decorative antiques.

M.J. Bowdery
12 London Road, Hindhead,
Surrey, GU26 6AF
Tel: 01428 606376
Eighteenth and nineteenth-
century furniture.

Patrick Boyd-Carpenter
(ref: P. Boyd-Carpenter)
Unit 331–332
Grays Antiques Market,
58 Davies Street,
London W1Y 2LP
Tel: 020 7491 7623
Fax: 020 7491 7623
Wide range of antiques, sixteenth
and eighteenth-century sculpture,
paintings and prints.

Elizabeth Bradwin
75 Portobello Road,
London W11 2QB
Tel: 020 7221 1121
Fax: 020 8947 2629
www.elizabethbradwin.com
Animal subjects.

Lesley Bragge
Fairfield House, High Street,
Petworth, West Sussex
Tel: 01798 342324
Wine-related items.

Augustus Brandt
Middle Street
Petworth
West Sussex GU28 0BE
Tel: 01798 344722
Fax: 01798 344772
e-mail: brandt@easynet.co.uk
www.augustus-brandt-
antiques.co.uk
*Scandinavian, French, Italian
and English 18th century
furniture, mirrors and lighting
and unusual decorative furnishing
and objects d'art.*

Brandt Oriental Art
(ref: Brandt)
First Floor, 29
New Bond Street,
London W1Y 9HD
Tel: 020 7499 8835
Fax: 020 7409 1882
*Chinese and Japanese works
of art.*

Bridge Bikes
137 Putney Bridge,
London SW15 2PA
Tel: 020 8870 3934
Bikes.

F.E.A. Briggs Ltd
(ref: Briggs)
5 Plaza Parade,
Winchester Road,
Romsey, Hampshire SO51 8JA
Tel: 01794 510061
*Victorian and Edwardian
furniture and textiles.*

Lynda Brine Antiques
(ref: Lynda Brine)
The Assembly Antiques
Centre
Saville Row
Bath BA1 2QP
Tel: 01225 448488
Fax: 01225 429661
e-mail: lyndabrine@yahoo.
co.uk
www.scentbottlesandsmalls.
co.uk
Scent bottles and bags.

Aubrey Brocklehurst
124 Cromwell Road,
London SW7 4ET
Tel: 020 7373 0319
Fax: 020 73737612
English clocks and barometers.

Gerald Brodie
Great Grooms Antique Centre
Hungerford
Berks RG17 0EP
*Fine furniture from the 18th
century.*

David Brower Antiques
(ref: David Brower)
113 Kensington Church Street,
London W8 7LN
Tel: 020 7221 4155
Fax: 020 7721 6211
www.davidbrower-antique.com
*Porcelain, European bronzes,
and Japanese works of art.*

Brown
First Floor, 533 Kings Road,
London SW10 0TZ
Tel: 020 7352 2046
Furniture.

I. and J. L. Brown Ltd
(ref: I. & J. L. Brown)
632–636 Kings Road,
London SW6 2DU
Tel: 020 7736 4141
Fax: 020 7736 9164
www.brownantiques.com
*English country and French
provincial antique and
reproduction furniture.*

Brown's Antique Furniture
(ref: Brown's)
First Floor, The Furniture
Cave,
533 Kings Road,
London SW10 0TZ
Tel: 020 7352 2046
Fax: 020 7352 6354
www.thecave.co.uk
*Library and dining, and
decorative objects from the
early eighteenth century.*

S. Brunswick
Alfie's Antiques Market,
13–25 Church Street,
London NW8 8DT
Tel: 020 7724 9097
Fax: 020 8902 5656
*Functional and decorative
furnishings for house, garden
and conservatory.*

Peter Bunting Antiques
(ref: Peter Bunting)
Harthill Hall, Alport,
Bakewell,
Derbyshire DE45 1LH
Tel: 01629 636203
Fax: 01629 636190
*Early oak and country furniture,
portraits and tapestries.*

**Butchoff Antiques
(ref: Butchoff)**
220 Westbourne Grove,
London W11 2RH
Tel: 020 7221 8174
Fax: 020 7792 8923
*English and continental furniture,
decorative items, porcelain and
mirrors.*

Butchoff Interiors
229 Westbourne Grove,
London W11 2SE
Tel: 020 7221 8163
Fax: 020 7792 8923
*One-off items, textiles,
collectables, dining tables, chairs,
consoles and accessories.*

Vincenzo Caffarella
Alfie's Antique Market,
13–25 Church Street,
London NW8 8DT
Tel: 020 7723 1513
Fax: 020 8731 8615
www.vinca.co.uk
*Twentieth-century decorative arts
and antiques.*

Cameo Gallery
151 Sydney Street,
London SW3 6NT
Tel: 020 7352 0909
Fax: 020 735 20066
Art Nouveau to Art Deco.

Jasmin Cameron
Antiquarias Antiques Market,
135 Kings Road,
London SW3 4PW
Tel: 020 7351 4154
Fax: 020 7351 4154
*Drinking glasses and decanters
1750–1910, vintage fountain
pens and writing materials.*

**Canonbury Antiques Ltd
(ref: Canonbury)**
174 Westbourne Grove,
London W11 2RW
Tel: 020 7229 2786
Fax: 020 7229 5840
www.canonbury-antiques.co.uk
*Eighteenth and nineteenth-
century furniture, reproduction
furniture and accessories.*

Vivienne Carroll
Stand N1, Antiquarius
135–141 Kings Road,
London SW3 4PW
Tel: 020 7352 8882
Fax: 020 7352 8734
*Silver, jewellery, porcelain and
ivory.*

**C.A.R.S. of Brighton
(ref: C.A.R.S.)**
4–4a Chapel Terrace Mews,
Kemp Town, Brighton BN2
1HU
Tel: 01273 622 722
Fax: 01273 601 960
www.carsofbrighton.co.uk
*Classic automobilia and regalia
specialists, and children's pedal
cars.*

**Cartoon Gallery, The
(ref: Cartoon Gallery)**
39 Great Russell Street,
London WC1 3PH
Tel: 020 7636 1011
Fax: 020 7436 5053
Comics.

**Mia Cartwright Antiques
(ref: Mia Cartwright)**
20th C. Theatre Arcade,
291 Westbourne Grove (Sats),
London W11
Tel: 01273 579700

**Castlegate Antiques
(ref: Castlegate)**
1-3 Castlegate, Newark, Notts
NG24 1AZ
Tel: 01636 701877
*18th and 19th-century furniture
and decorative objects.*

**Rupert Cavendish Antiques
(ref: R. Cavendish)**
610 Kings Road,
London SW6 2DX
Tel: 020 7731 7041
Fax: 020 7731 8302
www.rupertcavendish.co.uk
*European twentieth-century
paintings.*

Cekay
Stand 172, Grays Antique
Market,
58 Davies Street,
London W1Y 2LP
Tel: 020 7629 5130
Fax: 020 7730 3014
Antiques.

**Ronald G. Chambers Fine
Antiques
(ref: Ronald G. Chambers)**
Market Square, Petworth,
West Sussex GU28 0AH
Tel: 01798 342305
Fax: 01798 342724
www.ronaldchambers.com
*Eighteenth and nineteenth-
century furniture, paintings,
objets d'art, clocks and jewellery.*

Bill Chapman
Shop No. 11, Bourbon/
Hanby Antique Centre,
151 Sydney Street,
London SW3 6NT
Tel: 020 7351 5387
Collectables.

**Chelsea Gallery and II Libro
(ref: Chelsea Gallery)**
The Plaza, 535 Kings Road,
London SW10 0SZ
Tel: 020 7823 3248
Fax: 020 7352 1579
*Antique illustrated books,
literature, prints, maps,
specialising in natural history,
travel, architecture and history.*

**Chelsea Military Antiques
(ref: Chelsea (OMRS))**
Stands N13–14, Antiquarius,
131–141 Kings Road,
London SW3 4PW
Tel: 020 7352 0308
Fax: 020 7352 0308
www.chelseamilitaria.co.uk
*Pre-1945 militaria, edge
weapons, medals including British
and foreign campaign/gallantry
medals.*

Cine Art Gallery
759 Fulham Road
London SW6 5UU
Tel: 020 7384 0728
Fax: 020 7384 0727
www.cineartgallery.com
Vintage film posters.

Circa
L43, Grays Mews Antique
Market,
1–7 Davies Mews,
London W1Y 2LP
Tel: 01279 466260
Fax: 01279 466 260
Decorative and collectable glass.

**Clarke and Denny Antiques
Ref: Clarke & Denny**
Great Grooms Antiques
Centre
Billingshurst
West Sussex RH14 9EU
Antique furniture.

**Classic Fabrics with Robin
Haydock
(Ref: Classic Fabrics)**
Unit 18
Bourbon Hanby Antiques
Centre
151 Sydney Street
London SW3 6NY
Tel: 020 7349 9100
Mob: 07770 931240
Antique textiles and fabrics.

**John Clay Antiques
(ref: John Clay)**
263 New Kings Road,
London SW6 4RB
Tel: 020 7731 5677
*Furniture, objets d'art, silver and
clocks from the eighteenth and
nineteenth century.*

**Clock Clinic Ltd, The
(ref: Clock Clinic)**
85 Lower Richmond Road,
Putney,
London SW15 1EW
Tel: 020 8788 1407
Fax: 020 8780 2838
www.clockclinic.co.uk
*Antique clocks and barometers,
all overhauled and guaranteed.*

**Clock Workshop, The
(ref: Clock Workshop)**
17 Prospect Street, Caversham,
Reading, Berkshire RG4 8JB
Tel: 0118 947 0741
www.lapada.co.uk
*English clocks and French
carriage clocks.*

Cobwebs
73 Avery Hill Road,
New Eltham,
London SE9 2BJ
Tel: 020 8850 5611
*Furniture, general antiques and
collectables.*

Cohen & Cohen
101b Kensington Church
Street,
London W8 7LN
Tel: 020 7727 7677
Fax: 020 7229 9653
www.artnet.com
*Chinese export porcelain works
of art.*

**Garrick D. Coleman
(ref: G.D. Coleman)**
75 Portobello Road,
London W11 2QB
Tel: 020 7937 5524
Fax: 020 7937 5530
www.antiquechess.co.uk
*Antiques, fine chess sets and
glass paperweights.*

**J. Collins & Son
(ref: J. Collins)**
28 High Street, Bideford,
Devon EX39 2AN
Tel: 01237 473103
Fax: 01237 475658
*Georgian and Regency furniture,
Victorian oil paintings and
watercolours.*

**Rosemary Conquest
(ref: R. Conquest)**
4 Charlton Place,
London N1 8AJ
Tel: 020 7359 0616
*Continental and Dutch lighting,
copper, brass and decorative
items.*

Hilary Conqy
Antiquarias Antiques Market,
135 Kings Road,
London SW3 4PW
Tel: 020 7352 2099
Jewellery.

Marc Constantini Antiques
(ref: M. Constantini)
313 Lillie Road,
London SW6 7LL

Sheila Cook Textiles
(ref: Sheila Cook)
184 Westbourne Grove,
London W11 2RH
Tel: 020 7792 8001
Fax: 020 7229 3855
www.sheilacook.co.uk
*European costume, textiles
from the mid eighteenth century
to the 1970s.*

**Susie Cooper Ceramics
Gallery 1930**
(ref: Susie Cooper)
18 Church Street
Marylebone
London NW8 8EP
20th century ceramics.

Barry Cotton Antiques
(ref: Barry Cotton)
By appointment only
Tel: 020 8563 9899
Mob: 07831 354324
e-mail: barrycottonantiques@
tinyonline.co.uk
www.barrycottonantiques.fsnet.
co.uk
*Fine quality 18th and 19th
century period furniture.*

The Country Seat
Huntercome Manor Barn
nr. Henley on Thames
Oxon RG9 5RY
Tel: 01491 6431349
Fax: 01491 641533
e-mail: fery&clegg@
thecountryseat.com
www.thecountryseat.com
www.whitefriarsflass.com
*20th century furniture, ceramics
and glass.*

Sandra Cronan Ltd
(ref: Sandra Cronan)
18 Burlington Arcade,
London W1V 9AB
Tel: 020 7491 4851
Fax: 020 7493 2758
Art Deco jewellery.

Crowthers of Syon Lodge
(ref: Crowthers)
Architectural Antiques
for Interior and Exteriors
77/79 Pimlico Road
London SW1 W8PH
Tel: 020 7730 8668
*Architectural antiques and
sculpture.*

Curios Gardens & Interiors
(ref: Curios)
130c Junction Road,
Tufnell Park,
London N19 5LB
Tel: 020 7272 5603
Fax: 020 7272 5603
*Garden furniture, statuary,
reclaimed pine furniture and
antique furniture.*

Ronan Daly Antiques
Alfie's Antiques Market,
13–25 Church Street,
London NW8 8DT
Tel: 020 7723 0429

Andrew Dando
(ref: Dando)
4 Wood Street
Queen Square
Bath BA1 1JQ
Tel: 01225 422702
Fax: 012255 31017
e-mail:
andrew@andrewdando.uk
www.andrewdando/co.uk
English ceramics.

Michael Davidson
54 Ledbury Road,
London W11 2AJ
Tel: 020 7229 6088
Fax: 020 7792 0450
*Eighteenth-century furniture,
regency furniture, objects and
objets d'art.*

Jesse Davis Antiques
(ref: Jesse Davis)
Stands A9–11 Antiquarius,
131–141 Kings Road,
London SW3 4PW
Tel: 020 7352 4314
*Nineteenth-century pottery,
majolica, Staffordshire and other
collectable factories, and
decorative objects.*

Decodence
21 The Mall,
359 Upper Street,
London N1 0PD
Tel: 020 7354 4473
Fax: 020 7689 0680
*Classic plastics such as bakelite,
celluloid and catalin; vintage
radios, lighting, telephones and
toys.*

Deep, The
The Plaza, 535 Kings Road,
London SW10 0SZ
Tel: 020 7351 4881
Fax: 020 7352 0763
Recovered shipwrecked items.

Richard Dennis Gallery
(ref: Richard Dennis)
144 Kensington Church Street,
London W8 4BH
Tel: 020 7727 2061
Fax: 020 7221 1283
*Antique and modern studio
ceramics.*

Dial Post House
Dial Post, Near Horsham,
West Sussex RH13 8NQ
Tel: 01403 713388
Fax: 01403 713388
Furniture.

Dodo
Stand Fo73,
Alfie's Antiques Market,
13–25 Church Street,
London NW8 8DT
Tel: 020 7706 1545
Fax: 020 7724 0999
*Posters, tins and advertising signs,
1890–1940.*

Dolly Land
864 Green Lanes,
Winchmore Hill,
London N21 2RS
Tel: 020 8360 1053
Fax: 020 8364 1370
www.dollyland.com
Dolls.

Dolly Land (Steiff Club)
864 Green Lanes,
Winchmore Hill,
London N21 2RS
Tel: 020 8360 1053
Fax: 020 8364 1370
www.dollyland.com
*Dolls, Steiff bears, Scalextric,
trains and die-cast toys.*

Gavin Douglas
75 Portobello Road,
London W11 2QB
Tel: 020 7221 1121
www.antique-clocks.co.uk
*Clocks, bronzes, sculpture
and porcelain.*

**Drummonds Architectural
Antiques Ltd
(ref: Drummonds)**
The Kirkpatrick Buildings,
25 London Road, Hindhead,
Surrey GU26 6AB
Tel: 01428 609444
Fax: 01428 609445
www.drummonds-arch.co.uk
*Bathrooms, flooring, fireplaces,
statues, lighting, gates, railings,
doors, radiators, windows and
architectural features.*

H. Duffield
Unit So54
Alfie's Market
13/25 Church Street
London NW8 8DT
Tel: 020 7723 2548
Early 20th century telephones.

S. Duggan
First Floor, 533 Kings Road,
London SW10 0TZ
Tel: 020 7352 2046
Antiques.

Eastern Interiors
Bourbon Hanby Antiques
Centre
151 Sydney Street
London SW3 6NT
Tel: 020 7795 2658
Fax: 020 7565 0003
Mob: 07803 701 778
www.eastern-interiors.co.uk
Oriental boxes and furniture.

**Emanouel Corporation
U.K. Ltd.
(ref: Emanouel)**
64 South Audley Street,
London W1Y 5FD
Tel: 020 7493 4350
Fax: 020 7499 0996
*Important antiques and fine
works of art from the eighteenth
and nineteenth century, and
Islamic works of art.*

Emerson
Bourbon & Hanby Antiques
Centre,
Shop No. 2, 151 Sydney Street,
London SW3 6NT
Tel: 020 7351 1807
Fax: 020 7351 1807
Corkscrews and collectables.

Penny Fawcett at Tilings
High Street, Brasted,
Kent TN16 1JA
Tel: 01959 564735
Fax: 01959 565795

**Finchley Fine Art Galleries
(ref: Finchley)**
983 High Road, North
Finchley,
London N12 8QR
Tel: 020 8446 4848
*Watercolours, paintings, fine
eighteenth and nineteenth-century
furniture, pottery and porcelain.*

**J. First Antiques
(ref: J. First)**
Stand 310, 58 Davies Street,
London W1Y 1LB
Tel: 020 7409 2722
Fax: 020 7409 2722
www.firstsilver18@hotmail.com
*Antique English silver
collectables.*

Flower Antiques
Great Grooms Antique Centre
Hungerford
Berkshire RG17 0EP
Antique furniture.

David Ford
2 Queenstown Road, Battersea,
London SW8
Tel: 020 7622 7547

A. & E. Foster
Little Heysham, Forge Road,
Naphill, Buckinghamshire
HP14 4SU
Tel: 01494 562024
Fax: 01494 562024
*Antique treen works of art
and early treen.*

**Judy Fox Antiques
(ref: Judy Fox)**
81 Portobello Road/
176 Westbourne Grove,
London W11
Tel: 020 7229 8130/8488
Fax: 020 7229 6998
Furniture.

Lynda Franklin
25 Charnham Street,
Hungerford,
Berkshire, RG17 0EJ
Tel: 01488 682404
Fax: 01488 626089
*Antiques and interior design,
french furniture from the
seventeenth and eighteenth
centuries.*

**Vincent Freeman Antiques
(ref: Vincent Freeman)**
1 Camden Passage
Stand G 57
Islington
London N1 8EA
Tel: 020 7226 6178
Fax 020 7226 7231
Mob: 07889 966 880
*19th century musical boxes,
furniture and ceramics.*

**French Country Living
(ref: French Country)**
Rue des Remparts,
Mougins, France
Tel: 00 33 4 93 75 53 03
Fax: 00 33 4 93 75 63 03
Antiquities and decoration.

**French Glasshouse, The
(ref: French Glasshouse)**
P14–P16 Antiquarias
Antiques Market,
135 Kings Road,
London SW3 4PW
Tel: 020 7376 5394
Fax: 020 7376 5394
*Gallé and Daum glassware, and
Japanese works of art.*

French Room, The
5 High Street, Petworth,
West Sussex GU28 0AU
Tel: 01798 344454
Fax: 01403 269880
*French period furniture and
decorative wares.*

Freshfords
High Street, Freshford,
Bath BA3 6EF
Tel: 01225 722111
Fax: 01225 722991
www.freshfords.com
*Fine antique furniture and works
of art, specialising in dining and
library furniture.*

**Charles Frodsham & Co. Ltd
(ref: C. Frodsham)**
32 Bury Street,
London SW1Y 6AU
Tel: 020 7839 1234
Fax: 020 7839 2000
*Clocks, watches, marines
chronometers and other
horological items.*

**Fulham Antiques
(ref: Fulham)**
320 Munster Road,
London SW6 6BH
Tel: 020 7610 3644
Fax: 020 7610 3644
*Antique and decorative furniture,
lighting and mirrors.*

**Furniture Vault, The
(ref: Furniture Vault)**
50 Camden Passage,
London N1 8AE
Tel: 020 7354 1047
Fax: 020 7354 1047
*Eighteenth and nineteenth-
century furniture.*

Marilyn Garrow
The Farmhouse, Letheringham,
Woodbridge,
Suffolk IP13 7RA
Tel: 01728 746215
Fine and rare textiles.

**Rupert Gentle Antiques
(ref: Rupert Gentle)**
The Manor House,
Milton Lilbourne
nr Pewsey
Wiltshire SN9 5LQ
Tel: 01672 563344
Fax: 01672 563563
*Decorative antiques and works
of art.*

Geri
Unit S 057
Alfie's Antique Market
13-15 Church Street
Marylebone
London N W8 8DT
Tel: 020 7723 254
www.alfies.com
Antique telephones.

**Michael German Antiques
(ref: Michael German)**
38b Kensington Church Street,
London W8 4BX
Tel: 020 7937 2771
Fax: 020 7937 8566
www.antiquecanes.com
www.antiqueweapons.com
*Antique walking canes, antique
arms and armour.*

Get Stuffed
105 Essex Road,
London N1 2SL
Tel: 020 7226 1364
Fax: 020 7359 8253
www.thegetstuffed.co.uk
Taxidermy and natural history artefacts.

Ghaznavid
A30 Grays Antiques Market,
1–7 Davies Mews,
London W1Y 2LP
Tel: 020 7629 2813
Fax: 020 8896 2114
Roman.

Gabrielle de Giles
The Barn at Bilsington,
Swanton Lane, Bilsington,
Ashford, Kent TN25 7JR
Tel: 01233 720917
Fax: 01233 720156
Antique and country furniture, home interiors, designer for curtains and screens.

Glenda Antique Dolls and Collectables
(ref: Glenda Dolls)
Gray's Antique Market
Davies Street
London WI
Tel: 020 8367 2441
Dolls and collectables.

Gooday Gallery, The
(ref: Gooday Gallery)
14 Richmond Hill, Richmond,
Surrey TW10 6QX
Tel: 020 8940 8652
Arts and Crafts, Art Nouveau, Art Deco, post modernism, tribal art, and African and Oceanic masks.

John Goodison/Chris Paraskeva Antiques
(Ref: Goodison Paraskeva)
30 Camden Passage
London N1 8EA
Mob: 07711 839177
e-mail:goodison.paraskeva
@tinyworld.co.uk
Antique lighting and boxes and decorative items.

Gordon's Medals
(ref: Gordon's)
Stand 14–15 Grays Antiques
Market,
Davies Mews,
London W1Y 1AR
Tel: 020 7495 0900
Fax: 020 7495 0115
www.gordonsmedals.co.uk
Militaria, uniforms, headgear, badges, medals and documents.

Gosh
39 Great Russell Street,
London WC1B 3PH
Tel: 020 7436 5053
Fax: 020 7436 5053

Goya
Stand S002, Alfie's Market,
13–25 Church Street,
London NW8 8DT
Tel: 020 7723 6066
Twentieth-century glass.

Denzil Grant Antiques
(ref: Denzil Grant)
Drinkston House
Drinkston
Bury St. Edmunds
Suffolk IP30 9TT
Tel: 01449 736576
Fax: 01449 737679
mobile 07836 2233112
e-mail:denzil@denzilgrant.com
www.denzilgrant.com

Anita & Solveig Gray
(ref: A. & S. Gray)
58 Davies Street,
London W1Y 2LP
Tel: 020 7408 1638
Fax: 020 7495 0707
www.chinese-porcelain.com
Oriental and European porcelain works of art from the sixteenth to the eighteenth century.

Great Grooms Antique Centre
(ref: Great Grooms)
Great Grooms, Parbrook,
Billinghurst, West Sussex
RH14 9EU
Tel: 01403 786202
Fax: 01403 786224
www.great-grooms.co.uk
Furniture, porcelain, jewellery, silver, glass and pictures.

Anthony Green Antiques
ref: Anthony Green)
Unit 39, Bond Street
Antiques Centre,
124 New Bond Street,
London W1S 1DX
Tel: 020 7409 2854
Fax: 020 7409 2854
www.anthonygreen.com
Vintage wristwatches and antique pocket watches.

Henry Gregory
82 Portobello Road,
London W11 2QD
Tel: 020 7792 9221
Fax: 020 7792 9221
Silver-plate, silver, sporting goods and decorative antiques.

W. John Griffiths
Great Grooms Antique Centre
Hungerford
Berkshire RG17 OEP
Antique furniture.

Guest & Gray
Grays Mews Antique Market,
1–7 Davies Mews,
London W1Y 2LP
Tel: 020 7408 1252
Fax: 020 7499 1445
www.guest-gray.demon.co.uk
Oriental and European
ceramics and works of art,
and reference books.

Guinevere Antiques Limited
(ref: Guinevere)
574–580 Kings Road,
London SW6 2DY
Tel: 020 7736 2917
Fax: 020 7736 8267
Mirrors, cabinets, lights and
chandeliers.

Gurr and Sprake Antiques
(ref: Gurr & Sprake)
283 Lillie Road,
London SW6 7LL
Tel: 020 7381 3209
Fax: 020 7381 9502
Eighteenth and nineteenth-
century English and French
furniture, lighting and unusual
architectural pieces.

Gütlin Clocks and Antiques
(ref: Gütlin Clocks)
616 Kings Road,
London SW6
Tel: 020 7384 2439
Fax: 020 7384 2439
www.gutlin.com
Longcase clocks, mantle clocks,
furniture and lighting, all
eighteenth and nineteenth
century.

G Whizz
17 Jerdan Place,
London SW6 1BE
Tel: 020 7386 5020
Fax: 020 8741 0062
www.metrocycle.co.uk
Bikes.

J. de Haan & Son
(ref: J. de Haan)
PO Box 95, Newmarket,
Suffolk CB8 8ZG
Tel: 01440 821388
Fax: 01440 820410
Old English furniture,
barometers, gilt mirrors and fine
tea caddies.

Hadji Baba Ancient Art
(ref: Hadji Baba)
34a Davies Street,
London W1Y 1LG
Tel: 020 7499 9363
Fax: 020 7493 5504
Near and Middle East antiquities.

Robert Hales Antiques
(ref: Robert Hales)
131 Kensington Church Street,
London W8 7LP
Tel: 020 7229 3887
Fax: 020 7229 3887
Oriental and Islamic arms,
armour, from medieval
to nineteenth century.

Ross Hamilton Antiques Ltd
95 Pimlico Road,
London SW1W 8PH
Tel: 020 7730 3015
Fax: 020 7730 3015
www.lapada.uk/rosshamilton/
Seventeenth to nineteenth-century
fine English and continental
furniture, sixteenth to
twentieth-century paintings,
oriental porcelain, objets d'art
and bronzes.

Jim Hanson &
Argyll Etkin Ltd
(ref: Jim Hanson)
18 Claremont Field,
Ottery St Mary,
Devon EX11 1NP
Tel: 01404 815010
Fax: 01404 815224
Philatelist and postal historian.

Keith Harding's World of
Mechanical Music
(ref: Keith Harding)
The Oak House,
High Street, Northleach,
Gloucestershire GL54 3ET
Tel: 01451 860181
Fax: 01451 861133
www.mechanicalmusic.co.uk

Harpur Deardren
First Floor, 533 Kings Road,
London SW10 0TZ
Tel: 020 7352 2046
Furniture.

Adrian Harrington
Antiquarian Bookseller
(ref: Adrian Harrington)
64a Kensington Church Street,
London W8 4DB
Tel: 020 7937 1465
Fax: 020 7368 0912
www.harringtonbooks.co.uk
Antiquarian, rare and
secondhand books on literature,
children's illustrated and travel.

Peter Harrington
Antiquarian Bookseller
100 Fulham Road
London SW3 6HS
Tel: 020 7591 02220
Fax:020 7225 7054
www.peter-harrington-
book.com
Antique books and maps.

Kenneth Harvey Antiques
(ref: Kenneth Harvey)
Furniture Cave,
533 Kings Road,
London SW10 0TZ
Tel: 020 7352 8645
Fax: 020 7352 3759
www.kennethharvey.com
English and French furniture,
chandeliers and mirrors from the
late seventeenth to twentieth
century, and leather armchairs.

W.R. Harvey & Co. Ltd
86 Corn Street, Witney,
Oxfordshire OX8 7BU
Tel: 01993 706501
Fax: 01993 706601
www.wrharvey.co.uk
*Important stock of English
furniture, clocks, pictures,
mirrors and works of art from
1680–1830.*

**Victoria Harvey at Deuxieme
(ref: Victoria Harvey)**
44 Church Street,
London NW8 8EP
Tel: 020 7724 0738
Fax: 020 7724 0738
General decorative antiques.

**Hatchwell Antiques
(ref: Hatchwell)**
533 Kings Road
London SW10 OTZ
Tel: 020 7351 2344
Fax: 020 7351 3520
e-mail:hatchwell@callnetuk.
com
*Period furniture, fine furniture
and bronzes.*

**Gerard Hawthorn Ltd
(ref: Gerard Hawthorn)**
104 Mount Street,
London W1Y 5HE
Tel: 020 7409 2888
Fax: 020 7409 2777
*Chinese, Japanese and Korean
ceramics and works of art.*

Henry Hay
Unit 5054, 2nd floor,
Alfie's Market,
13–25 Church Street,
London NW8
Tel: 020 7723 2548
*Art Deco and twentieth-century
chrome and brass lamps and
bakelite telephones.*

**Hayman and Hayman
(ref: Hayman)**
Stand K3 Antiquarius
135 Kings Road
London SW3 4PW
Tel: 020 7351 6568
Fax: 020 8741 0959
e-mail:hayman@wahlgren.
demon.co.uk
*Art deco and brass photograph
frames, scent bottles and writing
equipment.*

**Heytesbury Antiques
(ref: Heytesbury)**
PO Box 222, Farnham,
Surrey GU10 5HN
Tel: 01252 850893
Antiques.

**Hill Farm Antiques
(ref: Hill Farm)**
at The Old Cinema
160 Chiswick High Road
London W4 IPR
Tel: 020 8994 2998 and 01488
638 541/361
e-mail:beesley@
hillfarmantiques.demon.co.uk
Antique furniture.

**Holland & Holland
(ref: H. & H.)**
31–33 Bruton Street,
London W1X 8JS
Tel: 020 7499 4411
Fax: 020 7409 3283
Guns.

Hope & Glory
131a Kensington Church
Street
(entrance in Peel Street),
London W8 7LP
Tel: 020 7727 8424
*Commemorative ceramics
including royal and political
subjects.*

**Paul Hopwell Antiques
(ref: Paul Hopwell)**
30 High Street
Westhaddon
Northamptonshire NN6 7AP
Tel: 01788 510636
Fax: 01788 510044
e-mail:
paulhopwell@antiqueoak.co.uk
www.antiqueoak.co.uk
*Seventeenth and eighteenth-
century English oak furniture.*

Jonathan Horne
66c Kensington Church Street,
London W8 4BY
Tel: 020 7221 5658
Fax: 020 7792 3090
www.jonathanhorne.co.uk
*Early English pottery, medieval
to 1820.*

**Howard & Hamilton
(ref: H. & H.)**
151 Sydney Street,
London SW3 6NT
Tel: 020 7352 0909
Fax: 020 7352 0066
Scientific instruments.

**Hulton Getty Picture Gallery
(ref: Hulton Getty)**
3 Jubilee Place
London SW3 3TD
Tel: 020 7376 4525
Fax: 0207 376 4524
www.getty-images.com
*Photographs from late
19th–20th century.*

**Huxtable's Old Advertising
(ref: Huxtable's)**
Alfie's Market,
13–25 Church Street,
London NW8 8DT
Tel: 020 7724 2200
*Advertising, collectables, tins,
signs, bottles, commemoratives
and old packaging from late
Victorian.*

**Hygra, Sign of the
(ref: Hygra)**
2 Middleton Road, London E8
4BL
Tel: 020 7254 7074   Fax: 0870
125 669
www.hygra.com
boxes@hygra.com

Iconastas
5 Piccadilly Arcade,
London SW1
Tel: 020 7629 1433
Fax: 020 7408 2015
Russian fine art.

**In Vogue Antiques
Martin Lister**
The Swan Antiques Centre
High Street
Tetsworth, Thame
Oxfordshire OX9 7AB
Tel: 01844 281777
Fax: 01844 281770
mobile 0773 786 103
e-mail:invogueantiques@aol.
com
www.theswan.co.uk
Antique furniture.

P.L. James
590 Fulham Road,
London SW6 5NT
Tel: 020 7736 0183
*Gilded mirrors, English and
oriental lacquer,
period objects and furniture.*

J.A.N. Fine Art
134 Kensington Church Street,
London W8 4BH
Tel: 020 7792 0736
Fax: 020 7221 1380
*Japanese, Chinese and Korean
ceramics, bronzes and works
of art.*

**Japanese Gallery Ltd
(ref: Japanese Gallery)**
66d Kensington Church Street,
London W8 4BY
Tel: 020 7729 2934
Fax: 020 7229 2934
*Japanese woodcut prints,
Japanese ceramics, swords,
armour and Japanese dolls.*

**Jessop Classic Photographica
(ref: Jessop Classic)**
67 Great Russell Street,
London WC1
Tel: 020 7831 3640
Fax: 020 7831 3956
*Classic photographic equipment,
cameras and optical toys.*

Juke Box Services
15 Lion Road,
Twickenham TW1 4JH
Tel: 020 8288 1700
www.jbs-ltd.co.uk
Juke boxes.

**Stephen Kalms Antiques
(ref: Stephen Kalms)**
The London Silver Vaults,
Chancery Lane,
London WC2A 1QS
Tel: 020 7430 1254
Fax: 020 7405 6206
*Victorian and Edwardian silver,
silver plate and decorative items.*

Kieron
K6 Antiquarias Antiques
Market,
135 Kings Rd,
London SW3 4PW
Tel: 020 7352 2099
Decorative arts.

Kitchen Bygones
13–15 Church Street,
Marylebone,
London NW8 8DT
Tel: 020 7258 3405
Fax: 020 7724 0999
Kitchenalia.

Shirly Knight
Antiques and Decorative
Furnishing
Great Grooms Antique Centre
Hungerford
Berkshire RG17 0RP
Tel: 01488 6823114
Fax: 01487 8233130
Antique furniture.

L. & E. Kreckovic
559 Kings Road,
London SW6 2EB
Tel: 020 7736 0753
Fax: 020 7731 5904
*Early eighteenth to nineteenth-
century furniture.*

La Boheme
c21 Grays Mews,
1–7 Davies Mews,
London W1Y 2LP
Tel: 020 7493 0675
Glass.

**Lacquer Chest, The
(ref: Lacquer Chest)**
75 Kensington Church Street,
London W8 4BG
Tel: 020 7937 1306
Fax: 020 7376 0223
*Military chests, china, clocks,
samplers and lamps.*

Lamberty
The Furniture Cave,
533 Kings Road,
London SW10 0TZ
Tel: 020 7352 3775
Fax: 020 7352 3759
www.lamberty.co.uk

Langfords
Vault 8–10,
London Silver Vaults,
Chancery Lane,
London WC2A 1QS
Tel: 020 7242 5506
Fax: 020 7405 0431
www.langfords.com
*Antique and modern silver
and silver plate.*

**Langfords Marine Antiques
(ref: Langfords Marine)**
The Plaza, 535 Kings Road,
London SW10 0SZ
Tel: 020 7351 4881
Fax: 020 7352 0763
www.langfords.co.uk
Nautical artefacts.

Judith Lassalle
7 Pierrepont Arcade,
Camden Passage,
London N1 8EF
Tel: 020 7607 7121
Optical toys, books and games.

Michael Laws
Bartlett Street Antiques
Centre
Bath BA1 2QZ
Tel: 01225 446322
Fax: 01249 658366
Antique fishing tackle and curios.

**Lennox Gallery Ltd
(ref: Lennox Gallery)**
4 Davies Mews,
London W1Y 1LP
Tel: 020 7491 0091
Fax: 020 7491 0657
Antiquities and numismatics.

Liberty plc
210–220 Regent Street,
London W1R 6AH
Tel: 020 7734 1234
Fax: 020 7578 9876
www.liberty.co.uk
*Twentieth-century furniture,
jewellery, ceramics, clothes
and kitchenware.*

**Libra Antiques
(ref: Libra)**
131D Kensington Church
Street
London W8 7PT
Tel: 020 7727 2990
English ceramics.

Libra Designs
34 Church Street,
London NW8 8EP
Tel: 020 7723 0542
Fax: 020 7286 8518
www.libradeco.com

**Linden & Co. (Antiques) Ltd
(ref: Linden & Co.)**
Vault 7, London Silver Vaults,
Chancery Lane,
London WC2A 1QS
Tel: 020 7242 4863
Fax: 020 7405 9946
Silver plate and works of art.

P. Lipitch
120 and 124 Fulham Road,
London SW3 6HU
Tel: 020 7373 3328
Fax: 020 7373 8888
General antiques.

**Little River Oriental Antiques
(ref: Little River)**
135 Kings Road,
London SW3 4PW
Tel: 020 7349 9080
*Chinese antiquities and domestic
ceramics.*

**London Antique Gallery
(ref: London Antique)**
66e Kensington Church Street,
London W8 4BY
Tel: 020 7229 2934
Fax: 020 7229 2934
*Meissen, Dresden, Worcester,
Minton, Shelley, Sèvrea, Lalique
and bisque dolls.*

Stephen Long
348 Fulham Road,
London SW10 9UH
Tel: 020 7352 8226
*Painted furniture, small
decorative items and English
pottery, from 1780–1850.*

Lotus House
Great Grooms
Hungerford
Berkshire RG17 OEP
Tel: 01488 6823114
Oriental antiques.

**M. Luther Antiques
(ref: M. Luther)**
590 Kings Road, Chelsea,
London SW6 2DX
Tel: 020 7371 8492
Fax: 020 7371 8492
*Eighteenth and nineteenth-
century English and continental
furniture, tables, chairs, mirrors
and lighting.*

**Pete McAskie Toys
(ref: P. McAskie)**
Stand A12–13, Basement,
1–7 Davies Mews,
London W1Y 2LP
Tel: 020 7629 2813
Fax: 020 7493 9344
*Tin toys from 1895–1980, die-
cast toys, robots, battery operated
toys and lead figures.*

Nicholas E. McAuliffe
(ref: N.E. McAuliffe)
First Floor, 533 Kings Road,
London SW10 0TZ
Tel: 020 7352 2046
Furniture.

Fiona McDonald
57 Galveston Road,
London SW15 2RZ
Tel: 020 2270 5559
*Mirrors, decorative furniture
and lighting.*

Mac Humble Antiques
(ref: Mac Humble)
7–9 Woolley Street, Bradford
on Avon,
Wiltshire BA15 1AD
Tel: 01225 866329
Fax: 01225 866329
www.machumbleantiques.co.uk
*Eighteenth and nineteenth-
century furniture, needlework,
samplers, metalware and
decorative items.*

Joyce Macnaughton-Smith
(ref: Macnaughton-Smith)
The Swan Antique Centre
Tetsworth
Thame
Oxfordshire
Berkshire OX9 7AB
Tel: 01884 281777
Antique furniture.

Mac's Cameras
262 King Street,
Hammersmith,
London W6 0SJ
Tel: 020 8846 9853
Antique camera equipment.

Magpies
152 Wandsworth Bridge Road,
London SW6 2UH
Tel: 020 7736 3738
*Small furniture, kitchenware,
door furniture, cutlery, lighting,
silver and silver-plate.*

C.H. Major
154 Kensington Church Street,
London W8 4BH
Tel: 020 7229 1162
Fax: 020 7221 9676
*Eighteenth and nineteenth-
century English furniture.*

E. & H. Manners
66a Kensington Church Street,
London W8 4BY
Tel: 020 7229 5516
Fax: 020 7229 5516
www.europeanporcelain.com
*Eighteenth-century European
porcelain and pottery.*

Map House, The
54 Beauchamp Place,
London SW3 1NY
Tel: 020 7584 8559
Fax: 020 7589 1041
www.themaphouse.com
*Antique maps from fifteenth to
nineteenth century, decorative
engravings from sixteenth to
nineteenth century.*

Marks Antiques
49 Curzon Street,
London W1Y 7RE
Tel: 020 7499 1788
Fax: 020 7409 3183
www.marksantiques.com
Antique silver.

David Martin-Taylor Antiques
(ref: D. Martin-Taylor)
558 Kings Road,
London SW6 2DZ
Tel: 020 7731 4135
Fax: 020 7371 0029
www.davidmartintaylor.com
*Eighteenth and nineteenth-
century continental and English
furniture, objets d'art, decorative
art, from the eccentric to the
unusual.*

Francesca Martire
Alfie's Antique Market
13-25 Church Street
London NW8 8DT
Tel: 020 7723 6066
www.@alfies.com
Open Tues-Sat 10-6.
*20th century lighting, glass,
furniture and jewellery.*

Megan Mathers Antiques
(ref: M. Mathers)
571 Kings Road,
London SW6 2EB
Tel: 020 7371 7837
Fax: 020 7371 7895
*Nineteenth-century continental
and English furniture, porcelain,
lighting and objets d'art.*

A.P. Mathews
283 Westbourne Grove,
London W11
Tel: 01622 812590
Antique luggage.

Gerald Mathias
Stands 3–6, Antiquarius,
131–141 Kings Road,
London SW3 4PW
Tel: 020 7351 1484
Fax: 020 7351 0484
www.geraldmathias.com
*Antique wooden boxes, tea
caddies and stationery cabinets.*

**Sue Mautner Costume
Jewellery
(ref: Sue Mautner)**
Stand P13, Antiquarius,
131–141 Kings Road,
London SW3 4PW
Tel: 020 7376 4419
*Costume jewellery from the
1940s and 1950s, including
Christian Dior, Miriam Haskell,
Schiaparelli and Coppolo Toppo.*

Metro Retro
1 White Conduit Street,
London N1 9EL
Tel: 020 7278 4884/
01245 442047
www.metroretro.co.uk
*Industrial-style furniture, lighting
and home accessories.*

**Midwinter Antiques
(ref: Midwinter)**
31 Bridge Street,
Newcastle under Lyme,
Staffordshire ST5 2RY
Tel: 01782 712483
Fax: 01630 672289
*Seventeenth and eighteenth-
century town and country
furniture, clocks and textiles.*

Arthur Millner
180 New Bond Street,
London W1S 4RL
Tel: 020 7499 4484
www.arthurmillner.com
*Indian and Islamic art and
related European material.*

Nicholas Mitchell
The Swan Antique Centre
Tetsworth
Thame
Oxfordshire
OX9 7AB
Tel: 01844 281777
Fax: 01844 281770
www/theswan.co.uk
English and continental furniture.

**Mora & Upham Antiques
(ref: Mora Upham)**
584 King's Road
London SW6 2DX
Tel: 020 7331 444
Fax: 020 7736 0440
e-mail: mora.upham@talk21.
com
*Fine English and continental
furniture, mirrors and lighting.*

**More Than Music
Collectables
(ref: More Than Music)**
C24–25 Grays Mews Antiques
Market,
1–7 Davies Mews,
London W1Y 2LP
Tel: 020 7629 7703
Fax: 01519 565510
www.mtmglobal.com
*Rock and popular music
memorabilia, specialising in
The Beatles.*

**Robert Morley and Company
Limited
(ref: Robert Morley)**
34 Engate Street, Lewisham,
London SE13 7HA
Tel: 020 8318 5838
Fax: 020 8297 0720
*Pianoforte and harpsichord
workshop.*

**Clive Morley Harps Ltd
(ref: Clive Morley)**
Unit 121,
Grays Antiques Market,
58 Davies Street,
London W1 5LP
Tel: 020 7495 4495
Fax: 01367 860 659
www.morleyharps.com
Harps.

**Terence Morse & Son
(ref: T. Morse & Son)**
237 Westbourne Gove,
London W11 2SE
Tel: 020 7229 4059
Fax: 020 7792 3284
*Eighteenth and nineteenth-
century fine English and
continental furniture, linen
presses and library furniture.*

**Motor Books
(ref: Motor)**
33 St Martin's Court,
London WC2N 4AN
Tel: 020 7836 3800
Fax: 020 7497 2539
Motoring books.

**Mousa Antiques
(ref: Mousa)**
B20 Grays Mews Antiques
Market,
1–7 Davies Mews,
London W1Y 1AR
Tel: 020 7499 8273
Fax: 020 7629 2526
Bohemian glass specialists.

**Murray Cards (International)
Ltd
(ref: Murray Cards)**
51 Watford Way,
London NW4 3JH
Tel: 020 8202 5688
Fax: 020 8203 7878
www.murraycards.com
Cigarette and trade cards.

**Music & Video Exchange
(ref: Music & Video)**
38 Notting Hill Gate,
London W11 3HX
Tel: 020 7243 8574
www.mveshops.co.uk
*CDs, memorabilia, vinyl –
deletions and rarities.*

Myriad Antiques
(ref: Myriad)
131 Portland Road,
London W11 4LW
Tel: 020 7229 1709
Fax: 020 7221 3882
French painted furniture, garden
furniture, bamboo, Victorian and
Edwardian upholstered chairs,
mirrors and objets d'art.

Stephen Naegel
Grays Antiques Market,
1–7 Davies Mews,
London W1Y 2LP
Tel: 020 7491 3066
Fax: 01737 845147
www.btinternet.com/~naegel
Toys.

Namdar Antiques
(ref: Namdar)
B22, Grays Mews Antiques
Market,
1-7 Davies Mews, London
W1Y 2LP
Tel: 020 7629 1183   Fax: 020
7493 9344
Metalware, Oriental and Islamic
ceramics, glassware
and silver.

Colin Narbeth and Son
(ref: C. Narbeth)
20 Cecil Court,
London WC2N 4HE
Tel: 020 7379 6975
Fax: 0172 811244
www.colin-narbeth.com
Banknotes, bonds and shares
of all countries and periods.

New Century
69 Kensington Church Street,
London W8 8BG
Tel: 020 7937 2410
Fax: 020 7937 2410
Design from 1860–1910.

New Kings Road Vintage
Guitar Emporium
(ref: Vintage Guitar)
65a New Kings Road,
London SW6 4SG
Tel: 020 7371 0100
Fax: 020 7371 0460
www.newkingsroadguitars.co.uk
Vintage guitars.

Chris Newland Antiques
(ref: C. Newland)
30–31 Islington Green,
Lower Level, Georgian Village,
London N1 8DU
Tel: 020 7359 9805
Fax: 020 7359 9805
Furniture.

John Nicholas Antiques
First Floor, 533 Kings Road,
London SW10 0TZ
Tel: 020 7352 2046
www.thecave.co.uk
Eighteenth to twentieth-century
furniture, accessories,
chandeliers, lighting and
tapestries.

North West Eight
(ref: North West 8)
36 Church Street,
London NW8 8EP
Tel: 020 7723 9337
Decorative antiques.

Oasis Ancient and
Islamic Arts
(ref: Oasis)
Stand E14, Grays Mews
Antiques Market,
1–7 Davies Mews,
London W1Y 1AR
Tel: 020 7493 1202
Fax: 020 8551 4487
Ancient and Islamic art from
2000BC to eighteenth century.

Ocean Leisure
11–14 Northumberland
Avenue,
London WC2N 5AQ
Tel: 020 7930 5050
Fax: 020 7930 3032
www.oceanleisure.co.uk

Old Advertising
Keith Gretton
26 Honeywell Road
London SW11 6EG
Tel: 020 7228 0741
Advertising items.

Old Cinema, The
160 Chiswick High Road
London W4 1PR
Tel: 020 8995 8801
Mob: 0777 5945482
Antique furniture from the 18th
and 19th century.

Old Cinema Antiques
Warehouse, The
(ref: Old Cinema)
157 Tower Bridge Road,
London SE1 3LW
Tel: 020 7407 5371
Fax: 020 7403 0359
www.antiques-uk.co.uk
Victorian, Edwardian,
reproduction furniture, babies'
chairs, telephone boxes, and
reproduction leather Chesterfields.

Old Father Time Clock
Centre
101 Portobello Road,
London W11 2QB
Tel: 020 8546 6299
Fax: 020 8546 6299
www.oldfathertime.net
Unusual and quirky clocks.

Old School
130c Junction Road,
Tufnell Park,
London N19
Tel: 020 7272 5603
Gardens and interiors.

Old Telephone Company, The
(ref: Old Telephone Co.)
The Battlesbridge Antiques
Centre,
The Old Granary,
Battlesbridge,
Essex SS11 7RE
Tel: 01245 400 601
www.theoldtelephone.co.uk
Antique and collectable
telephones.

Old Tool Chest, The
(ref: Old Tool Chest)
41 Cross Street,
London N1 0PG
Tel: 020 7359 9313
Ancient and modern tools of all
trades, woodworking, dentistry,
veterinary, mason's, and books.

Old World Trading Co
(ref: Old World)
565 Kings Road,
London SW6 2EB
Tel: 020 7731 4708
Fax: 020 7731 1291
Eighteenth and nineteenth-
century English and French
chimney places, fire dogs and
grates.

Oola Boola Antiques London
(ref: Oola Boola)
166 Tower Bridge Road,
London SE1 3LS
Tel: 020 7403 0794
Fax: 020 7403 8405
Victorian, Edwardian, Art
Nouveau, Art Deco, and Arts
and Crafts furniture.

Jacqueline Oosthuizen
Antiques
(ref: J. Oosthuizen)
23 Cale Street, Chelsea,
London SW3 3QR
Tel: 020 7352 6071
Fax: 020 7376 3852
Staffordshire pottery and
jewellery.

Pieter Oosthuizen
(ref: P. Oosthuizen)
Unit 4, Bourbon Hanby
Antiques Centre,
151 Sydney Street,
London SW3
Tel: 020 7460 3078
Fax: 020 7376 3852
Dutch and European Art
Nouveau pottery and
Boer War memorabilia.

Oriental Rug Gallery Ltd
(ref: Oriental Rug)
Eton Group Office
115-116 High Street
Eton
Berkshire SL4 6AN
Tel: 01753 623000
e-mail: rug@orientalruggallery.
com
Antique carpets, rugs and
cushions.

Ormonde Gallery
(ref: Ormonde)
156 Portobello Road
London W11 2EB
020 7229 9800
e-mail:frankormondegallery.
com
Oriental ceramics, furniture,
sculpture and works of art.

Paul Orssich
2 St Stephens Terrace,
London SW8 1DH
Tel: 020 7787 0030
Fax: 020 7735 9612
www.orssich.com
Maps and 20,000 rare
secondhand books.

Fay Orton Antiques
(ref: Fay Orton)
First Floor, 533 Kings Road,
London SW10 0TZ
Tel: 020 7352 2046
Furniture.

Anthony Outred Antiques
Ltd
(ref: Anthony Outred)
46 Pimlico Road
London SW1 8LP
Tel: 020 7730 4782
Fax: 020 7730 5643 fax
e-mail:antiques@outred.co.uk
www.outred.co.uk
English and continental antiques.

John Owen
(ref: John Owen)
Great Grooms Antiques
Centre
Hungerford
Berkshire RG17 OEP
Furniture from the 18th century.

Pacifica
Block 7, 479 Park West Place,
Edgware Road, London W2
Tel: 020 7402 6717
Tribal art.

Pars Antiques
(ref: Pars)
35 St George Street,
London W1R 9FA
Tel: 020 7491 9889
Fax: 020 7493 9344
Antiquities.

Pendulum of Mayfair
King House, 51 Maddox Street,
London W1R 9LA
Tel: 020 7629 6606
Fax: 020 7629 6616
*Clocks: including longcase,
bracket and wall,
and Georgian period furniture.*

Percy's Ltd
16 The London Silver Vaults,
Chancery Lane,
London WC2A 1QS
Tel: 020 7242 3618
Fax: 020 7831 6541
*Eighteenth and nineteenth-
century decorative silver and
plate.*

Period Pieces
Solihull
West Midlands
Tel: 0121 709 1205
Mob: 07778 452539
e-mail:susanshaw50@hotmail.
com
Antique boxes.

**Trevor Phillips & Son Ltd
(ref: T. Phillips)**
75a Jermyn Street,
London SW1Y 6NP
Tel: 020 7930 2954
Fax: 020 7321 0212
www.trevorphilip.demon.co.uk
*Early scientific instruments, and
seventeenth to nineteenth-century
globes.*

**Photographer's Gallery, The
(ref: Photo. Gallery)**
5 Great Newport Street,
London WC2H 7HY
Tel: 020 7831 1772
Fax: 020 7836 9704
www.photonet.org.uk

**David Pickup Antiques
(ref: David Pickup)**
115 High Street, Burford,
Oxfordshire OX18 4RG
Tel: 01993 822555
*Fine English furniture, emphasis
on the Cotswold Arts and Crafts
movement and early twentieth
century.*

**Pillows of Bond Street
(ref: Pillows)**
Bond Street,
London W11
Tel: 0468 947265
Pillows.

**Pimlico Antiques
(ref: Pimlico)**
Moreton Street,
London SW1
Tel: 020 7821 8448
*Furniture, works of art and
paintings.*

A. Piotrowski
Bourbon-Hanby Antiques
Centre
151 Sydney Street
London SW3 6NT
Tel: 020 7352 2106
Fax: 020 7565 0003
www.antiques-uk.co.uk/
bourbon-hanby
English ceramics.

**Nicholas S. Pitcher Oriental
Art
(ref: Nicholas S. Pitcher)**
1st Floor, 29 New Bond Street,
London W1Y 9HD
Tel: 020 7499 6621
Fax: 020 7499 6621
*Early Chinese ceramics and
works of art.*

Planet Bazaar
151 Drummond Street,
London NW1 2PB
Tel: 020 7387 8326
Fax: 020 7387 8326
www.planetbazaar.co.uk
*Designer furniture, art, glass,
lighting, ceramics, books and
eccentricities from the 1950s to
1980s.*

**Poppets Antiques
(ref: Poppets)**
Bourbon Hanby Antiques
Centre
151 Sydney Street
London SW3 6NT
Tel: 020 7352 2108
19th century furniture.

**Christopher Preston Ltd
(ref: C. Preston)**
The Furniture Cave,
533 Kings Road,
London SW10 0TZ
Tel: 020 7352 4229
*Antique furniture and decorative
objects.*

Annette Puttnam
Norton House,
Nr. Lewes, Iford,
Sussex BN7 3EJ
Tel: 01273 483366
Fax: 01273 483366

Radio Days
87 Lower Marsh,
London SE1 7AB
Tel: 020 7928 0800
Fax: 020 7928 0800
*Lighting, telephones, radios,
clothing, magazines and cocktail
bars from the 1930s–1970s.*

Raffety Walwyn
79 Kensington Church Street,
London W8 4BG
Tel: 020 7938 1100
Fax: 020 7938 2519
www.raffetyantiqueclocks.com
Fine antique clocks.

Rainbow Antiques
(ref: Rainbow)
329 Lillie Road,
London SW6 7NR
Tel: 020 7385 1323
Fax: 0870 052 1693
Italian and French period lighting from 1880–1940, chandeliers, lamps and lanterns.

Ranby Hall Antiques
(ref: Ranby Hall)
Barnby Moor, Retford,
Nottingham DN22 8JQ
Tel: 01777 860696
Fax: 01777 701317
www.ranbyhall.antiques-gb.com
Antiques, decorative items and contemporary objects.

R. & S. Antiques
Bourbon Hanby Antiques
Centre
151 SydneyStreet
Chelsea
London SW3 6NT
Tel: 020 73522106
Fax: 020 7565 0003

Mark Ransom Ltd
(ref: Mark Ransom)
62 and 105 Pimlico Road,
London SW1W 8LS
Tel: 020 7259 0220
Fax: 020 7259 0323
Decorative Empire and French furniture.

Rasoul Gallery
South Asian Antiques
K34/35 Grays Antiques
1-7 Davies Mews
London W1Y 2LP
Tel: 020 7495 7422
Mob: 07956 809760
e-mail:rasoulgallerya@hotmail.com
Islamic ceramics and antiquities.

RBR Group at Grays
(ref: RBR Group)
Stand 175, Grays Antiques
Market,
58 Davies Street,
London W1Y 2LP
Tel: 020 7629 4769
Jewellery and objects.

Red Lion Antiques
(ref: Red Lion)
New Street, Petworth,
West Sussex GU28 0AS
Tel: 01798 344485
Fax: 01798 342367
www.redlion-antiques.com
Seventeenth to nineteenth-century furniture.

Gordon Reece Gallery
(ref: Gordon Reece)
16 Clifford Street,
London W1X 1RG
Tel: 020 7439 0007
Fax: 020 7437 5715
www.gordonreecegalleries.com
Flat woven rugs and nomadic carpets, tribal sculpture, jewellery, furniture, decorative and non-European folk art especially ethnic and oriental ceramics.

Reel Poster Gallery
72 Westbourne Grove,
London W2 5SH
Tel: 020 7727 4488
Fax: 020 7727 4499
www.reelposter.com
Original vintage film posters.

Reel Thing, The
17 Royal Opera Arcade,
Pall Mall,
London SW1Y 4UY
Tel: 020 7976 1830
Fax: 020 7976 1850
www.reelthing.co.uk
Purveyors of vintage sporting memorabilia.

Retro Exchange
20 Pembridge Road,
London W11
Tel: 020 7221 2055
Fax: 020 7727 4185
www.l/fel.trade.co.uk
Space age-style furniture and 1950's kitsch.

Retro Home
20 Pembridge Road,
London W11
Tel: 020 7221 2055
Fax: 020 7727 4185
www.l/fel.trade.co.uk
Bric-a-brac, antique furniture and objects of desire.

A. Rezai Persian Carpets
(ref: A. Rezai Persian)
123 Portobello Road,
London W11 2DY
Tel: 020 7221 5012
Fax: 020 7229 6690
Antique oriental carpets, kilims, tribal rugs and silk embroideries.

John Riordan
Great Grooms Antique Centre
Charnham Street
Hungerford
Berkshire RG17 OEP
Tel: 01235 527698
Mob: 0780 8741823
e-mail: mrjohnriordan@
hotmail.com
www.bronzegriffin.com
Bronzes and antique furniture.

Riverbank Gallery Ltd
(ref: Riverbank)
High Street, Petworth,
West Sussex GU28 0AU
Tel: 01798 344401
Fax: 01798 343135
*Large English eighteenth and
nineteenth-century furniture,
decorative items, garden furniture
and decorative paintings.*

Rookery Farm Antiques and
Sara Lemkow
(ref: Rookery Farm Antiques)
12 Camden Passage
London N1 8ED
Tel: 020 7359 0190
Fax: 020 7704 2095
Mob: 07798 920060
e-mail: Rachel.lemko@
btinternet.com
www.antique-kitchenalia.co.uk
Kitchenalia and pine furniture.

Michele Rowan
V38 Antiquarias Antiques
Market,
135 Kings Road,
London SW3 4PW
Tel: 020 7352 8744
Fax: 020 7352 8744
Antique jewellery.

Malcolm Rushton
Studio 3, 13 Belsize Grove,
London NW3 4UX
Tel: 020 7722 1989
Early oriental art.

Russell Rare Books
81 Grosvenor Street,
London W1X 9DE
Tel: 020 7629 0532
Fax: 020 7499 2983
www.folios.co.uk
Rare books.

Salem Antiques
Great Grooms Antiques
Centre
Hungerford
Berkshire RG17 OEP
Tel: 01488 682314
Furniture from the 18th century.

Samiramis
M14–16 Grays Mews Antiques
Market,
1–7 Davies Mews,
London W1Y 1FJ
Tel: 020 7629 1161
Fax: 020 7493 5106
*Islamic pottery, silver, Eastern
items and calligraphy.*

Christopher F. Seidler
(ref: C.F. Seidler)
G13 Grays Mews Antiques
Market,
1–7 Davies Mews,
London W1Y 2LP
Tel: 020 7629 2851
Medals, arms and militaria.

Serendipity
Rosemary Ford
The Tythings
Preston Court
nr Ledbury
Herefordshire HR8 2LL
Tel: 01531 660245
Mob: 07836 7222411
*Traditional antiques, fine English
and continental furniture from the
18th and 19th century.*

Shahdad Antiques
(ref: Shahdad)
A16–17 Grays-in-Mews,
1–7 Davies Mews,
London W1Y 2LP
Tel: 020 7499 0572
Fax: 020 7629 2176
Islamic and ancient works of art.

Bernard J. Shapero Rare
Books
(ref: Bernard Shapero)
32 George Street,
London W1R 0EA
Tel: 020 7493 0876
Fax: 020 7229 7860
www.shapero.com
*Guide books from the sixteenth to
the twentieth century, antiquarian
and rare books, English and
continental literature, specialising
in travel, natural history and
colour plate.*

Sharif
27 Chepstow Corner,
London W2 4XE
Tel: 020 7792 1861
Fax: 020 7792 1861
*Oriental rugs, kilims, textiles and
furniture.*

Anthony Sharpe
16 Craven Hill Mews
London W2 3DY
Tel: 020 7706 2118
e-mail:s@anthonysharpe.com
*19th century lighting, bronzes,
screens and toile lighting. By
appt. only*

**Nicholas Shaw Antiques
(ref: N. Shaw)**
Great Grooms Antique Centre,
Parbrook, Billinghurst,
West Sussex RH14 9EU
Tel: 01403 786 656
Fax: 01403 786 656
www.nicholas-shaw.com
*Scottish and Irish fine silver, small
silver and collector's items.*

**Shiraz Antiques
(ref: Shiraz)**
1 Davies Mews,
London W1Y 1AR
Tel: 020 7495 0635
Fax: 020 7495 0635
*Asian art, antiquities, glass,
marble and pottery.*

Sieff
49 Long Street, Tetbury,
Gloucestershire, GL8 8AA
Tel: 01666 504477
Fax: 01666 504478
*Eighteenth and nineteenth-
century French provincial
fruitwood, and some twentieth-
century furniture.*

Sign of the Times
St Oswalds Mews,
London N6 2UT
Tel: 020 7584 3842
www.antiquesline.com
*Furniture, decorative metalware
and glass.*

B. Silverman
26 London Silver Vaults,
Chancery Lane,
London WC2A 1QS
Tel: 020 7242 3269
Fax: 020 7430 7949
www.silverman-london.com
*Seventeenth to nineteenth-century
fine English silverware and silver
flatware.*

**Jack Simons Antiques Ltd
(ref: Jack Simons)**
37 The London Silver Vaults,
Chancery Lane,
London WC2A 1QS
Tel: 020 7242 3221
Fax: 020 7831 6541
*Fine antique English and
continental silver and objets d'art.*

**Sinai Antiques
(ref: Sinai)**
219–221 Kensington Church
Street,
London W8 7LX
Tel: 020 7229 6190
Antiques and works of art.

Gloria Sinclair
Stand F023
Alfie's Antique Market
25 Church Street
London NW8 8DT
Tel: 020 7724 7118
European ceramics.

Sleeping Beauty
579–581 Kings Road,
London SW6 2DY
Tel: 020 7471 4711
Fax: 020 7471 4795
www.antiquebeds.com
Antique beds.

**Ruth Macklin Smith
(ref: R. Macklin Smith)**
Great Grooms Antiques
Centre
Hungerford
Berkshire RG17 OEP
Antique furniture.

**Julian Smith Antiques
(ref: Julian Smith)**
Bartlett Street Antique Centre
Bath.
Also
The Lodge
Wheelwrights Close
Sixpenny Handley
Dorset SP5 5SA
Tel: 01725 552 820
Mob: 07879 624734
*Luggage and gentlemen's
accessories.*

Solamani Gallery
Gray's Antiques Centre
Stand A20
1-7 Davies Mews
London W1Y 2LP
Tel: 020 7491 2562
Mob: 07956 546468
Islamic ceramics.

**Solaris Antiques
(ref: Solaris)**
170 Westbourne Grove,
London W11 2RW
Tel: 020 7229 8100
Fax: 020 7229 8300
*Decorative antiques from France
and Sweden, from all periods up
to 1970s*

**Somervale Antiques
(ref: Somervale)**
6 Radstock Road
Midsomer Norton
Bath BA3 2AJ
Tel: 01761 4122686
e-mail: ronthomas@
somervaleantiquesglass.co.uk
www.somervaleantiquesglass.
co.uk
*English, Bristol and Nailsea glass.
Shop open by appt. only, 24-hour
telephone service.*

Something Different
254 Holloway Road,
London N7 6NE
Tel: 020 7697 8538
Fax: 020 7697 8538
*Individually made African wood
and stone sculptures.*

**Somlo Antiques Ltd
(ref: Somlo)**
7 Piccadilly Arcade,
London SW1Y 6NH
Tel: 020 7499 6526
Fax: 020 7499 0603
www.somloantiques.com
*Vintage wristwatches and antique
pocket watches.*

Ian Spencer
17 Godfrey Street,
London SW3 3TA
*Large desks, sets of chairs and
dining tables.*

Sporting Times
Unit C 2A
Fitzaarland Road
Arundel
West Sussex BN18 9JS
Tel: 01903 885656
Mob: 07976 9422059
e-mail: MartinQ.Sportingtimes.
isnet.co.uk
www.sportingtimes.co.uk
Antique sporting items.

Star Signings
Unit A18–A19 Grays Mews
Antiques Market,
1–7 Davies Mews
London W1Y 2LP
Tel: 020 7491 1010
Fax: 020 7491 1070
*Sporting autographs and
memorabilia.*

**Steinway & Sons
(ref: Steinway)**
44 Marylebone Lane,
London W1M 6EN
Tel: 020 7487 3391
Fax: 020 7935 0466
New and refurbished pianos.

Jane Stewart
C 26–27, Grays Mews
Antiques Market,
1–7 Davies Mews,
London W1Y 2LP
*Early seventeenth to nineteenth-
century pewter, oak and writing
slopes.*

Constance Stobo
31 Holland Street,
London W8 4HA
Tel: 020 7937 6282
*Eighteenth and nineteenth-
century pottery, English lustre
ware, and Staffordshire animals.*

**Stockspring Antiques
(ref: Stockspring)**
114 Kensington Church Street
London W8 4BH
Tel: 020 7727 7995
e-mail:stockspringand
porcelain.co.uk
www.antique-porcelain.co.uk
*Antique English and continental
porcelain.*

**June & Tony Stone
(ref: J. & T. Stone)**
75 Portobello Road,
London W11 2QB
Tel: 020 7221 1121
Fine antique boxes.

Succession
18 Richmond Hill, Richmond,
Surrey TW10 6QX
Tel: 020 8940 6774
*Art Nouveau, Art Deco,
furniture, bronzes, glass and
pictures.*

**Sugar Antiques
(ref: Sugar)**
8–9 Pierrepont Arcade,
Camden Passage,
London N1 8EF
Tel: 020 7354 9896
Fax: 020 8931 5642
www.sugarantiques.com
*Wristwatches, pocketwatches,
costume jewellery, lighters,
fountain pens and small
collectables.*

Mark Sullivan
14 Cecil Court,
London WC2N 4EZ
Tel: 020 7836 7056
Fax: 020 8287 8492
Antiques and decorative items.

**Sultani Antiques Ltd
(ref: Sultani)**
Unit K29, Gray's Antique
Centre
1-7 Davies Mews
London W1Y 1AR
Tel: 020 7491 3842
Mob: 07956 814 541
Islamic ceramics and antiquities.

**Swan at Tetsworth, The
(ref: The Swan)**
High Street, Tetsworth,
Thame,
Oxfordshire OX9 7AB
Tel: 01844 281777
Fax: 01844 281770
www.theswan.co.uk
*Seventy dealers in historic
Elizabethan coaching inn.*

Talbot
65 Portobello Road,
London W11 2QB
Tel: 020 8969 7011
Fine scientific instruments.

**Talking Machine, The
(ref: Talk. Mach.)**
30 Watford Way,
London NW4 3AL
Tel: 020 8202 3473
www.gramophones.endirect.co.
uk
*Mechanical antiques typewriters,
radios, music boxes, photographs,
sewing machines, juke boxes,
calculators and televisions.*

**Telephone Lines Ltd
(ref: Telephone Lines)**
304 High Street, Cheltenham,
Gloucestershire GL50 3JF
Tel: 01242 583699
Fax: 01242 690033
Telephones.

**Templar Antiques
(ref: Templar)**
28 The Hall Antiques Centre,
359 Upper Street,
London N1 0PD
Tel: 020 7704 9448
Fax: 01621 819737
www.templar-antiques.co.uk
*Eighteenth and nineteenth-
century glass, English, Irish
and Bohemian.*

Temple Gallery
6 Clarendon Cross,
Holland Park,
London W11 4AP
Tel: 020 7727 3809
Fax: 020 7727 1546
www.templegallery.com
*Russian and Greek icons, from
twelfth to sixteenth century.*

**Themes & Variations
(ref: Themes)**
231 Westbourne Grove,
London W11 2SE
Tel: 020 7727 5531
Post-War design.

**Thimble Society, The
(ref: Thimble Society)**
Geoffrey van Arcade, 107
Portobello Road, London W11
2QB
Tel: 020 7419 9562
*Thimbles, sewing items, snuff
boxes and lady's accessories.*

30th Century Comics
17 Lower Richmond Road
London SW15 1JP
Tel: 020 8788 2052
e-mail:rob@thirtiethcentury.
free-online.co.uk
www.thirtiethcentury.free-
online.co.uk

**Sue & Alan Thompson
(ref: S. & A. Thompson)**
Highland Cottage, Broomne
Hall Road,
Cold Harbout RH5 6HH
Tel: 01306 711970
Fax: 01306 711970
*Objects of vertu, antique
tortoiseshell items, period
furniture and unusual
collector's items.*

**Through the Looking Glass
(ref: Looking Glass)**
563 Kings Road,
London SW6 2EB
Tel: 020 7736 7799
Fax: 020 7602 3678
Nineteenth-century mirrors.

**Through the Looking Glass
(ref: Looking Glass)**
137 Kensington Church Street,
London W8 7LP
Tel: 020 7221 4026
Fax: 020 7602 3678
Nineteenth-century mirrors.

**Tin Tin Collectables
(ref: Tin Tin)**
Ground Units 38–42, Antiques
Market,
13–25 Church Street,
London NW8 8DT
Tel: 020 7258 1305
www.tintincollectables.com
*Handbags, from Victorian to
present day, decorative
evening bags and luggage.*

**Tool Shop, The
(ref: Tool Shop)**
High Street, Needham Market,
Suffolk IP6 8AW
Tel: 01449 722992
Fax: 01449 722683
www.toolshop.demon.co.uk
*Antique and usable carpenter's
and joiner's tools.*

Tool Shop Auctions
78 High Street,
Needham Market,
Suffolk IP6 8AW
Tel: 01449 722992
www.uktoolshop.com
*Auctioneers and dealers of
antique woodworking tools and
new Japanese, French and
American tools.*

Tower Bridge Antiques
(ref: Tower Bridge)
159–161 Tower Bridge Road,
London SE1 3LW
Tel: 020 7403 3660
Fax: 020 7403 6058

Town & Country Antiques
(ref: Town & Country)
88 Fulham Road,
London SW3 1HR
Tel: 020 7589 0660
Fax: 020 7823 7618
www.anthony-james.com
English furniture.

Travers Antiques
71 Bell Street,
London NW1 6SX
Tel: 020 7723 4376
*Furniture and decorative items
from 1820–1920.*

Tredantiques
77 Hill Barton Road, Whipton,
Exeter EX1 3PW
Tel: 01392 447082
Fax: 01392 462200
Furniture.

Trio/Teresa Clayton
(ref: Trio)
L24 Grays Mews Antiques
Market,
1–7 Davies Mews,
London W1Y 2LP
Tel: 020 7493 2736
Fax: 020 7493 9344
*Perfume bottles and Bohemian
glass.*

Turn On Lighting
116–118 Islington High Street,
Camden Passage,
London N1 8EG
Tel: 020 7359 7616
Fax: 020 7359 7616
Antique lighting specialists.

Vale Antiques
Great Grooms Antiques
Centre
Hungerford
Berkshire RG 17 OEP
Tel: 01488 682314
Antique furniture.

James Vanstone
Unit 66 Admiral Vernan
Arcade
147 Portobello Road
London W11 2QB
Tel: 020 8541 4707
Mob: 07050 153018
Specialist in coins and medals.

Ventesimo
Unit S001
Alfie's Antique Market
13-25 Church Street
London NW8 8DT
Mob: 07767 498766
*20th century ceramics, glass
and lighting.*

Vintage and Rare Guitars
(ref: Vintage Guitars)
68 Kenway Road
London SW5 ORA
Tel: 020 7370 7834/6828
Fax: 020 7240 7500
Vintage and rare guitars.

Vintage Wireless Shop
(ref: Vintage Wireless)
The Hewarths Sandiacre,
Nottingham NG10 5NQ
Tel: 0115 939 3139
Radios.

**Michael Wakelin & Helen
Linfield**
(ref: Wakelin Linfield)
PO Box 48, Billingshurst,
West Sussex RH14 0YZ
Tel: 01403 700004
Fax: 01403 700004
*Metalware, pottery, treen,
lighting, textiles and mirrors.*

Alan Walker
Halfway Manor, Halfway,
Newbury,
Berkshire, RG20 8NR
Tel: 01488 657 670   Fax:
01488 657 670
Mobile: 0370 728 397
Fine antique barometers.

Graham Walpole
The Coach House,
189 Westbourne Grove,
London W11 2SB
Tel: 020 7229 0267
Fax: 020 7727 7584
*Small furniture, eighteenth and
nineteenth-century dolls' houses,
equestrian items, bronzes,
pictures and decorative items.*

Westland & Company
(ref: Westland & Co.)
St. Michael's Church,
The Clergy House,
Mark Street,
London EC2A 4ER
Tel: 020 7739 8094
Fax: 020 7729 3620
www.westland.co.uk
*Period fireplaces, architectural
elements and panelling.*

Westminster Group Antique Jewellery
(ref: Westminster)
Stand 150, Grays Antiques Market,
58 Davies Street,
London W1Y 2LP
Tel: 020 7493 8672
Fax: 020 7493 8672
Victorian and Edwardian secondhand jewellery and watches.

Wheels of Steel
B10–11 Grays Mews Antiques Market,
1–7 Davies Mews,
London W1Y 2LP
Tel: 020 8505 0450
Fax: 020 7629 2813
Trains and toys.

Whitford Fine Art
(ref: Whitford)
6 Duke Street, St. James',
London SW1Y 6BN
Tel: 020 7930 9332
Fax: 020 7930 5577
Oil paintings and sculpture, from late nineteenth century to twentieth century; post-War abstract and pop art.

Wilde Ones
283 Kings Road, Chelsea,
London SW3 5EW
Tel: 020 7352 9531
Fax: 020 7349 0828
Jewellery.

Jeff Williams
Grays Antiques Market,
58 Davies Street,
London W1K 5LP
Tel: 020 7629 7034
Toy trains.

Peter Wills
Room 4
The Swan Antique Centre
High Street
Tetsworth
Thame
Oxfordshire OX9 7AB
Tel: 01844 281 777
Fax: 01844 281 770
Antique furniture.

Rod Wilson
Red Lion, New Street,
Petworth,
West Sussex, GU28 0AS
Tel: 01798 344485
Fax: 01798 342367
Furniture.

O.F. Wilson Ltd
(ref: O.F. Wilson)
Queen's Elm Parade, Old Church Street,
London SW3 6EJ
Tel: 020 7352 9554
Fax: 020 7351 0765
Continental furniture, French chimney pieces, English painted decorative furniture and mirrors.

Wimpole Antiques
Lynn Lindsay
Stand 349 Grays Antique Market
5-8 Davies Street
London W1K 5LP
Tel: 020 7499 2889
e-mail: 1430@compuserve.com
Antique jewellery.

Yacobs
Grays Mews Antiques Market,
1–7 Davies Mews,
London W1Y 2LP
Tel: 020 7629 7034
Fax: 020 7493 9344
Islamic art.

Yazdani Mayfair Gallery
(ref: Yazdani)
128 Mount Street, Mayfair,
London W1Y 5HA
Tel: 020 7491 2789
Fax: 020 7491 3437
Ancient and Islamic art, Islamic ceramics, sculpture and antiquities.

Younger Antiques
Bourbon Hanby Antiques Centre
151 Sydney Street
SW3 6NT
Tel: 020 7352 2106
Antique furniture.

Youll's Antiques
(ref: Youll's)
27–28 Charnham Street,
Hungerford,
Berkshire RG17 0EJ
Tel: 01488 682046
Fax: 01488 684335
www.youll.com
English/French furniture from seventeenth to twentieth century, porcelain, silver and decorative items.

Zakheim
52 Ledbury Road,
London W11
Tel: 020 7221 4977
Russian art from icons to Soviet, architectural, and decorator's items.

Zoom
Arch 65, Cambridge Grove,
Hammersmith,
London W6 OLD
Tel: 0958 372 975
Tel: 07000 966620
Fax: 020 8846 9779
www.retrozoom.com
Twentieth-century furniture, lighting, telephones and works of art.

There follows our selection of the best antiques centres and markets in the country. These present the best of both worlds, with several dealers showing their particular specialities at the fair prices we expect from the reputable retailer.

BEDFORDSHIRE, BUCKINGHAMSHIRE, HERTFORDSHIRE

Antiques at Wendover Antiques Centre
The Old Post Office, 25 High Street,
Wendover HP22 6DU
Tel: 01296 625335
Dealers: 30

Barkham Antiques Centre
Barkham Street, Barkham RG40 4PJ
Tel: 0118 9761 355 Fax: 0118 9764 355

Buck House Antiques Centre
47 Wycombe End, Old Town,
Beaconsfield HP9 1LZ
Tel: 01494 670714

Luton Antiques Centre
Auction House, Crescent Road,
Luton LU1 2NA
Tel: 01582 405281 Fax: 01582 454080

Woburn Abbey Antiques Centre
Woburn Abbey, Bedfordshire MK17 9WA
Tel: 01525 290350 Fax: 01525 290271
Dealers: 50

BRISTOL, BATH, SOMERSET

Bartlett Street Antiques Centre
5-10 Bartlett Street, Bath BA1 2QZ
Tel: 01225 466689 Fax: 01225 444146
Dealers: 50+

Bath Saturday Antiques Market
Walcot Street, Bath BA1 5BD
Tel: 01225 448263 Fax: 01225.317154
Mobile: 083653 4893
Dealers: 70+

CAMBRIDGESHIRE

Fitzwilliam Antique Centre
Fitzwilliam Street, Peterborough PE1 2RX
Tel: 01733 565415

Gwydir Street Antiques Centre
Untis 1&2 Dales Brewery, Gwydir St,
Cambridge CB1 2LJ
Tel: 01223 356391

Hive Antiques Market, The
Unit 3, Dales Brewery, Gwydir St,
Cambridge CB1 2LG
Tel: 01223 300269

Old Bishop's, The Palace Antique Centre
Tower Road, Little Downham, Nr Ely
Cambridgeshire CB6 2TD
Tel: 01353 699177

CHESHIRE AND STRAFFORDSHIRE

Antique Furniture Warehouse
Unit 3-4 , Royal Oak Buildings, Cooper Street,
Stockport, Cheshire SK1 3QJ
Tel: 0161 429 8590 Fax: 0161 480 5375

Knutsford Antiques Centre
113 King Street, Knutsford, WA16 6EH
Tel: 01565 654092

CORNWALL

Chapel Street Antiques Market
61/62 Chapel Street, Penzance TR18 4AE
Tel: 01736 363267
Dealers: 30-40

Waterfront Antiques Complex
4 Quay Street, Falmouth, Cornwall TR11 3HH
Tel: 01326 311491
Dealers: 20-25

THE COTSWOLDS

Antique and Interior Centre, The
51A Long Street GL8 8AA
Tel: 01666 505083
Dealers: 10

CUMBRIA AND LANCASHIRE

Carlisle Antiques Centre
Cecil Hall, 46A Cecil Street,
Carlisle CA1 1NT
Tel: 0122 8536 910 Fax: 0122 8536 910
carlsle-antiques.co.uk

Cockermouth Antiques Market
Courthouse, Main Street,
Cockermouth CA15 5XM
Tel: 01900 826746

DERBYSHIRE AND NOTTINGHAMSHIRE

Alfreton Antiques Centre
11 King Street, Alfreton DE55 7AF
Tel: 01773 520781
alfretonantiques@supanet.com

Castle Gate Antiques Centre
55 Castle Gate, Newark NG24 1BE
Tel: 01636 700076 Fax: 01636 700144
Dealers: 10

Chappells and the Antiques Centre Bakewell
King Street DE45 1DZ
Tel: 01629 812 496   Fax: 01629 814 531
bacc@chappells-antiques.co.uk
Dealers: 30

Memory Lane Antiques Centre
Nottingham Road, Ripley DE5 3AS
Tel: 01773 570184
Dealers: 40-50

Portland Street Antiques Centre
Portland Street, Newark NG24 4XF
Tel: 01636 674397   Fax: 01636 674397

Top Hat Antiques Centre
70-72 Derby Road, Nottingham NG1 5DF
Tel: 0115 9419 143
sylvia@artdeco-fairs.co.uk

DEVONSHIRE
Abingdon House
136 High Street, Honiton EX14 8JP
Tel: 01404 42108
Dealers: 20

Antique Centre on the Quay, The
The Quay, Exeter EX2 4AP
Tel: 01392 493501
home free.emailamail.co.uk

Barbican Antiques Centre
82-84 Vauxhall Street, Barbican PL4 0EX
Tel: 01752 201752
Dealers: 40+

Honiton Antique Centre McBains Antiques
Exeter Airport, Industrial Est., Exeter EX5 2BA
Tel: 01392 366261   Fax: 01392 365572
mcbains@netcomuk.co.uk
Dealers:10

Newton Abbot Antiques Centre
55 East Street, Newton Abbot TQ12 2JP
Tel: 01626 354074
Dealers:40

Sidmouth Antiques and Collectors Centre
All Saints Road, Sidmouth EX10 8ES
Tel: 01395 512 588

DORSET
Bridport Antique Centre
5 West Allington, Bridport DT6 5BJ
Tel: 01308 425885

Colliton Antique Centre
Colliton Street, Dorchester DT1 1XH
Tel: 01305 269398 / 01305 260115

Emporium Antiques Centre
908 Christchurch Road, Boscombe,
Bournemouth, Dorset BH7 6DL
Tel: 01202 422380   Fax: 01202 433348
Dealers: 8

Mattar Antique Centre
Mattar Arcade, 17 Newlands DT9 3JG
Tel: 01935 813464   Fax: 01935 813464

ESSEX
Baddow Antique Centre
The Bringey, Church Street, Great Baddow,
Chelmsford, Essex CM2 7JW
Tel: 01245 476159

Finchingfield Antiques Centre
The Green, Finchingfield, Braintree,
Essex CM7 4JX
Tel: 01371 810258   Fax: 01371 810258
Dealers: 45

Harwich Antique Centre
19 King's Quay Street, Harwich, Essex
Tel: 01255 554719   Fax: 01255 554719
Dealers: 50
harwich@worldwideantiques.co.uk

Saffron Walden Antiques Centre
1 Market Row, Saffron Walden,
Essex CB10 1HA
Tel: 01799 524534   Fax: 01799 524703

HAMPSHIRE AND ISLE OF WIGHT
Antique Centre, The
Britannia Road, Southampton,
Hampshire SO14 0QL
Tel: 0238 0221 022
Dealers: 46

Antique Quarter, The
'Old' Northam Road, Southampton,
Hampshire SO14 0QL
Tel: 0238 0233 393
Dealers: 15

Dolphin Quay Antique Centre
Queen Street, Emsworth,
Hampshire PO10 7BU
Tel: 01243 379994   Fax: 01243 379251
enquiriesnancy@netscapeonline.co.uk

Eversley Antique Centre Ltd
Church Lane, Eversley, Hook,
Hampshire RG27 0PX
Tel: 0118 932 8518
Dealers: 11

Lyndhurst Antique Centre
19-21 High Street, Lyndhurst,
Hampshire SO43 7BB
Tel: 0238 0284 000
Dealers: 50

GLOUCESTERSHIRE
Struwwelpeter
The Old School House,
175 London Road, Charlton Kings,
Cheltenham Gloucester GL52 6HN
Tel: 01242 230088
Dealers: 7

HEREFORD AND WORCESTERSHIRE
Antique Centre, The
5-8 Lion Street, Kidderminster,
Worcestershire DY10 1PT
Tel: 01562 740389   Fax: 01562 740389
Dealers: 12

Hereford Antique Centre
128 Widemarsh Street, Hereford HR4 9HN
Tel: 01432 266242
Dealers: 35

Leominster Antique Centre
34 Broad Street, Leominster HR6 8BS
Tel: 01568 615505
Dealers: 22

Leominster Antique Market
14 Broad Street, Leominster HR6 8BS
Tel: 01568 612 189
Dealers: 15+

Linden House Antiques
3 Silver Street, Stansted CM24 8HA
Tel: 01279 812 373

Malvern Link Antique Centre
154 Worcester Road, Malvern Link,
Worcestershire WR14 1AA
Tel: 01684 575750
Dealers: 10

Ross on Wye Antique Gallery
Gloucester Road, Ross on Wye,
Herefordshire HR9 5BU
Tel: 01989 762290   Fax: 01989 762291
Dealers: 91

Worcester Antiques Centre
15 Reindeer Court, Mealcheapen Street,
Worcester WR1 4DF
Tel: 01905 610680/1   Fax: 01905 610681
Dealers: 45

KENT
Antiques Centre, The
120 London Road, Tubs Hill TN13 1BA
Tel: 01732 452104

Coach House Antique Centre
2a Duck Lane, Northgate, Canterbury,
Kent CT1 2AE
Tel: 01227 463117
Dealers: 7

Copperfield Antique & Craft Centre
Unit 4, Copperfield's Walkway, Spital Street,
Dartford, Kent DA1 2DE
Tel: 01322 281445
Dealer: 35

Corn Exchange Antiques Centre
64 The Pantiles, Tunbridge Wells, Kent TN2 5TN
Tel: 01892 539652   Fax: 01892 538454
Dealers: 11

Tenterden Antiques Centre
66 High Street TN30 6AU
Tel: 01580 765885   Fax: 01580 765655
Dealers: 20+

Tunbridge Wells Antique Centre
12 Union Square, The Pantiles,
Tunbridge Wells TN4 8HE
Tel: 01892 533708
twantique@aol.com

Village Antique Centre
4 High Street, Brasted, Kent TN16 1RF
Tel: 01959 564545
Dealers: 15

LEICESTERSHIRE, RUTLAND AND NORTHAMPTONESHIRE
Finedon Antique (Centre)
11-25 Bell Hill, Finedon NN9 5NB
Tel: 01933 681260   Fax: 01933 681779
sales@finedonantiques.com

Village Antique Market, The
62 High Street, Weedon NN7 4QD
Tel: 01327 342 015
Dealers: 40

LINCOLSHIRE
Astra House Antique Centre
Old RAF Helswell, Nr Caenby Corner,
Gainsborough, Lincolnshire DN21 5TL
Tel: 01427 668312
Dealers: 50

Guardroom Antiques
RAF Station Henswell,
Gainsborough DN21 5TL
Tel: 01427 667113
Dealers: 50

Henswell Antiques Centre
Caenby Corner Estate, Henswell Cliff
Gainsborough DN21 5TL
Tel: 01427 668 389   Fax: 01427 668 935
info@Hemswell-antiques.com
Dealers:270

St. Martin's Antique Centre
23a High Street, St Martin's, Stamford PE9 2LF
Tel: 01780 481158   Fax: 01780 766598

Stamford Antiques Centre
The Exchange Hall, Broad Street,
Stamford PE1 9PX
Tel: 01780 762 605   Fax: 01733 244 717
anoc1900@compuserve.com
Dealers: 40

LONDON
Alfie's Antique Market
13-25 Church Street NW8 8DT
Tel: 020 7723 6066   Fax: 020 7724 0999
alfies@clara.net

Antiquarius
131-41 King's Road SW3 4PW
Tel: 020 7351 5353 Fax: 020 7351 5350
antique@dial.pipex.com

Bermondsey
corner of Long Lane & Bermondsey Street
SE1 3UN
Tel: 020 7351 5353

Camden Passage
Upper Street, Islington N1
Tel: 020 7359 9969
www.camdenpassage.com

Grays Mews Antique Markets
58 Davis Street, and 1-7 Davis Mews WIY 2LP
Tel: 020 7629 7034
Dearlers: 300

Hampstead Antique and Craft Market
12 Heath Street, London NW3 6TE
Tel: 020 7431 0240 Fax: 020 7794 4620
Dealers: 20

Jubilee Market Hall
1 Tavistock Court, The Piazza
Covent Garden WC2 E8BD
Tel: 020 7836 2139

Lillie Road
237 Lillie Road, SW6
Tel: 020 7381 2500 Fax: 020 7381 8320

Portobello Road
In Notting Hill Gate W10 and W11
Tel: 020 7727 7684 Fax: 020 7727 7684
Dealers: 280

Spitalfields
65 Brushfield Street E1 6AA
Tel: 020 8983 3779 Fax: 020 7377 1783

NORFOLK
Fakenham Antique Centre,
The Old Congregational Church, 14 Norwich
Road, Fakenham, Norfolk NR21 8AZ
Tel: 01328 862941
Dealers: 20

NORTHUMBERLAND AND DURHAM
Village Antique Market, The
62 High Street, Weedon NN7 4QD
Tel: 01327 342015
Dealers: 40

OXFORDSHIRE
Antique on High Ltd
85 High Street, Oxford OX1 4BG
Tel: 01865 251075 Fax: 0129 665 5580
Dealers: 38

Country Markets Antiques and Collectables
Country Garden Centre, Newbury Road,
Chilton, nr. Didcot OX11 0QN
Tel: 01235 835125 Fax: 01235 833068
countrymarketsantiquesandcollectables
@breathnet.com
Dealers: 35

Old George Inn Antique Galleries
104 High Street, Burford, Oxfordshire OX18 4QJ
Tel: 01993 823319
Dealers: 22

Station Mill Antique Centre
Station Yard Industrial Estate, Chipping Norton,
Oxfordshire OX7 5HX
Tel: 01608 644563 Fax: 01608 644563
Dealers: 73

Swan at Tetsworth
High Street, Tetsworth, Oxfordshire OX9 7AB,
Tel: 01844 281777 Fax: 01844 281770
antiques@theswan.co.uk
Dealers: 80

SHROPSHIRE
Bridgnorth Antique Centre
Whitburn Street, Bridgnorth,
Shropshire WV16 4QP
Tel: 01746 768055
Dealers: 19

Old Mill Antique Centre
Mill Street, Shropshire WV15 5AG
Tel: 01746 768778 Fax: 01746 768944
Dealers: 90

Princess Antique Centre
14a The Square, Shrewsbury SY1 1LH
Tel: 01743 343701
Dealers: 100 stallholders

Shrewsbury Antique Centre
15 Princess House, The Square,
Shrewsbury SY1 1UT
Tel: 01743 247 704

Shrewsbury Antique Market
Frankwell Quay Warehouse,
Shrewsbury SY3 8LG
Tel: 01743 350619
Dealers: 30

Stretton Antiques Market
36 Sandford Avenue, Stretton SY6 6BH
Tel: 01694 723718 Fax: 01694 723718
Dealers: 60

K.W. Swift
56 Mill Street, Ludlow SY8 1BB
Tel: 01584 878571 Fax: 01746 714407
Dealers: 20, book market.

STAFFORDSHIRE
Lion Antique Centre
8 Market Place, Uttoxeter, Staffordshire ST14 8HP
Tel: 01889 567717
Dealers: 28

SUFFOLK
Church Street Centre
6e Church Street, Woodbridge, Suffolk IP12 1DH
Tel: 01394 388887
Dealers: 10

Long Melford Antiques Centre
Chapel Maltings, CO10 9HX
Tel: 01787 379287 Fax: 01787 379287
Dealers: 40

Woodbridge Gallery
23 Market Hill, Woodbridge, Suffolk IP12 4OX
Tel: 01394 386500 Fax: 01394 386500
Dealers: 35

SURREY
Antiques Centre, The
22 Haydon Place, Corner of Martyr Road,
Guildford GU1 4LL
Tel: 01483 567817
Dealers: 6

Antiques Warehouse, The
Badshot Farm, St George's Road,
Runfold GU9 9HY
Tel: 01252 317590 Fax: 01252 879751
Dealers: 40

Enterprise Collectors Market
Station Parade, Eastbourne, East Sussex BN21 1BD
Tel: 01323 732690
Dealers: 15

Hampton Court Emporium, The
52-54 Bridge Road, East Molesey,
Surrey KT8 9HA
Tel: 020 8941 8876
Dealers: 16

Kingston Antiques Market, The
29-31 London Road, Kingston-upon-Thames,
Surrey KT2 6ND
Tel: 020 8549 2004 Fax: 020 8549 3839
webmaster@antiquesmarket.co.uk
Dealers: 90

Packhouse Antique Centre
Hewetts Kilns, Tongham Road, Runfold,
Farnham, Surrey GU10 1PQ
Tel: 01252 781010 Fax: 01252 783876
hewett@cix.co.uk
Dealers: 80

Victoria and Edward Antique Centre
61 West Street, Dorking, Surrey RH4 1BS
Tel: 01306 889645
Dealers: 26

SUSSEX
Almshouses Arcade
19 The Hornet PO19 4JL
Tel: 01243 771994

Brighton Flea Market
31A Upper Street, James's Street BN2 1JN
Tel: 01273 624006 Fax: 01273 328665
arwilkinson@aol.com

Eastbourne Antiques Market
80 Seaside, Eastbourne BN22 7QP
Tel: 01323 642233
Dealers: 25

Lewes Antique Centre
20 Cliff High Street, Lewes BN7 2AH
Tel: 01273 476 148 / 01273 472 173
Dealers: 60

Old Town Antiques Centre, The
52 Ocklynge Road, Eastbourne, East Sussex
BN21 1PR
Tel: 01323 416016
Dealers: 16

Olinda House Antiques
South Street, Rotherfield, Crowborough,
East Sussex TN6 3LL,
Tel: 01892 852609

Petworth Antiques Market
East Street, Petworth, GU28 0AB
Tel: 01798 342073 Fax: 01798 344566

WARWICKSHIRE
Barn Antique Centre
Long Marston Ground, Station Road, Long
Marsden, Stratford-upon-Avon CV37 8RB
Tel: 01789 721399 Fax: 01789 721390
barnantiques@aol.com
Dealers: 50

Bridford Antique Centre
Warwick House, 94-96 High Street, Bidford on
Avon, Alcester, Warwickshire B50 4AF
Tel: 01789 773680
Dealers: 7

Dunchurch Antique Centre
16a Daventry Road, Dunchurch, Rugby,
CV22 6NS
Tel: 01788 522450
Dealers: 10

Malthouse Antique Centre
4 Market Place, Alcester, Warwickshire B49 5AE
Tel: 01789 764032
Dealers: 20

Stables Antique Centre, The
Hatton Country World, Dark Lane CV35 8XA
Tel: 01926 842405
Dealers: 25

Stratford Antiques and Interiors Centre Ltd
Dodwell Trading Estate, Evesham Road
CV37 9SY
Tel: 01789 297729   Fax: 01789 297710
info@stratfordantiques.co.uk
Dealers: 20

Vintage Antiques Centre
36 Market Place, Warwick CV34 4SH
Tel: 01926 491527
vintage@globalnet.co.uk
Dealers: 20

Warwick Antiques Centre
22 High Street, Warwick CV34 4AP
Tel: 01926 491382 / 01926 495704
Dealers: 32

WILTSHIRE
Brocante Antiques Centre
6 London Road, Marlborough SN8 1PH
Tel: 01672 516512   Fax: 01672 516512
brocante@brocanteantiquescentre.co.uk
Dealers: 20

Marlborough Parade Antique Centre, The
The Parade, Marlborough SN8 1NE
Tel: 01672 515331
Dealers: 70

YORKSHIRE
Arcadia Antiques Centre
12-14 The Arcade, Goole,
East Yorkshire DN14 5PY
Tel: 01405 720549
Dealers: 20

Banners Collectables
Banners Business Centre, Attercliffe Road,
Sheffield, South Yorkshire S9 3QS
Tel: 0114 244 0742
Dealers: 50

Barmouth Road Antique Centre
Barmouth Court
off Abbeydale, Sheffield, South Yorkshire S7 2DH
Tel: 0114 255 2711   Fax: 0114 258 2672
Dealers: 60

Cavendish Antique & Collectors Centre
44 Stonegate, York YO1 8AS
Tel: 01904 621666   Fax: 01904 644400
Dealers: 60

Halifax Antique Centre
Queens Road, Halifax,
West Yorkshire HX1 4OR
Tel: 01422 366 657   Fax: 01422 369 293
antiques@halifaxac.u-net.com
Dealers: 30

Harrogate Antiques Centre, The
The Ginnel, off Parliament Street HG1 2RB
Tel: 01423 508857   Fax: 01423 508857
Dealers: 50

Malton Antique Market
2 Old Maltongate, Malton YO17 0EG
Tel: 01653 692 732

Pickering Antique Centre
Southgate, Pickering,
North Yorkshire YO18 8BN
Tel: 01751 477210   Fax: 01751 477210
Dealers: 35

Stonegate Antique Centre
41 Stonegate, York, North Yorkshire YO1 8AW
Tel: 01904 613888   Fax: 01904 644400
Dealers: 120

York Antiques Centre
2a Lendal, York YO1 8AA
Tel: 01904 641445 / 641582
Dealers: 16+

SCOTLAND
Clola Antiques Centre
Shannas School House,
Clola by Mintlaw AB42 8AE
Tel: 01771 624584   Fax: 01771 624584
Dealers: 10

Scottish Antique & Arts Centre
Abernyte PH14 9SJ
Tel: 01828 686401   Fax: 01828 686199

WALES
Antique Market
6 Market Street, Hay-on-Wye HR3 5AD
Tel: 01497 820175

Cardiff Antiques Centre
10-12 Royal Arcade CF10 2AE
Tel: 01222 398891
Dealers: 13

Chapel Antiques
Methodist Chapel, Holyhead Road, Froncysyllte,
Denbighshire, Llangollen LL20 7RA
Tel: 01691 777624   Fax: 01691 777624
Dealers: 20

Jacobs Antique Centre
West Canal Wharf, Cardiff C51 5DB
Tel: 01222 390939
Dealers: 50

Index

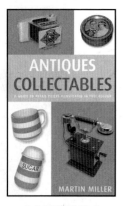